THE CRITICAL OPINIONS OF
WILLIAM WORDSWORTH

THE CRITICAL OPINIONS OF
WILLIAM WORDSWORTH

BY

MARKHAM L. PEACOCK, JR.

1969

OCTAGON BOOKS

New York

Reprinted 1969
by special arrangement with The Johns Hopkins Press

OCTAGON BOOKS
A DIVISION OF FARRAR, STRAUS & GIROUX, INC.
19 Union Square West
New York, N. Y. 10003

AM

LIBRARY OF CONGRESS CATALOG CARD NUMBER: 70-86282

Printed in U.S.A. by
TAYLOR PUBLISHING COMPANY
DALLAS, TEXAS

To

RAYMOND DEXTER HAVENS

CONTENTS

PREFACE

THE CATALOGUE in this book is divided into three sections which contain Wordsworth's critical comments: (1) on literary principles and subjects; (2) on various authors and their works; and (3) on his own verse and prose. Although the first two sections are arranged alphabetically, the third follows, as does the de Selincourt and Darbishire edition, the order of the one volume *Oxford Wordsworth*, edited by Thomas Hutchinson, except that the last part dealing with Wordsworth's prose is generally chronological.

As this work was revised for wartime publication, in the final version numerous short passages were converted to cross references, and the regrouping of these references left in the numbering many gaps, which, however, should cause no confusion. I also decided to conserve space by printing some abnormally long passages to which many cross references could be made. I regret the number of these references, but any other plan would have doubled the bulk of the catalogue.

All the important critical material which has appeared since 1944, when the manuscript of this work was sent to the printers, I have added to the catalogue. I fear, however, I may have considered some of the poet's comments non-critical which slightly, or indirectly, are related to literary criticism; particularly, this misjudgment may appear under these subjects: Infinity, Intellect, Nature, Primitivism, Realism and Wonder. On the other hand, I may have erred by including some noncritical statements, but I am more concerned about the possible omissions. For some notations in Wordsworth's handwriting, though probably dictated by Coleridge, see E. A. Shearer's "Wordsworth and Coleridge Marginalia in a Copy of Richard Payne Knight's *Analytical Inquiry into the Principles of Taste*," *The Huntington Library Quarterly*, I (October, 1937), 63-94; and J. I. Lindsay's answer, "A Note on the Marginalia," in the same number, pp. 95-9. I have been told that there are marginalia attributed to Wordsworth in a copy of Sir John Suckling's works, edited by William Carew Hazlitt. I shall appreciate learning the whereabouts of this copy, or of any other volume containing the poet's marginal notes.

Every student of Wordsworth is grateful to the late Professor Ernest de Selincourt for the wealth of new material presented so admirably in his editions of *The Prelude*, of the correspondence, and of the poetry (completed by Miss Helen Darbishire); but I am also greatly indebted to Miss Edith J. Morley, Professor Leslie N. Broughton, Miss Edith C. Batho; and to many others whose contributions are listed in the table of abbreviations preceding the catalogue. These scholars and their publishers, especially the Oxford Press, J. M. Dent and Sons, and the Cornell University Press, made this compilation possible. With variations the general plan of the catalogue is modeled after the late Professor Joseph Epes Brown's *The Critical Opinions of Samuel Johnson*, which did for that robust critic what Professor A. A. Murphree's compilation, when published, will do for Dryden.

My thanks are due the librarians and their associates at the Virginia Polytechnic Institute, and the Johns Hopkins, Columbia, Cornell, Virginia and North Carolina Universities for many kindnesses. But, especially, I wish to thank my colleague, Dr. Tench Tilghman, whose discriminating judgment I have relied on heavily. Also, Professor Kemp Malone and the late Professor Hazelton Spencer, of the Johns Hopkins University, offered very helpful advice during the early stages of the cataloguing.

This work was originally suggested to me by Professor Raymond Dexter Havens who has followed its growth with the intense concern he gives all his students' efforts and welfare. For his sake I wish this book more nearly met the standards of scholarship Professor Havens has always encouraged in his students and upheld in his own works.

To my mother and father for their encouragement and for the pleasant surroundings they gave me to work in, I am very thankful. Finally, to my wife, for proofreading and correcting this compilation, and for gentle understanding and unfailing patience with the compiler, I am most affectionately grateful.

MARKHAM PEACOCK, JR.

Blacksburg, Virginia
July 24, 1950

INTRODUCTION

THIS STUDY falls into two unequal parts: a catalogue of Wordsworth's literary opinions, and a brief discussion of Wordsworth as a critic. It is hoped that this compilation will be of general value in making readily available the opinions on various writers and literary questions of a great poet and critic of the romantic faith. Also, without some such collection it is impossible to make any sound and complete analysis of Wordsworth's literary beliefs. Therefore, it is hoped that this work will be of value to students of the poet in revealing: (1) the amount of his criticism; (2) the extent of his critical limitations; (3) the breadth of many of his critical attitudes; (4) the originality or independence of his views; and (5) the keenness and penetration of his comments.

1. The Amount of his Criticism

Until recent years a considerable body of Wordsworth's criticism has been closed to us, but, since Professor de Selincourt has published the final volume of the letters of the poet and his sister, it is possible now to provide a relatively complete catalogue of his opinions on literature. In addition to this previously unavailable material, there are several prefaces and prefatory letters that are rarely utilized by students of Wordsworth; even the Grosart (now superseded by the de Selincourt) edition of the prose, containing reports of the poet's conversations and the invaluable notes on his poems, dictated to Isabella Fenwick in 1843, is often overlooked. I have tried to collect every remark Wordsworth wrote or dictated, or was heard to utter on literary subjects; memoirs, biographies, reported conversations, letters, prefaces, and notes have been culled. The size of the catalogue indicates how considerable is the body of Wordsworth's criticism.

2. Limitations

The quantity of Wordsworth's criticism, however, would furnish a poor argument for making such a compilation were it not the criticism of a deep, intense, and creative mind. It was a mind of lofty ideals, and its very loftiness resulted in impatience with works not satisfying the highest artistic standards, and not fulfilling his concept of a worthy purpose. Wordsworth told his nephew, Christopher Wordsworth:

When I began to give myself up to the profession of a poet for life, I was impressed with a conviction, that there were four English poets whom I must have continually before me as examples—Chaucer, Shakespeare, Spenser, and Milton. These I must study, and equal *if I could*; and I need not think of the rest.[1]

These four were great artists, who spoke to men of " really important things," who fulfilled the obligations of poets to mankind.[2] Less significant poets, inferior in artistry and inspirational force, were often summarily dismissed rather than discussed. Wordsworth's opinions of Walter Scott and Byron illustrate his impatience. Though he admired Scott's character, he deplored Byron's; though he felt Scott's works lacked a worthy purpose, he felt Byron's had a viciously evil influence. Their metrical romances, and their verse in general, provided reading matter for their day, but neither as literature nor as inspiring, instructive works would they hold a permanent place. Every age would see the birth and death of such productions. Neither poet was a careful composer and neither satisfied Wordsworth's conception of the function of art to " uplift and feed in quiet " the minds and spirits of men. " Byron has the great power and genius, but there is something so repugnant to my moral sense that I abhor " his poems. Poetry should be " free from rank and corrupt passion . . . should refine and purify . . . [men's] natures; not make them worse . . . there is always a moral lesson . . . in Shakespeare's pictures [of passions, but not in Byron's]." Byron's influence was a positive force for evil; Scott erred on the negative side, for in dealing almost exclusively in externals (manners, trappings, and description), he failed to refine and purify the hearts of readers. Wordsworth's attitude put less emphasis on the question,

---

[1] A list of abbreviations precedes the catalogue, in which, see Chaucer 5.

[2] See in catalogue under Aim of Writing; Moral Element; Chaucer; Milton; Shakespeare; and Spenser.

" Has the author done what he tried to do? " than on " Was it worth doing? " [3]

There are other more decided limitations. First, though it is now generally recognized that Wordsworth was more widely-read than was previously thought, most of his reading was done in his earlier years. A combination of circumstances in his middle and later years tended to shut him off from books: (1) a growing preoccupation with composition and, especially, with revision of his own poems; (2) a recurring infection of his eyes often made writing or reading impossible for weeks; and (3) the distressing illness of Dorothy prevented her reading to him.[4] Though these circumstances limited his criticism in so far as they threw him out of contact with much good contemporary literature, the more limiting factor was that he was not a bookish man, certainly not in the sense that T. S. Eliot is, or that Milton, Pope, Shelley, and Coleridge were, and it seems clear that he never thought of himself as a critic, or set a high value on criticism.[5] He made no effort to keep up with the literature or criticism of his own day and displayed no great interest in it. Furthermore, he was surprisingly indifferent to certain important *genres*, the drama, the novel, and the epic. His remarks on the drama are not significant though he had some affection for it, experimented with it in *The Borderers*, and felt that " The works of the old English dramatists are the gardens of our language," and that " The poetic genius of England, with [a few exceptions] . . . is to be sought in her drama." [6] But neither comment is concerned with the drama as drama, that is, as something to be acted and seen, not as something to be read. Of the novel, excepting a few comments on Scott's novels, which he rightly placed above his verse, and his disapproval of Jane Austen's naturalism, of " modern novels of the Radcliffe school," of

[3] See under Aim of Writing; Composition; Moral Element; Byron; Scott, W.

[4] We must not forget that Dorothy reintroduced him to Jonson (see in catalogue), and aroused his interest in the sonnet by rereading Milton's to him (Landor 11 and Moxon 3).

[5] " I never cared a straw about the ' theory ' and the ' preface [to *L. B.*]' was written at the request of Mr. Coleridge." " I am not a critic and set little value upon the art." Regretted having written the Preface to *L. B.*, "though I do not reckon the principles then advanced erroneous." See W. 382 and Criticism 57 (also 58-9, 76-7).

[6] See under Drama.

" the metrical Novel," and of " frantic novels " of his day, he had almost nothing to add. He did, however, ask how the public could read Dickens and allow " the classics " to suffer, and he recognized Fielding and Smollett as " great masters of romance." But with the exception of his references to Dickens we find little evidence that he read a novel after 1827.[7] Stranger than his apparent indifference to the drama and the novel is his almost complete silence as to the epic. For heroic poetry abounded between 1775 and 1830, and Wordsworth himself considered attempting the type. Indeed, *The Prelude*, as Professor Havens has said, " was conceived as . . . a kind of philosophic epic." Besides, Milton, his favorite, was an epic poet. Yet his only significant remarks on this popular *genre* were written to Southey in 1815.[8]

In concluding this section, we should admit that Wordsworth is often stubborn, narrow, intolerant, as are most innovators. " The nemesis of intensity is narrowness," and, since Wordsworth cared a great deal, had strong convictions about poetry, and had suffered for them, some narrowness was inevitable. The surprising thing is the penetration, unexpected tolerance and insight often evidenced. He is unpredictable. The mass of his letters is dull, as are many of his poems, and parts of most of them, but—then comes the flash that rewards our patience.

3. BREADTH

But Wordsworth's narrowness has been exaggerated; he often showed surprising breadth and tolerance. Basically, his precept and practice were directed toward extending the themes of poetry to " every subject which could interest the human mind," and to a medium that was generally understood by men,[9] and not to a code known only to poets. The restricted conception that only certain subjects and types of expressions were suitable for poetry he strongly opposed. As to the purpose of poetry, he did not use " moral " in the narrow sense of conventional morality, and did not use " re-

---

[7] Under Narrative; Novel; and Mackenzie 2.

[8] Raymond Dexter Havens, *The Influence of Milton* (Cambridge, Mass., 1922), pp. 285-315, 271; see also Epic; Narrative Poetry 2; and Poetry 78.

[9] Style 6 and Subjects 2.

ligion " to refer to a special creed, or even to Christianity, when he said that Shakespeare's characters were not actuated sufficiently by religious impulses.[10] Though intolerant of triviality, superficiality, cheapness, or deliberate wrongdoing, such as the immoral teaching of Byron's works, Wordsworth had sympathy for human frailty. In fact, in the realm of moral judgments, he was at times unpredictable. Some of his translations from Chaucer, including the *Manciple's Tale*, Wordsworth withheld from publication only because several friends and relatives objected to them on moral grounds, "which though I cannot sympathize with. . . . I am bound to respect." Again, he remarked that in translating Boccaccio's tale of the illicit love of Ghismonda (Sigismonda in Dryden's version) and Guiscardo, Dryden in having the pair marry before consummating their love " has much injured the story by the marriage, and degraded Sigismunda's character by it. He has also . . . degraded her character still more by making her love absolute sensuality and appetite (Dryden has no other notion of the passion)." [11] " His tolerance of sexual irregularities shocked Miss Fenwick [and Harriet Martineau], and his apparent indifference to lying in ' Beggars ' and its sequel ' Where are they now?,' to stealing in ' The Two Thieves,' and ' The Farmer of Tilsbury Vale,' and to drunkenness in ' The Waggoner ' may have shocked others." His defence of Burns came "very near antinomianism," and his admiration for Rob Roy came very near " enjoyment of lawlessness." [12]

Wordsworth rightly believed that great art satisfies the needs of man's inner being, and that the relationship between art and life

---

[10] See under Aim of Writing; Moral Element; and Shakespeare 32.

[11] See Chaucer 15 (also 13, 14, 20, 21); and Dryden 18. The parenthetical comment on Dryden's idea of love recalls Wordsworth's marginal note (not in the catalogue) to a copy of Spenser's *Epithalamion*—see Robert Sencourt, "Letters to the Editor," *TLS*, 2517 (April 28, 1950), 261:

" All that could be wished to raise this admirable composition from its present rank, i. e., among the very best 3 or 4 odes in our language, to an undoubted supremacy is that Spenser had substituted two or three stanzas of moral tenderness from moral anticipations relative to marriage and life for two or three of the least beautiful of those relating to things and feelings purely bodily. [Mr. Sencourt adds that] He [W.] erased from the *Epithalamion* the references to Jove's amour with Alcmena and that to croaking frogs, and the charming passage which begins: ' But let still silence the true night watches keep.' "

[12] *Mind of a Poet*, pp. 147 and 154 n. 68; *Batho*, pp. 70-1.

must be close; this standard is the basis of much of his criticism, but his conception of the poet as a teacher of men never permitted him to forget that the poet must first be an artist.[13]   Neither did his conception of the poet as a teacher prevent his insistence on pleasure as an important poetic objective, though this insistence may seem especially surprising in him, for pleasure was not generally recognized as a worthy poetic purpose when Wordsworth wrote in 1800. " The Poet writes under one restriction only, namely, the necessity of giving immediate pleasure to a human Being possessed of that information which may be expected of him . . . as a Man. . . ."   The poet modifies his language because " he describes for a particular purpose, that of giving pleasure."   But do not " let this necessity of producing immediate pleasure be considered as a degradation of the Poet's art " for Wordsworth is not one to " talk of Poetry as a matter of amusement and idle pleasure. . . ."   Wordsworth partly justifies his use of meter because of the charm it lends humble subjects treated in a " naked and simple style," and, very originally, suggests that " metrical language " allows a reader to derive pleasure from strong passions, or pathetic scenes, which might be unbearable in prose. By tempering and restraining the passion, meter contributes to " The end of Poetry [which] is to produce excitement in co-existence with an overbalance of pleasure. . . ." [14]

Furthermore, few critics have been willing to admit so readily, as Wordsworth did, that age had rendered them incompetent to judge the works of younger writers, and that age was a decided deterrent to a critic's appreciation and understanding of younger artists:

I ought frankly to avow that the time is past with me for bestowing that sympathy to which they [new productions in verse] are entitled.   For many reasons connected with advanced life, I read but little of new works. . . .   But certain it is that old men's literary pleasures lie chiefly among the books they were familiar with in their youth; and this is still more pointedly true of men who have practised composition themselves.   They have fixed notions of style and of versification and their thoughts have moved on in a settled train so long that novelty in each or all of these, so far from being a recommendation, is distasteful to them, even though, if hard put to it, they might

---

[13] Under Aim of Writing, especially 7, 10, 11, 19, 28, 38A, 42; Moral Element; Dryden 18; Poetry 58, 120, 136, 138.
[14] See under Pleasure; Poetry 20; Passion 8; Versification 2.

be brought to confess that the novelty was all improvement. . . . I have many times, when called upon to give an opinion on works sent, felt obliged to recommend younger critics as more to be relied upon, and that for the reason I have mentioned.

Again:

As I advance in life I feel myself more and more incapable of doing justice to the attempts of young authors. The taste and judgment of an old man have too little of aptitude and flexibility for new things; and I am thoroughly convinced that a young writer cannot do worse than lean upon a veteran.[15]

These are not the comments of a dogmatist, though made long after that period in life when most of us have become rather arbitrary.

Wordsworth is commonly thought of as self-centered, and indifferent to the works of others. Though there is a sound basis for such an opinion, yet there is considerable evidence of his interest in poets of the past: Drayton, Daniel, Thomson, the Dyers, Collins, Lady Winchilsea, and many others. That disapproval of a poet's objectives or methods did not preclude his realizing the poet's ability is manifest in his criticism of Pope, to whom he attributed more imagination and power than to any other man of Pope's day, and whom he named among the greater English poets. Concerning writers of his own age, he recognized Tennyson as the coming poet, and, at a time when Shelley and Keats were reviled or neglected, he realized their greatness, different as their works were from his own. The irregularities of Shelley's life and opinions did not blind Wordsworth to his poetic powers. Neither did Wordsworth's moral outlook weaken his admiration for Burns, and even his objections to Byron are chiefly against the poet, as a dangerous guide and a careless workman, rather than against the man.[16] Interested as he was in the moral and spiritual well-being of man, Wordsworth at the same time managed generally to criticize on artistic rather than on moralistic grounds, and, in so far as the two attitudes blended in his views of the purpose of art and the relation of a poet to society, his criticism seems well-founded, and not the outgrowth of a narrow mind.

[15] Criticism 76, 77; see also Literature 15.
[16] See under these subjects and authors in catalogue.

4. ORIGINALITY

Wordsworth's greatness as a poet and as a critic was due in part to his independence. He thought for himself; he brushed aside the conventions of his day and dug down to first principles. His originality is best seen in the light of the hostility he aroused, especially through the Preface to *Lyrical Ballads (1800)*, which, however one-sided, is one of the really significant critical utterances made by any Englishman. A strong independent mind was needed to cut through the veil of decadent neoclassicism, which had risen after 1750 and which blurred or obscured the precepts and practices of greater writers of the past. Further, and more significantly, Wordsworth in attacking the misconceptions of certain schools of his day at the same time wisely retained the essential principles which these schools and the healthier neoclassicists held in common with important writers of all ages. His concern for the finished form, for universality, for the language of universal effectiveness and appeal, his belief that though poetry was passion it should be produced only by one who had " thought long and deeply," and his disapproval of emotional lawlessness, or his insistence on restraint in dealing with powerful emotions, are all ideas held by neoclassicists, and carried over from the best practice of previous great writers. Wordsworth also emphasized accurate observation, looking steadily at the object,—qualities usually associated with neoclassicism.[17]

But in evolving his philosophy of art, Wordsworth made three contributions, eminently original: (1) he stressed the poetic possibilities of humble and rustic life, as a source of both the subjects and the language of serious poetry; (2) he found a deep significance, and at times somewhat original themes for poetry in man's relation to nature; and (3) he emphasized more strongly than any previous writer, or critic, the place and value of the imagination in creative literature. Since in Wordsworth's views no subject or " language," either of the humble and rustic or of the more elevated social groups, had poetic force unless colored by the imagination,[18]

[17] See under Composition; Finish; Revisions; Universality; Wordiness 1 and Passion 6; Aim of Writing 10; Restraint and Love Poetry; Description and Observation.
[18] Under Imagination; Austen 1; Crabbe 1, 2, 5; W. 23; Realism.

and since nature often stimulated the imaginative faculty and almost always was modified by the imagination, we can see the close inter-relationship of these three contributions.[19]

No previous critic or poet had combined so clear a conception of the power of the imagination, and such clarification of its working processes with better poetic examples of its effects. In speaking of his intention to employ subjects and language from the humble and rustic, Wordsworth said:

The princpal object . . . proposed in these Poems was to choose incidents and situations from common life, and to relate or describe them, throughout, as far as was possible in a selection of language really used by men, and, at the same time, to throw over them a certain colouring of the imagination, whereby ordinary things should be presented to the mind in an unusual aspect.

For " the imagination [is the] . . . faculty which produces impressive effects out of simple elements." [20]

5. PENETRATION

Wordsworth's penetration and critical acumen are best shown in his prefaces, especially in the epoch-making preface to the *Lyrical Ballads*, but they may also be seen in brief passages such as this comment on Dryden:

I admire his talents and genius greatly, but he is not a poetical genius. The only qualities I can find in Dryden that are *essentially* poetical are a certain ardour and impetuosity of mind with an excellent ear: it may seem strange that I do not add to this great command of language; *that* he certainly has, and of such language, too, as it is most desirable that a Poet should possess, or rather, that he should not be without; but it is not language that is, in the high sense of the word poetical, being neither of the imagination nor of the passions; I mean of the amiable the ennobling or intense passions; I do not mean to say that there is nothing of this in Dryden, but as little . . . as is possible, considering how much he has written.

Concerning Shakespeare, Wordsworth warned against the neo-classic conception of " his wild irregular genius," and, on the other hand, attacked the romanticists' idolatry of " the unapproached first of poets." His views are a good corrective. Great artist that Shake-

---

[19] *Mind of a Poet*, pp. 88-125 and 203-65.
[20] See W. 354 and 345A; Imagination 1A.

speare was in handling and unifying his materials, and admirable as were " his imagination, his invention, and his intuitive knowledge of Human nature . . . ," " He had serious defects and not those only proceeding from carelessness. . . ." *Pericles*, he thought, should be admitted to the Shakespearean canon on internal evidence alone, though he admitted that internal evidence generally offered a very shaky basis of judgment. Furthermore, he was one of the first, after two centuries of neglect, to admire " Shakespeare's fine sonnets," and listed a number whose " merits of thought and language " impressed him.[21]

His remarks on *Ossian* reveal his acute psychological insight,[22] his powers of observation, and his ideas of artistic, imaginative descriptions of external nature:

born and reared in a mountainous country, from my very childhood I have felt the falsehood that pervades . . . *Ossian*. From what I saw with my own eyes, I knew that the imagery was spurious. In nature everything is distinct, yet nothing defined into absolute independent singleness. In Macpherson's work, it is exactly the reverse; everything (that is not stolen) is in this manner defined, insulated, dislocated, deadened,—yet nothing distinct. It will always be so when words are substituted for things.

This criticism supports part of his statement to Graves " that there were three callings for success in which Nature had furnished him with qualifications—the callings of poet, landscape-gardener, and critic of pictures and works of art." [23]

In general, his opinions on the more important writers are accurate

---

[21] Dryden 2; Shakespeare 27, 14, 32, 46, 56; Criticism 67. Shakespeare's sonnets were generally depreciated in Wordsworth's day, even by such enthusiasts as Hazlitt (*Hazlitt*, i, 357-61; vi, 175).

[22] Professors Legouis and Havens have indicated Wordsworth's power of analyzing states of mind and his absorbing interest in psychology which prompted many of his poems:

" As M. Legouis remarks, in the *Lyrical Ballads* Wordsworth ' almost gave the precedence to psychology over poetry. . . . Poetical psychology is his triumph [*CHEL*, xi, 101, and 111].' See the original preface to *The Borderers*, the 1805 note to ' The Thorn ' (which includes the striking utterance, ' Poetry is passion: it is the history or science of feelings [*Oxf. W.*, p. 899]') and the passages quoted by Legouis (trs., pp. 405-6) from the Preface to *Lyrical Ballads*. It may be significant that all of these comments were later suppressed." [*Mind of a Poet*, pp. 293-4.]

See also in the catalogue: Aim of Writing 7; Character Analysis 1-8; and Fletcher 2.

[23] See Macpherson 2; Criticism 61A.

and just, and, especially, is he able to point out the failures of men of power who did not utilize their faculties to the fullest advantage, or in the right direction. For example, he thought highly of Pope's abilities, but felt that he had been satisfied with " the Plain when the Heights were within his reach." Since poetry was passion, any evidence of insincerity on the part of a writer called down Wordsworth's strongest reproaches. This attitude governed his intense opposition to poets addicted to a " poetic diction"; their faults lay in failure to take seriously the poet's calling and his obligations to humanity.[24]

The same discriminatiton and keenness of judgment is evidenced in the catalogue under *Subjects*, where many of Wordsworth's most worthwhile opinions appear: on poetry he not only says much but is often penetrating (e. g., " Poetry is passion: it is the history or science of feelings "); on truth, observation, description, realism, and style, especially in relation to poetry, he has interesting, pertinent and original ideas; on nature he has more to say than any other English poet; on the imagination, the baffling subject concerning which his predecessors had said little that he found helpful, he displayed discerning powers of analysis, and provided excellent illustrations of its effects; on the sonnet, no previous, and few later, poets offer so much worthwhile criticism; on scholarly matters and editing (e. g., the " importance I attach to following strictly the last Copy of the text of an author "), he shows a surprising amount of interest and awareness; and on composition and revisions he reveals that he had " thought long and deeply," with respect both to style and form, for no poet had a higher regard for " the vital spirit of a perfect form," or spent more time attempting to achieve this perfection.[25] Indeed, one of his more subtle remarks is on the power of the metrical form to temper and restrain violent passion:

Now the co-presence of something regular, something to which the mind has been accustomed in various moods and in a less excited state, cannot but have great efficacy in tempering and restraining the passion by an intertexture of ordinary feeling, and of feeling not strictly and necessarily connected with the passion. [Meter makes bearable the tragic themes of ballads and

[24] In catalogue under Collins 5; Style; Aim of Writing; Moral Element and Passion.
[25] See in the catalogue under each of these headings.

the pathetic scenes of Shakespeare's plays, but a reader may be reluctant to re-persue] the distressful parts of " Clarissa Harlowe," or the " Gamester." . . . [26]

In conclusion, it is well to remember that Wordsworth never thought of himself as a critic; however, he had strong convictions on literary subjects, and he expressed them. He planned no formal system of criticism and much that he said was only explanatory of the purpose and method of his own poetic composition. He may have realized that some of his ideas were true for himself alone and were not to be imposed on other creative artists. On the other hand, his own poetic objectives and methods were usually based on broad, general laws, which he thought all writers should follow. It is these general principles which we must discover and explain if we are to understand or formulate a clear, unified conception of his critical opinions.

If, therefore, the question be asked, why we should study the critical utterances of Wordsworth, the reply might be made that his criticism is worth studying for the understanding it brings to his poetry and to all poetry, for he saw deeply into the nature and principles of the art he practised with intense devotion for over sixty years. And we hardly need to be reminded that when the poet turns critic we see more clearly into his conception of the poet's art than would be possible through the eyes of an intervening critic.

[26] See all of this passage under Versification 2.

TABLE OF ABBREVIATIONS, ETC.

A Day with Wordsworth: "A Day with Wordsworth," James Patrick Muirhead, *Blackwood's Magazine*, June, 1927, pp. 728-44.

Adv. L. B.: "Advertisement to *Lyrical Ballads*" (1798), *K. Prose*, i, 31-2.

Ans. to Mathetes: *Answer to the Letter of Mathetes* [1809], *Grosart*, i, 309-26.

App. L. B.: "Appendix to *Lyrical Ballads*" (1802), *Oxf. W.*, pp. 942-44.

Aubrey de Vere: *Aubrey de Vere*, Wilfrid Ward, London and N. Y., 1904.

Batho: The Later Wordsworth, Edith C. Batho, Cambridge, 1935. Miss Batho gives several quotations without references; when the compiler cannot find elsewhere, he refers to her work.

Biog. Lit.: *Biographia Literaria*, S. T. Coleridge, ed. J. Shawcross, 2 vols., Oxford, 1907.

Brothers Wiffen: *The Brothers Wiffen*, ed. S. R. Pattison, London, 1880.

Collier's Preface: *Seven Lectures on Shakespeare and Milton*, S. T. Coleridge, ed., with a preface, by J. Payne Collier, London, 1856.

Corr. C. R.: *The Correspondence of Henry Crabb Robinson with the Wordsworth Circle*, ed. Edith J. Morley, 2 vols., Oxford, 1927.

Corr. Taylor: *Correspondence of Henry Taylor*, ed. Edward Dowden, London, 1888.

C. Miscellaneous Criticism: *Coleridge's Miscellaneous Criticism*, ed. Thomas Middleton Raysor, Cambridge, Mass., 1936.

C. R. and T. R.: Henry Crabb and Thomas Robinson.

C. W., Jr.: "Conversations and Reminiscences recorded by the Bishop of Lincoln [Christopher Wordsworth, Jr.]," *Grosart*, iii, 458-67.

De Quincey's Reminiscences: *Literary Reminiscences*, 2 vols., Boston, 1851, vols. [v and vi] in *Thomas De Quincey's Writings*, ed. J. T. Fields, [24 vols.], Boston, 1850-72.

De Quincey's Letters to a Young Man: "Letters to a Young Man whose Education has been Neglected," *De Quincey's Writings*, [xv].

De Quincey's Essays on the Poets: *Essays on the Poets*, vol. [ix], in *De Quincey's Writings*.

De Sel.: Ernest de Selincourt.

De Vere: "Recollections of Aubrey de Vere," *Grosart*, iii, 486-99.

De Vere's Essays: *Essays, Chiefly on Poetry*, Aubrey de Vere, 2 vols., London, 1887.

De Vere's Recollections: *Recollections of Aubrey de Vere*, Aubrey de Vere, New York, 1897.

Diary of W. Scott: "Anecdote of Crabbe. From 'Diary of Sir Walter Scott,'" *Grosart*, iii, 503-4.

Early Wordsworth: *The Early Wordsworth*, Ernest de Selincourt, Presidential Address to The English Association, London, November, 1936.

E. L.: *The Early Letters of William and Dorothy Wordsworth* (*1787-1805*), ed. E. de Selincourt, Oxford, 1935.

English Traits: *English Traits*, Ralph Waldo Emerson, ed. E. W. Emerson, Boston and New York, 1903.

Epitaphs (1): *Oxf. W.*, pp. 928-33.

Epitaphs (2): *Grosart*, ii, 41-59.

Epitaphs (3): *Grosart*, ii, 60-75.

E. Q.: Edward Quillinan.

Essays in Criticism: *Essays in Criticism*, second series, Matthew Arnold, New York, 1924.

xxiii

E. Supp. Pref.: "Essay, Supplementary to *The Preface*," (1815), *Oxf. W.*, pp. 944-53.
Exc.: The Excursion, Oxf. W., pp. 756-896.
Farington Diary: The Farington Diary, Joseph Farington, ed. James Greig, 8 vols., London, 1922-28.
Gladstone: Life of William Ewart Gladstone, John Morley, 3 vols., New York, 1903.
Graves: "Reminiscences of the Rev. R. P. Graves," "On the Death of Coleridge," and "Further Reminiscences and Memorabilia, by R. P. Graves," *Grosart*, iii, 467-75.
Graves's Recollections: "Recollections of Wordsworth and the Lake Country," Robert Perceval Graves, *The Afternoon Lectures on Literature and Art*, Dublin, 1869.
Greville Memoirs: The Greville Memoirs 1814-60, ed. by L. Strachey and Roger Fulford, 8 vols., London, 1938.
Grosart: The Prose Works of William Wordsworth, ed. Alexander B. Grosart, 3 vols., London, 1876.
Hamilton: Life of William Rowan Hamilton, R. P. Graves, 3 vols., Dublin, 1882-89.
Haydon: The Autobiography and Memoirs of Benjamin Robert Haydon, 1786-1846, ed. Tom Taylor. New Edition with Introduction by Aldous Huxley, 2 vols., London, 1926.
Hazlitt: The Collected Works of William Hazlitt, ed. Waller and Glover, 12 vols., London, 1905.
H. C. R.: Henry Crabb Robinson on Books and Their Writers, ed. Edith J. Morley, 3 vols., London, 1938.
Henry Taylor: Autobiography of Sir Henry Taylor, 2 vols., London, 1885.
Hunt: The Autobiography of Leigh Hunt, 2 vols., New York, 1850.
I. F.: "Isabella Fenwick Notes," *Grosart*, iii, 3-211.
J. J. Tayler: "From Letters of Professor Tayler," *Grosart*, iii, 502-3.
Journals: Journals of Dorothy Wordsworth, ed. E. de Selincourt, 2 vols., New York, 1941.
Justice Coleridge: "Personal Reminiscences of the Hon. Mr. Justice Coleridge," *Grosart*, iii, 423-33.
K. and W. Railway: Kendal and Windermere Railway: two letters reprinted from the *Morning Post*, *Grosart*, ii, 321-41.
Knight: The Poetical Works of William Wordsworth, ed. William Knight, 8 vols., London, 1896.
K. Prose: Prose Works of William Wordsworth, ed. William Knight, 2 vols., London, 1896.
Lakes: A Guide through the District of the Lakes, Grosart, ii, 215-319.
L.: Letters. All letters are from de Selincourt's six volume edition, unless otherwise indicated.
Lady R., and *Mrs. D.*: "Reminiscences of Lady Richardson and Mrs. Davy," *Grosart*, iii, 435-58.
Letters (Coleridge): Letters of Samuel Taylor Coleridge, ed. Ernest Hartley Coleridge, 2 vols., Boston and New York, 1895.
Letters K.: Letters of the Wordsworth Family, ed. William Knight, 3 vols., Boston and London, 1907.
Letters of Scott: Familiar Letters of Sir Walter Scott, ed. David Douglas, 2 vols., Boston, 1894.
Life of Alaric Watts: Alaric Watts, Mrs. Alaric Watts, London, 1884.
Life of Dickens: Life of Charles Dickens. R. Shelton Mackenzie, Philadelphia, 1870.
Life of Southey: The Life and Correspondence of Robert Southey, ed. Charles Cuthbert Southey, 6 vols., London, 1850.
L. of Coleridge: Unpublished Letters of Samuel Taylor Coleridge, ed. Earl Leslie Griggs, 2 vols., London, 1932.

L. of Keats: The Letters of John Keats, ed. Maurice Buxon Forman, 2nd ed. (enlarged), London, 1935.

L. of Lamb: The Letters of Charles and Mary Lamb, ed. E. V. Lucas, 3 vols., London, 1935.

L. of W. Family: Some Letters of the Wordsworth Family, ed. Leslie Nathan Broughton, Ithaca, N. Y., 1942.

Longman MSS: A Description of the Wordsworth and Coleridge Manuscripts in the Possession of Mr. T. Norton Longman, ed. W. Hale White, New York and Bombay, 1897.

L. Sara Coleridge: Memoir and Letters of Sara Coleridge, ed. by her daughter, 2 vols., London, 1873.

L. to Friend of Burns: A Letter to a Friend of Robert Burns, Grosart, ii, 5-19.

Literary Veteran: Memoirs of a Literary Veteran, R. P. Gillies, 3 vols., London, 1851.

L. Y.: The Letters of William and Dorothy Wordsworth, The Later Years (1821-50), ed. E. de Selincourt, 3 vols., Oxford, 1939.

Martineau Autobiography: Harriet Martineau's Autobiography, ed. Maria W. Chapman, 2 vols., Boston, 1877.

Maurice: The Life of Frederick Denison Maurice, Frederick Maurice, with notes by Sir E. Strachey, 2 vols., New York, 1884.

Memoirs: Memoirs of William Wordsworth, Christopher Wordsworth, 2 vols., Boston, 1851.

Memoir of C. M. Young: A Memoir of Charles Mayne Young, Tragedian, With Extracts from his Son's Journal, Julian Charles Young, 2 vols., London and N. Y., 1871.

Memoirs of E. V. Kenealy: Memoirs of Edward Vaughan Kenealy, ed. Arabella Kenealy, London, 1908.

Memoirs of Scott: Memoirs of the Life of Sir Walter Scott, J. G. Lockhart, 2nd ed., Edinburgh, 1842.

Moore's Diary: Tom Moore's Diary, ed. J. B. Priestley, Cambridge, 1925.

Mrs. D.: see *Lady R.,* above.

Mrs. Fletcher: Autobiography, Edinburgh, 1874.

Mrs. Hemans: Memorials of Mrs. Hemans, Henry F. Chorley, 2 vols., N. Y. and London, 1836.

M. Y.: The Letters of William and Dorothy Wordsworth, The Middle Years (1806-20), ed. E. de Selincourt, 2 vols., Oxford, 1937.

Mind of a Poet: The Mind of a Poet, Raymond Dexter Havens, Baltimore, 1941.

Old Friends: Memories of Old Friends, being Extracts from the Journals and Letters of Caroline Fox, ed. Horace N. Pym, second edition (enlarged), Philadelphia, 1884.

Oxf. W.: The Poetical Works of William Wordsworth, ed. Thomas Hutchinson, Oxford, 1933. Titles of all poems in the catalogue will be in italics; first lines in quotation marks.

Postscript (1835): "Postscript, 1835," *Oxf. W.,* pp. 959-66.

Pref. 1815: Preface to *Poems* (1815), *Oxf. W.,* pp. 954-58.

Pref. L. B.: Preface to *Lyrical Ballads* (1800), *Oxf. W.,* pp. 934-42.

Pref. Exc.: Preface to *The Excursion* (1814), *Oxf. W.,* pp. 754-55.

Prel.: The Prelude, *Oxf. W.,* pp. 631-752; all references to 1850 text are to this edition.

Prel.: The Prelude, ed. Ernest de Selincourt, Oxford, 1926; used for references to the various MSS other than the 1850 text.

Reed: Wordsworth and Reed, The Poet's Correspondence with his American Editor: 1836-50, ed. L. N. Broughton, Ithaca, N. Y., 1933.

Remains: Blake, Coleridge, Wordsworth, Lamb, etc., being Selections from the Remains of Henry Crabb Robinson, ed. Edith J. Morley, Manchester, 1932.

Rogers and his Contemporaries: Rogers and his Contemporaries, Peter W. Clayden, 2 vols., London, 1889.

Reminiscences of S. and C.: Reminiscences of Samuel Taylor Coleridge and Robert Southey, Joseph Cottle, New York, 1847.

Sara Coleridge and Reed: Sara Coleridge and Reed, ed. L. N. Broughton, Cornell Studies in English, XXVII, Ithaca, N. Y., 1937.

Smith: The Poems of William Wordsworth, ed. N. C. Smith, 3 vols., London, 1908.

Table-Talk of Rogers: Recollections of the Table-Talk of Samuel Rogers, compiled by Alexander Dyce, New York, 1856.

Tennyson: Alfred Lord Tennyson—a Memoir, by His Son [Hallam Tennyson], 2 vols., New York, 1897.

Thomas Cooper: The Life of Thomas Cooper, written by himself, 2nd ed., London, 1872.

Trelawny: Recollections of the Last Days of Shelley and Byron, E. J. Trelawny, 2nd ed., London, 1859.

W.'s Works: Wordsworth's Poetical Works, ed. E. de Selincourt, Oxford, vol. I (1940), and vol. II (1944).

Whately: Personal and Family Glimpses of Remarkable People, Edward Whately, London, 1889.

W. W., C. W., C. W., Jr., Dora W. (Dora Quillinan after May 11, 1941), D. W., J. W., M. W., R. W: William, Christopher, Christopher, Jr., Dora, Dorothy, John, Mary, and Richard Wordsworth.

Yesterdays with Authors: Yesterdays with Authors, James T. Fields, Boston and New York, 1900.

* : an asterisk indicates that Wordsworth's opinion was recorded by others.

Where exact dates are available, the month will be indicated by a Roman numeral (e. g., September 13, 1818 will appear as IX. 13, 1818).

[ ]: Brackets are used in the conventional manner to indicate material supplied by previous editors or by the present compiler, and especially for paraphrases, which have been resorted to as little as possible and within which have been preserved many of Wordsworth's words and expressions, though usually without quotation marks.

1843 [K.]: Additional Fenwick notes in *Knight*.

PART ONE

SUBJECTS

SUBJECTS

Abstract, The. See under Abstractions

Abstractions. See Metaphysical. Contrast Realism; Sensitiveness
to Sense Impressions

1. See Imagination 33G, 34, 35; Poetry 58; Archimedes 1

2. [Abstract character of his poetry.] . . . my wish is, to be read as widely
as is consistent with reasonable pecuniary return. . . . That is the place [the
heart] I would fain occupy among the People of these Islands. And I am not
at all sure that the abstract character of no small portion of my own poetry
will at all stand in the way of that result. Though it would in *itself* recommend them to the mass of the people. *To Moxon,*   II. 5, 1838

3.   . . . So was it then with me, and so will be
                  With Poets ever. Mighty is the charm
                  Of those abstractions to a mind beset
                  With images, and haunted by herself,
                  And specially delightful unto me
                  Was that clear synthesis built up aloft
                  So gracefully. . . .
                  Prel., vi, 157-63.   1804-39

Abuse. See under Criticism, Effect of

Accidents. See Imagination 32A; Nature 20; Poetry 111; Realism
52; also under Incidents. Contrast Universality

Accuracy. See Description; Diction; Nature (External); Realism;
Style; Truth

1. See De Vere, Sir Aubrey 1; Dryden 17B; Hamilton, W. R. 4

Action. See also Plot; Subjects

1. See Imagination 32A; Passion 7, 31; Poetry 78; Coleridge 61B;
Lyttleton 1; W. 20, 21, 195, 202, 204

Adverse Self-criticism. See under Criticism, Unfavorable Self-

Affections. See under Passion

Aim of Writing. See Moral Element; Pleasure;

1. See W. 17, 23, 28, 43-4, 48-9, 67, 91, 117, 124, 166, 169, 173, 176,
202, 204-5, 232-3, 255, 287, 300A, 311, 331, 339-40, 345A, 346, 350A,
352-6, 364, 368A-69, 372, 385-6, 392, 395-6, 403-4

3

2.   See Abstractions 2; Ballads 3; Books 28; Composition 13, 14; Gardening 1; Passion 7, 8, 43; Periodical Planning 1, 2; Pleasure 2; Poetry 20, 21, 75, 138, 139; Realism 52; Style 1, 6; Versification 2

3.   We must then look for protection entirely amongst the dispassionate advocates of liberty and discussion. These, whether male or female, we must either amuse or instruct; nor will our end be fully obtained unless we do both. *To Mathews,*   VI, 1794

4.   See Burns 26; Crabbe 12; Pope 19; Reynolds, J. 3; Scott, W, 23; Spenser 21-2; Tennyson 8; Wieland 2

7.   I have also informed my reader what this purpose will be found principally to be: namely, to illustrate the manner in which our feelings and ideas are associated in a state of excitement. But speaking in language somewhat more appropriate, it is to follow the fluxes and refluxes of the mind when agitated by the great and simple affections of our nature. This object I have endeavoured in these short essays to attain by various means; by tracing the maternal passion through many of its more subtle windings, as in the poems of *The Idiot Boy* and *The Mad Mother* [in the editions of 1836-43, W. writes, " and the one beginning ' Her eyes are wild ' "]; by accompanying the last struggles of a human being, at the approach of death, cleaving in solitude to life and society, as in the Poem of the Forsaken Indian; by showing, as in the stanzas entitled *We are Seven*, the perplexity and obscurity which in childhood attend our notion of death, or rather our utter inability to admit that notion; or by displaying the strength of fraternal, or to speak more philosophically, of moral attachment when early associated with the great and beautiful objects of nature, as in *The Brothers*; or, as in the incident of Simon Lee, by placing my reader in the way of receiving from moral sensations another and more salutary impression than we are accustomed to receive from them. It has also been part of my general purpose to attempt to sketch characters under the influence of less impassioned feelings as in the *Two April Mornings, The Fountain, The Old Man Travelling, The Two Thieves,* etc., characters of which the elements are simple, belonging rather to nature than to manners, such as exist now, and will probably always exist, and which from their constitution may be distinctly and profitably contemplated. . . . it is proper that I should mention one other circumstance [see under Passion 7] . . . feeling. My meaning will be rendered perfectly intelligible by referring my Reader to the Poems entitled *Poor Susan* and the *Childless Father*, particularly the last stanza of the latter Poem.
Pref. L. B. (K. Prose, i, 50-1).   1800-1836

10.   From such verses [see Poetry 17] the Poems in these volumes will be found distinguished at least by one mark of difference, that each of them has a worthy *purpose*. Not that I always began to write with a distinct purpose formally conceived; but habits of meditation have, I trust, so prompted and regulated my feelings, that my descriptions of such objects as strongly excite those feelings, will be found to carry along with them a *purpose*. If this opinion be erroneous, I can have little right to the name of a Poet. For all good poetry is the spontaneous overflow of powerful feelings: and though this be true, Poems to which any value can be attached were never produced

on any variety of subjects but by a man who, being possessed of more than usual organic sensibility, had also thought long and deeply. For our continued influxes of feeling are modified and directed by our thoughts, which are indeed the representatives of all our past feelings; and, as by contemplating the relation of these general representatives to each other, we discover what is really important to men, so, by the repetition and continuance of this act, our feelings will be connected with important subjects, till at length, if we be originally possessed of much sensibility, such habits of mind will be produced, that, by obeying blindly and mechanically the impulses of those habits, we shall describe objects, and utter sentiments, of such a nature, and in such connexion with each other, that the understanding of the Reader must necessarily be in some degree enlightened, and his affections strengthened and purified. *Pref. L. B.*, p. 935. 1800

11. But, as the pleasure which I hope to give by the Poems [*L. B.* (1800)] now presented to the Reader must depend entirely on just notions upon this subject, and, as it is in itself of high importance to our taste and moral feelings, I cannot content myself with these detached remarks. . . . whatever be the language outwardly holden by men, a practical faith in the opinions which I am wishing to establish is almost unknown. If my conclusions are admitted, and carried as far as they must be carried if admitted at all, our judgments concerning the works of the greatest Poets both ancient and modern will be far different from what they are at present, both when we praise, and when we censure: and our moral feelings influencing and influenced by these judgments will, I believe, be corrected and purified. *Pref. L. B.*, p. 937. 1800

13. And this leads me to what gave me great concern, I mean the very unreasonable value which you set upon my writings, compared with those of others. You are young and ingenuous, and I wrote with a hope of pleasing the young, the ingenuous and the unworldly, above all others; but sorry indeed should I be to stand in the way of the proper influence of other writers. You will know that I allude to the great names of past times, and above all to those of our own Country.

I have taken the liberty of saying this much to hasten on the time when you will value my poems not less, but those of others, more.
To De Quincey. VII. 29, 1803

15. [Trusted] that I might leave
    Some monument behind me which pure hearts
    Should reverence.
    Prel., vi, 54-7. 1804-39

16. [He will teach and inspire through his treatment of nature and the]
        very heart of man,
    As found among the best of those who live,
    Not unexalted by religious faith,
    Not uninformed by books, good books, though few. . . .
    Prel., xiii, 241-4 (see also 224-56). 1804-39

18. Trouble not yourself upon their [*Poems in Two Volumes*, 1807] present reception; of what moment is that compared with what I trust is their

destiny, to console the afflicted, to add sunshine to daylight by making the happy happier, to teach the young and the gracious of every age, to see, to think and feel, and therefore to become more actively and securely virtuous; this is their office, which I trust they will faithfully perform long after we (that is, all that is mortal of us) are mouldered in our graves. I am well aware how for it would seem to many I overrate my own exertions. . . .
To Lady Beaumont,   V. 21, 1807

19. Every great Poet is a Teacher: I wish either to be considered as a Teacher, or as nothing. *To Beaumont,*   I or II, 1808

21. . . . the Convention of Cintra . . . is in my mind, an action dwelt upon only for the sake of illustrating principles, with a view to promote liberty and good policy; in the manner in which an anatomist illustrates the laws of organic life from a human subject placed before him and his audience.
To D. Stuart,   III. 26, 1809

22.* [Wordsworth resolved] to write upon public affairs in the *Courier*, or some other newspaper, for the sake of getting money; not wholly, however, on that account, for unless he were animated by the importance of his subject and the hope of being of use he could do nothing in that way.
D. W. to De Quincey,   V. 1, 1809

23. [The origin of epitaphs.] And, verily without the consciousness of a principle of immortality in the human soul, Man could never have had awakened in him the desire to live in the remembrance of his fellows: mere love, or the yearning of kind towards kind, could not have produced it. [See *Oxf. W.*, pp. 928-29 for an amplification of the principle of immortality, and its relation to the origin of epitaphs] . . . Accordingly, recurring to the twofold desire of guarding the remains of the deceased and preserving their memory, it may be said that a sepulchral monument is a tribute to a man as a human being; and that an epitaph (in the ordinary meaning attached to the word) includes this general feeling and something more; and is a record to preserve the memory of the dead, as a tribute due to his individual worth, for a satisfaction to the sorrowing hearts of the survivors, and for the common benefit of the living: which record is to be accomplished, not in a general manner, but, where it can, in *close connexion with the bodily remains of the deceased.* . . . *Epitaph 1* (*Oxf. W.*, pp. 928-29).   1810

26.   As to my occupations they look little at the present age—but I live in hope of leaving some thing behind me, that by some minds will be valued. *To F. Wrangham,*   early spring, 1812

27.   Of Poesy thus courteously employed
           In framing models to improve the scheme
           Of Man's existence, and recast the world. . . .
           Exc., iii, 335-7.   1814

28. . . . innumerable analogues and types of infinity, insensible to the countless awakenings to noble aspiration, which I have transferred into that poem [*Excursion*] from the Bible of the Universe, as it speaks to the ear of the intelligent; as it lies open to the eyes of the humbleminded. . . .
To Mrs. Clarkson (Corr. C. R., i, 78-9),   1814

29. I am sending to the press a collection of poems, that conclude the third and *last* Vol: of my miscellaneous pieces.—In more than one passage their publication will evince my wish to uphold the cause of Christianity. *To Haydon,*   I. 24, 1820

30.   Go forth, my little Book! pursue thy way;
             Go forth, and please the gentle and the good;
             Nor be a whisper stifled, if it say
             That treasures, yet untouched, may grace some future Lay.
             Desultory Stanzas, 87-90.   1822

31.   If these brief Records, by the Muses' art
             Produced as lonely Nature or the strife
             That animates the scenes of public life
             Inspired, may in thy leisure claim a part;
             And if these Transcripts of the private heart
             Have gained a sanction from thy falling tears;
             Then I repent not.
             " If these brief Records," 1-7.   1827

33. It is gratifying to one whose aim as an author has been to reach the hearts of his fellow-creatures of all ranks and in all stations to find that he has succeeded in any quarter; and still more must he be gratified to learn that he has pleased in a distant country men of simple habits and cultivated taste, who are at the same time widely acquainted with literature. *Reed,* p. 4.
                                                                    VIII. 19, 1837

34.   [Hopes] to enshrine in Verse
             Accordant meditations, which in times
             Vexed and disordered, as our own, may shed
             Influence, at least among a scattered few,
             To soberness of mind and peace of heart
             Friendly. . . .
             Aquapendente, 363-8.   1837

36.   You tell me that my writings have been your comfort and solace in sickness and affliction; it was kind in you to do so; for I meet with no reward comparable to such assurances. *To Mrs. J. M. Muleen,* III. 28, 1838

37.   My last words let them be—
             If in this book [*Sonnets,* 1838] Fancy and Truth agree;
             If simple Nature trained by careful Art
             Through It have won a passage to thy heart;
             Grant me thy love, I crave no other fee!
             " Serving no haughty Muse," 10-14.   1838

38A. [Poetry should put forth great truths.] See Moral Elements 22

39.* It was long . . . before he had ventured to hope himself a poet; from the beginning he felt his own poetic vocation to be the expounding of the symbolic Bible of nature. *Aubrey de Vere,* p. 69.   III. 9, 1841

40.* . . . spoke with contempt of A. B.'s low ambition [to make money by his writing]. *Aubrey de Vere,* pp. 69-70.   III. 9, 1841

42.* Once he said to me, ' It is indeed a deep satisfaction to hope and

2

believe that my poetry will be, while it lasts, a help to the cause of virtue and truth—especially among the young. As for myself, it seems now of little moment how long I may be remembered.
De Vere (*Grosart*, iii, 493).   1842-46

46.* He spoke with much regret of Scott's careless views about money, and said that he had often spoken to him of the duty of economy, as a means to insure literary independence. Scott's reply always was, ' Oh, I can make as much as I please by writing.' ' This,' said Mr. W., ' was marvellous to me, who had never written a line with a view to profit.'
Mrs. D. (*Grosart*, iii, 457).   I. 10, 1849

Alexandrines. See Versification 11, 12

Allegory. See Criticism 82; Imagination 33G; Spenser 21

Alterations. See under Composition; Revisions

Alliteration

1. *By* is certainly a better word than *through* [" By Art's bold privilege "], but I fear it cannot be employed on account of the subsequent line, ' But, *by* the Chieftain's look.'
To me the two ' bys ' clash both to the ear and understanding, and it was on that account I changed the word. I have also a slight objection to the alliteration ' By bold ' occurring so soon. *To Haydon*,   IX. 10, 1840

2. See Shakespeare 55

Analysis. See Reason

Ancients and Moderns. See Primitivism; Progress

***Ancient Writers* (Classical).** See under Authors and Works (Second Section)

Animation. See under Passion; Vigor

Anonymity

1. Two rules *we* ought to lay down; never to retort by attacking private character, and never to notice the particulars of a personal calumny, or any allegation of a personal nature proceeding from an anonymous quarter. We ought to content ourselves by protesting in the strongest terms against the practice, and pointing it out to indignation and contempt. *To ?*, X. 6, 1818

2. See Oxford Movement 2; Satire 7

Annuals. See also Books; Periodicals

1. See Hervey 2; Rogers 7

2. Alan Cunningham talked about making his Annual reflect the Literature of the Age—and Southey told him . . . the best you can make of these things, is picturebooks for grown Children.—I am something of his mind. . . . *To Reynolds*,   I. 28, 1829

Anthologies. See Anderson; Chalmers; Chambers: Dyce

1. See Thornton, B. 1

2. As to the Selection [i. e. the selection of W.'s poems made by Hine, *v.* Letter 971, De Sel.], I think you are a little too sanguine: a Collection from different Authors will always be preferred for schools, and if well done ought to be. *To Moxon,*　　　　　　　　　　　　　　　　　　　V. 14, 1833

3. The subject which I had thought of is much more limited than you suppose—being nothing more than an Account of the Deceased Poetesses of Great Britain—with an Estimate of their Works—but upon more mature Reflection I cannot persuade myself that it is sufficiently interesting for a separate subject, were I able to do it justice. The Dramatic and other imaginative female Writers might be added—the interest would thereby be encreased, but unity of subject would be sacrificed. . . .

I still am of opinion that something is wanted upon the subject—neither Dr. Johnson, nor Dr. Anderson, nor Chalmers, nor the Editor I believe of any other Corpus of English Poetry takes the least notice of female Writers—this, to say nothing harsher, is very ungallant. The best way of giving a comprehensive interest to the subject would be to begin with Sappho and proceed downwards through Italy antient and Modern, Spain, Germany, France and England. . . . *To D. Lardner,*　　　　　　　　　I. 12, 1838

Anthropomorphism. See Imagination 33 G

Anti-intellectualism. See under Intellect

Antiquarianism. See Camden Society 1; Poetry 128; W. 198

Antique Style

1. See Coleridge 59, 61

2. [In Chaucerian translations some] sprinklings of antiquity would be admitted, by persons of taste, to have a graceful accordance with the subject. *Grosart,* iii, 185.　　　　　　　　　　　　　　　　　　　　1820

Anti-rationalism. See under Reason

Anti-realism. See under Realism

Antithesis. See also Imagery; Style

1. . . . unmeaning antithesis [in Pope's epitaphs]. *Epitaph 3* (*Grosart,* ii, 60).　　　　　　　　　　　　　　　　　　　　　　　　　1810

2. See Byron 6A; Gillies 6; Lyttleton 1; Winchilsea 5

Aposthrophe, The

1. See Elegy 2; Armstrong 1; Rogers 2

Arrangement, Basis of

1. [Of poems.] See Imagination 48; Poetry 49, 58, 113-4, 134, 139; Hervey 2; W. 167, 194, 205, 322, 340, 383, 388-90A

2. [Of letters.] See Montagu, B. 3

Art.   See Composition; Practice; Revisions; Rules; Style

1.   [An author's] endeavor to excite admiration of himself by arts [indicates the meanness of the subject]. See Poetry 21

2.   . . . the outward help of art can facilitate the progress of nature. . . . *Ans. to Mathetes* (*Grosart*, i, 324).   1810

4.   [Lack of art and training forces many poets of nature to remain inarticulate.] See Poetry 65

5.   [W. removed from "Lucy Gray"] all that pertained to art. . . . *H. C. R.*, i, 190. IX. 11, 1816

6.   See Aim of Writing 37; Biography 2A; Copyright 4; Creative 3; Nature 16; Poetry 126; Rules 13; Taste 11; Versification 2; Gillies 5; Godwin, C. Grace 1; Gomm 1; Gray 6; Hamilton, Eliza M. 1, 3, 4; Hamilton, W. R. 4; W. 117

7.   . . . rules of art and workmanship . . . must be applied to imaginative literature, however high the subject, if it is to be permanently efficient. *To Hayward*,   1828

13.   [Practice will supply skill in workmanship.] See Practice 6

Artificial, The.   See "Poetic Diction" under Style

1.   [Manufactured lines.] See Blank Verse and Rhyme 1

1A.   [Artifices.] See Taste 11; Milton 53

2.   See Imagery 5; Goethe 7; W. 242

3.   [Artificial *vs.* artful.] See Brydges, E. 1

4.   . . . structure of the Sonnet is so artificial. *To C. R.* (*Corr. C. R.*, i, 354),   II, 1838

Artistical.   See W. 135

Artful.   See under Art; Brydges, E. 1

Authority.   See Ancient Writers; Imitation; Models; Rules

1.   See Criticism 49; Reynolds, J. 3; W. 355

Authors, Self-confidence of.   See also under Criticism: The Author
as Self-critic

1.   . . . nothing but confidence and resolution is necessary. *To W. Matthews*,   V, 17, 1792

2.   [To make alterations, a poet must have considerable faith in his own judgment.] See W. 355

Authors: Modern.   See under Literature, Opinion of Modern

Author vs. Critic.   See Criticism 39A; W. 189, 355

Authors: Women

1.   Female authorship is to be shunned. . . . See Hamilton, Eliza M. 4

2.   See Hemans, Felicia 1A; Thornton, B. 1

3. [Anthology] of Deceased Poetesses of Great Britain [needed, as Johnson, Anderson, Chalmers, and others have taken no notice of women writers]. See Anthologies 3

4. . . . dislike of Literary Ladies. . . . See Sedgewick 1

5. Women observe many particulars of manners and opinions [that escape the notice of men]. *To Moxon,*   X, 1, 1846

Autobiographical Element in an Author's Work. See Biography; Letters; Burns, R.; Field, B.

Autobiography. See under Biography

Baldness. See also Style

1. . . . in which I include all that takes from dignity. . . . See Translation 4

2. See Virgil 10

Ballads. See also under Percy

1. The meter of the old ballads is very artless. . . . See Versification 2

2. See Books 10; Poetry 69; Scotch Writers 2; Hogg 2; Percy 1; Pope 1A; W. 142

3. [Wordsworth recommends religious books for the poor, but finds some ballads hawked among them are good, though not religious; he objects to many] either for the superstition in them (such as prophecies, fortune-telling, etc.) or more frequently for indelicacy. [He admits, however, that he has] so much felt the influence of these straggling papers, that I have many a time wished I had talents to produce songs, poems, and little histories, that might circulate among other good things in this way. . . . Indeed, some of the Poems which I have published were composed, not without a hope that at some time or other they might answer this purpose. *To Wrangham* (pp. 223-4),   VI. 5, 1808

Beautiful, The. See Picturesque 3; Dryden 14

Beauty. See Passion 27; Reason 31; Subjects 17

Biographical Criticism. See Criticism, Biographical

Biography

1. See Knowledge 6; Moral Element 17; Poetry 20; Allsop 1; Burns 16-18; Currie 2; De Quincey 7; Dyer, G. 1; Lockhart 1, 2

2. [(A) Biography of intimate details.] . . . biography, though differing in some essentials from works of fiction, is nevertheless, like them, an *art,*—an art, the laws of which are determined by the imperfections of our nature, and the constitution of society. Truth is not here, as in the sciences, and in natural philosophy, to be sought without scruple, and promulgated for its own sake, upon the mere chance of its being serviceable; but only for obviously justifying purposes, moral or intellectual.

[Silence about the dead may be broken to prevent the suppression of profitable truth. The modern taste seeks for all the most intimate facts about an author, and is losing the balance between the claims of the deceased and the claims of the world to knowledge about the deceased.] Intelligent lovers of freedom are from necessity bold and hardy lovers of truth; but, according to the measure in which their love is intelligent, is it attended with a finer discrimination, and a more sensitive delicacy. The wise and good . . . respect, as one of the noblest characteristics of Englishmen, that jealousy of familiar approach. . . . [It is not necessary for the biographer of an author to pry into the life of his subject, as becomes necessary to the biographer of a statesman or leader whose public conduct can be explained only through weighing his good and bad qualities.] Our business is with their books,— to understand and to enjoy them. And, of poets more especially, it is true—that, if their works be good, they contain within themselves all that is necessary to their being comprehended and relished. It should seem that the ancients thought in this manner; for of the eminent Greek and Roman poets, few and scanty memorials were . . . ever prepared; and fewer still are preserved. It is delightful to read what, in the happy exercise of his own genius, Horace chooses to communicate of himself and his friends; but I confess I am not so much a lover of knowledge, independent of its quality, as to make it likely that it would much rejoice me, were I to hear that records of the Sabine poet and his contemporaries, composed upon the Boswellian plan, had been unearthed among the ruins of Herculaneum. You will interpret what I am writing, *liberally*. With respect to the light which such a discovery might throw upon Roman manners there would be reasons to desire it; but I should dread to disfigure the beautiful ideal of the memories of those illustrious persons with incongruous features, and to sully the imaginative purity of their classical works with gross and trivial recollections. The least weighty objection to heterogeneous details, is that they are mainly superfluous, and therefore an incumbrance. [(B) Biography of an objective writer.] . . . it is comparatively of little importance, while we are engaged in reading the *Iliad*, the *Eneid*, the tragedies of *Othello* and *King Lear*, whether the authors of these poems were good or bad men; whether they lived happily or miserably. Should a thought of the kind cross our minds, there would be no doubt, if irresistible external evidence did not decide the question unfavourably, that men of such transcendant genius were both good and happy: and if, unfortunately, it had been on record that they were otherwise, sympathy with the fate of their fictitious personages would banish the unwelcome truth whenever it obtruded itself, so that it would but slightly disturb our pleasure. [(C) Biography of a subjective writer.] Far otherwise is it with that class of poets, the principal charm of whose writings depends upon the familiar knowledge which·they convey of the personal feelings of their authors. This is eminently the case with the effusions of Burns;—in the small quantity of narrative that he has given, he himself bears no inconsiderable part, and he has produced no drama. Neither the subjects of his poems, nor his manner of handling them, allow us long to forget their author. On the basis of his human character he has reared a poetic one, which with more or less distinctness presents itself to view in almost every part of his earlier, and, in my estimation, his most valuable verses. This poetic fabric, dug out of the quarry of genuine human-ity, is airy and spiritual:—and though the materials, in some parts, are coarse, and the disposition is often fantastic and irregular, yet the whole is agreeable and strikingly attractive. Plague, then, upon your remorseless hunters after matter of fact (who, after all, rank among the blindest of human beings) when they would convince you that the foundations of this admirable edifice are hollow; and that its frame is unsound! Granting that all which has been raked up to the prejudice of Burns were literally true; and that it added, which it does not, to our better understanding of human nature and human life (for that genius is not incompatible with vice, and that vice leads to misery—the more acute from the sensibilities which are the elements of genius—we needed not those communications to inform us) how poor would have been the compensation for the deduction made, by this extrinsic knowl-edge, from the intrinsic efficacy of his poetry—to please, and to instruct! See Poetry 99. *L. to Friend of Burns* (*Grosart*, ii, 10-13). 1816

5. Poetically treated he [the Duke of Wellington] may pass for a Hero; and on that account I less regret what I wrote to you. But to the searching eye of the Historian, and still more of the Biographer, he will, I apprehend, appear as a man below the circumstances in which he moved. *To J. Scott,* II. 25, 1816

8. . . . nothing could be more bare of entertainment or interest than a biographical notice of me must prove if true. I referred him to Gagliani's [*sic*] Ed: which, as to the date and place of my birth, and the places of my education is correct—the date of my publications is easily procured—and beyond these I really see nothing that the world has to do with, in my life which has been so retired and uniform. *To S. C. Hall,* I. 15, 1837

10. Of idolatrous Biography I think very lightly. . . . See Gillman 1

11. [Autobiographical element in *The Prelude* prevents W. from pub-lishing it. See also W. 306, 311, 317.] *To T. Talfourd,* IV, 11, 1839

12. [Objections to publication of Barron Field's *Memoirs of the Life and Poetry of W. W.*, now in British Museum (MS add. 41325-7. De Sel.).] See Field, B. 3, 4

13. [Suggestion for collections of brief biographies of talented, but little known men.] See Way, B. 1

Blank Verse and Rhyme. See also Versification

1. Dr. Johnson observed, that in blank verse, the language suffered more distortion to keep it out of prose than any inconvenience to be apprehended from the shackles and circumspection of rhyme. This kind of distortion is the worst fault that poetry can have; for if once the natural order and con-nection of the words is broken, and the idiom of the language violated, the lines appear manufactured, and lose all that character of enthusiasm and inspiration, without which they become cold and insipid, how sublime soever the ideas and the images may be which they express. [*Alfoxden MS Notebook*, 1798. De Sel.] *Prel.* (De Sel.), p. xxx. n. 2. 1798

2.*   . . . nothing, especially for a poem of any continuance, was equal to blank verse. *Collier's Preface*, p. liii.   II. 10, 1814

Blasphemous Writings.   See also Moral Element

1.   [A general outcry] against the remissness of Government in permitting the free circulation of injurious writings. It has been especially felt in regard to the blasphemous parodies on the Liturgy. No one can comprehend why these things should not be suppressed and the authors or publishers punished. *To D. Stuart*,   IV. 7, 1817

Books.   See Intellect; Knowledge; Reading; Scholarly Interests

1.   See Composition 23; Imagination 11, 49; Knowledge 1A, 4, 6, 13; Poetry 55, 65; Style 33; Travel Literature 1-4; Lamb 12; Quillinan 5; Southey 12, 19; W. 28, 329

2.   Book-learning and books should be banished the land. . . . " O now that the genius," 6.   1800

3.*   Throw aside your books on chemistry . . . and read Godwin on Necessity. *Hazlitt*, iv, 201.   *c.* 1800

4.   Books, leisure, perfect freedom and [conversation]
                              . . . this is the stalk
            True Power doth grow on . . . .
            " I grieved for Buonaparte," 10, 13-14.   1802

5.   . . . love Nature and Books; seek these, and you will be happy. . . . *To De Quincey*,   III. 6, 1804

6.   [At Cambridge he] Read lazily in trivial books. . . .
            Prel., iii, 251 (see also A 524-30).   1804-39

7.   Not that I slighted books,—that were to lack
            All sense,—but other passions in me ruled,
            Passions more fervent, making me less prompt
            To in-door study than was wise or well,
            Or suited to those years.
            Prel., iii, 364-68.   1804-39

8.   Yes, that heartless chase
            Of trivial pleasures was a poor exchange
            For books and nature at that early age.
            'Tis true, some casual knowledge might be gained
            Of character or life; but at that time,
            Of manners put to school I took small note,
            And all my deeper passions lay elsewhere.
            Far better had it been to exalt the mind
            By solitary study, to uphold
            Intense desire through meditative peace. . . .
            Prel., iv, 297-306.   1804-39

9.   . . . Me hath such strong entrancement overcome,
            When I have held a volume in my hand,

Poor earthly casket of immortal verse,
Shakespeare, or Milton, labourers divine!
Great and benign, indeed, must be the power
Of living nature, which could thus so long
Detain me from the best of other guides
And dearest helpers, left unthanked, unpraised.
. . . Think not that I could pass along untouched
By these remembrances. Yet wherefore speak?
Why call upon a few weak words to say
What is already written in the hearts
Of all that breathe?—what in the path of all
Drops daily from the tongue of every child,
Wherever man is found? The trickling tear
Upon the cheek of listening Infancy
Proclaims it, and the insuperable look
That drinks as if it never could be full.
Prel., v, 162-69; 182-91.

1804-5

10.
                        Yet is it just
That here, in memory of all books which lay
Their sure foundations in the heart of man,
Whether by native prose, or numerous verse,
That in the name of all inspirèd souls—
From Homer the great Thunderer, from the voice
That roars along the bed of Jewish song,
And that more varied and elaborate,
Those trumpet-tones of harmony that shake
Our shores in England,—from those loftiest notes
Down to the low and wren-like warblings, made
For cottagers and spinners at the wheel,
And sun-burnt travellers resting their tired limbs,
Stretched under wayside hedge-rows, ballad tunes,
Food for the hungry ears of little ones,
And of old men who have survived their joys—
'Tis just that in behalf of these, the works,
And of the men that framed them, whether known,
Or sleeping nameless in their scattered graves,
That I should here assert their rights, attest
Their honours, and should, once for all, pronounce
Their benediction; speak of them as Powers
For ever to be hallowed; only less,
For what we are and what we may become,
Than Nature's self, which is the breath of God,
Or His pure Word by miracle revealed.
Prel., v, 197-222.

1804-39

10B.
                        . . . ye who pore
On the dead letter, miss the spirit of things;
Whose truth is not a motion or a shape
Instinct with vital functions, but a block

Or waxen image which yourselves have made,
And ye adore!
Prel., viii, 296-301.   1804-39

11.   [Imagination helped by] books and what they picture and record.
Prel., viii, 616.   1804-39

11A.   . . . How books mislead us. . . .
                Prel., xiii, 208 (see 208-20).   1804-39

11B.   [Has omitted in *The Prelude*]
                Of books how much!
                Prel., xiv, 313.   1804-39

12.   Dreams, books, are each a world; and books, we know
        Are a substantial world, both pure and good:
        Round these . . .
        Our pastime and our happiness will grow.
        There find I personal themes, a plenteous store,
        Matter wherein right voluble I am,
        To which I listen with a ready ear;
        Two shall be named, pre-eminently dear,—
        The gentle Lady married to the Moor;
        And heavenly Una with her milk-white Lamb.
        Personal Talk, 33-42.   1807

13.   But books will do nothing of themselves, nor institutions without
books. Two things are absolutely wanted in this Country; a thorough reform
in Parliament and a new course of education, which must be preceded by
some genuine philosophical writings from some quarter or other, to teach
the principles upon which that education should be grounded. We have
in our language better books than exist in any other, and in our land better
institutions, but the one nobody reads, and the others are fallen into disorder
and decay. *To D. Stuart*,   III. 26, 1809

14.   . . . books avail nothing *without institutions*—that is, of course,
institutions of civil liberty. *To D. Stuart*,   IV. 26, 1809

14A.   . . . their familiar voice
        Even to old age with unabated charm
        Beguiled his leisure hours, refreshed his thoughts,
        Beyond its natural elevation raised
        His introverted spirit, and bestowed
        Upon his life an outward dignity
        Which all acknowledged. The dark winter night,
        The stormy day had each its own resource;
        Song of the Muses, sage historic tale,
        Science severe, or word of Holy Writ
        Announcing immortality and joy . . . .
        Epitaph 3 (Grosart, ii, 74).   1810

15.   . . . books that explain
        The purer elements of truth involved
        In lines and numbers. . . .
        Exc., i, 252-4.   1814

16. [The boy] had small need of books; for [traditions and legends of the mountains nourished his imagination]. *Exc.*, i, 163-6.   1814

17.   . . . and books are yours,
    Within whose silent chambers treasure lies
    Preserved from age to age; more precious far
    Than that accumulated store of gold
    And orient gems, which, for a day of need,
    The Sultan hides deep in ancestral tombs.
    These hoards of truth you can unlock at will:
    . . . —furnished thus,
    How can you droop, if willing to be upraised?
    Exc., iv, 564-70 and 573-4.   1814

18.   With the ever-welcome company of books. . . .
             Exc., v, 57.
                                                                     1814

20. It is a disgrace to the age that Poetry won't sell without prints—I am a little too proud to let my Ship sail in the wake of the Engravers and drawing-mongers. *To Moxon,*   V. 14, 1833

23. The books which really improve the human mind are those that tempt to repeated perusal, and are read till they sink into it—and are even treasured up in the very shape they bore, when the reader first felt grateful to the Author for the good he had done him. *To T. Wyse,*   V. 3, 1838

25.* W. said when he got a bit of money and the choice was between using it for books or travel he chose the latter, for he thought he could find books " in *the running brooks* or even at a pinch *make for himself.*" *A Day with Wordsworth*, p .740.   VIII. 31, 1841

26. *Books* . . . [Southey's] *passion*; and *wandering* . . . was mine. . . . *I. F. (Grosart*, iii, 196).   1843

27.* No book-knowledge in the world can compensate you for such a loss [of health]. *Old Friends*, p. 213.   X. 6, 1844

28. [Illustrated books.]

             Discourse was deemed Man's noblest attribute,
             And written words the glory of his hand;
             Then followed Printing with enlarged command
             For thought—dominion vast and absolute
             For spreading truth, and making love expand.
             Now prose and verse sunk into disrepute
             Must lacquey a dumb Art that best can suit
             The taste of this once-intellectual Land.
             A backward movement surely have we here,
             From manhood—back to childhood; for the age—
             Back towards caverned life's first rude career.
             Avaunt this vile abuse of pictured page!
             Must eyes be all in all, the tongue and ear
             Nothing? Heaven keep us from a lower stage!
             Illustrated Books and Newspapers, 1-14.   1846

29. [W.'s interest in books dying fast.] *To I. Fenwick*, V. 13, 1846

Caesura, The. See Versification 11; Gillies 5; Rogers 5

Calmness, Moods of. See Nature 7

Camden Society. See also Antiquarianism; Scholarly Interests

1. . . . a vol. printed for the Camden Society entitled Plumpton Correspondence . . . the objects of the Camden Society are praiseworthy, and the specimens they have given not a little interesting. *To Moxon*, VII. 6, 1839

Capitals

1. See Bentley, Jr., Richard 1

2.* [Lines 1-205 of "Michael" were copied by Coleridge for L. B., (1800); but by W.] Many of the capitals Coleridge used are struck out. *Longman MSS*, pp. 32-3.   1800

Caricatures. See Scott, W. 37

Caroline Period, The. See Progress, Idea of 1

Catastrophe, The. See W. 195, 204

Character Analysis. See Epitaphs

1. See Discrimination 2; Crabbe 1; W. 21, 33, 43-4

2. [See analysis of the character in *The Thorn* (*Oxf. W.*, p. 899).]

3. [General analysis of idiots in relation to *The Idiot Boy*.] To John Wilson (pp. 295-8),   VI, 1802

5. [In an epitaph.] The character of a deceased friend or beloved kinsman is not seen, no—nor ought to be seen, otherwise than as a tree through a tender haze or a luminous mist, that spiritualizes and beautifies it; that takes away, indeed, but only to the end that the parts which are not abstracted may appear more dignified and lovely; may impress and affect the more. Shall we say, then, that this is not truth, not a faithful image; and that, accordingly, the purposes of commemoration cannot be answered?—It *is* truth, and of the highest order; for, though doubtless things are not apparent which did exist; yet, the object being looked at through this medium, parts and proportions are brought into distinct view which before had been only imperfectly or unconsciously seen: it is truth hallowed by love—the joint offspring of the worth of the dead and the affections of the living! . . .

It suffices, therefore, that the trunk and the main branches of the worth of the deceased be boldly and unaffectedly represented. Any further detail, minutely and scrupulously pursued, especially if this be done with laborious and antithetic discriminations, must inevitably frustrate its own purpose. . . . *Epitaph 1* (*Oxf. W.*, p. 931).   1810

6. [See Ernest de Selincourt, "The Hitherto Unpublished Preface to Wordsworth's 'Borderers,'" *The Nineteenth Century and After*, DXCVII (Nov., 1926), 723-41.]   1842

7. [See *I. F.* (*Grosart*, iii, 123-24) for an analysis of the heroine of *The White Doe*.]   1843

8. [Characters in *The Excursion* are discussed in *I. F.* (*Grosart*, iii, 196-201).]
1843

Characters. See also Biography; Character Analysis; Decorum; Drama; Imagination; Manners

1. . . . it is a living creature that must interest us [in an epitaph] and not an intellectual existence, which a mere character is. See Pope 19

3. [In *Ossian*] the characters never could exist . . . . *E. Supp. Pref.*, p. 950.
1815

4. See Aim of Writing 7; Drama 3; Imagination 32A, G; Poetry 66; Burger 2; Burns 1; Coleridge 61B; Defoe 3; Homer 4, 12, 13; Lamb 19; Shakespeare 14, 32, 33, 37A, 41; W. 21, 23, 33, 90-1

Chronicles. See also History

1.* . . . if you are fond of History read it in the old Memoirs or old Chronicles. *D. W. to C. Clarkson,*   Christmas Day, 1805

Circumlocution. See Translation 4

Circumstances. See Poetry 111; Godwin, C. Grace 1; W. 274

Cities and their Effect on the Imagination

1. [Cities dull the creative powers of a poet. See *Prel.*, vii, 678-81; xiii, 202-5; Passion 7; but contrast Imagination 24, and *Prel.*, vii, 722-39; viii, 639-75; A751-8, A796-9.]
1804-39

Coherence. See under Form; Style; Unity; and Blank Verse and Rhyme 1

Colloquial, The. See Diction 30

Comedy. See under Drama

Compensation, Principle of. See Translation 9

Common Sense. See under Good Sense; Judgment; Reason

Composition. See also Action; Art; Circumstances; Description; Finish; Form; Fancy; Imagination; Invention; Passion; Practice; Rules; Revisions; Sonnets; Style; Unity; Versification

1. See Aim of Writing 10; Criticism 39A; Infinity 4; Judgment 4; Moral Element 11; Nature 20; Passion 8; Picturesque 1; Poetry 24; Realism 52; Rules 13; Sonnets 2, 7; Style 48, 58; Versification 24A

2. [In the following passage from an (unpunctuated) autograph manuscript, W., according to Professor de Selincourt, realized "that an artist reveals his true power"]

> In that considerate and laborious work
> That patience which, admitting no neglect
> By slow creation, doth impart(s) to speach

Outline and substance even, till it has given
A function kindred to organic power,
The vital spirit of a perfect form.
Introduction to *Prel.* (*De Sel.*), p. xliii n.[1]   1798-1800

3. See W. 13, 17, 21, 46, 66, 78, 91, 109-10, 117, 124, 134, 142, 146, 152, 170, 180-2, 192, 202, 213, 241-42, 246, 249, 268, 279, 281-83, 286-87, 289-90, 308, 310, 319, 352, 368A, 373

4. See Burns 31; Chaucer 11; Coleridge, H. 6; Coleridge 74; Cowper 1; Crabbe 12; Dyer, J. 5; Faber 4; Gillies 6; Gomm 1; Gray 5, 6; Hamilton, W. R. 1; Hemans, Felicia 6; Milton 25; Reynolds, J. 3; Scott, J. 5; Scott, W. 15; Shakespeare 32

8.   Such facts as you have communicated to me are an abundant recompense for all the labour and pains which the profession of Poetry requires, and without which nothing permanent or good can be produced. *To De Quincey,*   III. 19, 1804

10.   Thus far, O Friend! did I, not used to make
A present joy the matter of a song,
Pour forth that day my soul in measured strains
. . . to the open fields I told
A prophecy: poetic numbers came
Spontaneously to clothe in priestly robe
A renovated spirit singled out,
Such hope was mine, for holy services.
Prel., i, 46-54.   1804-39

12.   The Poet, gentle creature as he is,
Hath, like the Lover, his unruly times;
His fits when he is neither sick nor well,
Though no distress be near him but his own
Unmanageable thoughts: his mind, best pleased
While she as duteous as the mother dove
Sits brooding, lives not always to that end,
But like the innocent bird, hath goadings on
That drive her as in trouble through the groves;
With me is now such passion, to be blamed
No otherwise than as it lasts too long.
Prel., i, 135-45.   1804-39

13.   Sometimes it suits me better to invent
A tale from my own heart, more near akin
To my own passions and habitual thoughts;
Some variegated story, in the main
Lofty, but the unsubstantial structure melts
Before the very sun that brightens it,
Mist into air dissolving! Then a wish,
My last and favourite aspiration, mounts
With yearning toward some philosophic song
Of Truth that cherishes our daily life;

> With meditations passionate from deep
> Recesses in man's heart, immortal verse
> Thoughtfully fitted to the Orphean lyre. . . .
> *Prel.*, i, 221-33.   1804-39

14.   At first I had a strong impulse to write a poem that should record my Brother's virtues, and be worthy of his memory. I began to give vent to my feelings, with this view, but I was overpowered by my subject and could not proceed: I composed much, but it is all lost except a few lines, as it came from me in such a torrent that I was unable to remember it. . . . This work must therefore rest awhile till I am something calmer. . . . *To Beaumont,*
                                                              V. 1, 1805

16.   [For the composition of epitaphs, see *Oxf. W.*, pp. 929-32.]

18.   Had I been as much delighted with the Story of the Beauty and the Beast as you appear to have been, and as much struck with its fitness for Verse, still your proposal would have occasioned in me a similar regret. I have ever had the same sort of perverseness, I cannot work upon the suggestion of others however eagerly I might have addressed myself to the proposed subject if it had come to me of its own accord. You will therefore attribute my declining the task of versifying the Tale to this infirmity, rather than to an indisposition to serve you. *To Wm. Godwin,*   III. 9, 1811

19.   For Fancy hath her fits both hot and cold. . . .
             " Far from our home," 86.   1811

[See lines 1-88 of this poem for comments on composition, poetic subjects, and fancy.]

20.   [The rulers of states should lay out their plans much as a] mighty Poet when he is determining the proportions and march of a Poem. Much is to be done by rule; the great outline is previously to be conceived in distinctness, but the consummation of the work must be trusted to resources that are not tangible, though known to exist.
To Captain Pasley (p. 440),   III. 28, 1811

21.   Your first position, that every idea which passes through a poet's mind may be made passionate, and therefore poetical, I am not sure that I understand. If you mean through a poet's mind when in a poetical mood, the words are nothing but an identical proposition. But a poet must be subject to a thousand thoughts in common with other men, and many of them must, I suppose, be as unsusceptible of alliance with poetic passion as the thoughts that interest ordinary men. But the range of poetic feeling is far wider than is ordinarily supposed, and the furnishing new proofs of this fact is the only incontestible demonstration of genuine poetic genius. 2dly, ' The moment a clear idea of any kind is conceived, it ought to be brought out directly and [as] rapidly as possible, without any view to any particular style of language.' I am not sure that I comprehend your meaning here. Is it that a man's thoughts should be noted down in prose, or that he should express them in any kind of verse that they most easily fall into? I think it well to make brief memoranda of our most interesting thoughts in prose; but to unite fragments of verse is an embarrassing practice. A similar course answers well

in painting, under the name of *Studies*; but in poetry it is apt to betray a writer into awkwardness, and to turn him out of his course for the purpose of lugging on these ready-made pieces by the head and shoulders. Or do you simply mean, that such thoughts as arise in the process of composition should be expressed in the first words that offer themselves, as being likely to be most energetic and natural? If so, this is not a rule to be followed without cautious exceptions. My first expressions I often find detestable; and it is frequently true of second words as of second thoughts, that they are the best. I entirely accord with you in your third observation, that we should be cautious not to waste our lives in dreams of imaginary excellence, for a thousand reasons, and not the least for this, that these notions of excellence may perhaps be erroneous, and then our inability to catch a phantom of no value may prevent us from attempting to seize a precious substance within our reach. *To Gillies*,   XII. 22, 1814

22.   In what I said upon the setting down thoughts in prose, I only meant, briefly, as memorandum, to prevent their being *lost*. It is unaccountable to me how men could ever proceed as Racine (and Alfieri I believe) used to do, first, writing their Plays in Prose, and then, turning them into Verse. It may answer with so slavish a language and so enslaved a Taste as the French have, but with us, it is not to be thought of. *To Gillies*,   II. 14, 1815

23.*   . . . he intends completely to plan the first part of the Recluse before he begins the composition, he must read many Books before he will fairly set to labor again. *D. W. to Sara Hutchinson*,   II. 18, 1815

25.   My verses have all risen up of their own accord. I was once requested to write an inscription for a monument which a friend proposed to erect in his garden, and a year elapsed before I could accomplish it. *To ?*,   1816

25A.   [Cannot join in commemorating the birth of Shakespeare, as] My verses have all risen up of their own accord. . . . Beside, I should have before me the tender explanation of Milton,

> . . . great Heir of Fame
> What need'st Thou such *weak* witness of thy Name.

L. of W. Family (p. 61),   III. 18, 1816

26A.   [*The Odes*] were poured out with much feeling, out from mismanagement of myself the labour of making some verbal corrections cost me more health and strength than anything of that sort ever did before. *To C. R.* (*Corr. C. R.*, i, 87),   VIII. 2, 1816

29.   . . . at no period of my life have I been able to write verses that do not spring up from an inward impulse of some sort or other; so that they neither seem proposed nor imposed. *To James Montgomery*,   I. 24, 1824

30.   *There is a pleasure in poetic pains*
Which only Poets know;—'twas rightly said;
Whom could the Muses else allure to tread
Their smoothest paths, to wear their lightest chains?
When happiest Fancy has inspired the strains,
How oft the malice of one luckless word
Pursues the Enthusiast to the social board,

Haunts him belated on the silent plains!
Yet he repines not, if his thought stand clear,
At last, of hindrance and obscurity,
Fresh as the star that crowns the brow of morn;
Bright, speckless, as a softly-moulded tear
The moment it has left the virgin's eye,
Or rain-drop lingering on the pointed thorn.
" There is a pleasure," 1-14.   1827

33.*   Many of my poems have been influenced by my own circumstances
when I was writing them. ' The Warning ' was composed on horseback, while
I was riding from Moresby in a snow-storm. Hence the simile in that poem,

'While thoughts press on and feelings overflow,
And quick words round him fall like *flakes* of *snow*.'

G. W., Jr. (Grosart, iii, 464).   *c.* 1827

34. [Does not understand] the passage your obliging note refers to,
viz., that society will hereafter tolerate no such thing as literature, considered
merely as a creation of art. If this be meant to say that any writer will be
disappointed who expects a place in the affections of posterity for works
which have nothing but their manner to recommend them, it is too obviously
true to require being insisted upon. But still such things are not without
their value, as they may exemplify with liveliness (heightened by the contrast
between the skill and perfection of the manner, and the worthlessness of the
matter as matter merely) rules of art and workmanship, which must be applied
to imaginative literature, however high the subject, if it is to be permanently
efficient. *To A. Hayward,*   [1828]

36. The Somnambulist [*Oxf. W.*, p. 478] is one of several Pieces, written
at a heat, which I should have much pleasure in submitting to your judgment
were the fates so favourable as that we might meet ere long.
To S. Rogers,   VII. 30, 1830

37. [" Chatsworth! "] fresh from the brain, make such allowance as you
can. . . . *To D. W.*,   XI. 8, 1830

38.* . . . He never wrote down as he composed, composed walking,
riding, or in bed, and wrote down after. . . .
Greville Memoirs, ii, 122.   II. 27, 1831

39. What I send is not ' warm ' but piping hot from the brain, whence it
came in the wood adjoining my garden not ten minutes ago, and was scarcely
more than twice as long in coming. *To Haydon,*   VI. 11, 1831

41. With regard to poetry, I must say that my mind has been kept this
last year and more in such a state of anxiety that all harmonies appear to
have been banished from it except those that reliance upon the goodness of
God furnishes. . . . *To W. R. Hamilton,*   II. 8, 1833

42. . . . I have begun to accustom my ear to blank verse in other Authors
with a hope they may put me in tune for my own. *To E. Q.*,   II. 23, 1833

44.* It was clear he thought he had achieved a high place among poets:
it had been the aim of his life, humanly speaking; and he had taken worthy

pains to accomplish and prepare himself for the enterprise . . . but he was a severe critic on himself, and would not leave a line or an expression with which he was dissatisfied until he had brought it to what he liked. He thought this due to the gift of poetry and the character of the poet. Carelessness in the finish of composition he seemed to look on almost as an offence. I remember well, that after speaking with love and delight of a very popular volume of poetry, he yet found great fault with the want of correctness and finish. Reciting one of the poems, and pointing out inaccuracies in it, he said ' I like the volume so much, that, if I was the author, I think I should never rest till I had nearly rewritten it.' *Justice Coleridge* (*Grosart*, iii, 424). summer, 1836

46.   Now as a masterly, or first rate Ode or Elegy, or piece of humour even, is better than a poorly or feebly executed epic Poem, so is the picture, tho' in point of subject the humblest that ever came from an easel better than a work after Michael Angelo or Raphael in choice of subject or aim of style if moderately performed. All styles down to the humblest are good, if there be thrown into the doing all that the subject is capable of, and this truth is a great honour, not only to painting, but in degree to every other fine art. Now it is well worth a Lecturer's while who sees the matter in this light first to point out through the whole scale of Art what stands highest, and then to shew what constitutes its appropriate perfection of all down to the lowest. *To Haydon,*   III. 12, 1840

47.   . . . your mother tells me she shrinks from Copies being spread of those Sonnets [the two sonnets on Mrs. Wordsworth's portrait, painted by Miss Gillies, *v. Oxf.* W., p. 279.]; . . . though I never poured out anything more truly from the heart. *To Dora and I. Fenwick,*   IV. 7, 1840

48.*   . . . Owed his success much to his unwearied labor in perfecting each poem to the utmost. *Aubrey de Vere,* p. 70.   III. 9, 1841

49.*   . . . He so feels the importance of high finish as not to begrudge a fortnight to a word, so he succeed at last in getting a competent one. *Old Friends,* p. 144,   VI. 28, 1841

57.*   . . . the stanzas [*The Widow on Windermere Side*] are written in sonnet-form; which was adopted when I thought the matter might be included in 28 lines. *I. F.* (*Grosart,* iii, 27).   1843

Conceit, The.   See Imagination 11, 16

Concentration.   See Unity

Conciseness.   See Rogers 4; Style.   Contrast Wordiness

Concreteness.   See Sensitiveness to Sense Impressions.   Contrast Abstractions

Congruity.   See also Proportion; Propriety; Taste 14

Connotation.   See Language 4

Consistency.   See Character Analysis; Characters; Decorum; W. 91

Contrariety. Contrast Proportion; Propriety

1. . . . quaintness and contrariety . . . quite out of keeping with a true poet. . . . See Coleridge, H. 6

Conventions, Literary. See under Rules

Copyright and Its Relation to Literature, The. See also Aim of Writing; Money, Writing for

1. This I think far too short a period [for twenty-eight years after the death of an author]; at least I am sure that it requires much more than that length of time to establish the reputation of original productions, both in Philosophy and Poetry, and to bring them consequently into such circulation that the authors, in the Persons of their Heirs or posterity, can in any degree be benefited, I mean in a pecuniary point of view, for the trouble they must have taken to produce the works. The law, as it now stands, merely consults the interest of the useful drudges in Literature, or of flimsy and shallow writers, whose works are upon a level with the taste and knowledge of the age; while men of real power, who go before their age, are deprived of all hope of their families being benefited by their exertions. Take, for instance, in Philosophy, Hartley's book upon Man, how many years did it sleep in almost entire oblivion! What sale had Collins' Poems during his lifetime, or during the fourteen years after his death, and how great has been the sale since? The product of it, if secured to his family, would have been an independence to them.

Take a still stronger instance, but this you may say proves too much, I mean Milton's minor Poems. It is nearly 200 years since they were published, yet they were utterly neglected till within these last 30 years; notwithstanding they had, since the beginning of the past century, the reputation of the Paradise Lost to draw attention towards them. Suppose that Burns or Cowper had left at their deaths each a child a few months old, a daughter for example, is it reasonable that those children, at the age of 28, should cease to derive benefit from their Father's works, when every Bookseller in the country is profiting by them? *To R. Sharp,* IX. 27, 1808

2. See Mediocrity 1

3. [Does not desire to sell the copyright of his works, for it is impossible to predict the value of works of imagination.] *To A. Watts,* VIII. 13, 1825

4. [W. quotes from *The Times:*] " . . . but who will suggest that if Shakespeare had not written *Lear,* or Richardson *Clarissa,* other poets or novelists would have invented them? In practical science every discovery is a step to something more perfect; and to give to the inventor of each a protracted monopoly would be to shut out all improvements by others. But who can improve or supersede (as is perpetually done in mechanical invention) these masterpieces of genius? They stand perfect, apart from all things else, self-sustained, the models for imitation, the source whence rules of art take their origin. And if we apply the analogy of mechanical invention to literature, we shall find that, in so far as it stands, there is really in the latter no monopoly at all, however brief. For example, historical or critical research

bears a close analogy to the process of mechanical discovery, and how does the law of copyright apply to the treasures it may reveal? The fact discovered, the truth ascertained, become at once the property of mankind, to accept, to state, to reason on; and all that remains to the author is the style in which it is expressed."

Of the broad distinctions I may not, perhaps, be an impartial judge, as I have had the honour of hearing them adopted from suggestions of my own, and they appear to have made an impression upon the public. The conclusion of the extract meets in fact the difficulty stated by you of determining what constitutes an original work, as distinguished from plagiarism. Dr. Arnold is now engaged in writing a *History of Rome*, in which I know that he will be greatly indebted to Niebuhr, but I have no doubt of the subject being treated by him in such a manner that neither Niebuhr—had he been an Englishman, and written in English—would be found, were he alive, to complain, nor could any competent tribunal to which the case might be referred condemn the subsequent writer for having made an unfair or illegal use of his predecessor's labours. So would it always be with the successful labours of men of honour and great talent employed upon the same subjects; and it is only upon the productions of such authors that the proposed extension of term has any bearing. Mere drudges and dishonest writers are sometimes protected by the law as it now exists; but their works, if not cried down at once, soon die of themselves, and the plundered author seldom thinks it worth while to complain, or seek a remedy by law. *To Sir Robert Peel,*   V. 3, 1838

5. . . . but I am sure that the time will come, and is not far distant, when the Legislature will be convinced, and act upon the conviction, that they who are so gifted as to produce works whether in Prose or Verse of lasting interest, should in their family and posterity be lastingly rewarded, out of the sale of their labours. *To Lady Monteagle,*   VI. 28, 1842

Correctness. See under Composition; Finish; Revisions

Creative, The. See Composition; Fancy; Genius; Imagination; Invention; Nature (External); Originality; Passion; Poetry; Power

1. See Cities 1; Elegy 2; Infinity 2, 4; Inspiration 3; Intuition 3; Moral Element 11; Poetry 19, 66, 77; Taste 14, 15; W. 29, 199

3. High is our calling, Friend!—Creative Art
    (Whether the instrument of words she use,
    Or pencil pregnant with ethereal hues,)
    Demands the service of a mind and heart,
    Though sensitive, yet, in their weakest part,
    Heroically fashioned—to infuse
    Faith in the whispers of the lonely Muse,
    While the whole world seems adverse to desert.
    And, oh! when Nature sinks, as oft she may,
    Through long-lived pressure of obscure distress,
    Still to be strenuous for the bright reward,

And in the soul admit of no decay,
Brook no continuance of weak-mindedness——
Great is the glory, for the strife is hard!
" High is our calling," 1-14.   1815

4.   . . . I had known
Too forcibly, too early in my life,
Visitings of imaginative power
For this to last: I shook the habit off
Entirely and for ever, and again
In Nature's presence stood, as now I stand,
A sensitive being, a *creative* soul.
Prel., xii, 201-7.   1804-39

Credibility.   See Dyer, J. 5; Gillies 1; W. 187; and Good Sense;
   Probability

Criticism: Author as Self-critic

1.   . . . I always deem the opinion of an able writer upon his own works
entitled to consideration. . . . *To Gillies,*   XI. 23, 1814

2.   See Heraud 1; Shakespeare 18; W. 117, 355

3.   Do not . . . be anxious about any individual's opinion concerning your
writings, however highly you may think of his genius or rate his judgment.
Be a severe critic to yourself; and depend upon it no person's decision upon
the merit of your works will bear comparison in point of value with your
own. You must be conscious from what feeling they have flowed, and how
far they may or may not be allowed to claim, on that account, permanent
respect; and, above all, I would remind you, with a view to tranquillise
and steady your mind, that no man takes the trouble of surveying and
pondering another's writings with a hundredth part of the care which an
author of sense and genius will have bestowed upon his own. Add to this
reflection another, which I press upon you, as it has supported me through
life, viz., that Posterity will settle all accounts justly, and that works which
deserve to last will last; and if undeserving this fate, the sooner they perish
the better. *To Robert Montgomery,*   II, 1835

4.   See Composition 44; Criticism 77

Criticism, Biographical

5.   [There are many things in a man's character] of which his writings,
however miscellaneous, or voluminous, will give no idea.
To De Quincey,   VII. 29, 1803

6.   See Biography 2A, B, C; Poetry 139; Byron 23

Criticism, Dramatic.   See under Drama

Criticism, Effect of.   See Invention; Publishing

7.   See Poetry 133; *Quarterly Review* 3; Talfourd 4; W. 22, 189, 197, 317

8.   . . . I am told that there has appeared in the said journal [*Critical
Review*] an article purporting to be a Review of those Poems which is a

miserable heap of spiteful nonsense, even worse than anything that has appeared hitherto, in these disgraceful days. I have not seen it, for I am only a Chance-Reader of reviews, but from what I have heard of the contents of this precious piece, I feel not so much inclined to accuse the author of malice as of sheer, honest insensibility, and stupidity. With what propriety did I select my motto for the Lyrical Ballads, which might have been continued with equal or greater propriety on the present occasion:

Quam nihil ad genium, Papiniane, tuum!

But Peace to this gentleman, and all his Brethren: as Southey neatly says ' they cannot *blast* our *laurels*, but they may *mildew* our *corn* '; and it is only on account of this latter power which to a certain degree they unfortunately possess that I troubled you, or deemed them worth a moment's thought.
To F. Wrangham,   XI. 4, 1807

9. . . . why don't you hire somebody to abuse you? and the higher the place selected for the purpose the better. For myself, I begin to fear that I should soon be forgotten if it were not for my enemies.
To Rogers,   V. 13, 1817

10. Perhaps also my own powers are gaining ground upon the public; but you cannot have failed to observe what pains are taken in many quarters to obstruct their circulation and to lower their character. Be it so, you would probably say; and that is a still stronger reason for their author putting them in the way of being more generally known. The misrepresentations—whether arising from incapacity, presumption, envy, or personal malice—would be best refuted by the books becoming as accessible as may be. I trust that it would be so; but still, having neither inherited a fortune, nor having been a maker of money, and being now advanced in life with a family to survive me, I cannot be indifferent to the otherwise base consideration of some pecuniary gain.
To J. Gardner,   IV. 5, 1830

11. Do not suppose, however, that I am not prepared for the language of censure and discouragement from many quarters. I hear of that also occasionally, and should be sorry were it otherwise; for I should then be sure that the igneus vigor and caelestis origo did not belong to me, but that I was of the world, worldly, and of the earth, earthy. . . .
To Kenyon,   late autumn, 1836

12.* I hold critical writings of very little use. They do rather harm.
H. C. R., ii, 479.   I. 7, 1836

14. I am not at all desirous that any one should write an elaborate critique on my poems. There is no call for it. If they be from above, they will do their own work in course of time; if not, they will perish as they ought. But scarcely a week passes in which I do not receive grateful acknowledgments of the good they have done to the minds of the several writers. They speak of the relief they have received from them under affliction and in grief, and of the calmness and elevation of spirit which the poems either give, or assist them in attaining. As these benefits are not without a traceable bearing upon the good of the immortal soul, the sooner, perhaps, they are pointed out and illustrated in a work like yours the better. *To H. Alford,*   II. 21, 1840

16.* [Would have gained an excellent income from his works] but for the stupidity of Mr. Gifford and the impertinence of Mr. Jeffrey. . . . This was the only kind of injury Mr. Jeffrey did me, for I immediately perceived that his mind was of that kind that his individual opinion on poetry was of no consequence to me whatever, that it was only by the influence his periodical exercised at the time in preventing my poems being read and sold that he could injure me; for feeling that my writings were founded on what was true and spiritual in human nature, I knew the time would come when they must be known, and I never therefore felt his opinion of the slightest value, except in preventing the young of that generation from receiving impressions which might have been of use to them through life. I say this, I hope not in a boasting spirit, but I am now daily surprised by receiving letters from various places at home and abroad expressive of gratitude to me from persons I never saw or heard of. As this occurs now, I may fairly conclude that it might have been so when the poems appeared, but for the tyranny exercised over public opinion by the *Edinburgh* and *Quarterly Reviews.*
Lady R. (Grosart, iii, 437). VIII. 28, 1841

17. I have no wish to see the Review ["Wordsworth's Poetical Works," *The North American Review,* CXXV (October, 1844), 352-84] of my Poems to which you allude, nor should I heed it if it fell in my way. It is too late in life for me to profit by censure, and I am indifferent to praise merely as such. *Reed,* p. 137. XI. 18, 1844

19. You mention an American review of my poems. There is nothing I am less disposed to read than things of that kind—in fact I never look at them, for if fault be found justly, I am too old to mend, and praise I care nothing about. *To S. Crompton,* I. 3, 1845

20. I am glad you approve my Railway Letter, but it has drawn upon me as I knew it would, from the low-minded and ill-bred a torrent of abuse through the Press—both in London, Glasgow and elsewhere, but as it has afforded me an opportunity of directing attention to some important truths I care little for such rancorous scurrility, the natural outbreak of self conceit and stupid ignorance. *To I. Fenwick,* early or mid I, 1845

21. . . . unpuffed publications have a poor chance of competing with puffed ones. *To Moxon,* III. 5, 1845

Criticism: Historical Method. See Manners Progress; Cotton

22. See Poetry 16, 21; Sonnets 7; Style 25, 33; Taste 11; Translation 4; Bacon 7; Bible 14; Chaucer 22-3; Crabbe 3; Donne 2; Godwin, C. G. 1; Homer 13; Locke 1; Macpherson 2; Michelangelo 6; Milton 52A; Thomson 9; W. 274.

25. [Influence of climate, and of social, sectional, and national prejudices upon appreciation of literature.] *To John Wilson,* VI, 1802

28. When we reflect that the father of this personage [unknown author of an epitaph on Sir George Vane] must have had his taste formed in the punning Court of James I., and that the epitaph was composed at a time when our literature was stuffed with quaint or out-of-the-way thoughts, it will seem not unlikely that the author prided himself upon what he might

call a clever hit: I mean his better affections were less occupied with the several associations belonging to the two ideas than his vanity delighted with that act of ingenuity by which they had been combined.
Epitaph 2 (Grosart, ii, 47).   1810

29.   [Use of mythology in an epitaph] an inexcusable fault for an inhabitant of a Christian country, yet admitting of some palliation in an Italian who treads classic soil and has before his eyes the ruins of the temples. . . . See Chiabrera 4

35.   . . . I know no test more to be relied upon than acknowledgments such as yours, provided the like have been received from persons of both sexes, of all ages, and who have lived in different latitudes, in widely different states of society, and in conditions little resembling each other.
Reed, p. 7.   II. 22, 1839

Criticism, Principles of; and General Remarks on Critics and Criticism.   See Art; Judgment; Rules; Taste

39.   See Criticism 81; Invention 4; Moral Element 11; Rules 13; Subjects 2; Byron 23, 23A; Gladstone 2; Macpherson 2; Milton 48; Wilson, J. 5; W. 9, 87, 282, 355, 364, 388-90A

39A.   [Reluctant] to censure so freely the writings of other Poets, and . . . I should not have done this, could I otherwise have made my meaning intelligible. The passages which I have condemned upon principle, and I have given my reasons, else I should have been inexcusable. Without an appeal to laws and principles there can be no criticism. What passes under that name is, for the most part, little more than a string of random and extempore judgments, a mode of writing more cheap than any other, and utterly worthless. When I contrast these summary decisions with the pains and anxiety of original composition, especially in verse, I am frequently reminded of a passage of Drayton on this subject which, no doubt, he wrote with deep feeling:

> Detracting what laborously we do
> Only by that which he but idly saith.

[This passage, cancelled in MS from the Appendix to *L. B.* (*1802*), came near the end, after the words " and the same language."]
Longman MSS, pp. 49-50.   1802

40.   . . . against a mode of false criticism which has been applied to Poetry, in which the language closely resembles that of life and nature. Such verses have been triumphed over in parodies, of which Dr. Johnson's stanza is a fair specimen:—

> I put my hat upon my head
> And walked into the Strand,
> And there I met another man
> Whose hat was in his hand.

Immediately under these lines let us place one of the most justly admired stanzas of the ' Babes in the Wood.'

> These pretty Babes with hand in hand
> Went wandering up and down;
> But never more they saw the Man
> Approaching from the Town.

In both these stanzas the words, and the order of the words, in no respect differ from the most unimpassioned conversation. [The words of both are] connected with none but the most familiar ideas; yet the one stanza we admit as admirable, and the other as a fair example of the superlatively contemptible. . . . [The difference arises not from the meter, the language, or the word-order] but the *matter* expressed in Dr. Johnson's stanza is contemptible. The proper method of treating trivial and simple verses, to which Dr. Johnson's stanza would be a fair parallelism, is not to say, this is a bad kind of poetry, or, this is not poetry; but, this wants sense; it is neither interesting in itself, nor can *lead* to anything interesting; the images neither originate in that sane state of feeling which arises out of thought, nor can excite thought or feeling in the Reader. *Pref. L. B.*, p. 941. 1800

41. [A method of criticism.] If an Author, by any single composition, has impressed us with respect for his talents, it is useful to consider this as affording a presumption, that on other occasions where we have been displeased, he, nevertheless, may not have written ill or absurdly; and further, to give him so much credit for this one composition as may induce us to review what has displeased us, with more care than we should otherwise have bestowed upon it. This is not only an act of justice, but, in our decisions upon poetry especially, may conduce, in a high degree, to the improvement of our own taste; for an *accurate* taste in poetry, and in all the other arts, as Sir Joshua Reynolds has observed, is an *acquired* talent, which can only be produced by thought and a long continued intercourse with the best models of composition. This is mentioned, not with so ridiculous a purpose as to prevent the most inexperienced Reader from judging for himself . . . but merely to temper the rashness of decision, and to suggest, that, if Poetry be a subject on which much time has not been bestowed, the judgment may be erroneous; and that, in many cases, it necessarily will be so.
Pref. L. B., pp. 941-42. 1800

42. [A plea for independent criticism.] This mode of criticism [judging by what others may think of a composition] so destructive of all sound unadulterated judgment, is almost universal: let the Reader then abide, independently, by his own feelings, and, if he finds himself affected, let him not suffer such conjectures to interfere with his pleasure.
Pref. L. B., p. 941. 1800

43. [A volume of small poems must be read] a few at once, or the book must remain some time by one [before an accurate judgment is possible].
To Beaumont, XI. 10, 1806

44. [Moral discipline as an aid to accurate criticism.] If it be a question of the fine arts (poetry for instance) the riper mind [morally disciplined by search for truth] not only sees that his opponent [of small intellectual and moral development] is deceived; but, what is of far more importance, sees how he is deceived. The imagination stands before him with all its imper-

fections laid open; as duped by shows, enslaved by words, corrupted by mistaken delicacy and false refinement, as not having even attended with care to the reports of the senses, and therefore deficient grossly in the rudiments of its own power. He has noted how, as a supposed necessary condition, the understanding sleeps in order that the fancy may dream. Studied in the history of society, and versed in the secret laws of thought, he can pass regularly through all the gradations, can pierce infallibly all the windings, which false taste through ages has pursued, from the very time when first, through inexperience, heedlessness, or affectation, the imagination took its departure from the side of truth, its original parent.
Ans. to Mathetes (*Grosart*, i, 323).   I. 4, 1810

45.   Minute criticism is in its nature irksome. . . . See Pope 19

48.*   . . . he is, however, so disgusted with critics. . . .
D. W. to C. Clarkson,   XII. 30, 1810

49.   So strange indeed are the obliquities of admiration, that they whose opinions are much influenced by authority will often be tempted to think that there are no fixed principles (This opinion seems actually to have been entertained by Adam Smith, the worst critic, David Hume not excepted, that Scotland, a soil to which this sort of weed seems natural, has produced) in human nature for this art to rest upon. I have been honoured by being permitted to peruse in MS. a tract composed between the period of the Revolution and the close of that century. It is the Work of an English Peer of high accomplishments, its object to form the character and direct the studies of his son. Perhaps nowhere does a more beautiful treatise of the kind exist. The good sense and wisdom of the thoughts, the delicacy of the feelings, and the charm of the style, are, throughout, equally conspicuous. Yet the Author, selecting among the Poets of his own country those whom he deems most worthy of his son's perusal, particularizes only Lord Rochester, Sir John Denham, and Cowley. Writing about the same time, Shaftesbury, an author at present unjustly depreciated, describes the English Muses as only yet lisping in their cradles. *E. Supp. Pref.*, pp. 947-48 and n. 1.   1815

53.   . . . the most profitable criticism is the record of sensations, provided the person affected be under no partial influence. See Reynolds, J. H. 1.
To J. H. Reynolds,   XI. 28, 1816

54.   Indeed I am heartily sick of even the best criticism, of course cannot humor an inclination to turn to the worst—*To Gillies,*   VI. 19, 1817

56.   Some will say, 'Did you ever know a poet who would agree with his critic when he was finding fault, especially if on the whole he was inclined to praise?' I will ask, 'Did you ever know a critic who suspected it to be possible that he himself might be in the wrong?' in other words, who did not regard his own impressions as the test of excellence? The author of these candid strictures [in the *Leeds Intelligencer*] accounts with some pains for the disgust or indifference with which the world received a large portion of my verse, yet without thinking the worse of this portion himself; but wherever the string of his own sympathies is not touched the blame is mine. *Goody Blake and Harry Gill* is apparently no favorite with the person who has transferred the article into the Leeds paper; yet Mr. Crabbe in my hearing said that

everybody must be delighted with that poem.' The *Idiot Boy* was a special favorite with the late Mr. Fox and with the present Mr. Canning. The South American critic quarrels with the *Celandine*, and no doubt would with the *Daffodils*, etc.; yet on this last the other day I heard of a most ardent panegyric from a high authority. But these matters are to be decided by principles; and I only mention the above facts to show that there are reasons upon the surface of things for a critic to suspect his own judgment.
To A. Watts,   XI. 16, 1824

57.   I am not a Critic—and set little value upon the art. The preface [to *L. B.*, 1800] which I wrote long ago to my own Poems I was put upon to write by the urgent entreaties of a friend, and heartily regret I ever had anything to do with it; though I do not reckon the principles then advanced erroneous. [See also W. 382.]   *To J. A. Heraud,*   XI. 23, 1830

58.*   I hold critical writings of very little use. They do rather harm. *H. C. R.*, ii, 479.   I. 7, 1836

59.   Though prevailed upon by Mr. Coleridge to write the first Preface to my Poems—which tempted, or rather forced, me to add a supplement to it—and induced by my friendship for him to write the Essay upon Epitaphs, now appended to The Excursion, but first composed for The Friend, I have never felt inclined to write criticism, though I have talked, and am daily talking, a great deal.

If I were several years younger I would, out of friendship to you mainly, sit down to the task of giving a body to my notions upon the essentials of Poetry, a subject which could not be properly treated without adverting to the other branches of fine art.   *To W. R. Hamilton,*   I. 4, 1838

60.   . . . that though it is principally matters of science in which publication through your Society would be serviceable, and indeed in that department eminently so, I concur with you in thinking that the same vehicle would be useful for bringing under the notice of the thinking part of the community critical essays of too abstract a character to be fit for popularity. There are obviously, even in criticism, two ways of affecting the minds of men: the one by treating the matter so as to carry it immediately to the sympathies of the many, and the other by aiming at a few select and superior minds, that might each become a centre for illustrating it in a popular way. Mr. Coleridge, whom you allude to, acted upon the world to a great extent through the latter of these processes; and there cannot be a doubt that your Society might serve the cause of just thinking and pure taste should you, as President of it, hold up to view the desirableness of first conveying to a few, through that channel, reflections upon Literature and Art which, if well meditated, would be sure of winning their way directly, or in their indirect results, to a gradually widening circle.   *To W. R. Hamilton,*   I. 4, 1838

61.   My Writings like those of any other Author who has given his to the World are open to the praise or censure of every one who thinks them of sufficient consequence to be noticed.   *To R. Bigsby,*   XII. 15, 1840

61A.*   . . . there were three callings for success in which Nature had furnished him with qualifications—the callings of poet, landscape-gardener, and critic of pictures and works of art.   *Graves (Grosart,* iii, 468).   *c.* 1840

64.* . . . a selection published by Moxon—to which W. gave his consent only on condition that certain poems should be included which had been the object he thought of unjust derision. C. R. (*Corr. C. R.*, ii, 836).
[*c.* 1845]

Criticism, Textual

65.   A correct text is the first object of an editor; then such notes as explain difficult or unintelligible passages, or throw light upon them; and lastly, which is of much less importance, notes pointing out passages or authors to which the Poet has been indebted, not in the piddling way of a phrase here and phrase there (which is detestable as a general practice), but where the Poet has really had essential obligations either as to matter or manner. *To W. Scott,*   XI. 7, 1805

66. See Editing 1; Scholarly Interests 21; Bentley, Jr., R. 1; Bible 14, Shakespeare 45

67.   I do not doubt that the lines in Bell's edition of the Highland Ode [" On Popular Superstitions "] are spurious; but on this opinion I am far less disposed to insist, than to maintain that the principle is decidedly bad of admitting anything as the genuine work of a deceased Author but upon substantial external evidence. There may be exceptions to this rule, but they are very rare; and in our Literature are almost confined to certain works of Shakespeare (Pericles for example) which ought to be admitted from internal evidence alone.
In the case of this ode of Collins there is not a jot of *external* evidence entitled to consideration. *To A. Dyce,*   X. 29, 1828

68.   A word or two about Collins—you know what importance I attach to following strictly the last Copy of the text of an Author; and I do not blame you for printing in the Ode to Evening ' brawling ' spring; but surely the epithet is most unsuitable to the time, the very worst . . . almost that could have been chosen. I have not been able to find my Copy of Martin's St. Kilda, but I am certain that the Bee not being known there is mentioned by him—and it is well that a negative which is so poetical, should rest upon the authority of fact. *To A. Dyce,*   IV. 30, 1830

Criticism, Time as an Aid to; and the Effect of Time on Critical Opinions

72. See Criticism 83; Literature 15; Poetry 70, 74, 76; Realism 29; W. 9, 369

73.   I am disposed strenuously to recommend to your habitual perusal the great poets of our own country, who have stood the test of ages. Shakespeare I need not name, nor Milton, but Chaucer and Spenser are apt to be overlooked. It is almost painful to think how far these surpass all others. *To A. Watts,*   XI. 16, 1824

74. [Fix your attention on literary guides that] have stood the test of time. See Hamilton, Eliza Mary 1

75. In fact thirty years are no adequate test for works of Imagination,

even from second or third-rate writers, much less from those of the first order, as we see in the instances of Shakespeare and Milton.
To J. Gardner,   V. 19, 1830

76. . . . I ought frankly to avow that the time is past with me for bestowing that sympathy to which they [new productions in verse] are entitled. For many reasons connected with advanced life, I read but little of new works either in prose or verse. . . . But certain it is that old men's literary pleasures lie chiefly among the books they were familiar with in their youth; and this is still more pointedly true of men who have practised composition themselves. They have fixed notions of style and of versification and their thoughts have moved on in a settled train so long that novelty in each or all of these, so far from being a recommendation, is distasteful to them, even though, if hard put to it, they might be brought to confess that the novelty was all improvement. . . . For myself, however, I have many times, when called upon to give an opinion on works sent, felt obliged to recommend younger critics as more to be relied upon, and that for the reason I have mentioned. *To De Vere* (p. 1386),   XI. 16, 1842

77. As I advance in life I feel myself more and more incapable of doing justice to the attempts of young authors. The taste and judgment of an old man have too little of aptitude and flexibility for new things; and I am thoroughly convinced that a young writer cannot do worse than lean upon a veteran. It was not my own habit to look out for such guidance. I trusted to myself, and to the principles of criticism which I drew from the practice of the great poets, and not from any observations made upon their works by professed censors. As you are so intimately acquainted with my poems, and as no change has taken place in my manner for the last forty-five years, you will not be at a loss to gather from them upon what principles I write, and what accordingly is likely to be my judgment of your own performances, either as to subject or style. *To ?,*   IV. 1, 1843

Criticism: Types of Critics

78. See Criticism 49; Poetry 25, 70, 72, 74, 75, 76; W. 135, 190

79. These people . . . do not *read* books, they merely snatch a glance at them that they may talk about them. See Taste 10.
To Lady Beaumont,   V. 21, 1807

79A. [The French do not appreciate Shakespeare.]
To Beaumont,   I or II, 1808

80. [German, French, and Italian critics on Shakespeare.] See Shakespeare 14

81. [The best and the worst critics among readers.] Whither then shall we turn for that union of qualifications which must necessarily exist before the decisions of a critic can be of absolute value? For a mind at once poetical and philosophical; for a critic whose affections are as free and kindly as the spirit of society, and whose understanding is severe as that of dispassionate government? Where are we to look for that initiatory composure of mind which no selfishness can disturb? For a natural sensibility that has been tutored into correctness without losing anything of its quickness; and for

active faculties, capable of answering the demands which an Author of original imagination shall make upon them, associated with a judgment that cannot be duped into admiration by aught that is unworthy of it?—among those and those only, who, never having suffered their youthful love of poetry to remit much of its force, have applied to the consideration of the laws of this art the best power of their understandings. At the same time it must be observed—that, as this Class comprehends the only judgments which are trustworthy, so does it include the most erroneous and perverse. For to be mistaught is worse than to be untaught; and no perverseness equals that which is supported by system, no errors are so difficult to root out as those which the understanding has pledged its credit to uphold. In this Class are contained censors, who, if they be pleased with what is good, are pleased with it only by imperfect glimpses, and upon false principles; who, should they generalize rightly, to a certain point, are sure to suffer for it in the end; who, if they stumble upon a sound rule, are fettered by misapplying it, or by straining it too far; being incapable of perceiving when it ought to yield to one of higher order. In it are found critics too petulant to be passive to a genuine poet, and too feeble to grapple with him; men, who take upon them to report of the course which *he* holds whom they are utterly unable to accompany,—confounded if he turn quick upon the wing, dismayed if he soar steadily ' into the region ';—men of palsied imaginations and indurated hearts; in whose minds all healthy action is languid, who therefore feed as the many direct them, or, with the many, are greedy after vicious provocatives;—judges, whose censure is auspicious, and whose praise ominous! In this class meet together the two extremes of best and worst.
E. Supp. Pref., pp. 945-46.   1815

82. [German Critics.] . . . a single Piece, which, from the very nature of it, as allegorical, and even imperfectly so, would horrify a German Critic; and, whatever may be thought of the Germans as Poets, there is no doubt of their being the best Critics in Europe. *To R. Sharp*,   IV. 16, 1822

82A. . . . the German People are such discerning judges. . . .
To John Bowring,   XII. 29, 1827

83. You advert to Critics that dont deal fairly with me—I do not blame them—they write as they feel—and that their feelings are no better they cannot help. The older part of Critics like Gifford had he been alive, have their classical prejudices and for the younger—I am not poetical enough, they require higher seasoning than I give.
To C. R. (Corr. C. R., i, 201),   I. 27, 1829

85. . . . judgments [of W.'s works] by friends given in this way [letters to W.] are mostly of little value. *To Moxon*,   XI. 20, 1835

86. [A friend as a critic.] . . . far from supposing that everyone who likes me shall think well of my poetry, yet I do think that openness of dealing is necessary before a friend undertakes to decry one's writings to the world at large. *To De Vere* (p. 1385),   XI. 16, 1842

Criticism, Unfavorable Self-

89. See Aim of Writing 13; Diction 1; Passion 7; Popular Judgment 8; Prose 5; Repetition 4; Sublime 4; Scott, W. 38; W. 3, 115, 311-2

91. The diction of that Poem [*Guilt and Sorrow*] is often vicious, and the descriptions are often false, giving proofs of a mind inattentive to the true nature of the subject. . . . *To Miss Taylor,* IV. 9, 1801

92. . . . uncertain about my success in *altering* Poems. . . .
To Mary and Sara, VI. 14, 1802

94. [Objects to publishing for then his faults] shine out.
To Rogers, V. 3, 1825

96. As to 'better canons of criticism, and general improvement of scholars,' I really, speaking without affectation, am so little of a Critic or Scholar that it would be presumptuous in me to write upon the subject to you. . . . I have been applied to to give lectures upon Poetry in a public institution in London, but I was conscious that I was neither competent to the office, nor the public prepared to receive what I should have felt it my duty to say, however [?inadequately]. *To W. R. Hamilton,* XI. 21, 1837

Decorum. See also Characters; Manners

1.* . . . he finds fault with Dryden's description of Bacchus in the *Alexander's Feast,* as if he were a mere good-looking youth, or boon companion—

> Flushed with a purple grace
> He shows his honest face—

instead of representing the God returning from the conquest of India, crowned with vine-leaves, and drawn by panthers, and followed by troops of satyrs. . . . *Hazlitt,* iv, 276. *c.* 1800

2. See Coleridge 61B

Dedications

1. The dedication [of *Specimens of English Sonnets,* selected by A. Dyce, 1833] which you propose I shall esteem as an honor; nor do I conceive upon what ground, but an over-scrupulous modesty, I could object to it.
To Dyce, Spring, 1833

2. You have submitted what you had intended as a Dedication for your Poems to me. I need scarcely say that as a *private letter* such expressions from such a quarter could not have been rec^d by me but with pleasure of *no ordinary kind,* unchecked by any consideration but the fear that my writings were overrated by you, and my character thought better of than it deserved. But I must say that a *public* testimony in so high a strain of admiration is what I cannot but shrink from—be this modesty true or false, it is in me— you must bear with it, and make allowance for it. And therefore as you have submitted the whole to my judgment, I am emboldened to express a wish that you would instead of this Dedication in which your warm and kind heart has overpowered you, simply inscribe them to me, with such expression of respect or gratitude as would come within the limits of the rule which after what has been said above, will naturally suggest itself.
To Mrs. Hemans, IV. 30, 1834

3 See Milnes, R. M. 2

Delicacy. See La Fontaine 1

Description. See Composition; Observation; Picturesque; Realism; Truth

1. See Nature 20; Poetry 66; Style 6, 17; Gray 6; Scott, W. 37; W. 87, 124, 396

3. [Too much description in Spenser's works.] See Spenser 21

4.* [*The Female Vagrant* one of] my worst poems . . . mere descriptive. . . . *Collier's Preface*, p. li.   II. 10, 1814

5. [The soul and essence of descriptive poetry.] See Truth 17

Descriptive Poetry. See under Description; Poetry

Details. See under Circumstances; Composition; Description; Realism; Truth

Dialogues

1. [Dialogues] ought always to have some little spice of dramatic effect. *To Landor*,   XII. 11, 1824

Diction. See Antique Style; Revisions; Style; Wordiness

1.* [D. W. says W. regretted not having submitted *The Evening Walk* and *The Descriptive Sketches* of 1793 to the inspection of some friend before publication. She adds that W.] is well aware that he would have gained considerably more credit if the Blemishes [obscurity of diction] of which I speak had been corrected. *D. W. to Jane Pollard* (p. 85),   II. 16, 1793

2. See Composition 30; Judgment 4; Style 40; Taste 11; Versification 2; Wordiness 1; Bible 14; Coleridge 61-2; Edgeworth 1; Gillies 1; Macpherson 2; Quillinan 7; Scott, J. 3; Tennyson 6; W. 88, 291, 355; Wrangham 4

8.   . . . when first my mind
        With conscious pleasure opened to the charm
        Of words in tuneful order, found them sweet
        For their own *sakes*, a passion, and a power;
        And phrases pleased me chosen for delight,
        For pomp, or love.
        Prel., v, 553-58.   1804-39

10.   O, wond'rous power of words, by simple faith
        Licensed to take the meaning that we love!
        Prel., vii, 119-20.   1804-39

11. Is your objection to the word 'immediately' or to its connection with the others? The word itself seems to have sufficient poetical authority, even the highest.
        Immediately a place
        Before his eyes appeared, sad, noisome, dark.
        [*P. L.*, XI, 477-8]

I am well aware that the *nimia simplicitas* of my diction will frequently be complained of. I am prepared for that, being confident that the more an intimacy with our best writers is cultivated, the less dislike of this kind shall I have to encounter. *To F. Wrangham,* VII. 12, 1807

12. [See letter to T. De Quincey, III, 26, 1809, *M. Y.*, p. 263-4.]

15. [See *H. C. R.*, i, 166 for interesting revisions in diction.]

18. [No objections to monosyllables in verse.]

To Hans Bush, VII. 6, 1819

20. [Faults in the diction of W. R. Hamilton's poems.] See Hamilton, W. R. 4 and 7

22. [See a long letter to B. Field, X, 24, 1828, *L. Y.*, pp. 307-13.]

24. Words . . . are powers either to kill or animate. See Hamilton, Eliza M. 4

25. [See letter to Moxon, II. 8, 1836, *L. Y.*, pp. 780-81.]

26. [See letter to J. Kenyon, Autumn, 1836, *L. Y.*, pp. 812-13.]

27. [See letters to Haydon, IX. 10 and 11, 1840, *L. Y.*, pp. 1035-37.]

30. [Approves the use of " so "; as it refers to] fireside feelings and intimate friends, there appears to me a propriety in an expression inclining to the colloquial. [See *L. Y.*, pp. 1187; also 1194.]

To J. T. Coleridge, XI. 2, 1843

31. . . . I have tried in vain to find a substitute for tenacious; but see no objection to change the passage thus [" How profitless the relics," 10 (*Oxf. W.*, p. 394)].

> Our fond regrets, all that our hopes would grasp?
> The sage's theory etc.—

To C. R. (Corr. C. R., ii, 573), IX. 29, 1844

32. Your suggestion of *is* for *was* etc. will be attended to [the reference is to " Is then no nook," 1 (*Oxf. W.*, p. 282)].

To C. R. (Corr. C. R., ii, 590), II. 2, 1845

33.* New thoughts, however deep . . . were not the staple of poetry, but old thoughts presented with immortal freshness, and a kind of inspired felicity of diction. Words . . . in poetry were more than the mere garments of thought. *Aubrey de Vere,* pp. 69-70, III. 9, 1845

35. [See letter to C. W., XI. 12, 1846, *L. Y.*, p. 1299.]

Didactic Poetry

1. . . . Didactic,—the principal object of which is direct instruction; as the Poem of Lucretius, the *Georgics of Virgil, The Fleece* of Dyer, Mason's *English Garden,* etc. *Pref.* (*1815*), p. 954. 1815

2. See Passion 51

Didacticism. See also Aim of Writing; Moral Element

1. See Aim of Writing 10, 11, 18; Poetry 125; Burns 18; Chaucer 21; W. 233, 369, 372

3

3. Every great Poet is a Teacher; I wish either to be considered as a Teacher, or as nothing. *To Beaumont,*   I or II, 1808

Dignified, The. See Sublime 4

Dignity. See Smoothness 1

Discrimination. Contrast Universality

1. [For a general discussion of discrimination in epitaphs, see his essays *Upon Epitaphs.*]

2. This want of discrimination has been ascribed by Dr. Johnson, in his Essay upon the epitaphs of Pope, to two causes: first, the scantiness of the objects of human praise; and, secondly, the want of variety in characters of men; or, to use his own words, ' to the fact, that the greater part of mankind have no character at all.' Such language may be holden without blame among the generalities of common conversation; but does not become a critic and a moralist speaking seriously upon a serious subject. The objects of admiration in human nature are not scanty, but abundant: and every man has a character of his own, to the eye that has skill to perceive it. The real cause of the acknowledged want of discrimination in sepulchral memorials is this: That to analyse the characters of others, especially of those whom we love, is not a common or natural employment of men at any time. We are not anxious unerringly to understand the constitution of the minds of those who have soothed, who have cheered, who have supported us: with whom we have been long and daily pleased or delighted. The affections are their own justification. . . . We shrink from the thought of placing their merits and defects to be weighed against each other in the nice balance of pure intellect; nor do we find much temptation to detect the shades by which a good quality or virtue is discriminated in them from an excellence known by the same general name as it exists in the mind of another. . . .
Epitaph 1 (Oxf. W., pp. 930-1).   1810

3. See Epitaphs 8; Gillies 5; Gomm 2; Pope 20; W. 274, 281

Dissimilitude. See Similitude

Diversity of Taste. See Criticism: Historical Method; Taste

Drama. See also under Dramatic Poetry; Manners 2; Versification 2; Aeschylus; Aristophanes; Baillie; Beaumont, F. and J.; Brooke; Brown, J. 1; Coleridge 41, 46, 59A, 66; Cunningham, A. 1; Dryden 19; Dyce 2, 4, 9; Euripides 1-3; Fletcher 1-2; Godwin, C. Grace 1; Goethe 7, 8, 16, 18; Homer 12; Johnson 11; Kotzebue; Lamb 7, 19; Landor 8-9; Lessing 2; Lewis 1-2; Procter; Racine 1; Scott, W. 18; Shakespeare; Shelley 1, 11; Sophocles; Talfourd 1-3; Taylor, Sir Henry 1-2; Winchilsea 5; W. 18-21.

1. If ever I attempt another drama, it shall be written either purposely for the closest, or purposely for the stage. There is no middle way.
To J. Tobin, III. 6, 1798

2. [Observation and a turn for dramatic writing.] See Periodicals 23

Drama: *Actors and Acting*

3. I hope the young Roscius, if he go on as he has begun, will rescue the English theatre from the infamy that has fallen upon it, and restore the reign of good sense and Nature. From what you have seen, how do you think he could manage a character of Shakespeare? Neither Selim [*Barbarossa*] nor Douglas requires much power; but even to perform them as he does talents and genius . . . must be necessary. I had very little hope, I confess, thinking it very natural that a theatre which had brought a dog upon the stage as a principal performer would catch at a wonder whatever shape it might put on. *To Beaumont,* XII. 25, 1804

4.* My Brother vows that if the Boy [Roscius] grows up as he has begun he will write a play on purpose for him, God granting *him* also life and health for so great a work.
D. W. to Lady Beaumont, Christmas Day, 1804

5. Enough is said to show
How casual incidents of real life,
Observed where pastime only had been sought,
Outweighed, or put to flight, the set events
And measured passions of the stage, albeit
By Siddons trod in the fulness of her power.
Yet was the theatre my dear delight. . . .
Prel., vii, 401-7. 1804-39

6. See Racine 1; Shakespeare 41

Drama: *Author and his Audience.* See Shakespeare 45

Drama, *English.* See Manners 2; Congreve 3; Shakespeare

8. [Drama of present day influenced by taste of the times.] See Passion 7; and 2A

9. [Infamy of English theatre.] See Drama 3

10. [See *Prel.,* vii, 260-97; 401-85, for W.'s experience during his residence in London with various kinds of dramatic performances.]

12.* The works of the old English dramatists are the gardens of our language. *C. W., Jr. (Grosart,* iii, 461). *c.* 1827

13. See Edgeworth 1; Fletcher, J. 1, 2; Lamb 19; Taylor, Sir Henry 1, 2; W. 19-21

15. The Poetic Genius of England with the exception of Chaucer, Spenser, Milton, Dryden, Pope, and a very few more, is to be sought in her Drama. How it grieves one that there is so little probability of those valuable authors being read except by the curious! *To Dyce,* IV. 30,1830

Drama, French.   See Racine; Shakespeare 14

Drama, General Remarks on.   See W, 189, 195, 301

Drama, German

20. . . . sickly and stupid German Tragedies [of present day].   See Passion 7; and also 2A

Drama, Language of.   See Poetry 23, 25

Drama: Restoration

21. [It does not appear from Lady Winchilsea's] Aristomenes that she would have been more successful than her contemporaries, if she had cultivated tragedy. See Winchilsea 5

Dramatic Poetry

1. The Dramatic,—consisting of Tragedy, Historic Drama, Comedy, and Masque, in which the Poet does not appear at all in his own person, and where the whole action is carried on by speech and dialogue of the agents; music being admitted only incidentally and rarely. The Opera may be placed here, inasmuch as it proceeds by dialogue; though depending, to the degree that it does, upon music, it has a strong claim to be ranked with the lyrical. The characteristic and impassioned Epistle, of which Ovid and Pope have given examples, considered as a species of monodrama, may, without impropriety, be placed in this class. *Pref.* (*1815*), p. 954.   1815

2. See Poetry 23, 25, 69; Godwin, C. Grace 1

Editing.   See Criticism, Textual; Letters, Objections to Publishing; Notes; Periodicals; Scholarly Interests; Dryden

1. . . . you know what importance I attach to following strictly the last Copy of the text of an Author. . . . *To Dyce,*   IV. 30, 1830

2. See Scholarly Interests 21; Hine 1, 2

4. Nothing can be more detestable and injurious to knowledge and taste than the inaccuracies in the low priced Editions, that are thrown out upon the world by Tegg, and others of his stamp. *To T. Wyse,*   V. 3, 1838

5. [Objects usually to notes to his poems;] the poems should be left to speak for themselves. . . . *To Moxon,*   XI. 5, 1845

Elegy

1. [To give way to] transports of mind, or to quick turns of conflicting passion . . . might constitute the life and beauty of a funeral oration or elegiac poem [but not of an epitaph]. *Epitaph 1* (*Oxf. W.,* p. 932).   1810

2.   [Conventions of pastoral elegies.]
          The Poets, in their elegies and songs
          Lamenting the departed, call the groves,
          They call upon the hills and streams to mourn,
          And senseless rocks; nor idly; for they speak,

In these their invocations, with a voice
Obedient to the strong creative power
Of human passion. Sympathies there are
More tranquil, yet perhaps of kindred birth,
That steal upon the meditative mind,
And grow with thought.
Exc., i, 475-84.   1814
3. See Lyric Poetry 2; W. 278

Elizabethan Period. See Progress 1; Anderson 1

Eloquence. See also Passion
1. [W. writes that his projected essays] must be written with eloquence, or not at all. My eloquence . . . will all be carried off, at least for some time, into my poem [the projected *Recluse*]. *To J. Tobin*,   III. 6, 1798
2. See Fancy 14

Embellishments. See Rogers 8; and also Imagery, and Style

Emendation, Textual. See under Criticism, Textual

Emotion. See under Passion.

Emphasis
1. [Pauses in verse for the sake of emphasis.] See Gillies 5

Emulation. See under Imitation

Encyclopedias. See Tegg, T. 1

English. See under Drama; History; Language; Literature; and Poetry

Enthusiasm. See also Passion; Vigor
1. See Blank Verse and Rhyme 1; Poetry 19

Epic, The. See Narrative Poetry 2; Poetry 78

Epigram. See Gillies 6; Gray 6

Epistles. See Pastoral Poetry 2

Epitaphs. See also Chiabrera; Pope
1. See Aim of Writing 23; Moral Element 11; Pastoral Poetry 2; Taste 11; Gray 13-4; Mason 1; W. 276, 279, 281-2; and W.'s essays *Upon Epitaphs* for a complete discussion.
8.   I wish Lady Frederick's mind were at ease on the subject of the Epitaph. Upon her own ideas, and using mainly her own language, I worked at it—but the production I sent was too long and somewhat too historical—yet assuredly it wanted neither discrimination nor feeling. . . .
To S. Rogers,   VII. 30, 1830

9.*   [Wordsworth agreed that certain changes in the diction of the early versions of his epitaph to Southey (*Oxf. W.*, p. 587) would be] more appropriate to the simplicity of an epitaph where you con every word, and where every word is expected to bear an exact meaning.
Lady R. (Grosart, iii, 438).   XII. 21, 1841

Epithets. See Criticism 68; Cowper 1

Etymology. See Imagination 33 A

Eulogy. See Dedications; Fame; Praise. Contrast Abuse

1. I find it difficult to speak publicly of good men while alive, especially if they are persons who have power; the world ascribes the eulogy to interested motives, or to an adulatory spirit, which I detest.
To F. Wrangham,   II, 19, 1819

Fable. See under Plot; Subject

Fables. See also Fiction; History; Legends; Romances

1. [Lady Winchilsea] unlucky in her models—Pindaric odes and French Fables. *To Dyce,*   IV. 30, 1830

Fact. See under Realism; Truth

False, The. See Macpherson. Contrast Truth

1. See Realism 29

Fame. See also Popular Judgment; Praise; Taste

1. See Poetry 46, 57A, 133, 148; Taste 15; Dyer, J. 1; Milton 37, 48; Shakespeare 14, 45; W. 166, 321, 368-9.

6. . . . no Poem of mine will ever be popular. . . .
To Beaumont,   I or II, 1808

8.*   If men are to become better . . . the poems will sooner or later find admirers: If society is not to advance in civilisation it would be wretched selfishness to deplore any want of personal reputation. The approbation of a few compensates for the want of popularity. But no one . . . has completely understood me—not even Coleridge. He is not happy enough. I am myself one of the happiest of men and no man who lives a life of constant bustle and whose happiness depends on the opinions of others can possibly comprehend the best of my poems. *Remains*, p. 49.   V, 1812

12. [Because of the small number of competent critics among readers (see Criticism 81), it followed that the best poetry suffered long neglect, while less worthy compositions flourished widely before passing into oblivion. Also, even when the best authors assumed their rightful positions, errors and prejudices have prevailed concerning their genius and works. Their fame is owed to the struggles they make, their vigor to their ability to overcome opposition.] *E. Supp. Pref.*, p. 946.   1815

13. A sketch of my own notion of the constitution of Fame has been

given; and, as far as concerns myself, I have cause to be satisfied. The love, the admiration, the indifference, the slight, the aversion, and even the contempt, with which these Poems have been received, knowing, as I do, the source within my own mind, from which they have proceeded, and the labour and pains, which, when labour and pains appeared needful, have been bestowed upon them, must all, if I think consistently, be received as pledges and tokens, bearing the same general impression, though widely different in value;—they are all proofs that for the present time I have not laboured in vain; and afford assurances, more or less authentic, that the products of my industry will endure. *E. Supp. Pref.*, p. 951.   1815

13A. The state of the public Mind is at present little adapted to relish any part of my poetical effusion on this occasion.—There is too much derangement in the taxation of the country; too much real distress, and above all too much imaginary depression, and downright party fury. But all this I disregard as I write chiefly for Posterity. *To C. W.*,   III. 25, 1816

14.   A volant Tribe of Bards on earth are found,
       Who, while the flattering Zephyrs round them play,
       On " coignes of vantage " hang their nests of clay;
       How quickly from that aery hold unbound,
       Dust for oblivion! To the solid ground
       Of nature trusts the Mind that builds for aye;
       Convinced that there, there only, she can lay
       Secure foundations.
       " A Volant Tribe," 1-8.   1823

15.   . . . but little known to fame. . . .
       Aquapendente, 94.   1837

16. . . . I feel & perhaps it may in some degree be the same with you, justified in attaching comparatively small importance to any literary monument that I may be enabled to leave behind. It is well however, I am convinced, that men think otherwise in the earlier part of their lives, and why it is so is a point I need not touch upon in writing to you.
Reed, p. 14.   XII. 23, 1839

17.* . . . he spoke of having long had a great desire for fame, but that that had now all ceased. . . . *Old Friends*, p. 286.   *c.* 1850

Fancy. See also Imagination

1. See Aim of Writing 37; Composition 19; History 6, 10; Imagination 11, 33A; Passion 8; Poetry 58, 66

2. . . . fancy, the power by which pleasure and surprise are excited by sudden varieties of situation and by accummulated imagery.
Oxf. W., p. 899.   1800-5

3.   Thus [see ll. 410-20] wilful Fancy, in no hurtful mood,
       Engrafted far-fetched shapes on feelings bred
       By pure Imagination: busy Power
       She was, and with her ready pupil turned
       Instinctively to human passions, then

Least understood.
Prel., viii, 421-6.   1804-39

5. . . . the understanding sleeps in order that the fancy may dream.
See Criticism 44

6. [Writer of epitaphs should be little disposed] to adopt phrases of
fancy. See Pope 18

7. See Chesterfield 1; Cotton 1; Reynolds, J. H. 1; W. 62-3, 67

9.* Wordsworth talked much about poetry. He was made to explain
fancy as opposed to *imagination*, from which it results that fancy forms
casual and fleeting combinations in which objects are united, *not* on a permanent relation which subsists and has its principle in the capacity of the
sensible produced to represent and stand in the place of the abstract intellectual conception, but in a voluntary power of combination which only
expresses the fact of the combination with little or no import beyond itself.
This is the best explanation I can give. Wordsworth quoted as instances a fine
description of cold from Cotton's *Winter* (his own *Kitten and the Falling
Leaves* I have mentioned before). *H. C. R.*, i, 93.   VI. 3, 1812

11.* I have heard Wordsworth speak of his poems of fancy as if he
deemed them not inferior to his poems of imagination. . . .
H. C. R., i, 96.   VI. 4, 1812

14. [Fancy and imagination.] To the mode in which Fancy has already
been characterized as the power of evoking and combining, or, as my friend
Mr. Coleridge has styled it, ' the aggregative and associative power,' my objection is only that the definition is too general. To aggregate and to associate,
to evoke and to combine, belong as well to the Imagination as to the Fancy;
but either the materials evoked and combined are different; or they are
brought together under a different law, and for a different purpose. Fancy
does not require that the materials which she makes use of should be sus-
ceptible of change in their constitution, from her touch; and, where they admit
of modification, it is enough for her purpose if it be slight, limited, and
evanescent. Directly the reverse of these, are the desires and demands of the
Imagination. She recoils from everything but the plastic, the pliant, and the
indefinite. She leaves it to Fancy to describe Queen Mab as coming,

> In shape no bigger than an agate-stone
> On the fore-finger of an alderman.

Having to speak of stature, she does not tell you that her gigantic Angel was
as tall as Pompey's Pillar; much less that he was twelve cubits, or twelve
hundred cubits high; or that his dimensions equalled those of Teneriffe or
Atlas;—because these, and if they were a million times as high it would be
the same, are bounded: The expression is, ' His stature reached the sky!' the
illimitable firmament!—When the Imagination frames a comparison, if it
does not strike on the first presentation, a sense of the truth of the likeness,
from the moment that it is perceived, grows—and continues to grow—upon
the mind; the resemblance depending less upon outline of form and feature,
than upon expression and effect; less upon casual and outstanding, than upon

inherent and internal, properties: moreover, the images invariably modify each other.—The law under which the processes of Fancy are carried on is as capricious as accidents of things, and the effects are surprising, playful, ludicrous, amusing, tender, or pathetic, as the objects happen to be appositely produced or fortunately combined. Fancy depends upon the rapidity and profusion with which she scatters her thoughts and images; trusting that their number, and the felicity with which they are linked together, will make amends for the want of individual value: or she prides herself upon the curious subtility and the successful elaboration with which she can detect their lurking affinities. If she can win you over to her purpose, and impart to you her feelings, she cares not how unstable or transitory may be her influence, knowing that it will not be out of her power to resume it upon an apt occasion. But the Imagination is conscious of an indestructible dominion:—the Soul may fall away from it, not being able to sustain its grandeur; but, if once felt and acknowledged, by no act of any other faculty of the mind can it be relaxed, impaired, or diminished.—Fancy is given to quicken and to beguile the temporal part of our nature, Imagination to incite and to support the eternal.—Yet is it not the less true that Fancy, as she is an active, is also, under her own laws and in her own spirit, a creative faculty? In what manner Fancy ambitiously aims at a rivalship with Imagination, and Imagination stoops to work with the materials of Fancy, might be illustrated from the compositions of all eloquent writers, whether in prose or verse; and chiefly from those of our own Country. Scarcely a page of the impassioned parts of Bishop Taylor's Works can be opened that shall not afford examples. See Chesterfield 1; Cotton 1. *Pref. 1815*, pp. 957-58.   1815

14A.   Awe-stricken as I am by contemplating the operations of the mind of this truly divine Poet [Milton], I scarcely dare venture to add that *An Address to an Infant* [" Address to my Infant Daughter, Dora "], which the reader will find under the class of Fancy in the present volumes, exhibits something of this communion and interchange of instruments and functions between the two powers [imagination and fancy]; and is accordingly placed last in the class, as a preparation for that of imagination, which follows. See Fancy 14; Imagination 33A-G. *Pref., 1815* (*K. Prose*, ii, 218-9). Omitted ed. 1845.   1815-36

Feeling. See under Passion

Felicity. See also Style

1.   [No] quantity of good verses can ever be produced by mere felicity. . . . See Gray 5

2.   See Wrangham 10; Coleridge 61B

3.*   . . . old thoughts presented with . . . a kind of inspired felicity of diction [are the staple of poetry]. *Aubrey de Vere*, p. 69.   III. 9, 1845

Feminine Endings. See also Versification

1.   [Trochaic endings for drama.] See Taylor, Sir Henry 2

Fiction.   See under Realism; also Fables; Legends; Mythology; Novel, The; Romances

   1.   [Avoid all modes of fiction in writing epitaphs.] See Pope 18
   2.   [Remoteness of place equivalent to distance of time.] See Currie 2
   3.   [Fiction and biography.] See Biography 2A
   4.   [Dante's fictions] often struck me as offensively grotesque and fantastic. . . . *To Landor,*   I. 21, 1824
   5.   See History 11, 12, 13

Figures of Speech.   See under Imagery

Finish.   See under Composition; Labor; Revisions; Style

   1.   [Finish of execution as a test of a sonnet's merit.] See Sonnet 7
   2.*   Carelessness in the finish of composition he seemed to look on almost as an offence. *Justice Coleridge (Grosart,* iii, 424).   Summer, 1836

Footnotes.   See under Notes

Forgeries, Literary.   See Cottle, J. 3; Macpherson 2

Form.   See under Composition; Finish; Proportion; Revisions; Sonnet; Unity; Versification; Wholeness

   1.   See Composition 2; Poetry 113; Heraud 1; W. 170

French.   See Criticism 79 A; Fables 1; Language 7-9; Literature 20, 22; Patronage 3; Taste 16; Shakespeare 14. For individual authors, see Beranger; Boileau; Bonaparte, L.; Brugiere; Cottin; De Lille; Du Bartas; Guizot; La Fontaine; Racine; Ramond; Rosset; Rousseau; Staël; Voltaire

Freshness.   See Diction; Poetry 158; Style

Funeral Oration

   1.   [To give way to] transports of mind, or to quick turns of conflicting passions . . . might constitute the life and beauty of a funeral oration or elegiac poem [but not of an epitaph]. *Epitaph 1 (Oxf. W.,* p. 932).   1810

Gardening.   See also Nature (External); Picturesque, The

   1.   Painters and Poets have had the credit of being reckoned the Fathers of English gardening. . . . It was a misconception of the meaning and principles of poets and painters which gave countenance to the modern system of gardening [*E. L.,* pp. 523-4]. . . . Laying out grounds, as it is called, may be considered as a liberal art, in some sort like Poetry and Painting; and its object, like that of all the liberal arts, is, or ought to be, to move the affections under the controul of good sense; that is, of the best and wisest, but speaking with more precision, it is to assist Nature in moving the affections; and surely,

as I have said, the affections of those who have the deepest perception of the beauty of Nature, who have the most valuable feelings, that is, the most permanent, the most independent, the most ennobling, connected with Nature and human life. No liberal art aims merely at the gratification of an individual or a class, the Painter or Poet is degraded in proportion as he does so; the true servants of the Arts pay homage to the human kind as impersonated in unwarped and enlightened minds. If this be so when we are merely putting together words or colours, how much more ought the feeling to prevail when we are in the midst of the realities of things. . . .
To Beaumont (*E. L.*, pp. 523-4 and 527),   X. 17, 1805

   2. See Criticism 61A; Taste 8; Addison 2

General and the Particular, The. See under Universality

Genius. See also Creative; Imagination; Originality; Power

   1. See Biography 2A-C; Moral Element 17; Nature 7; Reason 31; Burke 3A; Hamilton, Eliza M. 3; Pope 4, 6, 14

   2A.* [W. said he had] little talent; genius was his peculiar faculty. [See also White, H. K. 1.] *Remains*, p. 49.   V, 1812

   3. Of genius the only proof is, the act of doing well what is worthy to be done, and what was never done before: Of genius, in the fine arts, the only infallible sign is the widening the sphere of human sensibility, for the delight, honour, and benefit of human nature. Genius is the introduction of a new element into the intellectual universe: or, if that be not allowed, it is the application of powers to objects on which they had not before been exercised, or the employment of them in such a manner as to produce effects hitherto unknown. What is all this but an advance, or a conquest, made by the soul of the poet? . . . he [the reader] is invigorated and inspirited by his leader, in order that he may exert himself; for he cannot proceed in quiescence, he cannot be carried like a dead weight. Therefore to create taste is to call forth and bestow power, of which knowledge is the effect; and *there* lies the true difficulty. *E. Supp. Pref.*, p. 952.   1815

German. See Criticism 82-A; Drama 20; Language 10-13; Literature 22-4; Poetry 107; Transcendentalism 2; Shakespeare 14; W. 135. For individual authors, see Bucer; Burger; Busk; Fichte; Goethe; Grimm; Kant; Klopstock; Klopstock, Margareta; Kotzebue; Mosheim; Niebuhr; Schelling; Schiller; Stolberg; Voss; Winckelmann

Good Sense. See Credibility; Judgment; Probability; Reason

   1. See Criticism 49; Gardening 1; Imagery 15; Poetry 74; Style 6, 22, 24; Hamilton, Eliza M. 4; Jewsbury 1

   2. [Good sense a] property of all good poetry. . . . *Pref. L. B.*, p. 936.
                          1800

Gothic Novels. See Scott, W. 37

Grand, The. See Sublime 4

Greek. See under Ancient Writers (Classical)

Harmony. See Gillies 5; and also under Versification

Harsh, and Harshness. See Translation 4; Hamilton, Eliza M. 4; Shakespeare 56; and also Diction; Style; Versification

Hebrews, The
 1. . . . the Hebrews were preserved [from the bondage of definite form] by their abhorrence of idolatry. See Imagination 33G

Heroic Poetry. See Narrative Poetry 2; Poetry 78

Historical Method of Criticism. See under Criticism, Historical Method

Historical Research. See under History

Historic Poem, The. See Narrative Poetry 2

History. See also Biography
 1. [Historian *vs.* poet.] See Poetry 20
 2. See Biography 5; Knowledge 6; Legends 3; Passion 22; Arnold, T. 2; Homer 13; W. 171
 3.   'Tis true, the history of our native land,
           With those of Greece compared and popular Rome,
           And in our high-wrought modern narratives
           Stript of their harmonising soul, the life
           Of manners and familiar incidents,
           Had never much delighted me. And less
           Than other intellects had mine been used
           To lean upon extrinsic circumstances
           Of record or tradition. . . .
           Prel., viii, 617-25.   1804-39
 4.   . . . even the historian's tale
           Prizing but little otherwise than I prized
           Tales of the poets, as it made the heart
           Beat high, and filled the fancy with fair forms,
           Old heroes and their sufferings and their deeds. . . .
           Prel., ix, 204-8 (see also 168-80).   1804-39
 4A.   Above all
           Were reestablished now those watchful thoughts
           Which, seeing little worthy or sublime
           In what the Historian's pen so much delights
           To blazon—power and energy detached
           From moral purpose. . . .
           Prel., xiii, 39-44.   1804-39

5. . . . if you are fond of History read it in the old Memoirs or old Chronicles. *D. W. to C. Clarkson,* Christmas Day, 1805

6. [History] enslaves the Fancy. *To R. Sharp,* IV. 16, 1822

8. . . . a Worcester paper sent me that gives, what it calls the *real* History of Miserrimus—[*A Gravestone upon the floor in the Cloisters of Worcester Cathedral, v. Oxf. W.,* p. 275] spoiling, as *real* Histories generally do, the Poem altogether. . . . *To B. Field,* XII. 20, 1828

. . .

10.   Thus everywhere to truth Tradition clings,
Or Fancy localises Powers we love.
Were only History licensed to take note
Of things gone by, her meagre monuments
Would ill suffice for persons and events:
There is an ampler page for man to quote,
A reader book of manifold contents,
Studied alike in palace and in cot.
"The Lovers," 7-14.   1833

11.   Complacent Fictions were they, yet the same
Involved a history of no doubtful sense,
History that proves by inward evidence
From what a precious source of truth it came.
Ne'er could the boldest Eulogist have dared
Such deeds to paint, such characters to frame,
But for coeval sympathy prepared
To greet with instant faith their loftiest claim.
None but a noble people could have loved
Flattery in Ancient Rome's pure-minded style:
Not in like sort the Runic Scald was moved;
He, nursed 'mid savage passions that defile
Humanity, sang feats that well might call
For the blood-thirsty mead of Odin's riotous Hall.
"Complacent Fictions," 1-14.   1837

12.   [Historical research.]
Those old credulities, to nature dear,
Shall they no longer bloom upon the stock
Of History, stript naked as a rock
'Mid a dry desert? What is it we hear?
The glory of Infant Rome must disappear,
Her morning splendours vanish, and their place
Know them no more. If Truth, who veiled her face
With those bright beams yet hid it not, must steer
Henceforth a humbler course perplexed and slow;
One solace yet remains for us who came
Into this world in days when story lacked
Severe research, that in our hearts we know
How, for exciting youth's heroic flame,

Assent is power, belief the soul of fact.
[See *Knight*, viii, 60 note.]
"Those old credulities," 1-14.　　　　　　　　　　1837

13.　　[Historical research.]
Forbear to deem the Chronicler unwise,
Ungentle, or untouched by seemly ruth,
Who, gathering up all that Time's envious tooth
Has spared of sound and grave realities,
Firmly rejects those dazzling flatteries,
Dear as they are to unsuspecting Youth,
That might have drawn down Clio from the skies
To vindicate the majesty of truth.
Such was her office while she walked with men,
A Muse, who, not unmindful of her Sire
All-ruling Jove, whate'er the theme might be
Revered her Mother, sage Mnemosyne,
And taught her faithful servants how the lyre
Should animate, but not mislead, the pen.
"Forbear to deem," 1-14.　　　　　　　　　　　1837

14.*　　. . . desired a really great History of England. . . .
De Vere (*Grosart*, iii, 492).　　　　　　　1842-46

16.*　. . . Mr. Wordsworth has small value for anything but contemporary history. [Contrast *Prel.* (De Sel.), pp. 503-4.]
Mrs. D. (*Grosart*, iii, 443).　　　　　　　VII. 11, 1844

History Drama.　See Dramatic Poetry 1

Hymns, Devotional

1.　See Lyric Poetry 2

2.*　　He was in favour of a collection of metrical hymns, more peculiarly Christian in character than the Psalter, being set forth by authority for use in the Church; and for the choice of such hymns he thought a Committee should be appointed in which the knowledge of divine, of poet, and of laymen trusted for common sense and experience in life should be severally and conjointly engaged. As a practical suggestion of moment in the *composition* of such hymns he advised that composers should not in the four-line stanza do more than make the second and fourth lines rhyme; leaving the other two unrhymed, he said, would give an important addition of freedom both to the sense and the style. *Graves* (*Grosart*, iii, 473).　　　　*c.* 1840

3.　I am pleased to hear what you are about, but I am far too advanced in life to venture upon anything so difficult to do as hymns of devotion.
The one of mine which you allude to [*The Labourer's Noon-Day Hymn* (*Oxf. W.*, p. 506)] is quite at your service, only I could wish the first line of the fifth stanza to be altered thus:

Each field is then a hallowed spot.

Or you might omit the stanza altogether . . . the piece being long enough without it. *To H. Alford*,　　　　　　　　II. 28, 1844

Hyberbole. See Publishing 2; Graham, J. 1

Idealism. See under Realism

Idiom. See Blank Verse and Rhyme 1; Diction; Style

Idyls. See under Pastoral Poetry

Imagery. See also Description; Passion; Style; Truth

1. [Variety of] forms and imagery [ought]. See also Meter 1. *Pref. L. B.*, p. 939.
1800

2. See Criticism 40; Elegy 2; Fancy 2, 14; Translation 4; Setting 1

3. . . . passages, which with propriety abound with metaphors and figures, will have their due efect. . . . See Poetry 25

4. [In avoiding conventional poetic diction, W. was cut] off from a large portion of phrases and figures of speech which . . . have long been regarded as the common inheritance of Poets. *Pref. L. B.*, p. 936.   1800

5. [Discussion of style that the reader] may not censure me for not having performed what I never attempted. The Reader will find that personifications of abstract ideas rarely occur in these volumes; and are utterly rejected, as an ordinary device to elevate the style, and raise it above prose. My purpose was to imitate, and, as far as possible, to adopt the very language of men; and assuredly such personifications do not make any natural or regular part of that language. They are, indeed, a figure of speech occasionally prompted by passion, and I have made use of them as such; but have endeavoured utterly to reject them as a mechanical device of style, or as a family language which Writers in metre seem to lay claim to by prescription. [In 1800: " Except in a very few instances the Reader will find no personifications of abstract ideas in these volumes, not that I mean to censure such personifications; they may well be fitted for certain sorts of composition, but in these Poems I propose to myself to imitate, and, as far as possible, to adopt the very language of men, and I do not find that such personifications make any regular or natural part of that language."] I have wished to keep the Reader in the company of flesh and blood, persuaded that by so doing I shall interest him. Others who pursue a different track will interest him likewise; I do not interfere with their claim, but wish to prefer a claim of my own. *Pref. L. B.*, p. 936.
1802

6. See Coleridge 61B; Edgeworth 1; Graham, James 1; Macpherson 2; Rogers 2; Shakespeare 24; Watts, A. 1; W. 89, 170, 329

7. [Feeling powerfully as the earliest poets did] their language was daring, and figurative. *App. L. B.*, p. 942.
1802

8.   Brook! whose society the Poet seeks,
                    . . . I would not do
          Like Grecian Artists, give thee human cheeks,
          Channels for tears; no Naiad shouldst thou be,—
          Have neither limbs, feet, feathers, joints, nor hairs:
          It seems the Eternal Soul is clothed in thee

With purer robes than those of flesh and blood,
And hath bestowed on thee a safer good;
Unwearied joy, and life without its cares.
" Brook! whose," 1, and 7-14.   1806

9. [Writers of epitaphs should be little disposed] to enter into the more remote regions of illustrative imagery. See Pope 18

10. [Illustrative imagery may be " so impure " as to obscure depth of sincere feeling, but this fault is not so great as evidence of lack of feeling.] *Epitaph 3* (*Grosart*, ii, 62).   1810

15. [Personification must meet the test of good sense.] See Hamilton, Eliza M. 4

Images.   See Fancy; Imagination 33; Sensitiveness; W. 329.

Imagination.   See Creative, The; Fancy; Genius; Infinity; Invention; Nature; Originality; Passion; Style

1. See Aim of Writing 10, 28; Creative 4; Criticism 44, 81; Fancy 3, 9, 11, 14, 14A; Moral Element 11; Passion 8, 43; Poetry 34, 41, 49, 58, 66, 67, 68, 71, 111, 113, 114, 122, 138, 149; Progress 1; Realism 13, 47, 49; Reason 30; Style 40; Taste 14, 15, 23

1A. . . . imagination . . . the faculty which produces impressive effects out of simple elements. . . . *Oxf. W.*, p. 899.   1800-5

2.   Thus here [in London] imagination also found
             An element that pleas'd her, tried her strength,
             Among new objects simplified, arranged,
             Impregnated my knowledge, made it live. . . .
             Prel., viii. A 796-9.   1804-5

3. [The imagination is false when it goes beyond] The limits of experience and of truth. *Prel.*, x, A 842-49.   1804-5

4. [*The Prelude* has advanced with] imagination teaching truth. . . . *Prel.*, xi, A 42-5.   1804-5

5.   [Nature] upon the outward face of things,
             So moulds them, and endues, abstracts, combines,
             Or by abrupt and unhabitual influence
             Doth make one object . . . impress itself
             Upon all others and pervade them. . . .
             Prel., xiii, A 78-82; see W MS, *Prel.* (De Sel) pp. 475-7.   1804-5

6.   The Power . . .
                         which Nature thus
             Thrusts upon the senses, is the express
                              . . . Counterpart
             Which higher minds bear with them as their own.
             Prel., xiii, A 84-90; see also xiv, 86-90.   1804-5

7. See Austen, Jane 1; Bible 8; Cowper 1; Jeffrey 12; Miller 1; Pope 1A; Shakespeare 3; Thompson 7; Tickell 1A; W. 15, 23, 26, 89, 101A, 104, 117, 118, 195, 199, 345A, 352, 354, 364A, 386

8. My first creative sensibility . . . for the most [was dominated by the]
external things With which it communed. *Prel.*, ii, 360-8.   1804-39

8A.   Imagination—here the Power so called
           Through sad incompetence of human speech,
           That awful Power rose from the mind's abyss
           Like an unfathered vapour that enwraps,
           At once, some lonely traveller.
               . . .
           But to my conscious soul I now can say—
           " I recognize thy glory: " in such strength
           Of usurpation, when the light of sense
           Goes out, but with a flash that has revealed
           The invisible world, doth greatness make abode,
           There harbours; whether we be young or old,
           Our destiny, our being's heart and home,
           Is with infinitude, and only there. . . .
           Prel., vi, 592-96 and 598-605; see also vi, A 525-40.   1804-39

9.   . . . Nature works
           Herself upon the outward face of things
           As if with an imaginative power [alternative
           lines on another page of W MS].
           De Sel. (*Prel.*, p. 600n).   II-III, 1804

10.   More lofty themes [often made] the imaginative power
           Languish within me. . . .
           Prel., vii. 465-69.   1804-39

10A.   [The native shepherds were more exalted, had]
           Far more of an imaginative form
           Than the gay Corin of the groves [of pastoral poetry]. . . .
           Prel., viii. 282-5.   1804-39

11.   But when that first poetic faculty
           Of plain Imagination and severe,
           No longer a mute influence of the soul,
           Ventured, at some rash Muse's earnest call,
           To try her strength among harmonious words;
           And to book-notions and the rules of art
           Did knowingly conform itself; there came
           Among the simple shapes of human life
           A wilfulness of fancy and conceit:
           And Nature and her objects beautified
           These fictions, as in some sort, in their turn,
           They burnished her.
           Prel., viii, 365-76.   1804-39

19. [Influence of cities on the creative powers of a poet.] See Cities 1

20. [Higher minds] build up greatest things From least suggestions. . . .
[Such minds] need not extraordinary calls To rouse them . . . [and are able
to free themselves from the tyranny of the senses.] *Prel.*, xiv, 101-6.
[See also *Prel.*, xiv, 189-92.]   1804-39

22.   Imagination [and intellectual or spiritual love]
           . . . are each in each, and cannot stand
           Dividually.
           Prel., xiv, 206-9. [See also *Exc.*, iv, 1126-32.]   1804-39

23.   . . . the voice . . . of my Poetry without Imagination [in the
reader] cannot be heard. *To Lady Beaumont* (p. 126),   V. 21, 1807

24.   [A snowstorm in Fleet Street showed W.] what a blessing . . . there
is in habits of exalted imagination.   My sorrow was controlled, and my
uneasiness of mind—not quieted and relieved altogether—seemed at once to
receive the gift of an anchor of security. *To Beaumont,*   IV. 8, 1808

27.   . . . imagination almost always transcends reality.
To Gillies,   XI. 23, 1814

27A.   Happy for us that the imagination and affections in our own despite
mitigate the evils of that state of intellectural Slavery which the calculating
understanding is apt to produce. *Exc.*, iv, " Argument " (1814 ed.).   1814

28.   The imaginative faculty was lord
           Of observations natural. . . .
           Exc., iv, 707-8.   1814

29.   Is it well to trust
           Imagination's light when reason's fails,
           The unguarded taper where the guarded faints?
           Exc., iv, 771-3.   1814

30.   [Imagination of humble folk] a Man so bred
           (Take from him what you will upon the score
           Of ignorance or illusion) lives and breathes
           For noble purposes of mind: his heart
           Beats to the heroic song of ancient days;
           His eye distinguishes, his soul creates.
           Exc., iv. 828-33.   1814

32A.   This subject may be dismissed with observing—that, in the
series of Poems placed under the head of Imagination, I have begun with one
of the earliest processes of Nature in the development of this faculty. Guided
by one of my own primary consciousnesses, I have represented a commutation
and transfer of internal feelings, co-operating with external accidents to plant,
for immortality, conjoined impressions of sound and sight in the celestial
soil of the Imagination. The Boy, there introduced, is listening, with something of a feverish and restless anxiety, for the recurrence of the riotous
sounds which he had previously excited; and, at the moment when the intenseness of his mind is beginning to remit, he is surprised into a perception of
the solemn and tranquillising images which the Poem describes.—The Poems
next in succession exhibit the faculty exerting itself upon various objects of
the external universe; then follow others, where it is employed upon feelings,
characters, and actions [W.'s note: " Such of these as were furnished by
Scottish subjects have since been arranged in a cl₂˙s, entitled, ' Memorials

of Tours in Scotland ' "] ; and the class is concluded with imaginative pictures
of moral, political, and religious sentiments.

Pref. 1815 (K. Prose, ii, 215-16). 1815-36

33. [A] 'A man,' says an intelligent author, 'has imagination in proportion as he can distinctly copy in idea the impressions of sense: it is the
faculty which *images* within the mind the phenomena of sensation. A man has
fancy in proportion as he can call up, connect, or associate, at pleasure, those
internal images (φαντάζειν is to cause to appear) so as to complete ideal
representations of absent objects. Imagination is the power of depicting,
and fancy of evoking and combining. The imagination is formed by patient
observation; the fancy by a voluntary activity in shifting the scenery of the
mind. The more accurate the imagination, the more safely may a painter, or
a poet, undertake a delineation, or a description, without the presence of
the objects to be characterized. The more versatile the fancy, the more
original and striking will be the decorations produced.'—*British Synonyms
discriminated, by W. Taylor.*

Is not this as if a man should undertake to supply an account of a building,
and be so intent upon what he had discovered of the foundation, as to conclude his task without once looking up at the superstructure? Here, as in
other instances throughout the volume, the judicious Author's mind is en-
thralled by Etymology; he takes up the original word as his guide and escort,
and too often does not perceive how soon he becomes its prisoner, without
liberty to tread in any path but that to which it confines him.. It is not easy to
find out how imagination, thus explained, differs from distinct remembrance
of images; or fancy from quick and vivid recollection of them: each is nothing
more than a mode of memory. If the two words bear the above meaning,
and no other, what term is left to designate that faculty of which the Poet is
' all compact '; he whose eye glances from earth to heaven, whose spiritual
attributes body forth what his pen is prompt in turning to shape; or what is
left to characterize Fancy, as insinuating herself into the heart of objects with
creative activity?—

[B] Imagination, in the sense of the word as giving title to a class of the
following Poems, has no reference to images that are merely a faithful copy,
existing in the mind, of absent external objects; but is a word of higher
import, denoting operations of the mind upon those objects, and processes
of creation or of composition, governed by certain fixed laws. [W. illustrates
uses of the imagination in the word " hang " with reference to the goats in
Vergil (*First Eclogue*)]:

> " Non ego vos posthac viridi projectus inantro
> Dumosa *pendere* procul de rupe videbo."
>
> . . . . " half way down
> *Hangs* one who gathers samphire,"

is the well-known expression of Shakespeare [*Lear,* IV, vi, 14-5. Kittredge
ed.] delineating an ordinary image upon the cliffs of Dover. . . .

[From *Paradise Lost,* ii, 636-43, W. points out " hangs in the clouds "
as the height of imaginative power.]

[(C) illustrations of imagination in recording impressions of sound, in *Poems* (*1815*):]

> "Over his own sweet voice the Stock-dove *broods*;"

of the same bird,

> "His voice was *buried* among trees,
> Yet to be come at by the breeze;"
>
> "O, Cuckoo! shall I call thee *Bird*,
> Or but a wandering *Voice*?"

The stock-dove is said to *coo*, a sound well imitating the note of the bird; but, by the intervention of the metaphor *broods*, the affections are called in by the imagination to assist in marking the manner in which the bird reiterates and prolongs her soft note, as if herself delighting to listen to it, and participating of a still and quiet satisfaction, like that which may be supposed inseparable from the continuous process of incubation. 'His voice was buried among trees,' a metaphor expressing the love of *seclusion* by which this Bird is marked; and characterizing its note as not partaking of the shrill and the piercing, and therefore more easily deadened by the intervening shade; yet a note so peculiar and withal so pleasing, that the breese, gifted with that love of the sound which the Poet feels, penetrates the shades in which it is entombed, and conveys it to the ear of the listener.

> "Shall I call thee Bird,
> Or but a wandering Voice?"

This concise interrogation characterizes the seeming ubiquity of the voice of the cuckoo, and dispossesses the creature almost of a corporeal existence; the Imagination being tempted to this exertion of her power by a consciousness in the memory that the cuckoo is almost perpetually heard throughout the season of spring, but seldom becomes an object of sight.

Thus far of images independent of each other, and immediately endowed by the mind with properties that do not inhere in them, upon an incitement from properties and qualities the existence of which is inherent and obvious. These processes of imagination are carried on either by conferring additional properties upon an object, or abstracting from it some of those which it actually possesses, and thus enabling it to re-act upon the mind which hath performed the process, like a new existence.

[(D) The modifying power of imagination.] The Reader has already had a fine instance before him in the passage quoted [see (B)] from Virgil, where the apparently perilous situation of the goat, hanging upon the shaggy precipice, is contrasted with that of the shepherd contemplating it from the seclusion of the cavern in which he lies stretched at ease and in security. Take these images separately, and how unaffecting the picture compared with that produced by their being thus connected with, and opposed to, each other!

> "As a huge stone is sometimes seen to lie
> Couched on the bald top of an eminence,
> Wonder to all who do the same espy
> By what means it could thither come, and whence,

So that it seems a thing endued with sense,
Like a sea-beast crawled forth, which on a shelf
Of rock or sand reposeth, there to sun himself.

Such seemed this Man; not all alive or dead
Nor all asleep, in his extreme old age.

Motionless as a cloud the old Man stood,
That heareth not the loud winds when they call,
And moveth altogether if it move at all."
[*Resolution and Independence*, 57-65; and 75-77.]

In these images, the conferring, the abstracting, and the modifying powers of the Imagination, immediately and mediately acting, are all brought into conjunction. The stone is endowed with something of the power of life to approximate it to the sea-beast; and the sea-beast stripped of some of its vital qualities to assimilate it to the stone; which intermediate image is thus treated for the purpose of bringing the original image, that of the stone, to a nearer resemblance to the figure and condition of the aged Man; who is divested of so much of the indications of life and motion as to bring him to the point where the two objects unite and coalesce in just comparison. After what has been said, the image of the cloud need not be commented upon.

[(E) How the imagination shapes and creates.] By innumerable processes; and in none does it more delight than in that of consolidating numbers into unity, and dissolving and separating unity into number,—alternations proceeding from, and governed by, a sublime consciousness of the soul in her own mighty and almost divine powers. Recur to the passage already cited from Milton [see B, above]. When the compact Fleet, as one Person, has been introduced ' sailing from Bengala,' ' They,' *i. e.* the ' merchants,' representing the fleet resolved into a multitude of ships, " ply " their voyage towards the extremities of the earth: ' So ' (referring to the word ' As ' in the commencement) ' seemed the flying Fiend '; the image of his Person acting to recombine the multitude of ships into one body,—the point from which the comparison set out. ' So seemed,' and to whom seemed? To the heavenly Muse who dictates the poem, to the eye of the Poet's mind, and to that of the Reader, present at one moment in the wide Ethiopian, and the next in the solitudes, then first broken in upon, of the infernal regions!

" Modo me Thebis, modo ponit Athenis."

Hear again this mighty Poet,—speaking of the Messiah going forth to expel from heaven the rebellious angels,

" Attended by ten thousand thousand Saints
He onward came: far off his coming shone,"—

the retinue of Saints, and the Person of the Messiah himself, lost almost and merged in the splendour of that indefinite abstraction ' His coming! '

[(F) Imagination as a unifying process.] I will not consider it (more than I have already done by implication) as that power which, in the language of one of my most esteemed Friends [Lamb], ' draws all things to one;

which makes things animate or inanimate, beings with their attributes, subjects with their accessories, take one colour and serve to one effect.'

[(G) Imagination, poetical distinguished from human and dramatic.] The grand store-houses of enthusiastic and meditative Imagination, of poetical, as contra-distinguished from human and dramatic Imagination, are the prophetic and lyrical parts of the Holy Scriptures, and the works of Milton; to which I cannot forbear to add those of Spenser. I select these writers in preference to those of ancient Greece and Rome, because the anthropomorphitism of the Pagan religion subjected the minds of the greatest poets in those countries too much to the bondage of definite form; from which the Hebrews were preserved by their abhorrence of idolatry. This abhorrence was almost as strong in our great epic Poet, both from circumstances of his life, and from the constitution of his mind. However imbued the surface might be with classical literature, he was a Hebrew in soul; and all things tended in him towards the sublime. Spenser, of a gentler nature, maintained his freedom by aid of his allegorical spirit, at one time inciting him to create persons out of abstractions; and, at another, by a superior effort of genius, to give the universality and permanence of abstractions to his human beings, by means of attributes and emblems that belong to the highest moral truths and the purest sensations,—of which his character of Una is a glorious example. Of the human and dramatic Imagination the works of Shakespeare are an inexhaustible source. *Pref. 1815*, pp. 955-57.   1815

34. [De Selincourt says: In 1815 ' There was a boy ' stands first among the *Poems of the Imagination* and is referred to in the Preface in the following passage (omitted in 1845).] I dismiss this subject with observing that in the series of Poems placed under the head of Imagination, I have begun with one of the earliest processes of Nature in the development of this faculty. Guided by one of my own primary consciousnesses, I have represented a commutation and transfer of internal feelings, co-operating with external accidents to plant, for immortality, images of sound and sight, in the celestial soil of the Imagination. The Boy, there introduced, is listening, with something of a feverish and restless anxiety, for the recurrence of the riotous sounds which he had previously excited; and, at the moment when the intenseness of his mind is beginning to remit, he is surprised into a perception of the solemn and tranquillizing images which the Poem describes.
Pref. 1815 (*Prelude*, p. 531, ed. De Selincourt).   1815

34A.   Who wants the glorious faculty assigned
             To elevate the more-than-reasoning Mind,
             And colour life's dark cloud with orient rays.
             Imagination is that sacred power,
             Imagination lofty and refined. . . .
             " Weak is the will of Man," 6-10.   1815

35.* . . . by the imagination the mere fact is exhibited as connected with that infinity without which there is no poetry . . . that imagination is the faculty by which the poet conceives and produces—that is, images—individual forms in which are *embodied universal ideas or abstractions.* See also Realism 49. *H. C. R.*, i, 191.   IX. 11, 1816

36. The value of works of imagination it is impossible to predict.
To A. Watts, VIII. 13, 1825

37.* S - - -, in the work you mentioned to me, confounds *imagery* and *imagination*. Sensible objects really existing, and felt to exist, are *imagery*; and they may form the materials of a descriptive poem, where objects are delineated as they are. Imagination is a subjective term: it deals with objects not as they are, but as they appear to the mind of the poet.

The imagination is that intellectual lens through the medium of which the poetical observer sees the objects of his observation, modified both in form and colour; or it is that inventive dresser of dramatic *tableaux*, by which the persons of the play are invested with new drapery, or placed in new attitudes; or it is that chemical faculty by which elements of the most different nature and distant origin are blended together into one harmonious and homogeneous whole.

A beautiful instance of the modifying and *investive* power of imagination may be seen in that noble passage of Dyer's ' Ruins of Rome [I, 37],' where the poet hears the voice of Time; and in Thomson's description of the streets of Cairo, expecting t_e arrival of the caravan which had perished in the storm [*Summer*, 980]. *C. W., Jr.* (*Grosart*, iii, 464-65). *c.* 1827

38. . . . wherein does it [the Bell System of education] encourage the imaginative feelings, without which the practical understanding is of little avail, and too apt to become the cunning slave of the bad passions?
To H. J. Rose, XII. 11, 1828

39. . . . the soul of poetry, Imagination. See Godwin, C. Grace 1

42A. . . . an iron age,
Where Fact with heartless search explored
Shall be Imagination's Lord. . . .
Smith, iii, 439 (*To the Utilitarians*, 2-4). 1833

46.* Whatever is addressed to the imagination is essentially poetical, but very pleasing verses deserving all praise, but not so addressed, are not poetry.
H. C. R., ii, 608. I. 6, 1842

47. Sight is at first a sad enemy to imagination, and to those pleasures belonging to old times with which some exertions of that power will always mingle. Nothing perhaps brings this truth home to the feelings more than the city of Rome, not so much in respect to the impression made at the moment when it is first seen and looked at as a whole, for then the imagination may be invigorated, and the mind's eye quickened to perceive as much as that of the imagination; but when particular spots or objects are sought out, disappointment is . . . invariably felt. Ability to recover from this disappointment will exist in proportion to knowledge, and the power of the mind to reconstruct out of fragments and parts, and to make details in the present subservient to more adequate comprehension of the past.
Grosart, iii, 89-90. 1843 [K.]

48. I do not remember whether I have mentioned to you that following your example I have greatly extended the class entitled Poems of the Imagination, thinking as you must have done that if Imagination were pre-dominant

in the class, it was not indispensable that it sh[o]uld pervade every poem which it contained. Limiting the class as I had done before seemed to imply, and to the uncandid or observing did so, that the faculty which is the primum mobile in Poetry had little to do, in the estimation of the author, with Pieces not arranged under that head. I therefore feel much obliged to you for suggesting by your practise the plan which I have adopted.

Reed, p. 152.   IX. 27, 1845

49. . . . too little attention is paid to books of imagination which are eminently useful in calling forth intellectual power. We must not only have Knowledge but the means of wielding it, and that is done infinitely more thro' the imaginative faculty assisting both in the collection and application of facts than is generally believed. *To Seymour Tremenheere*, XII. 16, 1845

Imitation. See also under Models

1. [Imitation of popular ballads.] See Percy 1
2. See Brydges 1
3. . . . yet still I cannot help being afraid of encouraging emulation—it proves too often closely akin to envy, in spite of the christian spirit you recommend. My own case is, I am aware, a peculiar one in many respects, but I can sincerely affirm, that I am not indebted to emulation for my attainments whatever they be. I have from my Youth down to this late day cultivated the habit of valuing knowledge for its own sake and for the good that may and ought to come out of it, the unmixed pure good.

To Charles Wordsworth,   III. 12, 1846

Incidents

1. See Passion 7; Burger 2; Coleridge 61B and C; W. 329

Individuality. See Genius; Originality. Contrast Universality

1.   Points have we all of us within our souls
            Where all stand single; this I feel, and make
            Breathings for incommunicable powers;
            But is not each a memory to himself?
            Prel., iii, 185-88 (see also *Recluse* I, i. 86-8).   1804-39

2. See Burger 2; Goethe 7; Intuition 3; Rules 13

Inevitable, The. See Goethe 10

Infinity. See Imagination; Inspiration; Power

1. See Aim of Writing 28; Criticism 11, 14; Intuition 3, 4; Observation 2; W. 104, 329

2. [W. speaks of the transforming, creative power of the imagination] Trafficking with immeasurable thoughts. *Prel.*, W variant of xiii, A 93-96 [see also xii, A 145-51].   II-III, 1804

3.   The perfect image of a mighty Mind,
            Of one that feeds upon infinity,

That is exalted by an underpresence,
The sense of God. . . .
Prel., xiii. A 69-72. 1804-5

4. Such minds are truly from the Deity,
For they are Powers . . .
                by communion raised
From earth to heaven from human to divine. . . .
Prel., xiv. 112-18. 1804-39

5.   . . . the great thought
By which we live, Infinity and God.
Prel., xiii, A 183-4.
[His poetry is] the spousal verse
Of this great consummation. . . .
Recluse, " Prospectus," 47-58. 1814

6.   But descending
From these imaginative heights, that yield
Far-stretching views into eternity. . . .
Exc., iv, 1187-9. 1814

7. . . . Imagination [is given] to incite and support the eternal.
Pref. 1815, p. 958. 1815

12.* . . . by the imagination the mere fact is exhibited as connected with
that infinity without which there is no poetry. *H. C. R.*, i, 191. IX. 11, 1816

Inscriptions. See under Epitaphs

Inspiration. See Genius; Infinity; Intuition; Power

1. See Blank Verse and Rhyme 1; Infinity 4; Poetry 111, 124, 126, 128;
Fisher 3; Gomm 1; W. 238

2.   . . . Some called it madness—so indeed it was,
If child-like fruitfulness in passing joy,
If steady moods of thoughtfulness matured
To inspiration, sort with such a name;
If prophecy be madness; if things viewed
By poets in old time, and higher up
By the first men, . . .
May in these tutored days no more be seen
With undisordered sight.
Prel., iii, 146-54. 1804-39

3. Descend, prophetic Spirit! that inspir'st
The human Soul of universal earth,
Dreaming on things to come; and dost possess
A metropolitan temple in the hearts
Of mighty Poets; upon me bestow
A gift of genuine insight; that my Song
With star-like virtue in its place may shine,
Shedding benignant influence, and secure,
Itself, from all malevolent effect

Of those mutations that extend their sway
Throughout the nether sphere!
"Prospectus," *Exc.*, 83-93 (see also "If thou
    indeed derive," 1-3).   1814

4.*   Goethe's poetry is not inevitable enough [Arnold quotes W.].
Essays in Criticism, p. 155.   *c.* 1840

Instruction. See under Aim of Writing; Didacticism; Moral Element

Intellect, The. See also Books; Knowledge; Reading; Scholarly
    Interests

1.   See Imagination 49; Passion 7; Sensitiveness to Sense Impressions 3
2.   There is no happiness in this life but in intellect and virtue.
To Beaumont,   VII. 20, 1804

3.   . . . the majestic intellect. . . .
      Prel., xi, A 145.   1804-5

4.   . . . those palms achieved,
      . . . by patient exercise
      Of study and hard thought. . . .
      Prel., v, 8-10.   1804-39

5.   [Though depressed, he could not brook an] utter waste
      Of intellect . . .
      (Too well I loved . . .
      Pains-taking thoughts, and truth, their dear reward). . . .
      Prel., xi, 323-27.   1804-39

6.   The mind is lord and master—[of] outward sense. . . .
      Prel., xii, 222.   1804-39

7.   . . . the Mind of Man—
      My haunt, and the main region of my song.
      "Prospectus," *Exc.*, 40-1.   1814

8.   [Men who dedicate themselves to natural philosophy, painting, and
poetry, and refined taste, which are great acquisitions to society, are usually
not so happy as the more ignorant members of the laboring classes.] I do
not mean by this to be understood to derogate from intellectual pursuits,
for that would be monstrous.
I. F. (Grosart, iii, 154). [See Poetry 59.]   1843

Anti-intellectualism. See also Anti-rationalism

11.   Nor less I deem that there are Powers
      Which of themselves our minds impress;
      That we can feed this mind of ours
      In a wise passiveness.
      Expostulation and Reply, 21-4 (see also
      Prel. (DeSel.), p. 548).   1798

12.   One impulse from a vernal wood
             May teach you more of man,
             Of moral evil and of good,
             Than all the sages can.
             The Tables Turned, 21-4.   1798

12A. . . . intellect [among the things which constitute] the very little-
ness of life. *Prel. (De Sel.)*, p. 512.   1798-1800

13. . . . How little those formalities [which we call ' education '] have
to do With real feeling and just sense. . . . *Prel.*, xiii, 169-72.   1804-39

13A.   . . . soothed with a conception of delight
             Where meditation cannot come, which thought
             Could never heighten.
             Prel., xiii, A 304-6.   1804-5

14.   Haply the untaught Philosopher may speak
             Of the strange sight, nor hide his theory
             That satisfies the simple and the meek,
             Blest in their pious ignorance, though weak
             To cope with Sages undevoutedly free.
             " Ranging the heights of Scawfell," 10-14.   1833

15. [Pride of intellect.] See Reason 25

16. See Books 2, 3, 10B, 11A, 16, 25, 26, 27, 29; Inspiration 2; Intuition
3; Knowledge 10, 13; Poetry 142; W. 133A.

Intellectual

1. Since " fleeting moods Of shadowy exultation " [*Prel.*, ii, 312-13] are
not kindred to the intellect, " intellectual " must mean, as often in Wordsworth, lofty, spiritual, partaking of the nobler part of our nature. This is
akin to the first of the three meanings of " reason " distinguished in iv. A
296n. See i. 553n.; xii. 45n.; xiii. 178n.; xiv. A 96-7, A² B² variant, 168-
202n., and cf. *Borderers*, 1809-10 (" mighty objects do impress their forms
To elevate our intellectual being ") ; " Lie here," 32-3 (" in thee we saw A
soul of love, love's intellectual law ") ; *Recluse*, " Prospectus," 17-23 (" Of
moral strength, and intellectual Power . . . I sing ") ; *Excursion*, iv. 1273-4
(" raise, to loftier heights Of divine love, our intellectual soul "). Quoted
from *The Mind of a Poet*, pp. 329-30.

Interesting, The. See Knowledge 6; W. 115, 126, 195, 197, 330

Intuition. See also Infinity; Inspiration

1. See Infinity 2; Intellect 11, 12; Nature 5; Passion 2; Reason 1, 15,
18, 21 (and *The Mind of a Poet*, pp. 136-40) ; Rules 1

2. [An epitaph must not seem] spoken by rote, but perceived [by]
. . . an original intuition. See Pope 19

2C. [In contrast to] A reasoning . . . intellectual All-in-all [the poet
brings us]

                    The harvest of a quiet eye
                    That broods and sleeps on his own heart.
A Poet's Epitaph, 31-2; 51-2.   1799

2D.   . . . intuitive truths, [are]
                      The deepest and the best. . . .
                      Prel., vi, 39-40.   1804-39

3.   If thou partake the animating faith
            That Poets, even as Prophets, each with each
            Connected in a mighty scheme of truth,
            Have each his own peculiar faculty,
            Heaven's gift, a sense that fits him to perceive
            Objects unseen before, thou wilt not blame
            The humblest of this band who dares to hope
            That unto him hath also been vouchsafed
            An insight that in some sort he possesses,
            A privilege whereby a work of his,
            Proceeding from a source of untaught things,
            Creative and enduring, may become
            A power like one of Nature's.
            Prel., xiii, 300-12 (see also *Exc.*, iv, 631-46).   1804-39

4.   But when He who wore
            The crwon of thorns around his bleeding brow
            Warmed our sad being with celestial light,
            Then Arts, which still had drawn a softening grace
            From shadowy fountains of the Infinite,
            Communed with that Idea face to face:
            And move around it now as planets run,
            Each in its orbit round the central Sun.
            " Tranquility! the sovereign aim," 7-14.   1833

Invention. See Creative; Fancy; Imagination

   1. See Composition 13; Poetry 66; Macpherson 2

   4.* —Wordsworth holds the critical power very low, infinitely lower
than the inventive; and he said today that if the quantity of time considered
in writing critiques on the works of others were given to original composition,
of whatever kind it might be, it would be much better employed; it would
make a man find out sooner his own level, and it would do infinitely less
mischief. A false or malicious criticism may do much injury to the minds
of others; a stupid invention, either in prose or verse, is quite harmless.
Lady R. (*Grosart*, iii, 438-39).   XI, 1843

Invocations. See Apostrophe

Italian. See Sonnets 6, 7, 9; Versification 13 B, 24; Shakespeare 14.
       For individual authors, see Alfieri; Ariosto; Boccaccio; Chi-
       abrera; Dante; Manzoni; Mayer; Michelangelo; Petrarch;
       Tasso

Jacobean Age

1. [Jacobean Age had a taste for puns and quaint or out-of-the-way thoughts.] [Contrast Anderson 1.] *Epitaph* 2 (*Grosart*, ii, 47).   1810

Judgment. See Criticism; Popular Judgment; Reason; Taste

1. See Criticism 41; Gardening 1; Poetry 41, 66; Taste 1; W. 23, 268

2. See especially Reason 1 (subdivision 3); Good Sense 1-2

4.   My inner judgment
Not seldom differed from my taste in books,
As if it appertained to another mind,
And yet the books which then I valued most
Are dearest to me *now*; for, having scanned,
Not heedlessly, the laws, and watched the forms
Of Nature, in that knowledge I possessed
A standard, often usefully applied,
Even when unconsciously, to things removed
From a familiar sympathy.—In fine,
I was a better judge of thoughts than words,
Misled in estimating words, not only
By common inexperience of youth,
But by the trade in classic niceties,
The dangerous craft of culling term and phrase
From languages that want the living voice
To carry meaning to the natural heart;
To tell us what is passion, what is truth,
What reason, what simplicity and sense.
Prel., vi, 96-114.   1804-39

7. [Judgment and imagination.] See Moral Element 11

Knowledge. See also Books; Intellect; Passion; Reading; Reason; Scholarly Interests. Contrast Anti-intellectualism

1. See Genius 3; Imitation 3; Moral Element 11; Nature 5, 5A, 7A; Pleasure 2; Reason 23, 30-1; Taste 14; Burke 3A; Southey 33; W. 330, 391, 395

1A.   . . . the power that waits
On knowledge . . .
And strong book-mindedness . . .
Prel., iii, 388-95.   1804-39

2. [In his wanderings and in external nature, he could] find The knowledge which I love. . . . *Prel.*, xii, A 135-9.   1804-39

4.   May books and Nature be their early joy!
And knowledge, rightly honoured with that name—
Knowledge not purchased by the loss of power!
Prel., v, 423-5.   1804-39

5. [One who realizes] What knowledge can perform, is diligent to learn.
. . . *The Happy Warrior*, 9.   1805-6

6. [Your daughter can be trained and her faults overcome not] by over-
running her infancy with books about good boys and girls, and bad boys and
girls, and all that trumpery; but (and this is the only important thing I have
to say upon the subject) by putting her in the way of acquiring without
measure or limit such knowledge as will lead her out of herself, such knowledge as is interesting for its own sake; things known because they are
interesting, not interesting because they are known; in a word, by leaving her
at liberty to luxuriate in such feelings and images as will feed her mind in
silent pleasure. This nourishment is contained in fairy tales, romances, the
best biographies and histories, and such part of natural history relating to
the powers and appearances of the earth and elements, and the habits and
structure of animals, as belong to it, not as an art or science, but as a magazine
of form and feeling. This kind of knowledge is purely good, a direct anti-
dote to every evil to be apprehended, and food absolutely necessary to preserve
the mind of a child like yours from morbid appetites. Next to these objects
comes such knowledge as, while it is chiefly interesting for its own sake,
admits the fellowship of another sort of pleasure, that of complacence from
the conscious exertion of the faculties and love of praise. The accomplish-
ment of dancing, music, and drawing, rank under this head; grammar, learning of languages, botany probably, and out of the way knowledge of arts
and manufactures, &c. The second class of objects, as far as they tend to
feed vanity and self-conceit, are evil; but let them have their just proportion
in the plan of education, and they will afterwards contribute to destroy
these, by furnishing the mind with power and independent gratification: the
vanity will disappear, and the good will remain.

Lastly comes that class of objects which are interesting almost solely because
they are known, and the knowledge may be displayed; and this unfortunately
comprehends three fourths of what, according to the plan of modern
education, children's heads are stuffed with; that is, minute, remote, or
trifling facts in geography, topography, natural history, chronology, &c., or
acquisitions in art, or accomplishments which the child makes by rote, and
which are quite beyond its age; things of no value in themselves, but as they
show cleverness; things hurtful to any temper, but to a child like yours
absolute poison. *To a Friend* (pp. 103-5),   1806

7. . . . knowledge, efficacious for the production of virtue, is the ultimate end of all effort, the sole dispenser of complacency and repose.
Ans. to Mathetes (*Grosart*, i, 320).   I. 4, 1810
          . . .

9.   For knowledge is delight; and such delight
            Breeds love: yet, suited as it rather is
            To thought and to the climbing intellect,
            It teaches less to love, than to adore;
            If that be not indeed the highest love!
            Exc., iv, 346-50.   1814

10.   O grant the crown

That Wisdom wears, or take his treacherous staff
From Knowledge!
Aquapendente, 353-5.   1837

13. [Too much knowledge from books to the exclusion of that gained]
from intercourse with nature. . . . How much of what is precious comes
into our minds, in all ranks of society, not as Knowledge entering formally
in the shape of knowledge, but as infused thro' the constitution of things and
by the Grace of God. See Imagination 49.
To Seymour Tremenheere,   XII. 16, 1845

Labor. See Composition; Diction; Practice; Revisions; Style

Language. See Diction; Style

Language, Chaucerian

1. . . . the affecting parts of Chaucer are almost always expressed in
language pure and universally intelligible even to this day. [Probably added
to the Preface by Coleridge. See my note, "Variants to the Preface to
Lyrical Ballads," *MLN*, XLI (March, 1946), 175-7; Coleridge 59.]
Pref. L. B., p. 935 n¹.   1800

2. In the following Poem [*The Prioress's Tale*] no further deviation
from the original has been made than was necessary for the fluent reading
and instant understanding of the Author: so much, however, is the language
altered since Chaucer's time, especially in pronunciation, that much was to
be removed, and its place supplied with as little incongruity as possible. The
ancient accent has been retained in a few conjunctions, as *alsò* and *alwày*,
from a conviction that such sprinklings of antiquity would be admitted, by
persons of taste, to have a graceful accordance with the subject.
Grosart, iii, 185.   1820

3. [Purity of language of the Scotch poets after Chaucer.] See Scotch
Writers 6

Language, English

4.* Wordsworth was in excellent spirits, and conversed well on language;
he remarked on the advantage which a mixed language like English has over
one that is *single* like the German—in this, that the expressions do not so
closely and palpably give the sensual image and direct sense, but convey
indirect meanings and, faintly, allusions, by which poetry is favoured though
philosophy may be injured. *H. C. R.*, i, 359.   VI. 11, 1828

5. What do you think of an edition of 20,000 of my Poems being struck
off at Boston—as I have been told on good authority—An Author in the
English language is becoming a great Power for good or evil—if he writes
with spirit. *To C. R. (Corr. C. R.,* i, 335),   I. 28, 1837

5A. What a vast field is there open to the English mind, acting through
our noble language! *Reed*, p. 5.   VIII. 19, 1837

5B. See Translation 9; Versification 24A; Dryden 1

6.* . . . the spelling of our language was very much fixed in the time of

Charles the Second, and . . . the attempts which had been made since, and are being made in the present day, were not likely to succeed.
Lady R. (Grosart, iii, 452).   X, 1846

Language, French

7.   . . . the french language is peculiarly fitted for [indelicate tales].
See La Fontaine 1

8.   [French language] slavish . . . [and French taste] enslaved. . . .
To R. P. Gillies,   II. 14, 1815

9.*   . . . I hate the flimsiness of the French Language. . . .
Memoir of C. M. Young, i, 180.   *c.* 1830

9A.   See Dryden 1

Language, German

10.   I am not acquainted with the German language, a circumstance which I greatly regret, as the vast tract of country where that tongue is spoken cannot but produce daily performances which ought to be known amongst us.
To W. Mathews,   VI, 1794

11.   See Translation 2

12.   [English language has advantage over German.] See 4 above.

13.*   [W.] not at all favourable to the German language and opinions.
H. C. R., i, 430.   VI. 24, 1833

Language, Italian

14.   See Michelangelo 2; Versification 24A

Language, Latin

15.   [Opposes use of Latin] by moderns for works of taste and imagination. See Landor 10; and also 11

Latin. See Ancient Writers (Classical)

Latin Poetry. See Landor 10-11

Laureateship, The. See Southey 21, 22A

2.*   What think you of Mr Wordsworth's being the Laureat after all? He declined it, very decidedly though with all due respect, but another letter from the Lord Chamberlain, by return of post, has induced him to alter his decision. The duty will not be onerous, merely nominal . . . , but the acceptance of the appointment is urged upon him in a way that he could not resist without the utmost ungraciousness. Nothing will be *required* of him. It is a tribute to him ' as the first of living poets.'
E. Q. to C. R. (Corr. C. R., i, 484),   IV, 5, 1843

3.*   . . . he had refused the offer [of the laureateship] on account of his age (he is 73 this day). . . .
C. R. to T. R. (Corr. C. R., i, 486),   IV. 7, 1843

4. . . . and I was assured that it was offered me solely in consideration of that I had already done in Literature, and without the least view to future exertion as connected with the honor. It has since gratified me to learn from many quarters, that the Appointment has given universal satisfaction; and I need scarcely add that it has afforded me a melancholy pleasure to be thought worthy of succeeding my revered Friend. *To. ?*,   VI. 2, 1843

Laws. See under Rules

Learning. See Books; Knowledge; Reading; Scholarly Interests

Lectures

1. As to teaching Belles Lettres, Languages, Law, Political Economy, Morals, etc., by lectures, it is absurd. Lecturers may be very useful in Experimental Philosophy, Geology, and Natural History, or any Art or Science capable of illustration by experiments, operations, and specimens; but in other departments of knowledge they are, in most cases, worse than superfluous. Of course I do not include in the above censure *College Lectures*, as they are called, when the business consists not of haranguing the pupils, but in ascertaining the progress they have made. *To Lonsdale*,   VI, 1825

Lecturing. See Coleridge 18, 28

Legends. See also Mythology; Romance

1. See History 4, 10-13; Knowledge 6

2. [Legends, taking the place of books, nourished the imagination. See *Exc.*, i, 163-85.]   1814

3. [Imagination feels, and reason recognizes " the lasting virtue " of legends which]

created Powers
With attributes from History derived,
By Poesy irradiate. . . .
Aquapendente, 277-84.   1837

Letter-writing

A. . . . painfully conscious how poor a genius I possess for [composing letters. His are not] worth any body's acceptance. . . . Neither Cupid nor Minerva, nor Phoebus, nor Mercury, nor any of the Pagan Gods who presided over liberal and kindly inventions, deign to shed their influence over my endeavors in this field. *To Wrangham*,   I. 18, 1816

1.* . . . Mr. Wordsworth gave his opinion of the letters to this effect, judging from external as well as internal evidence, that though they came from one hand, they did not emanate from one and the same mind; that a man commencing to write letters might do so very badly, but as he advanced in life, particularly if he wrote many letters, he would probably improve in style; such improvement being constant and not capricious. That is, if he gradually learned to spell and write properly, he would not fall back at intervals into his original errors of composition and spelling—that if once he

4

had got out of his ignorance he could not fall back into it, except by design—that the human mind advances, but cannot recede, unless warped by insanity or weakened by disease. The conclusion arrived at, which facts afterwards proved, was, that the inequality in the letters arose from their being composed by different persons, some ignorant and some well-informed, while another person always copied them fairly for the post.
Life of Southey, vi, 299-300.   1836

2. For my own part it is my earnest wish that every Letter I have written may be restored to me or my Heirs or destroyed. My mind never took pleasure in showing itself off after that manner; and to say the truth I think that the importance of Letters in modern times is much overrated. If they be good and natural as Letters, they will seldom be found interesting to solid minds beyond the persons or the circle to which they are immediately addressed. I was struck the other day with an observation of the Poet Gray upon Pope's Epistles. As Letters, says he, 'they are not good but they are something better than Letters.' How far this may be true in respect to Pope I do not know, for it is long since I read his Letters, but the remark as of general application is far from being unimportant—*To C. R. (Corr. C. R.,* i, 366), VI. 18-24, 1838

3. [Good letters are expected of good verse writers.] See Crabbe 11

Letters, Objection to Publishing

1.* . . . You know we are very delicate upon the point of publishing the letters of private friends—but we feel that in the case of dear Ch. L[amb] the objections are not so forcible—The Essays he himself gave to the public are so much in the character of his letters.
M. W. to C. R. (Corr. C. R., i, 281),   XI, 1835

2. I have kept back several letters [Lamb's]—some because they relate merely to personal and domestic concerns, others, because they touch upon the character and manners of individuals who are now living, or too recently deceased to be brought under the public eye, without indelicacy. I have also thought proper to suppress every word of criticism upon my own Poems—though the strictures [?] are merely such, as might prove generally interesting—and occasionally lead to the pleasing strain of sentiment and descriptions which he has himself felt or observed. The suppressed letters shall not be destroyed.—Those relating to my works are withheld, partly because I shrink from the thought of assisting in any way to spread my own praises and still more as being convinced that the opinions or judgments of friends given in this way are mostly of little value. . . . *To Moxon,*   XI. 20, 1835

3.   I have been very uneasy since I sent off the selection of Lamb's Letters, as by so doing I seem to sanction a practice, which I hold, for the most part, in utter detestation—viz—that of publishing the casual effusions (and most letters are nothing more) of men recently dead—I was much pleased to learn from the life of Mackintosh that Sir Jas Scarlet destroyed all letters but those upon business, I wish this to be done towards myself and I would do it towards others, unless where I thought the Writer himself wished for their preservation. I earnestly desire you would get a sight of those of L., . . . strike out every passage which you think L. or his Sister would object

to—above all, such as you think would give pain to any living individual—or the Persons connections, after his death.
To C. R. (Corr. C. R., i, 288), XII. 16, 1835

4.* . . . had such a horror of having his letters preserved, that in order to guard against it he made them as bad and dull as possible.
Rogers and His Contemporaries, ii, 158. VIII, 1837

5. . . . grounds I am likely to have for regretting breaches of confidence in the publication of private Letters without the consent of the Writers or their Representatives. *To C. R. (Corr. C. R.,* i, 365), VI. 18-24, 1838

6. —But I will not conceal from you that I never set any value upon my Letters; and that it has ever been my wish that they should be destroyed as soon as read, and that I have frequently requested this should be done. Allow me further to say that publishing the Letters of a living Person without his consent previously obtained furnishes a precedent the effect of which, as far as it acts, cannot but be to check the free communication of thought between Man and Man. This is surely an evil; nor can I at all approve for this same and many other reasons the practice, now so prevalent, of publishing the Letters of distinguished persons, recently dead, without the consent of their representatives. [See also *L. Y.,* pp. 1024-25.]
To H. Bunbury, VII. 30, 1838

7. As to publishing any words from Mr. S's [Southey's] Letters, in his present state of mind and body, as he cannot be consulted, I think it ought not to be done. *To C. R. (Corr. C. R.,* i, 415), VI. 24, 1840

8. [Questioned about turning over Crabbe's letters to his biographer.] 'By no means,' was my answer, grounded not upon any objection there might be to publishing a selection from those letters, but from an aversion I have always felt to meet idle curiosity by calling back the recently departed to become the object of trivial and familiar gossip.
I. F. (Grosart, iii, 191). 1843

9. See Southey 53 and 54; Letter-writing 2

10. It appears from the preface to Taylor's correspondence that Mr. Southey had (very inconsiderately I think) given consent to the publication; but it also appears that Mr. S. must have looked to the Letters being revised by himself before they were given to the world, in which case many passages undoubtedly would have been struck out which the Editor [Robberds] most reprehensibly has not done. . . . But the licentious opinions in morals which Taylor engrafts upon his unbelief most ostentatiously displayed, are a still greater objection to the publication; and these ought to be exposed by some able journalist with the severest condemnation. *To Moxon,* III. 11, 1844

Literature. See also Poetry; Prose; Style; Subjects

1. [Political despotism would produce better literature in England.]
To D. Stuart, III. 26, 1809

2. I need scarcely say that literature has been the pursuit of my life; a life-pursuit, chosen (as I believe are those of most men distinguished by any

particular features of character) partly from passionate liking, and partly from calculations of the judgment; and in some small degree from circumstances in which my youth was placed, that threw great difficulties in the way of my adopting that profession to which I was most inclined, and for which I was perhaps best qualified. *To Lord Lonsdale,*   II. 6, 1812

3. [Suggestions for the general benefit of literature.] See Monuments 1
4. W.'s interest in literature dying fast.] *To I. Fenwick,*   V. 13, 1846

Literature, Opinion of Modern

5. [Asked for his opinion of modern literature, W. replied:] You might as well have solicited me to send you an account of the tribes inhabiting the central regions of the African Continent. God knows my incursions into the fields of modern literature—excepting in our own language three volumes of *Tristram Shandy,* and two or three papers of the *Spectator,* half subdued— are absolutely nothing. *To W. Mathews,*   VIII. 13, 1791

6. See W. 135, 346; Poetry 16, 17

7. [Literature of present day influenced by bad taste of the times.] See Passion 7; Burns 26A; under Authors and Works

9. [The best ancient and modern writers guilty of a false diction.] See Style 26

10. . . . I might as well live at St. Kilda for any commerce I have with passing Literature, especially bulky works. . . . [See Mackenzie 2.]
To F. Wrangham,   XI. 4, 1807

11. [Reads few modern books, but enjoys the old ones.]
To F. Wrangham,   Early Spring, 1812

12. [W. comments on the death of John Scott, ed. of *London Magazine,* in a duel with Christie, who intervened on Lockhart's behalf, when Scott attacked Lockhart for certain articles which he had printed in *Blackwood.*] It is an Innovation the effect of others which promise no good to the Republic of Letters or to the Country. We have had ribaldry, and sedition, and slanders enough in our Literature heretofore, but no epithet which those periods deserved is so foul as that merited by the present, viz.—the *treacherous.* . . . As to Poetry I am sick of it—it overruns the Country in all the shapes of the plagues of Egypt—frog-poets (the Croakers) mice-poets (the Niblers), a class *rhyming* to mice that shall be nameless, and fly-poets. (Gray in his dignified way calls flies the ' Insect Youth,' a term wonderfully applicable upon this occasion!) But let us desist or we shall be accused of envying the rising generation. *To C. R. (Corr. C. R.,* i, 99-100),   III. 13, 1821

13. I am surprized, and rather sorry, when I hear you say you read little, because you are removed from the pressure of the trash which hourly issuing from the Press in England, tends to make the very name of writing and books disgusting. I am so situated as to see little of it, but one cannot stop one's ears, and I sometimes envy you that distance which separates you altogether from this intrusion. *To Landor,*   IV. 20, 1822

14. . . . deal little with modern writers. . . . See Hamilton, Eliza M. 1

15.* . . . but Wordsworth in addition remarked: ' You know how I love and quote, not even Shakespeare and Milton, but Cowper, Burns, etc. As to the modern poets—Byron, Scott, etc.—I do not quote them because I do not love them. Byron has great power and genius, but there is something so repugnant to my moral sense that I abhor them. Besides, even as works of mere taste, there is this material circumstance, they came too late, my taste was formed, for I was forty-five when they appeared, and we cannot after that age love new things. New impressions are difficult to make. Had I been young I should have enjoyed much of them, I have no doubt! '

H. C. R., ii, 486-7.   I. 31, 1836

16. If I had been assured that he [Sergeant Talfourd] would have given it to the world, that letter [W.'s letter on the Copyright Bill] would have been written with more care, and with the addition of a very few words upon the *policy* of the bill as a measure for raising the character of our literature,— a benefit which, heaven knows, it stands much in need of.

To C. R. (*Corr. C. R.*, i, 360),   V. 9, 1838

17.*   Wordsworth's estimate of his contemporaries . . . ' I have known many that might be called very *clever* men, and a good many of real and vigorous *abilities*, but few of genius; and only one whom I should call " wonderful." That one was Coleridge. At any hour of the day or night he would talk by the hour, if there chanced to be *any* sympathetic listener, and talk better than the best page of his writings; for a pen half paralysed his genius. A child would sit quietly at his feet and wonder, till the torrent had passed by. The only man like Coleridge whom I have known is Sir William Hamilton, Astronomer Royal of Dublin.' I remember, however, that when I recited by his fireside Alfred Tennyson's two political poems, ' You ask me why, though ill at ease,' and ' Of old sat Freedom on the heights,' the old bard listened with a deepening attention, and when I had ended said after a pause, ' I must acknowledge that those two poems are very solid and noble in thought. Their diction also seems singularly stately.' He was a great admirer of *Philip van Artevelde*. In the case of a certain poet since dead, and never popular, he said to me, ' I consider his sonnets to be the best of modern times; " adding, ' Of course, I am not including my own in any comparison with those of others.' He was not sanguine as to the future of English Poetry. He thought that there was much to be supplied in other departments of our literature, and especially he desired a really great History of England; but he was disposed to regard the roll of English poetry as made up, and as leaving place for little more except what was likely to be eccentric or imitational. *De Vere* (*Grosart*, iii, 492).   1842-46

18.   It has been said that the English, though their country has produced so many great poets, is now the most unpoetical nation in Europe. It is probably true; for they have more temptation to become so than any other European people. Trade, commerce, and manufactures, physical science and mechanic arts, out of which so much wealth has arisen, have made our countrymen infinitely less sensible to movements of imagination and fancy than were our forefathers in their simple state of society.

I. F. (*Grosart*, iii, 35).   1843

19.* [Quillinan mentions W.'s failure to praise rival celebrities of his day.] *E. Q. to C. R. (Corr. C. R.*, ii, 779),   V. 15, 1851

Literature, French

20.* He condemns all French writers (as well of poetry as prose) in the lump. *Hazlitt*, iv, 277.   *c.* 1800

21.   [Literature of the French Revolution.] France . . .
               Hath brought forth no such souls as we had then
               [Oliver Cromwell's time].
               Perpetual emptiness! unceasing change!
               No single volume paramount, no code,
               No master spirit, no determined road;
               But equally a want of books and men!
               " Great men," 9-14.   1802

Literature, German

22.   We should have far better *books* circulated among us, if we were as thoroughly enslaved as the Romans under their Emperors. Witness the state of literature in Germany till within these two or three years, when it has been overrun by the French. The voice of reason and nature was uttered and listened to under the Prussian Despotism, and in the Courts of the Princelings. *To D. Stuart*,   III. 26, 1809

23.* Those petty courts of Germany have been injurious to its literature. They who move in them are too prone to imagine themselves to be the whole world, and compared with the whole world they are nothing more than these little specks in the texture of this hearth-rug. [See also Burns 26A.] *C. W., Jr. (Grosart*, iii, 466).   *c.* 1827

24.*   [Talked of the effect of German literature on the English mind.] We must wait to find out what it is; my hope is that the good will assimilate itself with all the good in the English character, and the mischievous element will pass away like so much else. [The only special criticism which he offered on German literature was] They often sacrifice Truth to Originality, and, in their hurry to produce new and startling ideas, do not wait to weigh their worth. When they have exhausted themselves and are obliged to sit down and think, they just go back to the former thinkers, and thus there is a constant revolution without their being quite conscious of it. Kant, Schelling, Fichte; Fichte, Schelling, Kant: all this is dreary work and does not denote progress. However, they have much of Plato in them, and for this I respect them: the English, with their devotion to Aristotle, have but half the truth; a sound Philosophy must contain both Plato and Aristotle. *Old Friends*, p. 215.   X. 6, 1844

Literature, Italian. See Versification 13 B, 24 A

Literature, Latin. See Landor 10-11

Literature for Children. See Legends; Romances

26.   Oh! give us once again the wishing-cap
Of Fortunatus, and the invisible coat
Of Jack the Giant-killer, Robin Hood,
And Sabra in the forest with St. George!
The child, whose love is here, at least, doth reap
One precious gain, that he forgets himself.
These mighty workmen of our later age,
Who, with a broad highway, have overbridged
The froward chaos of futurity,
Tamed to their bidding; they who have the skill
To manage books, and things, and make them act
On infant minds as surely as the sun
Deals with a flower. . . .
Prel., v, 341-53.   1804-39

27. See Knowledge 6; W. 28

Literature, Roman Catholic

28.   Shun the insidious arts
That Rome provides, less dreading from her frown
Than from her wily praise, her peaceful gown,
Language, and letters;—these, though fondly viewed
As humanising grace, are but parts
And instruments of deadliest servitude!
1 Ecc. Sonn., vii, 9-14.   1821

Literary Forgery. See Cottle, J. 3; Macpherson 2

Loco-descriptive Writers. See also Description; Pastoral Poetry

1. Crowe 1; Dyer, J. 5; Graves, J. 1; Gray 6; Whitaker 1-5; White, G. 1-2; Wrangham 8; W. 396, 398

Logic. See under Intellect; Reason

Love Poetry

1. [Others have handled themes of love more skilfully than he can.] See Subjects 13; also 21

2.* The absence of love-poetry in Wordsworth's works has often been remarked upon, and indeed brought as a charge against them. He once told me that if he had avoided that form of composition, it was by no means because the theme did not interest him, but because, treated as it commonly has been, it tends rather to disturb and lower the reader's moral and imaginative being rather than to elevate it.
De Vere (*Grosart*, iii, 491). (See also *Exc.*, vii, 367-73).   1842-46

3. See Poetry 37, 99; Restraint 1, 2; Burns 27; Wieland 2; Winchilsea 5

Lyric Poetry

1. See Poetry 69

2. . . . The Lyrical,—containing the Hymn, the Ode, the Elegy, the Song, and the Ballad; in all which, for the production of their *full* effect, an accompaniment of music is indispensable. *Pref. (1815)*, p. 954.   1815

Machinery of Epic Poetry. See Poetry 78

Magazines and Magazine-writers. See under Periodicals

Magnificence. See Style 40

Manner. See Poetry 157; Style 69

Manners. See also Characters; Universality

1. . . . I should principally wish our attention to be fixed upon Life and Manners [in a projected periodical]. *To W. Mathews,*   V. 23, 1794

2. I do not so ardently desire character in poems like Burger's, as manners, not transitory manners reflecting the wearisome unintelligible obliquities of city life, but manners connected with the permanent objects of nature and partaking of the simplicity of those objects. Such pictures must interest when the original shall cease to exist. The reason will be immediately obvious if you consider yourself as lying in a valley on the side of mount Etna reading one of Theocritus's Idylliums or on the plains of Attica with a comedy of Aristophanes in your hand. Of Theocritus and his spirit perhaps three fourths remain, of Aristophanes a multilated skeleton; at least I suppose so, for I never read his works but in a most villainous translation. But I may go further, read Theocritus in Ayrshire or Merionethshire and you will find perpetual occasions to recollect what you see daily in Ayrshire or Merionethshire, read Congreve Vanbrugh and Farquhar in London and though not a century has elapsed since they were alive and merry, you will meet with whole pages that are uninteresting and incomprehensible. Now I find no manners in Burger. . . . *D. W. and W. to Coleridge (E. L.,* pp. 221-2), II. 27, 1799

3. See Aim of Writing 7; History 3; Style 3; Burns 1; W. 21

6. [*The Lay of the Last Minstrel*] is throughout interesting and entertaining, and the picture of manners as lively as possible.
To W. Scott,   III. 7, 1805

7. [Manners in *Ossian*] are impossible. . . .
E. Supp. Pref., p. 950.   1815

8. [Opposes] accidents of manners and character produced by times and circumstances. . . . See Poetry 111

9. [The two senses in which W. uses the term.] See Homer 13; and also 12

Marvelous, The. See also Strangeness; Supernatural; Coleridge 31;
      W. 266

Mask, The. See Dramatic Poetry 1

Matter. See Plot; Subjects; Style 69

Matter of Fact, The. See under Realism

Meanness of Language. See under Style; Poetry 17

Mediocrity

1. That law [copyright] at present acts as a premium upon mediocrity, by tempting authors to aim only at immediate effect.
To J. Gardner,   IV. 5, 1830

Melancholy

1. See Poetry 32, 132

2.   How sweet at such a time, with such delight
       On every side, in prime of youthful strength,
       To feed a Poet's tender melancholy
       And fond conceit of sadness. . . .
       Prel., vi, 364-7.   1804-39

3.* [Coleridge] not happy enough [to understand my poems completely]. See Fame 8

4. [No great poem ever written by an unhappy man.] See Coleridge 31

Memoirs. See Biography; Chronicles 1

Metaphors. See under Imagery

Metaphysical, The. See Abstractions; Poetry 73; Realism; Coleridge 30, 35-6, 39, 46, 54, 56; Hamilton, Eliza M. 4; Shakespeare 32, (?) 56

Meter. See also Blank Verse and Rhyme; Poetry; Style; Versification

1. . . . the distinction of metre is regular and uniform, and not, like that which is produced by what is usually called POETIC DICTION, arbitrary, and subject to infinite caprices upon which no calculation whatever can be made. In the one case, the Reader is utterly at the mercy of the Poet, respecting what imagery or diction he may choose to connect with the passion; whereas, in the other, the metre obeys certain laws, to which the Poet and Reader both willingly submit because they are certain, and because no interference is made by them with the passion, but such as the concurring testimony of ages has shown to heighten and improve the pleasure which co-exists with it. *Pref. L. B.,* p. 939.   1800

2. [The causes of pleasure in meter. As there is in all the arts] the pleasure which the mind derives from the perception of similitude in dissimilitude. . . . and upon the accuracy with which similitude in dissimilitude, and dissimilitude in similitude are perceived, depend our taste and our moral feelings. [Thus meter is enabled to afford much pleasure.]
Pref. L. B., p. 940.   1800

3. See Pleasure 3; Poetry 16, 23-25, 29, 69; Versification 2; Cowper 1; W. 350

7. [Meter] separated the genuine language of [earliest] Poetry still further from common life. . . . *App. L. B.*, p. 943.   1802

9. . . . the choice of meter . . . in preference to prose. See Pope 18.

10. . . . irregular frame of meter [may be excused in] a dramatised ejaculation. . . . See W. 170

Middle Ages, The. See Chaucer; Gower; Romance

Mind, The. See under Intellect

Models. See Authority; Imitation

1. [Examples.] . . . long continued intercourse with the best models of composition. See Taste 1

2. . . . keep . . . to the great models. . . . *To Gillies,*   XI. 23, 1814

3. See Hamilton, Eliza M. 1

4.* . . . I was impressed with a conviction, that there were four English poets whom I must have continually before me as examples—Chaucer, Shakespeare, Spenser and Milton. These I must study, and equal *if I could*; and I need not think of the rest. *C. W., Jr.* (*Grosart*, iii, 459-60).   c. 1827

5.* [Learn from the first-class poets] how to observe and how to interpret Nature. *De Vere* (*Grosart*, iii, 489).   1842-46

Moderns vs. Ancients. See Ancient Writers; Primitivism; Progress, Idea of

Mock-heroic. See Narrative Poetry 2

Mock-sublime. See Coleridge 65 A

Money, Writing for. See also Aim of Writing; Copyright; Periodicals; Publishing, Aim of and Objections to

1. See Aim of Writing 22; Criticism 10, 16; Hemans, F. 6; Scott, W. 29; Shand 1; W. 3, 12, 197, 317, 321

5.* W. spoke with contempt of A. B.'s low ambition [to make money by his writing]. *Aubrey de Vere*, p. 70.   III. 9, 1841

Monody. See also Elegy; Funeral Oration

1. [Expression too poignant and transitory would be better in a Monody than in an epitaph.] *Epitaph 3* (*Grosart*, ii, 63).   1810

2. See W. 274

Monosyllabics. See also Style; Versification

1. [No objection to monosyllabic lines in verse.]
To Hans Busk,   VII. 6, 1819

Monuments to Poets

1. In the first place, Eminent poets appear to me to be a Class of men

who, less than any others, stand in need of such marks [monuments] of distinction, and hence I infer that this mode of acknowledging their merits is one for which they would not, in general, be themselves solicitous. . . .

[Furthermore, W. objects to the admirers of a poet erecting a monument to his memory.] If this may be justly objected to, and in my opinion it may, it is because the showy Tributes [monuments] to Genius are apt to draw off attention from those efforts by which the interests of Literature might be substantially promoted; and to exhaust public spirit in comparatively unprofitable exertions, when the wrongs of literary men are crying out for redress on all sides. [Wordsworth felt that the English copyright laws constituted the greatest wrong done to a writer. See this letter (to Mitchell) for W.'s statement of the case.]

[Erect monuments for heroes because] their noble Actions cannot speak for themselves, as the Writings of Men of genius are able to do. . . . Let our great Statesmen and eminent Lawyers, our learned and eloquent Divines, and they who have successfully devoted themselves to the obstruser Sciences, be rewarded in like manner; but toward departed Genius, exerted in the fine Arts, and more especially in Poetry, I humbly think, in the present state of things, the sense of our obligation to it may more satisfactorily be expressed by means pointing directly to the general benefit of Literature.

To J. F. Mitchell, IV. 21, 1819

Moral Element. See also Aim of Writing; Blasphemous Writings; Didacticism; Truth; Byron; Shelley

1. See Aim of Writing 10, 11; Imagination 33G; Knowledge 7; Meter 2; Pleasure 3; Poetry 47, 67, 75, 78; Style 13; Taste 11; Truth 3

2. See Bible 11; Burns 16-19, 26, 34-37, 45; Byron, 3, 7, 9, 17, 19, 21, 23; Chaucer 10, 15-16, 21-23; Dryden 2, 18; La Fontaine 1; Pope 20; Shakespeare 32; W. 37, 44, 124, 200, 232-33, 250, 269, 321, 353, 369

11. [Our estimate of the worth of an epitaph depends upon our feeling that sincerity, earnestness, and moral interest are the main objects of the writer.] Insensibility here shocks us, and still more so if manifested by a Writer going wholly out of his way in search of supposed beauties, which if he were truly moved he could set no value upon, could not even think of. We are struck in this case not merely with a sense of disproportion and unfitness, but we cannot refrain from attributing no small part of his intellectual to a moral demerit. And here the difficulties of the question begin, namely in ascertaining what errors in the choice of or the mode of expressing the thoughts, most surely indicate the want of that which is most indispensable. Bad taste, whatever shape it may put on, is injurious to the heart and the understanding. If a man attaches much interest to the faculty of taste as it exists in himself and employs much time in those studies of which this faculty (I use the word taste in its comprehensive though most unjustifiable sense) is reckoned the arbiter, certain it is his moral notions and dispositions must either be purified and strengthened or corrupted and impaired. How can it be otherwise, when his ability to enter into the spirit of works in literature must depend upon his feelings, his imagination and his understand-

ing, that is upon his recipient, upon his creative or active and upon his judging powers, and upon the accuracy and compass of his knowledge, in fine upon all that makes up the moral and intellectual man.

Epitaph 2 (Grosart, ii, 54).   1810

12. [Moral discipline as an aid to criticism.] See Criticism 44

17. The queries you put to me upon the connection between genius and irregularity of conduct may probably induce me to take up the subject again, and yet it scarcely seems necessary. No man can claim indulgence for his transgressions on the score of his sensibilities, but at the expense of his credit for intellectual powers. All men of *first* rate genius have been as distinguished for dignity, beauty, and propriety of moral conduct. But we often find the faculties and qualities of the mind not well balanced; something of prime importance is left short, and hence confusion and disorder. On the one hand it is well that dunces should not arrogate to themselves a pharisaical superiority, because they avoid the vices and faults which they see men of talent fall into. They should not be permitted to believe that they have more understanding merely on that account, but should be taught that they are preserved probably by having less feeling, and being consequently less liable to temptation. On the other hand, the man of genius ought to know that the cause of his vices is, in fact, his deficiencies, and not, as he fondly imagines, his superfluities and superiorities. All men ought to be judged with charity and forbearance after death has put it out of their power to explain the motives of their actions, and especially men of acute sensibility and lively passions. This was the scope of my letter to Mr. Gray [*A Letter to a Friend of Robert Burns* (1816)]. Burns has been cruelly used, both dead and alive. [See also Burns 26A.] *To John Scott,*   VI. 11, 1816

18. . . . genius is not incompatible with vice. . . . See Biography 2C

19. [W. found Goethe defective in religious sentiment.] See Goethe 8; also 7, 9, 12

20.* Goethe's writings cannot live . . . because *they are not holy.*
Mrs. Hemans, ii, 120.   1830

22.* [W. and De Vere] agreed that poetry ought to put forth great truths, full-forced and singly, without trying to adjust the balance between opposite truths. *Aubrey de Vere,* p. 69.   III. 8, 1841

25.* . . . considering this extension of our language, it behoved those who wrote to see to it, that what they put forth was on the side of virtue. *Ellis Yarnall (Grosart,* iii, 478).   VIII. 18, 1849

Music

1. [Music in drama.] See Dramatic Poetry 1

2. [The older poets represent themselves as singing their tales.] See Narrative Poetry 2

3. See Poetry 69

4. [In " Yes, it was the mountain echo," the word " rebounds " (l. 17) is introduced] for the imaginative warning turns upon the echo, which ought

to be revived as near the conclusion as possible. This rule of art holds [good to the theme of a piece of music, as well as to a poem].
To B. Field (*M. Y.*, pp. 311-12),   X. 24, 1828

Mythology. See also Fiction; Legends; Realism; Truth

1. [W. laments that he has no mythology that "in perfect confidence" he might use.] *Prel.*, i, 158-65.   1804-39

2. [Not to be used in epitaphs.] See Chiabrera 4

3.   Say why
That ancient story of Prometheus chained
To the bare rock, on frozen Caucasus;
The vulture, the inexhaustible repast
Drawn from his vitals? Say what meant the woes
By Tantalus entailed upon his race,
And the dark sorrows of the line of Thebes?
Fictions in form, but in their substance truths,
Tremendous truths! familiar to the men
Of long-past times, nor obsolete in ours.
Exchange the shepherd's frock of native grey
Robes with regal purple tinged; convert
The crook into a sceptre; give the pomp
Of circumstance; and here the tragic Muse
Shall find apt subjects for her highest art.
Exc., vi, 539-52.   1814

4.   . . . the gross fictions chanted in the streets
By wandering Rhapsodists. . . .
Exc., iv, 732-33.   1814

5.   . . . idle songs of wandering gods,
Pan or Apollo. . . .
Exc., vii, 729-30.   1814

8. See History 11, 12, 13; W. 104

7. No doubt the hackneyed and lifeless use into which mythology fell towards the close of the 17th century, and which continued through the 18th, disgusted the general reader with all allusion to it in modern verse. See W. 242. *I. F.* (*Grosart*, iii, 168).   1843

Narrative. See Ballads; Epics; Fiction; History; Legends; Mythology; Novels; Romance

1. . . . our high-wrought modern narratives [not liked by W.]. See History 3

2. [Spenserian stanza] unfit for narrative. *To C. Grace Godwin*, 1829

3. See W. 17

Narrative Poetry. See also Poetry

1. [Narrative poetry *vs.* drama.] See W. 195

2.   The narrative,—including the Epopoeia, the Historic Poem, the Tale, the Romance, the Mock-heroic, and, if the spirit of Homer will tolerate such neighbourhood, that dear production of our days, the metrical Novel.   Of this Class, the distinguishing mark is, that the Narrator, however liberally his speaking agents be introduced, is himself the source from which everything primarily flows.   Epic Poets, in order that their mode of composition may accord with the elevation of their subject, represent themselves as *singing* from the inspiration of the Muse, "Arma virumque *cano*;" but this is a fiction, in modern times, of slight value: the *Iliad* or the *Paradise Lost* would gain little in our estimation by being chanted.   The other poets who belong to this class are commonly content to *tell* their tale;—so that of the whole it may be affirmed that they neither require nor reject the accompaniment of music.   *Pref.* (*1815*), p. 954.   1815

Natural and Sensual School of Poetry.   See under Realism

1.   See Barrett, E. 3; Coleridge 36A; Goethe 12

Naturalness.   See under Realism

Nature (EXTERNAL).   See Description; Imagination; Observation; Poetry; Realism; Truth

1.   See Aim of Writing 7; Gardening 1; Imagination 5, 6, 9, 11, 32A; Knowledge 2, 4, 13; Picturesque 1; Poetry 42, 65, 65A, 121, 148; Progress, Idea of 2; Versification 2; Gray 6, 19; Macpherson 2, 3; Smith, Charlotte 2; Thomson 9, 13; Tickell 1A; W. 1, 5, 29, 189, 329, 345A

4.   . . . Love Nature and Books . . . and knowledge of mankind [will follow]. . . . *To De Quincey,*   III. 6, 1804

5.   . . . he, who in his youth
      A daily wanderer among woods and fields
      With living Nature hath been intimate,
      Not only in that raw unpractised time
      Is stirred to ecstasy, as others are,
      By glittering verse; but further, doth receive,
      In measure only dealt out to himself,
      Knowledge and increase of enduring joy
      From the great Nature that exists in works
      Of mighty Poets. Visionary power
      Attends the motions of the viewless winds,
      Embodied in the mystery of words:
      There, darkness makes abode, and all the host
      Of shadowy things work endless changes,—there,
      As in a mansion like their proper home,
      Even forms and substances are circumfused
      By that transparent veil with light divine,
      And, through the turnings intricate of verse,
      Present themselves as objects recognised,
      In flashes, and with glory not their own.
      Prel., v, 586-605.   1804-39

5A.   . . . Nature's self,
   By all varieties of human love
   Assisted, led me back . . .
   To those sweet counsels between head and heart
   Whence grew that genuine knowledge,
   Which . . . upholds me now. . . .
   Prel., xi, 350-6.
                 1804-39

6. [Nature offers through its laws and forms a standard of judgment.]
See Judgment 4

7.   From Nature doth emotion come, and moods
   Of calmness equally are Nature's gift:
   This is her glory; these two attributes
   Are sister horns that constitute her strength.
   Hence Genius, born to thrive by interchange
   Of peace and excitation, finds in her
   His best and purest friend; from her receives
   That energy by which he seeks the truth,
   From her that happy stillness of the mind
   Which fits him to receive it when unsought.
   Prel., xiii, 1-10.
                 1804-39

7A.   Long time in search of knowledge did I range
   The field of human life, in heart and mind
   Benighted; but, the dawn beginning now
   To re-appear, 'twas proved that not in vain
   I had been taught to reverence a Power
   That is the visible quality and shape
   And image of right reason; that matures
   Her processes by steadfast laws; gives birth
   To no impatient or fallacious hopes,
   No heat of passion or excessive zeal,
   No vain conceits; provokes to no quick turns
   Of self-applauding intellect; but trains
   To meekness, and exalts by humble faith;
   Holds up before the mind intoxicate
   With present objects, and the busy dance
   Of things that pass away, a temperate show
   Of objects that endure. . . .
   Prel., xiii, 16-32.
                 1804-39

11. . . . not a single image from Nature in the whole body of his
[Dryden's] works. . . . *To W. Scott,*
                XI. 7, 1805

12. I vindicate the rights and dignity of Nature. . . .
Epitaphs 3 (*Grosart*, ii, 60).
                 1810

14. [Use of images from] rural nature. See Shakespeare 24

16. . . . simple Nature trained by careful Art. . . .
   " Serving no haughty muse,"
   [see also *Prel.*, vi, 670-5.]
                 1838

18. Thy Art be Nature. . . . See Rules 13

19.* . . . that there were three callings for success in which Nature had furnished him with qualifications—the callings of poet, landscape-gardner, and critic of pictures and works of art.

Graves (*Grosart*, iii, 468).   *c.* 1840

20.* He expatiated . . . on the mode in which Nature had been described by one of the most justly popular of England's modern poets [Scott?]—one for whom he preserved a high and affectionate respect. 'He took pains,' Wordsworth said; 'he went out with his pencil and note-book, and jotted down whatever struck him most—a river rippling over the sands, a ruined tower on a rock above it, a promontory, and a mountain ash waving its red berries. He went home, and wove the whole together into a poetical descrip-tion.' . . . 'But Nature does not permit an inventory to be made of her charms! He should have left his pencil and note-book at home; fixed his eye, as he walked, with a reverent attention on all that surrounded him, and taken all into a heart that could understand and enjoy. Then, after several days had passed by, he should have interrogated his memory as to the scene. He would have discovered that while much of what he had admired was preserved to him, much was also most wisely obliterated. That which re-mained—the picture surviving in his mind—would have presented the ideal and essential truth of the scene, and done so, in a large part, by discarding much which, though in itself striking, was not characteristic. In every scene many of the most brilliant details are but accidental. A true eye for Nature does not note them, or at least does not dwell on them.' . . . He proceeded to remark that many who could descant with eloquence on Nature cared little for her, and that many more who truly loved her had yet no eye to discern her—which he regarded as a sort of 'spiritual discernment.' He continued, 'Indeed I have hardly ever known any one but myself who had a true eye for Nature, one that thoroughly understood her meanings and her teach-ings. . . .' *De Vere* (*Grosart*, iii, 487-8).   1842-46

21. [Limitations of Burns's sensitiveness to nature.] See Burns 29; also 27, 28

Nature (HUMAN). See Characters; Epitaphs; Satire

1. See Fancy 3; Passion 8; Periodicals 23; Poetry 47, 111, 133, 148; Reclaim 17-25; Versification 2; Byron 17; Carlyle 7; Coleridge 73; Lang-horne 2

2. [A poet] has a greater knowledge of human nature. . . .
Pref. L. B., p. 937.   1800

4. [Human and external nature are] adapted to each other. . . . See Pleasure 2

8.* [Young poets must study] human nature and material nature. . . .
De Vere (*Grosart*, iii, 488-89).   1842-46

Nature Poetry. See under Loco-descriptive Writers; Poetry

Neologisms. See Diction; Hamilton, W. R. 7

Newspapers. See under Periodicals; Periodical Planning

1. But certain I am, that the last thing that could have found its way into my thoughts would have been to enter into an engagement to write for any newspaper. . . . *To D. Stuart,* V. 17, 1838

Notes. See Hine 1, 2; Landor 10, 12; Todd 1; W. 109, 404

Novel, The. See Books; Narrative; Reading; Romance

1. . . . frantic novels [modern]. See Passion 7; Literature 1-19; Poetry 119; Bulwer-Lytton 1; Dickens 1.

2. [Metrical novels.] See Narrative Poetry 2.

3. See Fielding 1; Mackenzie 2; Richardson 1-2; Scott, W. 14, 36-7; Sedgwick 1

Novelty. See Quaintness; Strangeness; Taylor, I.

1. See Criticism 76; Literature 24; Passion 7; Poetry 17, 29; W. 345A

2. . . . meagre novelties Of colour and proportion . . .
Prel., xii, 117-18. 1804-39

Obscurity. See also Style

1. See Diction 1; Milton 37; Shakespeare 56

2.* The mind often does not think, when it thinks that it is thinking. If we were to give our whole soul to anything, as the bee does to the flower, I conceive there would be little difficulty in any intellectual employment. Hence there is no excuse for obscurity in writing.
C. W., Jr. (Grosart, iii, 460). *c.* 1827

Observation. See also Composiition; Description; Imagery; Imagination; Nature; Passion; Realism; Sensitiveness to Sense
Impressions; Style; Truth

1. See Imagination 33A; Nature (Human) 20; Poetry 66; Style 6, 17; Burns 28-9; Byron 9; Hamilton, Eliza M. 4; Thomson 13

2.* I have remarked, from my earliest days, that, if under any circum-
stances, the attention is energetically braced up to an act of steady observation, or of steady expectation, then, if this intense condition of vigilance should suddenly relax, at that moment any beautiful, any impressive visual object, or collection of objects, falling upon the eye, is carried to the heart with a power not known under other circumstances. Just now, my ear was placed upon the stretch, in order to catch any sound of wheels that might come down upon the lake of Wythburn from the Keswich road: at the very instant when I raised my head from the ground, in final abandonment of hope for this night, at the very instant when the organs of attention were all at once relaxing from their tension, the bright star hanging in the air above those outlines of massy blackness, fell suddenly upon my eye, and penetrated my capacity of apprehension with a pathos and a sense of the Infinite, that would not have arrested me under other circumstances.
De Quincey's Reminiscenses, i, 308-9. *c.* 1805

3. [Observation and a turn for dramatic writing.] See Periodicals 23

Occasional Poems. See also Composition

1. [*Lycidas* as a good illustration.] See Poetry 115

Odes. See also Pindaric Odes

1. See Lyric Poetry 2; Gray 6; W. 98

2. [Irregularity of versification in *Thanksgiving Ode* not to be encouraged.] See W. 166

Opera

1. [Opera might also be placed among lyric poetry.] See Dramatic Poetry 1

2. See W. 262

Opposition to Realism. See under Realism

Original Genius. See under Genius

Originality. See Creative; Genius; Imagination; Individuality

1. See Copyright 1, 4; Literature 24; Poetry 77; Taste 14; Coleridge, H. 6; Langhorne 2

2. [Poets] Have each his own peculiar faculty. . . .
Prel., xiii, 303.   1804-39

Ornaments. See also Style

1. [No embellishments promised in projected periodicals.] See Periodical Planning 2

2. See Poetry 21; Style 40; Moore, T. 1; Thomson 13; Virgil 10; W. 293

Overwrought, The. See also Style; Realism 29

Oxford Movement, The

1.* The poet is a *high* churchman, but luckily does not go all lengths with the Oxford School—He praises the *reformers* (for they assume to be such) for inspiring the age with deeper reverence for antiquity and a more cordial conformity with ritual observances—As well as a warmer piety— But he goes no further—Nevertheless he is claimed by them as *their* poet. And they have published a selection from his works with a dishonest preface from which one might infer he went all lengths with them.
C. R. to T. R. (Corr. C. R., i, 472),   XII. 29, 1842

2. To what you have so justly said upon Tractarianism much in the same spirit might be added. It was a grievous mistake that these Tracts issued from the same place were *numbered*, and at the same time anonymous. Upon the mischief that unavoidably attaches to publications without name, especially, you might have added, corporate publications, you have written with much truth and feeling. But the whole proceeding was wrong, and has led to errors, doubts, and uncertainties, shiftings and ambiguities, not to

say abolute double-dealing, injurious to Readers and perilous to those in whom they originated. First, it has caused the great and pernicious error of the Movement being called the Oxford Movement, as if it *originated* there, and had sprung up in a moment. But this opinion, which is false in fact, detracts greatly from its dignity, and tends much to narrow and obstruct its range of operation. There is one snare into which it was impossible that Writers so combined should not fall, that of the Individual claiming support for his opinion from the body when it suited him so to do, and rejecting it and resting upon his individuality when that answered his purpose better.
To W. E. Gladstone, III. 21, 1844

Painters. See Gardening 1; Passion 4; Poetry 55; Taste 8; Unity 5

Painting and Poetry. See Poetry 1

Parallel Passages. See also Plagiarism
1. [Principles for studying them.] See Byron 23
2. See Criticism 65; Peace 1

Passion. See also Aim of Writing; Love Poetry; Pathetic; Pleasure; Poetry; Restraint; Style

1. See Aim of Writing 7, 10, 11; Biography 2c; Composition 12-14, 21; Criticism 40, 81; Diction 8; Elegy 2; Fancy 3; Gardening 1; Genius 3; Imagery 5; Imagination 20, 22, 27A, 32A; Intellect 13; Intuition 2C; Knowledge 6; Meter 2; Nature 7, 7A; Picturesque 1; Poetry 19, 21, 24-6, 28, 34, 37, 42, 61-2, 66-7, 71, 74, 113, 117, 122-5; Reason 4, 6, 23, 31; Romance 2; Style 3, 13, 22, 40; Subjects 13, 14, 17; Taste 11, 14; Unity 4; Wordiness 1

2. —— It is the hour of feeling.
One moment now may give us more
Than years of toiling reason . . . .
To My Sister, 24-26. 1798

2A.* . . . the power of exciting tears [in tragedy]—I said that nothing was more easy than to deluge an audience, that it was done every day by the meanest writers. *Biog. Lit.* (" Satyrane's Letters "), ii, 179. [*c.* IX, 1798]

2B. See Coleridge 31, 61B; Cowper 1; Dryden 2; Hamilton, W. R. 4; Heraud 1; Lyttleton 1; Pope 1A, 18-21; Shakespeare 37A; Taliesin 2; Watts 1, 2; Wieland 2; Winchilsea 5; W. 1A, 21, 33, 44, 87, 91, 96, 98, 345A, 354-5, 364-A, 372, 386, 391

3. [The regularity of meter] cannot but have great efficacy in tempering and restraining the passion by an intertexture of ordinary feeling, and of feeling not strictly and necessarily connected with the passion. *Pref. L. B.,* p. 940. [The portion from the comma to the period added in 1802.] 1800

4.* [In the way Rembrandt works] something out of nothing, and transforms the stump of a tree, a common figure into an *ideal* object, by the gorgeous light and shade thrown upon it, he [W.] perceives an analogy to his own mode of investing the minute details of nature with an atmosphere of sentiment. . . . *Hazlitt,* iv, 277. *c.* 1800

6.   . . . all good poetry is the spontaneous overflow of powerful feelings. . . . *Pref. L. B.*, p. 935.   1800

7.   It has been said that each of these poems [*L. B.*, 1800] has a purpose. Another circumstance must be mentioned which distinguishes these Poems from the popular Poetry of the day; it is this, that the feeling therein developed gives importance to the action and situation, and not the action and situation to the feeling. . . . The subject is indeed important! For the human mind is capable of being excited without the application of gross and violent stimulants; and he must have a very faint perception of its beauty and dignity who does not know this, and who does not further know, that one being is elevated above another, in proportion as he possesses this capability. It has therefore appeared to me, that to endeavour to produce or enlarge this capability is one of the best services in which, at any period, a Writer can be engaged; but this service, excellent at all times, is especially so at the present day. For a multitude of causes, unknown to former times, are now acting with a combined force to blunt the discriminating powers of the mind, and, unfitting it for all voluntary exertion, to reduce it to a state of almost savage torpor. The most effective of these causes are the great national events which are daily taking place, and the increasing accumulation of men in cities, where the uniformity of their occupations produces a craving for extraordinary incident, which the rapid communication of intelligence hourly gratifies. To this tendency of life and manners the literature and theatrical exhibitions of the country have conformed themselves. The invaluable works of our elder writers, I had almost said the works of Shakespeare and Milton, are driven into neglect by frantic novels, sickly and stupid German Tragedies, and deluges of idle and extravagant stories in verse.— When I think upon this degrading thirst after outrageous stimulation, I am almost ashamed to have spoken of the feeble endeavour made in these volumes to counteract it; and, reflecting upon the magnitude of the general evil, I should be oppressed with no dishonourable melancholy, had I not a deep impression of certain inherent and indestructible qualities of the human mind, and likewise of certain powers in the great and permanent objects that act upon it, which are equally inherent and indestructible; and were there not added to this impression a belief, that the time is approaching when the evil will be systematically opposed, by men of greater powers, and with far more distinguished success. *Pref. L. B.*, pp. 935-36.   1800

8.   [Poet's language in conveying passion.] However exalted a notion we would wish to cherish of the character of a Poet, it is obvious, that while he describes and imitates passions, his employment is in some degree mechanical, compared with the freedom and power of real and substantial action and suffering. So that it will be the wish of the Poet to bring his feelings near to those of the persons whose feelings he describes, nay, for short spaces of time, perhaps, to let himself slip into an entire delusion, and even confound and identify his own feelings with theirs; modifying only the language which is thus suggested to him by a consideration that he describes for a particular purpose, that of giving pleasure. Here, then, he will apply the principle of selection which has been already insisted upon. He will depend upon this for

removing what would otherwise be painful or disgusting in the passion; he will feel that there is no necessity to trick out or to elevate nature: and, the more industriously he applies this principle, the deeper will be his faith that no words, which *his* fancy or imagination can suggest, will be to be compared with those which are the emanations of reality and truth.

But it may be said by those who do not object to the general spirit of these remarks, that, as it is impossible for the Poet to produce upon all occasions language as exquisitely fitted for the passion as that which the real passion itself suggests, it is proper that he should consider himself as in the situation of a translator, who does not scruple to substitute excellencies of another kind for those which are unattainable by him; and endeavours occasionally to surpass his original, in order to make some amends for the general inferiority to which he feels that he must submit. But this would be to encourage idleness and unmanly despair. *Pref. L. B.*, pp. 937-38. 1800

13. [Meter heightens the pleasure of the passion.] See Meter 1

20. [Was early taught] To love those unassuming things . . . that live in passion. (*Prel.*, xii, JJ41-7), p. 608E. 1802

21. . . . feeling powerfully as they [earliest poets] did, their language was daring, and figurative. *App. L. B.*, p. 942. 1802

22.   Zealously [I did] labour to cut off my heart
From all the sources of her former strength;
And, as by simple waving of a wand
The wizard instantaneously dissolves
Palace or grove, even so did I unsoul
As readily by syllogistic words
Some charm of Logic, ever within reach,
Those mysteries of passion which have made,
And shall continue evermore to make,
(In spite of all that Reason hath perform'd
And shall perform to exalt and to refine)
One brotherhood of all the human race
Through all the habitations of past years
And those to come, and hence an emptiness
Fell on the Historian's Page, and even on that
Of Poets, pregnant with more absolute truth.
The works of both wither'd in my esteem
Their sentence was, I thought, pronounc'd; their rights
Seem'd mortal, and their empire pass'd away.
Prel., xi, A 77-95.   1804-5

23.   . . . passion, which itself
Is highest reason in a soul sublime. . . .
Prel., v, 40-1.   1804-39

24. [Conjunction of reason and passion constitutes excellence in writing.] See Taste 11; also Reason 6 and 33

26.   So feeling comes in aid
Of feeling. . . .
Prel., xii, 269-70.   1804-39

27.   All truth and beauty, from pervading love. . . .
             Prel., xiii, A 151.   1804-5

30.   [In future years, W. promises to make verse]
             Deal boldly with substantial things; in truth
             And sanctity of passion. . . .
             Prel., xiii, 233-6.   1804-39

31.   I seemed about this time to gain clear sight
             Of a new world—a world, too, that was fit
             To be transmitted, and to other eyes
             Made visible; as ruled by those fixed laws
             Whence spiritual dignity originates,
             Which do both give it being and maintain
             A balance, an ennobling interchange
             Of action from without and from within;
             The excellence, pure function, and best power
             Both of the object seen, and eye that sees.
             Prel., xiii, 369-78.   1804-39

34. [A writer's feelings must be controlled in an epitaph.] *Epitaph 1*
(*Oxf. W.*, p. 932). See also Imagery 10.   1810

35. [Feeling and judgment.] See Moral Element 11; Picturesque 2

37. . . . truth is the soul of passion. . . . See Chiabrera 4

40.   Poetic passion, Dennis has well observed is of two kinds, imaginative and enthusiastic, And merely human and ordinary; of the former it is only to be feared that there is too great a proportion. . . .

One word upon ordinary or popular passion—Could your Correspondent [a Unitarian] read the description of Robert and the fluctuations of hope and fear in Margaret['s] mind and gradual [decay?] of herself and her dwelling without a bedimmed eye then I pity her. Could she read the distress of the Solitary after the loss of his family and the picture of his quarrel with his own conscience (though this tends more to meditative passion) without some agitation then I envy not her tranquility—Could the anger of Ellen before she sate down to weep over her Babe, tho' she were but a poor serving maid, be found in a book And that book said to be without passion, then, thank Heaven! [she is no kin of mine].

To Mrs. Clarkson (*Corr. C. R.*, i, 78, and 80-81),   1814

41. Passion, it must be observed, is derived from a word which signifies *suffering*; but the connexion which suffering has with effort, with exertion, and *action*, is immediate and inseparable. How strikingly is this property of human nature exhibited by the fact that, in popular language, to be in a passion is to be angry! But,

> Anger in hasty *words* or *blows*
> Itself discharges on its foes.

To be moved, then, by a passion is to be excited, often to external, and always to internal, effort; whether for the continuance and strengthening of the passion, or for its suppression, accordingly as the course which it takes may be painful or pleasurable. If the latter, the soul must contribute to its support, or it never becomes vivid,—and soon languishes and dies. And this brings us to the point. If every great poet with whose writings men are familiar, in the highest exercise of his genius, before he can be thoroughly enjoyed, has to call forth and to communicate *power*, this service, in a still greater degree, falls upon an original writer, at his first appearance in the world. *E. Supp. Pref.*, p. 952. 1815

43. In the higher poetry, an enlightened Critic chiefly looks for a reflection of the wisdom of the heart and the grandeur of the imagination.

E. Supp. Pref., p. 944. 1815

44. [Affections, free and kindly, necessary for a critic.] See Criticism 81

46.* [Proud that] his sensibility is excited by objects which produce no effect on others. . . . He says that he cannot be accused of being insensible to the real concerns of life. He does not waste his feelings on unworthy objects. *H. C. R.*, i, 166. V. 9, 1815

47.* [Probably referring to *The Prelude*, W. said "last night"] how small a portion of what he has felt or thought has he been able to reveal to the world; and he will leave it, his tale still untold.

Corr. Taylor, p. 94. VIII. 18, 1838

51.* He preferred such of his poems as touched the affections, to any others; for whatever is didactic—what theories of society, and so on—might perish quickly; but whatever combined a truth with an affection was . . . [a gain forever], good today and good forever. He cited the sonnet, On the feelings of a highminded Spaniard, which he preferred to any other (I so understood him), and the Two Voices, and quoted with evident pleasure, the verses addressed To the Skylark.

English Traits, pp. 23-4. VIII. 28, 1833

53.* . . . it is the *feeling* that instructs the *seeing*.
Old Friends, pp. 173-4. VI. 4, 1842

Past, The. See also Primitivism; Romance

1. See Progress, Idea of 1; Coleridge, Hartley 6

3. Some people are selfish enough to say, What has posterity done for me? but the past does much for us. *Lady R.* (*Grosart*, iii, 436). V. 2, 1841

Pastoral Poetry. See also Gay; Pope

1. [The shepherds of Wordsworth's hills were "more exalted far" and more appealing to the imagination "Than the gay Corin of the groves" of pastoral poetry.] *Prel.*, viii, 275-301. 1804-39

2. . . . The Idyllium,—descriptive chiefly either of the processes and appearances of external nature, as the *Seasons* of Thomson; or of characters, manners, and sentiments, as are Shenstone's *Schoolmistress*, *The Cotter's Saturday Night* of Burns, *The Twa Dogs* of the same Author; or of these in conjunction with the appearances of Nature, as most of the pieces of Theocritus, the *Allegro* and *Penseroso* of Milton, Beattie's *Minstrel*, Goldsmith's *Deserted Village*. The Epitaph, the Inscription, the Sonnet, most of

the epistles of poets writing in their own persons, and all loco-descriptive poetry, belong to this class. *Pref.* (*1815*), p. 954.   1815

  3.   See Gillies 6; Gray 6; Pope 6; Smith, C. 2; W. 300A

Pathetic, The.   See also Passion

  1.   See Poetry 24; Sublime 1; Taste 14; Versification 2; Cottle, J. 1A; Dryden 22; Heywood, T. 1; W. 20

  5.   As the pathetic participates of an *animal* sensation, it might seem— that, if the springs of this emotion were genuine, all men, possessed of competent knowledge of the facts and circumstances, would be instantaneously affected. And, doubtless, in the works of every true poet will be found passages of that species of excellence which is proved by effects immediate and universal. But there are emotions of the pathetic that are simple and direct, and others—that are complex and revolutionary; some—to which the heart yields with gentleness; others—against which it struggles with pride; these varieties are infinite as the combinations of circumstance and the con- stitutions of character. Remember, also, that the medium through which, in poetry, the heart is to be affected, is language; a thing subject to endless fluctuations and arbitrary associations. The genius of the poet melts these down for his purpose; but they retain their shape and quality to him who is not capable of exerting, within his own mind, a corresponding energy. There is also a meditative, as well as a human, pathos; an enthusiastic, as well as an ordinary, sorrow; a sadness that has its seat in the depths of reason, to which the mind cannot sink gently of itself—but to which it must descend by treading the steps of thought. *E. Supp. Pref.*, p. 952.   1815

  9.*   I have heard him pronounce that the Tragedy of *Othello*, Plato's records of the last scenes of the career of Socrates, and Isaac Walton's *Life of George Herbert*, were in his opinion the most pathetic of human composi- tions. *Graves* (*Grosart*, iii, 468).   *c.* 1845

Pathetic Fallacy, The.   See Description; Imagery; Realism; Style;
      Truth

  1.   See Imagery 8; Chesterfield 1; Hamilton, Eliza M. 4

  2.   [For a discussion of the pathetic fallacy in W.'s poetry, see Professor Havens's chapter on " Animism," *The Mind of a Poet*, pp. 68-87.]

Patronage

  1.   And first let me say that it is no part of my creed that money may not be received from a Friend without a return equivalent in the way of bargain; I think it may, just as well as advice, consolation, preferment, recommendations to serve worldly advancement, or any thing else; I go further than this and do not think that a Man of Letters or Science forfeits anything of his dignity by receiving pecuniary assistance even from those who are not his personal Friends; I mean in this as in the other case if he can justify the thing to himself by the circumstances under which he is placed, and the end to be answered.—Thus much for my notion whether right or wrong upon the general position: next comes the application to particular

instances: and here with regard to money received from strangers or those with whom a Man of Letters has little personal connexion, nothing can justify this but strong necessity, for the thing is an evil in itself; the right or wrong in this case will be regulated by the importance of the object in view, and the inability to attain it without this, or other means being resorted to.—With regard to personal Friends; according to the degree of love between them and the value they set upon each other, the necessity will diminish of weighing with scrupulous jealousy and fear whether such gifts should be received and to what amount: nevertheless in this as in every other species of communication good sense, strict moral principle, and the greatest delicacy on both sides ought to prevail. *To Beaumont,*   III. 12, 1805

2. See Poetry 118; Cowley 5; Horace 8; Whewell 1

3. . . . As to patronage, you are right in supposing that I hold it in little esteem for helping genius forward in the fine arts, especially those whose medium is words. Sculpture and painting *may* be helped by it, but even in these departments there is much to be dreaded. The French have established an Academy at Rome upon an extensive scale, and so far from doing good, I was told by every one that it had done much harm. The plan is this: they select the most distinguished students from the school or academy at Paris and send to Rome, with handsome stipends by which they are tempted into idleness and of course into vice. So that it looks like a contrivance for preventing the French nation and the world at large profiting by the genius which nature may have bestowed, and which left to itself would in some cases, perhaps, have prospered. . . .

Genius in poetry, or any department of what is called the Belles-Lettres, is much more likely to be cramped than fostered by public support; better wait to reward those who have done their work, tho' even here national rewards are not necessary, unless the labourers be, if not in poverty, at least in narrow circumstances. *To W. R. Hamilton,*   XII. 21, 1837

4.   You are right in your recollection that I named to you the subject of foreign piracy as injurious to English authors, and I may add now that, if it could be put a stop to, I believe that it would rarely happen that successful writers, in works of imagination and feeling at least, would stand in need of pensions from Government, or would feel themselves justified in accepting them. *To W. R. Hamilton,*   I. 4, 1838

Perfection. See under Composition; Form; Revisions; Style; Gray 6

Perfectibility. See Progress, Idea of 1

Periodicals and Magazines. See *Blackswood's Magazine*; Brougham 1; Byron 23-23A, 30; *Christian Keepsake; Courier*; Criticism; De Quincey 4, 5; De Sismondi 1; *Edinburgh Review*; Gifford; Jeffrey; Le Grice 1; *Liberal; Monthly Mirror*; Moxon 5; *Quarterly Review*; Roscoe; Scott, J. 4; Wilson 3, 7; W. 200

Periodicals, Opposition to, and Objections to Publishing in. See
also Periodical Planning

1. I am astonished that you can find no better use for your money than
spending it on those silly Reviews. *To S. Hutchinson* (p. 640), II. 18, 1815

2. [Mention of a public man's private affairs degrades an author to the
level of a magazine-writer.] See Southey 45

3. See Periodical Planning 1; Macaulay 1; Quillinan 9; Southey 42

4. The writers in these publications, while they prosecute their inglorious
employment, cannot be supposed to be in a state of mind very favourable for
being affected by the finer influences of a thing so pure as genuine poetry;
and as to the instance which has incited you to offer me this tribute of your
gratitude, though I have not seen it, I doubt not but that it is a splenetic
effusion of the conductor of that Review who has taken a perpetual retainer
from his own incapacity to plead against my claims to public approbation.
To B. Barton.   I. 12, 1816

5. I would gladly be instrumental in drawing the attention of the
Public to your [C. W.'s] valuable Sermons, if I knew how—but I have not
access to any periodical Publications. Besides if I had it would be little avail;
for unless a Person makes himself the humble Servt of the Editors, it is
quite impossible that the dew of their regards should fall upon him.—I never
had to take any steps to ensure for my own Publications a favorable introduction. Critiques upon my Poems have I know been sent to some of the
Reviews, the Quarterly in particular, by admirers of mine, who were Strangers
to my Person; but refused admittance; and if one of them had been admitted,
it would have been so garbled and sophisticated by the stupidity of the Editor,
as scarcely to have been recognizable by the author. This was actually done
in Lamb's review of the Excursion. *To C. W.*,   III. 12, 1816

6. I have no intention to print any of my little pieces in periodical
works, a practice I never had recourse to, except in the case of poems which
have a political bearing—*To Gillies*,   VI. 19, 1817

7. The critiques to which you allude I have not [?] and if, as is probable
they be such, as some good natured person forwarded to me, the Literary
Gazette, I should indeed thorough (ly) despise them. It is now 20 years since
the 'Duncery' of the periodical Press first declared war against me; and they
have kept it up with laudable perseverance; I wish I could praise any other
quality which they have evinced—*To Hans Busk*,   VII. 6, 1819

8. My determination has been thus far, to have no connection with any
periodical Publication—if ever I set it aside it will be probably in the instance
of the Retrospective Review; which if it kept to its title would stand apart
from Contemporary Literature, and the injurious feelings which are too apt
to mix with the critical part of it. *To Hervey*,   late 1825

8. Your having taken the *Souvenir* into your own hands makes me still
more regret that the general rule [of not contributing to periodicals] I have
laid down precludes my endeavouring to render you any service in that way.
To A. Watts,   VI. 18, 1826

9. I have since had applications, I believe, from nearly every Editor, but complied with none. I have, however, been smuggled into the 'Winter's Wreath' to which I contributed three years ago; it being then intended as a solitary Publication for charitable purposes. (The two pieces of mine [*To a Skylark* (*Oxf. W.*, p. 209) and *Memory* (*Oxf. W.*, p. 499)] which appeared there had some months before been published by myself in the last Edition of the Poems.) This having broken the ice, I had less reluctance to close with a proposal the other day made me by Mr. Reynolds, the terms of which were too liberal to be easily resisted, especially as coming from a Gentleman who had put me on the use of an application to my eyes, from which, I believe, I derived very great benefit. *To A. Cunningham,*   II. 26, 1828

10. . . . The proprietors of some of these works have made large sums by them, and it is reasonable that the writers should be paid in some proportion. . . . It is a matter of trade. All my natural feelings are against appearing before the public in this way. *To A. Cunningham,* III. 7, 1828

11. [If W. writes for a periodical,] let me remind you that I consider myself quite at liberty to contribute to any of these works that will pay me as you have done, and have engaged to do so. I care not a straw whether they will or no, but that liberty I reserve, also the right of reprinting the Pieces in any New Edition of my Works that may be called for.
To Reynolds,   XII. 19, 1828

12. [Writing for money.] . . . they pay for my name fully as much as for my verses; and this would sink in value, according to the frequent use made of it. . . . it is right that poets should get what they can, as these annuals cannot but greatly check the sale of their works, from the large sums the public pay for them, which allows little for other poetry.
To Allan Cunningham (pp. 344-5),   Monday, 1828

14. . . . mentioned your name to him [Reynolds, ed. of *The Keepsake*] in such terms as I am accustomed to use in speaking of you. He replied to my recommendation that their object was Authors of prime celebrity—and persons distinguished by rank or fashion, or station or anything else that might have as little to do with good writing. . . . I think you do quite right in connecting yourself with these light things. An Author has not fair play who has no share in their Profits—for the money given for them leaves so much less to spare for separate volumes.
To Maria Jewsbury (pp. 349-51),   I, 1829

15. My only excuse is, that they offered me a very liberal sum, and that I have laboured hard through a long life without more pecuniary emolument than a lawyer gets for two special retainders, or a public performer sometimes for two or three songs. *To G. H. Gordon,*   VII. 29, 1829

16. . . . I am rightly served for having degraded [in writing for *The Keepsake*] the Muses by having anything to do with the venal.
To E. Q.,   VIII. 4, 1829

17. I have an aversion little less than insurmountable to having anything to do with periodicals—and nothing but a sense of duty to my family would have induced me to treat with Mr. Hill. . . . I put away all thoughts of

looking for pecuniary emolument from that way of publication, which is tantamount to abandoning such expectation from any other.
To Moxon,   VII. 21, 1831

18.   The Sonnets [eleven] upon Capital Punishment. . . . I cannot print them in a Magazine for reasons you are aware of.
To Moxon,   I, 27, 1840

19.   The liability to these errors [misprints] is a very strong reason why poetry composed with care should never be first published in Newspapers, unless the author has an opportunity of correcting the press.
To I. Fenwick,   IX. 17, 1840

20.   I do not like to publish ∴ . . in a Newspaper, nor in any periodical . . . , for with any of these I have carefully abstained from connecting myself. *To Moxon,*   II. 4, 1841

22.   But I have particularly to request that no Copies be sent to any Reviewer or Editor of Magazines or Periodicals whatever. I shall send one myself to Mr. Lockhart as a token of private Friendship, but not as editor of the ʻ Quarterly Review.ʼ *To Moxon,*   III. 23, 1842

23.   You will perhaps have thought that I was splenetic, in insisting upon this volume not being sent to the Reviews.—It is a thing which I exceedingly dislike, as done, seemingly, to propitiate.

If any work comes from an Author of distinction, they will be sure to get hold of it, if they think it would serve their publication so to do; and if they be inclined to speak well of it, either from its own merits or their good opinion of the Author in general, sending the book is superfluous; and if they are hostile, it would only gratify the Editor's or Reviewer's vanity, and set an edge upon his malice. These are secrets of human nature which my turn for dramatic writing (early put aside) taught me—or rather that turn took its rise from the knowledge of this kind with which observation had furnished me. *To Moxon,*   III. 27, 1842

24.   I see no reason for changing my mind about sending to the Reviews. . . . I cannot tolerate the idea of courting the favour (or seeming to do so) of any critical tribunal in this country, the House of Commons not excepted. I suppose by this time my volume is out. You need not fear its not being noticed enough, whether for praise or censure.
To Moxon,   IV. 3, 1842

Periodical Planning.   See Editing

1.   But I should principally wish our attention to be fixed upon Life and Manners, and to make our publication a vehicle of sound and exalted Morality.

All the periodical Miscellanies that I am acquainted with, except one or two of the Reviews, appear to be written to maintain the existence of prejudice and to disseminate error. To such purposes I have already said I will not prostitute my pen. Besides were we ignorant or wicked enough to be so employed, in our views of pecuniary advantage (from the public at least) we should be disappointed. *To W. Mathews,*   V, 23, 1794

2. [A suggested periodical.] Do you think any objection can be made to the following ' *The Philanthropist, a monthly Miscellany* '? This title I think would be noticed. It includes everything that can instruct and amuse mankind; and, if we exert ourselves, I doubt not that we shall be able to satisfy the expectations it will raise. . . . Next should follow essays upon Morals, and Manners, and Institutions whether social or political. These several departments entirely for such as read for instruction.

Next should come essays partly for instruction and partly for amusement, such as biographical papers exhibiting the characters and opinions of eminent men, particularly those distinguished for their exertions in the cause of liberty, as Turgot, Milton, Sydney, Michiavel, Bucaria, etc. etc. etc. It would perhaps be advisable that these should, as much as possible form a Series, exhibiting the advancement of the human mind in moral knowledge. In this department will be included essays of taste and criticism, and works of imagination and fiction. Next should come a review of those publications which are particularly characterized by inculcating recommendations of benevolence and philanthropy. Some Poetry we should have. For this part of our plan we ought to have no dependence on original communications. The trash which infests the magazines strongly impresses the justice of this remark; from new poetical publications of merit, and such *old* ones as are not generally known, the pages allotted to verse may generally be filled. Next come Parliamentary Debates, detailed as you have specified, and State-Papers as are of importance.

. . . We should by no means *promise* any embellishments; and, as our work will relate rather to moral than natural knowledge, there will not often be occasion for them. I am far from thinking that we should not vary it by occasionally introducing topics of physical science. They should however be as popular, and as generally interesting as we can collect. We should print in the review form. *To W. Mathews* (*E. L.*, pp. 121-2, and 124), VI, 1794

Personification. See under Imagery

Picturesque, The. See Poetry 1

1. I had once given to these sketches [*Descriptive Sketches*] the title of Picturesque; but the Alps are insulted in applying to them that term. Whoever, in attempting to describe their sublime features, should confine himself to the cold rules of painting would give his reader but a very imperfect idea of those emotions which they have the irresistible power of communicating to the most impassive imaginations. The fact is, that controlling influence, which distinguishes the Alps from all other scenery, is derived from images which disdain the pencil. Had I wished to make a picture of this scene I had thrown much less light into it. But I consulted nature and my feelings. The ideas excited by the stormy sunset I am here describing owed their sublimity to that deluge of light, or rather of fire, in which nature had wrapped the immense forms around me; any intrusion of shade, destroying the unity of the impression, had necessarily diminished its grandeur.
Oxf. W., p. 608 n[1]. 1793

2. [It was "a strong infection of the age"; see *The Mind of a Poet*,

pp. 569-70, where Professor Havens says that, in *Prelude*, xii, 111-22, 144-5, 154-6, and 185-9, "he criticizes the devotees of the picturesque for their analytical, critical attitude, their superficiality, their preoccupation with esthetics to the neglect of the moral and spiritual ministry of nature, their judging nature in accordance with preconceptions derived from painting, and their slighting its appeal to the emotions and the imagination."]

Prel., xii, 111-22, 144-5, 154-6, and 185-9.   1804-39

3. . . . since it reached me I have carefully perused the whole essay with much pleasure, but neither by the remarks, nor by the explanation in your letter have I been able to gain a distinct understanding of your notion of the picturesque as something separate from what is suited to the pencil. But first let me correct an error respecting my own meaning, into which I have led you. When I observed that many objects were fitted for the pencil without being picturesque, I did not mean to allude, as you infer, to the Dutch School but to the higher order of the Italian Artists, in whom beauty and grace are predominant; and I was censurably careless in not marking, that my eye was less [?directed] upon landscape than upon their mode of treating the human figure, in their Madonnas, Holy families, and all their pieces of still life. These materials as treated by them, we feel to be exquisitely fitted for the pencil—yet we never think of them as picturesque—but shall I say as something higher—something that realizes the idealisms of our nature, and assists us in the formation of new ones. Yet I concur with you that the Dutch School has made excellent use of Objects which in life and nature would not by a superficial Observer be deemed picturesque, nor would they with any propriety, in popular language, be termed so—this however I suspect is, because our sense of their picturesque qualities is overpowered by disgust which some other properties about them create: I allude to their pictures of insides of stables—dung carts—dunghills and foul and loathsome situations, which they not infrequently are pleased to exhibit. But strip objects of these qualities— or rather take such as are found without them, and if they produce a more agreeable effect upon canvas than in reality, then I think it may be safely said, that the qualities which constitute the picturesque, are eminently inherent in such objects. I will dismiss this, I fear, tedious subject with one remark which will be illustrated at large, if I execute my intention—viz.—that our business is not so much with objects as with the law under which they are contemplated. The confusion incident to these disquisitions has I think arisen principally from not attending to this distinction. We hear people perpetually disputing whether this or that thing be beautiful or not—sublime or otherwise, without being aware that the same object may be both beautiful and sublime, but it cannot be felt to be such at the same moment. . . .

To J. Fletcher,   II. 25, 1825

4. See Gardening 1; Sublime 4; Taste 1, 8; Unity 5; Burns 29; Price, U. 1; Scott, W. 37

Pindaric Odes

1. [Lady Winchilsea] unlucky in her models—Pindaric odes and French Fables. *To Dyce,*   IV. 30, 1830

2. See Gray 4

Piracy, Literary. See Copyright; Forgeries; Plagiarism

Plagiarism. See also Parallel Passages

1. See Copyright 4; Bayley 2, 3; Byron 6A, 23; Coleridge 46; Gillies 5; Landor 7; Milton 47; Scott, W. 33; Wilson, J. 7

9. . . . the 4 [sonnets] upon Italy shall be sent you, upon one condition that you do not read them to *verse-writers*. We are all in spite of ourselves a parcel of thieves. I had a droll instance of it this morning—for while Mary was writing down for me one of these Sonnets, on coming to a certain line, she cried out somewhat uncourteously ' that's a plagiarism '—from whom? ' from yourself ' was the answer. I believe she is right tho' she could not point out the passage, neither can I. *To C. R. (Corr. C. R.,* i, 374), XII, 1838

Pleasure. See also Aim of Writing; Passion

1. See Aim of Writing 11, 18; Meter 1, 2; Passion 8; Poetry 20-1, 24, 99; Versification 2; Burns 18; W. 117, 346, 350, 368A, 369, 372

2. [The necessity of producing immediate pleasure is not a degradation of the poet's art.] It is an acknowledgement of the beauty of the universe, an acknowledgment the more sincere, because not formal, but indirect; it is a task light and easy to him who looks to the world in the spirit of love: further, it is a homage paid to the native and naked dignity of man, to the grand elementary principle of pleasure, by which he knows, and feels, and lives, and moves. We have no sympathy but what is propagated by pleasure: I would not be misunderstood; but wherever we sympathize with pain, it will be found that the sympathy is produced and carried on by subtle combinations with pleasure. [Knowledge is pleasure; where a man] has no pleasure he has no knowledge. What then does the Poet? He considers man and the objects that surround him as acting and re-acting upon each other, so as to produce an infinite complexity of pain and pleasure; he considers man in his own nature and in his ordinary life as contemplating this with a certain quantity of immediate knowledge, with certain convictions, intuitions, and deductions, which from habit acquire the quality of intuitions; he considers him as looking upon this complex scene of ideas and sensations, and finding everywhere objects that immediately excite in him sympathies which, from the necessities of his nature, are accompanied by an over-balance of enjoyment.

To this knowledge which all men carry about with them, and to these sympathies in which, without any other discipline than that of our daily life, we are fitted to take delight, the Poet principally directs his attention. He considers man and nature as essentially adapted to each other, and the mind of man as naturally the mirror of the fairest and most interesting properties of nature. And thus the Poet, prompted by this feeling of pleasure, which accompanies him through the whole course of his studies, converses with general nature, with affections akin to those, which, through labour and length of time [the scientist feels]. *Pref. L. B.,* p. 938. 1800

3. [W. admits that pleasure is] produced by metrical composition essentially different from that which I have here endeavoured to recommend: for the Reader will say that he has been pleased by such composition; and

what more can be done for him? The power of any art is limited; and he will suspect, that, if it be proposed to furnish him with new friends, that can be only upon condition of his abandoning his old friends. Besides, as I have said, the Reader is himself conscious of the pleasure which he has received from such composition, composition to which he has peculiarly attached the endearing name of Poetry; and all men feel an habitual gratitude, and something of an honourable bigotry, for the objects which have long continued to please them: we not only wish to be pleased, but to be pleased in that particular way in which we have been accustomed to be pleased. . . . to enjoy the Poetry which I am recommending, it would be necessary to give up much of what is ordinarily enjoyed. But, would my limits have permitted me to point out how this pleasure is produced, many obstacles might have been removed, and the Reader assisted in perceiving that the powers of language are not so limited as he may suppose; and that it is possible for poetry to give other enjoyments, of a purer, more lasting, and more exquisite nature. This part of the subject has not been altogether neglected, but it has not been so much my present aim to prove, that the interest excited by some other kinds of poetry is less vivid, and less worthy of the nobler powers of the mind, as to offer reasons for presuming, that if my purpose were fulfilled, a species of poetry, would be produced, which is genuine poetry; in its nature well adapted to interest mankind permanently, and likewise important in the multiplicity and quality of its moral relations. *Pref. L. B.*, p. 942.   1800

8. [The poet] Whose aim is pleasure light and fugitive [ill serves the muse]. Dedication to *The White Doe*, ll. 57-8.   IV. 20, 1815

Pleonasm.   See under Wordiness

Plot.   See Action; Subjects

1. See Coleridge 61B; Cottle, J. 1A; Lamb 19; W. 13, 16, 20-1

Plumpton Correspondence.   See Camden Society 1

Poet Laureates.   See Laureateship

Poetic Diction.   See Diction; Imagery; Passion; Style

Poetry.   See also Aim of Writing; Diction; Drama; Dramatic
      Poetry; Epic, The; Imagination; Literature; Love Poetry;
      Meter; Moral Element; Narrative Poetry; Pastoral Poetry;
      Style; Subjects; Versification

1. [Poetry and painting.] See Composition 46; Creative 3; Gardening 1; Nature 19, 20; Passion 4; Picturesque 1-4; Poetry 25, 55, 133A, 146; Publishing 7; Taste 1, 8; Haydon 2; Reynolds, J. 3; W. 192, 227.

2. See W. 5, 79, 104, 135, 189, 192, 199, 227, 249, 260, 345A, 350, 353-5, 364A, 369, 389, 390

3. See Abstractions 3; Composition 19, 21, 44; Criticism 40, 41, 59; Didactic Poetry 1; Dramatic Poetry 1; Elegy 2; Gardening 1; Genius 3; Imagination 33A-G; Intuition 2C, 3, 4; Literature 17, 18; Lyric Poetry 2;

Monuments 1; Narrative Poetry 2; Nature 5, 19, 20; Pastoral Poetry 2; Pathetic 5; Pleasure 2, 3; Passion 7, 8, 22, 41, 43; Popular Judgment 4; Realism 52; Reason 4, 31; Rhapsodists 1; Satirical Poetry 1; Style 6, 13, 24-40; Taste 14-5; Versification 2, 24A.

3A.* In speaking of music, and the difference there is between the poetical and musical ear, Wordsworth said he was totally devoid of the latter, and for a long time could not distinguish one tune from another. *Memoirs, Journal and Correspondence of Thomas Moore*, ed. Lord John Russell, 8 vols. (Boston, 1853), iv, 48. N. D.

4. . . . all good poetry is the spontaneous overflow of powerful feelings. . . . See Aim of Writing 10

5. See Burke 3A; Chiabrera 2; Dryden 2; Dyer, John 5; Goethe 12; Gomm 1; Gray 5, 6; Pope 6, 14, 18; Smith, Charlotte 2; Tennyson 9; Watts 1

10. . . . transitory and accidental ornaments [destroy sanctity and truth of pictures.] See Poetry 21

11. [Poetry as opposed to " Science," and to the " Matter of Fact."] See Poetry 25

13. [Bad poets have improperly used many beautiful phrases that, consequently, now arouse disgust.] See Style 6; also 24 and 26

15. . . . Writers in meter seem to lay claim to [personifications] by prescription. See Imagery 5

16. [A poet's obligation to the reader.] It is supposed, that by the act of writing in verse an Author makes a formal engagement that he will gratify certain known habits of association; that he not only thus apprises the Reader that certain classes of ideas and expressions will be found in his book, but that others will be carefully excluded. This exponent or symbol held forth by metrical language must in different eras of literature have excited very different expectations: for example, in the age of Catullus, Terence, and Lucretius, and that of Statius or Claudian; and in our own country, in the age of Shakespeare and Beaumont and Fletcher, and that of Donne and Cowley, or Dryden, or Pope. I will not take upon me to determine the exact import of the promise which, by the act of writing in verse, an Author in the present day makes to his reader: but it will undoubtedly appear to many persons that I have not fulfilled the terms of an engagement thus voluntarily contracted. They who have been accustomed to the gaudiness and inane phraseology of many modern writers, if they persist in reading this book to its conclusion, will, no doubt, frequently have to struggle with feelings of strangeness and awkwardness: they will look round for poetry, and will be induced to inquire by what species of courtesy these attempts can be permitted to assume that title. I hope therefore the reader will not censure me for attempting to state what I have proposed to myself to perform; and also (as far as the limits of a preface will permit) to explain some of the chief reasons which have determined me in the choice of my purpose: that at least he may be spared any unpleasant feeling of disappointment, and that I myself may be protected from one of the most dishonourable accusations which can

be brought against an Author; namely, that of an indolence which prevents him from endeavouring to ascertain what is his duty, or, when his duty is ascertained, prevents him from performing it. *Pref. L. B.*, 934-5.   1800

17. [Meanness in poetry.] I cannot, however, be insensible to the present outcry against the triviality and meanness both of thought and language, which some of my contemporaries have occasionally introduced into their metrical compositions; and I acknowledge that this defect, where it exists, is more dishonourable to the Writer's own character than false refinement or arbitrary innnovation, though I should contend at the same time, that it is far less pernicious in the sum of its consequences. *Pref. L. B.*, p. 935.   1800

19. [Analysis of a poet.] He is a man speaking to men; a man, it is true, endowed with more lively sensibility, more enthusiasm and tenderness, who has a greater knowledge of human nature, and a more comprehensive soul, than are supposed to be common among mankind; a man pleased with his own passions and volitions, and who rejoices more than other men in the spirit of life that is in him; delighting to contemplate similar volitions and passions as manifested in the goings-on of the Universe, and habitually impelled to create them where he does not find them. To these qualities he has added a disposition to be affected more than other men by absent things as if they were present; an ability of conjuring up in himself passions, which are indeed far from being the same as those produced by real events, yet (especially in those parts of the general sympathy which are pleasing and delightful) do more nearly resemble the passions produced by real events, than anything which, from the motions of their own minds merely, other men are accustomed to feel in themselves:—whence, and from practice, he has acquired a greater readiness and power in expressing what he thinks and feels, and especially those thoughts and feelings which, by his own choice, or from the structure of his own mind, arise in him without immediate external excitement. *Pref. L. B.*, p. 937.   1800

20. [The poet *vs.* the biographer and historian. There are men] who talk of Poetry as a matter of amusement and idle pleasure; who will converse with us as gravely about a *taste* for Poetry, as they express it, as if it were a thing as indifferent as a taste for rope-dancing, or Frontiniac or Sherry. Aristotle, I have been told, has said, that Poetry is the most philosophic of all writing: it is so: its object is truth, not individual and local, but general, and operative; not standing upon external testimony, but carried alive into the heart, by passion; truth which is its own testimony, which gives competence and confidence to the tribunal to which it appeals, and receives them from the same tribunal. Poetry is the image of man and nature. The obstacles which stand in the way of the fidelity of the Biographer and Historian, and of their consequent utility, are incalculably greater than those which are to be encountered by the Poet who comprehends the dignity of his art. The Poet writes under one restriction only, namely, the necessity of giving immediate pleasure to a human Being possessed of that information which may be expected from him, not as a lawyer, a physician, a mariner, and astronomer, or a natural philosopher, but as a Man. Except this one

restriction, there is no object standing between the Poet and the image of things; between this, and the Biographer and Historian, there are a thousand. *Pref. L. B.*, p. 938. 1800

21. [A poet, too, feels the affections the scientist] has raised up in himself, by conversing with those particular parts of nature which are the objects of his studies. The knowledge both of the Poet and the Man of science is pleasure; but the knowledge of the one cleaves to us as a necessary part of our existence, our natural and unalienable inheritance; the other is a personal and individual acquisition, slow to come to us, and by no habitual and direct sympathy connecting us with our fellow-beings. The Man of science seeks truth as a remote and unknown benefactor; he cherishes and loves it in his solitude; the Poet, singing a song in which all human beings join with him, rejoices in the presence of truth as our visible friend and hourly companion. Poetry is the breath and finer spirit of all knowledge; it is the impassioned expression which is in the countenance of all Science. Emphatically may it be said of the Poet, as Shakespeare hath said of man, 'that he looks before and after.' He is the rock of defence for human nature; an upholder and preserver, carrying everywhere with him relationship and love. In spite of difference of soil and climate, of language and manners, of laws and customs: in spite of things silently gone out of mind, and things violently destroyed; the Poet binds together by passion and knowledge the vast empire of human society, as it is spread over the whole earth, and over all time. The objects of the Poet's thoughts are everywhere; though the eyes and senses of man are, it is true, his favourite guides, yet he will follow wheresoever he can find an atmosphere of sensation in which to move his wings. Poetry is the first and last of all knowledge—it is as immortal as the heart of man. If the labours of Men of science should ever create any material revolution, direct or indirect, in our condition, and in the impressions which we habitually receive, the Poet will sleep then no more than at present; he will be ready to follow the steps of the Man of science, not only in those general indirect effects, but he will be at his side, carrying sensation into the midst of the objects of the science itself. . . . If the time should ever come when what is now called science, thus familiarized to men, shall be ready to put on, as it were, a form of flesh and blood, the Poet will lend his divine spirit to aid the transfiguration, and will welcome the Being thus produced, as a dear and genuine inmate of the household of man.—It is not, then, to be supposed that any one, who holds that sublime notion of Poetry which I have attempted to convey, will break in upon the sanctity and truth of his pictures by transitory and accidental ornaments, and endeavour to excite admiration of himself by arts, the necessity of which must manifestly depend upon the assumed meanness of his subject. *Pref. L. B.*, pp. 938-9. 1800

23. [Dramatic language of men.] What has been thus far said [see Poetry 21] applies to Poetry in general; but especially to those parts of composition where the Poet speaks through the mouth of his characters; and upon this point it appears to authorize the conclusion that there are few persons of good sense, who would not allow that the dramatic parts of composition are defective, in proportion as they deviate from the real language

of nature, and are coloured by a diction of the Poet's own, either peculiar to him as an individual Poet or belonging simply to Poets in general; to a body of men who, from the circumstance of their compositions being in metre, it is expected will employ a particular language. *Pref. L. B.*, p. 939.   1800

24. [Poetic process.] I have said that poetry is the spontaneous overflow of powerful feelings: it takes its origin from emotion recollected in tranquillity: the emotion is contemplated till, by a species of reaction, the tranquillity gradually disappears, and an emotion, kindred to that which was before the subject of contemplation, is gradually produced, and does itself actually exist in the mind. In this mood successful composition generally begins, and in a mood similar to this it is carried on; but the emotion, of whatever kind, and in whatever degree, from various causes, is qualified by various pleasures, so that in describing any passions whatsoever, which are voluntarily described, the mind will, upon the whole, be in a state of enjoyment. If nature be thus cautious to preserve in a state of enjoyment a being so employed, the Poet ought to profit by the lesson held forth to him, and ought especially to take care, that, whatever passions he communicates to his Reader, those passions, if his Reader's mind be sound and vigorous, should always be accompanied with an overbalance of pleasure. Now the music of harmonious metrical language, the sense of difficulty overcome, and the blind association of pleasure which has been previously received from works of rhyme or metre of the same or similar construction, an indistinct perception perpetually renewed of language closely resembling that of real life, and yet, in the circumstance of metre, differing from it so widely—all these imperceptibly make up a complex feeling of delight, which is of the most important use in tempering the painful feeling always found intermingled with powerful descriptions of the deeper passions. This effect is always produced in pathetic and impassioned poetry; while, in lighter compositions, the ease and gracefulness with which the Poet manages his numbers are themselves confessedly a principal source of the gratification of the Reader. [Of two pieces of writing, otherwise alike, readers will greatly prefer the one in verse.]
Pref. L. B., pp. 940-1.   1800

25. [Poetry and prose.] If in a poem there should be found a series of lines, or even a single line, in which the language, though naturally arranged, and according to the strict laws of metre, does not differ from that of prose, there is a numerous class of critics, who, when they stumble upon these prosaisms, as they call them, imagine that they have made a notable discovery, and exult over the Poet as over a man ignorant of his own profession. Now these men would establish a canon of criticism which the Reader will conclude he must utterly reject, if he wishes to be pleased with these volumes. And it would be a most easy task to prove to him, that not only the language of a large portion of every good poem, even of the most elevated character, must necessarily, except with reference to the metre, in no respect differ from that of good prose, but likewise that some of the most interesting parts of the best poems will be found to be strictly the language of prose when prose is well written. The truth of this assertion might be demonstrated by innumerable passages from almost all the poetical writings, even of Milton

himself. To illustrate the subject in a general manner, I will here adduce a short composition of Gray [*Sonnet on the Death of West*] who was at the head of those who, by their reasonings, have attempted to widen the space of separation betwixt Prose and Metrical composition, and was more than any other man curiously elaborate in the structure of his own poetic diction.

. . . It will easily be perceived, that the only part of this Sonnet which is of any value is the lines printed in Italics [ll. 6-8; 13-14]; it is equally obvious, that, except in the rhyme, and in the use of the single word " fruit-less " [l. 13] for fruitlessly, which is so far a defect, the language of these lines does in no respect differ from that of prose. . . . We will go further. It may be safely affirmed, that there neither is, nor can be, any *essential* difference between the language of prose and metrical composition. [Poetry resembles painting] . . . but where shall we find bonds of connexion sufficiently strict to typify the affinity betwixt metrical and prose composition? They both speak by and to the same organs; the bodies in which both of them are clothed may be said to be of the same substance, their affections are kindred, and almost identical, not necessarily differing even in degree; Poetry (I here use the word ' Poetry ' (though against my own judgment) as opposed to the word Prose, and synonymous with metrical composition. But much confusion has been introduced into criticism by this contradistinction of Poetry and Prose, instead of the more philosophical one of Poetry and Matter of Fact, or Science. The only strict antithesis to Prose is Metre; nor is this, in truth, a *strict* antithesis, because lines and passages of metre so naturally occur in writing prose, that it would be scarcely possible to avoid them, even were it desirable.) sheds no tears ' such as Angels weep,' but natural and human tears; she can boast of no celestial ichor that distinguishes her vital juices from those of prose; the same human blood circulates through the veins of them both.

. . . [Rhyme and metrical arrangement do not essentially affect this theory.] I answer that the language of such Poetry as is here recommended is, as far as is possible, a selection of the language really spoken by men; that this selection, wherever it is made with true taste and feeling, will of itself form a distinction far greater than would at first be imagined, and will entirely separate the composition from the vulgarity and meanness of ordinary life; and, if metre be superadded thereto, I believe that a dissimili-tude will be produced altogether sufficient for the gratification of a rational mind. What other distinction would we have? Whence is it to come? And where is it to exist? Not, surely, where the Poet speaks through the mouths of his characters: it cannot be necessary here, either for elevation of style, or any of its supposed ornaments: for, if the Poet's subject be judiciously chosen, it will naturally, and upon fit occasion, lead him to passions the language of which, if selected truly and judiciously, must necessarily be dignified and variegated, and alive with metaphors and figures. I forbear to speak of an incongruity which would shock the intelligent Reader, should the Poet inter-weave any foreign splendour of his own with that which the passion naturally suggests: it is sufficient to say that such addition is unnecessary. And, surely, it is more probable that those passages, which with propriety abound with metaphors and figures, will have their due effect, if, upon other occasions where the passions are of a milder character, the style also be subdued and temperate. *Pref. L. B.*, p. 936-37.   1800

26. . . . Poetry is passion; it is the history or science of feelings. . . . See Wordiness 1

28. [Language of earliest poetry.] The earliest poets of all nations generally wrote from passion excited by real events; they wrote naturally, and as men: feeling powerfully as they did, their language was daring, and figurative. *App. L. B.*, p. 942.   1802

29. [Language of later poetry.] This [that the language of poetry, as different from that of men, had an unusual appeal] was the great temptation to all the corruptions which have followed: under the protection of this feeling succeeding Poets constructed a phraseology which had one thing, it is true, in common with the genuine language of poetry, namely, that it was not heard in ordinary conversation; that it was unusual. But the first Poets, as I have said, spake a language which, though unusual, was still the language of men. This circumstance, however, was disregarded by their successors; they found that they could please by easier means; they became proud of modes of expression which they themselves had invented, and which were uttered only by themselves. In process of time metre became a symbol or promise of this unusual language, and whoever took upon him to write in metre, according as he possessed more or less of true poetic genius, introduced less or more of this adulterated phraseology into his compositions, and the true and the false were inseparably interwoven until, the taste of men becoming gradually perverted, this language was received as a natural language: and at length, by the influence of books upon men, did to a certain degree really become so. Abuses of this kind were imported from one nation to another, and with the progress of refinement this diction became daily more and more corrupt, thrusting out of sight the plain humanities of nature by a motley masquerade of tricks, quaintnesses, hieroglyphics, and enigmas. See Style 26. *App. L. B.*, p. 943.   1802

30. [Poets] the happiest of all men. . . . *D. W. and W. to Mary and Sara Hutchinson* (E. L. p. 305),   1802

31. [Strange abuses poets have introduced into their language.] See Cowper 1

32.   By our own spirits are we deified:
           We Poets in our youth begin in gladness;
           But thereof come in the end despondency and madness.
           Resolution and Independence, ll. 47-9.   1802

32A.   If thou indeed derive thy light from Heaven,
           Then, to the measure of that heaven—born light,
           Shine, Poet! in thy place, and be content. . . .
           " If thou indeed derive thy light," 1-3.   1802-27

33. [Cities and their influence on the creative powers of a poet.] See Cities 1

34.   [To the child feeling imparts power]
           That through the growing faculties of sense

Doth like an agent of the one great Mind
Create, creator and receiver both,
Working but in alliance with the works
Which it beholds.—Such, verily, is the first
Poetic spirit of our human life,
By uniform control of after years,
In most, abated or suppressed; in some,
Through every change of growth and of decay,
Pre-eminent till death.
[See also ii, 358-86, A 247-50, and A 265-73.]
Prel., ii, 256-64.   1804-39

35.   . . . A dignity, a smoothness, like the works
Of Grecian art, and purest poesy.
Prel., v, 458-9.   1804-39

37.   To a strain
More animated I might here give way,
And tell, since juvenile errors are my theme,
What in those days through Britain was performed
To turn *all* judgments out of their right course;
But this is passion over-near ourselves,
Reality too close and too intense,
And intermixed with something, in my mind,
Of scorn and condemnation personal,
That would profane the sanctity of verse.
Prel., xi, 52-61.   1804-39
. . .

39.   Go to the Poets, they will speak to thee
More perfectly of purer creatures;—yet
If reason be nobility in man,
Can aught be more ignoble than the man
Whom they delight in, blinded as he is
By prejudice, the miserable slave
Of low ambition or distempered love?
Prel., xii, 68-74.   1804-39

41.   . . . and I may not speak
Thus wrongfully of verse, however rude,
Which on thy [Coleridge's] young imagination, trained
In the great City, broke like light from far.
Moreover, each man's Mind is to herself
Witness and judge; and I remember well
That in life's every-day appearances
I seemed about this time to gain clear sight
Of a new world—a world, too, that was fit
To be transmitted, and to other eyes
Made visible; as ruled by those fixed laws
Whence spiritual dignity originates,
Which do both give it being and maintain

A balance, an ennobling interchange
Of action from without and from within;
The excellence, pure function, and best power,
Both of the object seen, and eye that sees.
Prel., xiii, 362-78.   1804-39

42.   I felt that the array
Of act and circumstance, and visible form,
Is mainly to the pleasure of the mind
What passion makes them; that meanwhile the forms
Of Nature have a passion in themselves,
That intermingles with those works of man
To which she summons him; although the works
Be mean, have nothing lofty of their own;
And that the Genius of the Poet hence
May boldly take his way among mankind
Wherever Nature leads; that he hath stood
By Nature's side among the men of old,
And so shall stand for ever.
Prel., xiii, 287-99.   1804-39

45. There is no forming a true estimate of a volume of *small* poems by
reading them all together; one stands in the way of the other. They must
either be read a few at once, or the book must remain some time by one,
before a judgment can be made of the quantity of thought and feeling and
imagery it contains, and what (and what variety of) moods of mind it can
either impart or is suited to. *To Beaumont,*   XI. 10, 1806

46.   Blessings be with them—and eternal praise,
Who gave us nobler loves, and nobler cares—
The Poets, who on earth have made us heirs
Of truth and pure delight by heavenly lays!
Oh! might my name be numbered among theirs,
Then gladly would I end my mortal days.
Personal Talk, iv, 51-6.   1807

47.* . . . spoke freely and praisingly of his own poems, which I never
felt to be unbecoming, but the contrary. He said he thought of writing an
essay, " Why bad poetry pleases.' . . . He spoke at length on the connection
of poetry with moral principles as well as with a knowledge of the principles
of human nature. He said he could not respect the mother who could read
without emotion his poem, *Once in a lonely hamlet I sojourned.* He said he
wrote his *Beggars* to exhibit the power of physical beauty and health and
vigour in childhood even in a state of moral depravity. He wished popularity for his *Two voices are there, one is of the Sea* as a test of elevation and
moral purity. *H. C. R.,* i, 10-11.   III. 15, 1808

48. . . . sincerity compels me to say that my poems must be more nearly
looked at before they can give rise to any remarks of much value, even from
the strongest minds.
[With respect to criticism offered of several poems] let the Poet first

consult his own heart, as I have done, and leave the rest to posterity;—to, I hope, an improving posterity. The fact is, the English *public* are at this moment in the same state of mind with respect to my poems, if small things may be compared with great, as the French are in respect to Shakespeare; and not the French alone, but almost the whole Continent. In short, in your friend's letter, I am condemned for the very thing for which I ought to have been praised; viz., that I have not written down to the level of superficial observes and unthinking minds. Every great Poet is a Teacher: I wish either to be considered as a Teacher, or as nothing. *To Beaumont,*   I or II, 1808

49.   The principle of the arrangement is that there should be a scale in each class and in the whole, and that each poem should be so placed as to direct the Reader's attention by its position to its *primary* interest. [In this letter to Coleridge, W. states the intended arrangement of his poems in the next edition. An ascending scale of imagination will govern the arrangement of each class.] *To Coleridge,*   early V, 1809

53.   [Prose and verse.] . . . betrayed by a common notion that what was natural in prose would be out of place in verse; that it is not the Muse which puts on the garb but the garb which makes the Muse. See Moral Element 11. *Epitaph 2 (Grosart,* ii, 52).   1810

54.   [W. feels a disgust toward bad poetry that only a poet can feel.] *To Lady Beaumont,*   V. 10, 1810

55.   I do not doubt that I shall like Arnald's picture; but he would have been a better painter, if his genius had led him to *read* more in the early part of his life. Wilkie's style of Painting does not require that the mind should be fed from Books; but I do not think it possible to *excel* in *Landscape* painting without a strong tincture of the Poetic Spirit. *To Beaumont,*   XI. 16, 1811

57.   [Processes in Dyer's *Fleece*] unsusceptible of being poetically treated. *To Lady Beaumont,*   XI. 20, 1811

57A.*   He spoke of his own poems with the just feelings of confidence that a sense of his own excellence gives him. He is now convinced that he never can derive emolument from them; but being independent now, he willingly gives up all idea of deriving profit from them. He is convinced that if men are to become better and wiser, the poems will sooner or later find their admirers; but if we are to perish and society is not to advance in civilization it would be wretched selfishness, said he, ' to deplore the want of any personal reputation.' The approbation he has met with from *some* superior persons compensates for the loss of popularity, though no man has completely understood him—Coleridge not excepted, who is not happy enough to enter into his feelings. *H. C. R.,* i, 73.   V. 8, 1812

58.*   Speaking of his own poems, Wordsworth said he principally valued them as being *a new power* in the literary world. . . . Wordsworth said he himself looked to the powers of the mind his poems call forth, and the energies they presuppose and excite, as the standard by which they are to be estimated. Wordsworth purposes as soon as the two last volumes are out of print to reprint the four volumes, arranging the poems with some reference either to the fancy, imagination, reflection, or mere feeling contained in them. *The Kitten and the Falling Leaves* he spoke of as merely fanciful, *The Highland Girl* as of the highest kind being imaginative, *The Happy Warrior* as appertaining to reflection. In illustration of his principle of imaginative power he quoted his *Cuckoo*, and in particular the ' wandering voice,' as giving local habitation to an abstraction. I stated as a compression of Wordsworth's rather obscure account of poetic abstraction the following as the operation. The poet first conceives the essential nature of his object and strips it of all its casualties and accidental individual dress, and in this he is a philosopher; but to exhibit his abstraction nakedly would be the work of a mere philosopher; therefore he reclothes his *idea* in an individual dress which expresses the essential quality, and has also the spirit and life of a sensual object, and this transmutes the philosophic into a poetic exhibition. Wordsworth quoted the picture of the Old Man in his Leech Gatherer and the simile of the stone on the eminence as an instance of an imaginative creation.

H. C. R., i, 89-90.   V. 31, 1812

59.* W. on the other hand, valued them [his poems] only according to the powers of mind they presupposed in the writer or excited in the hearer.

Remains, p. 53.   V. 31, 1812

61.* He talked much of poetry and with great and, to me, laudable freedom of his own poems. He said that perhaps there is as *intense* poetical feelings in *his* as Shakespeare's works, but in Shakespeare the poetical elements are mixed up with other things and wrought into greater works. In him the poetry is *reiner* [more pure]. He contrasted some fine lines from his verses on the Wye, with a popular passage from Lord Byron on solitude. . . .

Wordsworth asserted that Southey was no judge of *his* poems, writing too many of his own to enter into his mind. And on my saying that Southey had praised his unpublished poems as superior to those published, Wordsworth seemed to resent this rather as a depreciation of the latter than a praise of the former. He could not surpass what he had already written. They are the utmost energies of his mind. Before his ballads were published Tobin implored Wordsworth to leave out *We are Seven* as a piece that would damn the book. It became one of the most popular. He related this in answer to a remark that by only leaving out certain poems at the suggestion of someone who knows the public taste he might avoid giving offense. Rogers has said the same, but Wordsworth gives no credit to the assertion. His sonnet in which the wild rose is compared to a village girl [*How sweet it is, when mother Fancy rocks*] he says is almost the only one of pure fancy. I also mentioned the one on the ship [*Where lies the Land to which yon Ship must go?*]. He said it expressed the delight he had felt on thinking of the first feelings of men before navigation had so completely made the world known, and while a ship exploring unknown regions was an object of high interest and sympathy. *H. C. R.*, i, 93-4.   VI. 3, 1812

62. [Philosophy more spiritless and dull than poetry.] *Exc.*, iii, 333-40.
See also Language 4; Poetry 58, 125, 135; Reason 31   1814

64. [Poetic passion of two kinds, imaginative and enthusiastic.] See Passion 40

65.   Oh! many are the Poets that are sown
           By Nature; men endowed with highest gifts,
           The vision and the faculty divine;
           Yet wanting the accomplishment of verse,
           (Which, in the docile season of their youth,
           It was denied them to acquire, through lack
           Of culture and the inspiring aid of books. . . .
           Exc., i, 77-83.   1814

65A. . . . you attribute more influence to Nature and to Poetry than they can justly claim! *To R. P. Gillies.*   II. 14, 1815

66. The powers requisite for the production of poetry are: first, those of Observation and Description,—*i. e.* the ability to observe with accuracy things as they are in themselves, and with fidelity to describe them, unmodified by any passion or feeling existing in the mind of the describer; whether the things depicted be actually present to the senses, or have a place only in the memory. This power, though indispensable to a Poet, is one which he employs only in submission to necessity, and never for a continuance of time: as its exercise supposes all the higher qualities of the mind to be passive, and in a state of subjection to external objects, much in the same way as a translator or engraver ought to be to his original. 2ndly, Sensibility,—which, the more exquisite it is, the wider will be the range of a poet's perceptions; and the more will he be incited to observe objects, both as they exist in themselves and as re-acted upon by his own mind. (The distinction between poetic and human sensibility has been marked in the character of the Poet delineated in the original preface [see *Oxf. W.*, p. 937]). 3rdly, Reflection, —which makes the Poet acquainted with the value of actions, images, thoughts, and feelings; and assists the sensibility in perceiving their connexion with each other. 4thly, Imagination and Fancy,—to modify, to create, and to associate. 5thly, Invention,—by which characters are composed out of materials supplied by observations; whether of the Poet's own heart and mind, or of external life and nature; and such incidents and situations produced as are most impressive to the imagination, and most fitted to do justice to the characters, sentiments, and passions, which the Poet undertakes to illustrate. And, lastly, Judgment,—to decide how and where, and in what degree, each of these faculties ought to be exerted; so that the less shall not be sacrificed to the greater; nor the greater, slighting the less, arrogate, to its own injury, more than its due. By judgment, also, is determined what are the laws and appropriate graces of every species of composition. (As sensibility to harmony of numbers, and the power of producing it, are invariably attendants upon the faculties above specified, nothing has been said upon those requisites [Eds. 1836-45]). *Pref. 1815*, p. 954 and n[1].   1815

67. . . . justified by recollection of the insults which the ignorant, the incapable, and the presumptuous, have heaped upon these and my other writings, I may be permitted to anticipate the judgment of posterity upon

myself, I shall declare . . . that I have given in these unfavorable times, evidence of exertions of this faculty [imagination] upon its worthiest objects, the external universe, the moral and religious sentiments of Man, his natural affections, and his acquired passions; which have the same ennobling tendency as the productions of men, in this kind, worthy to be holden in undying remembrance. *Pref. 1815*, p. 957.   1815

68. [Basis for arrangement.] . . . poems, apparently miscellaneous, may with propriety be arranged either with reference to the powers of mind *predominant* in the production of them; or to the mould in which they are cast; or, lastly, to the subjects to which they relate. From each of these considerations, the following Poems have been divided into classes; which, that the work may more obviously correspond with the course of human life, and for the sake of exhibiting in it the three requisites of a legitimate whole, a beginning, a middle, and an end, have been also arranged, as far as it was possible, according to an order of time, commencing with Childhood, and terminating with Old Age, Death, and Immortality. My guiding wish was, that the small pieces of which these volumes consist, thus discriminated, might be regarded under a twofold view; as composing an entire work within themselves, and as adjuncts to the philosophical Poem, *The Recluse*. [W. feels that his arrangement takes nothing from the value of any individual poem. He trusts each class has enough variety for the unreflecting reader; for the thoughtful reader the arrangement will point out the particular and general purpose. But to avoid misleading it is proper to point out] that certain poems are placed according to the powers of mind, in the Author's conception, predominant in the production of them; *predominant*, which implies the exertion of other faculties in less degree. Where there is more imagination than fancy in a poem, it is placed under the head of imagination, and *vice versa*. Both the above classes might without impropriety have been enlarged from that consisting of 'Poems founded on the Affections'; as might this latter from those, and from the class 'proceeding from Sentiment and Reflection.' The most striking characteristics of each piece, mutual illustration, variety, and proportion, have governed me throughout.

Pref. 1815, pp. 954-55.   1815

69. [Poetry and Music.] All Poets, except the dramatic, have been in the practice of feigning that their works were composed to the music of the harp or lyre: with what degree of affectation this has been done in modern times, I leave to the judicious to determine. For my own part, I have not been disposed to violate probability so far, or to make such a large demand upon the Reader's charity. Some of these pieces are essentially lyrical; and, therefore, cannot have their due force without a supposed musical accompaniment; but, in much the greatest part, as a substitute for the classic lyre or romantic harp, I require nothing more than an animated or impassioned recitation, adapted to the subject. Poems, however humble in their kind, if they be good in that kind, cannot read themselves; the law of long syllable and short must not be so inflexible,—the letter of metre must not be so impassive to the spirit of versification,—as to deprive the Reader of all voluntary power to modulate in subordination to the sense, the music of the poem;—in the same

manner as his mind is left at liberty, and even summoned, to act upon its thoughts and images. But, though the accompaniment of a musical instrument be frequently dispensed with, the true Poet does not therefore abandon his privilege distinct from that of the mere Proseman;

> He murmurs near the running brooks
> A sweeter music than their own.
> *Pref. 1815*, p. 955.

1815

70. [Poetry and classes of readers.] With the young of both sexes, Poetry is, like love, a passion; but, for much the greater part of those who have been proud of its power over their minds, a necessity soon arises of breaking the pleasing bondage; or it relaxes of itself;—the thoughts being occupied in domestic cares, or the time engrossed by business. Poetry then becomes only an occasional recreation; while to those whose existence passes away in a course of fashionable pleasure, it is a species of luxurious amusement. In middle and declining age, a scattered number of serious persons resort to poetry, as to religion, for a protection against the pressure of trivial employments, and as a consolation for the afflictions of life. And, lastly, there are many, who, having been enamoured of this art in their youth, have found leisure, after youth was spent, to cultivate general literature; in which poetry has continued to be comprehended *as a study.*

Into the above classes the Readers of poetry may be divided; Critics abound in them all; but from the last only can opinions be collected of absolute value, and worthy to be depended upon, as prophetic of the destiny of a new work. *E. Supp. Pref.*, p. 944.

1815

71. [Business of poetry.] The appropriate business of poetry (which, nevertheless, if genuine, is as permanent as pure science), her appropriate employment, her privilege and her *duty*, is to treat of things not as they *are*, but as they *appear*; not as they exist in themselves, but as they *seem* to exist to the *senses*, and to the *passions*. *E. Supp. Pref.*, p. 944.

1815

72. [Poetry and religion.] The religious man values what he sees chiefly as an ' imperfect shadowing forth ' of what he is incapable of seeing. The concerns of religion refer to indefinite objects, and are too weighty for the mind to support them without relieving itself by resting a great part of the burthen upon words and symbols. The commerce between Man and his Maker cannot be carried on but by a process where much is represented in little, and the Infinite Being accommodates himself to a finite capacity. In all this may be perceived the affinity between religion and poetry; between religion—making up the deficiencies of reason by faith; and poetry—passionate for the instruction of reason; between religion—whose element is infinitude, and whose ultimate trust is the supreme of things, submitting herself to circumscription, and reconciled to substitutions; and poetry—ethereal and transcendent, yet incapable to sustain her existence without sensuous incarnation. In this community of nature may be perceived also the lurking incitements of kindred error;—so that we shall find that no poetry has been more subject to distortion, than that species, the argument and scope of which is religious; and no lovers of the art have gone farther astray than the pious and the devout. *E. Supp. Pref.*, p. 945.

1815

73. . . . the productions of that class of curious thinkers whom Dr. Johnson has strangely styled metaphysical Poets, were beginning to lose something of that extravagant admiration which they had excited. . . .
E. Supp. Pref., p. 947.   1815

74. [Attitude of youthful readers toward poetry. The delusion of poetry (see Poetry 71) may lead the youthful reader astray, for he lacks the protective devices of experience, judgment, and common sense to warn him] that the realities of the Muse are but shows, and that her liveliest excitements are raised by transient shocks of conflicting feeling and successive assemblages of contradictory thoughts. . . . [W. adds that he does not wish to diminish a youth's confidence in his feelings and thus abridge his pleasures. He feels, however, that the ardent, confident youth will not be deterred, and that the modest and ingenuous will be warned by these remarks, will have his sensibilities and judgment better regulated.]
E. Supp. Pref., p. 944.   1815

75. [Attitude of religious men toward poetry.] As Poetry is most just to its own divine origin when it administers the comforts and breathes the spirit of religion, they who have learned to perceive this truth, and who betake themselves to reading verse for sacred purposes, must be preserved from numerous illusions to which the two Classes of Readers whom we have been considering, are liable. [This class is likely to furnish poor critics: (1) their serious nature, narrowness of interest and sympathies force them to overlook many excellencies. (2) Men who read from religious or moral inclinations are beset with misconceptions peculiar to themselves, and overrate authors who express their beliefs, and so are likely to impart more passion to the author's language than they receive. (3) They are dissatisfied by any opposition to their religious tenets; especially those whose Christianity is based solely upon cold reason, instead of upon humility, for these are naturally full of contradictions, now contemptuous, then troubled, or suspicious. And (4) see Poetry 72.]
E. Supp. Pref., p. 945.   1815

76. [Men of affairs, having ceased to read poetry after their youth, are not] . . . advanced in true discernment beyond the age of youth. If, then, a new poem fall in their way, whose attractions are of that kind which would have enraptured them during the heat of youth, the judgment not being improved to a degree that they shall be disgusted, they are dazzled; and prize and cherish the faults for having had power to make the present time vanish before them, and to throw the mind back, as by enchantment, into the happiest season of life. As they read, powers seem to be revived, passions are regenerated, and pleasures restored. [Having satisfied their desire for escape from burdens of business, they praise a poem. Retaining their youthful love for absurdities, extravagances, and misplaced ornaments, they also retain their youthful inaptitude to be moved by the unostentatious beauties of a pure style.] *E. Supp. Pref.*, p. 944.   1815

77. [Original poet and audience.] If there be one conclusion more forcibly pressed upon us thna another by the review [in *E. Supp. Pref.*]

which has been given of the fortunes and fate of poetical Works, it is this—that every author, as far as he is great and at the same time *original*, has had the task of *creating* the taste by which he is to be enjoyed: so has it been, so will it continue to be. This remark was long since made to me by the philosophical Friend for the separation of whose poems from my own I have previously expressed my regret. The predecessors of an original Genius of a high order will have smoothed the way for all that he has in common with them;—and much he will have in common; but, for what is peculiarly his own, he will be called upon to clear and often to shape his own road. . . . *E. Supp. Pref.*, p. 951.　　　　　　　　　　　　　　　　　　　　　1815

78.　Epic poetry, of the highest class, requires in the first place an action eminently influential, an action with a grand or sublime train of consequences; it next requires the intervention and guidance of beings superior to man, what the critics, I believe, call machinery; and lastly, I think with Dennis that no subject but a religious one can answer the demand of the soul in the highest class of this species of poetry. Now Tasso's [*Jerusalem Delivered*] is a religious subject, and in my opinion a most happy one; but I am confidently of opinion that the movement of Tasso's poem rarely corresponds with the essential character of the subject; nor do I think it possible that, written in stansas, it should. The celestial movement cannot, I think, be kept up, if the sense is to be broken in that despotic manner at the close of every eight lines. Spenser's stanza is infinitely finer than the *ottava rima*, but even Spenser's will not allow the epic movement as exhibited by Homer, Vergil, and Milton. How noble is the first paragraph of the *Aeneid* in point of sound, compared with the first stanza of the *Jerusalem Delivered*! The one winds with the majesty of the Conscript Fathers entering the Senate House in solemn procession; and the other has the pace of a set of recruits shuffling on the drill-ground, and receiving from the adjutant or drill-serjeant the command to halt at every ten or twenty steps. *To Southey,*　　　　1815

79.　[Poetry and prose.] See Poetry 69

80.　In the higher poetry, an enlightened Critic chiefly looks for a reflection of the wisdom of the heart and the grandeur of the imagination. *E. Supp. Pref.*, 944.　　　　　　　　　　　　　　　　　　　　　　　　　1815

81.　[The best and the worst critics among readers of poetry.] See Criticism 81

85.　[A poetical mind necessary for a good critic.] See Criticism 81

87.　[Poetry between *Paradise Lost* and the *Seasons*.] See Thomson 13

89.　[Poetry cramped by the pressing realities of life rarely achieves the sublime.] See Sublime 2

98.　I have heard of many who, upon their first acquaintance with my poetry, have had much to get over before they could thoroughly relish it; but never of one who, having once learned to enjoy it, had ceased to value it or survived his admiration. This is as good an external assurance as I can desire that my inspiration is from a pure source, and that my principles of composition are trustworthy. *To B. Barton,*　　　　　　　　　　　　I. 12, 1816

99.　. . . it is the privilege of poetic genius to catch, under certain restrictions of which perhaps at the time of its being exerted it is but dimly conscious, a spirit of pleasure wherever it can be found,—in the walks of nature, and in the business of men.—The poet, trusting to primary instincts, luxuriates among the felicities of love and wine, and is enraptured while he describes the fairer aspects of war: nor does he shrink from the company of the passion of love though immoderate—from the convival pleasure though intemperate—nor from the presence of war though savage, and recognized as the handmaid of desolation. Frequently and admirably has Burns given way to these impulses of nature; both with reference to himself and in describing the condition of others. See also Burns 36-7.

L. to Friend of Burns (*Grosart*, ii, 13).   1816

100. [Poetic comprehension of historical events.] See " The Bard— whose soul is meek," 1-14.

102. [Probably a reference to Restoration poets; see *Knight*, vi, 203 n.]

> For deathless powers to verse belong,
> And they like Demi-gods are strong
> On whom the Muses smile:
> But some their function have disclaimed,
> Best pleased with what is aptliest framed
> To enervate and defile.
> " Departing summer," 25-30.   1819

103. [These lines may refer to Caedmon's *Paraphrase*; see *Knight*, vi, 203 n.]

> Not such [defiled] the initiatory strains
> Committed to the silent plains
> In Britain's earliest dawn:
> Trembled the groves, the stars grew pale,
> While all-too-daringly the veil
> O nature was withdrawn!
> " Departing summer," 31-36.   1819

105. [English Poetesses.]

> Lady! I rifled a Parnassian Cave
> (But seldom trod) of mildly-gleaming ore;
> And culled, from sundry beds a lucid store
> Of genuine crystals, pure as those that pave
> The azure brooks, where Dian joys to lave
> Her spotless limbs; and ventured to explore
> Dim shades—for reliques, upon Lethe's shore,
> Cast up at random by the sullen wave.
> To female hands the treasures were resigned;
> And to this Work!—a grotto bright and clear
> From stain or taint; in which thy blameless mind
> May feed on thoughts though pensive not austere;
> Or, if thy deeper spirit be inclined
> To holy musing, it may enter here.
> " Lady! I rifled," 1-14.   1820

106. The power of waters over the minds of Poets has been acknowledged from the earliest ages; through the ' Flumina amem sylvasque inglorius ' of Virgil, down to the sublime apostrophe to the great rivers of the earth, by Armstrong, and the simple ejaculation of Burns, (chosen, if I recollect right, by Mr. Coleridge, as a motto for his embryo ' Brook,') . . . .

Grosart, iii, 98.   1820

106A. [Poetry suffers from] the matter of fact. . . .

To R. Sharp,   IV. 16, 1822

107. . . . whatever may be thought of the Germans as Poets [they are] the best Critics in Europe. *To R. Sharp*,   IV. 16, 1822

111. The ground upon which I am disposed to meet your anticipation of the spread of my poetry is, that I have endeavoured to dwell with truth upon these points of human nature in which all men resemble each other, rather than on those accidents of manners and character produced by times and circumstances; which are the favourite seasoning (and substance too often) of imaginative writings. If, therefore, I have been successful in the execution of my attempt, it seems not improbable that as education is extended, writings that are independent of an over (not to say vicious) refinement will find a proportionate increase of readers, provided there be found in them a genuine inspiration. *To A. Cunningham*,   XI. 23, 1823

113. There is no material change in the classification . . . except that the Scotch Poems have been placed all together, under the Title of Memorials of Tours in Scotland; this has made a gap in the poems of Imagination which has been supplied by Laodamia, Ruth, and one or two more, from the close of Affections etc.—But I need not trouble you with these minutiae—Miscellaneous poems ought not to be jumbled together at *random*—were this done with mine the passage from one to another would often be insupportably offensive; but in my judgment the only thing of much importance in arrangement is that one poem should shade off happily into another . . . and the contrasts where they occur be clear of all harshness or abruptness—I differ from you and Lamb as to the classification of Imagination &c—it is of slight importance as matter of Reflection, but of great as matter of *feeling* for the Reader by making one Poem smooth the way for another—if this be not attended to classification by subject, or by mould or form, is of no value, for nothing can compensate for the neglect of it.

To C. R. (Corr. C. R., i, 160-1),   IV. 6, 1826

114. One word on the subject of arrangement—Lamb's order of time is the very worst that could be followed; except where determined by the course of public events; or if the subject be merely personal—in the case of Juvenile Poems, or those of advanced Age. For example I place the Ode to Enterprize among the Imaginative Poems, which class *concludes* with the Tintern Abbey—as being more admired than any other—according to my present arrangement the Enterprize immediately precedes it,—but this is objectionable. The Author cannot be supposed to be more than 6 or 8 and 20 when Tintern was written; and he must be taken for about 50 when he produced the other. So that it would perhaps be better placed elsewhere.

To C. R. (Corr. C. R., i, 164-5),   IV. 27, 1826

115.   Some of my friends . . . doubt whether poetry on contemporary persons and events can be good.   But I instance Spenser's 'Marriage,' and Milton's 'Lycidas.'   True, the 'Persae' is one of the worst of Aeschylus's plays; at least in my opinion.   *C. W., Jr. (Grosart,* iii, 461).   *c.* 1827

117.   . . . I am certain that, without conference with me, or any benefit drawn from my practice in metrical composition, your own high powers of mind will lead you to the main conclusions; you will be brought to acknowledge that the logical faculty has infinitely more to do with poetry than the young and the inexperienced, whether writer or critic, ever dreams of. Indeed, as the materials upon which that faculty is exercised in poetry are so subtle, so plastic, so complex, the application of it requires an adroitness which can proceed from nothing but practice; a discernment, which emotion is so far from bestowing that at first it is ever in the way of it.
To W. H. Hamilton,   IX. 24, 1827

118.   [W. discusses the poet's need and desire for freedom from restraints of court or patron, and from the complexities of life that destroy simplicity.] See *Oxf. W.* ("Those breathing Tokens," 60-132) ; also Horace 8; and Cowley 5; Literature 23; Patronage. Contrast Literature 22; Restraint. 1829

119.   My Poetry, less than any other of the day, is adapted to the taste of the Luxurious, and of those who value themselves upon the priviledge of wealth and station.   And though it be true that several passages are too abstruse for the ordinary Reader, yet the main body of it is as well fitted (if my aim be not altogether missed) to the bulk of the people both in sentiment and language, as that of any of my contemporaries.—I agree with you, (and for the same reason) that nothing can be inferred from failure of cheap publication in Kirke White's case. . . . It is not to be questioned that the perpetually supplied stimulus of Novels stands much in the way of the purer interest which used to attach to Poetry.   And although these poorer Narratives do but in very few instances retain more than the hold of part of a season upon public attention, yet a fresh crop springs up every hour.
To John Gardener,   V. 19, 1830

120.   The true standards of poetry is high as the soul of man has gone, or can go.   *To E. Hill Handley,*   X. 4, 1830

121.   Yea, what were mighty Nature's Self?
                    Her features, could they win us
                Unhelped by the poetic voice
                    That hourly speaks within us?
                "The Gallant Youth," 85-8.   1831

122.   Poetry, if good for anything, must appeal forcibly to the imagination and the feelings. . . . *To Mrs. Rawson,*   V. 1833

123.   Motions and Means, on land and sea at war
                    With old poetic feeling, not for this,
                    Shall ye, by Poets even, be judged amiss!
                    Nor shall your presence, howso'er it mar
                    The loveliness of Nature, prove a bar

> To the Mind's gaining that prophetic sense
> Of future change, that point of vision, whence
> May be discovered what in soul ye are.
> " Motions and Means," 1-8.   1833

123A.* . . . although he was known to the world only as a poet, he had given twelve hours thought to the condition and prospects of society, for one to poetry. . . . [Dewey said that in the great political agitation, poetry seemed to have died out entirely.] He [W.] said it had; but that was not the only cause; for there had been, as he thought, some years ago an over-production and a surfeit. Orville Dewey, *The Old World and the New*, 2 vols. (New York, 1836), i, 90.   VII. 30, 1833

124.   If Thought and Love desert us, from that day
> Let us break off all commerce with the Muse:
> With Thought and Love companions of our way,
> Whate'er the senses take or may refuse,
> The Mind's internal heaven shall shed her dews
> Of inspiration on the humblest lay.
> " Most Sweet it is," 9-14.   1833

125.* [Poetry touching the affections preferred to the didactic on theories of society which] might perish quickly; but whatever combined a truth with an affection was [a gain forever]. *English Traits*, pp. 23-4. VIII. 28, 1833

126. . . . *I* am complimented upon my *wisdom* and upon my *work-manship*—what more I say could a Poet desire—for no Man can be wise who writes verses to any extent without some degree of inspiration.

To C. R. (Corr. C. R., i, 259),   IV. 3, 1834

128.   While poring Antiquarians search the ground
> Upturned with curious pains, the Bard, a Seer,
> Takes fire:—The men that have been reappear;
> Romans for travel girt, for business gowned;
> And some recline on couches, myrtle-crowned,
> In festal glee: why not?
> " While poring," 1-6.   1835

131. [No great poem ever written by a young man or by an unhappy one.] See Coleridge 31

132. [Poetic treatment]

> Peace to their Spirits! why should Poesy
> Yield to the lure of vain regret, and hover
> In gloom on wings with confidence outspread
> To move in sunshine?
> *Aquapendente*, 85-8.   1837

133.* He repeated emphatically what he had said before to me, that he did not expect or desire from posterity any other fame than that which would be given him for the way in which his poems exhibit man in his essentially human character and relations—as child, parent, husband, the qualities which are common to all men as opposed to those which distinguish one man from another. His sonnets are not therefore the works that he esteems the most. Empson and I had both spoken of the sonnets as our favourites. He said: 'You are both wrong.' . . . Empson related that Jeffrey had lately told Empson that so many people had thought highly of Wordsworth that he was resolved to re-peruse his poems and see if he had anything to retract. Wordsworth on this said he had no wish now that Jeffrey should do anything of the kind. Jeffrey had done him all the injury he could by violent attacks, and the silence of the *Quarterly* had prevented the sale of his works—otherwise he might have made his Italian journey twenty years ago. *H. C. R.*, ii, 535.   VIII. 17, 1837

133A. . . . Poetry, a subject which could not be properly treated without adverting to the other branches of fine art. *To W. R. Hamilton*, I. 4, 1838

134.   You would find the breaking up of the miscellaneous sonnets into classes, I think, impracticable. I thought a good deal about upon [*sic*] your suggestion, but gave up the Idea. for example there are some 5 or 6 of a political character—these could not be incorporated with the political series; which begins in 1802; when Bonaparte was made Consul for life and ends with his overthrow. Others are local sonnets, yet too few for a separate class; nor could they be intermixed with Itinerary ones, others religious, yet could not go among the Ec[c]lesiastical, nor are they numerous enough for a separate class—and so on. . . .

To C. R. (*C. R.*, i, 369),   VII or VIII, 1838

135.   [A poet] ought chiefly to inculcate his lessons, not formally, but by implication. . . . See Chaucer 21

136.   For my own part, I have been averse to frequent mention of the mysteries of Christian faith; not from a want of a due sense of their momentous nature, but the contrary. I felt it far too deeply to venture on handling the subject as familiarly as many scruple not to do. I am far from blaming them, but let them not blame me, nor turn from my companionship on that account. Besides general reasons for diffidence in treating subjects of Holy Writ, I have some especial ones. I might err in points of faith, and I should not deem my mistakes less to be deprecated because they were expressed in metre. Even Milton, in my humble judgment, has erred, and grievously; and what poet could hope to atone for misapprehensions in the way in which that mighty mind has done? *To H. Alford*,   II. 21, 1840

137. . . . generally good writers of verse wrote good prose. See Crabbe 11

138.* [W. had not written] specifically religious poetry, involving definite Christian doctrine. . . . felt himself unworthy to deal with matters so high and holy. . . . [He insisted on the distinction] between religious poetry and versified religion; disclaiming the agreement with Dr. Johnson, he recognized such religious poetry as, being the expression of religious faith in vital movements, was also informed by the poetic imagination; [but the poet writing for his age and seeking to affect] the general heart, was debarred . . . from using an instrumentality of doctrine beyond what the condition of generally accepted truth determined; [and, second, what truths his own peculiar genius and opportunities fitted him to clothe in forms of art and to commend to others]. And he conceived that in limiting himself to this province he incurred no just reproach, as if he were necessarily unappreciative of others, which might be even higher truths. . . . He was willing to acknowledge that it [his poetry] was not sacred in the highest acceptation of the word, but he trusted that its influence would be ever such as would prepare the soul for truths holier than its own.

Graves's Recollections, pp. 319-21.   *c.* 1840

139.*   *Chronological Classification of Poems.*—Many years ago I expressed to Wordsworth a wish that his poems were printed in the order of their composition, assigning as reasons for the wish the great interest which would attach to observing the progressive development of the poet's thought, and the interpretative value of the light mutually reflected by poems of the same period. I remember being surprised by the feeling akin to indignation which he manifested at the suggestion. He said that such proceeding would indicate on the part of a poet an amount of egotism, placing interest in himself above interest in the subjects treated by him, which could not belong to a true poet caring for the elements of poetry in their right proportion, and designing to bring to bear upon the minds of his readers the best influences at his command in the way best calculated to make them effectual. *Graves (Grosart,* iii, 474).   *c.* 1840

140.   [Poetry should put forth great truths.] See Moral Elements 22

141.*   He [W.] makes no secret of his view that poetry stands highest among the arts. . . . *Old Friends,* p. 143.   VI. 28, 1841

142.*   And does such a man [Burns] deserve the name of a Bard, or a truly Great Poet? It would be a 'profanation of the term, and of all that is sacred in the noblest thoughts and feelings of man, to hold that mere intellect, so employed, could ever deserve, or commonly receive, that high appellation.' See Burns 26. *A Day With Wordsworth,* pp. 736-7.   VIII. 31, 1841

143.   [Highest tone best beseeming a poet.] See Burns 26

144.   . . . the degree in which poets dwell in sympathy with the past marks exactly the degree of their poetical faculty. See Coleridge, Hartley 6

145.   [Trochaic endings in drama.] See Taylor, Sir Henry 2

146.   The gentlest Poet, with free thoughts endowed,
             And a true master of the glowing strain,
             Might scan the narrow province with disdain
             That to the Painter's skill is here allowed.
             "The Gentlest Poet," 1-4.   1842

148.*   Wordsworth used to warn young poets against writing poetry remote from human interest. Dante he admitted to be an exception; but he considered that Shelley, and almost all others who had endeavoured to outsoar the humanities, had suffered deplorably from the attempt. I once heard him say, ' I have often been asked for advice by young poets. All the advice I can give may be expressed in two counsels. First, let Nature be your habitual and pleasurable study, human nature and material nature; secondly, study carefully those first-class poets whose fame is universal, not local, and learn from them: learn from them especially how to observe and how to interpret Nature.' *De Vere* (*Grosart*, iii, 488-9).   1842-46

149.* It has been observed also that the Religion of Wordsworth's poetry, at least of his earlier poetry, is not as distinctly 'Revealed Religion' as might have been expected from this poet's well-known adherence to what he has called emphatically. 'The lord, and mighty paramount of Truths.' He once remarked to me himself on this circumstance, and explained it by stating that when in youth his imagination was shaping for itself the channel in which it was to flow, his religious convictions were less definite and less strong than they had become on more mature thought, and that when his poetic mind and manner had once been formed, he feared that he might, in attempting to modify them, have become constrained. He added that on such matters he ever wrote with great diffidence, remembering that if there were many subjects too low for song, there were some too high.
De Vere (*Grosart*, iii, 491).   1842-46

150.   [Objections to writing love-poetry.] See Love Poetry 2

152.* He once said, speaking of a departed man of genius, who had lived an unhappy life and deplorably abused his powers, to the lasting calamity of his country, 'A great poet must be a great man; and a great man must be a good man; and a good man ought to be a happy man.'
De Vere (*Grosart*, iii, 494).   1842-46

154.   [The soul of poetry.] See Shakespeare 32

155.   [Future of English poetry not promising.] See Literature 17

156.   [Poets are often not so happy as ignorant members of the laboring classes.] *I. F.* (*Grosart*, iii, 154).   1843

157.   . . . no change has taken place in my [poetic] manner for the last forty-five years. . . . *To ?*,   IV. 1, 1843

158.* New thoughts, however deep, he said, were not the staple of poetry, but old thoughts presented with immortal freshness, and a kind of inspired felicity of diction. Words, he said, in poetry were more than the mere garments of thought. *Aubrey de Vere*, pp. 69-70.   III. 9, 1845

Popular Judgment. See Criticism; Fame; Judgment; Praise; Taste

1.* [*The Castle Spectre*] fitted the taste of the audience like a glove.
Hazlitt, xii, 271.   1798

4.   It is impossible that any expectations can be lower than mine concerning the immediate effect of this little work [*Poems in Two Volumes*, 1807] upon what is called the Public. I do not here take into consideration the envy and malevolence, and all the bad passions which always stand in the way of a work of any merit from a living Poet; but merely think of the pure absolute honest ignorance, in which all worldlings of every rank and situation must be enveloped, with respect to the thoughts, feelings, and images, on which the life of my poems depends.

[The poems have no appeal to the vanity of the selfish, materialistic people, striving to be " of consideration in society." We can have no thought without love of mankind.] This is a truth, and an awful one, because to be incapable of a feeling of Poetry in my sense of the word is to be without love of human nature and reverence for God. *To Lady Beaumont,* V. 21, 1807

6. Is it the result of the whole, that, in the opinion of the Writer, the judgment of the People is not to be respected? . . . The People have already been justified, and their eulogium pronounced by implication, when it was said, above—that, of *good* poetry, the *individual,* as well as the species, *survives.* And how does it survive but through the People? What preserves it but their intellect and their wisdom? [For the small, loud group, governed by factitious influence, the Public, W. has small use or hope] but to the People, philosophically characterized, and to the embodied spirit of their knowledge, so far as it exists and moves, at the present, faithfully supported by its two wings, the past and the future, his devout respect, his reverence, is due. *E. Supp., Pref.,* p. 953. 1815

7. See Fame 12; Passion 7; Poetry 70, 72, 74-7; Taste 15; Currie 2; Johnson 11; Scott, W. 38; Shakespeare 45, 46; Thomson 9; W. 166, 369.

8.* In remarking upon the causes of an author's popularity (with reference to his own failure, as he thought, in that respect), he mentioned, as one of them, the frequent occurrence of quotable passages,—of lines that dwelt in peoples memories, and passed into general circulation.
Moore's Diary, pp. 186-7. II. 20, 1835

12. [His popularity.] See Hamilton, Eliza M. 6

13. [*Paradise Lost,* as a poem, not appreciated by the masses.]
To E. Q. III. 9, 1840

15. In this country people who do not grudge laying out their money for new publications on personal or fugitive interests, that every one is talking about, are very unwilling to part with it for literature which is unindebted to temporary excitement. If they buy such at all it must be in some form, for the most part that has little to recommend it but low price.
Reed, p. 129. VII. 5, 1844

Power. See also Imagination; Passion

1. [He found verse] a passion, and a power. . . .
Prel., v. 555-6. 1804-39

4. [W. hoped his poetry might] become A power like one of Nature's [works]. *Prel.,* xiii, 312. (See also vii, 740-4; viii, 631-2; and *The Mind of a Poet,* pp. 472-3.) 1804-39

5. See Books 10; Diction 8; Fancy 3; Genius 3; History 4A; Imagination 9, 10, 21, 37, 49; Infinity 4; Knowledge 4; Nature 7A; Passion 41; Taste 14; W. 391

6. . . . there is life that breathes not; Powers there are
That touch each other to the quick in modes
Which the gross world no sense hath to perceive,
No soul to dream of.
Kilchurn Castle, 6-9. 1827

Practice. See Art; Composition; Diction; Revisions; Style

1. Fluency in writing will tread fast upon the heels of practice, and elegance and strength will not be far behind. *To W. Matthews,* V. 17, 1792

2. See Letter Writing 1; Godwin, W. 1; Crabbe 12; Reynolds, J. H. 1

3. [Practice essential in exercising the logical faculty in poetic composition.] See Poetry 117

4. . . . I am no ready master of prose writing, having been little practised in the art. *To J. K. Miller,*   XII. 17, 1831

6. The only deficiency [in the poems] respects skill in workmanship, of which however there is no want but what more practice would I doubt not supply. . . . [See also Gray 5; Reynolds, J. 3.] *To ?,*   I. 13, 1844

Praise. See Criticism, Effect of; Fame; Popular Judgment. Contrast Abuse

1. See Crabbe 12; Reynolds, John H. 1; W. 330, 369

3. [In private letters, praise may overflow; in dedications, must be restrained.] *To Mrs. Hemans,*   IV. 30, 1834

4. I hear from many quarters of the impression which my writings are making, both at home and abroad, and to an old man it would be discreditable not to be gratified with such intelligence; because it is not the language of praise for pleasure bestowed, but of gratitude for moral and intellectual improvement received. *To J. Kenyon,*   late Autumn, 1936

Precept. See under Criticism; Rules

Prefaces. See W. 389-90A

Prejudice. See under Criticism; Fame 12; Popular Judgment; Taste

Primitivism. See Anti-intellectualism; contrast Progress, Idea of

1. [See *Recluse,* I, i, 625-8; *Prel.,* viii, Y 194-213 (De Sel., p. 558); *Anecdote for Fathers;* and *Descriptive Sketches* (later text), 386-404 and 433-48; *Italian Itinerant,* 75-8; Poetry 28-9; Style 23-5.]

2.   [Shepherds] Not such as Saturn ruled 'mid Latian wilds,
         With arts and laws so tempered, that their lives
         Left, even to us toiling in this late day,
         A bright tradition of the golden age. . . .
         Prel., viii, 128-32 (see also i, 190-202; v, 223-425).   1804-39

3.   . . . I sang Saturnian rule
         Returned,—a progeny of golden years
         Permitted to descend, and bless mankind.
         Exc., iii, 756-58; see also 918-55.   1814

Probability. See also Credibility; Good Sense; Procter

1. See Poetry 69; W. 117, 187

2.* . . . he purposely made the narrative [of *Fidelity*] as prosaic as possible in order that no discredit might be thrown on the truth of the incident. *H. C. R.*, i, 191. IX. 11, 1816

Progress, Idea of

1. [Whether or not the present is inferior to the past in moral dignity and intellectual power, the main part of the dangers and impediments Wilson portrays in his " Letter to Mathetes " would not cease to exist for minds like his] as they arise out of the constitution of things, from the nature of youth, from the laws that govern the growth of the faculties, and from the necessary condition of the great body of mankind. . . . [In the times of Elizabeth, and of Charles I] though great actions were wrought, and great works in literature and science produced, yet the general taste was capricious, fantastical, or grovelling; and in this point, as in all others, was youth subject to delusion, frequent in proportion to the liveliness of the sensibility, and strong as the strength of the imagination. . . .

There are two errors, into which we easily slip when thinking of past times. One lies in forgetting, in the excellence of what remains, the large overbalance of worthlessness that has been swept away. . . . The second habitual error is, that in this comparison of ages we divide time merely into past and present, and place these in the balance to be weighed against each other. . . . [The present is of thirty to fifty years; the past, of centuries.] . . .

These observations are not made as implying a dissent from the belief of my correspondent, that the moral spirit and intellectual powers of this country are declining; but to guard against *unqualified* admiration, even in cases where admiration has been rightly fixed, and to prevent that depression, which must necessarily follow, where the notion of the peculiar unfavourableness of the present times to dignity of mind has been carried too far. For in proportion as we imagine obstacles to exist out of ourselves to retard our progress, will, in fact, our progress be retarded. [We must remember that] it is not necessary . . . that there should be at all times a continuous advance in what is of highest worth. In fact it is not, as a writer of the present day has admirably observed, in the power of fiction to pourtray in words, or of the imagination to conceive in spirit, actions or characters of more exalted virtue, than those which thousands of years ago have existed upon earth, as we know from the records of authentic history. Such is the inherent dignity of human nature, that there belong to it sublimities of virtue which all men may attain, and which no man can transcend: and, though this be not true in an equal degree of intellectual power, yet in the persons of Plato, Demosthenes, and Homer,—and in those of Shakespeare, Milton, and Lord Bacon,— were enshrined as much of the divinity of intellect as the inhabitants of this planet can hope will ever take up its abode among them. But the question is not of the power or worth of individual minds, but of the general moral or intellectual merits of an age—or a people, or of the human race. Be it so—let us allow and believe that there is a progress in the species towards unattainable perfection, or whether this be so or not, that it is a necessity of a good and greatly-gifted nature to believe it—surely it does not follow, that this progress should be constant in those virtues and intellectual qualities, and in those departments of knowledge, which in themselves absolutely con-

sidered are of most value—things independent and in their degree indispensible. . . . It suffices to content the mind, though there may be an
apparent stagnation, or a retrograde movement in the species, that something
is doing which is necessary to be done, and the effects of which will in due
time appear;—that something is unremittingly gaining, either in secret preparation or in open and triumphant progress. . . . It is enough for complacency
and hope, that scattered and solitary minds are always labouring somewhere
in the service of truth and virtue; and that by the sleep of the multitude the
energy of the multitude may be prepared. . . . [After Chaucer and Wyclif
came the Wars of the Roses, which were a blessing in that they destroyed
institutions and laws] under the oppression of which, if they had continued
to exist, the virtue and intellectual prowess of the succeeding century could
not have appeared at all, much less could they have displayed themselves with
that eager haste, and with those beneficient triumphs which will to the end of
time be looked back upon with admiration and gratitude.

If the foregoing obvious distinctions be once clearly perceived, and steadily
kept in view,—I do not see why a belief in the progress of human nature
towards perfection, should dispose a youthful mind, however enthusiastic, to
an undue admiration of his own age, and thus tend to degrade that mind.
Ans. to Mathetes (Grosart, i, 309-14).   XII. 14, 1809 and I. 4, 1810

2.   In such disposition of mind [nature admonished by reason. See Nature
and Reason] let the youth return to the visible universe; and to conversation
with ancient books; and to those, if such there be, which in the present day
breathe the ancient spirit: and let him feed upon that beauty which unfolds
itself, *not* to his eye as it sees carelessly the things which cannot possibly
go unseen, and are remembered or not as accident shall decide, but to the
thinking mind; which searches, discovers, and treasures up,—infusing by
meditation into the objects with which it converses and intellectual life;
whereby they remain planted in the memory, now, and for ever.
Ans. to Mathetes (Grosart, i, 320).   I. 4, 1810

3.   See Whitaker 5

Proportion

1.   See Poetry 24, 66; Taste 14; W. 355

2.   [Proportion achieved by meter.] See Versification 2

Propriety.   See under Diction; Epithet; Language; Passion; Style;
    Truth

1.   See Poetry 25

2.   [Hopes that] my ideas are expressed in language fitted to their
respective importance. *Pref. L. B.,* p. 936.   1800

3.   [In later times poets adopted the figurative language of the earlier
poets] sometimes with propriety, but much more frequently applied them
to feelings and thoughts with which they had no natural connexion whatsoever. *App. L. B.,* p. 942.   1802

Prose. For the distinction between verse and prose, see under Poetry; Style

1. . . . lines and passages of meter so naturally occur in writing prose. . . . See Poetry 25

2. See Style 1, 68; Bible 14; Dryden 1; Pope 18; W. 389

3. [State of English prose.] See Scott, J. 5

4. The last six lines of this Sonnet ["Nor wants the cause"] are chiefly from the prose of Daniel; and here I will state (though to the Readers whom this Poem will chiefly interest it is unnecessary) that my obligations to other prose writers are frequent,—obligations which, even if I had not a pleasure in courting, it would have been presumptuous to shun, in treating an historical subject. I must, however, particularise Fuller, to whom I am indebted in the Sonnet upon Wycliffe and in other instances. And upon the acquittal of the Seven Bishops [*Oxf. W.*, p. 442] I have done little more than versify a lively description of that event in the MS. Memoirs of the first Lord Lonsdale. *Grosart*, iii, 131.   1822

5. . . . I am no ready master of prose writing, having been little practised in the art. *To J. K. Miller*,   XII. 17, 1831

6. [That Coleridge prevented his contributing more frequently to *The Friend*, W. lamented,] As I never was fond of writing prose, and required some incitement to do so.
Letters K., iii, 121 (see also *Grosart*, iii, 457-8).   1836 or after

Prosody. See under Versification

Provincialisms. See also Style; Realism 52

Psalter, The. See Hymns 2

Publishing, Aim of, and Objections to. See also Copyright; Money, Writing for; Periodicals

1. See W. 3, 168, 197, 255, 306, 317, 322

2. There is little need to advise me against publishing; it is a thing which I dread as much as death itself. This may serve as an example of the figure by rhetoricians called hyperbole, but privacy and quiet are my delight.
To J. Tobin,   III. 6, 1798

3. My aversion from publication increases every day, so much so, that no motives whatever, nothing but pecuniary necessity, will, I think, ever prevail upon me to commit myself to the press again.
To J. Cottle,   VII. 27, 1799

4.* It is true that he has sometimes talked of publishing a few of the longest of them; but he has now entirely given up the idea—he has a great dislike to all the business of publishing—but that is not his reason—he thinks that having been so long silent to the world he ought to come forward again with a work of greater labour; and has many other lesser objections.
D. W. to Lady Beaumont,   XI. 4, 1805

5. [W. wishes to keep his poems out of reviewers' hands] chiefly because the immediate sale of books is more under the influence of reviews than is generally supposed, and the sale of this work is of some consequence to me.
To Wrangham,   VII. 12, 1807

6. [Will publish *The Convention of Cintra*] first, I believe in a newspaper for the sake of immediate and wide circulation. . . .
To Wrangham,   XII. 3, 1808

7. At the same time my own feelings urge me to state in sincerity, that I naturally shrink from solicitation of public notice. I never publish any thing without great violence to my own disposition which is to shun, rather than court, regard. In this respect we Poets are much more happily situated than our Brother Labourers of the Pencil; who cannot, unless they be born to a Fortune, proceed in their employments without public countenance.
To B. Haydon,   I. 13, 1816

8. [Publication] for the most part very prejudicial to young writers.
To J. Fletcher,   II. 25, 1825

9. As long as any portion of the Public seems inclined to call for my Poems, it is my duty to gratify that inclination, and if there be the prospect of pecuniary gain, though small, it does not become me to despise it, otherwise I should not face the disagreeable sensations, and injurious, and for the most part unprofitable labours in which the preparing for a new edition always entangles me. . . . *To S. Rogers,*   III. 23, 1825

10. . . . the extreme dislike which I have ever had to publication, as it is then that the faults of my writings, to use a conversational expression of your own applied to beauties, ' shine out.' *To S. Rogers,*   V. 3, 1825

11.* . . . never was in haste to publish; partly because he corrected a good deal, and every alteration is ungraciously received after printing. . . .
English Traits, p. 23.   VIII. 28, 1833

12. . . . I cannot muster courage to publish them, or anything else. I seem to want a definite motive—money would be one, if I could get it, but I cannot. . . . *To J. Kenyon,*   IX. 23, 1833

13. . . . the reason why I withheld such minor pieces as I have written, is not what some have chosen to say— an over-weening conceit of their being above the taste of my countrymen: it is no such thing—but a humble sense of their not being of sufficient importance for a separate Publication; and a strong ground of apprehension that either my Publisher or myself might be a loser, by giving them to the world. My 4 or 5 last *separate* publications in verse, were a losing concern to the Trade; and I am not ashamed of saying that I cannot afford to give my Time, my Health and my Money, without something of a prudential reserve. *To Kelsall,*   X. 31, 1833

14. Owing to the state of the times I have been very slack and indifferent about pushing it [*Yarrow Revisited and Other Poems*] through the Press; and I care as little about its Publication. . . . *To Moxon,*   I. 12, 1835

Punctuation

1. . . . punctuation a business at which I am ashamed to say I am no adept. *To H. Davy,* VII. 28, 1800

2. See Landor 11; Peace 2

Quaintness. See Novelty; Style

1. See Poetry 29; Shakespeare 56

2. . . . quaintness and contrariety . . . quite out of keeping with a true poet. . . . See Coleridge, H. 6; and Jacobean Age 1

Quotable Passages. See Popular Judgment 8A

Reading. See also Books; Intellect; Knowledge; Scholarly Interests

1. I have read nothing this age, nor indeed did I ever [contrast D. W.'s statement, *E. L.*, p. 51]. *To W. Mathews,* XI. 23, 1791

1A.* [W. considered proximity to a library] absolutely *necessary* to his health, nay to his existence.
Letters (Coleridge), i, 297 (see also i, 270). V. 6, 1799

2.* He is very anxious to get forward with the *Recluse* and is reading for the nourishment of his mind, preparatory to beginning. . . . See also Cowper 2. *D. W. to Lady Beaumont,* Christmas Day, 1805

2A. See Poetry 55; Travel Literature 1-4

3. The only *modern* Books that I read are those of travels, or such as relate to matters of fact; and the only modern books that I care for; but as to old ones, I am like yourself; scarcely anything comes amiss to me.
To F. Wrangham, Early Spring, 1812?

4. My reading powers were never very great, and now they are much diminished, especially by candle light. And as to buying books, I can affirm that on *new* books I have not spent five shillings for the last 5 years. I include reviews, magazines, Pamphlets, etc., etc. . . . and as to old Books, my dealings in that way, for want of means, have been very trifling. Nevertheless (small and paltry as my Collection is) I have not read a fifth part of it. *To F. Wrangham,* II. 19, 1819

5. . . . it is not once in a hundred times, that for many years past, I have been able to find time for reading prose fiction in periodicals—and too seldom indeed for the most celebrated novels.
To R. S. Mackenzie, XI. 25, 1837

Realism. See Description; History; Metaphysical; Truth; Sensitiveness; Subjects. Contrast Fancy; Fiction; Imagination; Legends; Mythology; Passion; Romances; Supernatural

1. [Will deal with what he finds] in life's daily prospect; [not with the supernatural.] *Peter Bell,* 131-45. 1798

5. [A poet must use the language of men.] See Style 6, 13

8. See Imagery 5; Passion 41; Poetry 66, 72; Sensuality 1; Subjects 17;

Unity 5; Defoe 3; Gay 1; Macpherson 2; Shakespeare 32; W. 43-4; 48; 117; 235, 270, 272, 346, 350, 352, 354

12.   [W. recalls that he had gained clear sight of] life's every-day appearances [that were worthy] To be transmitted, and to other eyes Made visible. . . . *Prel.*, xiii, 367-72.   1804-39

13.   . . . imagination almost always transcends reality.
To Gillies,   XI. 23, 1814

17.   [Pope believed] that Nature was not to be trusted.
E. Supp. Pref., p. 948.   1815

18.   To the solid ground
                Of nature trusts the Mind that builds for aye;
                Convinced that there, there only, she can lay
                Secure foundations.
                " A Volant Tribe," 5-8.   1823

19.*   [Elizabeth Barrett's] poems are too ideal for me. I want flesh and blood. . . . *H. C. R.*, ii, 562.   I. 3, 1839

23.*   . . . against writing poetry remote from [the humanities].
De Vere (*Grosart*, iii, 488-9).   1842-46

24.   [*Ancient Mariner* too remote from humanity.] See Coleridge 73

25.*   . . . Shelley's works were too remote from the humanities.
De Vere's Essays, i, 201.   1842-46

Anti-realism. See Composition; Description; Fancy; History; Imagery; Imagination; Observation; Passion; Picturesque; Poetry; Romances; Selection; Sensuality; Subjects; Supernatural; Truth

27.*   He complains of the dry reasoners and matter-of-fact people for their want of *passion*. . . . *Hazlitt*, iv, 277.   *c.* 1800

29.   [So many poems he loved as a boy are now dead to him. Though these poems were often full of falseness and overwrought, their " airy fancies " inspired him as he sought for " that most noble attribute of man "]

                . . . something loftier, more adorned,
                Than is the common aspect, daily garb,
                Of human life.
                Prel., v, 545-77.   1804-39

30.   See Character Analysis 5; Composition 13; Literature 26; Nature 20; Poetry 21, 24, 37, 39, 41, 57, 71-2, 74, 128; Power 7; Austen 1; Barrett 3; Shakespeare 3, 32; Tennyson 8; W. 15, 23, 29, 87, 91, 117, 124, 173, 180, 187-8, 191, 195, 198-9, 202, 205, 207, 233, 287, 329

32.   . . . and add the gleam,
                The light that never was, on sea or land,
                The consecration, and the Poet's dream. . . .
                [Versions of 1820 and 1827 differ.]
                Peele Castle, 14-16.   1805

34. . . . if the Picture were true to Nature, what claim would it have to be called Poetry? . . . [The matter of fact] with which the Muses have just about as much to do as they have with a Collection of medical reports, or of Law Cases. See Crabbe 1

36. . . . imagination almost always transcends reality.
To Gillies, XI. 23, 1814

37. Plague . . . upon your remorseless hunters after matter of fact. . . .
L. to Friend of Burns (*Grosart*, ii, 13). 1816

38. [Poetry suffers from] the matter of fact. . . .
To R. Sharp, IV. 16, 1822

39. . . . the Verses taking so high a flight, and particularly in the line 'lies fixed for ages' [l. 4 in "By Art's bold privilege"), it would be injurious to put forward the cold matter of fact, and the sense and spirit of the Sonnet ["By Art's bold privilege"] both demand that it should be suggested at the sight of the *Picture*. *To Haydon,* IX. 10, 1840

40. . . . I could not otherwise get rid of the prosaic declaration of the matter of fact that the Hero was so much older [reference to Wellington in "By Art's bold privilege"]. *To Haydon* (p. 1036), IX. 11, 1840

44. The six last lines of this sonnet ["Go, faithful Portrait!"] are not written for poetical effect, but as a matter of fact, which [W. had observed in the servants]. *I. F.* (*Grosart*, iii, 64). 1843

45. . . . not an image in it [*Evening Walk*] which I have not observed. . . . [W. amplifies this statement at some length, but concludes] by observing that the plan of it has not been confined to a particular walk, or an individual place; a proof (of which I was unconscious at the time) of my unwillingness to submit the poetic spirit to the chains of fact and real circumstance. The country is idealized rather than described in any one of its local aspects.
I. F. (*Grosart*, iii, 4-5). 1843

47. . . . sometimes I in thee have loved
My fancy's own creation.
"Yes! thou art fair," 3-4 (see also ll. 5-12). 1845

Fact

48. This [*Evening Walk*, 215-18] is a fact of which I have been an eye-witness. *Oxf. W.*, p. 595 n[3]. 1793

49.* He stated, what I had before taken for granted, that most of his *Lyrical Ballads* were founded on some incident he had witnessed or had heard of, and in order to illustrate how facts are turned into poetry he mentioned the origin of several poems; *Lucy Gray*, that tender and pathetic narrative of a child mysteriously lost on a common, was occasioned by the death of a child who fell into the lock of a canal. He removed from his poem all that pertained to art, and it being his object to exhibit poetically entire *solitude*, he represents his child as observing the day-*moon* which no town or village girl would ever notice.

The Leech Gatherer he did actually meet near Grasmere, except that he gave to his poetic character powers of mind which his original did not possess. The fable of the *Oak and Broom* proceeded from his beholding a rose in just such a situation as he has described the broom to be in. . . .

He represented . . . that by the imagination the mere fact is exhibited as connected with that infinity without which there is no poetry.

He spoke of his tale of the dog called *Fidelity*. He says he purposely made the narrative as prosaic as possible in order that no discredit might be thrown on the truth of the incident. In the description at the beginning and in the moral at the end he has alone indulged in a poetic vein—and these parts he thinks he has peculiarly succeeded in. He quoted some of the latter passage and also from *The Kitten and the Falling Leaves* to show how he had *connected even the kitten with the great, awful and mysterious powers of nature.* H. C. R., i, 190-1.   IX. 11, 1816

51.   See Imagination 43A; Reason 30; W. 5, 16, 19, 21, 31, 41, 68, 90-1, 176, 191, 198, 214, 258, 347

52.*   The first verses from which he remembered to have received great pleasure, were Miss Carter's ' Poem on Spring,' a poem in the six-line stanza, which he was particularly fond of, and had composed much in, for example, ' Ruth.' He said there was some foundation in fact, however slight, for every poem he had written of a narrative kind; so slight indeed, sometimes, as hardly to deserve the name; for example, ' The Somnambulist' was wholly built on the fact of a girl at Lyulph's Tower being a sleep-walker; and ' The Water Lily,' on a ship bearing that name. ' Michael ' was founded on the son of an old couple having become dissolute and run away from his parents; and on an old shepherd having been seven years in building up a sheepfold in a solitary valley: ' The Brothers,' on a young shepherd, in his sleep, having fallen down a crag, his staff remaining suspended midway. Many incidents he seemed to have drawn from the narration of Mrs. Wordsworth, or his sister, ' Ellen' for example, in ' The Excursion'; and they must have told their stories well, for he said his principle had been to give the oral part as nearly as he could in the very words of the speakers, where he narrated a real story, dropping, of course, all vulgarisms or provincialisms, and borrowing sometimes a Bible turn of expression: these former were mere accidents, not essential to the truth in representing how the human heart and passions worked; and to give these last faithfully was his object. If he was to have any name hereafter, his hope was on this, and he did think he had in some instances succeded; that the sale of his poems increased among the classes below the middle. . . .

Justice Coleridge (*Grosart*, iii, 426-7).   IX. 22 (?), 1836

53.   [Fact as basis of characters in *The Excursion*.] See Character Analysis 8

54.   The character and story [of *The Waggoner*] from fact.

I. F. (*Grosart*, iii, 36)   1843

Matter of Fact, The.   Contrast Anti-realism

55.   . . . Matter of Fact or Science. . . . See Poetry 25; also 106 A

56.   See Pope 18; W. 23, 133-4, 187, 207

57. [Reads and cares only for books] of travels, or such as relate to matters of fact. . . . *To F. Wrangham,*   early spring, 1812?

58.* [Line in " The Thorn ":] Three feet long and two feet wide. . . . ought to be liked. *H. C. R.,* i, 166.   V. 9, 1815

Reason. See also Good Sense; Intellect; Intuition; Judgment

1. [In *The Mind of a Poet*, pp. 362-4, Professor Havens points out that " Wordsworth distinguished at least three kinds of reason: (1) ' the grand And simple Reason ' (xii. A 123-4) or ' Reason in her most exalted mood ' (xiv. 192), that is, intuition, the *Vernunft*; (2) ' that humbler power Which . . . work[s] By logic and minute analysis ' (xii. A 124-6) and which, when misapplied, carried too far, and unchecked by other faculties, becomes Godwinian rationalism; (3) ' right reason ' (xiii. 22), that is judgment, sanity, instinctive wisdom, common sense, ' the plain And universal reason of mankind ' (vi. 545-6). . . . In both (2) and (3), which correspond to *der Verstand*, reason is opposed both to ' nature ' in the sense of ' the pure and simple work of the senses ' (Garrod, p. 99) and to that higher intuition, *die Vernunft*."]

4. There comes a time when Reason, not the grand
    And simple Reason, but that humbler power
    Which carries on its no inglorious work
    By logic and minute analysis
    Is of all Idols that which pleases most
    The growing mind. A Trifler would he be
    Who on the obvious benefits should dwell
    That rise out of this process; but to speak
    Of all the narrow estimates of things
    Which hence originate were a worthy theme
    For philosophic Verse; suffice it here
    To hint that danger cannot but attend
    Upon a Function rather proud to be
    The enemy of falsehood, than the friend
    Of truth, to sit in judgment than to feel.
    Prel., xi, A 123-37.   1804-5

6. [Reason may control and restrain the passion: see *Happy Warrior,* 12-8, 27-34; *Prel.,* iii, 154-66; iv, A 295-8; and xiii, A 263-5; and *Descriptive Sketches,* 434-7.]

7. [Reason] is our human nature's highest dower. . . . *Happy Warrior,* 16; see also 15-8, 27-34.   1805-6

8. [Conjunction of Reason and Passion constitutes excellence in writing.] See Taste 11

10. Yet a rich guerdon waits on minds that dare,
    If aught be in them of immortal seed,
    And reason govern that audacious flight
    Which heavenward they direct.
    " From the dark," 7-10.   1814

6

12. . . . poetry—passionate for the instruction of reason. . . .
E. Supp. Pref., p. 945.   1815

13. [Trusts that in his writings his imagination is] exercised, under and *for* the guidance of reason. *Postscript, 1835*, p. 966.   1835

14. See Criticism 44, 81; Imagination 29; Nature 7A; Passion 22-3; Poetry 29, 117, 142; Chiabrera 4; Hamilton, Eliza M. 4

Anti-rationalism. See Anti-intellectualism

15.   Sweet is the lore which Nature brings;
             Our meddling intellect
             Mis-shapes the beauteous forms of things:—
             We murder to dissect.
             The Tables Turned, 25-8.   1798

16.* He complains of dry reasoners. . . . *Hazlitt*, iv, 277.   *c.* 1800

17.   [Analysis] a pest
             That might have dried me up, body and soul.
             Prel., v, 228-9 (see also ix, 258-61; ii, 203-32,
                 376-82).   1804-39

18.   [When will the presumptuous] learn
             That in the unreasoning progress of the world
             A wiser spirit is at work for us. . . .
             Prel., v. 358-60 (see 347-63).   1804-39

21.   . . . their reason seemed
             Confusion-stricken by a higher power
             Than human understanding. . . .
             Prel., ix, 258-60. (See also ii, 203-32; xi, 83-92,
                 113-16, A 134-7, 282-370; xii, 45-74; and
                 Intuition 2C.)   1804-39

22. ["Poetry like everything else was subjected to the test of reason . . . and failed, because the poets described with sympathy and often with admiration the imperfect men whom we see about us." Quoted from *The Mind of a Poet*, p. 565.]
Prel., xii, 67-74 (see xi, A 83, A 86, and A 121-37).   1804-39

23. [Youth's] appropriate calling is not to distinguish in the fear of being deceived or degraded, not to analyze with scrupulous minuteness, but to accumulate in genial confidence; its instinct, its safety, its benefit, its glory, is to love, to admire, to feel, and to labour. . . . the way to knowledge shall be long, difficult, winding. . . . *Ans. to Mathetes (Grosart*, i, 325).   1809

24. See Imagination 27A, 29, 30, 34A, 38; Passion 2; Poetry 39, 75; Romance 2, 3; Coleridge 31, 36, 39, 54
[Pride of intellect. A presumptuous confidence] In the transcendent wisdom of the age . . . in laws divine, Deduced by reason. . . . [See also: "Nay, Traveller," 50-2; *Prel.*, xii, 105-9, 146-7; " Alas! what boots," 9-14; *Prel.*, v, 287, 329, 358; and xiii, 26-7, 46-7. *Exc.*, iv, 991-2 (" to some the universe is ' no more than . . . a mirror that reflects To proud Self-love her

own intelligence ' ") ; " Desire we past illusions," 7 (" conquering Reason, if self-glorified ") ; " Musings near Aquapendente," 337-9 (" Elate with view Of what is won, we overlook or scorn The best that should keep pace with it ") ; " Old Cumberland Beggar," 70-2 (" ye proud, Heart-swoln, while in your pride ye contemplate Your talents, power, or wisdom ") ; " St. Bees' Heads," 154-62 (" the Genius of our age . . . Boastful Idolatress of formal skill "). These are quoted from *The Mind of a Poet*, pp. 145-6 and notes 59-63.] *Exc.*, ii, 235-40.   1814

26.   . . . those truths,
Which unassisted reason's utmost power,
Is too infirm to reach.
Exc., v, 520-22.   1814

27.   . . . the mind's repose
On evidence is not to be ensured
By act of naked reason.
Exc., v, 560-62.   1814

28.   One of the main objects of *The Recluse* is to reduce the calculating understanding to its proper level among the human faculties.
To Mrs. Clarkson (p. 619),   XII, 1814

29.   And trust that spiritual Creatures round us move,
Griefs to allay which Reason cannot heal. . . .
" When Philoctetes," 9-10 (see also
" Oh what a Wreck," 6-10)   1827

30.*   All science which waged war with and wished to extinguish Imagination in the mind of man, and to leave it nothing of any kind but the naked knowledge of facts, was, he thought, much worse than useless; and what is disseminated in the present day under the title of " useful knowledge," being disconnected, as he thought it, with God and everything but itself, was of a dangerous and debasing tendency. For his part, rather than have his mind engrossed with *this* kind of science, to the utter exclusion of Imagination, and of every consideration but what refers to our bodily comforts, power and greatness, he would much prefer being a superstitious old woman.
Hamilton, i, 313.   VIII, 1829

31.   Some are of opinion that the habit of analysing, decomposing, and anatomising, is inevitably unfavourable to the perception of beauty. People are led into this mistake by overlooking the fact that such processes being to a certain extent within the reach of a limited intellect, we are apt to ascribe to them that insensibility of which they are in truth the effect, and not the cause. Admiration and love, to which all knowledge truly vital must tend, are felt by men of real genius in proportion as their discoveries in Natural Philosophy are enlarged; and the beauty in form of a plant or an animal is not made less but more apparent as a whole by a more accurate insight into its constituent properties and powers. A *savant*, who is not also a poet in soul and a religionist in heart, is a feeble and unhappy creature. [Poetry *vs.* philosophy: see Poetry 62.]   *I. F.* (*Grosart*, iii, 169).   1843

31A. [Analysis opposed: *Prel.*, ii, 203-32, 376-82; xi, A 121-37; xii, 216-20; *Exc.*, iv, 957-68, 1126-55; Reason 15, 23; Rules 1.]

32. [Wordsworth's mysticism, and his awareness " of the mystery which lies at the heart of reality" account for much of his anti-rationalism. See *The Mind of a Poet*, pp. 140-46.]
    . . . conquering Reason . . . Can nowhere move uncrossed by some new wall Or gulf of mystery. [See also " Bold words affirmed," 9-14; and *The Mind of a Poet*, pp. 141-2.] " Desire we past illusions," 7-9.   1833

33. [W. emphasized the value of the heart, the affections, and the feelings as correctives " to the errors and limitations of analytical reasoning. . . ." See Imagination 27 A; *The Mind of a Poet*, pp. 129-34.]

34. [The instincts and animism in relation to rationalism. Professor Havens says the instincts, to W., are another " corrective to the errors and limitations of analytical reason. . . ." (*The Mind of a Poet*, pp. 134-5). Further, he adds that " the great illustration of the trust Wordsworth put in the non-rational part of our nature is furnished by his animism." (*Ibid.*, pp. 135-6; see also examples in these pages.)]

Recitation. See also Lyric Poetry; Rhapsodists
    1. [W.'s lyric poems require only animated or impassioned recitation as a substitute for the classic lyre.] See Poetry 69

Reconciliation of Opposites. See under Similitude and Dissimilitude

Redundancy. See under Wordiness

Refinement. See under Style
    1. [Vicious refinement.] See Poetry 17, 111
    2. [Prejudices of false refinement.] See Taste 14
    3. See Barrett, Elizabeth 3

Reflection. See Imagination; Intellect; Thought
    1. See Poetry 58, 66, 113
    2. [Not enough reflection in Spenser's works.] See Spenser 21

Relativity of Taste. See Criticism, Historical; Taste

Religious Poetry. See Bible; Moral Element; Poetry 67, 72, 75, 78, 136, 138, 148; Montgomery, J. 2; Shakespeare 32; W. 104, 269

Repetition. See also Style
    1. [Effective repetition.] See Wordiness 1
    2. [Substitute] this verse
            Bear this prime truth in constant memory,

reading so for

Good to promote or curb depravity
[" Not to the object," 3].

This alteration arises out of a wish to avoid repetition which to a *certain degree* was inevitable in treating the subject as I have done with a desire that each Sonnet should be without *absolute* or logical dependence on the one preceding it. *To H. Taylor,*   XI. 3, 1841

 3. See Shakespeare 55; W. 209

 4. In a very few instances [ed. 1845] I have altered the expression for the worse, on account of the same feeling and word occurring rather too near the passage. *Reed,* pp. 152-53.   IX. 27, 1845

Restoration Poetry. See Poetry 102

Restraint. See Love Poetry; Passion; Thelwall

 1. [Emotional restraint. See Composition 12, 14; Reason 6; Versification 2; Scott, J. 6; *Mind of a Poet,* pp. 114, 218, 272-3, 285.]

 2.

. . . the Gods approve
The depth, and not the tumult, of the soul. . . .
Laodamia, 74-5.   1814

Reviews and Reviewers. See under Criticism; Periodicals

Revisions. See Composition; Diction; Labor; Practice; Scholarly
   Interests; Style

 1. . . . uncertain about my success in *altering* Poems. . . .
To Mary and Sarah H.,   VI. 14, 1802

 2. [With reference to an insertion, W. says that he is generally] uncertain about his success in *altering* poems; but in this case . . . I am sure I have produced a great improvement. *Grosart,* ii, 207.   *c.* 1802

 2A. See Repetition 4; Scholarly Interests 19; Versification 24A; Burger 2; Field 1-2; Hamilton, W. R. 1; W. 166, 168, 213, 244, 281, 334, 355, 373

 3. [Dora wrote Miss Kinnaird, February 17, 1832:] Mother and he work like slaves from morning to night—an arduous work—correcting [the MS of *The Prelude*]. . . . [W.] often pores over his MSS. by candlelight. . . . [On October 15, 1832, she again wrote that W. was] still correcting the old poem. *Prel. (ed. De Sel.),* p. 608A (see also p. xliii and n.[1]). [II-X, 1832]

 4.* . . . corrected a great deal, and every alteration is ungraciously received after printing. . . . *English Traits,* p. 23.   VIII. 28, 1833

 5. [See letter to J. Kenyon, late autumn, 1836.]

 6. If you think it worth while to compare the pieces entitled ' Evening Walk,' ' Descriptive Sketches,' and ' The Waggoner,' you will find I have made very considerable alterations, which I trust will be found to be improvements—at all events they ought to be so, for they cost me much labour.
To T. J. Judkin,   X. 20, 1836

7.   The labour I have bestowed in correcting the style of these poems now revised for the last time according to my best judgment no one can ever thank me for, as no one can estimate it.   The annoyance of this sort of work is, that progress bears no proportion to pains, and that hours of labour are often entirely thrown away—ending in the passage being left, as I found it.
To Moxon,   late XII, 1836

8.   But after all, the value of this Ed. [1836-37] in the eyes of the judicious, as hereafter will be universally admitted, lies in the pains which has been taken in the revisal of so many of the old Poems, to the re-modelling, and often re-writing whole Paragraphs which you know have cost me great labour and I do not repent of it. In the Poems lately written I have had comparatively little trouble.   *To Moxon,*   I. 28, 1837

9.*   [A projected trip was postponed a week while W. finished revising the MS of *The Prelude.*]   At this time he has been labouring for the last month, seldom less than six or seven hours in the day, or rather one ought to say the whole day, for it seemed always in his mind—quite a possession; and much . . . he has done to it, expanding it in some parts, retrenching it in others, and perfecting it in all. I could not have imagined the labour that he has bestowed on all his works had I not been so much with him at this time.   *Corr. Taylor,* p. 117.   III. 28, 1839

10.   [For examples of W's careful composition and frequent revisions, see a series of letters written to Haydon, September 4, 7, 10, and 11, 1840.]

11.*   He [W.] himself had owed his success much to his unwearied labor in perfecting each poem to the utmost.   *Aubrey de Vere,* p. 70.   III. 9, 1841

Rhapsodists.   See also Recitation

1.*   . . . he is jealous of the rhetorical declaimers and rhapsodists as trenching on the province of poetry.   *Hazlitt,* iv, 277.   *c.* 1800

Rhyme.   See under Blank Verse and Rhyme; Versification

Roman Catholic Literature.   See under Literature, Roman Catholic

Romance.   See also Anti-realism; Marvelous; Strangeness; Super-
       natural.   Contrast Realism

1.   See History 3, 4; Knowledge 6; Literature 26; Narrative Poetry 2; Realism 29

2.   The tales that charm away the wakeful night
                    In Araby, romances; legends penned
                    For solace by dim light of monkish lamps;
                    Fictions, for ladies of their love, devised
                    By youthful squires; adventures endless, spun
                    By the dismantled warrior in old age,
                    Out of the bowels of those very schemes
                    In which his youth did first extravagate;
                    These spread like day, and something in the shape

Of these will live till man shall be no more.
Dumb yearnings, hidden appetites, are ours,
And *they must* have their food.
. . .

                       Ye dreamers, then,
Forgers of daring tales! we bless you then,
Impostors, drivellers, dotards, as the ape
Philosophy will call you: *then* we feel
With what, and how great might ye are in league,
Who make our wish, our power, our thought a deed,
An empire, a possession,—ye whom time
And seasons serve; all Faculties to whom
Earth crouches, the elements are potter's clay,
Space like a heaven filled up with northern lights,
Here, nowhere, there, and everywhere at once.
   Prel., v, 496-507; 523-33 [see also *Exc.*, i, 177-85].   1804-39

3. [Wordsworth's love of romance. See *Prel.*, i, 166-220; v, 55-140, 451-533; vi, 73-94; vii, 449-57; ix, 204-8, 298-302, 437-91; x, 17-24; xiii, 142-59, 312-49; *Prel.* (*De Sel.*), pp. 521-2, 555 (lines 80-98), 602-5 (lines 60-114); *Exc.*, i, 177-85. These references are quoted from *The Mind of a Poet*, p. 440 (see also pp. 39-53 and 480-92).]

5.   Nor deem that localised Romance
                    Plays false with our affections;
                Unsanctifies our tears—made sport
                    For fanciful dejections:
                Ah, no! the visions of the past
                    Sustain the heart in feeling
                Life as she is—our changeful Life,
                    With friends and kindred dealing.
        " The gallant Youth," 89-96.   1831

Rules.   See Art; Authority; Criticism; Models

1.   Far less did rules prescribed by passive taste,
                Or barren intermeddling subtleties,
                Perplexed her mind. . . .
                Prel., xii, 154-6.   1804-39

2. [Processes of composition] governed by certain fixed laws. See Imagination 33B; also 11; Judgment 4; Style 33

3. . . . a fixed resolution to steer clear of personal satire. . . . See Satire 3

4. [The poet finds] . . . much is to be done by rule. . . . See Composition 20, and 34

5. [The law of long syllable and short must not be inflexible.] See Poetry 69; and also 25, 66

7. [Laws of imagination and fancy.] See Fancy 14

8. [Laws of biography.] See Biography 2A.

10.   [Tests for selecting the best sonnets.] See Sonnet 7

11.   . . . the source whence rules of art take their origin. See Copyright Laws 4

12.   See Criticism 39A, 49, 81; Picturesque 3; Style 33; Sublime 4; Taste 14; Burns 25; Gray 6; W. 101A, 346

13.   A *Poet*!—He hath put his heart to school,
　　　Nor dares to move unpropped upon the staff
　　　Which Art hath lodged within his hand—must laugh
　　　By precept only, and shed tears by rule.
　　　Thy Art be Nature; the live current quaff,
　　　And let the groveller sip his stagnant pool,
　　　In fear that else, when Critics grave and cool
　　　Have killed him, Scorn should write his epitaph.
　　　How does the Meadow-flower its bloom unfold?
　　　Because the lovely little flower is free
　　　Down to its root, and, in that freedom bold;
　　　And so the grandeur of the Forest-tree
　　　Comes not by casting in a formal mould,
　　　But from its *own* divine vitality.
　　　" *A Poet*! " 1-14.　　　　　　　　　　　　　　　　　1842

Sacred Writings.   See under Bible; Religious Poetry

Satire.   Contrast Aim of Writing; Universality

1.   Not however entirely to forget the world, I season my recollection of some of its objects with a little ill-nature, I attempt to write satires; and in all satires, whatever the authors may say, there will be found a spice of malignity.   Neither Juvenal nor Horace were without it, and what shall we say of Boileau, and Pope, or the more redoubted Peter [John Wolcot (Peter Pindar), 1738-1819]?   These are great names, but to myself I shall apply the passage of Horace, changing the bee into a wasp to suit the subject.

　　　　　　　Ego apis Matinae
　　　More modoque, &c, &c. [Horace, *Carm.*, 4. 2. 27.]
To Mathews,　　　　　　　　　　　　　　　　　　III. 21, 1796

2.   [Satire] would profane the sanctity of verse.   See Poetry 37

3.   I have long since come to a fixed resolution to steer clear of personal satire; in fact I never will have any thing to do with it as far as concerns the *private* vices of individuals on any account; with respect to public delinquents or offenders I will not say the same; though I should be slow to meddle even with these.   This is a rule which I have laid down to myself, and shall rigidly adhere to; though I do not in all cases blame those who think and act differently.   It will, therefore, follow that I cannot lend any assistance to your proposed publication.   The verses which you have of mine I should wish to be destroyed.   I have no copy of them myself, at least none that I can find.   I would most willingly give them up to you, fame, profit, and every-thing, if I thought either true fame or profit could arise out of them: I should

even with great pleasure leave you to be the judge in the case if it were unknown to everybody that I had ever had a concern in a thing of this kind; but I know several persons are acquainted with the fact and it would be buzzed about; and my name would be mentioned in connection with the work, which I would on no account should be. Your imitations seem well done; but as I have not the intermediate passages, I could not possibly judge of the effect of the whole. *To F. Wrangham,* XI. 7, 1806

4. See Satirical Poetry 1; Crabbe 1; Pope 20

7.   I have sent you a sonnet [" Said Secrecy," *Oxf. W.,* p. 513] which I shall not print in my collection, because my poems are wholly as I wish them to continue without *Personalities* of a vituperative character. If you think it worth being printed, pray have it copied and sent to the *Cantabridge Chronicle,* without a name. *To John W.,* III. 10, 1838

Satirical Poetry. See under Satire

1. And, lastly, philosophical Satire, like that of Horace and Juvenal; personal and occasional Satire rarely comprehending sufficient of the general in the individual to be dignified with the name of poetry. *Pref. 1815,* p. 954. 1815

Scholarship. See under Scholarly Interests

Scholarly Interests. See Anthologies; Criticism, Textual; Editing; History; Beaumont, F. and J.; Bentley, R.; Dyce; Macpherson

1.   . . . in that glorious time
    When Learning, like a stranger come from far,
    Sounding through Christian lands her trumpet, roused
    Peasant and king. . . .
    Prel., iii, 461-64. 1804-39

2. [On notes.] See Dryden 3-4; Hine, J. 1-2; Todd, H. J. 1

2A. See Anthologies 2, 3; Camden Society 1; Criticism 65, 67-8, 96; Scotch Writers 2; Sonnets 7; Bacon 7; Barbauld 3, 4; Beaumont, Sir John 6; Bell, J. 1; Bentley, Jr., Richard 1; Bible 14; Chaucer 11-17, 20-3; Cottle, A. 1; Cottle, J. 3; Cunningham, A. 5; Dryden 2-4; 18-23; Dyce 1, 2, 4, 6; Dyer, John 7; Homer 12, 13; Horace 7; Landor 10, 11; Macpherson 2, 3, 5; Maitland 1; Montagu, B. 2, 3; Montagu, Mary W. 1; Price, U. 3; Shakespeare 41, 45; Sharpe, C. K. 1; Skelton 2; Thomson 5, 6; Winchilsea, Lady 3, 7; Wordsworth, C. 5-6

3. [Disappointed in Todd's *Spenser,* not with the biography, which has merit, though it is badly organized, but with the notes.] That style of compiling notes ought to be put an end to. *To W. Scott,* XI. 7, 1805

7.   And learning's solid dignity. . . .
    Exc., v, 112. 1814

12. [See *L. Y.,* X. 29, 1828, for W's criticism of Bell's edition of Collins's poems.] See also Collins 6

14. . . . I learned lately that you had made a Book of Extracts, which I had long wished for opportunity and industry to execute myself. I am happy it has fallen into so much better hands. I allude to your *Selections from the Poetry of English Ladies* [*Specimens of British Poetesses* (1825)]. I had but a glance at your work; but I will take this opportunity of saying, that should a second Edition be called for, I should be pleased with the honor of being consulted by you about it. *To Dyce,*   X. 16, 1829

15. [To J. W. Croker, for his projected edition of Boswell's *Life of Johnson*, W. offers proof of Boswell's concern for accuracy in every detail. See a new letter to Croker, *MLN*, LIX (March, 1944), pp. 168-70.]
                                                                      II. 24, 1830

18. And is there any prospect of a future edition of your Specimens of British Poetesses? If I could get at the original works of the elder Poetesses, such as the Duchess of Newcastle, Mrs. Behn, Orinda [*Poems By the most deservedly admired Mrs. Katherine Philips, The Matchless Orinda, to which is added Monsieur Corneille's Tragedies Pompey and Horace, with several other Translations out of French*, 1678], etc., I should be happy to assist you with my judgment in such a Publication, which, I think, might be made still more interesting than this first Ed: especially if more matter were crowded into a Page. The two volumes of Extracts of Poems by Eminent Ladies, Helen Maria William's Works, Mrs. Smith's Sonnets, and Lady Winchelsea's Poems, form the scanty materials which I possess for assisting such a Publication. It is a remarkable thing that the two best Ballads, perhaps, of modern times, viz. Auld Robin Grey [by Lady A. Lindsay (1750-1825), first published in Herd's *Scottish Songs*, 1776], and the Lament for the Defeat of the Scots at Floddenfield [that beginning " I've heard them lilting, at the ewe milking," by Jean Elliot (1727-1805), first published in Herd], are both from the Pens of Females. *To Dyce,*   XII. 4, 1833

19. . . . I shall now hasten to notice the edition which you have superintended of my poems. I have only to regret, in respect to this volume, that it should have been published before my last edition, in the correction of which I took great pains, as my last labour in that way, and which moreover contains several additional pieces. *Reed,* p. 4.   VIII. 19, 1837

21. Coleridge's earlier poems including the Ancient Mariner *have* been published as you forsee our own would be, exactly as they first appeared, but in all probability much deteriorated by reckless printing.
To Southey,   IV. 30, 1838

25.* The plan which he suggested as meeting the difficulties of the case was the following:
That by proper authority a Committee of Revision of the English Bible should be appointed, whose business should be, retaining the present authorised version as a standard to be departed from as little as possible to settle upon such indubitable corrections of meaning and improvements of expression as they agreed ought to be made, and have these printed *in the margin* of all Bibles published by authority. That, as an essential part of the scheme, this Committee of Revision should be renewed periodically, but not too fre-

quently—he appeared to think that periods of fifty years might serve—at which times it should be competent to the Committee to authorize the transference from the margin into the text of all such alterations as had stood the test of experience and criticism during the previous period, as well as to fix on new marginal readings.

He was of opinion that in the constitution of the Committee care should be taken to appoint not only divines of established reputation for sound theology, and especially for their knowledge in connection with the original languages of the sacred volume, but some one author at least noted for his mastery over the vernacular language. . . . Wordsworth conceived that fixing the duration of the period of revision was of great consequence, both as obviating all agitation in the way of call for such a process, and as tending in the matter of critical discussions respecting the sanctioning, cancelling, and proposing of amendments to bring them to something of definitiveness in preparation for each era of revision.

The same process, under certain modifications, he though applicable to the Book of Common Prayer. In this he deprecated all tampering with doctrine, considering that alterations ought to be confined to changes rendering the services more clearly understood or more conveniently used.

Graves (Grosart, iii, 472-3). *c.* 1845

Scotch Writers. See Authors and Works (Second Section)

Scriptures, The. See under Bible

Selection. See also Aim of Writing; Meter; Poetry (Verse and Prose); Style; Subjects; Versification

1.   See Imagery 5; Nature 20; Passion 8; Picturesque 1, 3; Poetry 19, 25; Style 6, 13; Lyttleton, G. 1; W. 346, 350, 354

3.   . . . a selection of the real language of men in a state of vivid sensation. . . . *Pref. L. B.*, p. 934. 1800

Self-criticism. See under Criticism, Unfavorable Self-; Poetry; Wordsworth

Sensation. See under Passion; Sensitiveness to Sense Impressions

Sense Impressions. See under Sensitiveness to Sense Impressions

Sense of Form. See under Form

Sensibility. See under Passion

Sensitiveness to Sense Impressions. See Realism

1.   See Imagination 8, 20, 32A, 33A-G, 34, 37, 47; Passion 41; Poetry 3A, 19, 21, 34, 66, 71, 72, 124; W. 199, 329

3.   . . . my delights
Such as they were, were sought insatiably,
Though 'twas a transport of the outward sense,
[unfortunately] Not of the mind. . . .
Prel., xi, A 186-9. 1804-5

4. . . . the eyes and the senses of man are . . . [the poet's] favourite guides. . . . *Pref. L. B.*, p. 939.   1800

5.   The mind is lord and master—[of] outward sense. . . .
Prel., xii, 222.   1804-39

10.* With regard to *fragrance*, Mr. Wordsworth spoke from the testimony of others: he himself had *no sense of* smell. . . .

(Wordsworth has no sense of smell. Once, and once only in his life, the dormant power was awakened; it was by a bed of stocks in full bloom, at a house which he inhabited in Dorsetshire, some five and twenty years ago; and he says it was like a vision of Paradise to him: but it lasted only a few minutes, and the faculty has continued torpid from that time. The fact is remarkable in itself, and would be worthy of notice, even if it did not relate to a man of whom posterity will desire to know all that can be remembered. He has often expressed to me his regret for this privation.)

Life of Southey, i, 63.   *c.* 1840

Sensuality. See also Realism

1. See Barrett 3; Coleridge 36A; Goethe 12; Keats 6; Reynolds, J. H. 1

Sentiment. See under Passion

Sermons. See Rose, H. 1; Wordsworth, C. 1-3

Setting

1. I will thank you for any notice from India, though I own I am afraid of an Oriental story. I know not that you will agree with me; but I have always thought that stories, where the scene is laid by our writers in distant climes, are mostly hurt, and often have their interest quite destroyed, by being overlaid with foreign imagery; as if the tale had been chosen for the sake of the imagery only. *To B. Field*,   I. 19, 1829

2. [Circumstances.] See Godwin, C. Grace 1

Simile. See under Imagery

Simplicity. See under Diction; Passion; Realism; Style; Subjects

1. See Poetry 118; Sincerity 3; Style 40; Versification 2; W. 354

Similitude and Dissimilitude

1. See Meter 2

2. [Meter will produce a pleasing dissimilitude.]

Pref. L. B., p. 937.   1800

Sincerity. See also Passion; Poetry; Truth; Style

1. [Writer's emotional sincerity essential in an epitaph. See the essays *Upon Epitaphs*.] See Moral Element 11

2. See Imagery 10

3. [Sincerity essential in an epitaph.] For, when a man is treating an interesting subject, or one which he ought not to treat at all unless he be

interested, no faults have such a killing power as those which prove that he is not earnest, that he is acting a part, has leisure for affectation, and feels that without it he could do nothing. This is one of the most odious of faults; because it shocks the moral sense, and is worse in a sepulchral inscription, precisely in the same degree as that mode of composition calls for sincerity more urgently than any other. And indeed where the internal evidence proves that the writer was moved, in other words where this charm of sincerity lurks in the language of a tombstone and secretly pervades it, there are no errors in style or manner for which it will not be, in some degree, a recompense; but without habits of reflection a test of this inward simplicity cannot be come at; and as I have said, I am now writing with a hope to assist the well-disposed to attain it. *Epitaph 2 (Grosart,* ii, 48-9). 1810

4. [Pope lacks sincerity in his epitaph upon Mrs. Corbet.] See Pope 19; also 18, 20

Situation. See Accidents; Incidents; Setting; Subjects

1. See Passion 7; Proctor, B. W. 1

Smoothness. See Style

1. . . . A dignity, a smoothness, like the works
Of Grecian art, and purest poesy.
Prel., v, 458-59. 1804-39

Song. See Lyric Poetry 2

Sonnet, The

1. [Restrictions on the range of thought imposed by the sonnet-form.] See W. 182

1A. See Pastoral Poetry 2; Poetry 133-4; Landor 11; Moxon 2-4, 6; W. 100

2. [Sonnet, limitation of the form.]
. . . and hence for me,
In sundry moods, 'twas pastime to be bound
Within the Sonnet's scanty plot of ground;
Pleased if some Souls (for such there needs must be)
Who have felt the weight of too much liberty,
Should find brief solace there, as I have found.
"Nuns fret not," 9-14. 1807

5. Scorn not the Sonnet; Critic, you have frowned,
Mindless of its just honours; with this key
Shakespeare unlocked his heart; the melody
Of this small lute gave ease to Petrarch's wound;
A thousand times this pipe did Tasso sound;
With it Camöens soothed an exile's grief;
The Sonnet glittered a gay myrtle leaf
Amid the cypress with which Dante crowned
His visionary brow: a glow-worm lamp,

It cheered mild Spenser, called from Faery-land
To struggle through dark ways; and when a damp
Fell round the path of Milton, in his hand
The Thing became a trumpet; whence he blew
Soul-animating strains—alas, too few!
" Scorn not," 1-14.   1827

5A.   Happy the feeling from the bosom thrown
In perfect shape (whose beauty Time shall spare
Though a breath made it) like a bubble blown
For summer pastime into wanton air
Happy the thought best likened to a stone
Of the sea-beach, when, polished with nice care,
Veins it discovers exquisite and rare,
Which for the loss of that moist gleam atone
That tempted first to gather it.   That here,
O chief of Friends! such feelings I present
To thy regard, with thoughts so fortunate,
Were a vain notion; but the hope is dear
That thou, if not with partial joy elate,
Wilt smile upon this gift with more than mild content!
" Happy the feeling from the bosom," 1-14.   1827

6.   Shakespeare's sonnets . . . are not upon the Italian model, which
Milton's are; they are merely quatrains with a couplet tacked to the end;
and if they depended much upon the versification they would unavoidably be
heavy. See also Shakespeare 46, 56. *To W. R. Hamilton,*   XI. 22, 1831

7.   You propose to give specimens of the best *Sonnet-writers* in our
language. May I ask if by this be meant a Selection of the *best Sonnets, best*
both as to *kind* and *degree*? A Sonnet may be excellent in its kind, but that
kind of very inferior interest to one of a higher order, though not perhaps in
every minute particular quite so well executed, and from the pen of a writer
of inferior Genius. It should seem that the best rule to follow, would be,
first to pitch upon the Sonnets which are best *both* in kind and perfectness
of execution, and, next, those which, although of a humbler quality, are
admirable for the finish and happiness of the execution, taking care to exclude all those which have not one or other of these recommendations, however striking they might be as characteristic of the age in which the author
lived, or some peculiarity of his manner. The tenth sonnet of Donne, beginning ' Death, be not proud,' is so eminently characteristic of his manner,
and at the same time so weighty in thought, and vigorous in the expression,
that I would entreat you to insert it, though to modern taste it may be
repulsive, quaint, and laboured. . . .

Do you mean to have a short preface upon the Construction of the Sonnet?
Though I have written so many, I have scarcely made up my own mind upon
the subject. It should seem that the Sonnet, like every other legitimate composition, ought to have a beginning, a middle, and an end—in other words,
to consist of three parts, like the three propositions of a syllogism, if such
an illustration may be used. But the frame of metre adopted by the Italians

does not accord with this view, and, as adhered to by them, it seems to be, if not arbitrary, best fitted to a division of the sense into two parts, of eight and six lines each. Milton, however, has not submitted to this. In the better half of his sonnets the sense does not close with the rhyme at the eighth line, but overflows into the second portion of the metre. Now it has struck me, that his is not done merely to gratify the ear by variety and freedom of sound, but also to aid in giving that pervading sense of intense Unity in which the excellence of the Sonnet has always seemed to me mainly to consist. Instead of looking at this composition as a piece of architecture, making a whole out of three parts, I have been much in the habit of preferring the image of an orbicular body,—a sphere—or a dew-drop. All this will appear to you a little fanciful; and I am well aware that a Sonnet will often be found excellent, where the beginning, the middle, and the end are distinctly marked, and also where it is distinctly separated into *two* parts, to which, as I before observed the strict Italian model, as they write it, is favorable. Of this last construction of Sonnet, Russell's upon Philoctetes is a fine specimen; the first eight lines give the hardship of the case, the six last the consolation, or the *per-contra*. *To Dyce*, spring, 1833

9.* . . . all Wordsworth has said about the sonnet lately—or record here the fine fourteen lines of Milton's *Paradise Lost* which he says are a perfect sonnet without rhyme. But I will hereafter find the passage. Wordsworth does not approve of uniformly closing the sense with a full stop and of giving a turn to the thought in the [sestet]. . . . Wordsworth does not approve of closing the sonnet with a couplet, and he holds it to be absolutely a vice to have a sharp turning at the end with an epigrammatic point. He does not, therefore, quite approve of the termination of Cowper's sonnet to Romney. . . . *H. C. R.*, ii, 484-85. I. 26, 1836

10. . . . the structure of the Sonnet is so artificial. *To C. R. (Corr. C. R.,* i, 354), II, 1838

12. [Double rhymes.] See Versification 32

13.* All good Sonnetteers (Wordsworth included) own the difficulty of that form of verse. *E. Q. to C. R. (Corr. C. R.,* ii, 705), X. 14, 1849

Source-hunting. See Criticism 65; Byron 23

Spelling

1. [Attempts to fix spelling of English not likely to succeed.] *Lady R. (Grosart,* iii, 452). X, 1846

Stanzas. See under Meter; Unity 12; Versification

Strangeness. See under Marvelous, Novelty; Romance; Style; Supernatural; Wonder

1. See Translation 4; Coleridge 61; Montrose 1

Structure. See under Form; Sonnet; Unity

Study. See under Books; Intellect; Knowledge; Reading; Scholarly Interests

Style.   See also Alliteration; Antique Style; Antithesis; Baldness; Composition; Description; Diction; Felicity; Finish; Harsh; Imagery; Language; Nature; Novelty; Obscurity; Ornaments; Passion; Poetry; Practice; Quaintness; Realism; Repetition; Revisions; Smoothness; Sonnets; Syntax; Translation; Truth; Unity; Versification; Vulgarisms; Wordiness; Bible; Dryden; Hamilton, E. M. and W. R.; Hogg; Jewsbury; La Fontaine; Landor; Langhorne; Michelangelo; Moxon; Powell; Quilliran; Rogers; Scotch Writers; Scott, J. and W.; Shelley; Southey; Tennyson

1.   I have not been much used to composition of any kind, particularly in prose; my style therefore may frequently want fluency, and sometimes perhaps perspicuity, but these defects will gradually wear off; an ardent wish to promote the welfare of mankind will preserve me from sinking under them.
To W. Mathews (p. 123),   VI, 1794

2.   See Alliteration 1; Composition 21; Criticism 40; Diction 10; Eloquence 1; Finish 1, 2; History 11; Imagery 5; Imagination 11, 33; Jacobean Age 1; Judgment 4; Language 4; Letter Writing 1; Moral Element 11; Passion 8; Pathetic 5; Pleasure 3; Poetry 16, 17, 23-5, 28, 29, 76, 119; Realism 29, 52; Smoothness 1; Sublime 4; Taste 11, 14; Transitions 1

2A.   See Beattie 1; Bible 14; Brydges 1; Coleridge 59, 61-61C, 65A; Collins 10; Cowper 1; Crabbe 4; Dante 3; Dryden 2, 7, 9; Edgeworth, F. 1; Gillies 1, 5, 6; Godwin 1; Gray 11, 13, 14, 19; Handley, E. H. 1; Lyttleton, G. 1; Macauley 1; Macpherson 2; Montrose 1; Moore, T. 1; Percy 1; Pope 4, 6, 17-20, 27; Prior 1; Rogers 4, 8; Scott, W. 14, 15; Shakespeare 55, 56; Southey 43; Thomson 9, 13; Virgil 10; Wilson, J. 9; Winchilsea 5; W. 1, 23, 88, 91, 104, 135, 142, 242, 250, 293, 329, 330, 346, 350, 353-5

3.   Readers of superior judgment may disapprove of the style in which many of these pieces are executed; it must be expected that many lines and phrases will not exactly suit their taste. It will perhaps appear to them, that wishing to avoid the prevalent fault of the day, the author has sometimes descended too low, and that many of his expressions are too familiar, and not of sufficient dignity.   It is apprehended that the more conversant the reader is with our elder writers, and with those in modern times who have been the most successful in painting manners and passions, the fewer complaints of this kind will he have to make.
Adv. L. B. (*K. Prose*, i, 31-2).   1798

5.   [Distorted word order] is the worst fault that poetry can have. . . .
See Blank Verse and Rhyme 1

6.   [Poetic diction.]   There will also be found in these volumes little of what is usually called poetic diction; as much pains has been taken to avoid it as is ordinarily taken to produce it; this has been done for the reason already alleged, to bring my language near to the language of men; and further, because the pleasure which I have proposed to myself to impart, is

of a kind very different from that which is supposed by many persons to be the proper object of poetry. Without being culpably particular, I do not know how to give my Reader a more exact notion of the style in which it was my wish and intention to write, than by informing him that I have at all times endeavoured to look steadily at my subject; consequently, there is I hope in these Poems little falsehood of description, and my ideas are expressed in language fitted to their respective importance. Something must have been gained by this practice, as it is friendly to one property of all good poetry, namely, good sense: but it has necessarily cut me off from a large portion of phrases and figures of speech which from father to son have long been regarded as the common inheritance of Poets. I have also thought it expedient to restrict myself still further, having abstained from the use of many expressions, in themselves proper and beautiful, but which have been foolishly repeated by bad Poets, till such feelings of disgust are connected with them as it is scarcely possible by any art of association to overpower.
Pref. L. B., p. 936.   1800

7. [Poetic diction subject to writer's caprice.] See Meter 1

8. [Artificial distinction of style.] See Versification 2; Refinement

13. [Language of men must be used in poetry.] Among the qualities there [see Poetry 19 and 21] enumerated as principally conducing to form a Poet, is implied nothing differing in kind from other men, but only in degree. The sum of what was said is, that the Poet is chiefly distinguished from other men by a greater promptness to think and feel without immediate external excitement, and a greater power in expressing such thoughts and feelings as are produced in him in that manner. But these passions and thoughts and feelings are the general passions and thoughts and feelings of men. And with what are they connected? Undoubtedly with our moral sentiments and animal sensations, and with the causes which excite these; with the operations of the elements, and the appearances of the visible universe. . . . These, and the like, are the sensations and objects which the Poet describes, as they are the sensations of other men, and the objects which interest them. The Poet thinks and feels in the spirit of human passions. How, then, can his language differ in any material degree from that of all other men who feel vividly and see clearly? It might be *proved* that it is impossible. But, supposing that this were not the case, the Poet might then be allowed to use a peculiar language when expressing his feelings for his own gratification or that of men like himself. But Poets do not write for Poets alone, but for men. . . . he must express himself as other men express themselves. To this it may be added, that while he is only selecting from the real language of men, or, which amounts to the same thing, composing accurately in the spirit of such selection, he is treading upon safe ground, and we know what we are to expect from him. *Pref. L. B.*, p. 939.   1800

16. [Deficiencies of language in conveying impassioned feeling.] See Wordiness 1

17. You flatter me . . . that my style is distinguished by a genuine simplicity. Whatever merit I may have in this way I have attained solely by

endeavoring to look, as I have said in my preface, steadily at my subject. If you read over carefully the Poem of the Female Vagrant, which was the first written of the Collection (indeed it was written several years before the others) you will see that I have not formerly been conscious of the importance of this rule. The diction of that Poem is often vicious, and the descriptions are often false, giving proofs of a mind inattentive to the true nature of the subject on which it was employed. Hoping that it may afford you some amusement I will write down a few corrections of this poem in which I have endeavoured to bring the language nearer to truth. I think, if you will take the trouble of comparing these corrections with the correspondent passages in the printed poem, you will perceive in what manner I have attempted gradually to purify my diction. *To Miss Taylor*,   IV. 9, 1801

21. . . . hubbub of words [in Johnson's metrical paraphrase of Proverbs]. See Johnson 4; also 2

22.   In order further to point out some of the ordinary and less disgusting shapes which Misdiction puts on at the present day, I will transcribe a poem published a few years ago, which, though of great merit, is crowded with these defects.

> Could then the Babes from yon *unshelter'd* cot
> Implore thy *passing charity* in vain?
> Too thoughtless Youth! what though *thy happier lot*
> *Insult their life* of poverty and pain.
> What though their Maker doom'd them thus forlorn
> To brook the mockery of the *taunting throng*
> Beneath the *Oppressor's iron scourge* to mourn
> To *mourn, but not to murmur* at *his wrong!*
> Yet when their *last late* evening shall decline
> Their evening chearful though their day distrest,
> A hope perhaps more *heavenly bright* than thine,
> A Grace by thee unsought, and unpossest,
> A faith more fix'd, a rapture more divine
> Shall gild their passage to eternal rest.

The Reader has only to translate this sonnet [x in *Sonnets and Miscellaneous Poems*, Thomas Russell] into such language as any person of good sense and lively sensibility, one, I mean who does not talk out of books—would use upon such an occasion in real life, and he will at once perceive in what manner the passages printed in italics are defective. [Contrast with Russell, T. 2-3.] *Longman MSS*, pp. 47-8. [Cancelled in MS from *App. L. B.*, 1802.]   1802

23. . . . feeling powerfully as they [earliest poets] did, their language was daring, and figurative. *App. L. B.*, p. 942.   1802

24. [Origin and characteristics of poetic diction.] In succeeding times, Poets, and Men ambitious of the fame of Poets, perceiving the influence of such language [daring, figurative language of earliest poets] and desirous of producing the same effect without being animated by the same passion, set themselves to a mechanical adoption of these figures of speech, and made

use of them, sometimes with propriety, but much more frequently applied them to feelings and thoughts with which they had no natural connexion whatsoever. A language was thus insensibly produced, differing materially from the real language of men *in any situation*. The Reader or Hearer of this distorted language found himself in a perturbed and unusual state of mind: when affected by the genuine language of passion he had been in a perturbed and unusual state of mind also: in both cases he was willing that his common judgment and understanding should be laid asleep, and he had no instinctive and infallible perception of the true to make him reject the false; the one served as a passport for the other. The emotion was in both cases delightful, and no wonder if he confounded the one with the other, and believed them both to be produced by the same, or similar causes. Besides, the Poet spake to him in the character of a man to be looked up to, a man of genius and authority. Thus, and from a variety of other causes, this distorted language was received with admiration; and Poets, it is probable, who had before contented themselves for the most part with misapplying only expressions which at first had been dictated by real passion, carried the abuse still further, and introduced phrases composed apparently in the spirit of the original figurative language of passion, yet altogether of their own invention, and characterized by various degrees of wanton deviation from good sense and nature. *App. L. B.*, p. 942. 1802

25. It is indeed true, that the language of the earliest Poets was felt to differ materially from ordinary language, because it was the language of extraordinary occasions; but it was really spoken by men, language which the Poet himself had uttered when he had been affected by the events which he described, or which he had heard uttered by those around him. To this language it is probable that metre of some sort or other was early superadded. This separated the genuine language of Poetry still further from common life, so that whoever read or heard the poems of these earliest Poets felt himself moved in a way in which he had not been accustomed to be moved in real life, and by causes manifestly different from those which acted upon him in real life. *App. L. B.*, pp. 942-3. 1802

26. It would not be uninteresting to point out the causes of the pleasure given by this extravagant and absurd diction [see Poetry 29]. It depends upon a great variety of causes, but upon none, perhaps, more than its influence in impressing a notion of the peculiarity and exaltation of the Poet's character, and in flattering the Reader's self-love by bringing him nearer to a sympathy with that character; an effect which is accomplished by unsettling ordinary habits of thinking, and thus assisting the Reader to approach to that perturbed and dizzy state of mind in which if he does not find himself, he imagines that he is *balked* of a peculiar enjoyment which poetry can and ought to bestow. *App. L. B.*, p. 943. 1802

33. [Effect of an epitaph destroyed by style of the age.] Nevertheless a man called to a task in which he is not practised, may have his expression thoroughly defiled and clogged by the style prevalent in his age, yet still, through the force of circumstances that have roused him, his under feeling may remain strong and pure; yet this may be wholly concealed from common

view. Indeed the favorite style of different ages is so different and wanders so far from propriety that if it were not that first rate Writers in all nations and tongues are governed by common principles, we might suppose that truth and nature were things not to be looked for in books; hence to an unpractised Reader the productions of every age will present obstacles in various degrees hard to surmount; a deformity of style not the worst in itself but of that kind with which he is least familiar will on the one hand be most likely to render him insensible to a pith and power which may be within, and on the other hand he will be the least able to see through that sort of falsehood which is most prevalent in the works of his own time. Many of my Readers, to apply these general observations to the present case, must have derived pleasure from the epitaph of Lord Lyttleton [see Lyttleton 1] and no doubt will be startled at the comparison I have made; but bring it to the test recommended it will then be found that its faults, though not in degree so intolerable, are in kind more radical and deadly than those of the strange composition with which it has been compared. [The three essays *Upon Epitaphs* must be read by any one seeking to understand Wordsworth's use of the term " poetic diction."] *Epitaph 2 (Grosart,* ii, 54-5).   1810

40. In the higher poetry, an enlightened Critic chiefly looks for a reflection of the wisdom of the heart and the grandeur of the imagination. Wherever these appear, simplicity accompanies them; Magnificence herself, when legitimate, depending upon a simplicity of her own, to regulate her ornaments. [Our estimates are governed by comparisons; therefore readers, excited by glaring hues of diction, will for the most part be repelled by an original work] the colouring of which is disposed according to a pure and refined scheme of harmony? It is in the fine arts as in the affairs of life, no man can *serve (i. e.* obey with zeal and fidelity) two Masters.   See Poetry 76. *E. Supp. Pref.,* pp. 944-5.   1815

41. [Immortal style gained only by hard work.] See Gray 5

42.* He himself says in vindication of his style that a poet to touch the reader must speak as he speaks. . . . *H. C. R.,* i, 181.   III. 30, 1816

44. [No objections to monosyllabic lines in verse.]
To Hans Busk,   VII. 6, 1819

48.* Now whatever may be the result of my experiment in the subjects which I have chosen for poetical composition—be they vulgar or be they not,—I can say without vanity, that I have bestowed great pains on my *style,* full as much as any of my contemporaries have done on theirs. I yield to none in *love for my art.* I, therefore, labour at it with reverence, affection, and industry. My main endeavour as to style has been that my poems should be written in pure intelligible English.
C. W., Jr. (Grosart, iii, 462).   summer, 1827

49. [See a long letter to B. Field, X. 24, 1828 in *L. Y.,* p. 307-13.]

50. . . . any writer will be disappointed who expects a place in the affections of posterity for works which have nothing but their manner to recommend them. . . . See Composition 34

51. [Suggested revisions to W. R. Hamilton.] See Hamilton, W. R., 1, 4-7, 9

55. [Over-frequency of inversions.] See Moxon 2

56. [See letter to C. R. (*Corr. C. R.*, i, 288-9) for revision of "How profitless the relics," *Oxf. W.*, p. 394.]   XII. 16, 1836

58. . . . all Poetry upon a domestic or personal subject especially if not helped by rhyme requires to be written with extreme care in all that concerns style or it offends without the reader knowing why.
To Moxon,   II. 8, 1836

62. [All styles are good if perfected as far as the subject permits.] See Composition 46

67.* [W. had objected to] the near position of *in* and *ing* [*To H. C. Robinson*, l. 2. (*Oxf. W.*, p. 353)]. *C. R. to M. W.* (*Corr. C. R.*, i, 457),
                                                             III. 15, 1842

68.* He entered his protest as usual against [Carlyle's] style, and said that since Johnson no writer had done so much to vitiate the English language. He considers Lord Chesterfield the last good English writer before Johnson. Then came the Scotch historians, who did infinite mischief to style, with the exception of Smollett, who wrote good pure English. He quite agreed to the saying that all great poets wrote good prose; he said there was not one exception. He does not think Burns's prose equal to his verse, but this he attributes to his writing his letters in English words, while in his verse he was not trammelled in this way, but let his numbers have their own way. *Lady R.* (*Grosart*, iii, 452-3).   X. 26, 1846

69.* In speaking of I know not what style, he [W.] said, "to be sure, it was the manner, but then you know the matter always comes out of the manner." *English Traits*, p. 295.   III, 1848

Subjects. See Aim of Writing; Biography; History; Passion; Poetry

1. This tradition [see *Descriptive Sketches* (Quarto), l. 475] of the golden age of the Alps . . . is highly interesting not less to the philosopher than to the poet. *Oxf. W.*, p. 610, n. 4.   1793

2. It is the honourable characteristic of Poetry that its materials are to be found in every subject which can interest the human mind. The evidence of this fact is to be sought, not in the writings of Critics, but in those of Poets themselves. *Adv. L. B.* (*K. Prose*, i, 31).   1798

3. See Biography 11; Composition 21, 34; Criticism 40; Passion 31, 46; Poetry 21, 57, 67, 78, 113, 115; Realism 12; Reason 4; Versification 2; Pope 1A, 20; Watts 1; W. 13, 17-23, 29, 182, 195, 204, 260, 301, 345A, 354, 364

7. [A poet's subjects and audience.] See Style 13

8. . . . imagination . . . the faculty which produces impressive effects out of simple elements. . . . *Oxf. W.*, p. 899.   1800-5

9.   For seeing little worthy or sublime
                    In what we blazon with the pompous names

> Of power and action I was early taught
> To love those unassuming things that hold
> A silent station in this beauteous world
>
> . . .
>
> The things that live in passion. . . .
>
> (*Prel.*, xiii, JJ 41-7), p. 608E.   1802

10.   And showed my youth
>   How Verse may build a princely throne
>   On humble truth.
>   *At the Grave of Burns*, 34-6.   1803

10A.   [List of possible subjects for his projected work; see *Prel.*, i, 166-237.]   1804-39

11.   Rarely and with reluctance would I stoop
>   To transitory themes. . . .
>   *Prel.*, v, 223-4.   1804-5

12.   More lofty themes . . . [made] the imaginative
>   power Languish within me. . . .
>   *Prel.*, vii, 465-69.   1804-39

13.   [W. passes by the raptures of Vaudracour and Julia, for other poets have handled such themes better than he can, especially]
>   . . . that darling Bard
>   Who told of Juliet and her Romeo. . . .
>   'Tis mine to tread
>   The humbler province of plain history. . . .
>   *Prel.*, ix, A 633-41; See *Vaudracour and Julia*, 87-91.   1804-5

14.   [Will make] verse
>   Deal boldly with substantial things; in truth
>   And sanctity of passion. . . .
>   *Prel.*, xiii, 234-6.   1804-5

17.   [No subject worked up] By help of dreams [can arouse such awe as a study of] the Mind of Man . . . the main region of my song. [Why should we deal with] A history only of departed things, Or a mere fiction of what never was? Beauty [is] a living Presence of the earth [and surpasses] the most fair ideal Forms. . . .

>   For the discerning intellect of Man,
>   When wedded to this goodly universe
>   In love and holy passion, shall find these
>   A simple produce of the common day [ll. 52-5].

[To show how exquisitely the external world and the mind of man are fitted to each other is my purpose.] " *Prospectus* " to *Exc.*, 35-71. (See also Passion 31.)   1814

19.   [With certain restrictions the poet may seek the spirit of pleasure whenever it may be found.] See Poetry 99

20.* . . . not fond of drawing the subjects of his poems from occur-
rences in themselves interesting. . . . *H. C. R.*, i, 249.   VIII. 18, 1820

21.   Not Love, not War, nor the tumultuous swell
                 Of civil conflict, nor the wrecks of change,
                 Nor Duty struggling with afflictions strange—
                 Not these *alone* inspire the tuneful shell;
                 But where untroubled peace and concord dwell,
                 There also is the Muse not loth to range,
                 Watching the twilight smoke of cot or grange. . . .
                 "Not Love, not War," 1-7.   1823

23.* . . . poetry on contemporary persons and events can be good.
C. W., Jr. (*Grosart*, iii, 461).   *c.* 1827
                               . . . does aught meet your ken
                 More fit to animate the Poet's pen,
                 Aught that more surely by its aspect fills
                 Pure minds with sinless envy, than the Abode
                 Of the good Priest. . . .
                 "Say, ye," 6-10.   1831

25.   [Importance of choice of subjects.] See Quillinan 6

27.   [If poetry deals with the simplest objects of nature]
                 Her functions are they therefore less divine,
                 Her thoughts less deep, or void of grave intent
                 Her simplest fancies?
                 "Though the bold," 9-11.   1842

28.   [Some subjects too low, some too high for poetry.] See Poetry 149

29.* New thoughts, however deep, were not the staple of poetry, but
old thoughts presented with immortal freshness, and a kind of inspired
felicity of diction. *Aubrey de Vere*, p. 69.   III. 9, 1845

Subjective Writing. See Biography; Burns; Field, B. 4; Goethe 7

Sublime, The. See also Passions; contrast Pathetic

1.   [Primary sensations of the human heart are the vital springs of sublime
and pathetic compositions.] *Epitaph 2* (*Grosart*, ii, 48).   1810

2.   And for the sublime,——if we consider what are the cares that
occupy the passing day, and how remote is the practice and the course of life
from the sources of sublimity, in the soul of Man, can it be wondered that
there is little existing preparation for a poet charged with a new mission to
extend its kingdom, and to augment and spread its enjoyments?
E. Supp. Pref., p. 952.   1815

3.   See Picturesque 1, 3; Taste 14; Coleridge 65A; Dryden 14

4.   You have been successful in clearing up my doubts as to your
meaning upon the picturesque: it would occupy more paper than I have
before me, and require more exertion than this languid *Summer's day* in
April . . . would allow to establish my position—' the sublime and beautiful

cannot be felt in the same instant of time '—attaching such meaning to the words as I think they ought to bear. One is surprised that it should have been supposed for a moment, that *Longinus* writes upon the Sublime, even in our vague and popular sense of the word—What is there in Sappho's ode that has any affinity with the sublimity of Ezekiel or Isaiah, or even Homer or Eschylus? Longinus treats of animated, impassioned, energetic or if you will, elevated writing—of these, abundant instances are to be found in Eschylus and Homer—but nothing would be easier than to show, both by positive and negative proof, that his ὕψους when translated sublimity deceives the english Reader, by substituting an etymology for a translation. Much of what I observe you call sublime, *I* should denominate grand or dignified. But as I wrote before we shall never see clearly into this subject unless we turn from objects to laws—I am far from thinking that I am able to write satisfactorily upon matters so subtile—yet I hope to make a trial and must request your patience till that time. *To J. Fletcher*,   IV. 6, 1825

Supernatural, The. See Legends; Marvelous; Mythology; Realism
(Anti-realism); Romance; Strangeness
   1. See Realism 1; Coleridge 61B; W. 87, 117, 345A

Sympathy. See also Criticism; Taste
   1. See Pleasure 2; Poetry 21; W. 43, 44, 87, 345A; 364A

Syntax. See also Blank Verse and Rhyme; Meter; Style; Versification
   1. [Byron's line, "Minions of splendour shrinking from distress"
(*Childe Harold*, II. xxvi, 5)] in defiance of all syntax is foisted in for the
sake of the rhyme. *To R. P. Gillies*,   VI. 9, 1817
   2. See Scott, W. 10

Talent. See Genius 2A; Coleridge 21; White, H. K. 1

Tales. See under Mythology; Narrative Poetry; Realism; Romance

Taste. See Criticism; Fame; Popular Judgment; Praise; Rules;
Selection
   1. An accurate taste in poetry, and in all the other arts, Sir Joshua
Reynolds has observed, is an acquired talent which can only be produced by
severe thought, and a long continued intercourse with the best models of
composition. This is mentioned not with so ridiculous a purpose as to prevent
the most inexperienced reader from judging for himself; but merely to temper
the rashness of decision, and to suggest that if poetry be a subject on which
much time has not been bestowed, the judgment may be erroneous, and that
in many cases it necessarily will be so. *Adv. L. B.* (*K. Prose*, i, 32).   1798
   5. [Causes which blunt] the discriminating powers of the mind, [and
unfit it for] all voluntary exertion. See Passion 7
   6. See Books 28; Criticism 28, 41, 44, 49; Genius 3; Intellect 8; Meter
2; Poetry 20, 29, 70, 74-7, 119; Popular Judgment 4; Praise 4; Style 3;
Donne 1-3; Rogers 6, 8; Scott, W. 27; Shakespeare 45; W. 166, 353-4, 369

8. Painters and Poets have had the credit of being reckoned the Fathers of English gardening; they will also have, hereafter, the better praise of being fathers of a better taste. Error is in general nothing more than getting hold of good things, as everything has two handles, by the wrong one. It was a misconception of the meaning and principles of poets and painters which gave countenance to the modern system of gardening, which is now, I hope, on the decline; in other words, we are submitting to the rule which you at present are guided by, that of having our houses belong to the country, which will of course lead us back to the simplicity of Nature.

To Beaumont (pp. 523-24), X. 17, 1805

9. . . . the sickly taste of the public in verse.

To Beaumont, I or II, 1808

10. I am not . . . afraid of such censure, insignificant as probably the majority of those poems would appear to very respectable persons; I do not mean London wits and witlings, for these have too many bad passions about them to be respectable, even if they had more intellect than the benign laws of providence will allow to such a heartless existence as theirs is; but grave, kindly-natured, worthy persons, who would be pleased if they could. I hope that these Volumes [*Poems, 1807*] are not without some recommendations, even for Readers of this class, but their imagination has slept; and the voice which is the voice of my Poetry without Imagination cannot be heard.

To Lady Beaumont (p. 126), V. 21, 1807

11. Where the soul has been thoroughly stricken . . . there is never a want of *positive* strength; but because the adversary of Nature (call that adversary Art or by what name you will) is *comparatively* strong. The far searching influence of the power, which, for want of a better name, we will denominate Taste, is in nothing more evinced than in the changeful character and complexion of that species of composition which we have been reviewing. [In an epitaph, one would expect to find " genuine language," but there the faults of the age have been more prominent. Especially in verse do the epitaphs take on the notion of " art " and show the influence of the most esteemed works of " art " of that age. The volume, *Elegant Extracts in Verse,* illustrates the " artifices " which have] over-run our writings in metre since the days of Dryden and Pope. Energy, stillness, grandeur, tenderness, those feelings which are the pure emanations of Nature, those thoughts which have the infinitude of truth, and those expressions which are not what the garb is to the body but what the body is to the soul, themselves a constituent part and power or function in the thought—all these are abandoned for their opposites,—as if our countrymen, through successive generations, had lost the sense of solemnity and pensiveness (not to speak of deeper emotions) and resorted to the tombs of their forefathers and contemporaries, only to be tickled and surprised. [The general literature of the period weakens our sensibilities and judgment; only great misfortunes will elicit the truths of Nature in our writings.] Words are too awful an instrument for good and evil, to be trifled with; they hold above all other external powers a dominion over thoughts. If words be not . . . an incarnation of the thought, but only a clothing for it, then surely will they prove an ill gift. . . . Language, if

it do not uphold, and feed, and leave in quiet, like the power of gravitation or the air we beathe, is a counter-spirit, unremittingly and noiselessly at work, to subvert, to lay waste, to vitiate, and to dissolve. From a deep conviction then that the excellence of writing, whether in prose or verse, consists in a conjunction of Reason and Passion, a conjunction which must be of necessity benign; and that it might be deduced from what has been said that the taste, intellectual power and morals of a country are inseparably linked in mutual dependence, I have dwelt thus long upon this argument.

Epitaph 3 (Grosart, ii, 63-5).   1810

13. [Bad taste and morality.] See Moral Element 11

14. And where lies the real difficulty of creating that taste by which a truly original poet is to be relished? Is it in breaking the bonds of custom, in overcoming the prejudices of false refinement, and displacing the aversions of inexperience? [Or must the reader divest himself of the pride in dwelling on the unlikenesses rather than on the likenesses of men; and must the reader be shamed into recognizing the excellences of a talented man who may stand below him in the scale of society? Or can the spirits of the readers be humbled and humanized, that they may be purified and exalted?]

If these ends are to be attained by the mere communication of *knowledge,* it does *not* lie here.—Taste, I would remind the reader, like Imagination, is a word which has been forced to extend its services far beyond the point to which philosophy would have confined them. It is a metaphor, taken from a *passive* sense of the human body, and transferred to things which are in their essence *not* passive,—to intellectual *acts* and *operations.* The word, Imagination, has been overstrained, from impulses honourable to mankind, to meet the demands of the faculty which is perhaps the noblest of our nature. In the instance of Taste, the process has been reversed; and from the prevalence of dispositions at once injurious and discreditable, being no other than that selfishness which is the child of apathy,—which, as Nations decline in productive and creative power, makes them value themselves upon a presumed refinement of judging. Poverty of language is the primary cause of the use which we make of the word, Imagination; but the word, Taste, has been stretched to the sense which it bears in modern Europe by habits of self-conceit, inducing that inversion in the order of things whereby a passive faculty is made paramount among the faculties conversant with the fine arts. Proportion and congruity, the requisite knowledge being supposed, are subjects upon which taste may be trusted; it is competent to this office— for in its intercourse with these the mind is *passive,* and is affected painfully or pleasurably as by an instinct. But the profound and the exquisite in feeling, the lofty and universal in thought and imagination; or, in ordinary language, the pathetic and the sublime;—are neither of them, accurately speaking, objects of a faculty which could ever without a sinking in the spirit of Nations have been designated by the metaphor *Taste.* And why? Because without the exertion of a co-operating *power* in the mind of the Reader, there can be no adequate sympathy with either of these emotions: without this auxiliary impulse, elevated or profound passion cannot exist.

E. Supp. Pref., pp. 951-2.   1815

15. [That men run to poetry as if urged by an appetite is not a test of its excellence. Audacity and extravagance, a superficial picture of surface manners, or an appeal to curiosity and fancy, all without requiring thought, will make a work popular.] But in everything which is to send the soul into herself, to be admonished of her weakness, or to be made conscious of her power;—wherever life and nature are described as operated upon by the creative or abstracting virtue of the imagination; wherever the instinctive wisdom of antiquity and her heroic passions uniting, in the heart of the poet, with the meditative wisdom of later ages, have produced that accord of sublimated humanity which is at once a history of the remote past and a prophetic enunciation of the remotest future, *there*, the poet must reconcile himself for a season to few and scattered hearers.—Grand thoughts (and Shakespeare must often have sighed over this truth), as they are most naturally and most fitly conceived in solitude, so can they not be brought forth in the midst of plaudits without some violation of their sanctity. [In every period vicious poetry has more readers than the best poetry. The individual and the species of good poetry live; of the vicious poetry the individual dies, but the species continues] with adaptation, more or less skilful, to the changing humours of the majority of those who are most at leisure to regard poetical works when they first solicit their attention.

E. Supp. Pref., pp. 952-53. 1815

16. [French taste] enslaved. . . . *To R. P. Gillies*, II. 14, 1815

21. [Little] genuine relish for poetical Literature in Cumberland; if I may judge from the fact of not a copy of my Poems having sold there by one of the leading Booksellers, though Cumberland is my native County. *To Moxon*, VIII, 1833

23. These things [the University of Durham had conferred a degree upon W.] are not worth adverting to, but as signs that imaginative Literature notwithstanding the homage now paid to Science is not wholly without esteem. To C. R. (Corr. C. R., i, 374), XII, 1838

24. [Taste in style in the Popean era.] See Thomson 9

Tautology. See under Wordiness

Tedious, The

1. . . . everything is tedious when one does not read with the feelings of the Author—*D. W. and W. to Mary and Sara* (p. 306), VI. 14, 1802

2. See Chaucer 20; Lessing 2

Tenderness. See Sympathy; W. 364A

Textual Criticism. See under Criticism, Textual

Thought. See also Intellect; Reflection

1. See Criticism 40; Poetry 17, 74, 124; Style 13; Dryden 7; W. 1A, 124

4. [Thoughts] are indeed the representatives of all our past feelings. . . . See Aim of Writing 10; also 7; Pope 19

6. . . . the inherent superiority of contemplation to action. The Friend does not in this contradict his own words [Coleridge. See *The Friend*, i, 163, ed. Henry Nelson Coleridge (London, 1837)], where he has said heretofore, that 'doubtless to act is nobler than to think.' In those words, it was his purpose to censure that barren contemplation, which rests satisfied with itself in cases where the thoughts are of such quality that they may, and ought to, be embodied in action. But he speaks now of the general superiority of thought to action; as proceeding and governing all action that moves to salutary purposes; and, secondly, as leading to elevation, the absolute possession of the individual mind, and to a consistency or harmony of the being within itself, which no outward agency can reach to disturb or to impair; and lastly, as producing works of pure science; or of the combined faculties of imagination, feeling, and reason; works which, both from their independence in their origin upon accident, their nature, their duration, and the wide spread of their influence, are entitled rightly to take place of the noblest and most beneficient deeds of heroes, statesmen, legislators, or warriors. *Ans. to Mathetes* (*Grosart*, i, 320-21).   II. 4, 1810

Time. See under Criticism, Time as an Aid to

Titles

1. See Periodical Planning 2; Rogers 3; Wilson, J. 6; W. 11, 269

3. Mr. Carter is making an Index of first lines which I hope will be of some use, for it is impossible to give titles to a third part of this multifarious collection of Poems. *To Moxon,*   XI. 4, 1845

Topographical Writings. See Loco-descriptive Writers

Tradition. See History; Mythology; Realism; Romance

1. See History 8, 10-13

Tragedy. See under Drama; Dramatic Poetry; Shakespeare

Tranquillity. See Passion; Poetry 24; Restraint; Ancient Writers 16

Transcendentalism

1. See Emerson 1

2. German transcendentalism which you say this Critic [John Sergeant] is infected by, would be a woeful visitation for the world were it not sure to be as transitory as it is pernicious. *Reed*, p. 14.   XII. 23, 1839

Transitions. See also Style, Unity; W. 98

1. Where I have a large amount of Sonnets in series I have not been unwilling to start sometimes with a logical connection of a 'Yet' or a 'But.' Here, however, as the series is not long, I wished that each Sonnet should stand independent of such formal tie; and therefore, tho' with some loss, I have not followed your alteration, 'Yet not alone, nor chiefly.' Besides, and this by-the-by, 'Not alone' is less neat that 'solely,' or 'only' rather.
To H. Taylor,   XI. 8, 1841

Translation. See Chaucer; Dryden

1. I am not conscious of any want of ability for translating from the French or Italian Gazettes. . . . *To Wm. Mathews,* late XII, 1794

2.* William thinks it will be a great advantage to him to be acquainted with the German language; besides that translation is the most profitable of all works. *D. W. to R. W.,* IV. 30, 1798

4. We seem pretty much of opinion upon the subject of rhyme. Pentameters, where the sense has a close of some sort at every two lines, may be rendered in regularly closed couplets; but hexameters (especially the Virgilian, that run the lines into each other for a great length) cannot. . . . I should have attempted Virgil in blank verse, had I not been persuaded that no ancient author can be with advantage so rendered. Their religion, their warfare, their course of action and feeling, are too remote from modern interest to allow it. We require every possible help and attraction of sound, in our language, to smooth the way for the admission of things so remote from our present concerns. My own notion of translation is, that it cannot be too literal, provided three faults be avoided: *baldness,* in which I include all that takes from dignity; and *strangeness,* or *uncouthness,* including harshness; and lastly, attempts to convey meanings which, as they cannot be given but by languid circumlocutions, cannot in fact be said to be given at all. I will trouble you with an instance in which I fear this fault exists. Virgil, describing Aeneas's voyage, third book, verse 551, says—

> Hinc sinus Herculei, si vera est fama, Tarenti Cernitur.

I render it thus:

> Hence we behold the bay that bears the name
> Of proud Tarentum, proud to share the fame
> Of Hercules, though by a dubious claim.

I was unable to get the meaning with tolerable harmony into fewer words, which are more than to a modern reader, perhaps, it is worth. See Dryden 22; W. 293. *To Lord Lonsdale,* II. 5, 1819

5. See Ancient Writers 15; Language 2; Passion 8; Chaucer 11-17, 19-23; Macpherson 6; Michelangelo 2-4, 6; Virgil 10; Wrangham 7, 10; W. 177-8, 266, 291, 293-4, 296

9. . . . for I had abandoned the thought of ever sending into the world any part of that experiment—for it was nothing more—an experiment begun for amusement, and I now think a less fortunate one than when I first named it to you. Having been displeased in modern translations with the additions of incongruous matter, I began to translate with a resolve to keep clear of that fault, by adding nothing; but I became convinced that a spirited translation can scarcely be accomplished in the English language without admitting a principle of compensation. *Aeneid (Oxf. W.,* pp. 623-24). 1832

Travel Literature

1. See Hearne 1; W. 301

2.*   . . . likes books of voyages and travels. . . .
Hazlitt, iv, 277.   *c.* 1800

3. [See *De Sel.* (*Prel.*, W MS, 48-114, and notes, pp. 602-4): Ferdinand Columbus, *The Life and Actions of C. Columbus*; Edward Haie, *Report of the Voyage . . . 1583 . . . by Sir Humphrey Gilbert*; Mungo Park, *Travels in the Interior of Africa*. See *The Mind of a Poet*, pp. 306; especially 350-1, and 484.]

4. The only *modern* Books that I read [or care for] are those of travels. . . . *To F. Wrangham,*   early spring, 1812

Triteness. Contrast Genius; Individuality; Originality; Style

1. See Mythology 7; Pope 19

Trivial, The. Contrast Imagination; Infinity

1. [Trivial verses are not poetry.] See Criticism 40

2. [See Books 6, 8; Passion 46; Poetry 17; Subjects; also *The Mind of a Poet*, pp. 241-2 (for the trivial *vs.* the infinite), and 351, 362.]

Truth. See Description; Nature; Observation; Realism; Style

1. See Aim of Writing 37; Character Analysis 5; Criticism 40; History 11-13; Intuition 2D; Literature 24; Passion 8, 22, 37, 51; Poetry 20, 21, 111; Realism 49; Reason 4, 26; Subjects 10; Barrett, E. 3; Chiabrera 2; Chaucer 21; Macpherson 2, 3, 5-7; Scott, W. 27; Shakespeare 32; W. 5, 233, 245A, 330, 395

3.   . . . that religious dignity of mind,
        That is the very faculty of truth. . . .
        Prel., iv, A 297-8.   1804-5

4. [*The Prelude* has advanced with] imagination teaching truth. . . .
Prel., xi, A 45 (see also *Prel.*, x, A 842-9).   1804-5

7. . . . original parent [of good taste]. See Criticism 44

10. [Pope believed] that Nature was not to be trusted. . . . See Pope 6, also 18-20; Epitaphs; Imagination; Sincerity

11. [Truth serves in a biography to justify purposes, moral and intellectual.] See Biography 2A

12A.   To the solid ground
        Of nature trusts the Mind that builds for aye. . . .
        " A volant Tribe," 5-6.   1823

Understanding, The. See under Intellect; Moral Element 11

1. . . . the understanding sleeps in order that the fancy may dream. See Criticism 44; Imagination 38

2. [Understanding, severe and dispassionate, necessary for a critic.] See Criticism 81

3. [W. does not understand] those lines. Imagine not, however, that I think the worse of them on that account. *To E. H. Handley,*   X. 4, 1830

Uniformitarianism. See also Imagination; Passions; Unity; Universality

1. See Style 33; Unity 10; Pope 19, 20

6. [W.'s poems will please because] ' we have all of us one human heart! ' [For further evidence of emotional uniformitarianism, see *Prel.*, xiii, 216-20; *Epitaph 1*, pp. 931-2; *Epitaph 3*, p. 69; Poetry 111, 133; Taste 14; Universality 7; Versification 2; Pope 19-20.] W. 189

Unity. See also Form; Imagination; Uniformitarianism; Universality; Wholeness; Lyttleton

1. See Poetry 25, 68, 78, 113, 114; Repetition 2; Sonnet 7; Transitions 1; Chiabrera 3; Coleridge 61B; Homer 13; Macpherson 2; Shakespeare 32; W. 13, 17, 185, 187, 191, 194, 199, 205, 207, 246, 249, 250, 340

2. [Of impressions.] See Picturesque 1; Coleridge 54, 68-70

4. . . . the Poet binds together by passion and knowledge the vast empire of human society, as it is spread over the whole earth, and over all time. *Oxf. W.*, pp. 938-9. 1800

5.* We have known him to enlarge with a noble intelligence and enthusiasm on Nicolas Poussin's fine landscape-composition, pointing out the unity of design that pervades them, the superintending mind, the imaginative principle that brings all to bear on the same end, and declaring he would not give a rush for any landscape that did not express the time of day, the climate, the period of the world it was meant to illustrate, or had not this character of *wholeness* in it. [Cf. *Prel.*, xii, 106-21.] *Hazlitt*, iv, 277. 1800

6. . . . the mind can have no rest among a multitude of objects, of which it either cannot make one whole, or from which it cannot single out one individual, whereupon may be concentrated the attention divided among or distracted by a multitude? See W. 124

8. [Unity of materials.] See Shakespeare 14

9. [Unifying power of the imagination.] See Imagination 33 F

10. [See Professor Havens's chapter on the unifying power of the imagination, *The Mind of a Poet*, pp. 203-65; he also lists other instances of Wordsworth's belief in " the unity of all " on p. 319: *Prelude*, " i, 341-4; vi, 636-40; X variant of vii. A432-4; viii, 608-11, 665-72; xiii. 216-18 (see note) ; xiv. A 253-5. See also de. S. 512-13 and *Excursion*, ix. 1-15. . . . The unifying power of the imagination is discussed on pp. 207, 210, 212-15 " in *The Mind of a Poet*. See also *Prel.*, ii, 203-32, and xiii, A 254-5.]

11. [Unity and imagination.] See Imagination 47

12. [Stanzas destroy unity of a grand subject.] See Versification 13B; and also Parkinson, R. 1A

Universality. See also Discrimination; Imagination; Manners; Passion; Style; Uniformitarianism; Unity. Contrast Accidents; Individuality

1. [Universality of manners.] See Manners 2

4. [Men and poets submit to the regular and uniform laws of meter.] See Meter 1

5. [Poets affect the general thoughts and feelings of men.] See Style 13; also 33

6. See Character Analysis 5; Criticism 35; Imagination 33G, 35; Poetry 20, 21, 111, 133, 148; Satirical Poetry 1; Taste 14; Versification 2; Chaucer 1; Chiabrera 4-6; Gillies 3, 5; Goethe 7, 8; Newton 3; W. 189, 354-5

7. [W. hopes his poems show] that our best qualities are possessed by men whom we are too apt to consider, not with reference to the points in which they resemble us, but to those in which they manifestly differ from us. *To Charles James Fox* (*E. L.*, p. 262),   I. 14, 1801

8.   [He does not lack] that first great gift, the vital soul
            Nor general Truths, which are themselves a sort
            Of Elements and Agents, Under-powers
            Subordinate helpers of the living mind. . . .
            Prel., i, 150-3.   1804-39

9.   Rarely and with reluctance would stoop
            To transitory themes. . . .
            Prel., v, 223-4.   1804-39

10. No liberal art aims merely at the gratification of an individual or a class. . . . See Gardening 1

11. [Universality demanded in the treatment of an epitaph; it must be in] the general language of humanity as connected with the subject of death. . . . *Epitaph 1* (*Oxf. W.*, p. 931).   1810

11A. [Pope's epitaph] destitute of those universal feelings. . . . See Pope 20; also 19

12. . . . Your mind does not look sufficiently out of itself. . . . *To R. P. Gillies,*   IV. 9, 1816

18.* [Young poets should study] poets whose fame is universal, not local. . . . *De Vere* (*Grosart*, iii, 489).   1842-46

Unusual, The. See also Marvelous; Strangeness; Supernatural. Contrast Style; Subjects

1. . . . ordinary things should be presented to the mind in an unusual aspect. . . . *Pref. L. B.*, p. 935 (see also W. 345A).   1800

Variety. See also Discrimination

1. See Fancy 2; Sonnets 7; Versification 1, 2; Coleridge 61A and B; Dryden 1; Gillies 5; Milton 55; Peace 1; Shakespeare 56; W. 5, 21, 60, 120, 294

4. [Want of variety in Gillies's poems; and his sonnets] stand in each other's way from not being sufficiently diversified.

To R. P. Gillies,

IV. 9, 1816

Versification. See Blank Verse and Rhyme; Diction; Meter; Sonnets; Style; Syntax

1. I have not been sufficiently accustomed to the metre [hexameters] to give any opinion which can be depended upon. One thing strikes me in common with the German ladies that the two last feet are what principally give the character of Verse to the hexameters—the sum of my feeling is that the two last are more than verse, and all the rest not so much. I mean to say that there should be more of the sensation of metre in the whole of the verse to break the monotony of the two last feet. The lines also are not sufficiently run into each other, but that might be easily remedied.

To Coleridge (pp. 203-4),

I, 1799

2. [Why W. wrote in verse. First, to achieve] the most valuable object of all writing, whether in prose or verse; the great and universal passions of men, the most general and interesting of their occupations, and the entire world of nature before me—to supply endless combinations of forms and imagery. Now, supposing for a moment that whatever is interesting in these objects may be as vividly described in prose, why should I be condemned for attempting to superadd to such description the charm which, by the consent of all nations, is acknowledged to exist in metrical language? [Let the many who underrate the pleasure derived from meter, and demand that it be accompanied by the expected artificial distinctions of style, lest the reader be shocked by the deviation,] observe, that poems are extant, written upon more humble subjects, and in a still more naked and simple style, which have continued to give pleasure from generation to generation. Now, if nakedness and simplicity be a defect, the fact here mentioned affords a strong presumption that poems somewhat less naked and simple are capable of affording pleasure at the present day; and, what I wished *chiefly* to attempt, at present, was to justify myself for having written under the impression of this belief.

[A manly style, a subject of some importance, and words metrically arranged will produce pleasure.] The end of Poetry is to produce excitement in co-existence with an overbalance of pleasure; but, by the supposition, excitement is an unusual and irregular state of the mind; ideas and feelings do not, in that state, succeed each other in accustomed order. [If the words or images produce undue pain, the co-presence of something regular, as meter, will temper or restrain the undue proportion of pain by partly divesting the language of its reality. More pathetic situations and sentiments thus may be endured] in metrical composition, especially in rhyme, than in prose. The metre of the old ballads is very artless; yet they contain many passages which would illustrate this opinion; and, I hope, if the following Poems [*L. B.*, 1800] be attentively perused, similar instances will be found in them. [The pathetic parts of *Clarissa Harlowe*, and of *The Gamester* lack meter to relieve the undue proportion of pain; but meter allows us to bear the pathos of Shakespeare's writing. More frequently, however, meter will add pleasure and impart the proper mood to words] incommensurate with the passion, and inadequate to raise the Reader to a height of desirable excitement. . . . [See Translation 4.]   *Pref. L. B.*, pp. 939-40.   1800

3.   See Diction 8, 10; Hymns 2; Poetry 23-5, 65-6, 69, 78; Sonnets 6-9; Style 58; Burger 2; Coleridge 40, 61B; Dryden 1; Gillies 5, 6; Hamilton, W. R. 5, 6, 9; Hogg 2, 4; Landor 10; Longfellow 2; Milton 53; Pope 1A, 27; Rogers 4, 5; Scott, J. 5; Scott, W. 15; Smith, Charlotte 2; Southey 50; Sympson, J. 1; Tennyson 9; Virgil 4, 5; Winchilsea, Lady 5; W. 1, 36, 51, 91, 98, 142, 166, 170, 181, 205, 241, 289, 293-4, 329; Wrangham 10

11.*   [Alexandrines.] It was Southey's opinion, somebody said, that the Alexandrine could never be written and read properly without a pause. Wordsworth took the contrary side and repeated several twelve-syllable lines of his own [*The Female Vagrant*], where there could be no pause after the sixth syllable. . . . *Collier's Preface*, p. xxxvi.   X. 20, 1811

12.*   W. admitted that it [the Spenserian] was the best form of stanza in our language; but he seemed to think any set form comparatively bad, and that nothing, especially for a poem of any continuance, was equal to blank verse. *Collier's Preface*, pp. li-lii.   II. 10, 1814

13.*   [W. is] rather disposed to pity the poet who is so barren of thoughts, that he is obliged to owe them to the accidental recurrence of the same sound. He believed that Dryden had not done himself justice by the observation [that a poet was sometimes indebted to rhyme for a thought] for, though he was not a great poet, in the sense of invention and imagination; his thoughts were not unfrequently new and noble, and his language, in point of strength, fulness, and idiomatic freedom, incomparable.
Collier's Preface, p. liii.   II. 10, 1814

13B.   It [*Thanksgiving Ode*] is a *dramatised ejaculation*; and this, if anything can, must excuse the irregular frame of the metre. In respect to a *stanza* for a grand subject designed to be treated comprehensively, there are great objections. If the stanza be short, it will scarcely allow of fervour and impetuosity, unless so short that the sense is run perpetually from one stanza to another, as in Horace's Alcaics; and if it be long, it will be as apt to generate diffuseness as to check it. Of this we have innumerable instances in Spenser and the Italian poets. The sense required cannot be included in one given stanza, so that another whole stanza is added not unfrequently for the sake of matter which would naturally include itself in a very few lines.
To Southey (p. 717),   1816

14.   [Couplets.] I have indeed, a detestation of couplets running into each other, merely because it is convenient to the writer;—or from affected imitation of our elder poets. Reading such verses produces in me a sensation like that of toiling in a dream, under the *nightmair*. The Couplet promises rest at agreeable intervals; but here it is never attained—you are mocked and disappointed from paragraph to paragraph. *To Hans Bush*,   VII. 6, 1819

15.   [Monosyllabic lines.] In regard to monosyllabic lines, I do not think that there lies any objection to them merely as such; I mean any objection on

musical considerations. For the words, if well *chosen* and suitably united, blend into each other upon the ear, as readily almost as if the feet of the verse were composed of polysyllables. *To Hans Bush,* VII. 6, 1819

16. . . . I should have attempted Virgil in blank verse, had I not been persuaded that no ancient author can be with advantage so rendered. See Translation 4

21. [Blank verse and the Spenserian stanza.] See Godwin, C. Grace 1

24A.* Spoke of the immense time it took him to write even the shortest copy of verses,—sometimes whole weeks employed in shaping two or three lines, before he can satisfy himself with their structure. Attributed much of this to the unmanageableness of the English as a poetical language: contrasted it with the Italian in this respect, and repeated a stanza of Tasso, to show how naturally the words fell into music of themselves. It was one where the double rhymes, " ella," " nella," " quella," occurred, which he compared with the meagre and harsh English words " she," " That," " this," &c. &c. Thought, however, that, on the whole, there were advantages in having a rugged language to deal with; as in struggling with words one was led to give birth to and dwell upon thoughts [contrast Versification 13], while, on the contrary, an easy and mellifluous language was apt to tempt, by its facility, into negligence, and to lead the poet to substitute music for thought. *Moore's Diary,* p. 185.
II. 20, 1835

25. [Form of stanza suitable for dialogue.] See Percy 4

27. [Opposes sacrifice of sense to sound.] See Chaucer 20; and also Gillies 5; Hamilton, Eliza M. 4; Hamilton, W. R. 5; Peace 2; W. 36

29. . . . fond of the six line stanza [which he used in " Ruth "]. *Justice Coleridge (Grosart,* iii, 426).
IX. 22, 1836

29A. . . . print for ' Still were they faithful ' ' Still they were faithful.' You will notice the reason in the previous *inversion* of ' were they.' *To Moxon,*
II. 8, 1836

30.* . . . (' A Night Piece'; 'Yew Trees.') (In Wordsworth's own opinion, his best specimens of blank verse.) *C. R. to J. Mottram (Corr. C. R.,* ii, 820),
[c. 1840]

32. As to double rhyme, I quite agree with Mr. L. [Lockhart], that in the case disapproved by him, their effect is weak, and I believe will generally prove so in a Couplet at the close of a Sonnet. But having written so many I do not scruple, but rather like to employ them occasionally, tho' I have done it much less in proportion than my great Masters, especially Milton, who has two out of his 18 with double rhymes. *To H. Taylor,*
XI. 8, 1841

34. [Trochaic endings in the verse of drama.] See Taylor, Sir Henry 2

35.* . . . the versification of the Excursion, with some parts of which he is dissatisfied. . . . *E. Q. to C. R. (Corr. C. R.,* ii, 548), III. 19, 1844

36.* . . . what he deems to be faults (*chiefly in the versification*) of the Excursion. *M. W. to C. R. (Corr. C. R.,* ii, 551), IV. 7, 1844

Vigor

1.   . . . no Poetry can be good without animation. See Brydges 1

2.   See Language 5; Literature 17; Barrett, E. 4; De Vere, A. 2; Gillies 1; Hamilton, Eliza M. 1-3; Hamilton, W. R. 4, 5; Handley, E. H. 1; Jewsbury, Maria 1; Keats 2; Kenyon 2; Landor 11; Mackenzie 2; Manzoni 1; Southey 29; Winchilsea 5

4.   Your poem is vigorous, and that is enough for me. . . .
To Heraud,   XI. 23, 1830

Vocabulary.   See under Diction; Style

Vulgarisms.   See also Diction; Style

1.   [Vulgarisms in a story] were mere accidents, not essential to the truth in representing how the human heart and passions worked. See Realism 52

Wholeness.   See under Form; Unity

1.*   . . . he would not give a rush for any landscape that did not express the time of day, the climate, the period of the world it was meant to illustrate, or had not this character of *wholeness* in it. *Hazlitt*, iv, 277.   *c.* 1800

Women Writers.   See under Authors: Women

Wonder.   See Legends; Marvelous; Romance; Strangeness; Supernatural; Unusual; Thomson 13; W. 345A

1.   [See " The Ministry of Wonder," *Mind of a Poet,* pp. 480-92.]

Wordiness

1.   Upon this occasion I will request permission to add a few words closely connected with ' The Thorn ' and many other poems in these volumes. There is a numerous class of readers who imagine that the same words cannot be repeated without tautology; this is a great error; virtual tautology is much oftener produced by using different words when the meaning is exactly the same. Words, a Poet's words more particularly, ought to be weighed in the balance of feeling, and not measured by the space which they occupy upon paper. For the Reader cannot be too often reminded that Poetry is passion; it is the history or science of feelings. Now every man must know that an attempt is rarely made to communicate impassioned feelings without something of an accompanying consciousness of the inadequateness of our powers, or the deficiencies of language. During such efforts there will be a craving in the mind, and as long as it is unsatisfied the speaker will cling to the same words, or words of the same character. There are also various other reasons why repetition and apparent tautology are frequently beauties of the highest kind. Among the chief of these reasons is the interest which the mind attaches to words, not only as symbols of the passion, but as *things*, active and efficient, which are of themselves part of the passion. And further, from a spirit of fondness, exultation and gratitude, the mind luxuriates in the repetition of words which appear successfully to communicate its feelings.

The truth of these remarks might be shown by innumerable passages from the Bible, and from the impassioned Poetry of every nation. " Awake, awake, Deborah! " &c. Judges, chap. v., verses 12th, 27th, and part of 28th. See also the whole of that tumultuous and wonderful Poem. Note to *The Thorn (Oxf. W.,* pp. 899-900). 1800-1805

2. See W. 311

3. [Avoid] *revive again* this is a Tautology. *To Gillies,* VI. 9, 1817

4. As the Sonnet [" By Art's bold privilege "] first stood, there was a pleonasm. . . . *To Haydon* (p. 1038), IX. 11, 1840

Workmanship. See under Art; Composition; Finish; Form; Revision

PART TWO

AUTHORS AND WORKS

AUTHORS AND WORKS

Addison, Joseph

1. [*The Vision of Mirza.*] . . . a sublime allegory. . . .
Grosart, i, 3.   1793

2. . . . a pleasing paper in the *Spectator* (in the 7th vol., No. 477) upon this subject. The whole is well worth reading, particularly that part which relates to the winter garden.
To Beaumont,   XI. 10, 1806

3.   The most numerous class of sepulchral inscriptions do indeed record nothing else but the name of the buried person; but that he was born upon one day and died upon another. Addison in the *Spectator* . . . [objects to this type] "as a kind of satire upon the departed persons who had left no other memorial of them than that they were born and that they died." In certain moods of mind this is a natural reflection; yet not perhaps the most salutary which the appearance might give birth to.
Epitaphs 3 (*Grosart*, ii, 73).   1810

4. See Scotch Writers 2

Aeschylus

1. [Abundance of sublimity.] See Sublime 4

2.* . . . the 'Persae' is one of the worst of Aeschylus's plays. . . .
C. W., Jr. (*Grosart*, iii, 461).   *c.* 1827

3.* [Where is there] finer dramatic poetry, next to Shakespeare, than that of Aeschylus and Sophocles, not to speak of Euripides?
Ellis Yarnall (*Grosart*, iii, 479).   VII. 18, 1849

Aiken, John

1. [Bitter toward his critical editions of the poets.] See Barbauld 4

Akenside, Mark

1. [*Ode V, Against Suspicion*, viii] a fine stanza. . . . *Oxf. W.*, p. 626.

2. . . . stirred my mind agreeably in the same way, by recalling an Ode ["On recovering from a fit of sickness"] of Akenside's. . . .
To C. R. (*Corr. C. R.*, i, 272),   spring, 1835

Alcaeus

1.   Nor such [defiled] the spirit-stirring note
                     When the live chords Alcaeus smote,

175

Inflamed by sense of wrong;
Woe! woe to Tyrants! from the lyre
Broke threateningly, in sparkles dire
Of fierce vindictive song.
" Departing Summer," 37-42.   1819

Alfieri, Vittorio.   See Composition 22

Alford, Henry

1. . . . highly gratifying to me to learn that my writings are prized so
highly by a poet and critic of your powers. The essay upon them which you
have so kindly sent me seems well qualified to promote your views in writing
it. I was particularly pleased with your distinction between religion in poetry
and versified religion. . . . we have read your poems with no common
pleasure. Your ' Abbot of Muchelnaye ' also makes me curious to hear more
of him. *To H. Alford,*   II. 21, 1840

Allsop, Thomas

1. . . . the two vols: about Coleridge. The Editor is a man without
judgment, and therefore appears to be without feeling. His rule is to publish
all the truth that he can scrape together about his departed Friend, not perceiving the difference between the real truth, and what *appears to him* to be
true. The maxim nil de mortuis nisi *verum* was never meant to imply that
all truth was to be told, only nothing but what *is* true. This distinction also
has escaped his sagacity and ever will escape those of far superior talents to
Mr A. who care not what offense or pain they give to living persons provided
they have come to a conclusion however inconsiderately that they are doing
justice to the dead. *To Moxon,*   I. 9, 1836

Ancient Writers (Classical).   *Greek*: see Aeschylus; Alcaeus;
    Archimedes; Arion; Aristarchus; Aristophanes; Aristotle;
    Demosthenes; Euripides; Herodotus; Homer; Longinus;
    Musaeus; Pindar; Plato; Plutarch; Sappho; Simonides; Soph-
    ocles; Theocritus; Thucydides; Zoilus. *Latin*: see Catullus;
    Cicero; Horace; Juvenal; Lucretius; Ovid; Vergil

1.   There have I loved to show the tender age
           The golden precepts of the classic page;
           To lead the mind to those Elysian plains
           Where, throned in gold, immortal Science reigns;
           Fair to the view is sacred Truth display'd. . . .
           " And has the Sun," 67-71.   1784-5

2. [The best ancient and modern writers guilty of a false diction.]
App. L. B., p. 943.   1802

4.   Here, too, were " forms and pressures of the time,"
           Rough, bold, as Grecian comedy displayed
           When Art was young. . . .
           Prel., vii, 288-90.   1804-39

5. See Biography 2A; History 3, 11; Progress 1; Smoothness 1; Translation 4; W. 108, 242

7. [Mythology] . . . the gross fictions chanted in the streets
By wandering Rhapsodists. . . .
Exc., iv, 732-3.   1814

8. [Mythology] As old bards
Tell in their idle songs of wandering gods,
Pan or Apollo, veiled in human form. . . .
Exc., vii, 728-30.   1814

9. . . . the anthropomorphitism of the Pagan religion subjected the minds of the greatest poets in those countries too much to the bondage of definite form. . . . See Imagination 33G

11. [To unearth long-buried Greek MSS]
That were, indeed, a genuine birth
Of poesy; a bursting forth
Of genius from the dust:
What Horace gloried to behold
What Maro loved, shall we enfold?
Can haughty Time be just!
" Departing summer," 55-60.   1819

12. [Classical lore preserved by Christianity.]
. . . but classic lore glides on
By these Religious saved for all posterity.
1 Ecc. Sonn., xxv, 13-4.   1821

14. [The Greek dramatists and Homer differed in their methods of handling characters.] See Homer 12

15.* . . . first read the ancient classical authors; *then* come to *us*; and you will be able to judge for yourself which of us is worth reading. . . .
Catullus translated literally from the Greek; succeeding Roman writers did not so, because Greek had then become the fashionable, universal language. They did not translate, but they paraphrased; the ideas remaining the same, their dress differed. Hence the attention of the poets of the Augustan age was principally confined to the happy selection of the most appropriate words and elaborate phrases, and hence arises the difficulty of translating them.
C. W., Jr. (Grosart, iii, 458-59).   *c.* 1827

16. [Ancient writers before Christ had tranquility as their sovereign aim.]
" Tranquillity! the," 1-14.   1833

18.* . . . highly indignant with the Ancients for representing the nightingale as a sad bird, as well as attributing cowardice to the fox, ferocity to the wolf, etc.; maintained that they had cruelly wronged Nature.
Aubrey de Vere, p. 72.   IV. 28, 1841

20.* He spoke with great animation of the advantage of classical study, Greek especially. Where . . . would one look for a greater orator than Demosthenes; or finer dramatic poetry, next to Shakespeare, than that of

Aeschylus and Sophocles, not to speak of Euripides? [Herodotus] the most interesting and instructive book, next to the Bible, which had ever been written. Modern discoveries had only tended to confirm the general truth of his narrative. Thucydides he thought less of.

Ellis Yarnall (*Grosart*, iii, 479).   VIII. 18, 1849

Anderson, Robert

1. . . . passionately fond of poetry . . . [un]discriminating judgment, as the volumes he edited [show, through which W. became familiar with Chaucer,] Drayton, Daniel, and other distinguished [Elizabethan and Jacobean poets.] [See Anthologies 3.] *I. F.* (*Grosart*, iii, 70).   1843

Arabian Nights' Entertainments, The

1.   A precious treasure had I longed possessed,
             A little yellow, canvas-covered book,
             A slender abstract of the Arabian tales;
             And, from companions in a new abode,
             When first I learnt, that this dear prize of mine
             Was but a block hewn from a mighty quarry—
             That there were four large volumes, laden all
             With kindred matter, 'twas to me, in truth
             A promise scarcely earthly.
             Prel., v, 460-8.   1804-39

Archimedes

1.   Call Archimedes from his buried tomb
             Upon the grave of vanished Syracuse,
             And feelingly the Sage shall make report
             How insecure, how baseless in itself,
             Is the Philosophy whose sway depends
             On mere material instruments;—how weak
             Those arts, and high inventions, if unpropped
             By virtue.—He sighing with pensive grief,
             Amid his calm abstractions, would admit
             That not the slender privilege is theirs
             To save themselves from blank forgetfulness!
             Exc., viii, 220-30.   1814

Arion

1.   . . . thy skill, Arion!
             Could humanize the creatures of the sea. . . .
             On the Power of Sound, ix, 131-2.   1828

Ariosto, Ludovico

1. See Michelangelo 2
2. [Even Ariosto has less genius than Spenser.]

E. Supp. Pref., p. 946.   1815

3.*   Ariosto and Tasso are very absurdly depressed in order to elevate Dante. Ariosto is not always sincere; Spenser always so.

C. W., Jr. (*Grosart*, iii, 465).   *c.* 1827

Aristophanes. See Manners 2

Aristotle

1.   Aristotle, I have been told, has said, that poetry is the most philosophic of all writing: it is so. . . . *Pref. L. B.*, p. 938.   1800

2.   . . . the English, with their devotion to Aristotle, have but half the truth; a sound Philosophy must contain both Plato and Aristotle. See Literature 24

Aristarchus. See Jeffrey 10

Armstrong, John

1.   [Armstrong's] sublime apostrophe [*Art of Preserving Health*, iii, 355-64] to the great rivers of the earth. . . .

Grosart, iii, 98.   1820

Arnold, Thomas

1.   [*History of Rome.*] See Copyright Laws 4

2.*   He laments that Dr. Arnold should have spent so much of his time and powers in gathering up and putting into imaginary shape the scattered fragments of the history of Rome.

Mrs. D. (*Grosart*, iii, 443).   VII. 11, 1844

3.   [Dr. Arnold's Life.] He was a truly good man; of too ardent a mind however to be always judicious on the great points of secular & ec[c]lesiastical politics that occupied his mind and upon which he often wrote and acted under strong prejudices, and with hazardous confidence. But the Book, notwithstanding these objections, must do good, and *great* good.

To C. R. (*Corr. C. R.*, ii, 565),   VII. 14, 1844

4.   See Milton 63

Austen, Jane

1.*   . . . though he admitted that her novels were an admirable copy of life, he could not be interested in productions of that kind; unless the truth of nature were presented to him clarified, as it were, by the pervading light of imagination, it had scarce any attractions in his eyes; and for this reason he took little pleasure in the writings of Crabbe.

L. Sara Coleridge, i, 75.   VIII, 1834

Babes in the Woods. See Criticism 40

Bacon, Francis

1.   Britain, who thought to stain the field was fame,
           Now honour'd Edward's less than Bacon's name.
           " And has the Sun," 55-6.   1784-5

2.*   . . . you cannot be wrong, he says, if you read the best old writers, Lord Bacon's *Essays*, his *Advancement of Learning*, etc., for instance. . . .
D. W. to C. Clarkson,   Christmas Day, 1805

3.   . . . in the persons of Plato, Demosthenes, and Homer, and . . . of Shakespeare, Milton and Lord Bacon, were enshrined as much of the divinity of intellect as the inhabitants of this planet can hope will ever take up its abode among them. *Ans. to Mathetes* (*Grosart*, i, 312).   1809

4.   See Knight, Chas. 1; Montagu, B. 1, 2, 5, 6; Shakespeare 45

6.*   Scientific men are often too fond of aiming to be men of the world. They crave too much for titles, and stars, and ribbons. If Bacon had dwelt only in the court of Nature, and cared less for that of James the First, he would have been a greater man, and a happier one too.
C. W., Jr. (*Grosart*, iii, 465-6).   *c.* 1827

7.   I am glad that you are proceeding with the life of Bacon. You say that he was sacrificed to Buckingham. Have you read a letter of Buckingham's to him in which he charges him with the intention of sacrificing him (Buckingham) as he had betrayed all his patrons and friends in succession? Buckingham enumerates the cases. It has always appeared to me that much of the odium attached to Lord Bacon's name on account of corrupt practices arose out of ignorance respecting the spirit of those times, and the way in which things were carried on. *To B. Montagu,*   X. 22, 1831

8.*   . . . the figure of the great Lord Bacon. . . .
Lady R. (*Grosart*, iii, 450).   III. 6, 1845

9.*   But the most singular thing . . . is, that in all the writings of Bacon there is not one allusion to Shakespeare.
Mrs. D. (*Grosart*, iii, 457).   I. 11, 1847

Bailey, Benjamin

1.   . . . carefully read with great pleasure, the poems of your friend Baillie. *To J. Kenyon,*   I. 26, 1832

Baillie, Joanna

1.*   Read *Edinburgh* review of Miss Baillie's third volume of plays, which is written in an offensive tone, but in the main I think the criticism just. Miss Baillie is allowed to have much talent for observation and good sense, but she is denied to have poetic sense. . . . Though he [W.] admires Miss Baillie as a woman, concurs in this judgment, and says he could not read the later volumes. *H. C. R.*, i, 92.   VI. 3, 1812

Bamford, Robert

1.   . . . extracts from a paper in the *Christian Remembrancer*, October 1819 . . . known to be the work of the Rev. Robert Bamford . . . a great-grandson of Mr. Walker, whose worth it commemorates, by a record not the less valuable for being written in very early youth. *Grosart*, iii, 117.   1820

Barbauld, Anna Letitia

1.* In the opinion of Wordsworth she was the first of our literary women —and he was not bribed to that judgment by any congeniality of taste or concurrence in speculative opinions. . . . 'I am not in the habit of grudging people their good things, but I wish I had written those lines' [" Life! We have been long together "]. *H. C. R.*, i, 8,   1805

2.* He asserts for instance that Mrs. B[arbauld] has a bad heart; that her writings are absolutely insignificant, her poems are mere trash and specimens of every fault may be selected from them He quoted, to satirise, a Stanza [in *Ode to Content*] you & I have certainly admired—

> But thou o Nymph retired & coy!
> In what brown hamlet dost thou joy
> To tell thy tender tale?
> The lowliest children of the ground
> Moss-rose & Violet, blossom round
> And lily of the vale—

here he says, there is no genuine feeling or truth. Why is the hamlet *brown*? Because Collins in a description of exquisite beauty describing the introduction of Evening says " And hamlets brown & dim discovered Spires " Mrs. B. therefore sets down brown hamlets with[ou]t either propriety or feeling—And who are the lowliest children of the ground . . . ? Moss-rose—a Shrub! *C. R. to T. R.* (*Corr. C. R.*, i, 53-4),   III, 1808

3.* Wordsworth is not reconciled to Mrs. Barbauld; his chief reproach against her now is her having published pretty editions of Akenside, Collins, etc., with critical prefaces which have the effect of utterly forestalling the natural feeling and judgment of young and ingenuous readers. This practice he considers as absolutely shocking. *H. C. R.*, i, 74.   V. 8, 1812

4.* He had not then expressed the esteem for Mrs. Barb[auld]. wh. he late in life avowed. At this time W. was accustomed to express something like bitterness towards both Mrs. B. & Dr. Aiken on account of their critical Editions of the poets, by which they intercepted, he said, the natural judgments of unaffected readers. *Remains*, p. 52.   V. 13, 1812

5. . . . her [Anna Seward's] verses please me with all their faults better than those of Mrs. Barbauld, who with much higher powers of mind was spoiled as a Poetess by being a Dissenter, and concerned with a dissenting Academy. One of the most pleasing passages in her Poetry is the close of the lines upon life, written, I believe, when she was not less than 80 years of age: 'Life, we have been long together,' etc. *To Dyce*,   V. 10, 1830

6. See W. 26

Barrett, Elizabeth

1. I have been so much pleased with the power and knowledge displayed in Miss Barrett's volume of poems [*The Seraphim*, published 1838] . . . that I am desirous of seeing her translation of Aeschylus.
W. and M. W. to Kenyon,   VIII. 17, 1838

2. Miss Barrett appears to be a very interesting person, both for genius and attainments. *To J. Kenyon,*   II. 26, 1839

3.* . . . Her poems are too ideal for me. I want flesh and blood; even coarse nature and truth, where there is a want of refinement and beauty, is better than the other extreme. At the head of this natural and sensual school is Chaucer, the greatest poet of his class. Next comes Burns; Crabbe, too, has great truth, but he is too far removed from beauty and refinement.
H. C. R., ii, 562.   I. 3, 1839

4.   The conception of your Sonnet [on Haydon's portrait of W.] is in full accordance with the Painter's intended work, and the expression vigorous; yet the word ' ebb' though I do not myself object to it, nor wish to have it altered, will I fear prove obscure to nine readers out of ten.

> ' A vision free
> And noble, Haydon, hath thine Art released,—

Owing to the want of inflections in our language the construction here is obscure. Would it not be better thus?—I was going to write a small change in the order of the words, but I find it would not remove the objection. The verse as I take it, would be some what clearer thus, if you could tolerate the redundant syllable

> By a vision free
> And noble, Haydon, is thine Art released—

I had the gratification of receiving a good while ago, two copies of a volume of your writing, which I have read with much pleasure. . . .
To E. Barrett,   X. 26, 1842

5. See Browning 1

Barton, Bernard

1.   I differ from you in thinking that the only poetical lines in your address are ' stolen from myself.' The best verse, perhaps, is the following:

> Awfully mighty in his impotence,

which, by way of repayment, I may be tempted to steal from you on some future occasion. *To B. Barton,*   I. 12, 1816

Bayley, Peter

1. . . . a long dull poem [*The Fisherman's Wife*] in ridicule of the Idiot Boy, and in which Squire Bayley has mentioned by name ' Mr Wordsworth that most simple of all simple Poets.' . . . *To W. Scott,*   X. 16, 1803

2.* Do not on any account William says omit to speak of the plagiarisms from other Poets [in Bayley's poems]; Akenside, Cowper, Bowles etc. etc. This will interest them in the cause.
[De Sel. adds: *On the same sheet of paper are quotations from* ' Anct. Mar.' *showing plagiarisms from that poem in* ' Forest Fay ' (24th stanza), *and adding* ' there are several unnoticed verbal thefts such as " fiendish faces " from the Mad Mother, " The very breath suspended " from the Wye. The

plagiarisms in spirit are endless, and cannot be exhibited by quotations, but a person well-read in the L. B. will meet them every where. I cannot help adding, however, that the metre of this poem is taken from the Forsaken Indian Woman in L. B., a thing not worth noticing were it not that even so slight a circumstance would have prevented a man of any delicacy from abusing a person to whom he was indebted, even for such a trifle.']
D. W. to Coleridge,   XII, 1803

3.   I cannot forbear mentioning to you the way in which a wretched creature of the name of Peter Bailey has lately treated the author of your favorite book, the 'Lyrical Ballads.'   After pillaging them in a style of Plagiarism, I believe unexampled in the history of modern Literature, the wretched creature has had the baseness to write a long poem in ridicule of them, chiefly of *The Idiot Boy*; and, not content with this, in a note annexed to the same poem, has spoken of me, *by name*, as the *simplest*, i. e. the most contemptible of all Poets.   The complicated baseness of this (for the plagiarisms are absolutely by wholesale) grieved me to the heart for the sake of poor human Nature; that anybody could combine (as this man in some way or other must have done) an admiration and love of those poems, with moral feelings so detestable, hurt me beyond measure. If this Unhappy Creature's Volume should ever fall in your way, you will find the Plagiarisms chiefly in two Poems, one entitled *Evening in the Vale of Festiniog*, which is a wretched Parody throughout of *Tintern Abbey*, and the other *The Ivy Seat*, also *The Forest Fay*, and some others. *To De Quincey,*   III. 6, 1804

Baxter, Richard

1.   . . . Baxter's most interesting review of his own opinions and sentiments in the decline of life. *Grosart*, iii, 214.   1814

Beattie, James

1.   But I confess if there is to be an Error in style, I much prefer the *Classical* model of Dr. Beattie to the insupportable slovenliness and neglect of syntax and grammar, by which Hogg's writings are disfigured.
To Gillies,   II. 14, 1815

2.*   . . . [spoke] well of the earlier portion of Beattie's ' Minstrel,' not so much for originality of thought, as for the skilful manner in which he had employed the nine-line stanza.
Collier's Preface, p. lii.   II. 10, 1814

3.   [*The Minstrel.*] See Godwin, C. Grace 1

4.   [Very fine stanza from Beattie's *Ode to Retirement* (1758), 49-56 (The Aldine Edition of *The British Poets*, 1866, pp. 63-4).] See W. 297

Beaumont, Francis.   See also under Beaumont, Sir John

1.   The verses of your ancestor, Francis Beaumont, the younger, are very elegant and harmonious, and written with true feeling. Is this the only poem

of his extant? There are some pleasing Verses (I think by Corbet, Bishop of Norwich) on the death of Francis Beaumont the elder.

To Beaumont,   VII. 29, 1805

2.   And of that famous Youth, full soon removed
          From earth, perhaps by Shakespeare's self approved,
          Fletcher's Associate, Jonson's Friend beloved.
          " The embowering rose," 19-21.   1808

3.   Sang youthful tales of shepherds and their flocks;
          Unconscious prelude to heroic themes,
          Heart-breaking tears, and melancholy dreams
          Of slighted love, and scorn, and jealous rage,
          With which his genius shook the buskined stage.
          " Beneath yon eastern ridge," 12-16.   1811

Beaumont, Sir John

1.   . . . where that illustrious and most extraordinary man, Beaumont the Poet, and his Brother, were born. One is astonished when one thinks of that man having been only eight-and-twenty years of age, for I believe he was no more, when he died. Shakespeare, we are told, had scarcely written a single play at that age. I hope, for the sake of Poets, you are proud of these men.

To Beaumont,   V. 1, 1805

2.   I like your ancestor's verses the more, the more I see of them; they are manly, dignified, and extremely harmonious. I do not remember in any author of that age such a series of well-tuned couplets.

To Beaumont,   IX, 1806

3.   . . . where Francis Beaumont the Dramatist and his Brother Sir John Beaumont, also an admirable Poet, . . . were born. . . .

To W. Scott,   I. 20, 1807

4.   This line [*Brougham Castle,* 27] is from " The Battle of Bosworth Field," by Sir John Beaumont (brother to the Dramatist), whose poems are written with much spirit, elegance, and harmony; and have deservedly been reprinted lately in Chalmers' " Collection of English Poets."

Oxf. W., p. 900.   1807

5.   Not mindless of that distant age renowned
          When Inspiration hovered o'er this ground,
          The haunt of him who sang how spear and shield
          In civil conflict met on Bosworth-field. . . .
          " The embowering rose," 15-18.   1808

6.   The second [see *M. Y.,* pp. 470-1] has brought Sir John Beaumont and his brother Francis so livelily to my mind, that I recur to the plan of republishing the former's Poems, perhaps in connection with those of Francis. Could any further *search* be made after the Crown of Thorns [not extant, ascribed by Wood to Beaumont]? . . . The best way, perhaps, of managing this Republication would be to print it in a very elegant Type and Paper, and

not many copies, to be sold high so that it might be prized by the Collectors as a curiosity. Bearing in mind how many excellent things there are in Sir John Beaumont's little Volume, I am somewhat mortified at this mode of honouring his memory; but in the present state of the Taste of this Country, I cannot flatter myself that poems of that character would win their way into general circulation. Should it appear adviseable, another edition might afterwards be published, upon a plan which would place the Book within the reach of those who have little money to spare. *To Beaumont,*   XI, 1811

7.   . . . those illustrious Poets of your [Sir Geo. Beaumont's] name and family. . . . Dedication to *Pref., 1815*, p. 953.   1815

8.   See Wither 1

Bede

1.   O venerable Bede!
The saint, the scholar, from a circle freed
Of toil stupendous, in a hallowed seat
Of learning. . . .
        1 Ecc. Sonn., xxiii, 4-7.   1821

2.   This hill [see *1 Ecc. Sonn.,* vi, 13-4] at St. Alban's must have been an object of great interest to the imagination of the venerable Bede, who thus describes it, with a delicate feeling, delightful to meet with in that rude age, traces of which are frequent in his works:—' Variis herbarum floribus depictus imò usquequaque vertitus, in quo nihil repentè arduum, nihil praeceps, nihil abruptum, quem lateribus longè latèque deductum in modum aequoris natura companat, dignum videlicet eum pro insita sibi specie venustatis jam olim reddens, qui beati martyris cruore dicaretur.'
Oxf. W., p. 920.   1822

3.   The Conversion of Edwin, as related by him [Bede], is highly interesting—and the breaking up of this Council accompanied with an event so striking and characteristic, that I am tempted to give it at length in a translation [see *Oxf. W.,* p. 921] . . . [1822]. The last expression is a pleasing proof that the venerable monk of Wearmouth was familiar with the poetry of Virgil [1832]. *Oxf. W.,* p. 921.   1822 and 32

Behn, Mrs. Aphra. See Thornton, B. 1

Bell, Andrew

1.   [Bell's *An Experiment in Education*] is a most interesting work and entitles him to the fervent gratitude of all good men. . . .
To F. Wrangham,   X, 2, 1808

Bell, J.

1.   [Additions in Bell's text of Collins's *Ode on Popular Superstitions*] are spurious. . . . *To A. Dyce,*   X. 29, 1828

Bentley, Richard (1662-1742)

1.   . . . I have neither learning nor eyesight thoroughly to enjoy Bentley's

masterly *Dissertation on the Epistles of Phalaris*; many years ago I read the work with infinite pleasure. As far as I know, or rather am able to judge, it is without a rival in that department of literature; a work of which the English . . . may be proud as long as acute intellect, and vigorous powers, and profound scholarship shall be esteemed in the world.
To Dyce,   XII. 23, 1837

Bentley, Richard (1708-82)

1.   My copy of the Ode [*The Ode on a Distant Prospect of Eton College* (ll. 11, 22, 61) : the edition of 1768 read hills . . . shade; sprightly; fury Passions. De Sel.], in Gray's own handwriting, has

Ah, happy Hills, ah, pleasant Shade.

I wonder how Bentley could ever have substituted ' Rills,' a reading which has no support in the context. The common copies read, a few lines below,

Full many a *sprightly* race.

Gray's own copy has,

Full many a *smiling* race.

Throughout the whole poem the substantives are written in Capital Letters. He writes ' Fury-Passion,' and not, as commonly printed, the ' fury-passions.' What is the reason that our modern compositors are so unwilling to employ Capital Letters? *To J. Moultrie* (pp. 1271-2),   1845

Beranger, Pierre-Jean de

1.*   [Beranger praised]; he is eminently popular.
H. C. R., ii, 517.   III. 27, 1837

2.   There is a French Poet now living by name Beranger who would do justice to the Poems of Burns as far as that is possible. He is a man of extraordinary genius, and the french language under his management seems equal to any thing which Lyrical Poetry requires. *To J. Gibson,*   XII, 1848

Bible, The

1.   [Effective repetition in the song of Deborah (Judges, 5: 27-28).] See Wordiness 1   1800-1805

2.   See Books 10; Scholarly Interests 25; Johnson 4; Young 1; W. 242

5.   [The poetical imagination exemplified in the prophetic and lyrical parts of the Holy Scriptures.] See Imagination 33 G

6.   [Ezekiel and Isaiah.] See Sublime 4

7.   . . . I am unequal to the task [of enlarging the collection of translations and paraphrases from the Bible]. My own devotional feelings have never taken in verse a shape that connected them with scripture in a degree that would encourage me to an effort of this kind. The sacred writings have a majesty, a beauty, a simplicity, an ardour, a sublimity, that awes and over-powers the spirit of Poetry in uninspired men, at least this is my feeling; and if it has deterred me in respect to compositions that might have been entered upon without any view of their seeing the light, how much more

probable is it that I should be restrained, were I to make the endeavour under a consciousness that I was writing with a national purpose! . . . I dare not attempt it. *To Baird,*   VI. 15, 1827

8. . . . it is the habit of my mind inseparably to connect loftiness of imagination with that humility of mind which is best taught in Scripture. *To J. K. Miller,*   XII. 17, 1831

9.   . . . His pure Word by miracle revealed.
Prel., v. 222.   1832-39

10. The consolation which Children and very young Persons who have been religiously brought up, draw from the holy Scripture ought to be habitually on the minds of adults of all ages for the benefit of their own souls, and requires to be treated in a loftier and more comprehensive train of thought and feeling than by writers has usually been bestowed upon it. . . . I wish I were equal to any thing so holy, but I feel that I am not. *To C. H. Parry,*   V. 21, 1840

11. If it were not that we learn to talk and think of the lion and the eagle, the palm-tree, and even the cedar, from the impassioned introduction of them so frequently in Holy Scripture, and by great poets, and divines who write as poets, the spiritual part of our nature, and therefore the higher part of it, would derive no benefit from such intercourse with such subjects. *I. F. (Grosart,* iii, 49).   1843

13.* . . . of St. Paul, he said, ' Oh, what a character that is! how well we know him! How human, yet how noble! How little outward sufferings moved him! It is not in speaking of these that he calls himself wretched; it is when he speaks of the inward conflict. Paul and David,' he said, ' may be called the two Shakspearian characters in the Bible; both types, as it were, of human nature in its strength and its weakness. Moses is grand, but then it is chiefly from position, from the office he had entrusted to him. We do not know Moses as a man, as a brother man.' *Mrs. D. (Grosart,* iii, 455).   I. 15, 1845

14.* . . . a plan suggested by Wordsworth, for the revision of the authorised version of the Bible and the Book of Common Prayer.

With regard to the former, no one, he said, could be more deeply convinced of the inestimable value of its having been made when it was, and being what it is. In his opinion it was made at the happy juncture when our language had attained adequate expansion and flexibility, and when at the same time its idiomatic strength was unimpaired by excess of technical distinctions and conventional refinements; and these circumstances, though of course infinitely subordinate to the spiritual influence of its subject-matter, he considered to be highly important in connection with a volume which naturally became a universally recognized standard of the language; for thus the fresh well of English undefiled was made a perennial blessing to the nation, in no slight degree conducive to the robust and manly thinking and character of its inhabitants. He was satisfied, too, as to its general and most impartial accuracy, and its faithfulness in rendering not only the words but the style, the strength, and the spirit and the character of the original records. He attached too the value one might suppose he would attach to the desirableness of leaving undisturbed the sacred associations which to the feelings of aged Christians belonged to the *ipsissima verba* which had been their support under the trials of life.

And so with regard to the Prayer Book, he reverenced and loved it as the Church's precious heritage of primitive piety, equally admirable for its matter and its style. It may be interesting to add, that in reference to this latter point I have heard him pronounce that many of the collects seemed to him examples of perfection, consisting, according to his impression, of words whose signification filled up without excess or defect the simple and symmetrical contour of some majestic meaning, and whose sound was a harmony of accordant simplicity and grandeur; a combination, he added, such as we enjoy in some of the best passages of Shakespeare.

But notwithstanding that he held these opinions, which will evince that he was not one who would lightly touch either sacred volume, he did not think that plain mistakes in the translation of the Bible, or obsolete words, or renderings commonly misunderstood, should be perpetually handed down in our authorized version of the volume of inspiration, or that similar blemishes in the Prayer Book, which, as being of human composition, would admit of freer though still reverential handling, should be permitted to continue as stumbling-blocks interfering with its acceptableness and usefulness.

Graves (Grosart, iii, 471-72).   *c.* 1845

16.*   [Old Testament influenced Milton in *Samson Agonistes*.]
Graves (Grosart, iii, 461).   *c.* 1845

17.*   Herodotus . . . the most interesting and instructive book, next to the Bible, which had even been written.
Ellis Yarnall (Grosart, iii, 479).   VIII. 18, 1849

Blackwood's Magazine

1.   I know little of Blackwood's Magazine, and wish to know less. I have seen in it articles so infamous that I do not chuse to let it enter my doors. The Publisher sent it to me some time ago, and I begged (civilly you will take for granted) not to be troubled with it any longer.
To F. Wrangham,   II. 19, 1819

Blair, Alexander

1.   [Co-author, with John Wilson, of the " Letter to Mathetes." See Alan L. Strout, " Samuel Taylor Coleridge and John Wilson of *Blackwood's Magazine*," *PMLA*, XLVIII (March, 1933), 100-1.]

2.   [Blair's election to] the Professorship of English Literature in the London University. This information gave me much pleasure, and I heartily wish you success, persuaded as I am that this employment will be gratifying to yourself, and convinced that you are eminently qualified by your talents and attainments to do credit to it. I am lately come down from a neighborhood which reminded me of the pleasure which many years ago I enjoyed in

your society, talking over with you the principles of taste, and discussing the merits of different Authors. . . .

We were agreed I think upon everything of importance, and I do not think it likely that your subsequent studies will have made any very important change in your notions, so that if you are elected to this important office, I am persuaded you will deal with our Mother tongue feelingly and reverently. *To A. Blair,*   XII. 11, 1827

Blake, William

1.*   [Blake had] the elements of poetry a thousand times more than either Byron or Scott, but Scott he thinks superior to Campbell. . . . R[oger]s has an effeminate mind, but he has not the obscure writing of C[ampbell]. Introduction to *Corr. C. R.*, i, 24.   V. 24, 1812

2.*   Wordsworth & Lamb like his poems. *Remains*, p. 6.   *c.* 1815

3.*   . . . ' Songs of Innocence & Experience,' showing the two opposite states of the human soul. *Remains*, p. 18.   *c.* 1825

4.*   . . . some poems in M.S. by him [Blake] & they interested him [W.]— *Remains*, p. 14.   *c.* 1826

Boccaccio. See Dryden 18

Boileau

1.   [Malignity in his satires.] *To W. Mathews,*   III. 21, 1796

Bonaparte, Lucien

1.   See Macpherson 2

2.   [His epic *Charlemagne*] the first three Stanzas *convinced* me that L. B. was no *poet*. *To Gillies,*   II. 14, 1815

Book of Common Prayer. See Scholarly Interests 25; and also Bible

Boswell, James

1.   See Biography 2A; Scholarly Interests 15; Currie 2; Macpherson 2

Bourne, Vincent. See Landor 10

Bowles, William Lisle. See Moxon 2

Bowering, John

1.   It gives me pleasure to see that you continue transplanting the flowers of foreign Poetry into our tongue. *To John Bowering,* XII. 29, 1827

Brooke, Henry

1.   The tragedy [*Gustavus Vasa* (1793)] is a strange composition of genius and absurdity. . . . *To James Tobin,*   III. 6, 1798

Broome, William. See Johnson 11

Brougham, Henry Peter, Baron

1.   Mr. B. [Brougham] is not content with scribbling in the *Edinburgh Review* to the praise and glory of the Corsican. . . .
To J. Scott,   III. 21, 1816

2.*   . . . whose talents and moral virtues he greatly admires.
Greville Memoirs, ii, 122-23.   II. 27, 1831

3.   See Jeffrey 12

Brown, John [" Estimate "]

1.   [*Barbarossa* requires little power in actor.] See Drama, Actors and Acting 3

2.   See Scotch Writers 2

3.   [One of the first writers] who led the way to a worthy admiration of this country. *Lakes* (*Grosart,* ii, 255).   1809-35

4.   [Published a letter to a friend, in which the attractions of the vale of Keswick] were delineated with a powerful pencil, and the feeling of a genuine Enthusiast. [See Tickell 1A.] *Lakes* (*Grosart,* ii, 269).   1809-35

Brown, Phoebe Hindal

1.   [*The Mother's Hymn-Book.*] See Mackenzie 2

Browne, Sir Thomas

1.   You have gratified me by what you say of Sir Thomas Browne. I possess his *Religio Medici, Christian Morals, Vulgar Errors,* etc., in separate publications, and value him highly as a most original author. I almost regret that you did not add his treatise upon *Urn Burial* to your publication; it is not long, and very remarkable for the vigour of mind that it displays.
To J. Peace,   IV. 8, 1844

Browning, Robert

1.   Her choice [Elizabeth Barrett's] is a very able man, and I trust that it will be a happy union, not doubting that they will speak more intelligibly to each other than (notwithstanding their abilities) they have yet done to the public. *To Moxon,*   X. 12, 1846

Bruce, Michael

1.   . . . was called away too early to leave behind him more than a few trustworthy promises of pure affections and unvitiated imagination.
To J. F. Mitchell,   IV. 21, 1819

Bruce, Peter Henry

1.   Peter Henry Bruce, having given in his entertaining Memoirs the substance of this Tale [*The Russian Fugitive*]. . . .
Oxf. W., p. 925.   1835

Brugière, Amable-Guillaume, Baron de Barante

1.* The essay on the French literature . . . by Barante [*Tableau de la littérature française au XVIII siecle*. By Amable-Guillaume Prosper Brugière, Baron de Barante. 1808], which Wordsworth so strongly praises.

H. C. R., i, 248. X. 9, 1820

Bryant, William Cullen

1. . . . several of Mr. B's pieces have fallen in my way from time to time, some of which had merit of a very superior kind.

To Mackenzie, XI. 25, 1837

Brydges, Sir Egerton

1. . . . feebleness . . . is diffused through such of his writings as I have seen. Nor does the present Essay constitute, to me an exception, though it becomes me, in some respects, to approve of it, as no small portion of the sentiments it contains, have already been publicly expressed by me, in the preface to the L. B., and in the supplementary Essay to my last two Vols. It is plain that Sir E - - cannot have read them, or he would not have so formally quoted a publication from Mr Leigh Hunt, of yesterday [*The Feast of the Poets*, 1814, 2nd ed. 1815], for a sentiment which I announced 15 years ago, and took some pains to enforce and illustrate, as being the fundamental principle of my own style. . . . The fault of the Essay in question is, not that the opinions are in general erroneous; but they are brought forward in a loose straggling manner; there is no necessary succession in the thoughts, no development from a seminal principle.—Sir E. is quite correct in stating that no Poetry can be good without animation. But when he adds, ' that the position will almost exclude whatever is very highly and artificially laboured, for great artifice must destroy animation,' he thinks laxly, and uses words inconsiderately.—Substitute for the word ' artificially ' the word, ' artfully,' and you will at once see that nothing can be more erroneous than the assertion. The word, ' artificially ' begs the question (There is the same fault in the use of the word ' apes ' in what is said upon imitation. Studious imitators are not in general affected; but I have not room for my thoughts), because that word is always employed in an unfavourable sense. See Gray 5

To Gillies, IV. 15, 1816

2. . . . I found additional proofs of your regard in two valuable volumes from the labours of your learned Father [Sir Egerton Brydges (1762-1837)] . . . the greater part of which is new to me, contained in the Polyanthea and Cimelia. *To Capt. Barrett,* XI. 19, 1824

3. See Dyce 1

4. . . . Sir E's great merits [see also a letter to Dyce, VI. 22, 1830].
To E. Q., IV. 28, 1930

5. [Pleased by the sonnet upon Echo and Silence.]
To Dyce, Spring, 1833

6. . . . could not but feel honoured by such notice from so able and interesting an Author. *To Dyce,* XII. 4, 1833

7.   Accept my thanks for the life of Milton [*Poetical Works of John Milton*, ed. by Sir Egerton Brydges] which you have sent me, and my sincere acknowledgements of the honor done me by the Dedication which is more acceptable as uniting my name with Mr Southey's. This mark of respect to us both will I trust meet with the approbation of our common Friend, the Author, who is well fitted to do justice to the arduous task which he has undertaken. *To J. Macrone,*   VI. 2, 1835

Bucer, Martin.   See Erasmus 1

Buchanan, George

1.   See Macpherson 2

2.*   I think Buchanan's 'Maiae Calendae' equal in sentiment, if not in elegance, to anything in Horace. . . .

C. W., Jr. (*Grosart*, iii, 459).   *c.* 1827

3.   . . . his beautiful Ode to the first of May. . . .
Lakes (*Grosart*, ii, 254).   1809-35

Bull, George.   See Rose 1

Bulwer-Lytton, Edward George

1.*   Certainly *Dandy-Saints* are worse than even Literary Dandies whom Wordsworth (alluding to Litton Bulwer) declared to be the worst. . . .
C. R. to T. R. (*Corr. C. R.*, ii, 787),   III. 19, 1852

Bürger, Gottfried August

1.   See Manners 2; Percy 1

2.*   We [W., and D. W.] have read *Lenore* and a few little things of Bürger; but upon the whole we were disappointed, particularly in *Lenore*, which we thought in several passages inferior to the English translation [William Taylor's]. 'Wie donnerten die Brücken'—how inferior to
> 'The bridges thunder as they pass,
> But earthly sound was none, etc., etc.'

. . . As to Bürger, I am yet far from that admiration of him which he has excited in you; but I am by nature slow to admire; and I am not yet sufficiently master of the language to understand him perfectly. In one point I entirely coincide with your feeling concerning his versification. In *Lenore* the concluding double rhymes of the stanza have both a delicious and *pathetic* effect—
> Ach! aber für Lenoren
> War Gruss und Kuss verloren.

I accede too to your opinion that Bürger is always the poet; he is never the mobbist, one of those dim drivellers with which our island has teemed for so many years. Bürger is one of those authors whose book I like to have in my hand, but when I have laid the book down I do not think about him. I remember a hurry of pleasure, but I have few distinct forms that people my mind, nor any recollection of delicate or minute feelings which he has either communicated to me, or taught me to recognise. I do not perceive the presence of character in his personages. I see everywhere the character of Bürger himself; and even this, I agree with you, is no mean merit. But yet I wish him sometimes at least to make me forget himself in these creations. It seems to me, that in poems descriptive of human nature, however short they may be, character is absolutely necessary etc.: incidents are among the lowest allurements of poetry. Take from Bürger the *incidents* which are seldom or ever of his own invention, and much will still remain; there will remain a manner of relating which is almost always spirited and lively, and stamped and peculiarized with genius. Still, I do not find those higher beauties which can entitle him to the name of a great poet. I have read *Susan's Dream*, and I agree with you that it is the most perfect and Shaksperian of his poems, etc., etc. Bürger is the poet of the animal Spirits. I love his *Tra ra la* dearly; but less of the horn, and more of the lute—and far, far more of the pencil. *L. of Coleridge*, i, 133-4.   I. 25, 1800

Burke, Edmund

1.   See Reynolds, Joshua 3

2.*   . . . you always went from Burke with your mind filled. . . .
Haydon, i, 210.   V. 23, 1815

3.   Genius of Burke! forgive the pen seduced
             By specious wonders, and too slow to tell
             Of what the ingenuous, what bewildered men,
             Beginning to mistrust their boastful guides,
             And wise men, willing to grow wiser, caught,
             Rapt auditors! from thy most eloquent tongue—
             Now mute, for ever mute in the cold grave.
                 . . .
             While he forewarns, denounces, launches forth,
             Against all systems built on abstract rights,
             Keen ridicule; the majesty proclaims
             Of Institutes and Laws, hallowed by time;
             Declares the vital power of social ties
             Endeared by Custom; and with high disdain,
             Exploding upstart Theory, insists
             Upon the allegiance to which men are born—
                 . . .
             But memorable moments intervened,
             When Wisdom, like the Goddess from Jove's brain,
             Broke forth in armour of resplendent words,
             Startling the Synod. Could a youth, and one
             In ancient story versed, whose breast had heaved
             Under the weight of classic eloquence,
             Sit, see, and hear, unthankful, uninspired?
             Prel., vii, 512-18; 523-30; 537-43.   1820-39

3A.*   Spoke of the very little real knowledge of poetry that existed now;

so few men had time to study. For instance, Mr. Canning; one could hardly select a cleverer man; and yet, what did Mr. Canning know of poetry? What time had he, in the busy political life he had led, to study Dante, Homer, &c. as they ought to be studied, in order to arrive at the true principles of taste in works of genius. Mr. Fox, indeed, towards the latter part of his life, made leisure for himself, and took to improving his mind; and accordingly, all his later public displays bore a greater stamp of wisdom and good taste than his early ones. Mr. Burke alone was an exception to this description of public men; by far the greatest man of his age; not only abounding in knowledge himself, but feeding, in various directions, his most able contemporaries; assisting Adam Smith in his *Political Economy*, and Reynolds in his *Lectures on Painting*. Fox, too, who acknowledged that all he had ever learned from books was nothing to what he had derived from Burke.
Moore's Diary, pp. 30-1.   X. 27, 1820

4. I am averse (with that wisest of the Moderns Mr Burke) to all *hot* Reformations; i. e. to every sudden change in political institutions upon a large scale. *To Haydon*,   VII. 8, 1831

Burnet, Gilbert

1. See Burnet, who [in *The History of the Reformation*] is unusually animated on this subject [see *3 Ecc. Sonn.* xxxvii, 5-6]; the east wind, so anxiously expected and prayed for, was called the " Protestant wind."
Oxf. W., p. 923.   1822

Burnet, Thomas

2. [*Life of Bishop Bedell.*] See Jebb 1

1.   Since this paragraph [see *Exc.*, iii, 78-112] was composed, I have read with so much pleasure, in Burnet's " [Sacred] Theory of the Earth," a passage [see *Oxf. W.*, pp. 926-7] expressing corresponding sentiments, excited by objects of a similar nature, that I cannot forbear to transcribe it.
Oxf. W., p. 926.   1814

2. [In the *Theory of the Earth*] Nothing can be worthier of the magnificent appearances [of scenery] he describes than his language.
K. and W. Railway (*Grosart*, ii, 327).   1835

Burney, Frances

1. See Lamb 21

2. . . . I had read a good deal of it [*The Diary and Letters of Madame D'Arblay* (Frances Burney)] before and liked it better than the preceding ones. Her vanity is provoking, but when one has got over that, there is a great deal of interest to be found in it. *To Ellen Rickets*,   X. 22, 1842

Burns, Gilbert. See Burns 16, 17

Burns, Robert (General Criticism)

1. . . . in Burns you have manners everywhere. Tam O'Shanter I do not deem a character, I question whether there is any individual character in all

Burns' writing except his own. But every where you have the presence of human life. The communications that proceed from Burns come to the mind with the life and charm of recognitions. But Burns also is energetic solemn and sublime in sentiment, and profound in feeling. His Ode to Despondency I can never read without the deepest agitation. *To Coleridge,*   II. 27, 1799

2.   . . .
          Of Him who walked in glory and in joy
          Following his plough, along the mountain-side. . . .
          Resolution and Independence, 45-6.   1802

3.   . . .
          With chastened feelings would I pay
                    The tribute due
          To him, and aught that hides his clay
                    From mortal view.
          Fresh as the flower, whose modest worth
          He sang, his genius " glinted " forth,
          Rose like a star that touching earth,
                    For so it seems,
          Doth glorify its humble birth
                    With matchless beams.

                    . . .
          I mourned with thousands, but as one
          More deeply grieved, for He was gone
          Whose light I hailed when first it shone,
                    And showed my youth
          How Verse may build a princely throne
                    On humble truth.

                    . . .
          Might we together
          Have sate and talked where gowans blow,
                    Or on wild heather.
          What treasures would have then been placed
          Within my reach; of knowledge graced
          By fancy what a rich repast!
          At the Grave of Burns, 15-24; 31-36; and 52-57.   1803-7

4.   His judgment with benignant ray
          Shall guide, his fancy cheer, your way;
          But ne'er to a seductive lay
                    Let faith be given;
          Nor deem that " light which leads astray
                    Is light from Heaven."
          To the Sons of Burns, 37-42.   1803

5. See Biography 2A, B, C; Copyright 1; Moral Element 17; Poetry 99; Style 68; Barrett, E. 3; Coleridge 31; Currie 2; Gillies 2; Jeffrey 10; Macpherson 2; Smith, Charlotte 2; W. 401

14.   The service [*L. to a Friend of Burns*] I have lately rendered to Burns's genius will one day be performed to mine. The quotations, also, are

printed with the most culpable neglect of correctness: there are lines turned into nonsense. *To Southey* (p. 718),   1816

15. . . . the metropolis of his native country,—to which his writings have done so great honour. . . . *To J. Scott,*   VI. 11, 1816

16. [Suggested biography of Burns by his brother.] . . . the most odious part of the charges [against Burns] owed its credit to the silence of those who were deemed best entitled to speak and who, it was thought, would not have been mute, had they believed that they could speak beneficially. Moreover, it may be relied on as a general truth, which will not escape his [Gilbert Burns's] recollection, that tasks of this kind are not so arduous as, to those who are tenderly concerned in their issue, they may at first appear to be; for, if the many be hasty to condemn, there is a re-action of generosity which stimulates them—when forcibly summoned—to redress the wrong; and, for the sensible part of mankind, *they* are neither dull to understand, nor slow to make allowance for, the aberrations of men, whose intellectual powers do honour to their species.

L. to Friend of Burns (*Grosart*, ii, 19).   1816

17. . . . from the gratitude which, as a lover of poetry, I owe to the genius of his [Gilbert Burns's, who had asked W. the best mode of defending Burns's reputation] departed relative, I should most gladly comply with this wish; if I could hope that any suggestions of mine would be of service to the cause. But really, I feel it a thing of much delicacy, to give advice upon this occasion, as it appears to me, mainly, not a question of opinion, or of taste, but a matter of conscience. [Burns's brother, Gilbert, is the logical person either to strike out the offensive passages in Dr. Currie's *Life of Burns,* or to attach notes correcting the misrepresentations or exposing the exaggerations. If the arrangement of Currie's *Life* is changed], in my judgment, it would be best to copy the example which Mason has given in his second edition of Gray's works. There, inverting the order which had properly been adopted, when the Life and Letters were new matter, the poems are placed first; and the rest takes its place as subsidiary to them. [Using this method, Gilbert Burns, who has given proof of his ability, should prefix a concise life of the poet. In its proportion, degree of detail, and general execution, no better model exists than Fenton's *Life of Milton.* In this prefatory memoir Gilbert Burns must not allow fraternal partiality to destroy its trustworthiness. When one recalls the frightful things written and insinuated against this great poet, perhaps it would be well to state explicitly the pernicious habits of Burns, and the point to which his moral character had been degraded. It is a disgraceful feature of the times that this measure should be necessary, but the errors in Currie's *Life* impose this duty on any biographer of Burns.]

L. to Friend of Burns (*Grosart*, ii, 5-6).   1816

18. [Subjectivity of early poems.] But, in those early poems [see Burns 36 and 37] through the veil of assumed habits and pretended qualities, enough of the real man appears to shew that he was conscious of sufficient cause to dread his own passions, and to bewail his errors! [Though many testimonies against Burns are false, his own words prove that the order of

his life corresponded little with the clearness of his views. Had he better controlled his weaknesses, he would have been a greater poet, but of a different
class. Too, many peculiar beauties, which enrich his verses, and many acces-
sory influences, which contribute to their effect, would be wanting.] For
instance, the momentous truth of the passage already quoted, ' One point
must still be greatly dark,' &c. could not possibly have been conveyed with
such pathetic force by any poet that ever lived, speaking in his own voice;
unless it were felt that, like Burns, he was a man who preached from the text
of his own errors; and whose wisdom, beautiful as a flower that might have
risen from seed sown from above, was in fact a scion from the root of
personal suffering. [The poet thought of himself occupying the grave—
" Thoughtless follies laid him low."] Here is a sincere and solemn avowal—
a public declaration *from his own will*—a confession at once devout, poetical,
and human—a history in the shape of a prophecy! What more was required
of the biographer than to have put his seal to the writing, testifying that the
foreboding had been realized, and that the record was authentic?—Lastingly
is it to be regretted in respect to this memorable being, that inconsiderate
intrusion has not left us at liberty to enjoy his mirth, or his love; his wisdom
or his wit; without an admixture of useless, irksome, and painful details
[Currie's *Life of Burns*], that take from his poems so much of that right—
which, with all his carelessness, and frequent breaches of self-respect, he
was not negligent to maintain for them—the right of imparting solid instruction through the medium of unalloyed pleasure.

L. to Friend of Burns (Grosart, ii, 15-16).   1816

19. [A Monument for Burns.] . . . I cannot unite my humble efforts
with theirs in promoting this object. . . . In the first place, Eminent poets
appear to me to be a Class of men, who less than any others stand in need
of such marks of distinction; and hence I infer that this mode of acknowledging their merits is one for which they would not, in general, be themselves
solicitous. Burns did, indeed, erect a monument to Ferguson; but I apprehend his gratitude took this course because he felt that Ferguson had been
prematurely cut off, and that his fame bore no proportion to his deserts.
In neither of these particulars can the fate of Burns justly be said to resemble
that of his Predecessor: his years were indeed few, but numerous enough to
allow him to spread his name far and wide, and to take permanent root in
the affections of his Countrymen; in short, he has raised for himself a Monument so conspicuous, and of such imperishable materials, as to render a local
fabric of Stone superfluous, and therefore comparatively insignificant.

To J. F. Mitchell,   IV. 21, 1819

21.   Well sang the Bard [see *Knight*, vii, 295 n.]
                who called the grave, in strains
             Thoughtful and sad, the " narrow house."
             " Well sang the Bard," 1-2.   1831

             . . .

25.   Our pleasure varying at command
                Of each sweet Lay.

. . .
And ask of Nature from what cause
  And by what rules
She trained her Burns to win applause
  That shames the Schools.
Through busiest street and loneliest glen
Are felt the flashes of his pen;
He rules 'mid winter snows, and when
  Bees fill their hives;
Deep in the general heart of men
  His power survives.

What need of fields in some far clime
Where Heroes, Sages, Bards sublime,
And all that fetched the flowing rhyme
  From genuine springs,
Shall dwell together till old Time
  Folds up his wings?
" Too frail to keep the lofty vow," 29-30; 39-54.   1839

25A.* . . . a limited inferior creature, any genius he had a theme for one's pathos rather. . . . *Carlyle's Reminiscences,* ed. Norton (London, 1887), p. 302.   1840

26.* He thinks that Burns, in his own sphere, is unrivalled, and that as raising himself into such fame by the study of the objects which constantly met his eye in his daily life he is worthy of all praise; but he made a curious remark. . . . He said that Burns is the poet of human passions, and of the social enjoyments and rough friendships and little incidents of the life of a man in his own grade; but that he never assumes the highest tone which best beseems a poet; that he never spiritualizes, much less sanctifies his conceptions; that he never appears in the priestly robes or with the majestic authority of a Bard; that while his most beautiful effusions are on a daisy and a mouse, which met his eye as he followed the plough, and which he has embalmed for ever in immortal strains, yet that he nowhere in all his poems mentions the mountains of Arran, which lay constantly before him, had he raised either his eye or his mind so high. [W. considered the outline of the Northern mountains of Arran unsurpassed in beauty.] . . . "How could Carlyle call *him* [Burns] a *hero,* who was self-degraded and destroyed to a degree that made his life a continual misery? . . ." [See Carlyle 9]. He then returned to Burns, . . . reciting, the whole of ' the Poet's epitaph on himself ' and added, as a moral at the end of it, that instead of ' thoughtless follies laid him low,' it should be ' reckless vices laid him low.' [W. spoke of letters from Burns, then in Pickering's possession, as so profane and low as to be unpublishable] . . . "And does such a man deserve the name of a Bard, or a truly Great Poet? It would be ' profanation of the term, and of all that is sacred in the noblest thoughts and feelings of man, to hold that mere intellect, so employed, could ever deserve, or commonly receive, that high appellation." *A Day with Wordsworth,* pp. 735-7.   VIII. 31, 1841

26A.   Familiarity with the dialect of the border counties of Cumberland and Westmoreland made it easy for me not only to understand but to feel them [Burns's poems]. It was not so with . . . Cowper, as appears from one of his letters. . . . the simplicity, the truth and the vigour of Burns would have strongly recommended him, notwithstanding occasional coarseness, to the sympathies of Cowper, and ensured the approval of his judgment. It gives me pleasure, venial I trust, to acknowledge at this late day my obligations to these two great authors, whose writings in conjunction with Percy's *Reliques*, powerfully counteracted the mischievous influence of Darwin's dazzling manner, the extravagance of the earlier dramas of Schiller, and that of other German writers upon my taste and natural tendencies. May these few words serve as a warning to youthful Poets who are in danger of being carried away by the inundation of foreign literature, from which our own is at present suffering so much, both in style and points of far greater moment. True it is that in the poems of Burns, as now collected, are too many reprehensible passages; but their immorality is rather the ebullition of natural temperament and a humour of levity than a studied thing: whereas in these foreign Writers, and in some of our own country not long deceased (and in an eminent deceased Poet of our own age), the evil, whether voluptuousness, impiety, or licentiousness, is courted upon system, and therefore is greater, and less pardonable.

W.'s Works, iii, 441-2.   1842

27.*   [The great genius who had brought poetry back to nature.] Of course I [W.] refer to his serious efforts, such as the ' Cotter's Saturday Night '; those foolish little amatory songs of his one has to forget. [Hallam Tennyson here quotes from Aubrey de Vere.]   *Tennyson*, i, 211.   1842-46

28.   [Burns's failure to describe the scenes around Mosgiel.] Yet this is easily explained. In one of his poetical effusions he speaks of describing ' fair Nature's face,' as a privilege on which he sets a high value; nevertheless, natural appearances rarely take a lead in his poetry. It is as a human being, eminently sensitive and intelligent, and not as a poet clad in his priestly robes and carrying the ensigns of sacerdotal office, that he interests and affects us.

Whether he speaks of rivers, hills, and woods, it is not so much on account of the properties with which they are absolutely endowed, as relatively to local patriotic remembrances and associations, or as they are ministerial to personal feelings, especially those of love, whether happy or otherwise; yet it is not *always* so. Soon after we had passed Mosgiel Farm we crossed the Ayr, murmuring and winding through a narrow woody hollow. His line,

' Auld hermit Ayr staw thro' his woods,'

came at once to my mind, with Irwin, Lugar, Ayr, and Doon, Ayrshire streams over which he breathes a sigh, as being unnamed in song; and, surely, his own attempts to make them known were as successful as his heart could desire.

Grosart, iii, 154-55.   1843 [K.]

29.   [Burns's limitations in nature-appreciation. Dr. Adair, Burns's fellow-traveller said,] ' I doubt if he [Burns] had much taste for the picturesque.'

8

The personal testimony, however, upon this point is conflicting; but when Dr. Currie refers to certain local poems as decisive proofs that Burns' fellow-traveller [Adair] was mistaken, the biographer is surely unfortunate. How vague and tame are the poet's expressions in those few local poems, compared with his language when he is describing objects with which his position in life allowed him to be familiar! It appears, both from what his works contain, and from what is not to be found in them, that, sensitive as they abundantly prove his mind to have been in its intercourse with common rural images, and with the general powers of Nature exhibited in storm and stillness, in light or darkness, and in the various aspects of the seasons, he was little affected by the sight of one spot in preference to another, unless where it derived an interest from history, tradition, or local associations. . . . I am persuaded that, if he had been induced to ramble among our Lakes, by that time sufficiently celebrated, he would have seldom been more excited than by some ordinary Scottish stream or hill with a tradition attached to it, or which had been the scene of a favorite ballad or love song.

K. and W. Railway (Grosart, ii, 330).   1844

30. . . . always thought as highly of him as a poet as any perhaps of his countrymen may do. *To D. Williamson,*   VII. 27, 1844

32.* [Wordsworth spoke] with animation of Burns's poetry, but with qualified approval. . . . *Aubrey de Vere,* p. 99.   XII. 26, 1846

Burns (Works)

33.* . . . he had read it [*Poems, chiefly in the Scottish Dialect,* 1786] and admired many of the pieces very much. . . .
D. W. to Jane Pollard,   XII. 17, 1787

34.* He praised Burns for his introduction to *Tam o' Shanter.* He had given a poetical apology for drunkenness by bringing together all the circumstances which can serve to render excusable what is in itself disgusting, thus interesting our feelings and making us tolerant of what would otherwise be not endurable. . . . Wordsworth also praised the conclusion of *Death and Dr. Hornbook.* Wordsworth compared this with the abrupt prevention of the expected battle between Satan and the Archangel in Milton. . . .
H. C. R., i, 88-89.   V. 29, 1812

36. [*Tam o' Shanter.*] Who, but some impenetrable dunce or narrow-minded puritan in works of art, ever read without delight the picture which he has drawn of the convivial exaltation of the rustic adventurer, Tam o' Shanter? The poet fears not to tell the reader in the outset that his hero was a desperate and sottish drunkard, whose excesses were frequent as his opportunities. This reprobate sits down to his cups, while the storm is roaring, and heaven and earth are in confusion;—the night is driven on by song and tumultuous noise—laughter and jest thicken as the beverage improves upon the palate—conjugal fidelity archly bends to the service of general benevolence—selfishness is not absent, but wearing the mask of social cordiality—and, while these various elements of humanity are blended into one proud and happy composition of elated spirits, the anger of the tempest without doors

only heightens and sets off the enjoyment within.—I pity him who cannot perceive that, in all this, though these was no moral purpose, there is a moral effect.

> Kings may be blest, but Tam was glorious
> O'er a' the *ills* of life victorious.

What a lesson do these words convey of charitable indulgence for the vicious habits of the principal actor in this scene, and of those who resemble him!—Men who to the rigidly virtuous are objects almost of loathing, and whom therefore they cannot serve! The poet, penetrating the unsightly and disguesting surfaces of things, has unveiled with exquisite skill the finer ties of imagination and feeling, that often bind these beings to practices productive of so much unhappiness to themselves, and to those whom it is their duty to cherish;—and, as far as he puts the reader into possession of this intelligent sympathy, he qualifies him for exercising a salutary influence over the minds of those who are thus deplorably enslaved.

L. to Friend of Burns (Grosart, ii, 13-14). 1816

37. [*Death and Dr. Hornbook.*] Not less successfully does Burns avail himself of his own character and situation in society, to construct out of them a poetic self,—introduced as a dramatic personage—for the purpose of inspiriting his incidents, diversifying his pictures, recommending his opinions, and giving point to his sentiments. His brother can set me right if I am mistaken when I express a belief that, at the time when he wrote his story of *Death and Dr. Hornbook*, he had very rarely been intoxicated, or perhaps even much exhilarated by liquor. Yet how happily does he lead his reader into that track of sensations! and with what lively humour does he describe the disorder of his senses and the confusion of his understanding, put to test by a deliberate attempt to count the horns of the moon!

> But whether she had three or four
> He could na' tell.

Behold a sudden apparition that disperses this disorder, and in a moment chills him into possession of himself! Coming upon no more important mission than the grisly phantom was charged with, what mode of introduction could have been more efficient or appropriate? See Poetry 99.

L. to Friend of Burns (Grosart, ii, 14-15). 1816

38. [*Tam o' Shanter.*] See W. 119

39.* Burns's ' Scots wha hae ' is poor as a lyric composition.

C. W., Jr. (Grosart, iii, 465). *c.* 1827

40.* " Scots wha hae " " overrated!—trash!—stuff!—miserable inanity! without a thought—without an image! " etc. etc. etc.—then he recited the piece in a tone of unutterable scorn; and concluded with a *Da Capo* of " wretched stuff! " *Mrs. Hemans*, ii, 99. VI. 25, 1830

41. . . . less happy than the One [the daisy]
> That, by the unwilling ploughshare, died to prove
> The tender charm of poetry and love.

" There! said," 12-14. 1833

42. . . . a sight of Irwin and Lugar, which naebody sung till he named them in immortal verse. *To A. Cunningham,*   VI. 14, 1834

43. . . . many of Burns's [letters] are marvelous. See Crabbe 11

44.* [In "Scots wha hae" the only good line is "wha would fill a coward's grave."] *Whately,* p. 203.   *c.* 1840

45. How much is it to be regretted that, instead of writing such poems as the 'Holy Fair,' and others in which the religious observances of his country are treated with so much levity, and too often with indecency, Burns had not employed his genius in describing religion under the serious and affecting aspects it must so frequently take. *I. F. (Grosart,* iii, 69).   1843

46. He intended to reply, that Burns's lines to Fergusson would be a much more appropriate tribute than anything he could write; and he went on to say that Burns owed much to Fergusson, and that he had taken the plan of many of his poems from Fergusson, and the measure also. He did not think this at all detracted from the merit of Burns, for he considered it a much higher effort of genius to excel in degree, than to strike out what may be called an original poem.
Lady R. (Grosart, iii, 453).   XI, 1846

Busk, Hans

1. Your writings are not to be hurried over; this must plead my excuse for not having thanked you earlier for the 'Vestriad' . . . . The plan is more extensive than that of your former poems; and the execution equally good—I was particularly pleased with the descents into the submarine regions, and the infernal. These two Cantos I liked best; and the 'Council' is perhaps the least happy: in all councils there is something too quiescent—The serious passages, everywhere so gracefully interspersed, will excite a wish in many as they did in me, that you would favor the world with something in downright earnest—Your Portrait of Silene is eminently happy; and throughout the whole of your productions is an air of lively morality that most honourably distinguishes you among the multitude of candidates for poetic celebrity— . . . If you have erred at all in the movements of your couplets it is surely on the right side. . . .
I noticed in your Vestriad with particular pleasure, your flight in the Balloon. Rich in bold fictions as your Poem is, you were not called upon to make more of that vehicle than you have done—Judgement is shown in nothing more than the power to resist temptations of Fancy, especially where, as in your case, the gratification lies within easy reach.
[Not surprised that Busk liked *The Waggoner*] composing *widely* as you do from unborrowed feelings. . . . *To Busk,*   VII. 6, 1819

Byron, George Gordon (General Criticism)

1.* [Inferior poet to Blake.] *Remains,* p. 1.   V. 24, 1812

3.* . . . though cordially admitting his lordship's extraordinary power, and his claims as a man of genius, he yet firmly believed that his application of that power was reprehensible, perverted, and vicious.
Literary Veteran, iii, 144.   1814

6.* He reproached the author with the contradiction in the character of *The Corsair*, etc. *H. C. R.*, i, 168.   V. 28, 1815

6A.* Spoke of Byron's plagiarisms from him; the whole third canto of *Childe Harold* founded on his style and sentiments. The feeling of natural objects which is there expressed, not caught by B. from nature herself, but from him (Wordsworth), and spoiled in the transmission. *Tintern Abbey* the source of it all; from which same poem too the celebrated passage about Solitude, in the first canto of *Childe Harold*, is (he said) taken, with this difference, that what is naturally expressed by him, has been worked by Byron into a laboured and antithetical sort of declamation. *Moore's Diary*, p. 29.   X. 27, 1820

7. Southey . . . not quite so charitably disposed to Don Juan deceased as you evidently are . . . could not be expected from the Laureate, who, I will not say was his particular enemy, but who had certainly no friendship for him. Medwin makes a despicable Figure as the Salesman of so much trash. I do not believe there is a man living, from a Shoeblack at the corner of your street up to the Archbishop of Canterbury or the Lord Chancellor, of whose conversation so much worthless matter could be reported, with so little deserving to be remembered—as the result of an equal number of miscellaneous opportunities. Is this the fault of Lord B. or his Boswell? The truth is, I fear, that it may be pretty equally divided between them.

[Though Byron is dead], his spirit walks abroad, to do some good I hope, but a plaguy deal of mischief. I was much shocked when I heard of his death. . . . *To S. Rogers*,   I. 21, 1825

9.* He admitted the power of Byron in describing the workings of human passion, but denied that he knew anything of the beauties of Nature, or succeeded in describing them with fidelity. This he illustrated by examples. He spoke with deserved severity of Byron's licentiousness and contempt of religious decorum. He told us he thought the greatest of modern geniuses, had he given his powers a proper direction, and one decidedly superior to Byron, was Shelley, a young man, author of ' Queen Mab,' who died lately at Rome. *J. J. Taylor* (*Grosart*, iii, 503).   VII. 26, 1826

10.* Byron seems to me deficient in *feeling*. . . . I never read the ' English Bards' through. His critical prognostications have, for the most part, proved erroneous. *C. W., Jr.* (*Grosart*, iii, 462).   Summer, 1827

13. Byron and Scott are I am persuaded the only *popular* Writers in that line, perhaps the word ought rather to be that they are *fashionable* Writers. *To Moxon*,   VIII, 1833

14.* . . . looks on all things with an evil eye. *H. C. R.*, ii, 485.   I. 29, 1836

15. . . . but I was not a little glad when he gained the shore, though Shelley and Byron—one of them at least who seemed to have courted agitation from every quarter—would have probably rejoiced in such a situation. *Grosart*, iii, 87.   1843 [K.]

15A. See Literature 15; Poetry 61; Gillies 1, 6; Godwin, C. Grace 1; Hazlitt 2; *Liberal, The* 1; Scott, W. 7

16.   The lines following, 'Nor do words,' &c. ["Not in the lucid intervals," *Oxf. W.*, pp. 454-55], were written with Lord Byron's character as a poet before me, and that of others among his contemporaries, who wrote under like influences. *Grosart*, iii, 146.   1843 [K.]

17.*   . . . I could show you that Lord Byron was not so great a poet as you think him to be. . . .

I am pleased to find . . . that you preserve your muse chaste, and free from rank and corrupt passion. Lord Byron degraded poetry in that respect. Men's hearts are bad enough. Poetry should refine and purify their natures; not make them worse. [Cooper argues that] *Don Juan* was descriptive, and that Shakespeare had also described bad passions in anatomising the human heart, which was one of the great vocations of the poet.

But there is always a moral lesson, [W. said] . . . in Shakespeare's pictures. You feel he is not stirring man's passions for the sake of awakening the brute in them: the pure and the virtuous are always presented in high contrast; but the other riots in corrupt pictures, evidently with the enjoyment of the corruption. *Thomas Cooper*, p. 291.   1846

18.   You do me justice; I never spoke with acrimony of Lord Byron, notwithstanding the noble poet's public poetical attacks—perhaps the worst, because the most enduring of all.   His review of my poems was a very serious one, but Lord B. laughed at it, and thus disarmed me if I had been inclined to be angry—You say that Prof. Wilson declared 'that it was Wordsworth who first taught Byron to look at a mountain'—but I must disclaim the honour of being his lordship's poetical guide—notwithstanding the dictum of Christopher North. *To ?*,   III. 27, 1847

Byron (Works)

19.*   Wordsworth allowed him power, but denied his style to be English. Of his moral qualities we think the same.   He adds that there is insanity in Lord Byron's family, and that he believes Lord Byron to be somewhat cracked. *H. C. R.*, i, 85.   V. 24, 1812

21.   Let me only say one word upon Lord B.   The man is insane; and will probably end his career in a madhouse.   I never thought him anything else since his first appearance in public.   The verses on his private affairs excite in me less indignation than pity.   The latter copy is the Billingsgate of Bedlam.—Your Correspondent A. S. has written, begging his pardon, a very foolish Letter upon the Verses that appeared in the Chronicle—I have not seen them, but I have no doubt that what he praises so highly is contemptible as a work of Art, like the Ode to the Emperor Nap.—You yourself, appear to me to labour under some delusion as to the merits of Lord B's Poetry, and treat those wretched verses, The farewell, with far too much respect.   They are disgusting in sentiment, and in execution contemptible. 'Though my many faults deface me' etc.   Can worse doggerel be written than such a stanza?   One verse is commendable, 'All my madness none can know,' 'Sine dementia nullus Phoebus'; but what a difference between the amabillis insania of inspiration, and the fiend-like exasperation of these wretched productions.   It avails nothing to attempt to heap up indignation

upon the heads of those whose talents are extolled in the same breath. The true way of dealing with these men is to shew that they want genuine power. That talents they have, but that these talents are of a *mean* order; and that their productions have no solid basis to rest upon. Allow them to be men of high genius, and they have gained their point and will go on triumphing in their iniquity; demonstrate them to be what in truth they are, in all essential, Dunces, and I will not say that you will reform them; but by abating their pride you will strip their wickedness of the principal charm in their own eyes. I have read your late Champions with much pleasure. *To J. Scott,*   IV. 18, 1816

22. Have you heard of the attacks of Byron upon him and his answer? his L^dsp has lost as much by this affair as S. [Southey] has gained, whose letter was circulated in almost every newspaper in England. *To Landor,*   IV. 20, 1822

23. . . . I have not, nor ever had, a single poem of Lord Byron's by me, except the Lara . . . and therefore could not quote anything illustrative of his poetical obligations to me. As far as I am acquainted with his works, they are most apparent in the 3rd canto of Childe Harold; not so much in particular expressions, though there is no want of these, as in the tone (*assumed* rather than natural) of enthusiastic admiration of Nature, and a sensibility to her influences. Of my writings you need not read more than the blank verse poem on the river Wye to be convinced of this. . . . Nothing lowered my opinion of Byron's poetical integrity so much as to see 'pride of place' carefully noted as a quotation from Macbeth, in a work where contemporaries, from whom he had drawn by wholesale, were not adverted to. It is mainly on this account that he deserves the severe chastisement which you, or some one else, will undoubtedly one day give him, and may have done already, as I see by advertisement the subject has been treated in the 'London Mag.'

I remember one impudent instance of his thefts. In Raymond's translation of Coxe's travels in Switzerland, with notes of the translator, is a note with these words, speaking of the fall of Schaffhausen: 'Lewy, descendant avec moi sur cet échafaud, tomba à genoux en s'écriant: *Voilà un enfer d'eau!*' This expression is taken by Byron and beaten out unmercifully into two stanzas, which a critic in the Quarterly Review is foolish enough to praise. They are found in the 4th canto of Childe Harold. Whether the obligation is acknowledged or not I do not know, having seen nothing of it but in quotation.

Thank you for your parallels [in Taylor's 'Recent Poetical Plagiarisms']; I wished for them on Mr. Rogers' account, who is making a collection of similar things relating to Gray. There are few of yours, I think, which one could swear to as conscious obligations—the subject has three branches—accidental coincidences without any communication of the subsequent author; unconscious imitations; and deliberate conscious obligations. The cases are numerous in which it is impossible to distinguish these by anything inherent in the resembling passage, but external aid may be called in with advantage where we happen to know the circumstances of an author's life, and the direction of his studies. *To Henry Taylor,*   XII. 26, 1823

23A.   . . . You will probably see Gifford, the editor of the *Quarterly Review*. Tell him from me, if you think proper, that every true-born Englishman disallows the pretensions of the *Review* to the character of a faithful defender of the institutions of the country, while it leaves that infamous publication, *Don Juan*, unbranded. I do not mean by a formal critique, for it is not worth it—it would also tend to keep it in memory—but by some decisive words of reprobation, both as to the damnable tendency of such works, and as to the despicable quality of the powers requisite for their production.

What avails it to hunt down Shelley and leave Byron untouched? I am persuaded that *Don Juan* will do more harm to the English character than anything of our time; not so much as a book, but thousands, who will be ashamed to have it in that shape, will fatten upon choice bits of it in the shape of extracts.   *To ?* [De Sel. places in the group of 1826.   See *L. Y.*, p. 254.]   *c.* 1826

24.* Lord Byron has spoken severely of my compositions.   However faulty they may be, I do not think that I ever could have prevailed upon myself to print such lines as he has done; for instance,

> ' I stood at Venice on the Bridge of Sighs,
> A palace and a prison on each hand.'
>
> [*Childe Harold*, IV. i. 1-2]

Some person ought to write a critical review, analysing Lord Byron's language, in order to guard others against him in these respects.
C. W., Jr. (*Grosart*, iii, 462-63).   summer, 1827

24A. [Quillinan's poem *Mischief*, suggested by *Beppo*, contains lines] too pretty and pure to have been found in such company. [See Burns 26A.]
W. and Dora to E. Q.,   VII. 4, 1831

25.*   . . . Wordsworth used to say that he was too indolent to take due pains. *H. C. R.*, i, 417.   X. 30, 1832

26.   . . . that execrable Lampoon of Lord Byron [' To Lord Thurlow ']. What a monster is a Man of Genius whose heart is perverted!
To Miss Kinnaird,   I. 30, 1833

27. I saw Byron's execrable Lampoon [' To Lord Thurlow ']—what an unhappy mortal he was. . . . *To C. R.* (*Corr. C. R.*, i, 237),   V. 5, 1833

28.* Wordsworth related to me this evening the origin of Lord Byron's animosity to him. Wordsworth wrote a letter to a lady warning her against hoping for public favour as a poetess on account of her sensibility and true poetic feeling, and remarked that the only two poets of the day who enjoyed popularity were men *one of whom had no feeling*, and the other had none but perverted feelings. *H. C. R.*, i, 428-9.   VI. 17, 1833

29.*   Wordsworth says that Bunsen has informed him that from the particular friends of Byron he has learned that Lord Byron had an impression that he was the offspring of a demon. In a moment of disease he may have suffered such a thought to seize his imagination. [The last sentence seems to be Robinson's comment.] *H. C. R.*, ii, 521.   V. 17, 1837

30.* . . . of Wordsworth's expressing his disgust at the unhandsome treatment of the *minor* Lord poet by the *Edinburgh Review.* . . .
H. C. R., ii, 736.   [? (before 1834)]

31.* Do you call that [*The Prisoner of Chillon*] beautiful? . . . Why, it's nonsense. What means ' Eternal Spirit of the Chainless mind '?
Memoirs of E. V. Kenealy, p. 239.   *c.* 1840

Cædmon: [The Cædmonian School]

1. [*Paraphrase.*] See Poetry 103

Calderón, Pedro. See Rousseau 1

Camoëns, Luis. See Faber 4

Campbell, Thomas

1. See Blake 1; Hamilton, W. R. 7; Rogers 7; W. 329

3.* Wordsworth spoke with great contempt of Campbell as a poet, and illustrated his want of truth and poetic sense in his imagery by a close analysis of a celebrated passage in *The Pleasures of Hope,* ' Where Andes, giant of the Western star,' etc. [Part I, ll. 56-9], showing the whole to be a mere jumble of discordant images, meaning, in fact, nothing, nor conveying very distinct impression, it being first uncertain who or what is the giant, and who or what is the star. Then the giant is made to hold a meteor-standard and to sit on a throne of clouds and look (it is not apparent for what) on half the world. Gray's line, speaking of the bard's beard, which ' streamed like a meteor to the troubled air,' Wordsworth also considered as ridiculous, and both passages he represented to be unmeaningly stolen from a fine line by Milton, in which a spear is for its brightness only compared to a meteor.
H. C. R., i, 90.   V. 31, 1812

5.* Of Campbell, as a poet, he seemed to think very lightly, and blended his name with the nameless productions of other modern writers, whose extravagant fables, and guilty heroes, would be hid in oblivion in the next age, when the glare of novelty was worn off, and men found out that those conceptions were unnatural. *Brothers Wiffen,* p. 38.   1819

8.* [Campbell had] stolen his ' There is a change ' [*Oxf. W.,* p. 111].
Aubrey de Vere, p. 72 (see also *Lady R., Grosart,* iii, 445).   IV. 28, 1841

Canning, George

1.* [Had] no mind at all. *Letters of Scott,* ii, 339.   VIII. 25, 1825
2. See Burke 3A; W. 394

Carleton, George

1. Carleton's *Memoirs* . . . is a most interesting work.
To De Quincey,   III. 27, 1809

Carlyle, Thomas

1.* [Carlyle's critical articles and translations.] He said he thought him sometimes insane. . . . wrote most obscurely. He was clever and deep, but he defied the sympathy of every body. Even Coleridge wrote more clearly, though he had always wished Coleridge would write more to be understood.
English Traits, pp. 21-2.   VIII. 28, 1833

2.* Thinking Wordsworth, who could not forgive his not writing English, unjust to Carlyle on the score of language, I sent him Carlyle's admirable Petition to the House of Commons on behalf of the Copyright Bill. Wordsworth could not but praise it highly. He concluded his letter. 'And as to the style, *it is well calculated to startle dull men into attention.*'
H. C. R., ii, 542.   XI. 25, 1837

3.* . . . the Wordsworths . . . cannot endure it [*History of the French Revolution*]. H. C. R., ii, 560.   XII. 30, 1838

5.* . . . Wordsworth cannot enjoy Carlyle.
H. C. R., ii, 563.   I. 7, 1839

6.* . . . is intolerant of such innovations [in style] And cannot & will not read C. *C. R. to T. R. (Corr. C. R.,* i, 377),   I. 19, 1839

7.* I read with deep interest the third volume of Carlyle, of whom Wordsworth pronounces a harsh judgment. It is not only his style that he condemns, but his *inhumanity.* He says there is a want of due sympathy with mankind. Scorn and irony are the feeling and tone throughout.
H. C. R., ii, 566.   I. 26, 1839

8. Many thanks for the Examiner; it is well that the Copyright Question should be looked at from different points of view. Carlyle's petition and the extract from Landor's are both characteristic—Carlyle racy and may startle certain dull persons into attention to the subject—but the expression has often too much the air of burlesque, for my taste.
To C. R. (Corr. C. R., i, 382),   IV. 10, 1839

9.* How could Carlyle call *him* [Burns] a *hero*, who was self-degraded and destroyed to a degree that made his life a continual misery? But who would mind what Carlyle says, when he called Shakespeare and Milton 'things of shreds and patches?' True, he now says Shakespeare is the first of human intellects. But who can heed every such praise from the same judgment which could rashly and vainly and presumptuously endeavour to load the memory of such minds with such poor censure? Carlyle is an enthusiast, and nothing more; if pressed about his character, he [W.] would say he was less, or worse, than an ordinary enthusiast, because he is an audacious, inconsistent, and unlearned one. . . . 'And I,' said W., 'Say that he does not understand English Literature.' [See Burns 26.]
A Day with Wordsworth, pp. 736-7.   VII. 31, 1841

10.* When asked whether he would like to go hear Lord Monteagle (Mr. Spring Rice), Mr. Whewell, and Mr. Carlyle lecture on "Astronomy, Universal Philanthropy, &c." "Go!" said he, "I would as soon go to see so many carrion crows." *A Day with Wordsworth*, p. 740.   VIII. 31, 1841

11. See Emerson 1; Style 68

13.* [Carlyle], who is a pest to the English tongue, [cannot write English]. *English Traits*, 294 and note 1. III, 1848

Carter, Elizabeth

1.* The first verses from which he remembered to have received great pleasure, were Miss Carter's ' Poem on Spring.' . . .
Justice Coleridge (*Grosart*, iii, 426). IX. 22, 1836

Cary, Henry F.

1.* . . . I think his translation of Dante a great national work.
Recollections of Rogers, p. 282 note. *c.* 1825

Catullus

1.* Catallus translated literally from the Greek; succeeding Roman writers did not so. . . . *C. W., Jr.* (*Grosart*, iii, 458). *c.* 1827

Cavendish, Margaret. See under Newcastle, Duchess of

Cervantes. See Faber 4; Rousseau 1

Chalmers, Alexander. See Anthologies 3; Beaumont, Sir John 4

Chambers, Robert

1. . . . Chambers applied to me for permission to make extracts from my poems for his sickly-paddy [Chambers's *Encyclopaedia of English Literature*], as Coleridge used to call that class of publication.
To Moxon, XII, 1843

2. As to the Biographical Notices [Chambers's *Encyclopaedia of English Literature*], they are grossly erroneous; in particular, it is asserted that I was one of the Pantisocratic Society, though it has been publicly declared by Mr Southey that the project was given up years before I was acquainted either with himself or Mr Coleridge or any one belonging to the Scheme. One-half, at least, of what is said of Mr Coleridge, as to the facts of his life, is more or less erroneous; and, drolly enough, he marries me to one of my Cousins! He also affirms that my parents were able to send me to college though one died more than ten years before I went thither, and the other four; but these errors are trifles, the other, as to the Pantisocracy, is a piece of reprehensible negligence. *To Moxon*, IV. 20, 1844

3.* . . . Chambers's *Encyclopaedia of Literature*—a worthless book of extracts, chronologically arranged, in Wordsworth's opinion.
H. C. R., ii, 656. I. 7, 1846

Chapman, [?]

1. Mr Chapman's Verses give indications of a very poetical mind. He must much be deplored by all who knew him—are you aware that there are several lines word for word or nearly so from Verses of mine—the Author

being probably altogether unconscious of it. This gave me pleasure as a proof how familiar this interesting young Man must have been with my Poems. *To T. Powell,*   III, 1841

Chatterton, Thomas

1.   I thought of Chatterton, the marvellous Boy,
                  The sleepless Soul that perished in his pride. . . .
                  Resolution and Independence, 43-44.   1802

2. [*Ossian* influenced literature only in Chatterton's case.] See Macpherson 2

3. I would readily assist, according to my means, in erecting a Monument to the memory of Chatterton, who with transcendent genius was cut off by his own hand while he was yet a Boy in years; this, could he have anticipated the tribute, might have soothed his troubled spirit; as an expression of general belief in the existence of those powers which he was too impatient and too proud to develop. At all events it might prove an awful, and a profitable warning. *To J. F. Mitchell,*   IV. 21, 1819

4. . . . Thomson, Collins, and Dyer, had more poetic Imagination than any of their Contemporaries, unless we reckon Chatterton of that age—I do not name Pope, for he stands alone. . . . *To Dyce,*   I. 12, 1829

5.* . . . Chatterton was the most marvellous genius in his opinion; that he had produced greater fruits of poetic genius than any other man of his age. . . . *Maurice,* i, 199.   1836

6.* . . . Chatterton would have probably proved one of the very greatest poets in our language. *H. C. R.,* ii, 610.   I. 16, 1842

6A. See Cottle, J. 3; Homer 13

7. [Chatterton's] genius was universal; he excelled in every species of composition, so remarkable an instance of precocious talent being quite unexampled. His prose was excellent, and his powers of picturesque description and satire great. *H. C. R.,* ii, 611.   I. 17, 1842

8. Chatterton says of Freedom, ' Upon her head wild weeds were spread,' and depend upon it, if ' the marvellous boy ' had undertaken to give Flora a garland, he would have preferred what we are apt to call weeds to garden-flowers. True taste has an eye for both.
I. F. (*Grosart,* iii, 180).   1843

Chaucer, Geoffrey (General Criticism)

1. . . . the affecting parts of Chaucer are almost always expressed in language pure and universally intelligible to this day. [This note may be Coleridge's; see Language, Chaucerian 1.] *Pref. L. B.,* p. 935, n. 1.   1800

2.   Beside the pleasant Mill of Trompington
                  I laughed with Chaucer in the hawthorn shade;
                  Heard him . . . tell his tales
                  Of amorous passion.
                  Prel., iii, 275-78.   1804-39

3. . . . has rightly been called the morning star of her [England's] literature. . . . *Ans. to Mathetes* (*Grosart*, i, 314). I. 4, 1810

4. See Drama 15; Anderson 1; Barrett, E. 3; Dryden 2; Johnson 11; Shakespeare 24; W. 266, 268

5.* When I began to give myself up to the profession of a poet for life, I was impressed with a conviction, that there were four English poets whom I must have continually before me as examples—Chaucer, Shakespeare, Spenser, and Milton. These I must study, and equal *if I could*; and I need not think of the rest. *C. W., Jr.* (*Grosart*, iii, 459-60). *c.* 1827

6.* . . . Wordsworth, when he resolved to be a poet, feared competition only with Chaucer, Spenser, Shakespeare, and Milton.
H. C. R., ii, 776. [*c.* 1827]

7. [Chaucer's great works composed late in life.]
To T. Talfourd, XI. 28, 1836

8. I extol Chaucer and others, because the world at large knows little or nothing of their merits. *Letters K.*, iii, 121. 1836 or after

10. Chaucer was one of the greatest poets the world has ever seen. He is certainly, at times, in his comic tales indecent, but he is never, as far as I know, insidiously or openly voluptuous, much less would a stronger term, which would apply to some popular writers of our own day apply to him. He had towards the female sex as exquisite and pure feelings as ever the heart of man was blessed with, and has expressed them as beautifully in the language of his age, as ever man did. *To I. Fenwick* (p. 1002), 1840

11. He is a mighty Genius as you well know, and not lightly to be dealt with. For my own part, I am not prepared to incur any responsibility on the account of this project, which I much approve of, beyond furnishing my own little Quota; which I almost fear now must be confined to permission to reprint the Prioress's Tale, if thought worth while; and the Cuckoo and Nightingale which is ready. . . . It [W.'s MS] contained also, by the bye, a Translation of two Books of Ariosto's Orlando, and this and other of its contents, I should be sorry to lose altogether.

My *approbation* of the Endeavour to tempt people to read Chaucer by making a part of him intelligible to the unlettered, and tuneable to modern ears, will be sufficiently apparent by my own little Contributions to the intended Volume. But *beyond this* I do not wish to do any thing; or rather it could not be right that I should. Little matters in Composition hang about and teaze me awkwardly, and at improper times when I ought to be taking my meals or asleep. On this account, however reluctantly, I must *decline* even *looking over* the MSS either of yourself or your Friends. I am sure I should find some thing which I should attempt to change, and probably after a good deal of pains make the passage no better, perhaps worse—This is my infirmity, I have employed scores of hours during the course of my life in retouching favorite passages of favorite Authors, of which labour not a trace remains nor ought to remain—

. . . You could prefix an advertisement expressing how the Attempt came to be made, and upon what principles it was conducted.
To T. Powell, I. 18, 1840

12. . . . revising some verses of Chaucer, which I modernized some years ago—intending them as a gift to Mr. Powell a friend of mine, who in conjunction with some literary acquaintances, is engaged in doing other things of this Author upon my principle; as examplified in the Prioresses Tale. My love & reverence for Chaucer are unbounded, & I should like for the sake of unlearned readers to see the greatest part of his works done in the same way.   Dryden & Pope have treated these originals admirably in a manner of their own, which tho' good in itself is not Chaucers.

To C. R. (*Corr. C. R.*, i, 397-8),   I. 23, 1840

13.   Mr Powell . . . has some thought of preparing for Publication some portions of Chaucer modernized so far and no farther than is done in my treatment of the Prioress's Tale, that will in fact be his model. He will have Coadjutors, among whom I believe will be Mr Leigh Hunt, a man as capable of doing the work well as any living Author. I have placed at . . . Mr Powell's disposal in addition to the Prioress's Tale, three other pieces which I did long ago, but revised the other day. They are the Manciple's Tale, The Cuckoo and the Nightingale and 24 Stanzas of Troilus and Cressida. This I have done mainly out of my love and reverence for Chaucer, in hopes that whatever may be the merit of Mr Powell's attempt, the attention of other Writers may be drawn to the subject; and a work hereafter be produced by different pens which will place the treasures of one of the greatest of Poets within the reach of multitudes, which now they are not. . . . Had the thing been suggested to me by any number of competent Persons 20 years ago I would have undertaken the Editorship, done much more myself, and endeavoured to improve the several contributions where they seemed to require it.   *To Moxon,*   II. 21, 1840

14. . . . objections made to my publishing the specimens of Chaucer, nevertheless I have yielded to the judgments of others, and have not sent more than the Cuckoo and Nightingale. . . . The large and increasing instant demand for literature of a certain quality, holds out the strongest temptation to men, who could do better, writing below themselves, to suit the taste of the superficial Many.   What we want is not books to catch purchasers, Readers not worth a moment's notice, not light but solid matter, not things treated in a broad and coarse, or at best a superficial way, but profound or refined works comprehensive of human interests through time as well as space. Kotzebue was acted and read at once from Cadiz to Moscow; what is become of him now? But Tegg has the impudence to affirm, that another Paradise Lost, or a poem as good, would at once produce £10,000 from Mr Murray and others. ' Credat Judaeus Apella.' Paradise Lost is indeed bought because people for their own credit must now have it.   But how few, how very few, read it; when it is read by the multitude, it is almost exclusively not as a poem, but a religious Book.   *To E. Q.,*   III. 9, 1840

15.   Are you sure that it would answer to modernize the *whole* of Chaucer? I fear much would prove *tedious* and other parts to be objectionable upon the other grounds which I have formerly adverted to. You are welcome to my Cuckoo and Nightingale and to the small part of the Troilus and Cressida, and were my own judgment only to be consulted to the ' Manciples

tale,' but there is a delicacy in respect to this last among some of my Friends which though I cannot sympathize with it I am bound to respect. Therefore in regard to that piece you will consider my decision as at present suspended.
To T. Powell, V. 1, 1840

16.   Taking for granted that by every one indelicacy would be avoided; and also extreme lengthiness, to which Chaucer is sometimes prone, I felt that there was no call for my interference, and that it was best to leave every one to his own choice. On that letter therefore I have only to express my satisfaction that you are pleased with the contributions, especially with the Prologue which always appeared to me the most difficult thing to deal with. . . . my communications, given *solely* out of regard for you and reverence for Chaucer, should appear as unostentatiously as possible. . . .
To T. Powell, X. 16, 1840

17.   The attempt [W.'s translations from Chaucer] originated, I believe, in the Specimen I gave some years since, of the Prioresses Tale, and has no other object but to tempt the mere modern Reader to recur to the original.
To John Wilson, I. 11, 1841

Chaucer (Works)

19.   [This quotation is from Wordsworth's own *Selections from Chaucer Modernized*, stanza, IX. See *Knight*, vii, 59 n.]

> " Sweet is the holiness of Youth "—so felt
> Time-honoured Chaucer speaking through that Lay
> By which the Prioress beguiled the way,
> And many a Pilgrim's rugged heart did melt.
> Hadst thou, loved Bard! whose spirit often dwelt
> In the clear land of vision, but foreseen
> King, child, and seraph, blended in the mien
> Of pious Edward kneeling as he knelt
> In meek and simple infancy, what joy
> For universal Christendom had thrilled
> Thy heart! what hopes inspired thy genius, skilled,
> (O great Precursor, genuine morning Star)
> The lucid shafts of reason to employ,
> Piercing the Papal darkness from afar!
> 2 *Ecc. Sonn.*, xxxi, 1-14. 1821

20.   I am glad that you enter so warmly into the Chaucerian project, and that Mr L. Hunt is disposed to give his valuable aid to it. For myself I cannot do more than I offered, to place at your disposal the Prioresses Tale, already published, the Cuckoo and the Nightingale, the Manciples Tale, and I rather think but I cannot just now find it, a small portion of the Troilus and Cressida—you ask my opinion about that Poem—speaking from a recollection only of many years past, I should say it would be found too long and probably tedious. The Knights Tale is also very long, but tho' Dryden has executed it, in his own way observe, with great spirit and harmony, he has suffered so much of the simplicity, and with that of the beauty, and occasional pathos of the original to escape, that I should be pleased to hear that a new version

should be attempted upon my principle by some competent Person. It would delight me to read every part of Chaucer over again, for I reverence and admire him above measure, with a view to your work, but my eyes will not permit me to do so—who will undertake the Prologue to the C. Tales? For your publication that is indispensible, and I fear it will prove very difficult. It is written, as you know, in the couplet measure, and therefore I have nothing to say upon its metre—but in respect to the Poems in stanza, neither in the Prioresses Tale, nor in the Cuckoo and Nightingale have I kept to the rule of the original as to the form and number and position of the *rhymes*, thinking it enough if I kept the same number of lines in each stanza, and this I think is all that is necessary—and all that can be done without sacrificing the substance of sense, too often, to the mere form of sound.

To T. Powell (p. 992),　　　　　　　　　　　　　　　　　late 1839

21.　　Tell Mr. Quillinan, I think he has taken rather a *narrow* view of the spirit of the Manciple's Tale, especially as concerns its *morality*. The formal prosing at the end and the selfishness that pervades it flows from the genius of Chaucer, mainly as characteristic of the narrator whom he describes in the Prologue as eminent for shrewdness and clever Prudence. The main lesson, and the most important one, is inculcated as a Poet ought chiefly to inculcate his lessons, not formally, but by implication; as when Phoebus in a transport of passion slays a wife whom he loved so dearly. How could the mischief of telling truth, merely because it *is* truth, be more feelingly exemplified. The Manciple himself is not, in his understanding, conscious of this; but his heart dictates what was natural to be felt and the moral, without being intended forces itself more or less upon every Reader. Then how vividly is impressed the mischief of jealous vigilance and how truly and touchingly in contrast with the world's judgments are the transgressions of a woman in a low rank of life and one in high estate placed on the same level, treated. *To Dora*,　　　　　　　　　　　　　　　　　　　　spring, 1840

22.　　. . . but tho' I much admire the genius of Chaucer as displayed in this performance, I could not place my version at the disposal of the Editor, as I deemed the subject somewhat too indelicate for pure taste to be offered to the world at this time of day. Mr Horne has much hurt this publication by not abstaining from the Reeve's Tale—this, after making all allowance for the rude manners of Chaucer's age is intolerable, & by indispensable softening down the incidents he has killed the spirit of that humour, gross & farcical, that pervades the original. When the work was first mentioned to me, I protested as strongly as possible against admitting any coarseness or indelicacy —so that my conscience is clear of countenancing aught of that kind. So great is my admiration of Chaucer's genius, & so profound my reverence for him as an instrument in the hands of Providence for spreading the light of literature thro' his native land that notwithstanding the defects & faults in this Publication, I am glad of it, as a mean for making many acquainted with the original, who would otherwise be ignorant of every thing about him, but his name. *Reed*, 43.　　　　　　　　　　　　　　　　　　　I. 13, 1841

23.　　. . . glad to learn the Chaucer is doing so well . . . I am much pleased with the execution in general. Mr. Horne is particularly successful;

but in my opinion he ought not to have meddled with the Reve's Tale; it is far too gross for the present age, and, in consequence of the necessity of softening it down, the humour, such as it is, has evaporated. The Franklin's tale is as well done as need or can be. *To T. Powell,*   III, 1841

Chesterfield, Philip Dormer Stanhope, Fourth Earl of

1. . . . I will content myself with placing a conceit (ascribed to Lord Chesterfield) in contrast with a passage from the *Paradise Lost*:—

> The dews of the evening most carefully shun,
> They are the tears of the sky for the loss of the sun.

After the transgression of Adam, Milton, with other appearances of sympathizing Nature, thus marks the immediate consequence,

> Sky lowered, and, muttering thunder, some sad drops
> Wept at completion of the mortal sin.

The associating link is the same in each instance: Dew and rain, not distinguishable from the liquid substance of tears, are employed as indications of sorrow. A flash of surprise is the effect in the former case; a flash of surprise, and nothing more; for the nature of things does not sustain the combination. In the latter, the effects from the act, of which there is this immediate consequence and visible sign, are so momentous, that the mind acknowledges the justice and reasonableness of the sympathy in nature so manifested; and the sky weeps drops of water as if with human eyes, as ' Earth had before trembled from her entrails, and Nature given a second groan.' See Fancy 14

Pref. 1815, p. 958.   1815

2. See Style 68

Chiabrera

1. [Faults in Chiabrera's epitaphs.] See Pope 18

2. A similar sentiment [see Pope 19] is expressed with appropriate dignity in an epitaph by Chiabrera, where he makes the Archbishop of Albino say of himself, that he was

> —smitten by the great ones of the world,
> But did not fall; for virtue braves all shocks,
> Upon herself resting immoveably.

' So firm yet soft, so strong yet so refined': These intellectual operations (while they can be conceived of as operations of intellect at all, for in fact one half of the process is mechanical, words doing their own work and one half of the line manufacturing the rest) remind me of the motions of a Posture-master, or of a man balancing a sword upon his finger, which must be kept from falling at all hazards. ' The saint sustained it, but the woman died.' Let us look steadily at this antithesis: the *saint*, that is her soul strengthened by religion, supported the anguish of her disease with patience and resignation; but the *woman*, that is her body (for if anything else is meant by the word woman, it contradicts the former part of the proposition and the passage is nonsense), was overcome. Why was not this simply ex-

pressed; without playing with the Reader's fancy, to the delusion and dis-honour of his understanding, by a trifling epigrammatic point? But alas! ages must pass away before men will have their eyes open to the beauty and majesty of Truth, and will be taught to venerate Poetry no further than as she is a handmaid pure as her mistress—the noblest handmaid in her train!
Epitaph 2 (Grosart, ii, 58-9).   1810

3. Observe how exquisitely this [ideal treatment of the character of the deceased in an epitaph] is exemplified in the one beginning ' Pause, courteous stranger! Balbi supplicates,' . . . This composition is a perfect whole, there is nothing arbitrary or mechanical, but it is an organized body, of which the members are bound together by a common life and are all justly proportioned.
Epitaph 3 (Grosart, ii, 69).   1810

4. [Faults in his epitaphs] . . . if he had abstained from the introduc-tion of heathen mythology, of which he is lavish—an inexcusable fault for an inhabitant of a Christian country, yet admitting of some palliation in an Italian who treads classic soil and has before his eyes the ruins of the temples . . .—had omitted also some uncharacteristic particulars, and had not on some occasions forgotten that truth is the soul of passion, he would have left his Readers little to regret. I do not mean to say that higher and nobler thoughts may not be found in sepulchral inscriptions than his contain; but he understood his work, the principles upon which he composed are just. The Reader of *The Friend* has had proofs of this: one [see *Grosart*, ii, 70] shall be given of his mixed manner, exemplifying some of the points in which he has erred. . . . This epitaph is not without some tender thoughts, but a comparison of it with the one upon the youthful Pozzobonelli (see *Friend*) [" Not without hearing grief," *Oxf. W.*, p. 575] will more clearly shew that Chiabrera has here neglected to ascertain whether the passions expressed were in kind and degree a dispensation of reason, or at least com-modities issued under her licence and authority.
Epitaph 3 (Grosart, ii, 70).   1810

5. [Epitaphs on Raphael and on Tasso. In Chiabrera's epitaphs] the Reader is generally made acquainted with the moral and intellectual excellence which distinguished them by a brief history of the course of their lives or a selection of events and circumstances, and thus they are individualized; but in the two other instances, namely those of Tasso and Raphael, he enters into no particulars, but contents himself with four lines expressing one senti-ment upon the principle laid down in the former part [see *Epitaph 1 (Oxf. W.*, p. 932)] of this discourse, where the subject of an epitaph is a man of prime note.

> Torquato Tasso rests within this tomb;
> This figure weeping from her inmost heart
> Is Poesy: from such impassioned grief
> Let every one conclude what this man was.

Epitaph 3 (Grosart, ii, 70-1).   1810

6. The epitaph which Chiabrera composed for himself [" O Thou who," *Oxf. W.*, pp. 572-3] has also an appropriate brevity and is distinguished for

its grandeur, the sentiment being the same as that which the Reader has before seen so happily enlarged upon. *Epitaph 3* (*Grosart*, ii, 71).   1810

7. See W. 274

8. The Chiabrera [works of] is a great acquisition—

To C. R. (*Corr. C. R.*, i, 298),   IV, 1836

9.   A pure poetic Spirit—as the breeze,
            Mild—as the verdure, fresh—the sunshine, bright—
            Thy gentle Chiabrera!—not a stone,
            Mural or level with the trodden floor,
            In Church or Chapel, if my curious quest
            Missed not the truth, retains a single name
            Of young or old, warrior, or saint, or sage,
            To whose dear memories his sepulchral verse
            Paid simple tribute. . . .
            Yet in his page the records of that worth
            Survive, uninjured;—glory then to words. . . .
            Aquapendente, 234-42; 248-49.   1837

Chorley, Henry F.

1. In Mr Chorley's [*The Authors of England, a series of Medallion Portraits of Modern Literary Characters engraved by Achille Colas, with Illustrative Notices*, by Henry F. Chorley, 1838. (Preface dated Oct. 1837).] account of me in his ' living Authors ' just published, there are several gross errors—among others he says my appointment as Distributor of stamps took place no less than 11 years after the date he assigns it. [W. means that his appointment took place eleven years after the date to which Chorley assigns it. Chorley gives it as 1803. De Sel.] *To S. C. Hall*,   XII. 23, 1837

Christian Keepsake, The

1.   Accept my thanks for your valuable and elegant present, the Christian Keepsake; the purpose of the Work is excellent; and the execution, as far as I have seen, highly creditable to those concerned in it. I must confine my notice however, to the Memoir of that great and good Man, Thomas Clarkson: it is carefully compiled and the matter, as a piece of Biography, judiciously proportioned; if your limits would have allowed, the narrative might have been profitable extended, but my long and intimate acquaintance with Mr Clarkson enables me to say, that *any* report of his labours and perils in accomplishing his part of that great Work, the Abolition of the Slave Trade, must on account of his modesty and humility of mind fall very far short of the truth. *To the Ed. of ' The Christian Keepsake,'*   XII. 3, 1846

Cibber, Colley. See Dryden 19

Cicero

1. See Pope 20

2.*   Wordsworth had spoken of Cicero's Letters to Atticus as ' supremely interesting ' even in Dr. Heberden's English Translation. . . .
H. C. R., ii, 564.   I. 15, 1839

Clarke, James

1. . . . Clark's " Survey of the Lakes " . . . may amuse the reader
[W.'s note to *An Evening Walk*, 179-90; see *Knight*, i, 19, for the passage
from Clark's *Survey*]. *Oxf. W.*, p. 595 n. 2.   1793

Clarkson, Thomas

1.* Wm has read most of Mr. Clarkson's book [*A Portraiture of Quaker-
ism*] and has been much pleased, but he complains of the latter volume
being exceedingly disfigured by perpetual use of the word *tract*.
D. W. to C. Clarkson,   VII. 23, 1806

2.* William, I believe, made a few remarks upon paper, but he had not
time for much criticism, and in fact having only one perusal of the work
[*The History of the African Slave-Trade*] he was too much interested.
D. W. to C. Clarkson,   VIII. 30, 1807

3.* My Brother desires me especially to return his sincere thanks for the
letter contained in the Suffolk Chronicle. He was exceedingly pleased with
it, and thinks the Arguments unanswerable.
D. W. to C. Clarkson (p. 37),   V. 31, 1821

4.* . . . very civil about the *Strictures*, which he praised cordially.
H. C. R., ii, 559.   XII. 28, 1838

5.* I am glad to have found Wordw: quite pleased with the Strictures—
C. R. to T. R. (*Corr. C. R.*, i, 378),   I. 19, 1839

6. [In his *History of Abolition*] as an historian did not do justice to
Mr Stephen and Mr [Zachary] Macaulay & perhaps some others. But neither
Did Mr Southey nor any other candid person ever impute these deficiencies,
for such they were, in a book calling itself the History of the Abolition to
love of self or any cause more reprehensible than want of due inquiry and
consideration.—
For my own part I have many times expressed my regret, before I ever
interchanged a word with Mr S. [Southey] on the subject, that Mr C's book
was not what he Mr S recommended. . . .
To C. R. (*Corr. C. R.*, i, 413),   VI. 8, 1840

7. We have read with interest the unfinished Paper (so discreditably
published) which he [Thomas Clarkson] was writing upon Slavery in
America. The truths it contains cannot but prove galling to Numbers in
America. *To C. R.* (*Corr. C. R.*, ii, 637),   XI. 16, 1849

Cobbett, William. See Hamilton, T. 1

Coleridge, Hartley

1. . . . is a very able writer; but he also, like most men of genius, is
little to be depended upon. *To A. Watts*,   VI. 18, 1826

2. It is a pity that Mr Hartley Coleridge's Sonnets had not been published before your collection was made—as there are several well worthy of a
place in it. *To Dyce*,   XII. 4, 1833

3. I did the same to Mr Hartley Coleridge [request for epitaph on Lamb], and *asked* him to try his powers. Now as he is very ready, and has *great* powers, and retains a grateful affection for our deceased friend, we expect something good and appropriate. *To Moxon,*   XII. 6, 1835

4. . . . though he writes much and very ably, he is not to be depended upon for unfinished work. *To Moxon,*   I. 27, 1840

5. I admire his genius and talents far more than I could find words to express, especially for writing prose, which I am inclined to think, as far as I have seen, is more masterly than his Verse. The *work*manship of the latter seems to me not infrequently too hasty, has indeed too much the air of Italian improvizatore production. *To Moxon,*   II. 21, 1840

6.* [W. thinks] there is much talent but no genius in his poetry, and calls him an eminently clever man. One thing he has learnt,—that poetry is no pastime, but a serious earnest work, demanding unspeakable study. "Hartley has no originality; whenever he attempts it, it is altogether a mistake; he is so fond of quaintness and contrariety, which is quite out of keeping with a true poet: and then he is of that class of extreme Radicals who can never mention a bishop or a king, from King David downward, without some atrabilious prefix or other. Surely this is excessively narrow and excessively vain, to put yourself in opposition to the opinions and institutions which have so long existed with such acknowledged benefit; there must be something in them to have attracted the sympathies of ages and generations. I hold that the degree in which poets dwell in sympathy with the past marks exactly the degree of their poetical faculty. Shelley, you see, was one of these, and what did his poetry come to?" [Caroline Fox objected that poets would not be true to themselves unless they gave a voice to their yearnings after the Ideal rather than the Actual.] "Ah, but I object to the perpetual ill humor with things around them . . . and ill humor is no spiritual condition which can turn to poetry. Shakespeare never declaimed against kings or bishops, but took the world as he found it." *Old Friends*, p. 174.   VI. 4, 1842

7. . . . both his genius and talents are admirable.
To Moxon,   XII. 13, 1842

Coleridge, Henry Nelson. See Moutray 1

Coleridge, Samuel Taylor (General Criticism)

1. . . . his talent appears to me very great.
To Mathews (*L. Y.*, p. 1333),   X. 24, 1795

2. Take no pains to contradict the story that the L. B. are entirely yours. Such a rumour is the best thing that can befall them.
To Coleridge (p. 242),   1799

3. See Criticism 60; Fancy 14; Language 1; Literature 17; Poetry 57A, 77; Versification 1; Faber 4; Gillman 1; Lamb 13; W. 378A

4. I was much pleased with your verses in D.'s letter; there is an admirable simplicity in the language of the first fragment, and I wish there had been more of the 2nd; the fourth line wants mending sadly, in other respects the lines are good. *To Coleridge,*   IV. 16, 1802

5.   I am very anxious to have your notes for *The Recluse*. I cannot say how much importance I attach to this; if it should please God that I survive you, I should reproach myself forever in writing the work if I had neglected to procure this help.

D. W., W. W., and M. W. to Coleridge (p. 368),   III. 6, 1804

6.   . . . I would gladly have given 3 fourths of my possessions for your letter on *The Recluse* at that time. I cannot say what a load it would be to me, should I survive you and you die without this memorial left behind.

D. W. and W. to Coleridge,   III. 29, 1804

7.   Thou, my Friend! wert reared
            In the great city, 'mid far other scenes;
            But we, by different roads, at length have gained
            The self-same bourne.
                . . .
                            For thou has sought
            The truth in solitude, and, since the days
            That gave thee liberty, full long desired,
            To serve in Nature's temple, thou hast been
            The most assiduous of her ministers. . . .
            Prel., ii, 452-54; 460-64.   1804-39
                . . .

8.   And thou, O Friend! who in thy ample mind
            Hast placed me high above my best deserts. . . .
            Prel., iii, 317-18.   1804-39

9.   I have thought
            Of thee, thy learning, gorgeous eloquence,
            And all the strength and plumage of thy youth,
            Thy subtle speculations, toils abstruse
            Among the schoolmen, and Platonic forms
            Of wild ideal pageantry, shaped out
            From things well-matched or ill, and words for things,
            The self-created sustenance of a mind
            Debarred from Nature's living images,
            Compelled to be a life unto herself,
            And unrelentingly possessed by thirst
            Of greatness, love, and beauty.
            Prel., vi, 294-305.   1804-39

9A.   . . . Twins [W. and C.] almost in genius and in mind!
            Prel., vi, A 263.   1804-5

10.   Though mutually unknown, yea, nursed and reared
            As if in several elements, we were framed
            To bend at last to the same discipline,
            Predestined, if two beings ever were,
            To seek the same delights, and have one health,
            One happiness.
            Prel., vi, 254-9.   1804-39

11.   [Under Coleridge's influence, "thoughts and things" assumed more rational proportions.] *Prel.*, xiv, 275-301.   1804-39

12.   [Coleridge]

> Felt, that the history of a Poet's mind
> Is labour not unworthy of regard:
> To thee [Coleridge] the work shall justify itself.

Prel., xiv, 412-14.   1804-39

13.   Within this last month I have returned to the Recluse, and have written 700 additional lines.   Should Coleridge return, so that I might have some conversation with him upon the subject, I should go on swimmingly. *To Beaumont*,   VIII. 1, 1806

14.   . . . Coleridge, whose genius talents and comprehensive knowledge are well known. . . . *To Robert Grahme,*̅   XI. 26, 1808

15.   I cannot say that Coleridge has been managing himself well; and therefore I would not have you disappointed if the 'Friend' should not last long. . . . *To T. Poole*,   III. 30, 1809

16.   . . . Coleridge is not sufficiently master of his own efforts to execute anything which requires a regular course of application to one object. *To D. Stuart*,   V. 31, 1809

17.   I give it to you as my deliberate opinion, formed upon proofs which have been strengthening for years, that he [Coleridge] neither will nor can execute any thing of important benefit either to himself his family or mankind. Neither his talents nor his genius, mighty as they are, nor his vast information will avail him anything; they are all frustrated by a derangement in his intellectual and moral constitution.   In fact he has no voluntary power of mind whatsoever, nor is he capable of acting under any *constraint* of duty or moral obligation.   *To T. Poole*,   V. 31 or VI. 1, 1809

18.*   . . . I lament equally with the Wordsworths & yourself that such a man should be compelled to have recourse to such means [lecturing]. . . . *Remains*, p. 129.   I. 3, 1811

19.   Though with several defects, and some feeble and constrained expressions, it has great merit, and is far superior to the run, not merely of newspaper, but of modern poetry in general.   I half suspect it to be Coleridge's [the poem was not his], for though it is, in parts, inferior to him, I know no other writer of the day who can do so well.   It consists of five stanzas, in the measure of the 'Fairy Queene.'   *To Lady Beaumont*,   XI. 20, 1811

21.*   W. with no faint praise, then spoke of C.'s mind, the powers of which he declared to be greater than those of any man he ever knew.   From such a man, under favourable influences, everythg. might be looked for. His genius he thought to be great but his talent still greater, & it is in the union of so much genius with so much talent that C. surpasses all the men W. ever knew.   In a digression to wh. this remark led, W. observed of himself that he, on the contrary, has comparatively but little talent; genius is his characteristic quality.   *Remains*, pp. 149-50.   V. 8, 1812

22.* . . . they [W. and Coleridge] were warm admirers of each others genius & most ungrudgingly professed that admiration while, on the contrary, neither of them thought very highly of Southey's poetical genius, tho' his personal character & his talents as a prose writer & literator [*sic*] were very highly estimated. . . . *Remains*, p. 48.   V, 1812

23. I smiled at your notion of Coleridge reviewing the Ex. in the Ed. I much doubt whether he has read three pages of the poem. . . .
To C. Clarkson (p. 622),   XII. 31, 1814

24. . . . most distinguished for his knowledge and genius, and to whom the Author's Intellect is deeply indebted. . . . *Pref. Exc.*, p. 754.   1814

25. [Coleridge's irregularity of purpose prevented Wordsworth from writing more prose.] See Prose 6; contract Criticism 57, 59; W. 382, 389

27. [Coleridge's prose good.] *To J. Scott*,   III. 11, 1816

28. Coleridge, to whom all but certain reviewers wish well, intends to try the effect of another course of lectures in London on Poetry generally, and on Shakespeare's Poetry particularly. He gained some money and reputation by his last effort of the kind, which was, indeed, to him no effort, since his thoughts as well as his words flow spontaneously. He talks as a bird sings, as if he could not help it: it is his nature. . . . No man ever deserved to have fewer enemies, yet, as he thinks and says, no man has more, or more virulent. [De Sel: From the Preface to *Seven Lectures on Shakespeare and Milton*, by the late S. T. Coleridge, ed. by J. Payne Collier, 1856. There is no other authority for this letter, and its authenticity is not, therefore, above suspicion.] *To J. Payne Collier* (*L. Y.*, p. 1371),   late 1817

29. . . . the magnificent forehead of one of the first intellects that Great Britain has produced. . . . *To A. Cunningham*,   XI. 23, 1823

30.* After listening to Coleridge talk for two hours at his home, as they were leaving Rogers asked Wordsworth whether he had understood it. W. replied, "Not one syllable of it." [Dyce adds in a note that Wordsworth had said to him:] What is somewhere stated in print—that I said, "Coleridge was the only person whose intellect ever astonished me," is quite true. His conversation was even finer in his youth than in his later days; for, as he advanced in life, he became a little dreamy and hypermetaphysical
Table-Talk of Rogers, p. 203 and note .   *c.* 1825

31.* It is not enough for a poet to possess the power of mind; he must also have knowledge of the heart, and this can only be acquired by time and tranquil silence. No great poem has been written by a young man or by an unhappy one. It was poor dear Coleridge's constant infelicity that prevented him from being the poet that Nature had given him the power to be. He had always too much personal and domestic discontent to paint the sorrows of mankind. He could not

Afford to suffer
With those whom he saw suffer.

I gave him the subject of his Three Graves; but he made it too shocking and painful, and not sufficiently sweetened by any healing views. Not being able to dwell on or sanctify natural woes, he took to the supernatural, and hence his Ancient Mariner and Christabel, in which he shows great poetical power; but these things have not the hold on the heart which Nature gives, and will never be popular poems, like Goldsmith's or Burns's.

Early Wordsworth, p. 28. *c.* 1831

32. Surely these [Coleridge, W. Scott, and Sir Humphry Davy] are men of power, not to be replaced should they disappear. . . .

To Rogers, VII. 30, 1830

33. His mind has lost none of its vigour, but he is certainly in that state of bodily health that no one who knows him could feel justified in holding out the hope of even an introduction to him, as an inducement for your visiting London. Much do I regret this, for you may pass your life without meeting a man of such commanding faculties.

To W. R. Hamilton, I, 24, 1831

34. He and my beloved sister are the two beings to whom my intellect is most indebted. . . . *To W. R. Hamilton,* VI. 25, 1832

35.* [Wished Coleridge wrote more clearly.]

English Traits, pp. 21-2. VIII. 28, 1833

36.* . . . called him the most *wonderful* man that he had ever known— wonderful for the originality of his mind, and the power he possessed of throwing out in profusion grand central truths from which might be evolved the most comprehensive systems. Wordsworth, as a poet, regretted that German metaphysics had so much captivated the taste of Coleridge, for he was frequently not intelligible on the subject; whereas, if his energy and his originality had been more exerted in the channel of poetry, an instrument of which he had so perfect a mastery, Wordsworth thought he might have done more permanently to enrich the literature, and to influence the thought of the nation, than any man of the age. As it was, however, he said he believed Coleridge's mind to have been a widely fertilising one, and that the seed he had so lavishly sown in his conversational discourses, and the Sibyline leaves (not the poems so called by him) which he had scattered abroad so extensively covered with his annotations, had done much to form the opinions of the highest-educated men of the day; although this might be an influence not likely to meet with adequate recognition.

Graves (Grosart, iii, 469). [VII. 27, 1834]

36A.* . . . his prose would live and deserve to live; while, of the poetry, he thought by no means so highly. I had mentioned the *Genevieve* as a beautiful thing, but to this he objected: there was too much of the sensual in it. *Moore's Diary*, p. 187. II. 20, 1835

38. . . . every mortal power of Coleridge
Was frozen at its marvellous source;
The rapt One, of the godlike forehead,
The heaven-eyed creature sleeps in earth. . . .
" When first, descending," 15-18. 1835

39.* Latterly he [W.] thought he [Coleridge] had so much acquired the habit of analysing his feelings, and making them matter for a theory or argument, that he had rather dimmed his delight in the beauties of nature and injured his poetical powers.

Justice Coleridge (*Grosart*, iii, 427).   IX. 22, 1836

40.*   [W.] regretted that my uncle has written so little verse; he thought him so eminently qualified, by his very nice ear, his great skill in metre, and his wonderful power and happiness of expression. He attributed, in part, his writing so little, to the extreme care and labour which he applied in elaborating his metres. He said, that when he [Coleridge] was intent on a new experiment in metre, the time and labour he bestowed were inconceivable; that he was quite an epicure in sound.

Justice Coleridge (*Grosart*, iii, 427).   IX. 22, 1836

41.*   He [W.] remembered his [Coleridge's] writing a great part of the translation of ' Wallenstein,' and he said there was nothing more astonishing than the ease and rapidity with which it was done.

Justice Coleridge (*Grosart*, iii, 428).   IX. 22, 1836

43.*   Thought Coleridge admired Ossian only in youth. . . .

Gladstone, i, 136.   1836

46.   I have been much annoyed by a serious charge of Plagiarism brought against Coleridge in the last number of Blackwood [March, 1840]. I procured the number for the purpose of reading it—With the part concerning the imputation of the thefts from Schelling, having never read a word of German metaphysics, thank Heaven! though I doubt not they are good diet for some tastes I feel no disposition to meddle. But when in further disparagement of the object of his remarks he asserts that C. was indebted ' to Germans for the brightest gems of his poetic crown,' I feel myself competent to say a few words upon that subject. The Critic names Schiller and Stolber[g] as, among others, strong instances in support of his assertion—And what are the passages adduced, two Hexameter verses, and a hexameter and pentameter, word for word from Schiller, and passed off by Coleridge as his own. If it be true this was excessive folly on Coleridge's part, but it is beyond measure absurd to talk of this paltry stuff as the Magazinist has ventured to do. So far from such things being gems in his crown they would be much honoured by calling them farthings in his Pocket. But then C. produced the lines to shew that he was a great discoverer in metre, one who had for the first time found out and by these specimens exemplified in a modern language & that his own, the spirit of these several constructions of musical sound. But having admitted that it was silly if not worse in my Friend to claim what was not his own, I feel free to affirm that Coleridge had carefully studied and successfully practised English Hexameters before he knew a word of German. And I am astonished that he did not give specimens of his own, with which he had taken, in Hexameters, I know far more pains than anything of the sort is worth. These are the sole proofs of his robberies of Schiller, but if he had stolen ten times as freely, I could have added in explanation & partly in exculpation that he gave to Schiller 50 times more than he took without thinking worth while to let the world know what he had done.   C. translated

the 2nd part of Wallenstein under my roof at Grasmere from MSS.—about that time I saw the passages of the Astronomical Times and the antient Mythology, which, as treated in Coleridge's professed [?] translat[i]on, were infinitely superior.—As to the passage from Stolberg, it was begun, as I know, as a translation, and amplified. Coleridge took incredible pains with the execution and has greatly excelled the original; but why he did not in this case also speak the plain truth I am quite at a loss to conceive—Compare Chiabrera's epitaph upon Ambrosio Salinero, which I have translated, with Coleridge's tombless epitaph upon one he calls Satyrane and you will have another instance how unadvised was his way in these little matters. I used to beg he would take the trouble of noting his obligations, but half his time was passed in dreams, so that such hints were thrown away. I should not have thought it worth while to write so much, had not the unfairness with which the Blackwoodite treats the *Poet* C in this point led me to suspect that as a metaphysician he has been used somewhat in the same manner. . . .

To C. R. (Corr. C. R., i, 401-3),   III. 10, 1840

47.* . . . Sir W. Hamilton was the most remarkable man he [W.] had known except Coleridge. *Aubrey de Vere,* p. 70.   III. 9, 1841

48.* . . . the want of will which characterized both him and Hartley; the amazing effort which it was to him to will anything was indescribable: but he acknowledged the great genius of his poetry.
Old Friends, pp. 174-5.   VI. 4, 1842

49.* . . . Coleridge's twenty-sixth year was his " annus mirabilis," and that if he had not then suffered himself to be drawn aside from poetry he must have proved the chief poet of modern times.
De Vere's Recollections, p. 42.   1842-46

52. [C.] so much impressed [by *Guilt and Sorrow*] . . . , that it would have encouraged me to publish the whole as it then stood. . . .
I. F. (Grosart, iii, 11).   1843

53. . . . that great & good man. . . . *Reed,* p. 95.   III. 27, 1843

54.* . . . the liveliest and truest image he could give of Coleridge's talk was ' that of a majestic river, the sound or sight of whose course you caught at intervals, which was sometimes concealed by forests, sometimes lost in sand, then came flashing out broad and distinct, then again took a turn which your eye could not follow, yet you knew and felt that it was the same river: so,' he said, ' there was always a train, a stream, in Coleridge's discourse, always a connection between its parts in his own mind, though one not always perceptible to the minds of others.' . . . in his opinion Coleridge had been spoilt as a poet by going to Germany. The bent of his mind, which was at all times very much to metaphysical theology, had there been fixed in that direction. ' If it had not been so,' said Wordsworth, ' he would have been the greatest, the most abiding poet of his age. His very faults would have made him popular (meaning his sententiousness and laboured strain), while he had enough of the essentials of a poet to make him deservedly popular in a higher sense.' *Mrs. D. (Grosart,* iii, 441-42).   VII. 11, 1844

55.* . . . on some one observing that it was difficult to carry away a distinct impression from Coleridge's conversation, delightful as every one felt his outpourings to be. Wordsworth agreed, but said he was occasionally very happy in clothing an idea in words. . . .

Lady R. (Grosart, iii, 444).   VII. 12, 1844

56.* . . . Coleridge was not under the influence of external objects. He had extraordinary powers of summoning up an image or series of images in his own mind, and he might mean that his idea of Marathon was so vivid, that no visible observation could make it more so. A remarkable instance of this . . . is his poem, said to be "composed in the Vale of Chamouni." Now he never was at Chamouni, or near it, in his life.

Mrs. D. (Grosart, iii, 442).   VII. 11, 1844

58.* Coleridge, as Wordsworth once expressed it to me, had been "in blossom" only for four years—from 1796 to 1800. The plant was perennial, but the flowers were few. *Henry Taylor,* i, 188.   *c.* 1845

Coleridge (Works)

59. *The Rime of the Ancyent Marinere* was professedly written in imitation of the *style,* as well as of the spirit of the elder poets; but with a few exceptions, the Author believes that the language adopted in it has been equally intelligible for these three last centuries.

Adv. L. B. (K. Prose, i, 32).   1798

59A.* Wordsworth admires my tragedy *Osorio.* . . .

Letters (Coleridge), i, 221.   VI, 1797

60. (. . . I shall probably add some [other poems to *L. B.,* 1800] in Lieu of The Ancyent Marinere). . . . *To J. Cottle,*   VI. 2, 1799

61. . . . it seems that The Ancyent Marinere has upon the whole been an injury to the volume, . . . the old words and the strangeness of it have deterred readers from going on. If the volume should come to a second edition I would put in its place some little things which would be more likely to suit the common taste. [See *E. L.,* p. 174.] *To J. Cottle,*   VI. 24, 1799

61A. For the sake of variety and from a consciousness of my own weakness [here appeared the following passage, which was never printed (see *Longman MSS,* p. 19): "I have again requested the assistance of a Friend who contributed largely to the first volume, and who has furnished me with the long and beautiful" (the last three words were struck out, probably by Coleridge, who was correcting the MS of the *Pref. L. B., 1800)* "Poem of Christabel, without which I should not yet have ventured to present a second volume to the public"], I was induced to request the assistance of a Friend, who furnished me with the Poems of the *Ancient Mariner,* the *Foster-Mother's Tale,* the *Nightingale,* the *Dungeon* [omitted 1802-5], and the Poem entitled *Love.* I should not, however, have requested this assistance, had I not believed that the poems of my Friend would in a great measure have the same tendency as my own, and that, though there would be found a difference, there would be found no discordance in the colours of our style; as our opinions on the subject of poetry do almost entirely coincide. [This paragraph was omitted after the edition of 1805.]

Pref. L. B. (K. Prose, i, 46 n.[1]).   1800-5

61B. [Four great defects in "The Ancient Mariner":] first, that the principal person has no distinct character, either in his profession as Mariner, or as a human being who, having been long under controul of supernatural impressions, might be supposed himself to partake of something supernatural; secondly, that he does not act, but is constantly acted upon; thirdly, that the events, having no necessary connection, do not produce each other; and lastly, that the imagery is somewhat too laboriously accumulated. Yet the Poem contains many delicate touches of passion, and indeed the passion is everywhere true to nature; a great number of the stanzas present beautiful images and are expressed with unusual felicity of language; and the versification, though the metre is itself unfit for long poems, is harmonious and artfully varied, exhibiting the utmost powers of that metre, and every variety of which it is capable. It therefore appeared to me that these several merits (the first of which, namely that of the passion, is of the highest kind,) gave to the poem a value which is not often possessed by better poems. On this account I requested of my Friend to permit me to republish it. [This note to "The Ancient Mariner" in the *L. B.* was not reprinted.]

Longman MSS, pp. 22-3.   1800

61C.* The "Christabel" was running up to 1,300 lines, and was so much admired by Wordsworth, that he thought it indelicate to print two volumes with his name, in which so much of another man's was included; and, which was of more consequence, the poem was in direct opposition to the very purpose for which the lyrical ballads were published, viz., an experiment to see how far those passions which alone give any value to extraordinary incidents were capable of interesting, in and for themselves, in the incidents of common life [see also *L. of Coleridge,* i, 159].

Letters (Coleridge), i, 337   VIII. 14, 1800

62.   Thou in bewitching words, with happy heart,
             Didst chaunt the vision of that Ancient Man,
             The bright-eyed Mariner, and rueful woes
             Didst utter of the Lady Christabel.
             Prel., xiv, 398-401.   1804-39

63. [*Christabel.*] See Scott, W. 33, 38

64. See Thought 6; W. 148, 198A, 330

65.* [The *Biographia Literaria*] has given him no pleasure, and he finds just fault with Coleridge for professing to write about himself and writing merely about Southey and Wordsworth. . . . The praise [of W.'s poems] is extravagant and the censure inconsiderate. *H. C. R.,* i, 213.   XII. 4, 1817

65A.* [W.] censured the passage [line 23 of "A Hymn before Sunrise"] as strained and unnatural, and condemned the Hymn in toto . . . as a specimen of the Mock Sublime.

L. of Coleridge, ii, 261.   1820

66. See the beautiful Song in Mr. Coleridge's Tragedy, " The Remorse " [III, i]. Why is the harp of Quantock silent?

Oxf. W., p. 905.   1822

67.* Coleridge's *Christabel* no doubt gave him [Scott] the idea of writing long ballad-poems: Dr. Stoddart had a very wicked memory, and repeated various passages of it (then unpublished) to Scott.

Table-Talk of Rogers, p. 206 note.   *c.* 1824

68. The selection of Sonnets appears to me to be very judicious. If I were inclined to make an exception it would be in the single case of the sonnet of Coleridge upon Schiller [*To the Author of ' The Robbers'* (1794)], which is too much of a rant for my taste. The one by him upon Linley's music [*Lines to W. Linley, Esq., while he sang a song to Purcell's music* (1800)] is much superior in execution; indeed, as a strain of feeling, and for unity of effect, it is very happily done. *To Dyce,*   XII. 4, 1833

69.* . . . of Coleridge's far more equivocal incorrectnesses in talk, Wordsworth said he thought much of this was owing to a *school habit.* . . . There was in Coleridge a sort of dreaminess which would not let him see things as they were. He would talk about his own feelings and recollections and intentions in a way that deceived others, but he was first deceived himself. ' I am sure,' said Wordsworth, ' that he never formed a plan or knew what was to be the end of *Christabel,* and that he merely deceived himself when he thought, as he says, that he had had the idea quite clear in his mind. But I believe that at the school the boys had a habit very unfavourable to the practice of truth. . . .' *H. C. R.,* ii, 487.   II. 1, 1836

70.* He said he had no idea how ' Christabelle ' was to have been finished, and he did not think my uncle had ever conceived, in his own mind, any definite plan for it; that the poem had been composed while they were in habits of daily intercourse, . . . the most unreserved intercourse between them as to all their literary projects and productions, and he had never heard from him any plan for finishing it. Not that he doubted my uncle's *sincerity* in his subsequent assertions to the contrary; because, he said, schemes of this sort passed rapidly and vividly through his mind, and so impressed him, that he often fancied he had arranged things, which really and upon trial proved to be mere embryos. I omitted to ask him, what seems obvious enough now, whether, in conversing about it, he had ever asked my uncle how it would end. The answer would have settled the question. He regretted that the story had not been made to end the same night in which it begun. There was difficulty and danger in bringing such a personage as the witch to daylight, and the breakfast-table; and unless the poem was to have been long enough to give time for creating a second interest, there was a great probability of the conclusion being flat after such a commencement.

Justice Coleridge (Grosart, iii, 427).   IX. 22, 1836

72.* [The most ghastly incident in the *Ancient Mariner*—that of the dead men rising up to pull the ropes—was W.'s suggestion.]

Whately, p. 204.   *c.* 1840

73.* [W.] objected on the same ground [remoteness from humanities] to Coleridge's "Ancient Mariner," while he asserted notwithstanding that Coleridge's genius, aided by his unrivalled metrical faculty, ought to have rendered him the greatest poet of modern times. In poetic capability, though not in performance, he ranked him with those great ancient poets of wisdom and Truth who prophesied to their age and were unsubdued by adversity or neglect. . . . *De Vere's Essays*, i, 201-2.   1842-46

74.   . . . and in the course of this walk was planned the poem of the ' Ancient Mariner,' founded on a dream, as Mr. Coleridge said, of his friend ' Mr. Cruikshank. Much the greatest part of the story was Mr. Coleridge's invention; but certain parts I myself suggested; for example, some crime was to be committed which would bring upon the Old Navigator, as Coleridge afterwards delighted to call him, the spectral persecution, as a consequence of that crime and his own wanderings. I had been reading in Shelvocke's *Voyages*, a day or two before, that, while doubling Cape Horn, they frequently saw albatrosses in that latitude, the largest sort of sea-fowl, some extending their wings twelve or thirteen feet. ' Suppose,' said I, ' you represent him as having killed one of these birds on entering the South Sea, and that the tutelary spirits of these regions take upon them to avenge the crime.' The incident was thought fit for the purpose, and adopted accordingly. I also suggested the navigation of the ship by the dead men, but do not recollect that I had anything more to do with the scheme of the poem. The gloss with which it was subsequently accompanied was not thought of by either of us at the time, at least not a hint of it was given to me, and I have no doubt it was a gratuitous after-thought. We began the composition together, on that to me memorable evening: I furnished two or three lines at the beginning of the poem, in particular—

> ' And listen'd like a three years' child;
> The Mariner had his will.'

These trifling contributions, all but one, (which Mr. C. has with unnecessary scrupulosity recorded), slipt out of his mind, as they well might. As we endeavoured to proceed conjointly (I speak of the same evening), our respective manners proved so widely different, that it would have been quite presumptuous in me to do anything but separate from an undertaking upon which I could only have been a clog. . . . The ' Ancient Mariner ' grew and grew till it became too important for our first object, which was limited to our expectation of five pounds. . . . *I. F.* (*Grosart*, iii, 16-17).   1843

75.   To the instances named in this letter of the indifference even of men of genius to the sublime forms of Nature in mountainous districts, the author of the interesting Essays, in the *Morning Post*, entitled Table Talk has justly added Goldsmith, and I give the passage in his own words.
  " The simple and gentle-hearted Goldsmith, who had an exquisite sense of rural beauty in the familiar forms of hill and dale, and meadows with their hawthorn-scented hedges, does not seem to have dreamt of any such thing as beauty in the Swiss Alps, though he traversed them on foot, and had therefore the best opportunities of observing them. . . ."

K. and W. Railway (*Grosart*, ii, 333 n.).   1844

76. . . . and in order to defray his part of the expense, Coleridge on the same afternoon commenced his poem of the ' Ancient Mariner '; in which I was to have borne my part, and a few verses were written by me, and some assistance given in planning the poem; but our styles agreed so little, that I withdrew from the concern, and he finished it himself.

Grosart, iii, 223.   XI, 1847

Coleridge, Sara

1. I rather tremble for the Notice she is engaged in giving of her Father's life. Her opportunities of knowing any thing about him were too small for such an Employment, which would be very difficult to manage for any one, nor could her judgment be free from bias unfavourable to truth.

To I. Fenwick,   early XI, 1846

Collins, William (General Criticism)

1.* [W.] has a fondness for . . . Collins. *Hazlitt*, iv, 277.   c. 1800

2. See Copyright 1; Criticism 68

3. [Collins's poems now very popular, but only after long neglect.] See Fame 12. *E. Supp. Pref.*, p. 949.   1815

4.   I have to thank you for your elegant Edition of Collins, an Author who from the melancholy circumstances of his life, particularly the latter part of it, has a peculiar claim upon such attention as you have bestowed upon him and his works. *To Dyce*,   X. 29, 1828

5. These three Writers, Thomson, Collins, and Dyer, had more poetic Imagination than any of their Contemporaries, unless we reckon Chatterton as of that age—I do not name Pope for he stands alone—as a man most highly gifted; but unluckily he took the Plain when the Heights were within his reach. *To Dyce*,   I. 12, 1829

6. You are at perfect liberty to declare that you have rejected Bell's Copy [*Ode on Popular Superstitions*] in consequence of my opinion of it— and I feel much satisfaction in being the Instrument of rescuing the memory of Collins from this disgrace. I have always felt some concern that Mr Home, who lived several years after Bell's publication, did not testify more regard for his decreased friend's memory by protesting against this imposi- tion. Mr. Mackenzie is still living, and I shall shortly have his opinion upon the question—and if it be at all interesting I shall take the liberty of sending it to you. *To Dyce*,   I. 12, 1829

Collins, William (Works)

7. See Criticism 67-8

8. *Ode to the Death of Thomson*

> Yet be as now thou art,
> That in thy waters may be seen
> The image of a poet's heart,
> How bright, how solemn, how serene!
> Such as did once the Poet bless,

Who, murmuring here a later ditty,
Could find no refuge from distress
But in the milder grief of pity.
Now let us, as we float along,
For *him* [see *Knight*, i, 34 n.] suspend the
    dashing oar;
And pray that never child of song
May know that Poet's sorrows more.
Remembrance of Collins, 9-20.   1789

9. [*Ode to Evening.*] See Barbauld 2

10. [*Ode on Superstitions.*] Collins could at no period of his life have suffered so bad a line to stand as They mourned, in air, *fell fell* Rebellion *slain*, or such a one as *Pale red* Culloden where those hopes were *drowned*. See Bell, J. 1. *To Dyce*,   X. 29, 1828

Congreve, William

1. See Manners 2; Johnson 11

3. . . . his *Old Bachelor.* One can scarcely hit on any performance less in harmony with the scene; but it was a local tribute paid to intellect by those who had not troubled themselves to estimate the moral worth of that author's comedies. And why should they? he was a man distinguished in his day, and the sequestered neighbourhood in which he often resided was perhaps as proud of him as Florence of her Dante. It is the same feeling, though proceeding from persons one cannot bring together in this way without offering some apology to the shade of the great visionary. *I. F.* (*Grosart*, iii, 94).   1843

Cooper, Thomas

1.* [W. spoke kindly of Thomas Cooper's *Purgatory of Suicides.*] *Thomas Cooper*, pp. 289-90.   *c.* 1846

2.* . . . pleased . . . that you preserve your muse chaste, and free from rank and corrupt passion. *Thomas Cooper*, p. 291.   1846

Corbet, Richard

1. [Wrote] some pleasing verses . . . on the death of Francis Beaumont the elder. . . . *To Beaumont*,   VII. 29, 1805

Cornish, T. H.

1. . . . a wretched Author of the name of Cornish who has published a ' National Poem, The Thames,' and he has been dunning me for praise of it. . . . *M. W. and W. to Moxon*,   IV. 1, 1842

Cornwall, Barry. See Procter, Bryan Waller

Cottin, Marie. See Scott, W. 14

9

Cottle, Amos Simon

1. . . . a volume of Icelandic poetry [*Icelandic Poetry, or the Edda of Saemund*]. The volume has afforded me considerable pleasure. It is generally executed in spirit, though there are many inaccuracies which ought to have been avoided. *To J. Cottle,*   XII. 13, 1797

Cottle, Joseph

1. We have read them [? *Malvern Hills*] with pleasure. The volume contains . . . excellent passages. *To J. Cottle* (*L. Y.*, p. 1339),   V. 9, 1798

1A. . . . amused with the " Anthology." Your poem of the " Killcrop " we liked better than any; only we regretted that you did not save the poor innocent's life, by some benevolent art or other. You might have managed a little pathetic incident, in which nature appearing forcibly in the child, might have worked in some way or other, upon its superstitious destroyer. [Cottle is the only authority for this part of the letter.]
To J. Cottle,   VI. 2, 1799

2. *The Malvern Hills*, from which you gave me a valuable extract, I frequently look at. It was always a favourite of mine. some passages—and especially one, closing

>   To him who slept at noon and wakes at eve—
I thought super-excellent. *To J. Cottle,*   I. 27, 1829

3. I have read a good deal of your volumes with much pleasure, and in particular, the ' Malvern Hills,' which I found greatly improved, I have also read the ' Monody on Henderson,' both favourites of mine. And I have renewed my acquaintance with your observations on Chatterton, which I always thought very highly of, as being conclusive on the subject of the forgery. *To J. Cottle,*   VIII. 2, 1829

4. You have treated the momentous subject of socinianism [*Essays on Socinianism*] in a masterly manner, which is entirely and absolutely convincing. *To J. Cottle,*   XI. 24, 1843

5. Now for your little tract, *Heresiarch Church of Rome*. I have perused it carefully, and go the whole length with you in condemnation of Romanism, and probably much further, by reason of my having passed at least three years of life in countries where Romanism was the prevailing or exclusive religion; and if we are to trust the declaration, ' By their fruits ye shall know them,' I have stronger reasons, in the privilege I have named, for passing a severe condemnation upon leading parts of their faith and courses of their practice than others who have never been eyewitnesses of the evils to which I allude. *To J. Cottle,*   XII. 6, 1845

Cotton, Charles

1. Finally, I will refer to Cotton's *Ode Upon Winter*, an admirable composition, though stained with some peculiarities of the age in which he lived, for a general illustration of the characteristics of Fancy. The middle part of this ode contains a most lively description of the entrance of Winter,

with his retinue, as ' A palsied king,' and yet a military monarch,—advancing
for conquest with his army; the several bodies of which, and their arms and
equipments, are described with a rapidity of detail, and a profusion of *fanciful*
comparisons, which indicate on the part of the poet extreme activity of
intellect, and a correspondent hurry of delightful feeling. Winter retires
from the foe into his fortress, where

> a magazine
> Of sovereign juice is cellared in;
> Liquor that will the siege maintain
> Should Phoebus ne'er return again.

. . . I cannot resist the pleasure of transcribing what follows, as an instance
still more happy of Fancy employed in the treatment of feeling than, in its
preceding passages, the Poem supplies of her management of forms. [See
Oxf. W., p. 958 for this lengthy quotation (stanzas 40-49).]
Pref. 1815, p. 958.   1815

    2. See Currie 2

Courier, The

    1. And indeed there has appeared so much practical good sense in *The
Courier*, that I cannot but regret that you do not take the trouble of putting
together some of the most generally and permanently interesting of these
observations, in a separate shape which might ensure their duration.
To D. Stuart,   III. 26, 1809

Cowley, Abraham

    1. See Criticism 49; Johnson 11; Milton 48
    4.*   Read all Cowley; he is very valuable to a collector of English
sound sense. *C. W., Jr. (Grosart,* iii, 465).   *c.* 1827

    5.   In a deep vision's intellectual scene,
> Such earnest longings and regrets as keen
> Depressed the melancholy Cowley, laid
> Under a fancied yew-tree's luckless shade;
> A doleful bower for penitential song,
> Where Man and Muse complained of mutual wrong;
> While Cam's ideal current glided by,
> And antique towers nodded their foreheads high,
> Citadels dear to studious privacy.
> But fortune, who had long been used to sport
> With this his tried Servant of a thankless Court,
> Relenting met his wishes; and to you
> The remnant of his days at least was true;
> You, whom, though long deserted, he loved best;
> You, Muses, books, fields, liberty, and rest!

See Poetry 118. " Those breathing Tokens," 111-25.   1829
    6.   The summit of this mountain [see *Oxf. W.*, p. 471 (XXI, 9)] is
well chosen by Cowley as the scene of the ' Vision,' in which the spectral

angel discourses with him concerning the government of Oliver Cromwell. 'I found myself,' says he, 'on top of that famous hill in the Island Mona, which has the prospect of three great, and not long since most happy, kingdoms. As soon as I looked upon them, they called forth the sad representation of all the sins and all the miseries that had overwhelmed them these twenty years.' It is not to be denied that the changes now in progress, and the passions, and the way in which they work, strikingly resemble those which led to the disasters the philosophic writer so feelingly bewails.

Grosart, iii, 153.   1835

7. . . . I could not but smile at your Boston Critic [? John Sergeant], placing my name by the side of Cowley. I suppose he cannot be such a simpleton as to mean any thing more, than that the same measure of reputation, or fame, if that be not too presumptuous a word, is due to us both.

Reed, p. 14.   XII. 23, 1839

Cowper, William

1. It is from Cowper's Verses supposed to be written by Alexander Selkirk:—[ll. 24-40, p. 312 in Oxford edition, ed. H. S. Milford, (London, 1913)].
This passage is quoted as an instance of three different styles of composition. The first four lines are poorly expressed; some Critics would call the language prosaic; the fact is, it would be bad prose, so bad, that it is scarcely worse in metre. The epithet 'church-going' applied to a bell, and that by so chaste a writer as Cowper, is an instance of the strange abuses which Poets have introduced into their language, till they and their Readers take them as matters of course, if they do not single them out expressly as objects of admiration. The two lines 'Ne'er sigh at the sound,' &c., are, in my opinion, an instance of the language of passion wrested from its proper use, and, from the mere circumstance of the composition being in metre, applied upon an occasion that does not justify such violent expressions; and I should condemn the passage, though perhaps few Readers will agree with me, as vicious poetic diction. The last stanza is throughout admirably expressed: it would be equally good whether in prose or verse, except that the Reader has an exquisite pleasure in seeing such natural language so naturally connected with metre. The beauty of this stanza tempts me to conclude with a principle which ought never to be lost sight of, and which has been my chief guide in all I have said,—namely, that in works of *imagination and sentiment*, for of these only have I been treating, in proportion as ideas and feelings are valuable, whether the composition be in prose or in verse, they require and exact one and the same language. Metre is but adventitious to composition, and the phraseology for which that passport is necessary, even where it may be graceful at all, will be little valued by the judicious.

App. L. B., pp. 943-44. [See *W. Works* (*De Sel.*), ii, 409n.[1]]   1802-36

2.* [Dorothy writes that they had received pleasure from a poem by Cowper which Lady Beaumont mentioned.] I believe it did my Brother some good, and set him on to writing after a pause sooner than he would otherwise have done. *D. W. to Lady Beaumont* (*E. L.*, p. 418),   X. 7, 1804

3. See Copyright Laws 1; Burns 26A; Gillies 2; Smith, Charlotte 2

5. [*The Task* is a composite of satirical, didactic, and idyllic poetry.]
Pref. 1815, p. 954. 1815

7.* . . . a sharp turning at the end with an epigrammatic point [as in Cowper's sonnet to Romney, W. disapproves].
H. C. R., ii, 485. I. 26, 1836

8. [Cowper's great works composed late in life.]
To T. Talfourd, XI. 28, 1836

9. Cowper's letters are everything that letters can be. . . . See Crabbe 11

Coxe, William. See Ramond, Baron de Carbonnieres

Crabbe, George

1. . . . Crabbe's *verses*; for *poetry* in no sense can they be called. . . . I remember that I mentioned in my last that there was nothing in the last publication so good as the description of the Parish workhouse, Apothecary, etc. This is true—and it is no less true that the passage which I commended is of no great merit, because the description, at the best of no high order, is in the instance of the apothecary, inconsistent, that is, false. It, no doubt, sometimes happens, but, as far as my experience goes, very rarely, that Country Practitioners neglect, and brutally treat, their Patients; but what kind of men are they who do so?—not Apothecaries like Crabbe's Professional, pragmatical Coxcombs, ' generally neat, all pride, and business, bustle, and conceit,' no, but drunken reprobates, frequenters of boxing-matches, cock-fightings, and horse-races—these are the men who are hard-hearted with their Patients, but any man who attaches so much importance to his profession as to have strongly caught, in his dress and manner, the outward formalities of it, may easily indeed be much occupied with himself, but he will not behave towards his ' Victims,' as Mr. Crabbe calls them, in the manner he has chosen to describe. After all, if the Picture were true to nature, what claim would it have to be called Poetry? At the best, it is the meanest kind of satire, except the purely personal. The sum of all is, that nineteen out of 20 of Crabbe's Pictures are mere matters of fact; with which the Muses have just about as much to do as they have with a Collection of medical reports, or of Law Cases. *To S. Rogers,* IX. 29, 1808

2.* He also blamed Crabbe for his unpoetical mode of considering human nature and society. *H. C. R.*, i, 168. V. 28, 1815

3.* Of Crabbe, he spoke in terms of almost unmingled praise, conceiving that his works would be turned to, with curiosity and pleasure, when the rapid march of improvement, in another century, had altered the manners, and situation, of the peasantry of England. . . .
Brothers Wiffen, p. 38. 1819

4.* Wordsworth says Crabbe is always an addition to our classical literature, whether he be or be not a poet. He attributes his want of popularity to a want of *flow* of *feeling*,—a general dryness and knottiness of style and matter *which it does not soothe the mind to dwell upon*. . . .

Letters of Scott (*Lockhart to his wife*), ii, 343.　　　　VIII. 25, 1825

5.* . . . [W.] told Anne a story, the object of which, as she understood it, was to show that Crabbs had no imagination. Crabbe, Sir George Beaumont, and Wordsworth were sitting together in Murray's room in Albermarle Street. Sir George, after sealing a letter, blew out the candle which had enabled him to do so, and exchanging a look with Wordsworth, began to admire in silence the undulating thread of smoke which slowly arose from the expiring wick, when Crabbe put on the extinguisher. [Contrast Lockhart 2.] *Diary of W. Scott* (*Grosart*, iii, 503).　　　　　　*c.* 1831

6. See Austen, Jane 1; Barrett, E. 3; Langhorne 2; Lockhart 2; W. 23

7. . . . the extracts made such an impression upon me, that *I* can also repeat them. The two lines

> ' Far the happiest they
> The moping idiot and the madman gay '
> [*The Village*, i. 238-9]

struck my youthful feelings particularly—tho' facts, as far as they had then come under my knowledge, did not support the description; inasmuch as idiots and lunatics among the humbler Classes of society were not to be found in Workhouses—in the parts of the North where I was brought up,—but were mostly at large, and too often the butt of thoughtless Children. Any testimony from me to the merit of your revered Father's Works would I feel be superfluous, if not impertinent. They will last, from their combined merits as Poetry and Truth full as long as any thing that has been expressed in Verse since they first made their appearance. . . . P.S. In the year 1828, upon the application of Miss Hoare yr Father was so obliging as to write in my daughter's Album the following Verses, accompanied with a note in his own hand writing, which shall also be transcribed. [*Occasional Poems,* ' The World of Dreams,' stanza XIII]. . . . And I may add that she prizes them highly, as I, her Father do, they being evidence of that quietness of Spirit, and gentleness of feeling which marked his manners and conversation, as far as we had opportunities of intercourse with him.

To Geo. Crabbe (*L. Y.*, pp. 1376-7),　　　　　　　　　II, 1834

11.* Wordsworth considers him a dull man in conversation. He said he did not either give information, nor did he enliven any subject by discussion. He spoke highly of his writings as admirable specimens of the kind, but he does not like the misanthropic vein which runs through them. He was surprised to hear from my mother that Crabbe's prose style was stiff and artificial in his letters. He said that generally good writers of verse wrote good prose, especially good letters. " Cowper's letters are everything that letters can be, and many of Burns's are marvellous." *Mrs. Fletcher*, p. 216.　　1840

12. Crabbe obviously for the most part preferred the company of women to that of men; for this among other reasons, that he did not like to be put upon the stretch in general conversation. Accordingly, in miscellaneous society his talk was so much below what might have been expected from a man so deservedly celebrated, that to me it seemed trifling. It must upon other occasions have been of a different character, as I found in our rambles

together on Hampstead Heath; and not so much so from a readiness to communicate his knowledge of life and manners as of natural history in all its branches. His mind was inquisitive, and he seems to have taken refuge from a remembrance of the distresses he had gone through in these studies and the employments to which they led. Moreover such contemplations might tend profitably to counterbalance the painful truths which he had collected from his intercourse with mankind. Had I been more intimate with him I should have ventured to touch upon his office as a Minister of the Gospel, and how far his heart and soul were in it, so as to make him a zealous and diligent labourer. In poetry, tho' he wrote much, as we all know, he assuredly was not so. I happened once to speak of pains as necessary to produce merit of a certain kind which I highly valued. His observation was, ' It is not worth while.' You are right, thought I, if the labour encroaches upon the time due to teach truth as a steward of the mysteries of God; but if poetry is to be produced at all, make what you do produce as good as you can. Mr. Rogers once told me that he expressed his regret to Crabbe that he wrote in his late works so much less correctly than in his earlier. ' Yes,' replied he, ' but then I had a reputation to make; now I can afford to relax.' Whether it was from a modest estimate of his own qualifications or from causes less creditable, his motives for writing verse and his hopes and aims were not so high as is to be desired. After being silent for more than twenty years he again applied himself to poetry, upon the spur of applause he received from the periodical publications of the day, as he himself tells us in one of his Prefaces. Is it not to be lamented a man who was so conversant with permanent truth, and whose writings are so valuable an acquisition to our country's literature, should have *required* an impulse from such a quarter?

I. F. (Grosart, iii, 191-92).   1843

Crewdson, Jane

1.*   [W. never heard to] praise any poetry but his own, except a piece of Jane Crewdson's. *Old Friends,* p. 143.   VI. 28, 1841

Crowe, William

1.*   . . . (author of *Lewesdon Hill,* a poem Wordsworth speaks highly of). *H. C. R.,* i, 16.   1810

2.   [*Lewesdon Hill.*] See Dyer, John 5

Cunningham, Allan

1.   I have not yet been able to make myself acquainted with more than a few of the first scenes of your drama [*Sir Marmaduke Maxwell*], one of your ballads, and the songs. I am therefore prevented from accompanying my thanks with those notices which to an intelligent author give such an acknowledgment its principal value. The songs appear to me full as good as those of Burns, with the exception of a *very* few of his best; and *The Mermaid* is wild, tender, and full of spirit. The little I have seen of the play I liked, especially the speeches of the spirits, and that of Macgee, page 7.

To A. Cunningham,   VI. 12, 1822

2.   See Scotch Writers 2

3.   . . . the Maid of Elvar by A. Cunningham.—If you happen to see him let him know that we have lately read it aloud in my family, and that we were all exceedingly pleased with it. The beauties are innumerable, and it is much to be praised both for the general spirit of the narrative and a faithful description of rural scenes and manners. The faults are, an over luxuriance of style and something of a sameness, and occasional impossibility in the incidents.

To Moxon,   XII. 9, 1833

4.   In the work of Alan Cunningham to which you refer he has trifled with his own good name in Authorship. He is a man of distinguished talents, both as Poet and a Biographer and ought to be more careful than he has been in the work you criticize, were it only for considerations of pecuniary gain.

To Moxon,   I. 14, 1834

5.   The little audience of my family were as much pleased as myself; and indeed I can sincerely say that the poem [*Maid of Elvar*] is full of spirit and poetic movement. We have also read with pleasure the volume of your *Lives of the Painters,* containing that of my lamented friend, Sir George Beaumont. I wish I had seen the MS. before the book was printed, as I could have corrected some errors in matter of fact, and supplied some deficiencies. If this life should be reprinted shortly, I shall with pleasure do this for you. I have also a copy of verses inspired by his memory [*Elegiac Musings, Oxf. W.,* p. 583] which, if not too long—I think they amount to between fifty and sixty lines—I would place at your disposal for the same purpose.

To A. Cunningham,   I. 17, 1834

Cunningham, Peter

1.   I was gratified by learning from his handsome edition of Drummond which your son sent me, that he had taken a turn for letters. . . .

To Allan Cunningham,   I. 17, 1834

Currie, James

1.   See Burns 17, 18, 29

2.   [In reading some of Burns's letters, especially the later, W. felt pity for Burns, and strong indignation against the biographer, Currie.] If, said I, it were in the power of a biographer to relate the truth, the *whole* truth, and nothing *but* the truth, the friends and surviving kindred of the deceased, for the sake of general benefit to mankind, might endure that such heart-rending communication should be made to the world. But in no case is this possible; and, in the present, the opportunities of directly acquiring other than superficial knowledge have been most scanty; [for Currie hardly knew Burns, and his avocations did not allow him to take the pains necessary for ascertaining the authenticity of his information.] So much for facts and actions; and to what purpose relate them even were they true, if the narrative cannot be heard without extreme pain; unless they are placed in such a light, and brought forward in such order, that they shall explain their own laws, and leave the reader in as little uncertainty as the mysteries of our nature will allow,

respecting the spirit from which they derive their existence, and which governed the agent? But hear on this pathetic and awful subject, the poet himself, pleading for those who have transgressed! [Here follow the concluding twelve lines to " Address to the Unco Guid." Why did not the recollection of this affecting passage prevent Currie from revealing the infirmities of Burns? He must have known that men would eagerly judge the guilt or innocence of Burns on his testimony, or that many minds would be harmed by the incitements of these allegations. How can Currie compensate for the sorrow brought to the minds of the considerate few by testimony so unfavorable?] Here, said I, being moved beyond what it would become me to express, here is a revolting account of a man of exquisite genius, and confessedly of many high moral qualities, sunk into the lowest depths of vice and misery! But the painful story, notwithstanding its minuteness, is incomplete,—in essentials it is deficient; so that the most attentive and sagacious reader cannot explain how a mind, so well established by knowledge, fell— and continued to fall, without power to prevent or retard its own ruin.

[A bosom friend, a pure spirit, would have treated the downfall of Burns more sympathetically.] In this manner the venerable spirit of Isaac Walton was qualified to have retraced the unsteady course of a highly-gifted man, who, in this lamentable point, and in versatility of genius, bore no unobvious resemblance to the Scottish bard; I mean his friend COTTON—whom, notwithstanding all that the sage must have disapproved in his life, he honoured with the title of son. Nothing like this, however, has the biographer of Burns accomplished; and, with his means of information, copious as in some respects they were, it would have been absurd to attempt it. The only motive, therefore, which could authorize the writing and publishing matter so distressing to read—is wanting!

[Much of Currie's information is rendered unsatisfactory through lack of reserve, or through being coupled with improbable and irreconcilable facts. Few readers will compare the letters with each other or with other documents in the publication to reach an accurate knowledge of Burns's character.] The life of Johnson by Boswell had broken through many pre-existing delicacies, and afforded the British public an opportunity of acquiring experience, which before it had happily wanted; nevertheless, at the time when the ill-selected medley of Burns's correspondence first appeared, little progress had been [made, nor is likely ever to be made by the masses in distinguishing between those confidential communications said courteously to please a correspondent, or to amuse the writer's fancy, and those things fixed in his judgment, and cherished in his heart.] But the subject of this book was a man of extraordinary genius; whose birth, education, and employments had . . . kept him in a situation far below that in which the writers and readers of expensive volumes are usually found. Critics upon works of fiction have laid it down as a rule that remoteness of place, in fixing the choice of a subject, and in prescribing the mode of treating it, is equal in effect to distance of time;— restraints may be thrown off accordingly. Judge then of the delusions which artificial distinctions impose, when to a man like Doctor Currie, writing with views so honourable, the *social condition* of the individual of whom he was treating, could seem to place him at such a distance from the exalted reader, that ceremony might be discarded with him, and his memory sacrificed, as it were, almost without compunction.

[Currie's *Life* can harm Burns only in destroying his children's affection.] Ill-fated child of nature, too frequently thine own enemy,—unhappy favourite of genius, too often misguided,—this is indeed to be "crushed beneath the furrow's weight!' *L. to Friend of Burns* (*Grosart*, ii, 7-10).   1816

Daniel, Samuel

1.   And things of holy use unhallowed lie
                       [*Inscriptions*, iv. 18]

is taken from the following of Daniel,

                       Strait all that holy was unhallowed lies
                       [*Musophilus*, l. 289]

I will take this occasion of recommending to you . . . to read the epistle addressed to the Lady Margaret, Countess of Cumberland, beginning,

                       He that of such a height hath built his mind.

The whole poem is composed in a strain of meditative morality more dignified and affecting than anything of the kind I ever read. It is, besides, strikingly applicable to the revolutions of the present times.

To Lady Beaumont   XI. 20, 1811

2.   The last lines of this Sonnet [*1 Ecc. Sonn.*, XI] are chiefly from the prose of Daniel. . . . *Oxf. W.*, p. 921.   1822

3.   [Admired Daniel's poetry. See also Anderson 1.]

Reed, p. 96 (and p. 85).   III. 27, 1843

Dante

1.*   . . . his strong predilection for . . . Dante. . . .

Hazlitt, iv, 276.   *c.* 1800

2.   See Poetry 148; Burke 3A; Gray 18; Faber 4; Michelangelo 2

3.   Pray be so good as to let me know what you think of Dante—it has become lately—owing a good deal, I believe, to the example of Schlegel—the fashion to extol him above measure. I have not read him for many years; his style I used to think admirable for conciseness and vigour, without abruptness; but I own that his fictions often struck me as offensively grotesque and fantastic, and I felt the Poem tedious from various causes.

To Landor,   I. 21, 1824

4.*   Ariosto and Tasso are very absurdly depressed in order to elevate Dante. *C. W., Jr.* (*Grosart*, iii, 465).   *c.* 1827

5.*   [Dante, the third great poet.]

Graves's Recollections, p. 297.   *c.* 1840

6.   But in his breast the mighty Poet bore
                       A Patriot's heart, warm with undying fire.
                       "Under the shadow," 11-12.   1840-1

D'Arblay. See under Burney, Frances

Darwin, Erasmus

1.   You are quite correct in your notice of my obligation to Dr. Darwin. In the first edition of the Poem it was acknowledged in a note [to the poem *To Enterprise*, ll. 114-16], which slipped out of its place in the last, along with some others. [See also Burns 26A.] *To Dyce,*   IV. 30, 1830

Davidson, Lucretia

1.   . . . a very extraordinary young Creature. . . . Surely many things, not often bestowed, must concur to make genius an enviable gift. This truth is painfully forced upon one's attention in reading the effusions and story of this Enthusiast hurried to her grave so early.
To Mrs. Hemans,   XI. 22, 1831

Davies, Sneyd

1.   [His poem beginning] ' There was a time my dear Cornwallis, when ' . . . well merits preservation. *To Dyce,*   VI. 22, 1830

Davy, Sir Humphry

1.   Surely these are men of power, not to be replaced should they disappear, as one [Davy] has done. *To Rogers,*   VII. 30, 1830

Defoe, Daniel

1.*   . . . likes . . . Robinson Crusoe. *Hazlitt,* iv, 277.   *c.* 1800

2.   See Milton 41

3.*   He thought the charm of *Robinson Crusoe* mistakenly ascribed, as it commonly is done, to its *naturalness*. Attaching a full value to the singular yet easily imagined and most picturesque circumstances of the adventurer's position, to the admirable painting of the scenes, and to the knowledge displayed of the working of human feelings, he yet felt sure that the intense interest created by the story arose chiefly from the extraordinary energy and resource of the hero under his difficult circumstances, from their being so far beyond what it was natural to expect, or what would have been exhibited by the average of men; and that similarly the high pleasure derived from his successes and good fortunes arose from the peculiar source of these uncommon merits of his character. *Graves (Grosart,* iii, 468).   *c.* 1840

De Lille, Jacques

1.   The hand of false taste had committed on its banks [the Loire] those outrages which the Abbe de Lille so pathetically deprecates in those charming verses descriptive of the Seine. . . . *Oxf. W.,* p. 616n².   1793

Della Cruscans

1.   . . . the style is in imitation of the English garden, imitated as Della Crusca might imitate Virgil. *To T. Poole,*   X. 3, 1798

Demosthenes

1. See Bacon 3
2.* Where . . . would one look for a greater orator than Demosthenes.
. . . *Ellis Yarnall* (*Grosart*, iii, 479).   VIII. 18, 1849

Denham, John. See Criticism 49

Dennis, John. See Passion 40; Poetry 78

1.* I once collected his ridiculous pamphlets to oblige Wordsworth, who
(together with S. T. C.) had an absurd " craze " about him. [De Quincey's
letter to A. Blackwood, VII. 30, 1842 (quoted in E. N. Hooker's *The Critical
Works of John Dennis*, ii, lxxiii).]

De Quincey, Thomas

1.   I was reading . . . your note on Moore's Letters with great pleasure,
and expressing at the same time how well it was done: upon which she
[Mrs. W.] observed to me, ' How, then, did not you use stronger language
of approbation? ' When you wrote to Mr. De Quincey you merely said you
were ' satisfied with it.' I replied that this I considered as including everything; for said I, ' Mr. De Quincey will do me the justice to believe that, as
I knew he was completely master of the subject, my expectations would be
high; and if I told him that these were answered, what need I or could I
say more? ' *To De Quincey*,   V. 26, 1809

2. . . . being a man of great abilities and the best feelings. . . .
To D. Stuart,   V. 31, 1809

3.* . . . of whose talents as a writer W. thought highly.
Remains, p. 57.   before 1812

4. He is preparing a short series of Letters, to be addressed to the Editor
of some periodical Publication, say of *The Courier*; upon the subject of the
stupidities, the ignorance, and the dishonesties of *The Edinburgh Review*; and
principally as it relates to myself, whom, perhaps you know, the Editor has
long honoured with his abuse. My works have been a stumbling block to
him from the commencement of his Career. What I have to request is that,
if it consist with your plan, you would give these Letters a place in your
Columns. . . . You need not doubt but that the Letters will be a credit to
any Publication, for Mr. De Q. is a *remarkably* able man.
To D. Stuart (p. 630),   1815

5. In the same number of Blackwood [*Blackwood's Edinburgh Magazine*,
XXIV (December, 1828), 885-908] is an Article upon Rhetoric, undoubtedly
from De Quincey. Whatever he writes is worth reading—there are in it some
things from my Conversation—which the Writer does not seem aware of.
See also W. 391. *To C. R.* (*Corr. C. R.*, i, 201),   I, 27, 1829

6. [" Literature of Knowledge and Literature of Power."] See W. 391.

7.* [De Quincey's articles relating to Wordsworth] in ' Tait's Magazine.'
He forbade their entrance into his own house.
Corr. Taylor, p. 96.   VIII. 18, 1838

De Sismondi, M. J. L.

1. One of the ablest things I have read upon the character and tendency of the Reform Bill is in the *North American Review* of four or five months back [" The Prospect of Reform in Europe," *North American Review*, lxxii (July, 1831), pp. 154-90]. *To Lord Lonsdale,*   XI. 29, 1831

De Staël, Anne Louise Germaine. See Macpherson 2

De Vere, Aubrey

1.* . . . liked the poem from which I took them [lines from one of Aubrey de Vere's poems] . . . he thought it was your father's.
Hamilton, ii, 34.   1832-33

2. . . . Mr De Vere's ode ['May is the bridal of the year']. Pray assure him that I am duly sensible of the honor he has done me in his animated verses. . . . *To W. R. Hamilton,*   II. 8, 1833

De Vere, Sir Aubrey

1. If the expression, especially in point of truthfulness, were equal in your father's poems to the sanctity and weight of the thoughts, they would be all that one could desire in that style of writing.
To De Vere (*L. Y.*, p. 1386),   XI. 16, 1842

2.* . . . I consider his sonnets to be the best of modern times; . . . Of course I am not including my own in any comparison with those of others.
De Vere (*Grosart*, iii, 492).   1842-6

Dickens, Charles

1. Dr Arnold told me that his lads seemed to care for nothing but Bozzy's next NO., and the Classics suffered accordingly—Can that Man's public and others of the like kind materially affect the question—I am quite in the dark. . . . *M. W. and W. to Moxon,*   IV. 1, 1842

2.* . . . a very talkative, vulgar young person—but I dare say he may be clever . . . I have never read a line he has written.
Life of Dickens, p. 243.   *c.* 1843

Digby, Kenelm Henry

1.* Wordsworth made honourable mention of Digby's *Broad Stone of Honour. H. C. R.,* i, 357.   V. 28, 1828

2. The subject of the following poem [*Armenian Lady's Love*] is from the Orlandus of the author's friend, Kenelm Henry Digby: and the liberty is taken of inscribing it to him as an acknowledgment, however unworthy, of pleasure and instruction derived from his numerous and valuable writings, illustrative of the piety and chivalry of the olden time.
Oxf. W., p. 139.   1830

3. [Of line 32 of *Humanity*, W. says:] I am indebted, here, to a passage in one of Digby's valuable works [probably *Of Bodies and of Man's Soul*].
Oxf. W., p. 925.   1835

Disraeli, Benjamin

1.   How can any one when such trashy books as Disraeli's [*Coningsby* appeared in this year] are run after expect any portion of public attention, unless he confines himself to personalities or topics of the day.
To Moxon,   VII. 21, 1844

Doane, George W.

1.   . . . of no ordinary powers of mind and attainments. . . .
Reed, pp. 56-57.   VIII. 16, 1841

Dobson, Matthew

1.   [Approves Dobson's epitaph on his daughter.]
Epitaph 3 (*Grosart*, ii, 66).   1810

Dockray, Benjamin

1.   . . . some things which you have said upon the Church of England, and the relation in which its members stand to it, do not seem to me to be bourne out by the fact. [Mr. L. A. McIntyre suggests that these Papers are ' possibly Dockray's " Remarks on the Catholic emancipation, and on the former ascendancy and present state of the Roman Catholic Religion." ' London, 1829. De Sel.]   *To Dockray,*   XII. 2, 1828
2.   Your *Egeria* arrived. . . . The strain of your thoughts is . . . excellent, and the expression everywhere suitable to the thought. I have to thank you also for a most valuable paper on Colonial Slavery. In your view of this important subject I entirely coincide.   *To Dockray,*   IV. 25, 1833

Donne, John

1.   . . . I have been trying my skill upon one of Mr. Donne's [sermons], which I hope to make something of. I prefer this Writer because he is so little likely to be explored by others; and is full of excellent matter, though difficult to manage for a modern audience.   *To Dora W.,*   IV or V., 1830
2.   The tenth sonnet of Donne, beginning ' Death, be not proud,' is so eminently characteristic of his manner, and at the same time so weighty in thought, and vigorous in the expression, that I would entreat you to insert it, though to modern taste it may be repulsive, quaint, and laboured.
To Dyce,   spring, 1833
3.   [' Death, be not proud,' meets highest tests of a sonnet.]   See Sonnet 7

Douglas, Gavin

1.   [Excelled English poets after Chaucer.]   See Scotch Writers 6

Drayton, Michael

1.   [Admired Drayton's poetry. See also Anderson 1.]
Reed, p. 96 (and p. 85).   III. 27, 1843
2.   See Criticism 39A

Drummond, William

1.   . . . so elegant a Writer. . . . *To Peter Cunningham,*   IX. 24, 1833

Dryden, John (General Criticism)

1.*   [W. preferred Dryden's rhymes to Pope's], because his couplets had greater variety in their movement. [Pope's, however, were more exact in respect to] the final terminations . . . but . . . I thought it was easy to excuse some inaccuracy in the final sounds, if the general sweep of the verse was superior. . . . [The English are] not so exact with regard to the final endings of the lines as the French. . . . [The English make] no distinction between masculine and feminine (i. e. single and double) rhymes. . . . [The attempt to enrich a language by borrowing idioms from another tongue] was a very dangerous practice . . . Milton had often injured both his prose and verse by taking this liberty too frequently. I recommended to him [Klopstock] the prose works of Dryden as models of pure and native English. I was treading upon tender ground, as I have reason to suppose that he has himself liberally indulged in the practice.

Biog. Lit. (" Satyrane's Letters "), ii, 178.   [*c.* IX, 1798]

1A.*   [W. will allow none of the excellencies of poetry to Pope and Dryden.]   *Hazlitt,* iv, 277.   *c.* 1800

2.   I was much pleased to hear of your engagement with Dryden; not that he is, as a *Poet,* any great favourite of mine. I admire his talents and Genius greatly, but he is not a poetical genius. The only qualities I can find in Dryden that are *essentially* poetical are a certain ardour and impetuosity of mind with an excellent ear: it may seem strange that I do not add to this great command of language; *that* he certainly has, and of such language, too, as it is most desirable that a Poet should possess, or rather, that he should not be without; but it is not language that is, in the high sense of the word poetical, being neither of the imagination nor of the passions; I mean of the amiable the ennobling or intense passions; I do not mean to say that there is nothing of this in Dryden, but as little, I think, as is possible, considering how much he has written. You will easily understand my meaning when I refer to his versification of *Palamon and Arcite,* as contrasted with the language of Chaucer. Dryden has neither a tender heart nor a lofty sense of moral dignity: where his language is poetically impassioned, it is mostly upon unpleasing subjects; such as the follies, vices, and crimes of classes of men or of individuals. That his cannot be the language of imagination must have necessarily followed from this, that there is not a single image from Nature in the whole body of his works; and in his translations from Virgil, whenever Virgil can be fairly said to have his *eye* upon his object, Dryden always spoils the passage. *To W. Scott,*   XI. 7, 1805

3.   I am curious to see your notes on Dryden's political Poems, which are, in my opinion, far the best of his works. . . .

To W. Scott (*M. Y.,* p. 458c),   I. 18, 1808

4.   I had a peep at your edition of Dryden. I had not time to read the notes, which would have interested me much, namely the historical and illus-

trative ones; but some of the critical introductions I read, and am not surprised at the criticisms they contain, but rather surprized at them coming from you, who in your infancy and childhood must have had so many of the strains of native Poetry resounding in your ears. *To W. Scott,*   VIII. 4, 1808

5.   See Heywood, T. 1; Pope 20; Shakespeare 45; Thomson 13; W. 294

9.*   ['Language is the dress of thought.' Dryden (*Lives*, i, 58). Wordsworth told De Quincey that it was highly unphilosophical to call language the 'dress of thought.' He would call it the 'incarnation of thought.' (Quoted from Marjorie L. Barstow's *Wordsworth's Theory of Poetic Diction*, Yale Studies in English, XVII, New Haven, 1917, p. 36 n[1].)]

12.*   [W. denies that he has disparaged Pope and Dryden;] I have committed much of both to memory.

C. W., Jr. (Grosart, iii, 460).   *c.* 1827

13.   [Dryden one of the poetic geniuses of England.]

To Dyce,   IV. 30, 1830

14.*   I have ten times more knowledge of Pope's writings, and of Dryden's also, than ever this writer [Hazlitt] had. To this day I believe I could repeat, with a little previous rummaging of my memory, several thousand lines of Pope. But if the beautiful, the pathetic, and the sublime be what a poet should chiefly aim at, how absurd it is to place these men amongst the first poets of their country! Admirable are they in treading their way, but that way lies almost at the foot of Parnassus. [See *Prel.,* V, 546-52; possibly the lines refer to Pope and Dryden].

Letters K., iii, 122.   1836 or after

15.   [Dryden's great works composed late in life.]

To T. Talfourd,   XI. 28, 1836

16.*   . . . Dryden to have the most talent [compared with Pope]—the strongest understanding. *H. C. R.,* ii, 608.   I. 6, 1842

17.*   . . . it is most gratifying to fill the same station [laureateship] that Dryden and Southey have done.

Old Friends, p. 200.   VIII. 21, 1843

Dryden (Works)

17A.*   He [Klopstock] called Rousseau's Ode to Fortune a moral dissertation in stanzas. I [W.] spoke of Dryden's St. Cecelia. . . .

Biog. Lit. ("Satyrane's Letters"), ii, 176.   [*c.* IX, 1798]

18.   [*Fables.*] . . . if I can be of any use, do not fail to apply to me. . . . when you come to the Fables, might it not be advisable to print the whole of the *Tales* of Boccace in a smaller type in the original language? If this should look too much like swelling a Book, I should certainly make such extracts as would shew where Dryden had most strikingly improved upon or fallen below, his original. I think his translations from Boccace are the best, at least the most poetical of his Poems. It is many years since I saw Boccace, but I remember that Sigismunda is not married by him to Guiscard (the names are different in Boccace in both tales, I believe, certainly in Theodore,

etc.). I think Dryden has much injured the story by the marriage, and degraded Sigismunda's character by it. He has also, to the best of my remembrance, degraded her character still more by making her love absolute sensuality and appetite (Dryden has no other notion of the passion). With all these defects, and they are very gross ones, it is a noble Poem. Guiscard's answer, when first approached by Tancred, is noble in Boccace,—nothing but this: *Amor può molto più che ne voi ne io possiamo.* This, Dryden has spoiled: he says first very well, ' The faults of love by love are justified,' and then come four lines of miserable rant, quite *à la Maximin*.

To W. Scott,   XI. 7, 1805

19.[*Satires.*] . . . his political and satirical Poems may be greatly benefited by illustration, and even absolutely require it. It has struck me as being not impossible but that from your connection with the Buccleugh family you may be enabled to learn something about the Duke of Monmouth that may be interesting, and perhaps of Shaftesbury:—I wish it were in my power to do any service to your Book: I have read Dryden's Works (all but his plays) with great attention, but my observations refer entirely to matters of taste; and things of this kind appear better anywhere than when tagged to a Poet's works, where they are absolute impertinences. In the beginning of the *Absalom*, etc. you find an allusion to a freak or revel of the Duke of Monmouth of rather a serious kind (Ammon's murther). This I remember is mentioned in Andrew Marvel's Poems, which I have not seen these any years, but which I think you might peep into with advantage for your work. One or two of the Prologues may be illustrated from Cibber's *Apology*.

To W. Scott,   XI. 7, 1805

19A.* . . . Dryden's Ode is low, and vulgar, and stupid. *Noctes Ambrosianae*, John Wilson, ed. R. S. Mackenzie, 5 vols., New York, 1863, i, 165.   N. D.

20. [*Annus Mirabilis.*] I think the character of the Annus Mirabilis as a Poem might be illustrated by some extracts from a long sermon entitled ' God's terrible voice in the City,' in which the Fire of London is minutely described; Dryden's is a sorry Poem, and the Sermonist though with a world of absurdity has upon the whole greatly the advantage of him.

To W. Scott (*M. Y.*, p. 458c),   I. 18, 1808

21. [Translations.] . . . though there is very great merit in his two translations from Boccaccio. Chaucer, I think, he has entirely spoiled, even wantonly deviating from his great original, and always for the worse. . . . As a Translator from the antient classics he succeeds the best with Ovid, next with Juvenal, next with Virgil, and worst of all with Homer. He has, however done, some things with spirit from Horace, and in one or two passages, with first rate excellence.—I have a very high admiration of the talents both of Dryden and Pope, and ultimately, as from all good writers of whatever kind, their Country will be benefited greatly by their labours. But thus far . . . their writings have done more harm than good. It will require yet half a century completely to carry off the poison of Pope's Homer. . . .

To W. Scott,   I. 18, 1808

22. [Translation of the *Aeneid*.] . . . two passages from Dryden first, the celebrated appearance of Hector's ghost to Aeneas. Aeneas thus addresses him:

> O light of Trojans and support of Troy,
> Thy father's champion, and thy country's joy,
> O long expected by thy friends, from whence
> Art thou returned, so late for our defence?
> Do we behold thee, wearied as we are
> With length of labours and with toils of war?
> After so many funerals of thy own,
> Art thou restored to thy declining town?

This I think not an unfavourable specimen of Dryden's way of treating the solemnly pathetic passages. Yet, surely, here is *nothing* of the *cadence* of the original, and little of its spirit. The second verse is not in the original, and ought not to have been in Dryden; for it anticipates the beautiful hemistich,

> Sat patriae Priamoque datum.

By the by, there is the same sort of anticipation in a spirited and harmonious couplet preceding:

> Such as he was when by *Pelides slain*
> Thessalian coursers dragged him o'er the plain.

This introduction of Pelides here is not in Virgil, because it would have prevented the effect of

> Redit exuvias inductus Achillei.

There is a striking solemnity in the answer of Pantheus to Aeneas:

> Venit summa dies et ineluctabile tempus
> Dardaniae: fuimus Troës, fuit Ilium, et ingens
> Gloria Teucrorum, &c.

Dryden thus gives it:

> Then Pantheus, with a groan,
> Troy is no more, and Ilium was a town.
> The fatal day, the appointed hour is come
> When wrathful Jove's irrevocable doom
> Transfers the Trojan state to Grecian hands.
> The fire consumes the town, the foe commands.

To Lord Lonsdale [see W. 293],   II. 5, 1819

23. [Translation of the *Aeneid*.] See Virgil 10

24. See Chaucer 12, 20

Du Bartas, Guillaume Salluste

1. Who is there that now reads the *Creation* of Dubartas? [In its day more popular than Spenser's *F. Q.*] See Fame 12.

E. Supp. Pref., p. 946.   1815

Dubois, Edward

1. [Southey] believed it was he [Dubois] who had abused my last Poems, and this, too, in a most disingenuous manner! *To Coleridge,* IV. 19, 1808

Duke, Richard. See Johnson 11

Dunbar, William. See Macpherson 2

Dyce, Alexander

1. . . . the expression, in your Edition of Collins, of *shamefully* incorrect as applied to a Transcript made by Sir Egerton Brydges in the Sylvan Wanderer, is too harsh, or rather not sufficiently [?] to so distinguished a person who is at the same time so ardent an Admirer of Collins, though I think it the duty of an Editor to point out all faults of this kind if considerable. *To Dyce,* X. 16, 1829

2. English literature is greatly indebted to your Labours; and I have much pleasure on this occasion of testifying my respect for the sound judgement, and conscientious diligence, with which you discharge your duty as an Editor. Peele's works were well deserving of the care you have bestowed upon them, and as I did not previously possess a copy of any part of them, the beautiful book which you have sent me was very acceptable.
To Dyce, X. 16, 1829

3. Without flattery I may say that your editorial diligence and judgment entitle you to the highest praise. . . . *To Dyce,* VI. 22, 1830

4. . . . your valuable Present of Webster's D. [ramatic] Works [Dyce's ed. of Webster appeared in this year, in 4 vols.] and the Specimens [*Specimens of British Poetesses*]. Your Publisher was right in insisting upon the whole of Webster, otherwise the book might have been superseded, either by an entire Edition separately given to the world, or in some Corpus of the Dramatic Writers. *To Dyce,* IV. 30, 1830

5. See Scholarly Interests 14, 18

6. . . . Skelton, a Writer deserving of far greater attention than his works have hitherto received. Your Edition will be very serviceable, and may be the occasion of calling out illustrations perhaps of particular passages from others, beyond what your own Reading, though so extensive, has supplied. I am pleased also to hear that Shirley is out. *To Dyce,* I. 7, 1833

7. [*Specimens of English Sonnets* generally approved by W.]
To Dyce, XII. 4, 1833

8. Many sincere thanks for your elegant and valuable editions of *Akenside, Beattie,* and Shakespear, from the perusal of which I promise myself much pleasure. *To Dyce,* III. 2, 1835

9. . . . Skelton's Works edited with your usual industry, judgment and discernment. . . . I feel truly obliged by this and the like marks of your attention, and beg you to accept my sincere thanks for the same, which I offer

with unavoidable regret that, being so far advanced in years, I cannot make that profitable use of your labours, which at an earlier period of life I might have done. I am much in the same situation as Pope when Hall's Satires were first put into his hand [he wished he had seen them sooner].

To Dyce,   I. 5, 1844

Dyer, George

1.* . . . the *Life of Robert Robinson* (I have heard Wordsworth speak of it as one of the best books of biography in the language). . . .

H. C. R., i, 4.   1799

2.   This [see 3 *Ecc. Sonn.,* XXXV, 10] is borrowed from an affecting passage in Mr. George Dyer's History of Cambridge.

Grosart, iii, 137.   1822

Dyer, John

1.   Bard of the Fleece, whose skilful genius made
        That work a living landscape fair and bright;
        Nor hallowed less with musical delight
        Than those soft scenes through which thy childhood strayed,
        Those southern tracts of Cambria, " deep embayed,
        With green hills fenced, with ocean's murmur lulled; "
        Though hasty Fame hath many a chaplet culled
        For worthless brows, while in the pensive shade
        Of cold neglect she leaves thy head ungraced,
        Yet pure and powerful minds, hearts meek and still,
        A grateful few, shall love thy modest Lay,
        Long as the shepherd's bleating flock shall stray
        O'er naked Snowdon's wide aerial waste;
        Long as the thrush shall pipe on Grongar Hill!
        " Bard of the Fleece," 1-14.   1811

2. If you have not read *The Fleece*, I would strongly recommend it to you. The character of Dyer, as a patriot, a citizen, and a tender-hearted friend of humanity, was, in some respects, injurious to him as a poet, and has induced him to dwell, in his poem, upon processes which, however important in themselves, were unsusceptible of being poetically treated. Accordingly, his poem is, in several places, dry and heavy; but its beauties are innumerable, and of a high order. In point of *imagination* and purity of style, I am not sure that he is not superior to any writer in verse since the time of Milton.

[See also Tickell 1A.] *To Lady Beaumont,*   XI. 20, 1811

3.   In treating this subject [see *Exc.,* viii. 112-3], it was impossible not to recollect, with gratitude, the pleasing picture, which, in his Poem of the Fleece, the excellent and amiable Dyer has given of the influences of manufacturing industry upon the face of this Island. He wrote at a time when machinery was first beginning to be introduced, and his benevolent heart prompted him to augur from it nothing but good.

Grosart, iii, 216.   1814

4.* . . . strong in his admiration of Dyer's ' Fleece '. . . .
Collier's Preface, p. lii,   II. 10, 1814

5.   A poet, whose works are not yet known as they deserve to be, thus
enters upon his description of the ' Ruins of Rome:'

> ' The rising Sun
> Flames on the ruins in the purer air
> Towering aloft;'

and ends thus—

> ' The setting sun displays
> His visible great round, between yon towers,
> As through two shady cliffs.'

Mr. Crowe, in his excellent loco-descriptive Poem, ' Lewesdon Hill,' is
still more expeditious, finishing the whole on a May-morning, before breakfast.

> ' Tomorrow for severer thought, but now
> To breakfast, and keep festival to-day.'

No one believes, or is desired to believe, that those Poems were actually
composed within such limits of time; nor was there any reason why a prose
statement should acquaint the Reader with the plain fact, to the disturbance
of poetic credibility. *Grosart*, iii, 97.   1820

6.*   A beautiful instance of the modifying and *investive* power of
imagination . . .' Ruins of Rome ' [i, 37]. . . .
C. W., Jr. (Grosart, iii, 465).   *c.* 1827

7.   Dyer is another of our minor Poets—minor as to quantity—of whom
one would wish to know more.   Particulars about him might still be collected,
I should think, in South Wales—his native Country, and where in early life
he practised as a Painter. . . .   These three writers, Thomson, Collins, and
Dyer, had more poetic imagination than any of their contemporaries [except
Pope and Chatterton]. *To Dyce*,   I. 12, 1829

Echard, Lawrence

1.   [*History of England* contains a most laughable account of Ogilby.]
To W. Scott (M. Y., p. 458c),   I. 18, 1808

Edgeworth, Francis Beaufort

1.   The specimens of your young friend's [Francis B. Edgeworth's]
genius are very promising. His poetical powers are there strikingly exhibited;
nor have I any objections to make that are worthy of notice, at least I fear not.
I should say to him, however, as I said to you, that *style* is, in poetry, of
incalculable importance; he seems, however, aware of it, for his diction is
obviously studied. Thus the great difficulty is to determine what constitutes
a good style. In deciding this, we are all subject to delusions; not improbably
I am so, when it appears to me that the metaphor in the first speech of
his Dramatic Scene is too much drawn out; it does not pass off as rapidly as
metaphors ought to, I think, in dramatic writing. I am well aware that our
early dramatists abound with these continuities of imagery, but to me they

appear laboured and unnatural—at least, unsuited to that species of composition of which action and motion are the essentials. ' While with the ashes of a light that was ' and the two following lines are in the best style of dramatic writing; to every opinion thus given, always add, I pray you, *in my judgment*, though I may not, to save trouble or to avoid a charge of false modesty, express it. ' This over-perfume of a heavy pleasure,' etc., is admirable, and indeed it would be tedious to praise all that pleases me.

Shelley's *Witch of Atlas* I never saw; therefore the stanza referring to Narcissus and her was read by me to some disadvantage. One observation I am about to make will at least prove I am no flatterer, and will, therefore, give a qualified value to my praise:

> There was nought there
> But those three ancient hills *alone.*

Here the word ' alone,' being used instead of ' only,' makes an absurdity like that noticed in the *Spectator*—' Enter a king and three fiddlers, *solus.*'
To W. R. Hamilton,   II. 12, 1829

Edinburgh Review, The

1.   See De Quincey 4; Jeffrey 9; *Quarterly Review* 3; Townsend 1

3.*   . . . unhandsome treatment of the *minor* Lord poet. . . .
H. C. R., ii, 736.   *c.* 1830

5.*   [Wordsworth says that his poems would have had an earlier influence] but for the tyranny exercised over public opinion by the *Edinburgh* and *Quarterly Reviews. Lady R. (Grosart,* iii, 437).   VIII. 28, 1841

6.*   [The Edinburgh Reviewers could not write English.] The Edinburgh Review wrote what would tell and what would sell. It had however changed the tone of its literary criticism from the time when a certain letter was written to the editor by Coleridge. *English Traits,* pp. 294n[1]-295.   III, 1848

Edwards, John

1.   . . . expressed with true sensibility by an ingenious Poet of the present day. The subject of his poem is ' All Saints ' Church, Derby ': he has been deploring the forbidding and unseemly appearance of its burial-ground, and uttering a wish, that in past times the practice had been adopted of interring the inhabitants of large towns in the country. . . .
Epitaph 1 (Oxf. W., p. 930).   1810

Elliot, Jane

1.   [" I've heard them lilting, at the ewe milking " is one of the two best modern ballads.] *To Dyce,*   XII. 4, 1833

Elliott, Ebenezer

1.*   Wordsworth speaks highly of the author of *Corn Law Rhymes.* He says: ' None of us have done better than he has in his best, though there is a deal of stuff arising from his hatred of subsisting things. Like Byron, Shelley, etc., he looks on all things with an evil eye.' . . . The great merit of

Elliott, says Wordsworth, is his industry: he has laboured intensely and, like the Gladstonbury thorn, has flowered in winter; his later writings are the best. I asked for the name of some poem. Wordsworth says *The Ranter* contains some fine passages. ' Elliott has a fine eye for nature; he is a very extraordinary man.' *H. C. R.*, ii, 485.   I. 29, 1836

2.* [Praised Elliott] warmly. . . .

Corr. C. R., i, 328.   XII. 7, 1836

Emerson, Ralph Waldo

1. . . . Essays of Mr Emerson. Our Carlyle and he appear to be what the French used to call Esprits forts, though the French Idols shewed their spirit after a somewhat different Fashion. Our two present Philosophers, who have taken a language which they suppose to be English for their vehicle, are verily " Par nobile Fratrum," and it is a pity that the weakness of our age has not left them exclusively to the appropriate reward [,] mutual admiration. Where is the thing which now passes for philosophy at Boston to stop?

Reed, p. 57.   VIII. 16, 1841

Erasmus

1.   . . . when illustrious men,
                    Lovers of truth, by penury constrained,
                    Bucer, Erasmus, or Melancthon, read
                    Before the doors or windows of their cells
                    By moonshine through mere lack of taper light.

Prel., iii, 474-8.   1804-39

Euripides

1. See Heywood, T. 1; Homer 12

3.* [No] finer dramatic poetry, next to Shakespeare, than that of Aeschylus and Sophocles, not to speak of Euripides.

Ellis Yarnall (*Grosart*, iii, 479).   VIII. 18, 1849

Faber, Frederick W.

1.* W. told de Vere that Frederick William Faber (whose poem ' Sir Lancelot' won his high praise) ought not to be a clergyman, as poetry should claim the whole man. *Aubrey de Vere*, p. 72.   IV. 24, 1841

2.* [Had a better eye for nature than W.]

De Vere (*Grosart*, iii, 488).   1842-46

3.* [Faber] has, as W. thinks, considera[ble] talent even as a poet. . . .

C. R. to T. R. (*Corr. C. R.*, i, 474),   I. 12, 1843

4. It [Faber's poem] is a mine of description, and valuable thought and feeling; but too minute and diffusive and disproportioned; and in the workmanship very defective. The Poem was begun too soon and carried on too rapidly before he had attained sufficient experience in the art of writing, and this he candidly and readily admits. Some of his Friends wish and urge him to continue writing verse. . . . A man like him cannot serve two Masters.

He has vowed himself as a Minister of the Gospel to the service of God. He is of that temperament that if he writes verse the Spirit must *possess* him, and the practise master him, to the great injury of his work as Priest. Look at the case of Milton, he thought it his duty to take an active part in the troubles of his country, and consequently from his early manhood to the decline of his life he abandoned Poetry. Dante wrote his Poem in a great measure, perhaps entirely, when exile had separated him from the passions and what he thought the social duties of his native City. Cervantes, Camoens and other illustrious foreigners wrote in prison and in exile, when they were cut off from all other employments. So will it be found with most others, they composed either under similar circumstances, or like Virgil and Horace, at entire leisure, in which they were placed by Patronage, and charged themselves with no other leading duty than fulfilling their mission in their several ways as Poets. Now I do believe as I told Mr Faber, that no man can write verses that will live in the hearts of his Fellow creatures but through an overpowering impulse in his own mind, involving him often in labor that he cannot dismiss or escape from, though his duty to himself and others may require it. Observe the difference of execution in the Poems of Coleridge and Southey, how masterly is the workmanship of the former, compared with the latter; the one persevered in labour unremittingly, the other could lay down his work at pleasure and turn to anything else. But what was the result? Southey's Poems, notwithstanding the care and forethought with which most of them were planned after the material had been diligently collected, are read once but how rarely are they recurred to! how seldom quoted, and how few passages, notwithstanding the great merit of the works in many respects, are gotten by heart. *To I. Fenwick,*   X. 5, 1844

5.* W. respects F's poetic abilities. . . .

C. R. to T. R. (*Corr. C. R.*, ii, 616),   XII. 20, 1845

Farish, [?]

1. [See *Guilt and Sorrow*, 81.] From a short MS. poem . . . [by] a man of promising genius, who died young. *Oxf. W.*, p. 897.   1842

Farquhar, George.   Manners 2

Fawcett, Joseph

1. . . . Fawcett, who was an able and eloquent man. He published a poem on War, which had a good deal of merit, and made me think more about him than I should otherwise have done.

I. F. (*Grosart*, iii, 197-8).   1843

Fenton, Elijah

1. [*Life of Milton.*] See Burns 17

Ferguson, Robert

1. See Burns 19

2. . . . Burns owed much to Ferguson. . . . See Burns 46

3.* . . . [Robert] Ferguson's sonnets: *The Shadow of the Pyramids*— all on Egypt. Wordsworth praises them for their pure style.
H. C. R., ii, 672.   XII. 24, 1847

Fichte, Johann Gottlieb. See Literature 24

Field, Barron

1. [For W.'s confidence in Field's literary judgment see the long letter to Field, X. 24, 1828, in *L. Y.*, pp. 307-13.]

2. [Some of Barron Field's criticisms upon W.'s latest edition will be useful; others he cannot accept.]
To C. R. (*Corr. C. R.*, i, 350),   XII. 15, 1837

3.   I set my face entirely against the publication of Mr Field's MSS. [the MS of Barron Field's ' Memoirs of the Life and Poetry of W. W.,' still unpublished, is in the British Museum (MS add. 41325-7)]. I ought to have written to him several weeks ago, but feeling as I did truly sensible of the interest he took in my character and writings and grateful to him for having bestowed so much of his valuable time, upon the subject, I could not bring myself to tell him what I have just with all frankness stated to you. I must however do so. Mr Field has been very little in England, I imagine, for above twenty years and consequently is not aware, that much the greatest part of his labour would only answer the purpose of reviving forgotten theories and exploded opinions. Besides, there are in his notions things that are personally *disagreeable* (not to use a harsher term) to myself and those about me. And if such an objection did not lie against the publication, it is enough that the thing is *superfluous*. In the present state of this Country in general, how could this kind natured Friend ever be deceived into the thought that criticism and particulars so minute could attract attention even from a few? *To Moxon,*   I. 10, 1840

4.   . . . I am decidedly against the publication of your Critical Memoir; your wish is, I know, to serve me, and I am grateful for the strength of this feeling in your excellent heart. I am also truly proud of the pains of which you have thought my writings worthy; but I am sure that your intention to benefit me in this way would not be fulfilled. The hostility which you combate so ably is in a great measure passed away, but might in some degree be revived by your recurrence to it, so that in this respect your work would, if published, be either superfluous or injurious, so far as concerns the main portion of it. I shall endeavour, during the short remainder of my life, to profit by it, both as an author and a man, in private way; but the notices of me by many others which you have thought it worth while to insert are full of gross mistakes, both as to facts and opinions, and the sooner they are forgotten the better. Old as I am, I live in the hope of seeing you, and should in that event have no difficulty in reconciling you to the suppression of a great part of this work entirely, and of the whole of it in its present shape. One last word in matter of authorship: it is far better not to admit people so much behind the scenes, as it has been lately fashionable to do. *To Barron Field,*   I. 16, 1840

Fielding, Henry

1.* [W. regretted] that neither of those great masters [Fielding and Smollett] of romance appeared to have been surrounded with any due marks of respect in the close of life.
Memoirs of Scott, p. 731.   IX. 17, 1831

Fisher, Emmeline

1. We had some more of her smaller Poems read, which are really wonderful, so that I will repeat what I have often said in your hearing, that she is the greatest Prodigy I ever read or heard of.
To I. Fenwick,   VI, 1841

2. I have endeavoured to recommend and inculcate the merging of the Genius in the Woman, as much as she can. It is obvious that though most amiably disposed to love the qualities of heart and mind that are loveable in others, she attaches, as is natural for one so gifted, too much importance to intellect and literature, and leans too much towards those who, she thinks, are distinguished in that way. *To I. Fenwick*,   VIII. 5, 1841

3.* Spoke of her with enthusiasm; after what she wrote when a child, it was impossible she could go on progressing; her poetry was pure inspiration showered down direct from heaven, and did not admit of any further perfection. *Old Friends*, p. 214.   X. 6, 1844

4. I ought not to conclude this first portion of my letter without telling you that I have now under my Roof, a Cousin, who some time ago was introduced, improperly I think, she being then a child, to the notice of the public, as one of the English Poetesses, in an article of the Quarterly so Entitled.
Reed, p. 144.   VII. 1, 1845

Flatman, Thomas. See Milton 48

Fletcher, Jacob

1. I wish your Tragedies had been more successful, particularly if you are likely to be discouraged from a second adventure. . . .
To J. Fletcher,   II. 25, 1825

2. Your Tragedies I have read with much pleasure, they are in language, versification, and general propriety both as to sentiment, character, and conduct of story, *very much* above mediocrity—so that I think every one that reads must approve in no ordinary degree. Nevertheless I am not surprised at their not having attracted as much attention as they deserve. First, because they have no false beauties, or spurious interest, and next (and for being thus sincere I make no apology) the passions, especially in the former, are not wrought upon with so daring a hand as is desireable in dramatic composition. In the first play the tragic character of the story would lead you to expect that the interest would settle upon the father, who, in his joint character of Magistrate and Father became the Judge and executioner of his own Son—but it does not—the lady attached to Giovani undergoes the most dramatic feelings of any one in the Piece, there is a conflict in her mind in more than one scene

that is sufficiently animated; but the incident which is the hinge of the whole, viz. the death of Giovani, is produced without design, and the Play moves throughout with too little of a prospective interest—so that you do not hang trembling upon the course of events, in part foreseen. The 2nd Play, though less poetical and elegant, has I think much more of *dramatic* interest—some of the situations are pregnant with anxiety and strong emotions, in particular the point where the youth arrives unexpected by his Mother, and he himself being safe, has to blast her congratulatory joy by being the bearer of such miserable news as his Father's death. This is a fine reverse. The foster Brother's situation is also well suited to Tragedy, and indeed the general course of this story which involves in its nature a plot, things being done by design—an advantage in which, as I have already observed, I think the other deficient.—I am well pleased to possess your book, and more especially as coming from yourself.

Now for your MS.—I find no fault with your Scottish Tour, but that you have given us too little of it. I am reconciled to your comparative judgement of the two Countries—now understanding it, which I did not before.

To J. Fletcher,   IV, 6, 1825

3. . . . thanks for the pleasure your Journals have afforded me. . . .

To J. Fletcher,   IV. 30, 1827

Fontaine. See La Fontaine, Jean de

Fox, Charles James

1.* [To Fox] he denied the higher qualities of the mind, philosophy, and religion, and with reason denied his assertion of human rights in matters of religion to be a proof of religion. *H. C. R.*, i, 103.   VII. 6, 1812

2. See Burke 3A

Fuller, Thomas

1. [To Fuller] I am indebted in the Sonnet upon Wicliffe [2 *Ecc. Sonn.*, xvii] and in other instances. *Oxf. W.*, p. 921.   1822

Galt, John. See Hazlitt 2

Gauden, John. See Wordsworth, Christopher 5

Gay, John

1. [*Eclogues.*] The instigator of the work [see Pope 6], and his admirers, could perceive in them nothing but what was ridiculous. Nevertheless, though these Poems contain some detestable passages, the effect, as Dr. Johnson well observes, " of reality and truth became conspicuous even when the intention was to show them grovelling and degraded." The Pastorals, ludicrous to such as prided themselves upon their refinement, in spite of those disgusting passages, " became popular, and were read with delight, as just representations of rural manners and occupations."

E. Supp. Pref. (*Oxf. W.*, p. 948).   1815

Geoffrey of Monmouth. See W. 34 (and *Oxf. W.*, pp. 102-3).

Gessner, Soloman

1. [*The Death of Abel.*] See Young 1

Gibbon, Edward

1. My little Library had long been disgraced by want of Gibbons [? decline] a deficiency you have kindly supplied. . . .
To C. R. (Corr. C. R., i, 298),   IV, 1836

2. [Macaulay's style more gorgeous than Gibbon's.] See Macaulay 1

3.* [Gibbon cannot write English.] *English Traits,* p. 294.   III, 1848

Gifford, William

1. . . . the Bavius of the Quarterly Review has done for that sweet Composition [Lamb's review of *The Excursion*]. . . .
To Mrs. Clarkson (Corr. C. R., i, 81),   1814

2. Criticism 16; Periodicals 5; Byron 23A

Gilbert, William

1. This description [*The Brothers,* 47-64] of the Calenture is sketched from an imperfect recollection of an admirable one in prose, by Mr. Gilbert, author of the *Hurricane. Oxf. W.,* p. 96n[1].   1800

2. . . . the above quotation [see *Grosart,* iii, 213-14] . . . from a strange book [*Hurricane*], is one of the finest passages of modern English prose. *Grosart,* iii, 214.   1814

Gillies, Robert P.

1. . . . *Egbert,* which is pleasingly and vigorously written, and proves that with a due sacrifice of exertion, you will be capable of performing things that will have a strong claim on the regards of posterity. But keep, I pray you, to the great models; there is in some parts of this tale, particularly page fourth, too much of a bad writer—Lord Byron; and I will observe that towards the conclusion, the intervention of the peasant is not only unnecessary, but injurious to the tale, inasmuch as it takes away from that species of credibility on which it rests. I have peeped into *The Ruminator,* and turned to your first letter, which is well executed, and seizes the attention very agreeably. . . . As to style, if I had an opportunity I should like to converse with you thereupon. Such is your sensibility, and your power of mind, that I am sure I could induce you to abandon many favourite modes of speech; for example, why should you write, ' Where the lake gleams beneath the *autumn* sun, instead of ' autumnal,' which is surely more natural and harmonious? We say ' summer sun,' because we have no adjective termination for that season, but ' vernal ' and ' autumnal,' are both unexceptionable words. Miss Seward uses ' hybernal,' and I think it is to be regretted that the word is not familiar. *To Gillies,*   XI. 23, 1814

2. . . . your *Exile,* which pleased me more, I think, than anything that I have read of yours. There is, indeed, something of ' mystification ' about it, which does not enhance. its value with me; but it is, I think, in many

passages delightfully conceived and expressed. I was particularly charmed with the seventeenth stanza, first part. This is a passage which I shall often repeat to myself; and I assure you that, with the exception of Burns and Cowper, there is very little of recent verse, however much it may interest me, that sticks to my memory (I mean which I get by heart). The recommendation of your volume is, that it is elegant, sensitive, and harmonious,—a rare merit in these days; its defect, that it deals too much in pleasurable and melancholy generalities. But if you preserve your health of body, I am confident you will produce something in verse that will last. I have read *The Ruminator*, and I fear that I did not like it quite as much as you would wish. It wants depth and strength, yet it is pleasingly and elegantly written, and contains everywhere the sentiments of a liberal spirit.

To Gillies,   XII. 22, 1814

3. . . . first to the Poem. The lines which I liked best, I think, were (2nd and 3d pages) from ' I prayed for madness,' to ' and even that Image faded on my mind,' and page 12. [? Blandt] then &c to ' human voice ' inclusive—I fear that towards the conclusion you attribute more influence to Nature and to Poetry than they can justly claim! The style of Albert is spirited; but the Poem has the same defect as the other; in turning so much upon internal feelings, and those of a peculiar kind, without a sufficiency of incident or imagery to substantiate them.—We now understand each other with respect to the positions of your former letter, and there remains I think no difference of opinion between us upon the subject. . . . Impute it to any thing but a wish to say agreeable things for the sake of saying them, when I tell you that the harmony of your verses in the *Varia* in particular, does in my estimation entitle you to no mean praise; especially when it is considered what a hobbling pace the Scottish Pegasus seems to have adopted in these days. —You advert in your notes to certain stores of Highland character incident and manners which have been but slightly touched upon. Would not it be well to collect these as materials for some poetic story, which if you would set yourself to work in good earnest, I am confident you could execute with effect. Let me recommend this to you or to compose a Romance, founded on some one of the many works of this kind that exist, as Wieland has done in his Oberon: not that I should advise such a subject as he has chosen. You have an ear, and you have a command of diction, a fluency of style: and I wish, as your friend, that you would engage in some literary labour that would carry you out of yourself, and be the means of delighting the well-judging part of the world. *To Gillies,*   II. 14, 1815

4. . . . I found much that gave me considerable pleasure; nevertheless . . . these Compositions, while they possess the same beauties as those which I have formerly seen of yours, labour also under the same defects in full as great a degree. Your mind does not look sufficiently out of itself, and it is impossible that you should do justice to your Genius, till you have acquired more command over the current of your somewhat morbid sensibilities. I trust that you will not be hurt at my speaking thus without reserve; what would it avail to be insincere? Besides, you are thoroughly aware of your own infirmity, and what I say, if objectionable, must mainly be so on account

of being superfluous. Your Friends will value this little Volume; I assure you that I value it much, and should prize it still more, were I assured that it would not be given to the Public to be trampled under foot by every bestial hoof that it may happen to encounter; I mean to express a wish that its circulation should be confined to those who being capable of feeling its merits will also understand the true quality of its imperfections. As I have before said, the constitutional disease of your Poems is want of variety. I find, therefore, some difficulty in pointing out which has most pleased, or displeased me. Of the Tales, I shall not repeat what I wrote heretofore; the same praise and censure apply to the new, which I presumed to give to the old. The sonnets are more or less agreeable, separately considered; but they stand in each other's way from not being sufficiently diversified. I think I was most pleased with the 27th, but I could easily point out many that I liked. Nevertheless . . . I recommend that the work should not be published. . . .

To Gillies,   IV. 9, 1816

5. The 'Visionary' contains many good lines and well-written passages, for example, ' the never-dying leaves of ivy bright,'—' Fly when pursued, and when obtained expire.' The latter half of page 53 is finely conceived and expressed. So are many other passages as in page 30, ' Long was the way, and led o'er trackless heath '; but you are probably aware that the poem, as a whole, is objectionable—upon the same grounds as the other tales. It wants substance, and is rendered puzzling in the conduct by the succession of persons not sufficiently discriminated from each other in character or situation, and who engage in no course of action. So that upon the whole I cannot say that I think this piece superior to its predecessors, and in point of versification I think it inferior. Your rhyme has in general more harmony than your blank verse, which latter might in many instances be improved with little trouble. For example, at the top of page 100 are three lines, each having its pause on the sixth syllable. Read the second line thus: ' renews his wonted carol; stillness reigns,' and the sound will be improved without injury to the sense. You frequently introduce pauses at the second syllable, which are always harsh, unless the sense justify them and require an especial emphasis; but in such cases as the following observe their bad effect, page 21, ' the race;—the game of dice.'

I am sorry you should have been rendered uneasy by charges of plagiarism brought against you by your friends. I cannot deny that I have been frequently reminded of what I have written by your verses, but never under any circumstances which led me to any reflection discreditable to your ingenuousness of mind. The resemblances are such as you probably are for the most part wholly unconscious of, and were it otherwise, I do not see that they can be reckoned otherwise than as an indirect compliment to the original author. I therefore entreat of you, so far as I am concerned, to dismiss the matter wholly from your thoughts. Your poems are sufficiently original, and tinctured enough, perhaps too exclusively from your own mind. I cannot conclude without noticing the introductory poem to your tales. It is written with much liveliness, and, I think, furnishes good ground for expectation that you will succeed when you look out of yourself. Of most of the other poems you have heard my sentiments before. Both ' Lucia ' and ' Montalban ' contain agreeable stanzas, but as wholes they are too deficient in substance. If you write more blank verse, pray pay particular attention to your versification, especially as to the pauses on the first, second, third, eighth, and ninth syllables. These pauses should never be introduced for convenience, and not often for the sake of variety merely, but for some especial effect of harmony or emphasis. *To Gillies,* XI. 16, 1816

6. I like it [*Oswald*] better than any of the preceding ones. There is a strong family resemblance, no doubt, in them all—but this as a whole is to me the most interesting. It is natural throughout, and contains many pleasing passages, though I think that in the merits of particular parts some of the others are equal and perhaps superior to it. But the general impression of this last is to my mind much more agreeable than ony of the preceding ones. Oswald's feelings on learning that his first passion was hopeless, are given in an animated style—and his recovery.

> Even in an hour of sun-illumined Rain

is very fine, but observe that here are eight lines together all rhyming in the Vowel *A*, which gives a heaviness to the movement of this paragraph which every Reader will feel, without being aware of the cause. Lady Clara's character and Residence are very well described, and one is pleased to meet such a couplet as this, it is a sort of beauty that seems natural to you.

> All through the copse wood winding walks there were
> That led to many a natural parterre

But how could you write, ' at every step the scenery seemed improving '; this is a thorough bad verse; bad language even for prose—The apology for Oswald's second passion in the preceding Canto is well done. The 6 lines at the top of page 71—an excellent composition, the sentiment is natural to the character—Is there any thing like this in any of Lord Byron's Poems—the language is better than his for the most part appears to be—but the sentiment seems somewhat in his style. I could enumerate many couplets and passages that particularly pleased me, for example in the 36th stanza, ' Spring-tide came on,' and the six succeeding lines, particularly ' and long sweet evenings were when mellow dyes Of Twilight lingered in the western skies '—Your essay is desultory enough—of the soundness of the opinion it does not become me to judge—The famous passage on Solitude which you quote from Lord B. does not deserve the notice that has been bestowed upon it. As *composition* it is bad—particularly the line (Minions of grandeur shrinking from distress [' Minions of splendour shrinking from distress.' *Childe Harold,* II, xxvi. 5]) which in defiance of all syntax is foisted in for the sake of the rhyme. But the sentiment by being expressed in an *antithetical* manner, is taken out of the Region of high and imaginative feeling, to be placed in that of point and epigram. To illustrate my meaning and for no other purpose I refer to my own Lines on the Wye, where you will find the same sentiment not formally put as it is here, but ejaculated as it were fortuitously in the musical succession of preconceived feeling. Compare the paragraph ending ' **How** often has my spirit turned to thee ' and the one where occurs the lines.

> And greetings where no kindness is and all
> The dreary intercourse of daily life,

with the lines of Lord B—and you will perceive the difference. *You* will give me credit for writing for the sake of truth, and not from so disgusting a motive as self commendation at the expense of a man of Genius. Indeed if I had not known you so well, I would rather have suppressed the truth, than incurred the risk of such an imputation.

Page 20—you say ' my Rustic lyre I cast away, unable to *pourtray.*' We do not pourtray with a Lyre but with a pencil. You frequently use *revive again* this is a Tautology. *To Gillies,*   VI. 9, 1817

Gillman, James

1.   Mr Gillman's Book [a biography of Coleridge] is not better than I feared I should find it. It is full of mistakes as to facts, and misrepresentations concerning facts. Poor dear Coleridge from a hundred causes many of them unhappy ones was not to be trusted in his account either of particular occurences, or the general tenor of his engagements and occupations. Mr. G. may be more fortunate when he shall come to what he himself had an opportunity of observing, but there again I have my fears. Of idolatrous Biography I think very lightly: we have had too many examples of it lately; take Mr Wilberforce's life by his Sons as a specimen; and Coleridge I am afraid will not be dealt more wisely with. Observe in what I have said above I do not mean to impeach poor C.'s veraciousness, far from it, but his credibility. He deceived himself in a hundred ways; relating things according to the humor of the moment, as his spirits were up or down, or as they furnished employment for his fancy, or for his theories.
To ?,   VI. 9, 1838

Gladstone, William E.

1.*   . . . Gladstone *On the relation of the Church to the State.* . . . Even Wordsworth says he cannot distinguish its principles from Romanism.
C. R. to T. R. (Corr. C. R., i, 376),   I. 19, 1839

2.*   Wordsworth pronounced it [Gladstone's *The State in its Relation to the Church*] worthy of all attention, doubted whether the author had not gone too far about apostolical descent, but then . . . the poet admitted he must know a great deal more ecclesiastical history, be better read in the Fathers, and read the book itself over again, before he could feel any right to criticise.
Gladstone, i, 176.   1839

3.   Pray accept my thanks for your State and Prospects of the Church [' Present Aspects of the Church '] which I have carefully read. . . . You have approached the subject in a most becoming spirit, and treated it with admirable ability. From scarcely anything that you have said did I dissent; only felt some little dissatisfaction as to the limits of your Catholicity; for some limits it must have; but probably you acted wisely in not being more precise upon this point. *To W. E. Gladstone,*   III. 21, 1844

Godwin, C. Grace

1. I have . . . [read *The Wanderer's Legacy*], and with much pleasure. Wherever it is read, such poetry cannot but do you honour. It is neither wanting in feeling, nor in that much rarer gift which is the soul of poetry, Imagination. There is a great command of language also, and occasionally fine versification; but here and in some other points of workmanship, you are most defective, especially in the blank verse. Am I right in supposing that several of these pieces have been written at different periods of life? 'The Wanderer,' for example, though full of varied interest, appears to me, in point of versification, and in some respects of style, much inferior to 'Destiny,' a very striking poem. This and the 'Monk of Camaldoli' are, in my judgment, the best *executed* pieces in the volume. Both evince extraordinary powers.

The fault of your blank verse is that it is not sufficiently broken. You are aware that it is infinitely the most difficult metre to manage, as is clear from so few having succeeded in it. The Spenserian stanza is a fine structure of verse; but that is also almost insurmountably difficult. You have succeeded in the broken and more impassioned movement—of which Lord Byron has given good instances—but it is a form of verse ill adapted to conflicting passion; and it is not injustice to say that the stanza is spoiled in Lord Byron's hands; his own strong and ungovernable passions blinded him to its character. It is equally unfit for narrative. *Circumstances* are difficult to manage in any kind of verse, except the dramatic, where the warmth of the action makes the reader indifferent to those delicacies of phrase and sound upon which so much of the charm of other poetry depends. If you write more in this stanza, leave Lord Byron for Spenser. In him the stanza is seen in perfection. It is exquisitely harmonious also in Thomson's hands, and fine in Beattie's 'Minstrel'; but these two latter poems are merely descriptive and sentimental; and you will observe that Spenser never gives way to violent and conflicting passion, and that his narrative is bare of circumstances, slow in movement, and (for modern relish) too much clogged with description. Excuse my dwelling so much on this dry subject; but as you have succeeded so well in the arrangement of this metre, perhaps you will not be sorry to hear my opinion of its character. One great objection to it (an insurmountable one, I think, for circumstantial narrative) is the poverty of our language in rhymes.

But to recur to your volume. I was everywhere more or less interested in it. Upon the whole I think I like best 'Destiny' and the 'Monk,' but mainly for the reasons above given. The 'Wanderer's Legacy' being upon a large scale, and so true to your own feelings, has left a lively impression upon my mind; and a moral purpose is answered, by exhibiting youthful love under such illusion with regard to the real value of its object. The 'Seal Hunters' is an affecting poem, but I think you linger too long in the prelusive description. I could speak with pleasure of many other pieces. . . .

. . . to point out certain minutiae of phrase in your volume, where you have been mislead by bad example, especially of the Scotch. The popularity, of some of their writings has done no little harm to the English language, for the present at least. *To C. Grace Godwin,*   1829

10

2.*   . . . my Brother thinks highly of Mrs. Godwin's powers and attainments.   *D. W. to Moxon,*   X. 2, 1834

Godwin, William

1.   I have received from Montagu, Godwyn's second edition [the second edition of Godwin's *Political Justice* appeared in 1796]. I expect to find the work much improved. I cannot say that I have been encouraged in this hope by the perusal of the second preface, which is all I have yet looked into. Such a piece of barbarous writing I have not often seen. It contains scarce one sentence decently written. I am surprised to find such gross faults in a writer, who has had so much practice in composition.
To Wm. Mathews,   III. 21, 1796

2.   See W. 301

3.*   Throw aside your books of chemistry . . . and read Godwin on Necessity.   *Hazlitt,* iv, 201.   *c.* 1800

Goethe, Johann Wolfgang von (General Criticism)

1.   Of the excellence of Lessing I can form no distinct idea. My internal prejudgment concerning Wieland and Goethe (of Voss I knew nothing) were, as your letter has convinced me, the result of no *negligent* perusal of the different fragments which I had seen in England.
D. W. and W. to Coleridge (p. 221),   II. 27, 1799

2.*   Goethe's writings cannot live . . . because *they are not holy.*
Mrs. Hemans, ii, 120.   1830

3.*   . . . I have no pleasure in hearing Wordsworth talk—[on] Goethe, whom he depreciates in utter ignorance. *H. C. R.,* ii, 478.   I. 5, 1836

4.   See Voltaire 6

5.*   But where has he [W.] published that Göthe is an impostor? I believe he s[ai]d something of the kind in my chambers one morning.
C. R. to Landor (*Corr. C. R.,* i, 327),   XII. 7, 1836

It annoys me greatly to read your prose note that ' Impostor was the expression ' W: used of G: because I do not recollect his using the very words, but I know that he always talks ignorantly and therefore absurdly about G. and I fear he may have said so—
C. R. to Landor (*Corr. C. R.,* i, 331),   XII. 17, 1836

6.*   I [W.] there indict him [Goethe] for wantonly outraging the ܁ympathies of humanity.
Sara Coleridge and Reed, p. 106.   *c.* 1840

7.*   He thinks that the German poet [Goethe] is greatly overrated, both in this country and his own. He said, ' He does not seem to me to be a great poet in either of the classes of poets. At the head of the first class I would place Homer and Shakspeare, whose universal minds are able to reach every variety of thought and feeling without bringing their own individuality before the reader. They infuse, they breathe life into every object they approach, but you never find *themselves*. At the head of the second class, those whom you can trace individually in all they write, I would place Spenser and Milton. In all that Spenser writes you can trace the gentle affectionate spirit of the man; in all that Milton writes you can find the exalted sustained being that he was. Now in what Goethe writes, who aims to be of the first class, the *universal*, you find the man himself, the artificial man, where he should not be found; so that I consider him a very artificial writer, aiming to be universal, and yet constantly exposing his individuality, which his character was not of a kind to dignify. He had not sufficiently clear moral perceptions to make him anything but an artificial writer.

Lady R. (Grosart, iii, 435-36). VIII. 25, 1841

8.* Of Goethe Wordsworth spoke with his usual bitterness, and I cannot deny that his objection is well-founded—that is an extreme defect of religious sentiment, perhaps I should say, moral sense—and this suffices, says Wordsworth, to prove that he could be only a second-rate man. Wordsworth, however, does not deny that he is a great artist—but he adds this, in which I do not agree: In Shakespeare and Homer we are astonished at the universality of their penetration. They seem to embrace the whole world. Every form and variety of humanity they represent with equal truth. In Goethe you see that he attempts the same, but he fails. In Milton and Spenser there is not the attempt. You have admirable representations, and what the authors mean to do they actually do. Goethe's *Tasso* and his *Iphigenia* Wordsworth declares to be flat and insipid; but then he knows them only in translations. He has formerly said the same of *Herman and Dorothea*: he expressed disgust at the *Bride of Corinth*, which Herder called *scheusslich*.

H. C. R., ii, 627-28. I. 1, 1843

9.* [Goethe professed indifference to theology.]

Old Friends, p. 216. X. 6, 1844

10.* Goethe's poetry is not inevitable enough [Arnold quotes W.].

Essays in Criticism, p. 155. *c.* 1845

11.* [W.'s depreciation of Goethe's genius.]

E. Q. to C. R. (Corr. C. R., ii, 779), V. 15, 1851

Goethe (Works)

12.* [*Iphigenie.*] I have tried to read Goethe. I never could succeed. Mr. ―― [Crabbe Robinson?] refers me to his 'Iphigenia,' but I there recognize none of the dignified simplicity, none of the health and vigor which the heroes and heroines of antiquity possess in the writings of Homer. The lines of Lucretius describing the immolation of Iphigenia are worth the whole of Goethe's long poem. Again, there is a profligacy, an inhuman sensuality, in his works which is utterly revolting. I am not intimately acquainted with them generally. But I take up my ground on the first canto of 'Wilhelm Meister'; and, as the attorney-general of human nature, I there indict him for wantonly outraging the sympathies of humanity. Theologians tell us of the degraded nature of man; and they tell us what is true. Yet man is essentially a moral agent, and there is that immortal and unex-

tinguishable yearning for something pure and spiritual which will plead against these poetical sensualists as long as man remains what he is.
C. W., Jr. (Grosart, iii, 465).   *c.* 1827

13. [*Wilhelm Meister.*] See Goethe 12

14.* [Abused] Goethe's Wilhelm Meister heartily. It was full of all manner of fornication. It was like the crossing of flies in the air. He had never gone farther than the first part. . . .
English Traits, p. 21.   VIII. 28, 1833

15.* In reading *Die Braut von Korinth* translated, [W.] was more horrified than enchained, or rather altogether the first. Wondering how any one could translate it or the Faust, but spoke as knowing the original.
Gladstone, i, 136.   1836

16. [*Faust.*] See Goethe 15

17. [W.] expressed disgust at the *Bride of Corinth*. See Goethe 8

18. [*Iphigenie, Herman and Dorothea*, and *Tasso*] flat and insipid. . . .
See Goethe 8

Goldsmith, Oliver

1. See Coleridge 31, 75; Langhorne 2; Reynolds, Joshua 3; Tickell 2

2.   A Pastor such as Chaucer's verse portrays;
            Such as the heaven-taught skill of Herbert drew;
            And tender Goldsmith crowned with deathless praise!
            " Sacred Religion ! " 12-14.   1806-20

3.* . . . Wordsworth would not assent to the opinion [that Goldsmith stood too high as a poet]. *Farington Diary*, viii, 2.   V. 21, 1815

4.* . . . lines in *The Traveller* made an impression on him in his youth.
H. C. R., ii, 517.   III. 28, 1837

Gomm, William

1.   Your verses . . . are an additional proof of the truth which forced from me, many years ago, the exclamation—Oh! many are the poets that are sown—By Nature [*Excursion*, I, 77].
The rest of that paragraph also has some bearing upon your position in the poetical world. The thoughts and images through both the poems, and the feelings also, are eminently such as become their several subjects; but it would be insincerity were I to omit adding that there is here and there a want of that skill in *workmanship*, which I believe nothing but continued practice in the art can bestow. I have used the word *art*, from a conviction, which I am called upon almost daily to express, that poetry is infinitely more of an art than the world is disposed to believe. Nor is this any dishonour to it; both for the reason that the poetic faculty is not rarely bestowed, and for this cause, also, that men would not be disposed to ascribe so much to inspiration, if they did not feel how near and dear to them poetry is.
To Wm. Gomm,   IV. 16, 1834

2.   Your Sonnet addressed to the unfinished monument of Governor Malartie is conceived with appropriate feeling, and just discrimination.
To Wm. Gomm,   XI. 23, 1846

Graham, James. See Montrose, James Graham, First Marquis of

Grahame, James

1.   Few of the more minute rural appearances please me more than these, of one shrub or flower lending its ornaments to another. . . . Mr. Graham in his *Birds of Scotland* has an exquisite passage upon this subject, with which I will conclude [see ll. 8-9; 11-15, p. 23, in 1806 (Edinburgh) edition].
To Lady Beaumont (p. 99),   XII. 23, 1806

Granville, George, Baron of Lansdowne. See Johnson 11

Graves, John

1.   [W. regrets seeing works of this kind (topographical histories), which might be made so very interesting,] utterly marred by falling into the hands of wretched Bunglers, e. g. the *History of Cleveland* . . . by a Clergyman of Yarm of the name of Grave, the most heavy performance I ever encountered.
. . . *To F. Wrangham,*   X. 2, 1808

Graves, R. P.

1.   Many thanks for your Sonnet both on account of the affectionate sentiments it so well expresses, as for the proof it gave that you were going on well. *To Graves,*   I. 17, 1842

Gray, Thomas (General Criticism)

1.   See Poetry 25; Quillinan 6; Thomson 13; W. 237
2.*   . . . a great dislike to Gray. . . . *Hazlitt,* iv, 277.   *c.* 1800
4.   If Gray's plan [of ode] be adopted, there is not time to become acquainted with the arrangement, and to recognize with pleasure the recurrence of the movement. *To Southey* (p. 718),   1816
5.   Gray failed as a Poet, not because he took too much pains, and so extinguished his animation [see Brydges 2]; but because he had little of that fiery quality to begin with; and his pains were of the wrong sort. He wrote English Verses, as he and other Eton school-Boys wrote Latin; filching a phrase now from one author, and now from another. I do not profess to be a person of very various reading; nevertheless if were to pluck out of Grays tail all the feathers which, I know, belong to other Birds he would be left very bare indeed. Do not let any Body persuade you that any quantity of good verses can ever be produced by mere felicity; or that an immortal *style* can be the growth of mere Genius—Multa *tulit* fecitque, must be the motto of all those who are to last. There are Poems now existing which all the World ran after at their first appearance (and it will continue to run after their like) that do not deserve to be thought of as *literary* Works— every thing in them being skin deep merely, as to thought and feeling, the juncture or suture of the composition not a jot more cunning or more fitted

for endurance than the first fastening together of fig-leaves in Paradise. But, I need not press upon you the necessity of Labour, as you have avowed your convictions on this subject. *To Gillies,*   IV. 15, 1816

6. . . . Gray, in one of his letters . . . affirms that description (he means of natural scenery and the operations of Nature) though an admirable ornament, ought *never* to be the subject of poetry. How many exclusive dogmas have been laid down, which genius from age to age has triumphantly refuted! and grossly should I be deceived if, speaking freely to you as an old Friend, these local poems do not contain many proofs that Gray was as much in the wrong in this interdict, as any critical Brother who may have framed his canons without a spark of inspiration or poetry to guide him. I particularly recommend to your second perusal the Eclipse [*Oxf. W.*, p. 343], to be valued I think as a specimen of description in which beauty majesty and novelty, nature and art, earth and heaven are brought together with a degree of lyrical spirit and movement which professed Odes have, in our language at least, rarely attained. I am sure you cannot have overlooked this piece. But fearing that it may have failed to interest you as much as I could wish, I have thus adverted to it, being sure that your taste leads you to rate a perfect idyllicism or exquisite epigram higher than a moderate epic—perfection you will agree with me, in humble kinds, is preferable to moderate execution in the highest. *To R. Sharp.*   IV. 16, 1822

7. [W. approves Gray's remark on Pope's letters, "they are not good, but they are something better than Letters."] See Letter-writing 2

8.* His [Gray's] own remarks on the poetical habits which unfitted him for the production of a poem of large compass seem to me [Sara Coleridge] excellent and are just what I have often heard in other words from W. W. and H. Taylor. *Sara Coleridge and Reed,* p. 67.   *c.* 1840

Gray, Thomas (Works)

10.* [By W.'s conversation, Coleridge] had been induced to reexamine with impartial strictness Gray's celebrated elegy.
Biog. Lit., i, 26 n.   *c.* 1800

11. The sonnet [*Sonnet on the Death of Mr. Richard West. See Oxf. W.,* p. 936] quoted from Gray, in the Preface, except the lines printed in Italics, consists of little else but this diction, though not of the worst kind; and indeed, if one may be permitted to say so, it is far too common in the best writers both ancient and modern. *App. L. B.,* p. 943.   1802

12.   But now
        I thought, still traversing that widespread plain,
        With tender pleasure of the verses [from Gray's
                Elegy] graven
        Upon his tombstone, whispering to myself:
        He loved the Poets, and, if now alive,
        Would have loved me, as one not destitute
        Of promise, nor belying the kind hope
        That he had formed, when I, at his command,
        Began to spin, with toil, my earliest songs.
Prel., x, 544-52.   1804-39

13. [*Epitaph on Mrs. Jane Clerke.*] The latter part of the following by Gray is almost the only instance among the metrical epitaphs in our language of the last century, which I remember, of affecting thoughts rising naturally and keeping themselves pure from vicious diction; and therefore retaining their appropriate power over the mind. [Here follows the *Epitaph on Mrs. Clerke*] . . . I have been speaking of faults which are aggravated by temptations thrown in the way of modern Writers when they compose in metre. The first six lines of this epitaph are vague and languid, more so than I think would have been possible had it been written in prose. . . . Gray . . . was so happy in the remaining part, especially the last four lines. . . .
Epitaph 3 (Grosart, ii, 66-7).   1810

14. [Gray in *Epitaph on his Mother*] failed *in prose* upon a subject which it might have been expected would have bound him indissolubly to the propriety of Nature and comprehensive reason. I allude to the conclusion of the epitaph upon his mother, where he says, ' she was the careful tender mother of many children, one of whom alone had the misfortune to survive her.' This is a searching thought, but wholly out of place. [Had the child been helpless the thought would have been appropriate; otherwise, the thought is selfish and focuses attention on the author rather than upon the subject of the epitaph. Also the expression of so poignant and transitory a feeling is out of place in an epitaph, too morbid and " peculiar."]
Epitaphs 3 (Grosart, ii, 67-8).   1810

15.* [Line 20 of *The Bard*] ridiculous [and stolen from Milton].
H. C. R., i, 90.   V. 31, 1812

16. See Campbell 3; Landor 10

18. In a noble strain also does the Poet Gray address, in a Latin Ode, the *Religio Loci* at the Grande Chartruise. [Before Thomas Burnet (see Burnet 2), and Gray, all English travelers' writings expressed fear and dislike of " precipitous rocks and mountains," and even Gray in his *Journal* quotes Dante's " Let us not speak of them, but look and pass on."]
K. and W. Railway (Grosart, ii, 327).   1835

19. . . . the record [Gray's *Journal*] left behind him of what he had seen and felt in this journey, excited that pensive interest with which the human mind is ever disposed to listen to the farewell words of a man of genius. The journal of Gray feelingly showed how the gloom of ill health and low spirits had been irradiated by objects, which the Author's powers of mind enabled him to describe with distinctness and unaffected simplicity. Every reader of this journal must have been impressed with the words which conclude his notice of the Vale of Grasmere:—' Not a single red tile, no flaring gentleman's house or garden-wall, breaks in upon the repose of this little unsuspected paradise; but all is peace, rusticity, and happy poverty, in its neatest and most becoming attire.' *Lakes (Grosart, ii, 269-70).*   1810-35

20. . . . the vale of Grasmere . . . as touchingly described by the Poet Gray in his journal written 70 years ago.
To I. Fenwick,   VIII. 30, 1841

Green, William

1. Green's comprehensive *Guide to the Lakes.* . . .
Grosart, iii, 102.   1820

Grimm, Friedrich. See Shakespeare 14

Guizot, François Pierre Guillaume

1.* . . . Guizot and the few other men of real genius. . . .
Old Friends, p. 215.   X. 6, 1844

Hakewill, George. See Shakespeare 45

Halifax, Charles Montague, Earl of. See Johnson 11

Hall, Joseph. See Montagu 5

Hall, Samuel C.

1. The Embellishments [in Hall's ed. of the *Amulet*, 1827] are elegant
and the literary part is conducted upon a principle that cannot but be highly
approved, that of uniting *instruction* with amusement. [W. lists several
approved articles.]
To S. C. Hall (L. of W. Family, p. 65),   IV. 12, 1827

2. . . . satisfied with your notice of my writings and character [in *The
Book of Gems*]—All I can say further is that I have *wished* both to be what
you indulgently affirm they are. In the few facts of your Memoir, there is
only one mistake or rather inaccuracy. You say he was educated *with* his
almost equally distinguished Brother—My Br. Dr W—he it is true was
brought up at the same school—but being upwards of 4 years younger than
myself—we could scarcely be said to be educated together—and I had left
College before he came there.   *To S. C. Hall,*   XII. 23, 1837

Hallam, Arthur Henry

1. A sad case was that of my young friend Hallam. . . . He was a
young Man of genius, great acquirements and high promise.
To R. Jones,   X. 29, 1833

Hamilton, Eliza Mary

1. [Verses in the poem, *The Boy's School,*] are surprisingly vigorous for
a female pen, but occasionally too rugged, and especially for such a subject;
they have also the same fault in expression as your own, but not I think in
quite an equal degree. Much is to hoped from feelings so strong, and from
a mind thus disposed. I should have entered into particulars with these also,
had I seen you after they came into my hands. Your sister is, no doubt,
aware that in her poem she has trodden the same ground as Gray, in his Ode
upon a Distant Prospect of Eton College. What he has been contented to
treat in the abstract she has represented in particular, and with admirable
spirit. But again, . . . let me exhort you (and do you exhort your sister)

to deal little with modern writers, but fix your attention almost exclusively upon those who have stood the test of time.
To W. R. Hamilton,   IX. 24, 1827

2. . . . much gratified with your sister verses . . . they are well and vigorously expressed, and the feelings are such as one could wish should exist oftener than they appear to do in the bosoms of *male* astronomers.
To W. R. Hamilton,   II. 12, 1829

3. Your sister's [verses] have abundance of spirit and feeling; all that they want is what appears in itself of little moment, and yet is incalculably great; that is, workmanship—the art by which the thoughts are made to melt into each other, and to fall into light and shadow, regulated by distinct pre-conception of the best general effect they are capable of producing. This may seem very vague to you, but by conversation I think I could make it appear otherwise; it is enough for the present to say that I was much gratified, and beg you will thank your sister for favouring me with the sight of compositions so distinctly marked with that quality which is the subject of them [i. e. genius. W. W.]. *To W. R. Hamilton,*   VII. 24, 1829

4. They abound with genuine sensibility, and do her much honour; but, as I told you before, your sister must practise her mind in severer logic than a person so young can be expected to have cultivated; for example, the first words of the first poem, ' Thou *most companionless.*' In strict logic, ' being companionless ' is a positive condition not admitting of more or less, though in poetic feeling it is true that the sense of it is deeper as to one object than to another; and the *day* moon is an object eminently calculated for impressing certain minds with that feeling; therefore the expression is not faulty in itself absolutely, but faulty in its position—coming without preparation, and there-fore causing a shock between the commonsense of the words, and the impassioned imagination of the speaker. This may appear to you frigid criticism, but, depend upon it, no writings will live in which these rules are disregarded. In the next line,

Walking the blue but foreign fields of day,

the meaning here is walking blue fields which, though common to see in our observation by night, are not so by day, even to accurate observers. Here, too, the thought is just; but again there is an abruptness; the distinction is too nice, or refined, for the second line of a poem. [Next follow suggestions for improving the *harsh diction* of Mary Hamilton's poems] ' Breast ' is a sacrifice to rhyme, and is harsh in expression. We have had the *brow* and the *eye* of the moon before, both allowable; but what have we reserved for human beings, if their features and organs etc., are to be *lavished* on objects without feeling and intelligence? You will, perhaps, think this observation comes with an ill grace from one who is aware that he has tempted many of his admirers into *abuses* of this kind; yet, I assure you, I have never given way to my own feelings in personifying natural objects, or investing them with sensation, without bringing all that I have said to a rigorous after-test of good sense, as far as I was able to determine what good sense is. Your sister will judge, from my being so minute, that I have been much interested in

her poetical character; this very poem highly delighted me; the sentiment meets with my entire approbation, and it is feelingly and poetically treated. Female authorship is to be shunned as bringing in its train more and heavier evils than have presented themselves to your sister's ingenuous mind. . . . She will probably write less in proportion as she subjects her feelings to logical forms, but the range of her sensibilities, so far from being narrowed, will extend as she improves in the habit of looking at things through the steady light of words; and to speak a little metaphysically, words are not a mere *vehicle*, but they are *powers* either to kill or animate.
To W. R. Hamilton,   XII. 23, 1829

4A.   [Her] poetical genius is highly promising. . . .
To G. H. Gordon (*L. of W. Family*, p. 40),   VII or VIII, 1830

5.   I hope that my criticisms have not deterred your sister from poetical composition. The world has indeed had enough of it lately, such as it is; but that is no reason why a sensibility like hers should not give vent to itself in verse.   *To W. R. Hamilton,*   I. 24, 1831

6.   . . . we know not what favour her volume of poems [Dublin, 1838] may have met with from the public, but we are convinced that they merit a degree of approbation far beyond what it is too probable they will receive, poetry being so little to the taste of these times. I am strongly persuaded that in my own case, should I have first appeared before the public at this late day, my endeavours would have attracted little attention; forty years have been required to give my name the station (such as it is) which it now occupies.
To W. R. Hamilton,   I. 20, 1839

Hamilton, Thomas

1.   The subject is rather hackneyed—but I hope his Book [*Men and Manners in America*], of which I have read the first Vol: will be of some use in correcting the errors of those, who are inclined to think that a Government such as the American might be advantageously adopted in our Country. Hume may really believe this as he is a narrow-minded, stupid Fellow, but Cobbet who is a most able and sagacious Man [when] he talks in that strain is a wilful deceiver, for selfish purposes.
To C. R. (*Corr. C. R.*, i, 237),   V. 5, 1833

Hamilton, William Rowan (General Criticism)

1.   You send me showers of verses, which I receive with much pleasure, as do we all; yet have we fears that this employment may seduce you from the path of Science, which you seem destined to tread with so much honour to yourself and profit to others. Again and again I must repeat, that the composition of verse is infinitely more of an art than men are prepared to believe; and absolute success in it depends upon innumerable minutiae, which it grieves me you should stoop to acquire a knowledge of. Milton talks of ' pouring easy his unpremeditated verse.' It would be harsh, untrue, and odious, to say there is anything like cant in this; but it is not true to the letter, and tends to mislead. I could point out to you five hundred passages in

Milton upon which labour has been bestowed, and twice five hundred more to which additional labour would have been serviceable. Not that I regret the absence of such labour, because no poem contains more proofs of skill acquired by practice. These observations are not called out by any defects or imperfections in your last pieces especially: they are equal to the former ones in effect, have many beauties, and are not inferior in execution; but again I do venture to submit to your consideration, whether the poetical parts of your nature would not find a field more favorable to their exercise in the regions of prose: not because those regions are humbler, but because they may be gracefully and profitably trod with footsteps less careful and in measures less elaborate. And now I have done with the subject, and have only to add, that when you write verses you would not fail, from time to time, to let me have a sight of them; provided you will allow me to defer criticism on your diction and versification till we meet. *To W. R. Hamilton,*   XI. 22, 1831

2*. . . . Sir W. Hamilton was the most remarkable man he had known except Coleridge [see also Literature 17].

Aubrey de Vere, p. 70.   III. 9, 1841

Hamilton, William Rowan (Works)

4. . . . I can assure you that, in my judgment, your verses are animated with true poetic spirit, as they are evidently the product of strong feeling. The sixth and seventh stanzas affected me much, even to the dimming of my eye, and faltering of my voice while I was reading them aloud. Having said this, I have said enough; now for the *per contra.*

You will not, I am sure, be hurt, when I tell you that the workmanship (what else could be expected from so young a writer?) is not what it ought to be; even in those two affecting stanzas it is not perfect. . . .

> But shall despondence therefore *blench* my *brow,*
> Or pining sorrow sickly ardour o'er.

These are two of the worst lines in mere expression. 'Blench' is perhaps miswritten for 'blanch': if not, I don't understand the word. *Blench* signifies to flinch. If 'blanch' be the word, the next ought to be '*hair.*' You can't here use *brow* for the *hair* upon it, because a white brow or forehead is a beautiful characteristic of youth. 'Sickly ardour o'er' was at first reading to me unintelligible. I took 'sickly' to be an adjective joined with 'ardour,' whereas you mean it as a portion of a verb, from Shakespeare, 'Sicklied o'er with the pale cast of thought,' but the separation of the parts, or decomposition of the word, as here done, is not to be endured.

To W. R. Hamilton,   IX. 24, 1827

5. Your own verses are dated 1826. I note this early date with pleasure, because I think if they had been composed lately, the only objections I make to them would probably not have existed, at least in an equal degree. It is an objection that relates to style alone, and to versification; for example, the last line, 'And he was *the* enthusiast no more,' which is, in meaning, the weightiest of all, is not sinewy enough in sound—the syllable *the,* as the metre requires, should be long, but it is short, and imparts a langour to the

sense. The three lines, ' As if he were addressing,' etc., are too prosaic in movement. After having directed your attention to these minutiae, I can say, without scruple, that the verses are highly spirited, and interesting and poetical. The change of character they describe is an object of instructive contemplation, and the whole executed with feeling. . . .

The sonnet I like very much, with no drawback but what is, in a great measure, personal to myself. I am so accustomed, in my own practice, to pass *one* set of rhymes at least through the first eight lines, that the want of that vein of sound takes from the music something of its consistency—to my mind and ear. *To W. R. Hamilton,*   II. 12, 1829

6. Your own verses are to me very interesting, and affect me much as evidences of high- and pure-mindedness, from which humble-mindedness is inseparable. I like to see and think of you among the stars, and between death and immortality, where three of these poems place you. The *Dream of Chivalry* is also interesting in another way; but it would be insincere not to say that something of a style more terse, and a harmony more accurately balanced, must be acquired before the bodily form of your verses will be quite worthy of their living souls. You are probably aware of this, though perhaps not in an equal degree with myself; nor is it desirable you should be, for it might tempt you to labour, which would divert you from subjects of infinitely greater importance. *To W. R. Hamilton,*   VII. 24, 1829

7. . . . the poem you were so kind as to enclose gave me much pleasure, nor was it the less interesting for being composed upon a subject you had touched before. The style in this latter is more correct, and the versification more musical. Where there is so much of sincerity of feeling, in a matter so dignified as the renunciation of Poetry for Science, one feels that an apology is necessary for verbal criticism. I will therefore content myself with observing that *joying* for *joy,* or *joyance,* is not to my taste—indeed, I object to such liberties upon principle. We should soon have no language at all if the unscrupulous coinage of the present day were allowed to pass, and become a precedent for the future. One of the first duties of a writer is to ask himself whether his thought, feeling, or image cannot be expressed by existing words or phases, before he goes about creating new terms, even when they are justified by the analogies of the language. ' The cataract's steep flow ' is both harsh and inaccurate—' Thou hast seen me bend over the cataract ' would express one idea in simplicity, and all that was required; had it been necessary to be more particular, *steep flow* are not the words that ought to have been used. I remember Campbell says in a composition that is overrun with faulty language,

And dark as winter was the *flow*
Of Iser rolling rapidly—

that is, flowing rapidly. The expression ought to have been *stream* or *current.* *To W. R. Hamilton,*   XII. 23, 1829

8. . . . your letter and verses; for both of which I thank you, as they exhibit your mind under those varied phases which I have great pleasure in contemplating. *To W. R. Hamilton,*   X. 27, 1831

9.   The verses called forth by your love and the disappointment that followed I have read with much pleasure, tho' grieved that you should have suffered so much; as poetry they derive an interest from your philosophical pursuits, which could not but recommend the verses even to indifferent readers, and must give them in the eyes of your friends a great charm. The style appears to me good, and the general flow of the versification harmonious; but you deal somewhat more in dactylic endings and identical terminations than I am accustomed to think legitimate. . . .

To W. R. Hamilton,   VI. 25, 1832

10.   Your lecture I have read with much pleasure. It is philosophical and eloquent, and instructive, and makes me regret—as I have had a thousand occasions of doing—that I did not apply to mathematics in my youth. It is now, and has long been, too late to make up for the deficiency.

To W. R. Hamilton,   II. 8, 1833

11.   Your Sonnets, I think, are as good as anything you have done in verse. We like the 2nd best, and I single it out the more readily, as it allows me an opportunity of reminding you of what I have so often insisted upon, the extreme care which is necessary in the composition of poetry.

> The ancient images *shall not* depart
> From my soul's temple, the refined gold
> Already prov'd *remain*.

Your meaning is that it shall remain, but, according to the construction of our language, you have said it shall not.

> the refined gold,
> Well proved, shall then remain,

will serve to explain my objection.

To W. R. Hamilton,   V. 8, 1833

12.   Your own two sonnets . . . we read . . . with interest.

To W. R. Hamilton,   XII. 21, 1837

13.   . . . a few words to thank you for your poem on *Elysian Fields*, and that in which you have done me so much honour by the affectionate manner in which you speak of me. *To W. R. Hamilton,*   I. 20, 1839

14.   Thank you for your translations. The longer poem [referring to a translation by Sir W. R. H. of Schiller's *Die Ideale*, to which a stanza was added by Sir W. (Grosart)] would have given me more pain than pleasure, but for your addition, which sets all right.

To W. R. Hamilton (p. 1163),   IV. 1843

Hamilton of Bangour, William

1.   See the various Poems the scene of which is laid upon the banks of the Yarrow; in particular the exquisite Ballad of Hamilton beginning

> ' Busk ye, busk ye, my bonnie, bonnie Bride,
> Busk ye, busk ye, my winsome Marrow.'

Grosart, iii, 68.   1807

Hampden, Dickson

1. Of Dr Hampden's opinions [in 1827 he wrote *Essays of the Philo-sophical Evidences of Christianity*] I know no more than any one may have learned from the extracts from his Lectures in the newspapers—But surely it is astounding that he and others can remain in the Church at all.

To J. Watson,   II. 28, 1836

Handley, E. Hill

1. . . . your interesting Letter evinces an extraordinary power would be obvious to the dullest and the most insensible. Indeed I may declare with sincerity that great things may be expected from one capable of feeling in such a strain, and expressing himself with so much vigor and originality. With your verses upon Furness Abbey I am in sympathy when I look on the dark side of the subject—and they are well expressed except for the phrase that ' Superstitions damn ' (if I read aright) which is not to *my* taste.

And now for the short piece that ' contains the thoughts of your whole life.' Having prepared you for the conclusion that neither my own opinion nor that of any one else is worth much in deciding the point for which this document is given as evidence I have no scruple in telling you honestly that I do not understand those lines. Imagine not, however, that I think the worse of them on that account. Were any one to shew an acorn to a native of the Orcades who had never seen a shrub higher than his knee, and by way of giving him a notion or image of the oak should tell him that its ' latitude of boughs ' lies close folded in that ' auburn nut ' the Orcadian would stare and would feel that his imagination was somewhat unreasonably taxed. So it is with me in respect to this germ. I do not deny that the ' forest's Monarch with his army shade ' may be lurking there in embryo; but neither can I under-take to affirm it. Therefore let your mind, which is surely of a higher order, be its own oracle. . . .   The true standard of poetry is high as the soul of man has gone, or can go. How far my own falls below that, no one can have such pathetic conviction of as my poor self.

To E. Hill Handley,   X. 4, 1830

Hare, Julius C.

1. To the honour of Cambridge he is in the highest repute there, for his sound, and extensive learning. *To Landor,*   I. 21, 1824

2.* . . . Hare . . . very excellent and very learned; more valued by Wordsworth for his classical than for his German attainments.

Old Friends, p. 215.   X. 6, 1844

Harrington, James

1.   Great men have been among us; hands that penned
            And tongues that uttered wisdom—better none. . . .
            " Great men," 1-2.   1802

Harrison, Antony

1. . . . of facetious memory, and the whole family of Addison (certain

proof that the blood is adulterated, though the name continues to be spelt as formerly) found the Excursion not un peu but très pesant. It was too low in the subjects for their high-flying fancies.

To C. Clarkson, New Year's Eve, 1814

Harte, Walter H.

1. . . . In Harte's Poems, Anderson's edition, are two or three notes upon Dryden which might be worth looking at—Harte had read Dryden's work with exceeding care, but very little profit.

To W. Scott (p. 458c), I. 18, 1808

Hartley, David

1. [*Observations on Man.*] See Copyright Laws 1

Haydon, Benjamin R.

1. Haydon has done himself credit by his essay [*The Judgment of Connoisseurs upon Works of Art* (1816)] on the Elgin Marbles.

To J. Scott, III. 21, 1816

2. See Creative 3; Poetry 1; W. 126; and W.'s three sonnets to Haydon.

Hazlitt, William

1. The miscreant Hazlitt continues, I have heard, his abuses of Southey Coleridge and myself, in the Examiner.—I hope that you do not associate with the Fellow, he is not a proper person to be admitted into respectable society, being the most perverse and malevolent Creature that ill luck has ever thrown in my way. Avoid him—hic niger est—And this, I understand, is the general opinion wherever he is known in London.

To B. R. Haydon, IV. 7, 1817

2. There is another acquaintance of mine also recently gone—a person for whom I never had any love, but with whom I had for a short time a good deal of intimacy—I mean Hazlitt, whose death you may have seen announced in the papers. He was a man of extraordinary acuteness, but perverse as Lord Byron himself, whose life by Galt I have been skimming since I came here. Galt affects to be very profound, though [he] is in fact a very shallow fellow, —and perhaps the most illogical writer that these illogical days have produced. His 'buts' and his 'therefores' are singularly misapplied, singularly even for this unthinking age. He accuses Mr Southey of pursuing Lord B— with *rancour*. I should like a reference to what Mr. S— has written of Lord B—, to ascertain whether this charge be well founded. I trust it is not, both from what I know of my friend, and from the aversion which Mr G— has expressed towards the *Lakers*, whom in the plenitude of his ignorance he is pleased to speak of as a *class* or *school* of Poets.

To W. R. Hamilton, IX. 26, 1830

3. See Dryden 14

4.* . . . ranked [Hazlitt] very high as a prose-writer. . . .

Yesterdays with Authors, p. 255. 1847

Headley, Henry

1.   Headley was a most extraordinary young man—more remarkable for precocity of judgment than any one I ever read or heard of; in his Poems also are beautiful passages, especially in the ' Invocation to Melancholy.' . . . It would be well if you could obtain some account of so promising a genius which would appear with great propriety in an account of Dr Parr.
To E. H. Barker,   VII. 24, 1829

Hearne, Samuel

1.   See that very interesting work, Hearne's *Journey from Hudson's Bay to the Northern Ocean. Grosart,* iii, 24 (see also p. 25).   1798

Hemans, Felicia

1.   We like Mrs Hemans much—her conversation is what might be expected from her Poetry, full of sensibility. . . .
To Rogers,   VII. 30, 1830

1A.   [Her] conversation, like that of many literary Ladies, is too elaborate and studied. . . .
To G. H. Gordon (L. of W. Family, p. 40),   VII or VIII, 1830

2.*   . . . Mr Wordsworth was pleased with ' The St Cecilia,' particularly with the *nightingale* verse. *Mrs. Hemans,* ii, 106.   1830

3.   Never before did I feel such reason to be grateful for what little inspiration Heaven has graciously bestowed upon my humble Intellect. What you kindly wrote upon the interest you took during your travels in my verses could not but be grateful to me because your own show that in a rare degree you understand and sympathise with me. *To Mrs. Hemans,*   XI. 22, 1831

4.   [*The Pilgrim Song.*] . . . many of the Pieces had fallen in my way before they were collected; and had given me more or less pleasure—as all your productions do. . . . I can only say that whenever I have peeped into the volume—I have been well recompensed. This morning I glanced my eye over the Pilgrim Song to the evening Star with great pleasure.
To Mrs. Hemans,   IV. 30, 1834

5.   [*Scenes and Hymns of Life* (1834), dedicated to W.] Where there is so much to admire it is difficult to select; and therefore I shall content myself with naming only two or three pieces. And, first, let me particularise the piece that stands second in the volume, *Flowers and Music in a Room of Sickness.* This was especially touching to me, on my poor sister's account, who has long been an invalid confined almost to her chamber. The feelings are sweetly touched throughout this poem, and the imagery very beautiful; above all, in the passage where you describe the colour of the petals of the wild rose. This mourning I have read the stanzas upon *Elysium* with great pleasure. You have admirably expanded the thought of Chateaubriand.

    . . . I cannot conclude without thanking you for your sonnet upon a place so dear to me as Grasmere [*A Remembrance of Grasmere,* included in ' Records of the Spring of 1834 ']; it is worthy of the subject.
To Mrs. Hemans,   IX, 1834

6.   Mrs. Hemans was unfortunate as a Poetess in being obliged by circumstances to write for money, and that so frequently and so much, that she was compelled to look out for subjects wherever she could find them, and to write as expeditiously as possible. As a woman she was to a considerable degree a spoilt child of the world. She had been early in life distinguished for talents, and poems of hers were published whilst she was a girl. . . . I was not a little affected by learning that after she withdrew to Ireland a long and severe illness raised her spirit as it depressed her body. This I heard from her most intimate friends, and there is striking evidence of it in a poem entitled [Blank; and in Pencil on opposite page—Do you mean a Sonnet entitled ' Sabbath Sonnet,' composed by Mrs. Hemans, April 26th, 1835, a few days before her death? ' How many blessed groups this hour are wending! '] *I. F. (Grosart, iii, 193)*.   1843

Heraud, J. A.

1.   Your Poem [*The Descent into Hell*] is vigorous, and that is enough for me—I think it in some places diffuse, in others somewhat rugged, from the originality of your mind. You feel strongly; trust to those feelings, and your poem will take its shape and proportions as a tree does from the vital principle that actuates it. I do not think that great poems can be cast in a mould.—Homer's, the greatest of all, certainly was not. Trust, again I say, to yourself. *To Heraud*,   XI. 23, 1830

2.   . . . I much admire what I have been able to peruse of his work, and think very highly of his genius. *To Moxon*,   VIII. 25, 1834

3.*   . . . a man of great talent. . . . *H. C. R.*, ii, 565.   I. 20, 1839

Herbert, George

1.   A Pastor . . .
     Such as the heaven taught skill of Herbert drew. . . .
     " Sacred Religion ! " 12-13.   1806-20

Herodotus

1.   . . . I am in hopes that by & by she [Dora W.] will attack Herodotus & Thucydidees [*sic*].
W. W., M. W. and D. W. to C. R. (Corr. C. R., i, 268),   XI. 24, 1834

2.*   Herodotus he though, ' the most interesting and instructive book, next to the Bible, which have ever been written.' Modern discoveries had only tended to confirm the general truth of his narrative.
Ellis Yarnall (Grosart, iii, 479).   VIII. 18, 1849

Hervey, T. K.

1.   I read your Australia with much pleasure; it comprehends whatever is most interesting in the subject; and the verse is harmonious and the language elegant. The smaller pieces are not unworthy of their place.
To T. K. Hervey,   late 1825

2.   I have however read most of the Poetry [in *Friendship's Offering*]

and have been much pleased with several pieces both of the Editor [T. K. Hervey] and the Contributors. Your Book is designed principally for the sofa Table, and appears to me admirably adapted to that purpose—both in its embellishments and the mode in which the Authors have executed their part of the Task. It would be, as you will conjecture, something more to my particular taste, if it were less for that of the *fine* world—if it pressed closer upon common life—but this would not suit the market—therefore you will do well to go on as you have begun under the auspices of the present able Editor. Will he excuse me if I mention that the arrangement of the miscellaneous poems is of consequence—it either may greatly aid or much spoil their effect—For instance, Mr Montgomery's serious and even solemn Lines are unluckily followed by a smart jeu d'esprit of one of the Smith's, and the two poems, though both very good in their several ways, strangle each other. Another Poem, one of Mr. Hervey's has many sweet lines, but it is unfortunately entitled on a Picture of a *dead* Girl—instead of a Girl since dead. Such a title reminds one of Pictures of dead Game—these are trifles, but of most importance to the class of readers whom your Book will best suit. . . .
To L. Relfe,   VII. 25, 1826

Heywood, Thomas

1.   One passage in one of your notes I was grieved to see; not the language of praise applied to things which, according to my feelings, do not deserve it, but hard censure unjustly passed upon a great man, I mean Heywood, the dramatist. Only read (not to speak of any of his other things) his *Woman Killed with Kindness*. There is an exquisite strain of pathos in many parts of that play, which Dryden not only was utterly incapable of producing, but of feeling when produced. The praise which has been given to Otway, Heywood is far better entitled to. He does not indeed write like a poet, but his scenes are, many of then, as *pathetic* as any that have been produced since the days of Euripides.   *To W. Scott,*   VIII. 4, 1808

Hill, Thomas

1.   . . . a tag of literature, a drysalter of the name of Hill, *a proprietor* of a periodical publication of which you probably never heard, entitled the Monthly Mirror; and of the existence of which I should also have been ignorant if a good natured Friend had not told me that I had the honor of being abused in it.   *To W. Scott* (p. 458 f.),   V. 14, 1808

Hine, Joseph

1.   [On the selection of W.'s poems, made by Joseph Hine, and the presence of notes in the edition.] When you mentioned ' notes,' I was afraid of them, and I regret much the one at the end was not suppressed. . . .
To Moxon,   early VI, 1831

2.   . . . I could wish most to be cancelled . . . the note about the Excursion—it would hurt Mr Hine's feelings perhaps to tell him so—but really the note ought not to be there. As to improving the Selection in another Edition, I am very sceptical about that. Mr. Quillinan talks of omitting the

Idiot Boy—it was precisely for his perception of the merit of this Class of
Poems that I allowed Mr Hine to make the Selection. You would find no two
Persons agree with you what was best; and upon the whole tell Mr H. that
I think he has succeeded full as well if not better than most other Persons
could have done.—There is another Note which I also object to much—it is
about [?Edinbro and the ?]. . . . *To Moxon,*   VI. 13, 1831

Hogg, James

1. [*The Queen's Wake*] does Mr. Hogg great credit. Of the tales, I
liked best, much the best, *The Witch of Fife,* the former part of *Kilmenie,*
and the *Abbot Mackinnon.* Mr. Hogg himself, I remember, seemed most
partial to *Mary Scott,* though he thought it too long. For my own part,
though I always deem the opinion of an able writer upon his own works
entitled to consideration, I cannot agree with Mr. Hogg in this preference.
The story of *Mary Scott* appears to me extremely improbable, and not skilfully
conducted; besides, the style of the piece is often vicious. The intermediate
parts of *The Queen's Wake* are done with much spirit, but the style here,
also, is often disfigured with false finery, and in too many places it recalls
Mr. Scott to one's mind. Mr. Hogg has too much genius to require that support, however respectable in itself. *To Gillies,*   XI. 23, 1814

2.   Mr. Hogg's *Badlew* . . . I could not get through. There are two
pretty passages; the flight of the deer, and the falling of the child from the
rock of Stirling, though both are a little *outrè.* But the story is coarsely
conceived, and, in my judgment, as coarsely executed; the style barbarous,
and the versification harsh and uncouth. Mr. Hogg is too illiterate to write
in any measure or style that does not savour of balladism. This is much to
be regretted; for he is possessed of no ordinary power.
To Gillies,   XII. 22, 1814

3. See Scott, W. 10; W. 150

5. . . . H. had disgusted me not by his vulgarity, wh. he c^d not help, but
by his self-conceit in delivering confident opinions upon classical literature
and other points about wh. he c^d know nothing. The reviving this business
in this formal way after a lapse of nearly 18 years does little credit to Mr
Hogg and it affords another proof how cautious one ought to be in admitting
to one's house trading Authors of any description, Verse men or Prose men.
To E. Q.,   IV. 22, 1832

6. He was undoubtedly a man of original genius, but of coarse manners
and low and offensive opinions. *I. F. (Grosart,* iii, 191).   1843

Holcroft, Thomas

1. I have attempted to read Holcroft's *Man of Ten Thousand,* but such
stuff. *To Wm. Mathews,*   III. 21, 1796

Home, John

1. [Douglas requires little power in actor.] See Drama 3
2. See Collins 6

Homer (General Criticism)

1.   . . . in memory of all books which lay
            Their sure foundations in the heart of man . . .
            From Homer the great Thunderer. . . .
            Prel., v., 198-9, and 202.   1804-39

2.   And know we not that from the blind have flowed
            The highest, holiest, raptures of the lyre;
            And wisdom married to immortal verse?
            Exc., vii, 534-36.   1814

3.   [Abundance of sublimity.] See Sublime 4

4.* . . . but I there [Goethe's *Iphigenie*] recognize none of the dignified simplicity, none of the health and vigor which the heroes and heroines of antiquity possess in the writings of Homer.

C. W., Jr. (*Grosart*, iii, 465).   *c.* 1827

5.   Dim-gleaming through imperfect lore,
                 . . . blind
            Maeonides of ampler mind. . . .
                 Written in . . . Macpherson's Ossian, 79-80.   1827

6.   See Goethe 7, 8; Heraud 1

7.   [Homer's genius active in old age.] See Talfourd 2

8.* [Homer placed next to Shakespeare.]

Graves's Recollections, p. 297.   *c.* 1840

Homer (Works)

10.   *Iliad*. See Biography 2B; Narrative Poetry 2

12.*   The first book of Homer appears to be independent of the rest. The plan of the *Odyssey* is more methodical than that of the *Iliad*. The character of Achilles seems to me one of the grandest ever conceived. There is something awful in it, particularly in the circumstance of his acting under an abiding foresight of his own death. One day, conversing with Payne Knight and Uvedale Price concerning Homer, I expressed my admiration for Nestor's speech, as eminently natural, where he tells the Greek leaders that *they* are mere children in comparison with the heroes of *old* whom *he* had known. 'But,' said Knight and Price, 'that passage is spurious!' However, I will not part with it. It is interesting to compare the same characters (Ajax, for instance) as treated by Homer, and then afterwards by the Greek dramatists, and to mark the difference of handling. In the plays of Euripides, politics come in as a disturbing force: Homer's characters act on physical impulse. There is more *introversion* in the dramatist: whence Aristotle rightly calls him τραγικώτατος. The tower scene, where Helen comes into the presence of Priam and the old Trojans, displays one of the most beautiful pictures anywhere to be seen. Priam's speech on that occasion is a striking proof of the courtesy and delicacy of the Homeric age, or, at least, of Homer himself. *C. W., Jr.* (*Grosart*, iii, 458).   *c.* 1827

13.   My own judgement [on Homer's poems] I feel to be of no *especial*

value, for I cannot pretend to have read those Poems *critically*; and *scholastically* know little about them,—but speaking from general impression and results, I should say that the Books of the Iliad were never intended to make one Poem, and that the Odyssey is not the work of the same man or exactly of the same age. These are startling things to affirm, but as in respect to Ossian, to Rowley etc., etc. there is or may be on my mind a feeling and conviction, but slightly affected either for or against by such particulars of scholarship as I am at all competent to judge of. As to the merits of the Poetry, it is in my judgment only second to Shakespeare; at the same time I cannot but think that you in some points overrate the Homeric Poems, especially the manners. The manners are often to me an encumberance in reading Homer as a *Poet*, using here (not very justifiably) manners, for designating customs, rules, ceremonies, minor incidents and details, costumes etc. and for almost everything, except natural appearances, that is not passion or character, or leading incident. As *history* these particulars are always more or less interesting, but as Poetry, they are to me often barely tolerable and not for their own sakes, but for the evidence they give of a mind in a state of sincerity and simplicity. *To Henry N. Coleridge,*   late summer, 1830

14. . . . I was never weary of travelling over the scenes through which he [Homer] led me. *I. F. (Grosart,* iii, 168).   1843

Hooker, Richard. See Montagu 5

Horace

1.   Did Sabine grace adorn my living line,
          Bandusia's praise, wild stream, should yield to thine!
          Evening Walk, 72-3.   1787-89

2. [Malignity in his satires.] *To W. Mathews,*   III. 21, 1796

3.* [Gross deficiency in the plan of Horace's *Odes.*]
Biog. Lit. ("Satyrane's Letters"), ii, 176.   [*c.* IX, 1798]

4. [His Alcaics give a sense of unity.] See Versification 13B

5. See Ancient Writers 11; Biography 2A; Virgil 10

7.*   The characteristics ascribed by Horace to Pindar in his ode, 'Pindarum quisquis,' &c. are not found in his extant writings. Horace had many lyrical effusions of the Theban bard which we have not. How graceful is Horace's modesty in his 'Ego *apis* Matinae More modoque,' as contrasted with the Dircaean Swan! Horace is my great favourite: I love him dearly.
C. W., Jr. (Grosart, iii, 459).   *c.* 1827

8.   That life—the flowery path that winds by stealth—
          Which Horace needed for his spirit's health;
          Sighed for, and in heart and genius, overcome
          By noise and strife, and questions wearisome,
          And the vain splendours of Imperial Rome?—
          Let easy mirth his social hours inspire,
          And fiction animate his sportive lyre,
          Attuned to verse that, crowning light Distress

> With garlands, cheats her into happiness;
> Give *me* the humblest note of those sad strains
> Drawn forth by pressure of his gilded chains,
> As a chance-sunbeam from his memory fell
> Upon the Sabine farm he loved so well;
> Or when the prattle of Bandusia's spring
> Haunted his ear—he only listening—
> He proud to please, above all rivals, fit
> To win the palm of gaiety and wit;
> He, doubt not, with involuntary dread,
> Shrinking from each new favour to be shed,
> By the world's Ruler, on his honoured head!
> See Poetry 118. " Those breathing Tokens," 91-110.   1829

10.   . . . or I invoke
> His [Horace's] presence to point out the spot
>   where once
> He sate, and eulogised with earnest pen
> Peace, leisure, freedom, moderate desires;
> And all the immunities of rural life
> Extolled, behind Vacuna's crumbling fane.
> *Aquapendente*, 257-61.   1837

11.* From . . . Horace, who was an especial favourite, and Lucretius, he used to quote much. *Graves* (*Grosart*, iii, 469).   *c.* 1840

Horne, Richard H.

1. Let me however recommend to your notice, the Prologue, & the Franklin's tale . . . by Mr Horne, . . . the latter in particular, very well done. *Reed*, p. 43.   I. 13, 1841

2. See Chaucer 22-3

Howitt, Mary.   See Watts, A. 4

Hume, David.   See Criticism 49

Hume, Joseph.   See Hamilton, T. 1

Hunt, Leigh

1. [W.] heard with pleasure, that his writings were valued by Mr Hunt. *To L. Hunt,*   II. 12, 1815

2. . . . I have great respect for the *Talents* of its [the *Examiner's*] Editor. *To Gillies,*   IV. 9, 1816

3. . . . Mr Hunt being a Man of Genius and Talent. . . .
To J. Forster,   XII. 19, 1831

4. See Chaucer 13, 20

5. [Hunt] has not failed in the Manciple's tale which I myself modernized many years ago. . . . *Reed*, p. 43.   I. 13, 1841

6.* I have heard Wordsworth speak very kindly both of the writings and person of Leigh Hunt. *H. C. R.*, iii, 854. I. 22, 1846

Hutchinson, Lucy

1.* My brother speaks of it [*Life of Colonel Hutchinson*, by his widow] with unqualified approbation, and he intends to read it over again.
D. W. to Lady Beaumont, II. 17, 1807

Jameson, Anna

1. [*Diary of an Ennuyée*, a book] of mere amusement.
To Maria Jewsbury, VII-VIII, 1826

Jebb, John

1. . . . your Reprint of Burnet's Lives etc., with Preface and Notes, a valuable token of your regard for which I beg you to accept my sincere thanks.
The Prefaces by Mr Knox were new to me . . . was much delighted with his eloquent, philosophical and truly christian tone of conversation.
If Bishop Burnet's Life of Bishop Bedell [William Bedell (1571-1642)] could have been abridged without material injury, it would have given me pleasure to see it in the Collection. . . . I have often expressed to Dr W. my regret that Bp. Bedell's Life was not included in his ecclesiastical Biography. *To the Bishop of Limerick [John Jebb],* I. 28, 1833

Jeffrey, Francis

1. See Criticism 16; Poetry 133; De Quincey 4; Scott, W. 35

2.* It would be treating Mr. Jeffrey with too much respect to notice any of his *criticism*; but when he makes my Brother censure himself, by quoting words as from his poems which are not there, I do think it is proper that he should be contradicted and put to shame. I mentioned this to my Brother, and he agrees with me; not that he would do it himself; but he thinks it would be well for you, or some other Friend of his, to do it for him, but in what way? *D. W. To De Quincey,* V. 1, 1809

3. [W. agrees with Jeffrey's adverse criticism (see *Edinburgh Review*, xxxviii, 261-90) of Joanna Baillie's third volume of plays.]
See Baillie 1

4. I am delighted to hear that your Edinburgh Aristarch has declared against *The Excursion*, as he will have the mortification of seeing a book enjoy a high reputation, to which he has not contributed.
To Gillies, XII. 22, 1814

5. . . . Jeff. has already printed off a Review [of *The Excursion*]; beginning with these elegant and decisive words: ' This will not do.' The sage Critic then proceeding to show cause why. The precious farce is what the Coxcomb's Idolaters call a *crushing* Review. Therefore you see as the evil Spirits are rouzed it becomes the good ones to stir, or what is to become of the poor Poet and his Labours? *To C. Clarkson,* XII. 31, 1814

6. As to the Ed: Review I hold the Author of it in entire contempt

And therefore shall not pollute my fingers with the touch of it—There is one Sentence in the Ext [extract] ending in ' *Sublime Attractions* of the Grave ' which, if the poem had contained nothing else that I valued, would have made it almost a matter of religion with me to keep out of the way of the best stuff which so mean a mind as Mr. Jeffreys could produce in connection with it.—His impertinences, to use the mildest term if once they had a place in my memory would for a time at least stick there. . . . If the mind were under the power of the will I should read Mr. Jy merely to expose his stupidity to his still more stupid admirers—
To C. R. (Corr. C. R., i, 81),   1814

8.   Your opinion of Jeffrey is just—he is a depraved Coxcomb; the greatest Dunce, I believe, in this Island, and assuredly the Man who takes most pains to prove himself so. *To Gillies,*   II. 14, 1815

. 9.*   [Never reads the *Edinburgh Review.*] He does not wish to have the opinions and *ribaldry* of *Jeffries,* the author of it floating in His memory, for however much He may despise such matter He would not have it buz in His thoughts when occupied on any siubject when Poetry engages His mind.
Farington Diary, viii, 1.   V. 21, 1815

10.   The *Edinburgh* reviewer—and him I singled out because the author [Peterkin] of the vindication of Burns has treated his offences with comparative indulgence, to which he has no claim, and which, from whatever cause it might arise, has interfered with the dispensation of justice. . . . When a man, self-elected into the office of a public judge of the literature and life of his contemporaries, can have the audacity to go to these lengths in framing a summary of the contents of volumes that are scattered over every quarter in the globe, and extant in almost every cottage of Scotland, to give the lie to his labours; we must not wonder if, in the plenitude of his concern for the interests of abstract morality, the infatuated slanderer should have found no obstacle to prevent him from insinuating that the poet, whose writings are to this degree stained and disfigured, was [insincere in friendship and love, and did not pay his debts.]
It is notorious that his persevering Aristarch [that ' Zoilus ' should be substituted for Aristarchus, as a friend suggested, the question lies between spite and presumption; and it is not easy to decide upon a case where the claims of each party are so strong; but the name of Aristarch, who, simple man would allow no verse to pass for Homer's which he did not approve of, is retained, for reasons that will be deemed cogent (*Grosart,* ii, 17 note)], as often as a work of original genius comes before him, avails himself of that opportunity to re-proclaim to the world the narrow range of his own comprehension. [W. declares] the foregoing attack upon the intellectual and moral character of Burns, to be the trespass (for reasons that will shortly appear, it cannot be called the venial trespass) of a mind obtuse, superficial, and inept. . . . But, assuredly, we shall have here another proof that ridicule is not the test of truth, if it prevent us from perceiving, that *depravity* has no ally more active, more inveterate, nor, from the difficulty of divining to what kind and degree of extravagance it may prompt, more pernicious than

self-conceit. Where this alliance is too obvious to be disputed, the culprit ought not to be allowed the benefit of contempt—as a shelter from detestation; much less should he be permitted to plead, in excuse for his transgressions, that especial malevolence had little or no part in them. . . . It is a descent, which I fear you will scarcely pardon, to compare these redoubtable enemies of mankind [Napoleon and Robespierre] with the anonymous conductor of a perishable publication. But the moving spirit is the same in them all; and, as far as difference of circumstances, and disparity of powers, will allow, manifests itself in the same way; by professions of reverence for truth, and concern for duty—carried to the giddiest heights of ostentation, while practice seems to have no other reliance than on the omnipotence of falsehood. [Here are] hints for a picture of the intellectual deformity of one who has grossly outraged his [Burns's] memory. . . .

L. to Friend of Burns (Grosart, ii, 16-19).   1816

12. [*Apropos* of the copyright bill before the privy-council, W. asks what] those Stupes know about the merit of works of Imagination—are the judges likely to be better than Jeffrey or B [Brougham]—himself, and yet one of them so late as [18]22—had the folly to write in the E. Review, that my productions were despicable without thought, without feeling taste or judgment &c. &c. See Edin. Review, [Nov.] 1822—

To C. R. (Corr. C. R., i, 369),   VII or VIII, 1838

14.* [Jeffrey could not write English.]

English Traits, p. 294.   III, 1848

Jewsbury, Maria

1. [Greatly moved by her dedication of *Phantasmagoria* to him.]
I am afraid that it may give you some little pain to be told that upon the whole, I prefer your Prose to your Verse; but the lines 'to Love' are so excellent that you need not be discouraged even should you coincide with me in thinking this opinion is just. In this Poem is a Couplet that is obscure ' And I know what all have known ' should be ' I shall know ' etc.—the rest is admirable, both in thought and expression, and the conclusion from ' Bright-winged wanderer etc.' appears to me quite original. In the Lines to Death there is much strength, but I will point to your notice a faulty Couplet for the sake of summoning you to rigorous examination, which I look upon as indispensable in verse—

> Death thou are half disarm'd and even I
> Could find it then less terrible *to die*

There is confusion between *the Person of Death and act of dying*—the process under two conflicting views—it ought to be, to meet thy dart—or, to submit to thy might—or something of that kind. But I might have spared these notices, since you describe yourself as deeply regretting defects and imperfections. Though I wished in this letter to benefit you in another way than my writings have yet done—a thousand times more agreeable to me is it to express my admiration of the good sense, the vivacity, the versatility and the ease and vigour diffused thro' your very interesting volume. The Critical

Essays, and those that turn upon manners and the surface of life, are remarkable; the one for sound judgment, and the other for acute observation and delicate handling, without exaggeration or caricature, and the episode ' the Unknown,' highly to be commended for the conciseness and spirit of the style (as indeed is all you have written), shews an acquaintance with the human heart and a power over the feelings from which no common things may be augured. Yet while I express myself thus, let me caution you, who are probably young, not to rest your hopes or happiness upon Authorship. I am aware that nothing can be done in literature without enthusiasm, and therefore it costs me more to write in this strain—but of even successful Authors how few have become happier Men—how few I am afraid have become better by their labours. Why should this be? and yet I cannot but feel persuaded that it is so with our sex, and your's is, I think, full as much exposed to evils that beset the condition. It is obvious that you have a just sense of what female merit consists in—therefore I hope for you in a degree which I could not venture to do without this evidence of the depth of your feelings and the loftiness of your conceptions.

To Maria Jewsbury,   V. 4, 1825

2. . . . her two interesting volumes, *Phantasmagoria.* . . . It is impossible to foretell how the powers of such a mind may develop themselves, but my judgment inclines to pronounce her natural bent to be more decidedly toward life and manners than poetic work. *To A. Watts,*   VIII. 5, 1825

3.   Her enthusiasm was ardent, her piety steadfast; and her great talents would have enabled her to be eminently useful in the difficult path of life to which she had been called. The opinion she entertained of her own performances, given to the world under her maiden name, Jewsbury, was modest and humble, and, indeed, far below their merits; as is often the case with those who are making trial of their powers, with a hope to discover what they are best fitted for. In one quality, viz., quickness in the motions of her mind, she had, within the range of the Author's acquaintance, no equal. *Grosart,* iii, 179.   1835

Johnson, Samuel

1. See Blank Verse and Rhyme 1; Criticism 40; Discrimination 2; Poetry 73, 138; Style 68; Gay 1; Macpherson 2; Milton 48, 53; Percy 1; Tickell 2

2.*   . . . in the beginning of Dr. Johnson's *Vanity of Human Wishes*—

> ' Let observation with extensive view
> Survey mankind from China to Peru '—

he [W.] says there is a total want of imagination accompanying the words, the same idea is repeated three times under the disguise of a different phraseology: it comes to this—' let *observation*, with extensive *observation*, *observe* mankind '; or take away the first line and the second . . . literally conveys the whole. *Hazlitt,* iv, 277.   c. 1800

4. [W., in illustrating " poetic diction," contrasts Johnson's] hubbub of words [in his metrical paraphrase of Proverbs 6: 6-11 with the diction of the Bible]. *App. L. B.,* p. 943.   1802

6. [W. disagrees with Johnson's praise of Pope's *Mrs. Corbet*.] See Pope 19

7.* He spoke of Johnson's style, etc., and denied him style as well as poetry; allowed his excellence in conversation and considered his false notions concerning the dignity of writing as the cause of his bad writing.
H. C. R., i, 103.　　　　　　　　　　　　　　　　　　　　VI. 6, 1812

11. [In selecting the eminent English poets, the booksellers referred to the popular miscellanies, and to their account-books.] The Editor was allowed a limited exercise of discretion, and the Authors whom he recommended are scarcely to be mentioned without a smile. We open the volume of Prefatory Lives, and to our astonishment the *first* name we find is that of Cowley!— What is become of the morning-star of English Poetry? Where is the bright Elizabethan constellation? Or, if names be more acceptable than images, where is the ever-to-be-honoured Chaucer? where is Spenser? where Sidney? and, lastly, where he, whose rights as a poet, contradistinguished from those which he is universally allowed to possess as a dramatist, we have vindicated, —where Shakespeare?—These, and a multitude of others not unworthy to be placed near them, their contemporaries and successors, we have *not*. But in their stead, we have (could better be expected when precedence was to be settled by an abstract of reputation at any given period made, as in this case before us?) Roscommon, and Stepney, and Phillips, and Walsh, and Smith, and Duke, and King, and Spratt—Halifax, Granville, Sheffield, Congreve, Broome, and other reputed Magnates—metrical writers utterly worthless and useless, except for occasions like the present, when their productions are referred to as evidence what a small quantity of brain is necessary to procure a considerable stock of admiration, provided the aspirant will accommodate himself to the likings and fashions of his day.
E. Supp. Pref., pp. 950-51.　　　　　　　　　　　　　　　　　1815

14.* . . . Mr. Wordsworth was not acquainted with this Essay [Johnson's " Essay on Epitaphs "] when he wrote his own. He afterwards spoke of it with much commendation. *Memoirs*, i, 432 n. 3.　　　　　*c*. 1827

16. [Johnson rightly says Tickell was one of our best minor poets.]
To Dyce,　　　　　　　　　　　　　　　　　　　　　VII. 23, 1831

17. [*Lives of the English Poets*.] See Anthologies 3

Johnstone, Charles

1.* Wordsworth has, however, sanctioned the pleasure I took in them [Johnstone's sonnets]. *H. C. R.*, ii, 484.　　　　　　　　I. 25, 1836

Jonson, Ben

1.* [D. W. read some short poems of Jonson to W.] which were too *interesting* for him, and would not let him go to sleep.
Journals, i, 110.　　　　　　　　　　　　　　　　　　II. 11, 1802

2.* [D. W. and W.] much delighted with the poem *Penhurst*.
Journals, i, 111.　　　　　　　　　　　　　　　　　　II. 11, 1802

Juvenal. See Satire 1; W. 300A

Kant, Immanuel. See Literature 24

Keats, John

1.* . . . A very pretty piece of Paganism [" Ode to Pan " from *Endymion*]. . . .
William Sharp, *The Life and Letters of Joseph Severn* (London, 1892), p. 33.
1817

2. Your account of young Keats interests me not a little; and the sonnet [' Great spirits now on earth are sojourning,'] appears to be of good promise, of course neither you nor I being so highly complimented in the composition can be deemed judges altogether impartial—but it is assuredly vigorously conceived and well expressed; Leigh Hunt's compliment is well deserved, and the sonnet is very agreeably concluded.
To Haydon (*L. Y.*, p. 1367),   I. 20, 1817

3. How is Keates, he is a youth of promise too great for the sorry company he keeps. *To Haydon,* ——   I. 16, 1820

4.* [Having expressed previously in " Praised to the Art " almost the same thought as that of Keats's Ode *On a Grecian Urn,* W.] felt a peculiar satisfaction. Not that he suggested any borrowing of the idea on the part of Keats. *Graves's Recollections*, pp. 301-2.   *c.* 1840

5.* [Keats and Shelley] would ever be favorites with the young, but would not satisfy men of all ages. *Batho*, p. 101.   *c.* 1840

6.* The danger for both Keats and Tennyson . . . was overlusciousness. *Batho*, pp. 101-2.   *c.* 1840

Keble, John

1.* . . . he mentioned, with marked pleasure, a dedication written by Mr. Keble, and sent to him for his approval, and for his permission to have it prefixed to Mr. Keble's new volumes of Latin Lectures on Poetry delivered at Oxford. Mr. Wordsworth said that he had never seen any estimate of his poetical powers, or more especially of his aims in poetry, that appeared to him so discriminating and so satisfactory. *Mrs. D.* (*Grosart*, iii, 441).
III. 5, 1844

2. It gave me pleasure to be told that Mr Keble's dedication of his Praelectiones had fallen in your way, and that you had been struck by it. It is not for me to say how far I am entitled to the honor which he has done me, but I can sincerely say, that it has been the main scope of my writing to do what he says I have accomplished. And where could I find a more trustworthy judge? *Reed*, p. 128.   VII. 5, 1844

3. See Watts 5, 6

Kenyon, John

1. Mr Kenyon's book [*A Rhymed Plea for Tolerance,* 1833] has pleased me exceedingly, and surprised me still more. I never suspected him of being

a *sinner in verse*-writing. The work does him great credit, less as a whole than from the spirit of particular parts. Christians, however, will justly think that Tolerance is carried too far, by a philosophy that places all creeds so much upon the same footing.
To C. R. (Corr. C. R., ii, 838),   XI. 15, 1833

2. [Kenyon's *Plea for Tolerance*] is ably done and full of animation. . . .
To Moxon,   XII. 9, 1833

3.* [The *Plea for Tolerance*] I cannot say it is precisely poetry, but it is something as good [not poetry but gives great delight].
To C. R. (Corr. C. R., ii, 838),   *c.* 1833

4. . . . volumes of Poems &c from Mr [R. M.] Milnes [*Poems of Many Years*], Mr Kenyon and Mr Trench—[*Sabbation* (1838)] . . . all of them if we may judge from what we have read, of great merit. . . .
To C. R. (Corr. C. R., i, 362),   V. 9, 1838

5. . . . we value much, certain Vols of Poems that have been sent us, by Mr Kenyon, Mr Milnes & Mr Trench.
To C. R. (Corr. C. R., i, 364),   VI. 18-24, 1838

6. . . . Mrs W. begs me to say that some passages of your Vol. [*Poems, for the most part occasional,* 1838. The first was entitled *Moonlight*—its argument reads: Moon], the moonlight especially, remind her of parts of my own Work (still in MS) upon my early life. This is not the first instance where our wits have *jumped,* as great wits are apt to do.
To Kenyon,   VI, 1838

7. Mr Kenyon's [see 6 above] and Mr Milnes's [*Poems of Many Years,* 1838] and Mr Trench's [*Sabbation, Honor Neale,* and other Poems, 1838] . . . have all great merit and not a little originality. They have pleased us much. *To Moxon,*   VI-VII, 1838

Killigrew, Anne

1. The few lines upon St. John the Baptist . . . are pleasing.
To Dyce,   IV. 30, 1830

King, William. See Johnson 11

Klopstock, F. G.

1. There is nothing remarkable either in his conversation or appearance, except his extreme gaiety. . . . *To T. Poole,*   X. 3, 1798
2. See Dryden 1, 17A

Klopstock, Margareta Moler

1.* [Letters written by Mrs. Klopstock]—he was exceedingly affected by them, and said it was impossible to read them without loving the woman.
D. W. to Lady Beaumont,   I. 5, 1805

Knight, Charles

1. The Selections [*Half Hours with the Best Authors*] appear to be judiciously made; though I regret to find that there are no extracts from the Works of Lord Bacon, one of the greatest Writers that our Country has produced. *To Chas. Knight,*   V. 20, 1848

Knox, Alexander

1. See Jebb 1

2. I shall never forget . . . his eloquent and dignified conversation. *To W. R. Hamilton,*   I. 11, 1836

Kotzebue, August von

1. [Not a writer of profound works; once widely read and acted.] What is become of him now? *To E. Q.,*   III. 9, 1840

La Fontaine, Jean de

1. . . . in my opinion things of this sort [versifying a tale of the Beauty and the Beast, suggested to W. by Godwin] cannot be even decently done without great labour, especially in our language. Fontaine acknowledges that he found ' les narrations en vers très mal-aisées,' yet he allowed himself, in point of metre and versification, every kind of liberty, and only chose such subjects as (to the disgrace of his Country be it spoken) the french language is peculiarly fitted for. . . . I think the shape in which it appears in the little Book you have sent me has much injured the Story, and . . . I confess there is to me something disgusting in the notion of a human Being consenting to mate with a Beast, however amiable his qualities of heart. There is a line and a half in the Paradise Lost upon this subject which always shocked me [*P. L.*, viii, 593-4]. . . .
These are objects to which the attention of the mind ought not to be turned even as things in possibility. . . . Brute metaphorically used, with us designates ill-manners of a coarse kind, or insolent and ferocious cruelty—I make these remarks with a view to the difficulty attending the treatment of this story in our tongue, I mean in verse, where the utmost delicacy, that is, true philosophic permanent delicacy is required. *To Godwin,*   III. 9, 1811

Laing, Malcolm. See Macpherson 2

Laing, Samuel

1. Before you go to Norway don't fail to read Samuel Laing['s] . . . Journal of a residence in Norway 1836 published by Longman—for a book professing to be written in English, it is in style the worst I ever read; & the Author in some important points, is an ill reasoning & an inconsistent theorist. But his book contains a good deal of valuable information, respecting a Country little visited, & where there have existed for many many Centuries Institutions, & a state of Society worthy of being considered, by a more comprehensive mind than this Traveller's.
To C. R. (Corr. C. R., i, 354),   II, 1838

Lamb, Charles (General Criticism)

1. See Imagination 33F; Poetry 114; W. 148, 195, 279-84, 364A

3. [Lamb's prose is exquisite.] *To J. Scott,*   III. 11, 1816

4. [W. inscribes *The Waggoner* to Lamb] in acknowledgement of the pleasure I have derived from your Writings. . . .
Oxf. W., p. 173.   V. 20, 1819

5.* He read some recent compositions, which Wordsworth cordially praised. *H. C. R.*, i, 240.   VI. 2, 1820

7. The Poetic Genius of England with the exception of Chaucer, Spenser, Milton, Dryden, Pope, and a very few more, is to be sought in her Drama. How it grieves one that there is so little probability of those valuable authors being read except by the curious. I questioned my Friend Charles Lamb whether it would answer for some person of real taste to undertake abridging the plays [Elizabethan] that are not likely to be read as wholes, and telling such parts of the story in brief abstract as were ill managed in the Drama. He thought it would not—I, however, am inclined to think it would.
To Dyce,   IV. 30, 1830

8. Thanks for Charles Lamb's verses which are characteristic. . . .
To E. Q.,   II. 23, 1833

9. . . . most of the Essays I have read and with great pleasure. . . .
To Moxon,   V. 14, 1833

10. . . . tell L. [Lamb] that his Works are our delight, as is evidenced better than by words—by April weather of smiles & tears whenever we read them. *To C. R. (Corr. C. R.,* i, 252),   XI. 15, 1833

11. . . . discriminating verses. . . . C. Lamb's verses are always delightful, as is everything he writes, for he both feels and thinks. Will he excuse me for observing that the couplet,

like a signet signed
By a strong hand seemed burnt

appears to me incorrect in the expression, as a signet is a seal and not the impress of a seal; we do not burn by a seal, but by a branding iron.
To Moxon,   I. 14, 1834

12.   And when the precious hours of leisure came,
          Knowledge and wisdom, gained from converse sweet
          With books, or while he ranged the crowded streets
          With a keen eye, and overflowing heart:
          So genius triumphed over seeming wrong,
          And poured out truth in works by thoughtful love
          Inspired—works potent over smiles and tears.
          And as round mountain-tops the lightning plays,
          Thus innocently sported, breaking forth
          As from a cloud of some grave sympathy,
          Humour and wild instinctive wit, and all
          The vivid flashes of his spoken words.
          " To a good Man," 11-22.   1835

13. [Influential for their genius and talents were Lamb and Coleridge.]
To Henry Taylor,   last week of VI, 1835

14. [Essays and letters of the same character.] See Letters, Objections to Publishing 1; see also 2 and 3

15.   His submitting to that mechanical employment, placed him in fine moral contrast with other men of genius, his cotemporaries, who in sacrificing personal independence, have made a wreck of morality and honour to a degree which it is painful to consider. To me this was a noble feature in Lamb's life & furnishes an admirable lesson by which thousands might profit.
To C. R. (Corr. C. R., i, 288),   XII. 16, 1835

16.   Thanks for Lamb's Poems, and the Verses—they are now quite correct and I have no wish to alter them further: the only thing which I find amiss in them is the position of the words By God in the beginning of the line which gives them the appearance of an oath, but I cannot alter it without weakening the passage. *To Moxon,*   I, 9, 1836

17.* . . . Lamb's abuse of the country and his declared detestation of it was all affected; he enjoyed it and entered into its beauties; besides, Lamb had too kindly and sympathetic a nature to detest anything.
Old Friends, p. 174.   VI. 4, 1842

18.   Lamb was a good Latin scholar. . . . *I. F. (Grosart,* iii, 191). 1843

Lamb (Works)

19.   I liked your play [*The Wife's Trial*] marvellously, having no objection to it but one, which strikes me as applicable to a large majority of plays, those of Shakspear himself not entirely excepted, I mean a little degradation of character, for a more dramatic turn of Plot. Your present of Hone's Book [*The Table Book,* 1827, contained Lamb's extracts from the Garrick Plays] was very acceptable, and so much so, that your part of the book is the cause why I did not write long ago—I wished to enter a little more minutely into notice of the dramatic Extracts. . . .
To Lamb,   I. 10, 1830

20. . . . Lamb's pleasing verses upon your lamented Brother [Daniel Rogers,—for the Sonnet, *v.* Lamb, *Poems,* ed. Lucas, p. 56.—De Sel.]. . . .
To Rogers,   VI. 5, 1830

21. . . . a delightful Vol: your last, I hope not, of *Elia.* . . . I am not sure but I like the Old China and The Wedding as well as any of the Essays. I read Love me and love my Dog . . . I fell upon an Anecdote in Madame D'Arblayes' life of her father, where the other side of the question is agreeably illustrated. *To Lamb,*   V. 17, 1833

22. . . . I met with a few pleasing lines addressed by him [see *Poems* of Lamb, ed. E. V. Lucas, pp. 75, and 371] to the veteran Stoddart. . . .
To Moxon,   XII. 31, 1833

23. . . . his Letters. I agree with you they must be valuable.
To Moxon,   I. 12, 1835

24. . . . much pleased with several things in Lamb's Poems that I had not sufficiently noticed before, particularly with the latter part of Lines upon the death of a newborn infant. *To Moxon,* I. 9, 1836

25. [Lamb's beautiful sonnet, " The Family Name."] *Oxf. W.,* p. 926. 1837

Lamb, Mary

1. See W. 282

2. Were I to give way to my own feelings, I should dwell not only on her genius and intellectual powers, but upon the delicacy and refinement of manner which she maintained inviolable under most trying circumstances. *I. F. (Grosart,* iii, 190). 1843

Landor, Walter Savage (General Criticism)

1. See W. 104

2. His conversation is lively and original; his learning great, tho' he will not allow it. . . . *To W. R. Hamilton,* VI. 25, 1832

3. You are quite at liberty to send my Sonnets to Landor if you think it worth while—but his antipathies are strong, & I know he has a particular dislike to the *Sonnet. To C. R. (Corr. C. R.,* i, 259), IV. 3, 1834

4.* [Acknowledged Landor's genius.] *H. C. R.,* ii, 516. III. 22, 1837

5.* Mr W. tho no party to my act [defense of W. against Landor], is well satisfied. . . . *E. Q. to C. R. (Corr. C. R.,* i, 484), IV. 5, 1843

6. The attack upon W. S. L. [Landor's dialogue between Porson and Southey, attacking W., appeared in *Blackwood's Magazine* for Dec. 1842. Quillinan's reply was printed there in the following April. De Sel.] to which you allude was written by my son-in-law; but without any sanction from me, much less encour gement; in fact I knew no^thing about it or the preceding article of Landor, that had called it forth, till after Mr Q's had appeared. He knew very well that I should have disapproved of his condescending to notice anything that a man so deplorably tormented by ungovernable passion as that unhappy creature might eject. His character may be given in two or three words: a madman, a bad-man, yet a man of genius, as many a madman is. *To W. R. Hamilton,* IV, 1843

7. Sea-shells of many descriptions were common in the town [Cockermouth], and I was not a little surprised when I heard Mr. Landor had denounced me as a Plagarist from himself for having described a boy applying a sea-shell to his ear, and listening to it for intimation of what was going on in its native element. *I. F. (Grosart,* iii, 146). 1843

Landor (Works)

9.* He spoke with respect of Landor's power. The tragedy [*Count Julian*] which he is now publishing has very fine touches, he says. *H. C. R.,* i, 82. V. 13, 1812

10. I felt myself much honoured by the present of your book of Latin

11

Poems [*Idyllia Heroica Decem*, 1820] . . . and with great pleasure did I [peruse] . . . the dissertation annexed to your Poems. . . . You will not perhaps be surprized when I state that I differ from you in opinion as to the propriety of the Latin language being employed by Moderns for works of taste and imagination. Miserable would have been the lot of Dante, Ariosto, and Petrarch, if they had preferred the Latin to their Mother tongue (there is, by-the-way, a Latin translation of Dante which you do not seem to know), and what could Milton, who was surely no mean master of the Latin tongue, have made of his Paradise Lost, had that vehicle been employed instead of the Language of the Thames and Severn! Should we even admit that all modern dialects are comparatively changeable, and therefore limited in their efficacy, may not the sentiment which Milton so pleasingly expresses when he says he is content to be read in his Native Isle only, be extended to durability, and is it not more desirable to be read with affection and pride, and familiarly for five hundred years, by all orders of minds, and all ranks of people, in your native tongue, than only by a few scattered Scholars for the space of three thousand? My own special infirmity moreover gives me an especial right to urge this argument—had your Idylliums been in English I should long ere this have been as well acquainted with them as with your Gebir, and with your other Poems—and now I know not how long they may remain to me a sealed book.

I met with a hundred things in your Dissertation that fell in with my own sentiments and judgments; but there are many opinions which I should like to talk over with you. The ordonnance of your Essay might, I think, be improved, and several of the separate remarks, upon Virgil in particular, though perfectly just, would perhaps have been better placed in notes or an appendix; they are details that obstruct the view of the whole. Vincent Bourne surely is not so great a favourite with you as he ought to be, though I acknowledge there is ground for your objection upon the score of ultra *concinnity* . . . yet this applies only to a certain portion of his longs and shorts. Are you not also penurious in your praise of Gray? The fragment at the commencement of his fourth book, in which he laments the death of West, in cadence and sentiment, touches me in a manner for which I am grateful. The first book also of the same Poem appears to me as well executed as anything of that kind is likely to be. Is there not a speech of Solon to which the concluding couplet of Gray's sonnet bears a more pointed resemblance than to any of the passages you have quoted? He was told, not to grieve for the loss of his son, as tears would be of no avail; ' and for that very reason,' replied he, ' do I weep.' It is high time I should thank you for the honourable mention you have made of me. It could not but be grateful to me to be praised by a Poet who has written verses of which I would rather have been the Author than of any produced in our time. What I now write to you, I have frequently said to many. *To Landor*,   IX. 3, 1821

11.   In respect to Latin Poetry, I ought to tell you that I am no judge, except upon general principles. I never practised Latin verse, not having been educated at one of the Public Schools. My acquaintance with Virgil, Horace, Lucretius, and Catullus is intimate; but as I never read them with a critical view to composition, great faults in language might be committed which

would escape my notice; any opinion of mine, therefore, on points of classical nicety would be of no value, should I be so inconsiderate as to offer it. A few days ago, being something better in my sight, I read your *Sponsalia* [*Sponsalia Polyxenae*, translated by Landor and published in Hellenics, 1847, as *The Espousals of P.*]; it is full of spirit and animation, and is probably of that style of versification which suits the subject; yet, if you thought proper, you could produce, I think, a richer harmony; and I met some serious inaccuracies in the punctuation which, from the state of my eyes encreasing in the difficulty of catching the sense, took something from the pleasure of the perusal. The first book which I read unless it be one in large type, shall be these Poems. I must express a wish, however, that you would gratify us by writing in English—there are noble and stirring things in all that you have written in your native tongue, and that is enough for me. In your Simonidea . . . I was pleased to find rather an out-of-the-way image, in which the present hour is compared to the shade on the dial. It is a singular coincidence, that in the year 1793, when I first became an author, I illustrated the sentiment precisely in the same manner [*Evening Walk*, 37-42 (*Oxf. W.*, p. 592)]. In the same work you commend the fine conclusion of Russel's sonnet upon Philoctetes, and depreciate that form of composition. I do not wonder at this; I used to think it egregiously absurd, though the greatest poets since the revival of literature have written in it. Many years ago my sister happened to read to me the sonnets of Milton, which I could at that time repeat; but somehow or other I was singularly struck with the style of harmony, and the gravity, and republican austerity of those compositions. In the course of the same afternoon I produced 3 sonnets, and soon after many others; and since that time, and from want of resolution to take up anything of length, I have filled up many a moment in writing Sonnets, which, if I had never fallen into the practice, might easily have been better employed. The Excursion is proud of your approbation. *To Landor*,   IV. 20, 1822

12. . . . your admirable Dialogues. They reached me last May, at a time when I was able to read them, which I did with very great pleasure. . . . I concur with you in so much, and differ with you in so much also, that, though I could have easily disposed of my assent, easily and most pleasantly, I could not face the task of giving my reasons for my dissent! For instance, it would have required almost a pamphlet to set forth the grounds upon which I disagreed with what you have put into the mouth of *Franklin* on *Irish* affairs, the object to my mind of constant anxiety. What would I not give for a few hours' talk with you upon Republics, Kings, and Priests and Priestcraft. This last I *abhor*; but why spend our time declaiming against it? . . . Your Dialogues are worthy of you, and great acquisitions to literature. The classical ones I like best, and most of all that between Tully and his Brother. That which pleases me the least is the one between yourself and the Abbé de Lille. The observations are invariably just, I own, but they are fitter for illustrative notes than the body of a Dialogue, which ought always to have some little spice of dramatic effect. I long for the third volume. . . .

To Landor,   XII. 11, 1824

13. . . . Thank you for the Copy sent and also for the Trial of Wm

Shakespear [*Citation and Examination of William Shakespeare touching Deer-stealing*, by Walter Savage Landor, 1834]—very clever.

To Moxon,   I. 12, 1835

14. . . . thank him for Pericles and Aspasia, but tell him to leave the Church alone. *To C. R. (Corr. C. R.,* i, 302)   IV. 27, 1836

Langhorne, John

1. See Scotch Writers 2

2. . . . I have not had time for more than a glance at your part of the Volumes [*The Book of Gems*]—but I must say how much I was pleased with your notice of our Westmorland Poet, Langhorne—the Critique is very judicious, both as to his merits and his faults—I do not wonder that you are struck with his Poem of the Country Justice—You praise it, and with discrimination—but you might have said still more in its favour. As far as I know, it is the first Poem, unless perhaps Shenstone's Schoolmistress be excepted, that fairly brought the Muse into the Company of common life, to which it comes nearer than Goldsmith, and upon which it looks with a tender and enlightened humanity—and with a charitable, (and being so) philosophical and poetical construction that is too rarely found in the works of Crabbe. It is not without many faults in style from which Crabbe's more austere judgment preserved him—but these are to me trifles in a work so original and touching. *To S. C. Hall,*   I. 15, 1837

3.* . . . one of the poets who had not had justice done him. His *Country Justice* has true feeling and poetry.

H. C. R., ii, 517.   III. 27, 1837

Law, William. See Milton 41

Le Grice, C. V.

1.   Do not you write in the Critical Review occasionally? I know you are intimate with the publisher, Mawman. I put this question to you because there is a most malignant Spirit (his fleshly name is Legrice) whose gall and venom are discharged upon the public through that review. This wretch, for such I cannot but call him, has taken Coleridge, his quondam School-fellow at Christs hospital and contemporary at Cambridge, into his most deadly hatred, and persecutes him upon all occasions, in which hatred all Coleridge's friends have a share, and I among the rest. I have therefore to request that you would take so much trouble as to keep the review of my Poems in the Critical out of this Creature's hands, either by reviewing them yourself, which I should like best, or in any other way. I have requested this of you, not that I think the criticisms of this man [Le Grice] would have the slightest influence on the final destiny of these poems. . . .

To F. Wrangham,   VII. 12, 1807

2. He [Le Grice] left us . . . a speech of his upon Cottage Gardens, three or four copies of a sonnet (his own writing), of which you are the

subject. As you may not have seen the verses I send them. We were agreeably surprised by the sight of them after he was gone. . . .
To C. W.,   VIII. 11, 1841

Lessing, Gotthold Ephraim

1. See Goethe 1
2.* . . . Nathan . . . is tedious.
Biog. Lit. (" *Satyrane's Letters* "), ii, 176.   [*c.* IX, 1798]

Lewis, M. G.

1.* [*The Castle Spectre*] fitted the taste of the audience like a glove.
Hazlitt, xii, 271.   1789
2. I am perfectly easy about the theatre, if I had no other method of employing myself Mr. Lewis's success would have thrown me into despair. The Castle Spectre is a Spectre indeed. Clothed with the flesh and blood of £400 received from the treasury of the theatre it may in the eyes of the author and his friends appear very lovely. *To J. Tobin,*   III. 6, 1798

Leyden, John.   See Scotch Writers 2

Liberal, The

1. It is reported here that Byron, Shelley, Moore, Leigh Hunt (I do not know if you have heard of all these names) are to lay their heads together in some Town of Italy, for the purpose of conducting a Journal [*The Liberal, Verse and Prose from the South,* London 1822, printed by and for John Hunt. It opened with Byron's *Vision of Judgment*] to be directed against everything in religion, in morals and probably in government and literature, which our Forefathers have been accustomed to reverence,—the notion seems very extravagant but perhaps the more likely to be realized on that account.
To Landor,   IV. 20, 1822

Lindsay, Lady Anne

1. [*Auld Robin Grey* is one of the two best modern ballads.]
To Dyce,   XII. 4, 1833

Lloyd, Edward

1. Not approving Edward's lines [on Owen Lloyd] altogether, though the sentiments were sufficiently appropriate. . . . *To C. W.,* VIII. 11, 1841

Lloyd, Owen

1. [His] verses are not without merit, and would be read with pleasure in many a church, or [churchyard], but they are scarcely good or characteristic of the Subject [death of Charles Lamb]. *To Moxon,*   XII. 6, 1835

Locke, John

1.*   The influence of Locke's Essay was not due to its own merits, which are considerable; but to external circumstances. It came forth at a happy opportunity, and coincided with the prevalent opinions of the time. The Jesuit doctrines concerning the papal power in deposing kings, and absolving subjects from their allegiance, had driven some Protestant theologians to take refuge in the theory of the divine right of kings. This theory was unpalatable to the world at large, and others invented the more popular doctrine of a social contract, in its place; a doctrine which history refutes. But Locke did what he could to accommodate this principle to his own system. . . .

The best of Locke's works, as it seems to me, is that in which he attempts the least—his *Conduct of the Understanding.*

C. W., Jr. (Grosart, iii, 461-62).   *c.* 1827

Lockhart, John G.

1.*   . . . Scott's *Life.* I found the book, what Wordsworth declared it to be, a degradation of the literary character of our countryman.

H. C. R., ii, 534.   VIII. 14, 1837

2. [*Life of Sir Walter Scott.*] I congratulate you sincerely upon having brought to a conclusion so arduous an undertaking. . . . I need not say that I read them with lively interest—the other four [volumes] I have since perused, as they reached me, and with still deeper concern. A day or two before our Friend's last departure to the South, he told me that upon reviewing his life, he could not but reckon it a favored, and upon the whole, a very happy one; nor do I think that your Narrative, melancholy as in many respects it is, proves the contrary: the most painful part of his trials, and that which in my mind causes the strongest regret, is the burthen of Secrecy, for a burthen it must have been to one of his open genial nature, under which so great a portion of it was spent. If, as I suspect, his admirable Works would not, at least many of them, have been produced, but for the spur of worldly ambition, the world at large will, for the sake of those Works, be little disposed to blame what you yourself must have reckoned weaknesses, as is evident from the mode in which you account for, and with no inconsiderable success, palliate them. Again, in the misfortunes of the latter part of his life there is to be found much consolation both for those who loved him, and for Persons comparatively indifferent to his fate. How nobly does his character rise under his calamities, what integrity, what fortitude, what perseverance under pain both of body and mind—qualities which he himself would not have known he possessed to that degree, but for the very infirmities that were the origin and leading cause of his reverses of fortune—so that balancing one thing with another, and above all looking at his immortal Works, I feel at liberty after perusing your Memoir to accede to his own view that his was a favored and a happy life. For yourself, my dear Sir, and your friends it must be a matter of sincere pleasure to have your name thus associated with that of your Father-in-law. So much of Sir Walter's affairs having become objects of public investigation, nothing remained for you but to act as openly and sincerely as you have done in writing his Life. Whatever complaints may have been made upon this point will pass away, and ere long your mode of treating the delicate and difficult subject will meet with uni-

versal approbation. In your P. S. you allude to the length of the work as having been objected to, and I hope you will not be hurt when I say, that I have been somewhat of the same opinion. The Diary of his northern voyage ought, I think, to have been printed apart from the life; and some of the letters also would have been more in their place, if separated from the narrative. But all this is of little consequence.

You notice incorrect statements and express a wish that others may be pointed out for amendment in a future Edition. There are a few trifling inaccuracies relating to Mr. Southey and myself. Mr. Southey was not at Storrs when Sir W. S. and you were entertained there along with Mr. Canning, Prof. Wilson, and myself; nor did I accompany your Party to Lowther as you state—but only to Mr. Marshall's at Hallsteads. The anecdote of Crabbe and the candle smoke [*v.* Lockhart's *Scott,* ch. lxxiii, under date Jan. 1827] was often *told me* by Sir George Beaumont, and in the conclusion drawn from it by *him* I concurred, not so much as set down by Sir Walter that it was a proof of the Poet's *want of imagination* as of a sense of *beauty*, but I was not present when the thing occurred—whether at Murray's or elsewhere I do not recollect. *To Lockhart,*   IV. 27, 1838

3.* . . . we read part of an article on copyright by Lockhart in the *Quarterly.* . . . Wordsworth is . . . pleased with the article.
H.C.R., ii, 607.   I. 1, 1842

Lofft, Capell (1806-73)

1. The Author of Ernest . . . was a distinguished Scholar when at Trin: Coll. Cambridge—*To Cordelia Marshall,*   II. 19, 1840

Longfellow, Henry Wadsworth

1.* . . . Wordsworth spoke highly of Longfellow and regretted his name. *H. C. R.,* ii, 678.   VI. 17, 1848

2. Mr. Longfellow's poem [*Evangeline*] is obviously, in metre and in manner and matter, after the model of Voss's *Louise,* a poem which used to be as popular in Germany as the metre, which does not suit modern languages, would allow. In our own language we have no spondees, and are therefore obliged to substitute trochaics, or to make spondees out of the end of one word and the beginning of the next. *To J. P. Nichol,*   VIII, 1848

Longinus. See Sublime 4

Lonsdale. See Lowther, Sir John

Lowther, Sir John

1. [In the sonnet (3 *Ecc. Sonn, viii*)] upon the acquital of the Seven Bishops I have done little more than versify a lively description of that event in the MS. Memoirs [of *The Reign of James II*] of the first Lord Lonsdale, *Oxf. W.,* p. 921.   1822

Lucretius

1.* [The lines] of Lucretius describing the immolation of Iphigenia are worth the whole of Goethe's long poem.

C. W., Jr. (Grosart, iii, 465).   *c.* 1827

2.* [Wordsworth quoted much from Lucretius.]

Graves (Grosart, iii, 469).   summer, 1827

3.* Lucretius he esteems a far higher poet than Virgil; not in his system, which is nothing, but in his power of illustration.

English Traits, p. 21.   VIII. 28, 1833

Lyttleton, George

1. [An epitaph] taken from a celebrated Writer of the last century [see *Epitaph* 2 (*Grosart*, ii, 52-3) for this epitaph]. . . . The composition is in the style of those laboured portraits in words which we sometimes see placed at the bottom of a print to fill up lines of expression which the bungling Artist has left imperfect. . . . [No doubt Lord Lyttleton loved his wife, though his verses do not prove it.] This epitaph would derive little advantage from being translated into another style as the former was; for there is no under current; no skeleton or staminae of thought and feeling. The Reader will perceive at once that nothing in the heart of the Writer had determined either the choice, the order or the expression, of the ideas; that there is no interchange of action from within and from without; that the connections are mechanical and arbitrary, and the lowest kind of these—heart and eyes: petty alliterations, as meek and magnanimous, witty and wise, combined with oppositions in thoughts where there is no necessary or natural opposition. Then follow voice, song, eloquence, form, mind—each enumerated by a separate act as if the Author had been making a *Catalogue Raisonné*.

These defects run through the whole; the only tolerable verse is,

> Her speech was the melodious voice of love.

. . . We have therefore in him the example of a mind during the act of composition misled by false taste to the highest possible degree; and, in that of Lord Lyttleton, we have one of a feeling heart, not merely misled, but wholly laid asleep by the same power. Lord Lyttleton could not have written in this way upon such a subject, if he had not been seduced by the example of Pope. . . . *Epitaph* 2 (*Grosart*, ii, 52-3).   1810

Lytton.   See Bulwer-Lytton

Macaulay, Thomas Babington

1.*   Macauley, he [W.] says, is false in style, and in everything else; he is more gorgeous than Gibbon, fatiguing a reader by the constant straining after something bright, and content to pick up tinsel rather than want its glitter. This, he says, may partly be a consequence of writing much for periodicals, where a man must condense as much showy writing as possible into the smallest possible space; but the false hollow nature of the man's

mind he deduces from other things as much as that. . . . in literary style
. . . he equally oversteps *the Modesty of Nature.*
A Day with Wordsworth, pp. 737-38.   VII. 31, 1841

Mackenzie, Robert S.

1.   Your verses written under such affecting circumstances do great
honour both to your heart and head, especially the former copy, which is
indeed very touching. *To R. S. Mackenzie,*   II. 23, 1837

2. . . . the Poems in the Annual you have directed us to, . . . are
remarkable both for tenderness and poetical spirit; the one upon your departed
Child, is not unworthy of ranking with the Mother's lays of Miss Browne
which we have read, and been much pleased with; as also, the animated piece
in which the course of a river is traced from its fountain to the sea: this was
not less interesting to me on account of its reminding me, of Mr. Coleridge's
intention of writing a poem to be called ' the Brook ' [see the note to the
Duddon Sonnets; W. 182] and of my own Duddon. . . . not once in a
hundred times, that for many years past, I have been able to find time for
reading prose fictions in periodicals—and too seldom indeed for the most
celebrated novels.

What a pity a Man so wealthy did not provide in his will for the poor
orphan Mourner—the story, as you have given it, is truly affecting; and the
Sonnet gives the essence of the incident in a manner that does you much
credit, and it is much to be regretted that you have not more time to give to
the Muses, whom you serve so willingly and well. Are you aware that Cowper
has been beforehand with you in the Ice-palace [*The Task*, v, 127-176]?
To R. S. Mackenzie,   XI. 25, 1837

Mackintosh, Sir James

1. . . . Mackintosh's opinion of my Poems . . . tell him I was happy
to have given a man like him so much pleasure. . . .
To R. Short,   IX, 27, 1808

Macpherson, James

1. [*Ossian.*] See Young 1

2. [*Ossian.*] All hail, Macpherson! hail to thee, Sire of Ossian! The
Phantom was begotten by the snug embrace of an impudent Highlander
upon a cloud of tradition—it travelled southward, where it was greeted with
acclamation, and the thin Consistence took its course through Europe, upon
the breath of popular applause. The Editor of the *Reliques* had indirectly
preferred a claim to the praise of invention, by not concealing that his supplementary labours were considerable; how selfish his conduct, contrasted with
that of the disinterested Gael, who like Lear, gives his kingdom away, and is
content to become a pensioner upon his own issue for a beggarly pittance!—
Open this farfamed Book!—I have done so at random, and the beginning of
the *Epic Poem Temora*, in eight Books, presents itself. ' The blue waves of
Ullin roll in light. The green hills are covered with day. Trees shake their
dusky heads in the breeze. Grey torrents pour their noisy streams. Two
green hills with aged oaks surround a narrow plain. The blue course of a

stream is there. On its banks stood Cairbar of Atha. His spear supports the king; the red eyes of his fear are sad. Cormac rises on his soul with all his ghastly wounds.' Precious memorandums from the pocket-book of the blind Ossian! [In attacking a widely-popular work, a critic must offer irrefragable proof of its unworthiness. Born in the mountains, W. recognized the spurious imagery in *Ossian*.] In nature everything is distinct, yet nothing defined into absolute independent singleness. In Macpherson's work it is exactly the reverse; everything (that is not stolen) is in this manner defined, insulated, dislocated, deadened,—yet nothing distinct. It will always be so when words are substituted for things. [The characters are unreal, the manners impossible, and a dream has more substance.] Mr. Malcolm Laing has ably shown that the diction of this pretended translation is a motley assemblage from all quarters; but he is so fond of making out parallel passages as to call poor Macpherson to account for his ' *ands* ' and his ' *buts!* ' and he has weakened his argument by conducting it as if he thought that every striking resemblance was a *conscious* plagiarism. It is enough that the coincidences are too re-markable for its being probable or possible that they could arise in different minds without communication between them. Now as the Translators of the Bible, and Shakespeare, Milton, and Pope, could not be indebted to Mac-pherson, it follows that he must have owed his fine feathers to them; unless we are prepared gravely to assert, with Madame de Staël, that many of the characteristic beauties of our most celebrated English Poets are derived from the ancient Fingallian; in which case the modern translator would have been but giving back to Ossian his own.—It is consistent that Lucien Buonaparte, who could censure Milton for having surrounded Satan in the infernal regions with courtly and regal splendour, should pronounce the modern Ossian to be the glory of Scotland;—a country that has produced a Dunbar, a Buchanan, a Thomson, and a Burns! These opinions are of ill omen for the Epic ambition of him who has given them to the world.

[*Ossian* inspired only one English poet—Chatterton.] He had perceived, from the successful trials which he himself had made in literary forgery, how few critics were able to distinguish between a real ancient medal and a counterfeit of modern manufacture; and he set himself to the work of filling a magazine with *Saxon Poems*,—counterparts of those of Ossian, as like his as one of his misty stars is to another. This incapability to amalgamate with the literature of the Island is, in my estimation, a decisive proof that the book is essentially unnatural; nor should I require any other to demonstrate it to be a forgery, audacious as worthless.—Contrast, in this respect, the effect of Macpherson's publication with the *Reliques* of Percy, so unassuming, so modest in their pretensions!—I have already stated how much Germany is indebted to this latter work; and for our own country, its poetry has been absolutely redeemed by it. I do not think that there is an able writer in verse of the present day who would not be proud to acknowledge his obligations to the *Reliques*; I know that it is so with my friends; and, for myself, I am happy in this occasion to make a public avowal of my own.

Dr. Johnson, [was] more fortunate in his contempt of the labours of Macpherson than those of his modest friend. . . .

E. Supp. Pref., p. 950.   1815

3.* [Wiffin records that W. denounced *Ossian*] as a disgusting imposture, the manners, and imagery, designated as false, and unreal, condemned in toto, yet to the blind Bard himself he had some relentings. He was evidently giving his griefs, to the echoes of the hills; but all beyond,—the touching tenderness, and beauty, of the characters delineated, the lively descriptions of mountain scenery, and the ethereal spirit of melancholy, which pervades those singular compositions, were abandoned without a sigh.

Brothers Wiffin, p. 40.   1819

4.   See Scotch Writers 2

5.   [*Ossian.*]

> What need, then, of these finished Strains?
> Away with counterfeit Remains!
> . . .
> Spirit of Ossian! if imbound
> In language thou may'st yet be found,
> If aught (intrusted to the pen
> Or floating on the tongues of men,
> Albeit shattered and impaired)
> Subsist thy dignity to guard,
> In concert with memorial claim
> Of old grey stone, and high-born name
> That cleaves to rock or pillared cave
> Where moans the blast, or beats the wave,
> Let Truth, stern arbitress of all,
> Interpret that Original,
> And for presumptuous wrongs atone;—
> Authentic words be given, or none!

Written in . . . Macphersons's Ossian, 11-12; 17-30.   1827

6.   [In *Oxf. W.*, p. 950] you will find a notice of the Poetry printed by Macpherson under the name of Ossian, in which it is pronounced to be in a great measure spurious, and . . . [there] is a Poem [*Oxf. W.*, p. 472] in which the same opinion is given. I am not at present inclined, nor probably ever shall be, to enter into a detail of the reasons which have led me to this conclusion; something is said upon the subject in the first of the passages to which I have taken the liberty of referring you. Notwithstanding the censure of Mr Macpherson which is implied in this opinion you will see proofs . . . that I consider myself much indebted to Macpherson, as having made the English Public acquainted with the Traditions concerning Ossian and his age. Nor would I withhold from him the praise of having preserved many fragments of Gaelic Poetry, which without his attention to the subject might perhaps have perished. Most of these, however, are more or less corrupted by the liberties he has taken in the mode of translating them.

To E. H. Barker,   IV. 23, 1829

7.   . . . the interest which the poetic world must attach to the name of Ossian, for the knowledge of which we English are mainly indebted to Macpherson; it is therefore impossible for me not to feel towards him a

degree of gratitude which makes me regret the more that he should have ever mixed up so much untruth with the subject.
To E. H. Barker,   VII. 24, 1829

8.*   Thought Coleridge admired Ossian only in youth, and himself [W.] admired the spirit which Macpherson *professes* to embody.
Gladstone, i, 136.   1836

Maitland, Samuel R.

1.   . . . a Book which though somewhat over minute and consequently in parts tedious has interested us much. It is written by the Librarian at Lambeth, and entitled, the dark ages. It confirms, without alluding to any thing of mine all that I had previously thrown out upon the benefits conferred by monastic institutions, and exposing the ignorance of Robertson Milner Mosheim and others upon this subject—repels most successfully their calumnies. *To C. R. (Corr. C. R.,* ii, 579-80),   XII. 8, 1844

Mant, Richard

1.   . . . he was said to be the Author of a forgotten Poem called the Simpliciad—the principal butt of which was to ridicule me, so that I was somewhat drolly placed in such company. *To E. Q.,*   IX. 10, 1830

Manzoni, Alessandro

1.   Thanks for your animated stanzas from Manzoni.
To W. E. Gladstone,   VI, 1838

Marshall, Julia

1.   . . . we were all much delighted with the verses she put into my hands . . . they are *we think* eminently characteristic and tender.
To J. Marshall,   early IX, 1831

Martineau, Harriet

1.*   . . . all the Rydalites . . . have been quite charmed, affected & instructed by the Invalid's volume [H. Martineau's *Life in a Sick Room*] . . . Mr Wordsworth praised it with more unreserve, I may say with more *earnestness*, than is usual with him. . . .
E. Q. to C. R. (Corr. C. R., i, 533),   XII. 9, 1843

2.*   . . . the very warm praise of the Wordsworths of Harriet Martineau's *Life in* [*the*] *Sick Room. H. C. R.,* ii, 636.   XII. 12, 1843

Marvel, Andrew

1.   Great men have been among us; hands that penned
          And tongues that uttered wisdom—better none. . . .
          " Great men," 1-2.   1802

2.   See Dryden 19

Mason, William

1. [Mason's *Epitaph on Miss Drummond*] is very far from being the worst of its kind. . . . *Epitaph 3* (*Grosart*, ii, 66).   1810

2. See Burns 17

Matthias, J. T.

1. . . . Matthias's Gray . . . I hope for much pleasure and profit from the perusal of most of it, at *leisure*. *To S. Rogers*,   II. 18, 1836

Mayer, Enrico

1. I was sadly mortified that I had not an opportunity of thanking him [Mayer] personally for the elegant [Italian] sonnet which he addressed to me at Oxford, two lines of it were especially beautiful.

To C. R. (*Corr. C. R.*, i, 391),   VII. 7, 1839

Medwin, Thomas. See Byron 7

Melanchthon. See Erasmus 1

Melmoth, William. See Milton 41

Merewether, Frances

1. [Considered Merewether's pamphlet, *Thoughts on the Present State of Popular Opinion in Matters of Religion in England*, 1824] extremely well done. *To Merewether* (*L. of W. Family*, p. 63),   I. 10, 1825

Michelangelo, Buonarroti

1. I have peeped into the sonnets, and they do not appear at all unworthy of their great Author. *To Beaumont*,   XII. 25, 1804

2. I mentioned Michael Angelo's Poetry some time ago; it is the most difficult to contrue I ever met with, but just what you would expect from such a man, showing abundantly how conversant his soul was with great things. There is a mistake in the world concerning the Italian language; the Poetry of Dante and Michael Angelo proves, that if there be little majesty and strength in Italian verse, the fault is in the authors and not in the tongue. I can translate, and have translated, two Books of Ariosto at the rate, nearly, of 100 lines a day, but so much meaning has been put by Michael Angelo into so little room, and that meaning sometimes so excellent in itself, that I found the difficulty of translating him insurmountable. I attempted at least fifteen of the sonnets, but could not anywhere succeed, I have sent you the only one I was able to finish, it is far from being the best or most characteristic, but the others were too much for me. [*Yes: hope may with my strong desire keep pace* (*Oxf. W.*, p. 256)]. *To Beaumont* (pp. 528-9),   X. 17, 1805

3.* . . . I wish my Brother could have done more in testimony of his reverence for so great a man, but he finds so much thought in the poems and the Italian so difficult that he has tried in vain.

D. W. to Lady Beaumont,   XI. 7, 1805

4.   The following Sonnet ["No mortal object"], translated from Michael Angelo, is characteristic of him both as Man and as Artist.

To Beaumont,   IX. 8, 1806

5.   See W. 177-78

6.   However, at first, these two Sonnets ["Rapt above earth" and "Eternal Lord!"] from M. Angelo may seem in their spirit somewhat inconsistent with each other, I have not scrupled to place them side by side as characteristic of their great author, and others with whom he lived. I feel, nevertheless, a wish to know at what periods of his life they were respectively composed. The latter, as it expresses, was written in his advanced years, when it was natural that the Platonism that pervades the one should give way to the Christian feeling that inspired the other. Between both, there is more than poetic affinity. *I. F. (Grosart*, iii, 94-95).   1843

Mickle, William J.

1.   See Scotch Writers 2

2.   . . . as it appears from his poem on Sir Martin, was not without genuine poetic feelings. . . . *I. F. (Grosart*, iii, 141).   1843

Miller, J. K.

1.   I turn with pleasure to the sonnets you have addressed to me, and if I did not read them with unqualified satisfaction, it was only from consciousness that I was unworthy of the encomiums they bestowed upon me.

Among the papers I have lately been arranging, are passages that would prove, as forcibly as anything of mine that has been published, you were not mistaken in your supposition that it is the habit of my mind inseparably to connect loftiness of imagination with that humility of mind which is best taught in Scripture. *To J. K. Miller,*   XII. 17, 1831

Milman, Henry H.

1.   . . . spent the evening with us yesterday; and such is the variety of his information, that we found his conversation both entertaining and instructive, though his manner is much against him. [See also *L. Y.*, p. 1292.]

To Lady Bentinck,   VII-VIII, 1846

Milner, Joseph.   See Maitland 1

Milnes, R. Monckton

1.   See Kenyon 4, 5

2.   . . . Mr Milnes's Book [*Memorials of a Tour in Some Parts of Greece,* 1834], the Dedication of which is for its length one of the most admirable specimens of that class of composition to be found in the whole compass of English Literature. Of the Poems also I can say, tho' I have yet read but a few of them, that they add another to the proofs that much poetical genius is stirring among the youth of this Country. *To Moxon,*   I. 14, 1834

Milton, John (General Criticism)

1.   See Copyright 1; Criticism 75; Diction 11; Drama 15; Fancy 14A; Imagination 33E, G; Passion 7; Poetry 25, 136; Carlyle 9; Chaucer 5; Dryden 1; Faber 4; Goethe 7; Homer 2; Landor 10, 11; Macpherson 2; Peace 2; Shakespeare 26, 55; Tasso 2; W. 35, 241, 329, 339, 364A

3.   Thy soul was like a Star, and dwelt apart;
  Thou hadst a voice whose sound was like the sea;
  Pure as the naked heavens, majestic, free. . . .
  " Milton! thou," 9-11. [See *W.'s Works*, iii, 409.]   1802

4.   Those trumpet-tones of harmony. . . . See Books 10

5.   Yea, our blind Poet, who, in his later day,
  Stood almost single; uttering odious truth—
  Darkness before, and danger's voice behind,
  Soul awful—if the earth has ever lodged
  An awful soul—I seemed to see him here
  Familiarly, and in his scholar's dress
  Bounding before me, yet a stripling youth—
  A boy, no better, with his rosy cheeks
  Angelical, keen eye, courageous look,
  And conscious step of purity and pride.
  Prel., iii, 283-92.   1804-39

6.   . . . and that great Bard. . . .
  Prel., iii, 316.   1804-39

10.   See Bacon 3; Goethe 8; Hamilton, W. R. 1

11.*   . . . Milton [the finest writer] of blank verse. . . .
Collier's Preface, p. lii.   II. 10, 1814

  Among the hills
  He gazed upon that mighty orb of song,
  The divine Milton.
  Exc., i, 248-50.   1814

16.   I have long been persuaded that Milton formed his blank verse upon the model of the *Georgics* and the *Aeneid*. . . .
To Lord Lonsdale,   II. 5, 1819

17.   And One there is who builds immortal lays,
  Though doomed to tread in solitary ways,
  Darkness before and danger's voice behind
  Yet not alone, nor helpless to repel
  Sad thoughts; for from above the starry sphere
  Come secrets, whispered nightly to his ear;
  And the pure spirit of celestial light
  Shines through his soul—" that he may see and tell
  Of things invisible to mortal sight."
  3 Ecc. Sonn., iv, 6-14.   1821

18.   Such Milton, to the fountain-head
                    Of glory by Urania led!
                    Macpherson's Ossiam, 81-2.   1824

19.* Spenser, Shakespeare, and Milton are his favourites among the English poets, especially the latter, whom he almost idolises. He expressed one opinion . . . that he preferred the ' Samson Agonistes ' to ' Comus.'
J. J. Taylor (*Grosart*, iii, 502).   VII. 26, 1826

20.* [Chose Milton as one of his literary models.]
C. W., Jr. (*Grosart*, iii, 459-60)   *c.* 1827

26. [Poets succeed best where] the subject is most poetical but as to the Reform bill and Reform the genius of Milton himself could scarcely extract poetry from a theme so inauspicious. *To Merewether,*   VI. 18, 1832

27. [Milton's great works composed late in life.]
To T. Talfourd,   XI. 28, 1836

28.   Of that holiest of Bards. . . .
                    " Vallombrosa," 26.   1837

29.* . . . the narrowish limits visible in Milton. . . . See Carlyle 9.
Carlyle's Reminiscences, ed. Norton (London, 1887), p. 302.   1840

34. I had long been Well acquainted with them [Milton's sonnets], but I was particularly struck on that occasion [an afternoon in 1801] with the dignified simplicity and majestic harmony that runs through most of them— in character so totally different from the Italian, and still more so from Shakespeare's fine sonnets. See also Landor 11.
I. F. (*Grosart*, iii, 52-53).   1843

36.* [As a poet W. feared] competition . . . with . . . Milton.
H. C. R., ii, 776.   [*c.* 1845]

37.* . . . of Milton, whose poetry, he said, was earlier a favourite with him than that of Shakespeare. Speaking of Milton's not allowing his daughters to learn the meaning of the Greek they read to him, or at least not exerting himself to teach it to them, he admitted that this seemed to betoken a low estimate of the condition and purposes of the female mind. ' And yet, where could he have picked up such notions,' said Mr. W., ' in a country which had seen so many women of learning and talent? But his opinion of what women ought to be, it may be presumed, is given in the unfallen Eve, as contrasted with the right condition of man before his Maker:

                    " He for God only, she for God in him."

Now that,' said Mr. Wordsworth, earnestly, ' *is* a low, a very low and a very false estimate of woman's condition.' He was amused on my showing him the (almost) contemporary notice of Milton by Wycherly, and, after reading it, spoke a good deal of the obscurity of men of genius in or near their own times. ' But the most singular thing,' he continued, ' is that in all the writings of Bacon there is not one allusion to Shakespeare.'
Mrs. D. (*Grosart*, iii, 457).   I. 11, 1847

Milton (Works)

38.* . . . Wordsworth once said that he could read the description of Satan in Milton [*Paradise Lost,* i, 587 ff.], till he felt a certain faintness come over his mind from a sense of beauty and grandeur. . . .

Hazlitt, xi, 457. *c.* 1800

39.* . . . I read aloud the eleventh book of *Paradise Lost.* We [D. W. and W.] were much impressed, and also melted into tears.

Journals, i, 106. II, 2, 1802

40. But you have not done justice (who indeed could?) to that fine stanza ' Cultu simplici gaudens Liber, etc. etc.' it is untranslatable.

To F. Wrangham, IV. 17, 1808

41. My meaning is, that piety and religion will be best understood by him who takes the most *comprehensive* view of the human mind, and that for the most part, they will strengthen with the general strength of the mind. . . . For example Paradise Lost, and Robinson Crusoe might be as serviceable as Law's Serious Call, or Melmouth's Great Importance of a Religious Life. . . . *To Wrangham* (p. 225), VI. 5, 1808

42. The Friend cited . . . a passage from the prose works of Milton, eloquently describing the manner in which good and evil grow up together in the field of the world almost inseparably. . . .

Ans. to Mathetes (*Grosart,* i, 324). I. 4, 1810

43. [W. objects to lines 593-4 of *Paradise Lost,* viii, as indelicate.]
See La Fontaine 1

44. [*Paradise Lost.*] See Imagination 33B; Narrative Poetry 2; Chesterfield 1; Thomson 13

45. See Composition 25A; Sonnets 5, 7

47. [Milton's minor poems were so neglected that Pope could borrow from them without risk of its being known. Voss allowed their spirit to vanish, and changed their character in his translations. The poems are now loudly praised.] *E. Supp. Pref.,* p. 947. 1815

48. [*Paradise Lost,* had more readers than the petition, ' Fit audience find though few,' requested; but Dr. Johnson mistakenly says the English were ' *just* to it' in purchasing thirteen hundred copies in two years, despite the enemies Milton had made. W. replies that Milton's political ideas had also made him many friends. Many purchased this masterpiece only because they had revered the man, others purchased it as a religious work, but few for its poetical merits. Dr. Johnson states that there were few readers at this time; yet W. points out seven editions of Cowley poems by 1681, four of Flatmen's works by 1686, five of Waller's poems, and nine of Norris's works. Even in 1790 the poems of Cowley were very popular.] This is not mentioned in disparagement of that able writer and amiable man; but merely to show that, if Milton's work were not more read, it was not because readers did not exist at the time. [Only three thousand copies of an inexpensive edition

were sold; only about one thousand of Shakespeare's works between 1623 and 1664. There were plenty of readers, but their admiration led them elsewhere. The great writers are generally neglected for minor writers, for there are few genuine critics in any period who appreciate the original excellence of *Paradise Lost*.] [As further support, W. adds this note:] Hughes is express upon this subject: in his dedication of Spenser's Works to Lord Somers, he writes thus. " It was your Lordship's encouraging a beautiful edition of ' Paradise Lost ' that first brought that incomparable Poem to be generally known and esteemed." See also Criticism 49, 81.

E. Supp. Pref., p. 947 and n². 1815

49. [*Education.*] . . . martial qualities are the natural efflorescence of a healthy state of society. All great politicians seem to have been of this opinion; . . . and lastly Milton, whose tractate of education never loses sight of the means of making men perfect, both for contemplation and action, for civil and military duties. *To J. Scott,* VI. 11, 1816

51.* But I instance . . . Milton's ' Lycidas ' [as proof that good poetry can be written on contemporary persons and events].

C. W., Jr. (*Grosart*, iii, 461). *c.* 1827

52.* One of the noblest things in Milton is the description of that sweet, quiet morning in the ' Paradise Regained ' [iv, 431 ff.], after that terrible night of howling wind and storm. The contrast is divine.

C. W., Jr. (*Grosart*, iii, 461). *c.* 1827

52A.* ' Comus ' is rich in beautiful and sweet flowers, and in exuberant leaves of genius; but the ripe and mellow fruit is in ' Samson Agonistes.' When he wrote that, his mind was Hebraized. Indeed, his genius fed on the writings of the Hebrew prophets. This arose, in some degree, from the temper of the times; the Puritan lived in the Old Testament, almost to the exclusion of the New. *C. W., Jr.* (*Grosart*, iii, 461). *c.* 1827

53.* . . . Wordsworth was remarkably eloquent and felicitous in his praise of Milton. He spoke of the *Paradise Regained* as surpassing even the *Paradise Lost* in perfection of execution, though the theme is far below it and demanding less power. He spoke of the description of the storm [*Paradise Regained*, iv, 409 ff.] in it as the finest in all poetry, and he pointed out some of the artifices of versification by which Milton produced so great an effect as in passages like this:

> . . . pining atrophy,
> Marasmus, and wide-wasting pestilence,
> Dropsies and asthmas, and joint-racking rheums.
> [*Paradise Lost*, xi, 486-8.]

in which the power of the final ' rheums ' is heightened by the ' atrophy ' and ' pestilence.' ' But,' said he, ' I would not print this and similar observations, for it would enable ordinary verse-makers to imitate the practice, and what genius discovered mere mechanics would copy.' ' Hence,' I said, ' I hold critical writings of very little use. They do rather harm.' Wordsworth also praised, but not equally, the *Samson Agonistes*. He concurred, he said, with Johnson in this, that this drama has no *middle*, but the beginning and end are equally sublime. *H. C. R.*, ii, 479. I. 7, 1836

54.* . . . the fine fourteen lines of Milton's *Paradise Lost* which he says are a perfect sonnet without rhyme. *H. C. R.*, ii, 484. I. 26, 1836

55.* He talked of Milton, and observed how he sometimes indulged himself, in the ' Paradise Lost,' in lines which, if not in time, you could hardly call verse, instancing,

' And Tiresias and Phineus, prophets old; '

and then noticed the sweet-flowing lines which followed, and with regard to which he had no doubt the unmusical line before had been inserted.

' Paradise Regained ' he thought the most perfect in *execution* of anything written by Milton. . . .

Justice Coleridge (Grosart, iii, 430). X. 10, 1836

56.* [*Sonnets.*] My admiration of some of the Sonnets of Milton first tempted me to write in that form. The fact is not mentioned from a notion that it will be deemed of any importance by the reader, but merely as a public acknowledgent of one of the innumerable obligations, which, as a Poet and a man, I am under to our great fellow-countryman.

Memoirs, i, 192. V. 21, 1838

57. [Double rhymes in Milton's sonnets.] See Versification 32

58. [*Paradise Lost* not properly appreciated by the masses.]

To E. Q., III. 9, 1840

59. [*Lycidas.*] See W. 242

60.* [Of the finest elegiac compositions in English] Milton's *Lycidas* and my *Laodamia* are twin Immortals. *Alaric Watts*, i, 240. *c.* 1840

63.* He said he thought [Dr. Arnold] was mistaken in the philosophy of his view of the danger of Milton's Satan being represented without horns and hoofs; that Milton's conception was as true as it was grand; that making sin ugly was a common-place notion compared with making it beautiful outwardly, and inwardly a hell. It assumed every form of ambition and worldliness, the form in which sin attacks the highest natures.

Lady R. (Grosart, iii, 449). XII. 18, 1844

Montagu, Basil

1. . . . your advancing Edition of Lord Bacon's Works [Montagu's edition of Bacon's works was published 1825-36 in sixteen volumes, of which the first four had lately appeared. De Sel.] was brought me. . . . It is a beautiful Book, the Paper and print excellent, and promises to be every way worthy of its illustrious Author. . . . The only collection I have access to of Lord Bacon's works belongs to Coleridge. I possess indeed many of his best things in separate shapes, but I have long felt uncomfortable at having no complete Collection of my own; your Book will supply this deficiency and in the most agreeable way. *To B. Montagu*, VII. 25, 1826

2. I have nothing important to observe on your preface. It is judicious

and written with spirit. The head of ' Ignorance ' as an objection to change is not, I think, so well treated as the rest. ' Habit ' ought to have been distinctly stated as giving an undue weight to the reasons which may exist for continuing practices for which better might be substituted.

To B. Montagu,   III. 20, 1827

3. . . . the 12th vol of Lord Bacon, . . . and also for your little treatise on Laughter [*Thoughts on Laughter.* London, 1830] which has amused me much. You have rendered good service to the Public by this Edition of the Works of one of the greatest Men the world has produced. . . . Let me ask whether it would not have been better, to print the Letters of which the last Vol consists not as you have done, but in chronological order, only taking care to note from what Collection the several letters were taken. I should certainly have much preferred that Arrangement. . . .

To B. Montagu,   IV. 5, 1830

5.   If the books from which your *Selections* [*Selections from the Works of Taylor, Hooker, Hall, and Lord Bacon, with an Analysis of the Advancement of Learning*] are made were the favourite reading of men of rank and intelligence, I should dread little from the discontented in any class. But what hope is there of such a rally in our debilitated intellects?

To B. Montagu (p. 595),   1831

6.   I congratulate you sincerely on bringing to a close this important and laborious work [i. e. the last volume of M.'s edition of Bacon].

To B. Montagu,   I. 1, 1835

7. . . . your Tract upon Quaker funerals. . . . It gives me pleasure to add that I approve of the spirit in which it is written.

To B. Montagu,   X. 17, 1840

Montagu, Mary Wortley

1.   Could you tell me anything of Lady Mary Wortley Mont: more than is to be learned from Pope's Letters and her own? She seems to have been destined for something much higher and better than she became. A parallel between her genius and character and that of Lady Winchelsea her Contemporary (though somewhat prior to her) would be well worth drawing.

To Dyce,   IV. 30, 1830

Montgomery, James

1.   See Hervy 2; W. 57

2.   I can assure you with truth that from the time I first read your *Wanderer of Switzerland*, with the little pieces annexed, I have felt a lively interest in your destiny as a poet; and though much out of the way of new books, I have become acquainted with your works, and with increasing pleasure, as they successively appeared. It might be presumptuous in me were I to attempt to define what I hope belongs to us in common; but I cannot deny myself the satisfaction of expressing a firm belief that neither morality nor religion can have suffered from our writings; and with respect to *yours* I know that both have been greatly benefited by them. Without

convictions of this kind all the rest must, in the latter days of an author's life, appear to him worse than vanity. *To J. Montgomery,*   XI. 30, 1836

Montgomery, Robert

1.   With your ' Omnipresence of the Deity ' I was acquainted long ago, having read it and other parts of your writings with much pleasure, though with some abatement, such as you yourself seem sufficiently aware of, and which, in the works of so young a writer, were by me gently judged, and in many instances regarded, though in themselves faults, as indications of future excellence. In your letter, for which also I thank you, you allude to your Preface, and desire to know if my opinion concurs with yours on the subject of sacred poetry. That Preface has been read to me, and I can answer in the affirmative; but at the same time allow me frankly to tell you that what *most* pleased me in that able composition is to be found in the few concluding paragraphs, beginning ' It is now seven years since,' etc.

To R. Montgomery,   II, 1835

2.*   . . . a polite letter [see 1, above] to Montgomery on his Omnipresence of the Deity which I have heard him [W.] call " the omnipresence of folly & nonsense." . . . *Sara Coleridge and Reed,* p. 103.   *c.* 1840

3.*   I have heard him rejoice that he had thanked the author for it [see 2, above] before he had read it. *Sara Coleridge and Reed,* p. 74.   *c.* 1840

Monthly Mirror, The.   See Hill 1

Montrose, James Graham, First Marquis of

1.   [W. commends Montrose for the sincerity of his epitaph on Charles I.] . . . Hyperbole in the language of Montrose is a mean instrument made mighty because wielded by an afflicted soul, and strangeness is here the order of Nature. *Epitaph 2 (Grosart,* ii, 51).   1810

Moore, Thomas

1.*   . . . T. Moore has great natural genius; but he is too lavish of brilliant ornament. His poems smell of the perfumer's and milliner's shops. He is not content with a ring and a bracelet, but he must have rings in the ears, rings on the nose—rings everywhere.

C. W., Jr. (Grosart, iii, 462).   summer, 1827

Moran, E. R.

1.   . . . the thought that runs thro' the Sonnet [probably by Moran] gives it a great interest. I am writing where I have it not before me, or I should have taken the liberty of quoting one line towards the conclusion, in which the word *to* occurs twice causing an inelegance both of sound and construction which might be easily remedied. *To E. R. Moran,*   IX. 2, 1840

More, Thomas

1.   . . . More's gay genius played
With the inoffensive sword of native wit,
Than the bare axe more luminous and keen.
2 Ecc. Sonn., xxvi, 12-14.   1821

Mosheim, Johann Lorenz. See Maitland 1

Moutray [John Moultrie, probably; Henry Nelson Coleridge has been suggested. See *Corr. C. R.*, i, 100 n. 1]

1. Be assured however that it is not fear of such accusation which leads me to praise a Youngster who writes verses in the Etonian, to some of which our Cumberland Paper has introduced me, & some I saw at Cambridge. He is an Imp as hopeful I think as any of them—by name Moutray; if you should ever fall in with him tell him that he has pleased me much.
To C. R. (Corr. C. R., i, 100),   III. 13, 1821

Moxon, Edward

1.   Your poem I have read with no inconsiderable pleasure; it is full of natural sentiments and pleasing pictures: among the minor pieces, the last pleased me much the best, and especially the latter part of it. This little volume, with what I saw of yourself during the short interview, interest me in your welfare; and the more so, as I always feel some apprehension for the destiny of those who in youth addict themselves to the composition of verse. It is a very seducing employment, and, though begun in disinterested love of the Muses, is too apt to connect itself with self-love, and the disquieting passions which follow in the train of that our natural infirmity. Fix your eye upon acquiring independence by honourable business, and let the Muses come after rather than go before. Such lines as the latter of this couplet,

> Where lovely woman, chaste as heaven above,
> Shines in the golden virtues of her love.

and many other passages in your poem, give proof of no common-place sensibility. *To Moxon,*   XII. 8, 1826

1A.   . . . a very respectable Poet. . . .
To G. H. Gordon (L. of W. Family, p. 37),   VII. 10, 1830

2.   . . . thanks for your Sonnets [Moxon's *Sonnets* was published in 1833; a second volume appeared in 1835, dedicated to W. De Sel.] which we have both read with much pleasure. There is a great deal of sweet feeling and pleasing expression in them. In the 3d there is a mistake, the River that flows through Rydal is not the Brathay but the Rothay—This is a good Sonnet. Were I asked to Name a favorite or two, perhaps I should chuse 12,–18–23–28. In the cadence and execution of your Sonnets I seem to find more of the manner of Bowles than my own, and this you must not think a disparagement as Bowles in his sonnets has been very successful. The principal fault in your style is an overfrequency of inversion. For example at the close of the first—the fall of Man is a phrase of meaning so awful, and so much in the thoughts and upon the tongue of every religious Person that the Disclocation of the words is to me a little startling—not that I have any wish that it should be altered. *To Moxon,*   V. 14, 1833

3.   Thank you for the sonnets [Moxon's *Sonnets,* dedicated to W. W., were published in 1835. De Sel.]. I am not at all disappointed in them.

They are very pleasing; and we all like them much.—You need not apologize for dedicating them to me—for they aim at no rivalship with mine, being so different both in the unity of the subject, and in the metre and style of versification. Yours are of Elizabeth's and James's and the 1st Charles' time; mine rather after the model of Milton. *To Moxon,* V. 15, 1835

4.   If I had given way to my feelings I should have observed upon the beauty of many of the sonnets [i. e. Moxon's].

I have made a few verbal alterations, which I hope you will think improvements. *To Moxon,* VIII. 2, 1835

5.* . . . Wordsworth speaks with indignation of the *Quarterly Review* attack on Moxon as base. It is a mere attack on the publisher under pretence of attacking the poet. *H. C. R.,* ii, 534. VIII. 15, 1837

6.   We like the Sonnets [*Sonnets* of 1830 and 1835, reprinted] thinking them pleasing compositions—We shall not be offended if you do not adopt any of our alterations. *To Moxon,* VIII. 17, 1843

Muloch, T. S.

1.   Let Talfourd flagellate him when he becomes impertinent upon the Lake-School. . . .
To C. R. (Corr. C. R., i, 101), III. 13, 1821

Musaeus

1.   Musaeus, stationed with his lyre
          Supreme among the Elysian quire. . . .
          Ossian, 39-40. 1824

Newcastle, Margaret Cavendish, Duchess of

1.   The Mirth and Melancholy has so many fine strokes of Imagination that I cannot but think there must be merit in many parts of her writings. How beautiful those lines, from ' I dwell in groves,' towards the conclusion, ' Yet better loved the more than I am known,' excepting the 4 verses after ' Walk up the hills.' And surely the latter verse of the couplet,
          The tolling bell which for the dead rings out,
          A mill where rushing waters run about,
is very noticeable; no person could have hit upon that union of images without being possessed of true poetic feeling. *To Dyce,* IV. 30, 1830

2.   It pleased me to find that you sympathized with me in admiration of the Passage from the Dutchess of Newcastle's poetry. . . .
To Dyce, III. 20, 1833

Newton, Isaac

1.   Of Newton with his prism and silent face,
          The marble index of a mind for ever
          Voyaging through strange seas of Thought, alone.
          Prel., iii, 61-3. 1804-39

2.   Even the great Newton's own ethereal self. . . .
          Prel., iii, 267. 1804-39

3.* [Looked upon] him [Newton], considering both the magnitude and the universality of his genius, as perhaps the most extraordinary man that this country ever produced. . . . he was an excellent linguist, but never sought display, and was content to work in that quietness and humility both of spirit and of outward circumstances in which alone all that is truly good was ever done. *A Day with Wordsworth*, p. 741.   VIII. 31, 1841

4. . . . his evasion of the question about Poetry, and putting the answer into the mouth of Barrow makes it very probable that he would have been no very competent judge in any department of imaginative literature. . . .
To E. and Dora.   VIII-IX, 1841

Niebuhr, Barthold G.

1. [*History of Rome.*] See History 11-13

Norris of Bemerton, John.   See Milton 48

Osborne, Francis

1.* . . . Osborne's *Advice to his Son*, a book Wordsworth gave to Monkhouse, and which I supposed, therefore, a favourite. This I wondered at, but I found on inquiry that Wordsworth only respected the sagacity of detached remarks. . . . *H. C. R.*, i, 340.   X. 7, 1826

Ossian.   See under Macpherson

Otway, Caesar

1.   I have read with great pleasure the ' Sketches in Ireland ' which Mr Otway was kind enough to present me. . . .
To W. R. Hamilton,   VII. 24, 1829

Otway, Thomas.   See Heywood, T. 1

Ovid

1. [*Epistulae ex Ponto.*] See Dramatic Poetry 1

2. Before I read Virgil I was so strongly attached to Ovid, whose *Metamorphoses* I read at school, that I was quite in a passion whenever I found him, in books of criticism, placed below Virgil.
I. F. (*Grosart*, iii, 168).   1843

Page, Frederick

1. . . . an intelligent gentleman [W. wanted to read Page's projected work on Ireland]. *To G. H. Gordon,*   XII. 1, 1829

Paley, William

1.* He approves of [Paley's works].
Hazlitt, iv, 277   *c.* 1800

Parkinson, Richard

1A. [I have read] the agreeable Present of your Vol. of Poems [*Sacred and Miscellaneous*] . . . with much pleasure. . . .

The Legend of St Bega's Abbey is well treated, and with the concluding allusion to the College I was particularly pleased. The feeling and expression are both excellent. Permit me to observe that the agreeable lines upon the hermitage, would be improved by the omission of the stanza beginning Such was his life & also that which follows. They distort the quiet tenor of the Poem. The line, " Of [' Or '] friend untimely snatched above," is but a bad one, and might be altered with advantage.

To R. Parkinson (*L. of W. Family*, p. 70),   XII. 6, 1832

1.   Several traditions of miracles, connected with the foundation of the first of these religious houses, survive among the people of the neighborhood; one of which is alluded to in these Stanzas [*St. Bees' Head*]; and another, of a somewhat bolder and more peculiar character, has furnished the subject of a spirited poem by the Rev. R. Parkinson. . . . *Oxf. W.*, p. 924.   1835

2.   Accept my thanks for the 2nd Edition of your Old Church Clock; and my acknowledgment for the dedication, acceptable on many accounts.

You have fallen into a mistake respecting the drawing from which the view of Seathwaite Chapel is taken. It was not done by the Barber who married a granddaughter of Robert Walker, but by a young friend of mine since dead. *To R. Parkinson*,   IV. 8, 1844

Parr, Samuel

1.   Dr Parr (who you recollect gave a proof of his critical acumen in the affair of Ireland's MSS which he pronounced to be genuine Shakespear) has declared that it [*The Excursion*] is ' all *but* Milton.' . . .

To C. Clarkson (p. 622),   XII. 31, 1814

Pasley, Charles W.

1.   [*Military Policy* was written] too much under the influence of feelings similar to those of a Poet or novelist, who deepens the distress in the earlier part of his work, in order that the happy catastrophe which he has prepared for his hero and heroine may be more keenly relished [*M. Y.*, p. 432].

. . . I congratulate my country on the appearance of a book which, resting in this point our national safety upon the purity of our national character, will, I trust, lead naturally to make us, at the same time, a more powerful and a highminded nation [*M. Y.*, p. 440]. *To Captain Pasley*,   III. 28, 1811

Peabody, Elizabeth

1.   [Thank] you both for the interesting Contents of your Volume [*The Record of a School*], and for the account you are so obliging as to give me of the effects which some of my poems have produced upon the minds of young persons in your presence.

To Elizabeth Peabody,   IV, 7, 1836

Peace, John

1.   . . . but I have long wished to thank *you* for the *Apology for Cathedrals,* which I have learned is from your pen. The little work does you great credit; it is full of that wisdom which the heart and imagination alone could adequately supply for such a subject, and is, moreover, very pleasingly diversified by styles of treatment all good in their kind. . . . I entirely concur in the views you take. . . .

. . . I have lately been reading Cowper's ' Task ' aloud, and in so doing was tempted to look over the parallelisms, for which Mr Southey was, in his edition, indebted to you. Knowing how comprehensive your acquaintance with poetry is, I was rather surprised that you did not notice the identity of the thought, and accompanying illustrations of it, in a passage of Shenstone's ' Ode upon Rural Elegance,' compared with one in ' The Task ' [Book IV, ' It is a flame,' &c., compared with Shenstone's ' Ode to the Duchess of Somerset,' ' Her impulse nothing may restrain.'—W. W.] where Cowper speaks of the inextinguishable love of the country as manifested by the inhabitants of cities in their culture of plants and flowers, where the want of air, cleanliness, and light is so unfavourable to their growth and beauty. The germ of the main thought is to be found in Horace [Lib. 1, *Epist.* 10, v. 22. W.].   *To Peace,*   I. 19, 1841

2.   Your *Descant* amused me, but I must protest against your system, which would discard punctuation to the extent you propose. It would, I think, destroy the harmony of blank verse when skillfully written. What would become of the pauses at the third syllable, followed by an *and,* or any such word, without the rest which a comma, when consistent with the sense, calls upon the reader to make, and which being made, he starts with the weak syllable that follows, as from the beginning of a verse? I am sure Milton would have supported me in this opinion. Thomson wrote his blank verse before his ear was formed as it was when he wrote the ' Castle of Indolence,' and some of his short rhyme poems. It was, therefore, rather hard in you to select him as an instance of punctuation abused.

To J. Peace,   II. 23, 1842

Pearson, William

1.*   My brother was much interested by the information you had gathered from your vagrant neighbors, the Gipsies. . . . He intends, if you have no objection, to send the account to be inserted in the ' Naturalists' Magazine,' if the matter be thought new or sufficiently important.

D. W. to W. Pearson,   III. 25, 1830

2.*   My brother intends sending the ' Hedgehog ' [a poem by W. P.] to the Naturalists' Magazine. . . . *D. W. to W. Pearson,*   V. 5, 1830

Peele, George

1.   Peele's works are well deserving of the care you [Dyce edited Peele's works in 1828] have bestowed upon them. . . . *To Dyce,*   X. 16, 1829

2.   See Dyce 2

Percy, Thomas

1. Next in importance to the *Seasons* of Thomson . . . come the *Reliques of Ancient English Poetry*; collected, new-modelled, and in many instances (if such a contradiction in terms may be used) composed by the Editor, Dr. Percy. [The *Reliques* produced many poor imitations of ballads. Ill-suited to the prevailing taste, the *Reliques* sank into temporary neglect, under the scorn of Johnson. Bürger, and other able writers in Germany, composed under Percy's influence many delightful poems. Percy, writing under a mask, followed his genius into the regions of true simplicity and genuine pathos as evinced by the exquisite ballad *Sir Cauline*]; yet . . . in his own person and character as a poetical writer, he adopted, as in the tale of the *Hermit of Warkworth*, a diction scarcely in any one of its features distinguishable from the vague, the glossy, and unfeeling language of his day. I mention this remarkable fact with regret, esteeming the genius of Dr. Percy in this kind of writing superior to that of any other man by whom in modern times it has been cultivated. That even Bürger . . . had not the fine sensibility of Percy, might be shown from many passages, in which he has deserted his original only to go astray. For example: [see *Oxf. W.*, pp. 949-50, for a contrast between a ballad of Percy's and a translation by Bürger]. *E. Supp. Pref.*, pp. 949-50.   1815

2. [Poetry influenced by Percy's *Reliques*.] See Macpherson 2

3. See Burns 26A; Scotch Writers 2

4. See in Percy's Reliques that fine old ballad, " The Spanish Lady's Love; " from which Poem the form of stanza, as suitable to dialogue, is adopted. *Oxf. W.*, p. 139 n[1].   1835

Peterkin, Alexander

1. . . . I regret that you omitted . . . [her] *Sorrow*, or at least that you did not abridge it. The first and third Paragraph are very affecting. See also ' Expostulation ' . . . ; it reminds me strongly of one of the Penitential Hymns of Burns. *To Dyce*,   IV. 30, 1830

Petrarch

1. Is it not in fact obvious that many of his love-verses must have flowed, I do not say from a wish to display his own talent, but from a habit of exercising his intellect in that way, rather than from an impulse of his heart? It is otherwise with his Lyrical Poems, and particularly with the one upon the degradation of his country. There he pours out his reproaches, lamentations, and aspirations like an ardent and sincere patriot.
I. F. (Grosart, iii, 85).   1843

Philips, Katherine. See Scholarly Interests 18

Phillips, Ambrose. See Johnson 11

Pilkington, Laetitia

1. See Jeffrey 10

2. . . . the author [in his *Life of Burns*] has rendered a substantial service to the poet's memory; and the annexed letters are all important to the subject. *L. to Friend of Burns* (*Grosart*, ii, 5).   1816

Pindar. See Horace 7

Pindar, Peter. See under Wolcot, John

Plato

1. See Bacon 3

2.*   I have heard him pronounce that the Tragedy of *Othello*, Plato's records of the last scenes of the career of Socrates, and Isaac Walton's *Life of George Herbert*, were in his opinion the most pathetic of human compositions. *Graves* (*Grosart*, iii, 468).   *c.* 1840

3. . . . the Genius of Plato. See W. 109.

4. [German writers] have much of Plato in them, and for this I respect them . . . a sound Philosophy must contain both Plato and Aristotle. See Literature 24

5.*   [W. admitted that Plato's *Republic* published as a new book would not find readers] yet we have embodied it all.
English Traits, p. 295.   III, 1848

Plumpton, Sir William. See under Camden Society

Plutarch. [For W.'s interest in Plutarch, see *Prel.*, viii, 617-25, and ix, 408-17. See also *The Mind of a Poet*, pp. 474 and 504, and *Prel.*, ed. de Selincourt, p. 503.]

Poole, Thomas

1. . . . it gave me the highest pleasure to learn that in the Poems about which alone I was anxious, I had pleased you; and your praise was expressed with such discrimination as gave it a high value indeed.
To T. Poole,   VII, 1801

Pope, Alexander (General Criticism)

1. As to the idea of the decay of your mental powers, you may easily get rid of it, by reading Pope's description of the cave of spleens in the *Rape of the Lock.* *To Wm. Mathews,*   VIII. 13, 1791

1A. We see that Pope, by the power of verse alone, has contrived to render the plainest commonsense interesting, and even frequently to invest it with the appearance of passion. In consequence of these convictions I related in metre the tale of Goody Blake and Harry Gill, which is one of the rudest of this collection. I wish to draw attention to the truth that power of the human imagination is sufficient to produce such changes in our physical nature as might almost appear miraculous. The truth is an important one; the fact (for it is a fact) is a valuable illustration of it; and I have the satisfaction of knowing that it has been communicated to many hundreds of

people who would never have heard of it, had it not been narrated in a Ballad, and in a more impressive metre than is usual in Ballads.
Pref. L. B. (K. Prose, i, 69). [Omitted after ed. of 1837.]   1800-36

2.*   [W. will allow none of the excellencies of poetry to Pope and Dryden.]   *Hazlitt*, iv, 277.   *c*. 1800

3.   See Chaucer 12; Collins 5; Dryden 1, 14, 21; Milton 47; W. 1

4.   . . . whose sparkling and tuneful manner had bewitched the men of letters his contemporaries, and corrupted the judgment of the nation through all ranks of society. So that a great portion of original genius was necessary to embolden a man to write faithfully to Nature upon any affecting subject if it belonged to a class of composition in which Pope had furnished examples.
Epitaph 2 (Grosart, ii, 53-4).   1810

5.*   . . . Pope was a more finished and polished versifier than Dryden.
. . . *Collier's Preface*, p. lii.   II. 10, 1814

6.   The arts by which Pope, soon afterwards, contrived to procure himself a more general and a higher reputation than perhaps any English Poet ever attained during his lifetime, are known to the judicious.   And as well known is it to them, that the undue exertion of those arts is the cause why Pope has for some time held a rank in literature, to which, if he had not been seduced by an over-love of immediate popularity, and had confided more in his native genius, he never could have descended. He bewitched the nation by his melody, and dazzled it by his polished style, and was himself blinded by his own success. Having wandered from humanity in his Eclogues with boyish inexperience, the praise, which these compositions obtained, tempted him into a belief that Nature was not to be trusted, at least in pastoral Poetry. To prove this by example, he put his friend Gay upon writing those Eclogues which their author intended to be burlesque. See Gay 1. *E. Supp. Pref.*, p. 948.   1815

8.   [Pope's praise of Thomson not sincere.] See Thompson 13

9.*   I have been charged by some [see 2, above] with disparaging Pope and Dryden. This is not so. I have committed much of both to memory. As far as Pope goes, he succeeds; but his Homer is not Homer, but Pope. *C. W., Jr. (Grosart*, iii, 460).   *c* 1827

11.   The Poetic Genius of England with the exception of Chaucer, Spenser, Milton, Dryden, Pope, and a very few more, is to be sought in her Drama. *To Dyce*,   IV. 30, 1830

13.   [Classical diction and refinement of Pope.] See Thomson 9

14.*   . . . he held Pope to be the greatest poet, but Dryden to have the most talent—the strongest understanding. Genius and ability he opposed —as others do. He said his preface on poetical language had been misunderstood. Whatever is addressed to the imagination is essentially poetical, but very pleasing verses deserving all praise, but not so addressed, are not poetry. *H. C. R.*, ii, 608.   I. 6, 1842

Pope (Works)

16. [Malignity in his satires.]   *To W. Mathews,*   III. 21, 1796

17. [W. illustrates " poetic diction " by contrasting Pope's *Messiah* with the Biblical version.]   *App. L. B.,* p. 943.   1802

18. [Epitaphs.] The course which we have taken having brought us to the name of this distinguished Writer—Pope—I will in this place give a few observations upon his Epitaphs,—the largest collection we have in our language, from the pen of any Writer of eminence. As the epitaphs of Pope and also those of Chiabrera, which occasioned this dissertation, are in metre, it may be proper here to enquire how far the notion of a perfect epitaph, as given in a former Paper [*Epitaph* 1], may be modified by the choice of metre for the vehicle, in preference to prose. If our opinions be just, it is manifest that the basis must remain the same in either case; and that the difference can only lie in the superstructure; and it is equally plain, that a judicious man will be less disposed in this case than in any other to avail himself of the liberty given by metre to adopt phrases of fancy, or to enter into the more remote regions of illustrative imagery. For the occasion of writing an epitaph is matter-of-fact in its intensity, and forbids more authoritatively than any other species of composition all modes of fiction, except those which the very strength of passion has created; which have been acknowledged by the human heart, and have become so familiar that they are converted into substantial realities. When I come to the epitaphs of Chiabrera, I shall perhaps give instances in which I think he has not written under the impression of this truth; where the poetic imagery does not elevate, deepen, or refine the human passion, which it ought always to do or not to act at all, but excludes it. In a far greater degree are Pope's epitaphs debased by faults into which he could not I think have fallen if he had written in prose as a plain man and not as a metrical Wit. See Pope 19.

Epitaph 2 (*Grosart,* ii, 55-6).   1810

19. [W. disagrees with Johnson's approval of Pope's *Mrs. Corbet*; for the true impulse is wanting in that he aims only to give a favorable portrait of her character. Pope forgets that it is a living creature, not an intellectual existence, that must interest us. The treatment is cold and unfeeling.] . . . the thoughts have their nature changed and moulded by the vicious expression in which they are entangled, to an excess rendering them wholly unfit for the place they occupy.

> Here rests a woman, good without pretence,
> Blest with plain reason—

from which *sober sense* is not sufficiently distinguishable. This verse and a half, and the one ' so unaffected, so composed a mind,' are characteristic, and the expression is true to nature; but they are . . . the only parts of the epitaph which have this merit. Minute criticism is in its nature irksome, and as commonly practised in books and conversation, is both irksome and injurious. Yet every mind must occasionally be exercised in this discipline, else it cannot learn the art of bringing words rigorously to the test of thoughts; and these again to a comparison with things, their archetypes, contemplated first in themselves, and secondly in relation to each other; in all which processes the mind must be skilful, otherwise it will be perpetually imposed upon. In the next couplet the word *conquest* [is trite, and not appropriate in an epitaph. ' No arts essayed; but not to be admired,' suggests artifices to conceal her admirable qualities, and the context implies merit in this. But Pope simply is trying to say she shunned admiration with an unusual Modesty, and that she had an unaffected mind. The sense of love and peaceful admiration she inspires is disturbed by an oblique and ill-timed stroke of satire.] . . . She is not praised so much as others are blamed, and is degraded by the Author in thus being made a covert or stalking-horse for gratifying a propensity the most abhorrent from her own nature—' Passion and pride were to her soul unknown.' [Here, and in ' virtue only is our own,' the author appears to have no notion of his own meaning.] If she was ' good without pretence,' it seems unnecessary to say that she was not proud. Dr. Johnson, making an exception of the verse, ' Convinced that virtue only is our own,' praises this epitaph for ' containing nothing taken from common places.' . . . it is not only no fault but a primary requisite in an epitaph that it shall contain thoughts and feelings which are in their substance commonplace, and even trite. It is grounded upon the universal intellectual property of man,—[universal sensations and truths] . . . they should be uttered in such connection as shall make it felt that they are not adopted, not spoken by rote, but perceived in their whole compass with the freshness and clearness of an original intuition. . . . The line ' Virtue only is our own,'—is objectionable, not from the commonplaceness of the truth, but from the vapid manner in which it is conveyed. [See Chiabrera 2 for the rest of this passage.] *Epitaph 2* (*Grosart*, ii, 56-8). 1810

20. [*Epitaphs.*] If my notions are right, the epitaphs of Pope cannot well be too severely condemned; for not only are they almost wholly destitute of those universal feelings and simple movements of mind which we have called for as indispensible, but they are little better than a tissue of false thoughts, languid and vague expressions, unmeaning antithesis, and laborious attempts at discrimination. Pope's mind has been employed chiefly in observation upon the vices and follies of men. Now, vice and folly are in contradiction with the moral principle which can never be extinguished in the mind; and therefore, wanting the contrast, are irregular, capricious, and inconsistent with themselves. [Satire is opposed to the moral principle requisite to an epitaph. Virtue, not vice, is the subject of an epitaph.] . . .

It is reasonable then that Cicero, when holding up Cataline to detestation; and (without going to such an extreme case) that Dryden and Pope, when they are describing characters like Buckingham, Shaftsbury, and The Duchess of Marlborough, should represent qualities and actions at war with each other and with themselves; and that the page should be suitably crowded with antithetical expressions. But all this argues an obtuse moral sensibility and a consequent want of knowledge, if applied where virtue ought to be described in the language of affectionate admiration. In the mind of the truly great and good everything that is of importance is at peace with itself; all is stillness, sweetness and stable grandeur. Accordingly the contemplation of virtue is attended with repose. [Unity of tone or feeling is essential to an epitaph. The satirist, accustomed to portraying evil, or placing good and evil in contrasting positions, lacks the "nobler sympathies," essential to the writer of epitaphs. The subject of an epitaph must not be a bad man, and any weaknesses in the good must be disregarded.]

Epitaph 3 (Grosart, ii, 60-2).　　　　　　　　　　　　　　　　1810

21. . . . the epitaph of Pope upon Harcourt; of whom it is said that he never gave his father grief but when he died.' I need not point out how many situations there are in which such an expression of feeling would be natural and becoming; but in a permanent inscription things only should be admitted that have an enduring place in the mind; and a nice selection is required even among these. *Epitaphs 3 (Grosart,* ii, 68).　　　　1810

22. See Dramatic Poetry 1; Pope 6; Shakespeare 45; Thomson 13

26. [*Homer.*] See W. 294; Scotch Writers 2

27. [*Solitude,* and *Essay on Criticism.*] Pope, in that production of his Boyhood, the ode to Solitude, and in his Essay on Criticism, has furnished proofs that at one period of his life he felt the charm of a sober and subdued style, which he afterwards abandoned for one that is to my taste at least too pointed and ambitious, and for a versification too timidly balanced.
To Dyce,　　　　　　　　　　　　　　　　　　　　　　V. 10, 1830

Powell, Thomas

1. In the printed verses you sent me some time ago are several stanzas that pleased me much—I have this moment glanced my eye over them but of two that particularly touched me, I can only find one, it is
　　Know! those who find no peace on earth will find none in the grave—
To T. Powell,　　　　　　　　　　　　　　　　　　　III, 1841

2. They [Powell's poems in *The Monthly Chronicle*] all have the characteristic merits of your writing; but I should like to have an opportunity of noting vivâ voce some of the faults, as I take them to be, of style.
To Powell,　　　　　　　　　　　　　　　　　　　XII. 11, 1841

3. [A volume of poems read] with great pleasure. The thoughts and sentiments I find myself in sympathy with, every where I think, except page 315. Napoleon . . . was a false creature faithless in every object . . . . long ago . . . I found your workmanship as a Poet not equal to the beauty and grandeur of your thoughts and feelings. I still am of the same opinion notwithstanding the pleasure the perusal of your Vol. has given me; and how here to assist you I do not know. I can only then reflect that your bard has gratified me much. The divine History of the Earth, The invocation to the Earth etc etc are all in a high strain of thought and feeling, and other pieces are [?] for appropriate tenderness. *To T. Powell,*　　　　　IV. 2, 1842

Price, Uvedale

1.* My Brother thinks that Mr Price [through his *Essay on the Picturesque*] has been of great service in correcting the false taste of the layers out of Parks and Pleasure-grounds. *D. W. to Lady Beaumont,*　　I. 19, 1806

2. He is 77 years of age and truly a wonder both for body and mind. . . .
To S. Rogers,   I. 21, 1825

3. He has just written a most ingenious work on ancient metres, and the proper mode of reading Greek and Latin verse. If he is right, we have all been wrong; and I think he is. [In 1827 Price had published an *Essay on the Modern Pronunciation of Greek and Latin,* in which he contended that ' our system of pronouncing the ancient languages is at variance with the principles and established rules of ancient prosody and the practice of the best poets.' De Sel.] *To ?,*   I. 25, 1828

Prince, John C.

1. [W.] thanks Mr Prince for his Tribute [poem *On the Death of Southey*] to the memory of Mr Southey, protesting only however, as he does *strongly* against the censure passed on his departed Friend towards the conclusion of the Poem, which censure he knows to be utterly undeserved and most unjust. *To J. C. Prince,*   V. 15, 1843

Prior, Matthew

1. [As an illustration of "poetic diction," W. contrasts] Prior's ' Did sweeter sounds adorn my flowing tongue,' &c. &c. ' Though I speak with the tongues of men and of angels,' &c. &c., 1st Corinthians, ch. xiii.
App. L. B., p. 943.   1802

Procter, Bryan Waller (Barry Cornwall)

1. The feelings are cleverly touched in it [Cornwall's tragedy, *Mirandola*]; but the situations for exhibiting them, are produced not only by sacrifice of the respectability of the persons concerned, but with great, & I should have thought unnecessary violation or probability and common sense. But it does appear to me in the present late age of the world a most difficult task to construct a good tragedy free from stale & mean contrivances and animated by new & suitable Characters. So that I am inclined to judge Cornwall gently, and sincerely rejoice in his success.
To C. R. (Corr. C. R., i, 99),   III. 13, 1821

Quarterly Review, The

1. See Periodicals 5; Sewell 1; Whewell 1; W. 200

3.* . . . he thought he had more cause of complaint against the *Quarterly* than the *Edinburgh.* We can more easily forgive the open, rather ostentatious enemy, than the would-be-thought friend. *H. C. R.,* iii, 833.   [*c.* 1840]

4.* [His poems would have had an earlier influence] but for the tyranny exercised over public opinion by the *Edinburgh* and *Quarterly Reviews.*
Lady R. (Grosart, iii, 437).   VIII. 28, 1841

Quillinan, Edward

1.* The verses are very affecting—and I think they will set my Brother's mind to flow in numbers, as they have already wrought on his feelings. He has mused upon your lines. . . . *D. W. to E. Q.* (p. 99),   XI. 19, 1822

2.*   Dora read your verses to her Father, who just now tells me ' They are pretty verses ' if he may be allowed to say so of any so panegyrical of himself. *D. W. to E. Q.*,   V, 1824

3.   Thanks for your spritely verses. . . . *To E. Q.*,   XI. 16, 1830

4.   I hope you are not answerable for the sin of being the author of ' Mischief.' [' Mischief,' a tale of intrigue, obviously suggested by *Beppo*. . . . Q. published the first section (anonymously) with Moxon in 1831, the second in 1834. De Sel.]. [Dora adds] Father says there are some lines far too pretty and pure to have been found in such company.
W. and Dora to E. Q.,   VII. 4, 1831

5.   . . . much pleased with the second part of Mischief; it is written with great spirit and a variety of talent which does the Author no small credit. I cannot guess why this performance has not made more impression than I am aware it has done, but the political agitations of the times leave no leisure for any thing but 1d Mags and 5/– books with cuts which may be looked at but are seldom read. *To E. Q.*,   VI. 11, 1834

6.   This very day Dora read to me your Poem again; it convinces me along with your other writings that it is in your power to attain a permanent place among the poets of England, your thoughts, feelings, knowledge, and judgement in style, and skill in metre entitle you to it; if you have not yet succeeded in gaining it the cause appears to me mainly to lie in the subjects wh. you have chosen. It is worthy of note how much of Gray's popularity is owing to the happiness with which his subject is selected in three pieces—his Hymn to Adversity, his ode on the distant prospect of Eton College, and his Elegy. I ought however in justice to add that one cause of your failure appears to have been thinking too humbly of yourself, so that you have not reckoned it as worth while to look sufficiently round you for the best subjects or to employ as much time in reflecting, condensing bringing out and placing your thoughts and feelings in the best point of view, as is necessary. I will conclude this matter of poetry, my part of the letter, with requesting that as an act of friendship at your convenience you would take the trouble, a considerable one I own, of comparing the corrections in my last edition with the text in the preceding one. You know my principles of style better I think than any one else, and I should be glad to learn if anything strikes you as being altered for the worse. You will find the principal changes in The White Doe, in wh. I had too little of the benefit of your help and judgment: there are several also in the sonnets both miscellaneous and political—in the other poems they are nothing like so numerous, but here also I should be glad if you wd take the like trouble. *To E. Q.*,   IX. 20, 1837

7.   . . . read your verses [*Poems*, published by Moxon, London, 1853] with much pleasure; they want neither eye nor feeling, and are upon the whole . . . worthy of the subject. But the expression is here and there faulty, as I am pretty sure you must be yourself aware. [Next follow detailed suggestions for correcting the diction of the poems.] *To E. Q.*,   1841

8.   His [Quillinan's] inaction mortifies me the more because his talents are greatly superior to those of most men who earn a handsome livelihood by Literature. *To I. Fenwick,*   IX. 19, 1844

9.   It is a pity that Quillinan has not access to Books, or he might have been of great use to your Dictionary of Dates, for he is wonderfully industrious, a most pains-taking Man. I wish you could put into his hands some literary labour by which he could add to his very scanty Income. Do think about it. As to any light work of his own choice, I am sure it would never sell unless he would condescend, which he never will do, to traffic in the trade of praise with London Authorlings, who write in newspapers, Magazines and Reviews. You Publishers are quite at the mercy of these Knots and Cabals of Scribblers whose publications are of the day, the week, the month, or the Quarter. I do not mean their writing merely in Reviews, but also what they give to the World individually, whatever shape it may assume, or through whatever vehicle it may be offered to the public. It is a sad condition of things, but I see no remedy—*To Moxon,*   I. 23, 1845

10.   Mrs. Q. [Quillinan] is about finishing the copying of her Journal. Had she seen more of Portugal and Spain it would have been well worth sending to the press; but in regard to the former she was prevented by bad weather. Women observe many particulars of manners and opinions which are apt to escape the notice of the Lords of Creation. *To Moxon,* X, 1, 1846

11.   I have read in the proof the Article upon Gil Vincente: it is well done and I think it will be a pleasing variety in the Quarterly.
To J. G. Lockhart,   XI. 14, 1846

12.*   The first thing Mrs. W said to me when she came home was ' Quillinan, those are two fine sonnets on Rome '—therefore I infer that *the* Great Poet endured them.
E. Q. to C. R. (Corr. C. R., ii, 700),   VII. 9, 1849

Racine, Jean

1.*   . . . did not wish to see it [*Athalie*] acted, as it would never come up to the high imagination he had formed in reading it, of the prophetic inspiration of the priests. . . . *Moore's Diary,* p. 27.   X. 24, 1820

2.*   Racine lived in a court till it became necessary to his existence, as his miserable death proved. *C. W., Jr. (Grosart,* iii, 466).   *c.* 1827

3.   See Composition 22

Radcliffe, Ann

1.   [Objects to novels of her school.] See Scott, W. 37

Ramond, Baron de Carbonnières

1.   For most of the images in the next sixteen verses [*Descriptive Sketches* (Quarto), ll. 372 ff.] I am indebted to M. Raymond's interesting observations annexed to his translation of Coxe's Tour in Switzerland.
Oxf. W., p. 609 n. 2.   1793

2. I find in Monsieur Raimond's [Ramond's] translation of Coxe's Travels in Switzerland, that Mr Bodner, a German poet of Zurich, had presented him with a volume of amorous verses of the poets of the thirteenth century. This work is extracted from a manuscript which The King of France entrusted to the city of Zurich in the year 1752. I will transcribe a sentence which follows ' Il m'a encore donné (that is Mr Bodner) le receuil de ses tragedies historiques et politiques, ouvrage aussi savant qu' interessant.' If it had been *son* receuil the meaning of this sentence would have been evident, but the word *savant* seems to imply that it is a collection of which Mr Bodner is only the editor; unless being original tragedies they are accompanied with notes. *W. and D. W. to Coleridge*,   I, 1799

3. In the third stanza of the *Desultory Stanzas* [*Oxf. W.*, p. 350] I am indebted to Mr. Raymond who has written with genuine feeling on these subjects. *Knight*, vi, 383 n.   1822

4. Have you read Raymond's account of the former [Coxe's *Travels in Switzerland*]—it is well worth looking over, more for the beauty of particular passages, than its general interest, or its merit as far as I am able to judge, as an acquisition to Geology—It is however on this account that the Author seems to pride himself—His translation of Coxe, I think, I recommended to you before—*To C. R. (Corr. C. R.*, i, 191-2),   XI. 28, 1828

Reynolds, F. Mansel

1. . . . your own Verses upon the Coquette are too coarse for so fine dress'd a publication—and your Invitation is not so happy as some light things I have seen from your Pen. . . . *To F. M. Reynolds,*   I. 28, 1829

Reynolds, John H.

1. Your Poem [*Naiad*] is composed with elegance and in a style that accords with the subject; but my opinion on this point might have been of more value if I had seen the Scottish Ballad on which your work is founded. You do me the honour of asking me to find fault in order that you may profit by my remarks. I remember when I was young in the practice of writing praise was prodigiously acceptable to me and censure most distasteful, nay, even painful. For the credit of my own nature I would fain persuade myself to this day, that the extreme labour and tardiness with which my compositions were brought forth had no inconsiderable influence for exciting both these sensations. Presuming, however, that you have more philosophy than I was master of at that time, I will not scruple to say that your Poem would have told more upon me, if it had been shorter. . . . Your Fancy is too luxuriant, and riots too much upon its own creations. . . . your poem would be better without the first 57 lines (not condemned for their own sakes), and without the last 146, which nevertheless have much to recommend them. The Basis is too narrow for the super-structure; and to me it would have been more striking barely to have hinted at the deserted Fair One and to have left it to the Imagination of the Reader to dispose of her as he liked. Her fate dwelt upon at such length requires of the reader a sympathy which cannot be furnished without taking the Nymph from the unfathomable abyss of the

cerulean waters and beginning afresh upon gross Terra Firma. I may be wrong but I speak as I felt, and the most profitable criticism is the record of sensations, provided the person affected be under no partial influence.

To J. H. Reynolds, XI. 28, 1816

Reynolds, Joshua

1. See Criticism 41; Laste 1; Burke 3A

3. Several of the Discourses I had read before, though never regularly together: they have very much added to the high opinion which I before entertained of Sir Joshua Reynolds. Of a great part of them, never having had an opportunity of *studying* any pictures whatsoever, I can be but a very inadequate judge; but of such parts of the Discourses as relate to general philosophy, I may be entitled to speak with more confidence; and it gives me great pleasure to say to you . . . that they appear to me highly honourable to him. The sound judgment universally displayed in these Discourses is truly admirable,—I mean the deep conviction of the necessity of unwearied labour and diligence, the reverence for the great men of his art, and the comprehensive and unexclusive character of his taste. Is it not a pity . . . that a man with such a high sense of the *dignity* of his art, and with such industry, should not have given more of his time to the nobler departments of painting? . . . It is such an animating sight to see a man of genius, regardless of temporary gains, whether of money or praise, fixing his attention solely upon what is intrinsically interesting and permanent, and finding his happiness in an entire devotion of himself to such pursuits as shall most ennoble human nature. We have not yet seen enough of this in modern times; and never was there a period in society when such examples were likely to do more good than at present. The industry and love of truth which distinguished Sir Joshua's mind are most admirable; but he appears to me to have lived too much for the age in which he lived, and the people among whom he lived, though this is an infinitely less degree than his friend Burke, of whom Goldsmith said, with such truth, long ago, that—

> Born for the universe, he narrowed his mind,
> And to party gave up what was meant for mankind.
> [*Retaliation,* ll. 31-2.]

I should not have said thus much of Reynolds, which I have not said without pain, but because I have so great a respect for his character, and because he lived at a time when, being the first Englishman distinguished for excellence in the higher department of painting, he had the field fairly open for him to have given an example, upon which all eyes needs much have been fixed, of a man preferring the cultivation and exertion of his own powers in the highest possible degree to any other object of regard.

To Beaumont, VII. 20, 1804

4. . . . read the rest of his *Discourses,* with which I have been greatly pleased. . . . *To Beaumont,* XII. 25, 1804

Rice, Spring

1.*   When asked whether he would like to go hear Lord Monteagle (Mr. Spring Rice) Mr. Whewell, and Mr Carlyle lecture on " Astronomy, Universal Philanthropy, &c." " Go! " said he, " I would as soon go to see so many carrion crows." *A Day with Wordsworth*, p. 740.   VIII. 31, 1841

Richardson, Samuel

1.   [*Clarissa Harlowe.*] See Copyright 4; Versification 2

2.   See Scott, W. 14

Richmond, James C.

1.*   . . . Richmond's *Memorial to the Bench of Bishops*, which Wordsworth said was beautifully written—all but the allusions to his own eccentricities, and that was injudicious. *H. C. R.*, ii, 607.   I, 2, 1842

Ridpath, George

1.   [*History of the Borders.*] . . . it was difficult to conceive how so dull a book could be written on such a subject. *I. F.* (*Grosart*, iii, 13).   1843

Robberds, John W.

1.   [Reprehensible editing of Southey's letters.] See Letters 10

Robertson, William.   See Maitland 1; Scotch Writers 7; Thomson 9

Robinson, Anthony

1.*   W. had been pleased with a letter by Ant. Robinson on his *Convention of Cintra*, who, he said, had better understood him than I had in my review of it in the *London Review*. *Remains*, p. 56.   VI. 6, 1812

Robinson, Henry Crabb

1.*   My review [C. R. reviewed *The Convention of Cintra*, in *London Review*, 1809] gained me, I believe, very little credit—not with Wordsworth, though eulogistic. *H. C. R.*, i, 13.   1809

2.   See Poetry 113; Robinson, A. 1

3.*   The *Quarterly Review* [vol. 31, no. 62, April, 1825] is now in the House. My Brother has read your Article with great pleasure, & says you think too humbly of the style in which it is done. He thinks the metre excellent—the style good enough.
D. W. to C. R. (*Corr. C. R.*, i, 137),   IV. 12, 1825

4.   [W. agrees with C. R.'s criticism of the diction in " How profitless," 10 (*Oxf. W.*, p. 394).]   *To C. R.* (*Corr. C. R.*, i, 288-9),   XII. 16, 1835

Rochester, John Wilmot, Second Earl of.   See Criticism 49

Rogers, Samuel

1.   See Blake 1

2.   I have read it with great pleasure. The Columbus is what you intended,

it has many bright and striking passages, and Poems, upon this plan, please better on a second Perusal than the first. The *Gaps* at first disappoint and vex you.

There is a pretty piece [i. e. the lines " Written in the Highlands "] in which you have done me the honour of imitating me—towards the conclusion particularly, where you must have remembered the High-land Girl.— I like the Poem much; but the first paragraph is hurt by two apostrophes, to objects of different character, one to Luss, and one to your Sister; and the Apostrophe is not a figure, that like Janus, carries two faces with a good grace. *To Rogers,* V. 5, 1814

3. It [*Human Life, a Poem*] contained some very pleasing passages, but the title is much too grandiloquent for the performance, and the plan appeared to me faulty. *To F. Wrangham,* II. 19, 1819

4. . . . Italy . . . we all read with much pleasure. Venice, and The Brides of Venice, that was the title I think, pleased as much as any; some parts of the Venice are particularly fine. I had no fault to find but rather too strong a leaning to the pithy and concise, and to some peculiarities of versification which occur perhaps too often. *To Rogers,* IX. 16, 1822

5. I often read your Italy, which I like much, though there are quaintnesses and abruptnesses which I think might be softened down, and in the versification I would suggest that with so many Trochaic terminations to the lines, the final pauses in the middle of the verse should be more frequently on firm syllables on that account. *To Rogers,* III. 23, 1825

6. How goes on your Poem [*Italy*]? The Papers spoke of a new edition being intended with numerous engravings, which, if executed under your presiding taste cannot but be invaluable. *To Rogers,* IX. 20, 1827

7. [W. heard] that the *Sale* of your Pleasures of Memory, which had commanded public attention for 36 years, had greatly fallen off within the last two years. The Edinburgh Review tells another story, that you and Campbell (I am sorry to couple the names) are the only Bards of our day whose laurels are unwithered. Fools! I believe that yours have suffered in the common blight (if the flourishing of a Poet's Bays can fairly be measured by the sale of his Books or the buzz that attends his name at any given time) and that the ornamented annuals, those greedy receptacles of trash, those Bladders upon which the Boys of Poetry try to swim, are the cause. *To Rogers,* VI. 5, 1830

8. Your Italy can no where, out of your own family, be more eagerly expected than in this House. The Poetry is excellent we know, and the Embellishments, as they are under the guidance of your own taste, must do honor to the Arts. . . . *To Rogers,* VII. 30, 1830

9. . . . the Illustrations of the forthcoming Edition of Mr Rogers Miscellaneous Poems [*Poems*, with steel engravings by Turner, J. W. M., and Stothard, J., 1834; *v.* Letter of Dec. 31]. As far as I could judge from a hasty inspection, without opportunity for comparison, I am inclined to think that the embellishments will be reckoned fully equal to those of the *Italy*. *To Moxon,* VIII, 1833

10. These are bad times for publishing Poetry, in short nothing but low prices and utilitarian works seem to go down, with the exception of a few expensively illustrated works. Those of Mr R. [Rogers] have the advantage of being [? managed] under the direction of his own very fine taste.
To Moxon,   XII. 9, 1833

11. . . . we are charmed with the design and execution of the illustrations and with the taste of the whole work [the *Poems* of Rogers, 1834] which and its companion the Italy will shine as Brother stars, tho' not twin-born, in the hemisphere of literature for many centuries.
To Moxon,   I. 14, 1834

12. But I cannot forbear adding that as several of the Poems [1834] are among my oldest and dearest acquaintance in the Literature of our day, such an elegant edition of them, with their illustrations must to me be peculiarly acceptable. *To S. Rogers,*   I. 14, 1834

13. Rogers is a wonderful Man—his life is worthy of being written with care, & *copiously*—but I fear so valuable a work as that would be, will never be produced. *To C. R. (Corr. C. R., i, 373),*   XII, 1838

14. [One of the best judges of poetry, Rogers, approves of lines 10-11 of W.'s " By Art's bold privilege."] *To Haydon,*   IX. 23, 1840

15.* . . . Wordsworth is highly indignant that H. B. [John Doyle in *Political Sketches*] the clever caricaturist, should have so little respect for age and genius, as to make such a man as Mr Rogers the subject of that witless vulgar fun, & everybody here is disgusted to hear of it.
E. Q. to C. R. (Corr. C. R., i, 470),   XI. 28, 1842

Roscoe, W. S.

1. You remember the squabble I got into with young Roscoe [William Stanley Roscoe]—a very shallow fellow at Mrs. Charles Aikin's. He is suspected by a Scotch friend of mine to be the author of a vehement senseless and if I had not used the word before I should add virulent attack upon me in a publication now struggling into birth under the name of the Edinburgh Magazine [later called *Blackwood's Magazine*]. This stupid diatribe is occasioned by my Letter on the subject of the new edition of Burns.—If it tends to make my Publication enquired after—I should be thankful to this *Young Gentleman*—such he was, and young in brain he must ever be—but as to the substantive in any creditable sense, nothing can be left but what he may owe to his Tailor—*To C. R. (Corr. C. R., i, 93),*   VI. 24, 1817

Roscommon, Wentworth Dillon, Earl of. See Johnson 11

Rose, Hugh J.

1. I have read your excellent sermons delivered before the University [Hugh James Rose (1795-1838), of Trinity, Cambridge: a friend of Newman, Froude and Keble, and a prominent but moderate high Churchman] several times. In nothing were my notions different from yours as there expressed. It happened that I had been reading just before Bishop Bull's sermon [*The Priest's Office Difficult and Dangerous*] of which you speak so

highly; it had struck me just in the same way as an inestimable production. I was highly gratified by your discourses, and cannot but think that they must have been beneficial to the hearers, there abounds in them so pure a fervour. *To Rose,* XII. 11, 1828

Rosset, Pierre Fulcrand

1. In this description of the cock [*Evening Walk,* Quarto, 129-30], I remembered a spirited one of the same animal in the l'Agriculture, ou Les Georgiques Françoises of M. Rossuet. *Oxf. W.,* 594 n. 1. 1793

Rousseau, Jean Jacques

1. The Spaniards are a people with imagination: and the paradoxical reveries of Rousseau, and the flippancies of Voltaire, are plants which will not naturalize in the country of Calderon and Cervantes.
The Convention of Cintra (*Grosart,* i, 162). 1809

Ruskin, John

1.* I remember well the pleasure and admiring approval with which he greeted the first publication [*Modern Painters*] of Mr. Ruskin. . . . *Batho,* p. 38. *c.* 1845

2.* [*Modern Painters.*] Ruskin he thought a brilliant writer, but there was too much praise of Turner in his book, to the disparagement of others; he had hardly a word for any one else.
Knight's Life of Wordsworth, ii, 334 (see *Batho,* p. 49 n.). VIII. 18, 1849

Russell, Thomas

1. [Sonnet on] Philoctetes is a fine specimen. . . . See Sonnet 7; and Landor 11.

1A. See Style 22

2. There are two sonnets of Russell, which, in all probability, you may have noticed, ' Could, then, the Babes,' and the one upon Philoctetes, the last six lines of which are first rate. *To Dyce,* spring, 1833

3. The four last lines of this sonnet [" How sad a welcome "] are adopted from a well-known sonnet of Russel [*Sonnet* X; see ed. of Eric Partridge, London, 1925, p. 125], as conveying my feeling better than any words of my own could do.—*Oxf. W.,* p. 925. 1835

Sappho

1.   [*Ode to Aphrodite.*]
               And not unhallowed was the page
               By wingèd Love inscribed, to assuage
               The pangs of vain pursuit;
               Love listening while the Lesbian Maid
               With finest touch of passion swayed
               Her own Æolian lute.
               " Departing summer," 43-48. 1819

2. What is there in Sappho's ode that has any affinity with the sublimity of Ezekiel or Isaiah, or even of Homer or Eschylus?

To J. Fletcher,　　　　　　　　　　　　　　　　IV. 6, 1825

3. See Anthologies 3

Schelling, Friedrich Wilhelm Joseph von.　See Literature 24

Schiller, Johann Christoph Friedrich von

1. See Burns 26A; Coleridge 46; Hamilton, W. R. 14

3.*　Schiller had far more heart and ardor than Goethe, and would not, like him, have professed indifference to theology and politics, which are the two deepest things in man,—indeed, all a man is worth, involving duty to God and to man. *Old Friends,* p. 216.　　　　　　　　X. 6, 1844

Scotch Writers

1. See Criticism 49; Godwin, C. Grace 1

2. The collection of songs which you announce I had not heard of. Your own poetry shows how fit you are for the office of editing native strains; and may not one hope that the taste of the public in these matters is much improved since the time when Macpherson's frauds met with such dangerous success, and Percy's ballads produced those hosts of legendary tales that bear no more resemblance to their supposed models than Pope's Homer does to the work of the blind bard. Do not say I ought to have been a Scotchman. Tear me not from the country of Chaucer, Spenser, Shakespeare, and Milton; yet I own that since the days of childhood, when I became familiar with the phrase, ' They are killing geese in Scotland, and sending the feathers to England ' (which every one had ready when the snow began to fall), and when I used to hear, in the time of a high wind, that

> Arthur's bower has broken his band,
> And he comes roaring up the land;
> King o' Scots wi' a' his power
> Cannot turn Arthur's bower,

I have been indebted to the North for more than I shall ever be able to acknowledge. Thomson, Mickle, Armstrong, Leyden, yourself, Irving, (a poet in spirit), and I may add Sir Walter Scott were all Borderers. If they did not drink the water, they breathed at least the air of the two countries. The list of English Border poets is not so distinguished, but Langhorne was a native of Westmoreland, and Brown the author of the *Estimate of Manners and Principles,* etc.,—a poet as his letter on the vale of Keswick, with the accompanying verses, shows—was born in Cumberland. So also was Skelton, a demon in point of genius; and Tickell in later times, whose style is superior in chastity to Pope's, his contemporary. Addison and Hogarth were both within a step of Cumberland and Westmoreland. . . . It is enough for me to be ranked in this catalogue, and to know that I have touched the hearts of many by subjects suggested to me on Scottish ground; these pieces you will find classed together in the new edition. *To A. Cunningham,*　XI. 23, 1823

4. [Their want of a perfect English style.] See Thomson 9

5.* [The Scotch historians] did infinite mischief to style, with the exception of Smollett, who wrote good pure English.

Lady R. (Grosart, iii, 452-53).   X, 1846

6.* He [W.] spoke highly of the purity of language of the Scotch poets of an earlier period, Gavin Douglass and others, and said that they greatly excelled the English poets, after Chaucer, which he attributed to the distractions of England during the wars of York and Lancaster.

Lady R. (Grosart, iii, 453).   XI. 26, 1846

7.* No Scotchman . . . can write English. He detailed the two models, on one or the other of which all the sentences of the historian Robertson are framed. Nor could Jeffrey, nor the Edinburgh Reviewers write English, nor can [Carlyle], who is a pest to the English tongue. Incidentally he added, Gibbon cannot write English.

English Traits, pp. 294 and note 1.   III, 1848

Scott, John

1. . . . the pleasure and instruction which I have received from your *Visit to Paris*. . . . *To J. Scott,*   V. 14, 1815

2. There is also an excellent political essay of Scott at the head of the same number. *To Haydon,*   I. 13, 1816

3. Your *Paris Revisted* has been in constant use since I received it—a very welcome sight it was. Nothing in your works has charmed us more than the lively manner in which the painting of everything that passes before your eyes is executed. Every one of your words *tells*; and this is an art which few travellers, at least of our days, are masters of. *To J. Scott,*   II. 22, 1816

4. I hear what you say of the Champion [Scott's magazine] with regret. Pity that your other labours cannot proceed without injury to that periodical writing which has, I know, been very beneficial. Could not you procure assistance, relinquishing profit accordingly?

To J. Scott,   II. 25, 1816

5. In regard to your own announced adventure upon the sea of Poetry I may truly say that I was most glad to hear it; because your Prose has convinced me that you have a mind fitted to ensure your success.—Nevertheless my pleasure was not absolutely pure—for if you have not practised metre in youth, I should apprehend that your thoughts would not easily accommodate themselves to those chains, so as to give you a consciousness that you were moving under them and with them, gracefully and with spirit. I question not that you have written with rapidity; nothing is more easy; but in nothing is it more true than in composing verse that the nearest way home is the longest way about. In short I dreaded the labour which you were preparing for yourself. You are a Master of Prose; and your powers may be so flexible and fertile as to be equal to both exercises—so much the better!—I mean equal to them without injury to your health. But should it appear to me that the Specimens you send of your Poem require additional care and exertion, I shall

not scruple to tell you so; and with the less reluctance because I am confident that you may attain eminence in English prose which few of late have reached. That field is at present almost uncultivated; we have adroit living prose writers in abundance; but impassioned, eloquent, and powerful ones not any, at least that I am acquainted with. Our Prose taking it altogether, is a disgrace to the country. . . .

I fear what I have said on Prose as now produced, may be misunderstood. Charles Lamb, my friend, writes prose exquisitely; Coleridge also has produced noble passages, so has Southey. But I mean that there is no body, of philosophical, impassioned, eloquent, finished prose now produced.
To J. Scott,   III. 11, 1816

6. I am sorry that he [Scott] is about to publish upon so melancholy an occasion [had lost a child]—His verses I fear will have too large an infusion of pain in them to be either generally pleasing or serviceable whatever degree of genius they may exhibit. *To B. R. Haydon* (*L. Y.*, p. 1368),   I. 20, 1817

7. . . . I shall look for his book on Italy with impatience. . . . Scott and I disagree about many very important points; but I greatly admire his Talents, and respect him highly. *To Haydon,*   I. 24, 1820

Scott, Walter (General Criticism)

1. See Blake 1; Gillies 3; Hogg 1; Lockhart 2; Scotch Writers 2; W. 60, 204

2. [Scott's criticisms of Dryden.] See Dryden 4

3.* . . . Wordsworth spoke with great contempt of Scott, and illustrated his remarks on a phrase, 'kindling a spark'—it is with a spark we kindle a fire, etc. He assented to the observation ' that the secret of Scott's popularity is the vulgarity of his conceptions, which the million can at once comprehend.' *H. C. R.*, i, 82.   V. 13, 1812

4. [A criticism, probably of Scott's descriptive method.] See Nature 20

6. What you say of W. Scott reminds me of an Epigram something like the following—

> Tom writes his Verses with huge speed,
>   Faster than Printer's Boy can set 'en,
> Faster far than we can read,
>   And only not so fast as we forget 'en.
> *To Rogers,*   I. 12, 1813

7. . . . Mr. Scott and your friend Lord B. [Byron] flourishing at the rate they do, how can an honest *Poet* hope to thrive?
To Rogers,   V. 5, 1814

9. Do not imagine that my principles lead me to condemn Scott's method of pleasing the public, or that I have not a very high respect for his various talents and extensive attainments. *To R. P. Gillies,*   XII. 22, 1814

10. But I confess if there is to be an Error in style, I much prefer the *Classical* model of Dr. Beattie to the insupportable slovenliness and neglect

of syntax and grammar, by which Hogg's writings are disfigured. It is excusable in him from his education, but Walter Scott knows, and ought to do, better. They neither of them write a language which has any pretension to be called English; and their versification—who can endure it when he comes fresh from the Minstrel? *To Gillies,*   II. 14, 1815

12.* [W. illustrated the mechanical nature of Scott's poetry] by saying it was like a machine made to amuse children which turns round seeming to unravel something but to which there is no end. He said that in some of Scott's descriptions where there is much action to be expressed as in battles etc. Scott has shown energy. *Farington Diary*, viii, 2.   V. 2, 1815

14.* . . . the Scottish novels. Is sure they are Scott's. The only doubt he ever had on the question did not arise from thinking them too good to be Scott's, but, on the contrary, from the infinite number of clumsy things in them; commonplace contrivances, worthy only of the Minerva press, and such bad vulgar English as no gentleman of education ought to have written. When I mentioned the abundance of them, as being rather too great for one man to produce, he said, that great fertility was the characteristic of all novelists and story-tellers. Richardson could have gone on forever; his *Sir Charles Grandison* was, originally, in thirty volumes. Instanced Charlotte Smith, Madame Cottin, &c. &c. Scott, since he was a child, accustomed to legends, and to the exercise of the story-telling faculty; sees nothing to stop him as long as he can hold a pen. *Moore's Diary*, pp. 29-30.   X. 27, 1820

15.* . . . is not a careful composer. He allows himself many liberties, which betray a want of respect for his reader. For instance, he is too fond of inversions; *i. e.* he often places the verb before the substantive, and the accusative before the verb. W. Scott quoted, as from me,

> ' The swan on *Sweet* St. Mary's lake
> Floats double, swan and shadow,'

instead of *still*; thus obscuring my idea, and betraying his own uncritical principles of composition. *C. W., Jr. (Grosart*, iii, 462).   Summer, 1827

16. Surely these are men of power, not to be replaced. . . .
To Rogers,   VII. 30, 1830

17.   For Thou, upon a hundred streams,
                      By tales of love and sorrow,
              Of faithful love, undaunted truth,
                      Hast shed the power of Yarrow. . . .
              " The gallant Youth," 65-68.   1831

18. . . . has during the last six and twenty years diffused more innocent pleasure than ever fell to the lot of any human being to do in his own lifetime. . . . Voltaire, no doubt, was full as extensively known, and filled a larger space probably in the eye of Europe; for he was a great theatrical writer, which Scott has not proved himself to be, and miscellaneous to that degree, that there was something for all classes of readers: but the pleasure afforded by his writings, with the exception of his Tragedies and minor Poems, was not pure, and in this Scott is greatly his superior.
To W. R. Hamilton.   X. 27, 1831

19.   Great Minstrel of the Border!
           " The gallant Youth," 8.   1831

20.   The mighty Minstrel breathes no longer. . . .
           " When first, descending," 9.   1835

21. The newspapers are, as they did in Sheridan's case, extolling his genius, that is his poetical genius, most ridiculously—these follies pass away and truth only remains. *To Dora,*   early IV, 1838

23.* Mr. W. and my Uncle S. [Southey] could not but regret Scotts want of devotion to literature for its own sake—for its humanizing influences —his using it merely as means to a further end, far less important. *Sara Coleridge and Reed,* p. 103.   *c.* 1840

24.* . . . Scott, and indeed all but the highest poets, wanting in truthfulness of poetic logic. *Aubrey de Vere,* p. 70.   III. 9, 1841

25. I first became acquainted with this great and amiable man (Sir Walter Scott) in the year 1803. . . .
I. F. (Grosart, iii, 138).   1843

26.* . . . his reasons for thinking that as a poet Scott would not live. ' I don't like,' he said, ' to say all this, or to take to pieces some of the best reputed passages of Scott's verse, especially in presence of my wife, because she thinks me too fastidious; but as a poet Scott *cannot* live, for he has never in verse written anything addressed to the immortal part of man. In making amusing stories in verse, he will be superseded by some newer versifier; what he writes in the way of natural description is merely rhyming nonsense.' As a prose writer, Mr. Wordsworth admitted that Scott had touched a higher vein, because there he had really dealt with feeling and passion. As historical novels, professing to give the manners of a past time, he did not attach much value to those works of Scott's so called, because that he held to be an attempt in which success was impossible.
Mrs. D. (Grosart, iii, 442-43).   VII. 11, 1844

27.* He discoursed at great length on Scott's works. His poetry he considered of that kind which will always be in demand, and that the supply will always meet it, suited to the age. He does not consider that it in any way goes below the surface of things; it does not reach to any intellectual or spiritual emotion; it is altogether superficial, and he felt it himself to be so. His descriptions are not true to Nature; they are addressed to the ear, not to the mind. He was a master of bodily movements in his battle-scenes; but very little productive power was exerted in popular creations.
Lady R. (Grosart, iii, 445).   VII. 12, 1844

28.* [W. spoke of Scott's poetry] with contempt.
Aubrey de Vere, p. 99.   XII. 26, 1846

29.* He spoke with much regret of Scott's careless views about money, and said that he had often spoken to him of the duty of economy, as a means to insure literary independence. Scott's reply always was, ' Oh, I can make as much as I please by writing.' ' This,' said Mr. W., ' was marvellous to me, who had never written a line with a view to profit.'
Mrs. D. (Grosart, iii, 457).   I. 10, 1849

Scott, *Walter* (Works)

30.* He [Scott] partly read and partly recited, sometimes in an enthusiastic style of chant, the first four cantos of the *Lay of the Last Ministrel,* and the novelty of the manners, the clear picturesque descriptions, and the easy glowing energy of much of the verse, greatly delighted me [W.].
Memoirs of Scott (ed. 1842), p. 110. IX. 17, 1803

31. High as our expectations were, I have the pleasure to say that the poem [*Last Minstrel*] has surpassed them much. We think you have completely attained your object; the Book is throughout interesting and entertaining, and the picture of manners as lively as possible.
To W. Scott, III. 7, 1805

32.* We have the *Lay of the Last Minstrel* and have read it with great pleasure. *D. W. to Lady Beaumont,* V. 4, 1805

33.* We [D. W. and W.] were struck with the resemblance yet we were both equally convinced from the frankness of Walter Scott's manner that it was an unconscious imitation. Since *the Lay of the last Minstrel* has been published, William has blamed himself exceedingly for not having mentioned to Walter Scott the apprehension that he had that the style of his Poem had been, and would be in its future progress, influenced by this acquaintance with *Christabel,* and also that he did not point out one expression which was the same—he thought he could not do it with propriety, being self-introduced at S's house that very day and they having known nothing of each other before. . . . my Brother and Sister think that the Lay being published first, it will tarnish the freshness of *Christabel,* and considerably injure the first effect of it. *D. W. to Lady Beaumont,* X. 27, 1805

34. Thanks for your Song which I duly received; shall I be wicked enough to say ' materiam superabat opus? and will you *forgive* the slight difference '— 'tis your own phrase [I cannot identify the song: the words in quotation marks are probably taken from a criticism which Scott had passed on one of Wordsworth's poems. De Sel.] You see how malicious I can be. Joking apart I think the song well done and am glad it answered your purpose.
To W. Scott (p. 458 A), VIII. 18, 1806

35. . . . *Marmion,* which I have read with lively pleasure. I think your end has been attained. That it is not in every respect the end which I should wish you to propose to yourself, you will be well aware, from what you know of my notions of composition, both as to matter and manner. . . . the stupid nonsense which I am told he [Jeffrey] has written of me. With respect to your Poem I can say that in all the circle of my acquaintance, it seems as well liked as the *Lay.* . . . Had the poem been better than the *Lay* it could scarcely have satisfied the public, which, at best, has too much of the monster, the moral monster, in its composition. In the notes you have quoted two lines of mine from memory, and your memory, admirable as it is, has here failed you. The passage stands with you

The swa*ns* on *sweet* St. Mary's lake

The proper reading is

> The *swan* on *still* St. Mary's lake

I mention this that the erratum may be corrected in a future edition.

To W. Scott.   VIII. 4, 1808

36.* Wordsworth, I hear, is a great admirer of *Waverley*, and he ascribes it also to Scott. *H. C. R.*, iii, 850.   II. 6, 1815

37.* You mentioned *Guy Mannering* in your last. I have read it. I cannot say that I was disappointed, for there is very considerable talent displayed in the performance, and much of that sort of knowledge with which the author's mind is so richly stored. But the adventures I think not well chosen, or invented, and they are still worse put together; and the characters, with the exception of Meg Merrilies, excite little interest. In the management of this lady the author has shown very considerable ability, but with that want of taste which is universal among modern novels of the Radcliffe school; which, as far as they are concerned, this is. I allude to the laborious manner in which everything is placed before your eyes for the production of picturesque effect. The reader, in good narration, feels that pictures rise up before his sight, and pass away from it unostentatiously, succeeding each other. But when they are fixed upon an easel for the express purpose of being admired, the judicious are apt to take offence, and even to turn sulky at the exhibitor's officiousness. But these novels are likely to be much overrated on their first appearance, and will afterwards be as much undervalued. *Waverley* heightened my opinion of Scott's talents very considerably, and if *Mannering* has not added much, it has not taken much away. Infinitely the best part of *Waverley* is the pictures of Highland manners at Mac Ivor's castle, and the delineation of his character, which are done with great spirit. The Scotch baron, and all the circumstances in which he is exhibited, are too peculiar and *outré*. Such caricatures require a higher condiment of humour to give them a relish than the author of *Waverley* possesses.

To Gillies,   IV. 25, 1815

38.* . . . from Sir Walter Scott's earliest poems, the Eve of St. John, and etc. I [W.] did not suppose that he possessed the power which he afterwards displayed especially in his novels. Coleridge's *Christabel* no doubt gave him the idea of writing long ballad-poems: Dr. Stoddart had a very wicked memory, and repeated various passages of it (then unpublished) to Scott. Part of the *Lay of the Last Minstrel* was recited to me by Scott while it was yet in manuscript; and I did not expect that it would make much sensation: but I was mistaken; for it went up like a baloon.

Table-Talk of Rogers, p. 206 and note.   *c.* 1825

39. . . . he [Scott] composed a few lines for Dora's Album, and wrote them in it; we prize this Memorial very much, and the more so as an affecting testimony of his regard at the time, when as the verses prove, his health of body and powers of mind were much impaired and shaken.

To Mrs. Hemans,   VIII. 20, 1833

40. See W. 191, 235

Sedgwick, Catharine Maria

1. I quite agree with you about Miss Sedgewick's Book—such productions add to my dislike of Literary Ladies—indeed make me almost detest the name. *To E. and Dora Q.*   VIII-IX, 1841

Sergeant, John

1. . . . your Boston Critic. . . . See Cowley 7

Settle, Elkanah. See Shakespeare 45

Seward, Anna

1. . . . uses 'hybernal'; [W. regrets] that the word is not [more] familiar. *To Gillies,*   XI. 23, 1814

2. At the close of a sonnet of Miss Seward's are two fine verses:

> Come, that I may not hear the winds of night,
> Nor count the heavy eave-drops as they fall.

You have well characterized the Poetic powers of this Lady—but, after all, her verses please me with all their faults better than those of Mrs. Barbauld. . . . *To Dyce,*   V. 10, 1830

Sewell, William

1. Have you seen the last Quarterly—There is a well-intended but very feeble notice of me in it, and an ignorant and injurious one of Coleridge— The Passage occurs at the beginning of an article upon Carlyle; and it is said to be written by Sewell, a high Churchman of Oxford. *To C. R. (Corr. C. R., 1, 419),*   X. 27, 1840

Shadwell, Thomas. See Shakespeare 45

Shaftesbury, Anthony Ashley Cooper, Third Earl of

1. . . . at present unjustly depreciated. . . . See Criticism 49

Shakespeare, William (General Criticism)

1. See Biography 2B; Composition 25A; Criticism 75; Drama 15; Poetry 61; Sonnets 5, 6; Taste 15; Versification 2

2. The invaluable works of our elder writers, I had almost said the works of Shakespeare and Milton. . . . See Passion 7

3.   [W.'s imagination not touched]
> Save when realities of act and mien,
> The incarnation of the spirits that move
> In harmony amid the Poet's world,
> Rose to ideal grandeur, or, called forth
> By power of contrast, made me recognise,
> As at a glance, the things which I had shaped,
> And yet not shaped, had seen and scarcely seen,
> When, having closed the mighty Shakespeare's page,
> I mused, and thought, and felt, in solitude.

Prel., vii, 477-85.   1804-39

5.   Nor such [shepherds] as—when an adverse fate had driven,
          From house and home, the courtly band whose fortunes
          Entered, with Shakespeare's genius, the wild woods
          Of Arden. . . .
          Prel., viii, 136-39.   1804-39

6.   [Not appreciated by the French.]
To Beaumont,   I or II, 1808

7.*   He says he does not see much difficulty in writing like Shakespeare,
if he had a mind to try it. *L. of Lamb*, ii, 51.   II, 26, 1808

9.   See Bacon 3; Burger 2; Byron 17; Chaucer 5; Goethe 7, 8; Homer 13;
Johnson 11; Lamb 19; Milton 48; Young 1; W. 364A

11.[Shakespeare's works are an inexhaustible source of the human and
dramatic imagination.] See Imagination 33G

14.   [Reputation abroad and at home.
The French still averse to this darling of our Nation.] Baron Grimm is
the only French writer who seems to have perceived his infinite superiority to
the first names of the French Theatre; an advantage which the Parisian Critic
owed to his German blood and German education. The most enlightened
Italians, though well acquainted with our language, are wholly incompetent
to measure the proportions of Shakespeare. The Germans only, of foreign
nations, are approaching towards a knowledge and feeling of what he is. In
some respects they have acquired a superiority over the fellow countrymen of
the Poet: for among us it is a current, I might say, an established opinion,
that Shakespeare is justly praised when he is pronounced to be 'a wild
irregular genius, in whom great faults are compensated by great beauties.'
How long may it be before this misconception passes away, and it becomes
universally acknowledged that the judgment of Shakespeare in the selection
of his materials, and in the manner in which he has made them, heterogeneous
as they often are, constitute a unity of their own, and contribute all to one
great end, is not less admirable than his imagination, his invention, and his
intuitive knowledge of Human nature? *E. Supp. Pref.*, pp. 946-7.   1815

16.*   Spenser, Shakespeare, and Milton are his favourites among the English poets, especially the latter, whom he almost idolises.
J. J. Tayler (*Grosart*, iii, 502).   VII. 26, 1826

18.*   I cannot account for Shakespeare's low estimate of his own
writings, except from the sublimity, the superhumanity, of his genius. They
were infinitely below his conception of what they might have been, and
ought to have been. *C. W., Jr.* (*Grosart*, iii, 460).   *c.* 1827

24.   He [Hogarth] reminds me both of Shakespeare and Chaucer; but
these great Poets seem happy in softening and diversifying their views of life,
as often as they can, by metaphors and images from rural nature; or by
shifting the scene of action into the quiet of groves or forests. What an
exquisite piece of relief of this kind occurs in The Merchant of Venice—
where, after the agitating trial of Antonio, we have Lorenzo and Jessica
sitting in the open air on the bank on which the moonlight is sleeping—but
enough. *To J. Kenyon,*   I. 26, 1832

25. Modesty, and a deep feeling how superfluous a thing it is to praise Shakespeare, have kept me often, and almost habitually, silent upon that subject. Who thinks it necessary to praise the sun?

Letters K., iii, 121-2. 1836 or after

26. . . . how slowly did the poetry of Milton make its way to public favour; nor till very lately were the works of Shakespeare himself justly appreciated even within his own country. *To Robert Peel,* V. 3, 1838

27.* . . . the unapproached first of poets.

Graves's Recollections, p. 297. *c.* 1840

28. [Venerates] the genius of Shakespeare. . . .

L. of W. Family, VII. 21, 1840

29.* . . . Shakespeare himself had his blind sides, his limitations. . . . Compare Carlyle 9.

Carlyle's Reminiscences, ed. Norton (London, 1887), p. 302. 1840

30. Shakespeare never declaimed against kings or bishops, but took the world as he found it. See Coleridge, Hartley 6

32.* Truth, he used to say—that is, truth in its largest sense, as a thing at once real and ideal, a truth including exact and accurate detail, and yet everywhere subordinating mere detail to the spirit of the whole—this, he affirmed, was the soul and the essence not only of descriptive poetry, but of all poetry. He had often, he told me, intended to write an essay on poetry, setting forth this principle, and illustrating it by references to the chief representatives of poetry in its various departments. It was this twofold truth which made Shakespeare the greatest of all poets. 'It was well for Shakespeare,' he remarked, ' that he gave himself to the drama. It was that which forced him to be sufficiently human. His poems would otherwise, from the extraordinarily metaphysical character of his genius, have been too recondite to be understood. His youthful poems, in spite of their unfortunate and unworthy subjects, and his sonnets also, reveal this tendency. Nothing can surpass the greatness of Shakespeare where he is at his greatest; but it is wrong to speak of him as if even he were perfect. He had serious defects, and not those only proceeding from carelessness. For instance, in his delineations of character he does not assign as large a place to religious sentiment as enters into the constitution of human nature under normal circumstances. If his drama had more religion in them, they would be truer representations of man, as well as more elevated, and of a more searching interest.'

De Vere (Grosart, iii, 488). 1842-46

33. . . . two Shakesperian characters in the Bible. . . . See Bible 13

35.* [Milton's poetry] was earlier a favorite with him than that of Shakespeare. *Mrs. D. (Grosart,* iii, 457). I. 11, 1847

36.* [Shakespeare wrote the finest dramatic poetry.]

Ellis Yarnall (Grosart, iii, 479). VIII. 18, 1849

37.* [As a poet W. feared] competition . . . with . . . Shakespeare. . . .

H. C. R., ii, 776. [*c.* 1845]

Shakespeare (Works)

37A.*   [The Fool in *Lear* gave] a terrible wildness to the distress. . . .
Biog. Lit. (" Satyrane's Letters "), ii, 178.   [*c.* IX, 1798]

38.*   [W.] hates those interlocutions between Lucius and Caius.
Hazlitt, iv, 276   [*c.* 1800]

41.   [*Hamlet*, and *Richard III.*] I wish much to have your further opinion of the young Roscius, above all of his ' Hamlet.' It is certainly impossible that he should understand the character, that is, the composition of the character. But many of the sentiments which are put into Hamlet's mouth he may be supposed to be capable of feeling, and to a certain degree of entering into the spirit of some of the situations. I never saw *Hamlet* acted myself, nor do I know what kind of a play they make of it. I think I have heard that some parts which I consider among the finest are omitted; in particular, Hamlet's wild language after the ghost has disappeared. The Players have taken intolerable liberties with Shakespeare's plays, especially with *Richard the Third*, which, though a character admirably conceived, and drawn, is in some scenes bad enough in Shakespeare himself; but the play, as it is now acted, has always appeared to me a disgrace to the English stage. *Hamlet*, I suppose, is treated by them with more reverence. They are both characters far, far above the abilities of any actor whom I have ever seen.
To Beaumont,   V. 1, 1805

42.   [*Romeo and Juliet.*] See Subjects 13

43.   [*Othello.*] See Books 12

44.   [*Lear*, IV, vi, 14-15.] See Imagination 33B

45.   [The Plays.] A dramatic Author, if he write for the stage, must adapt himself to the taste of the audience, or they will not endure him; accordingly the mighty genius of Shakespeare was listened to. The people were delighted: [but probably they flocked also to the plays of the inferior dramatists, and would have awarded the prize to sorry dramatists—as often the Greeks did in the days of Sophocles and Euripides. Witness the numbers who reckoned Settle and Shadwell as talented as Dryden. Striking proof of Shakespeare's] almost omnipotent genius is, that he could turn to such glorious purpose those materials which the prepossessions of the age compelled him to make use of. Yet even this marvellous skill appears not to have been enough to prevent his rivals from having some advantage over him in public estimation; else how can we account for passages and scenes that exist in his works, unless upon a supposition that some of the grossest of them, a fact which in my own mind I have no doubt of, were foisted in by the Players, for the gratification of the many?

[Failure of Bacon and the learned Hakewill to mention Shakespeare indicates the lack of impression he made upon the ruling intellects of the day.] His dramatic excellence enabled him to resume possession of the stage after the Restoration; but Dryden tells us that in his time two of the plays of Beaumont and Fletcher were acted for one of Shakespeare's. And so faint and limited was the perception of the poetic beauties of his dramas in the time of Pope, that, in his Edition of the Plays, with a view of rendering to the general reader a necessary service, he printed between inverted commas those passages which he thought most worthy of notice. See Fame 12 and 13

E. Supp. Pref., p. 946 and n. 1. 1815

46. [Poems and Sonnets.] There is extant a small Volume of miscellaneous poems, in which Shakespeare expresses his own feelings in his own person. It is not difficult to conceive that the Editor, George Steevens, should have been insensible to the beauties of one portion of that Volume, the Sonnets; though in no part of the writings of this Poet is found, in an equal compass, a greater number of exquisite feelings felicituously expressed. But, from regard to the Critic's own credit, he would not have ventured to talk of an act of parliament not being strong enough to compel the perusal of those little pieces (This flippant insensibility was publicly reprehended by Mr. Coleridge in a course of Lectures upon Poetry given by him at the Royal Institution. For the various merits of thought and language in Shakespeare's *Sonnets*, see Nos. 27, 29, 30, 32, 33, 54, 64, 66, 68, 73, 76, 86, 91, 92, 93, 97, 98, 105, 107, 108, 109, 111, 113, 114, 116, 117, 129, and many others), if he had not known that the people of England were ignorant of the treasures contained in them: and if he had not, moreover, shared the too common propensity of human nature to exult over a supposed fall into the mire of a genius whom he had been compelled to regard with admiration, as an inmate of the celestial regions—" there sitting where he durst not soar."

E. Supp. Pref., p. 947 and n. 1. 1815

47. [*Romeo and Juliet*, I, iv, 54-5.] See Fancy 14

48. [*Othello.*] See Biography 2B

49.* 'Macbeth,' is the best conducted of Shakespeare's plays. The fault of ' Julius Caesar,' ' Hamlet,' and ' Lear,' is, that the interest is not, and by the nature of the case could not be, sustained to their conclusion. The death of Julius Caesar is too *overwhelming* an incident for *any* stage of the drama but the *last*. It is an incident to which the mind clings, and from which it will not be torn away to share in other sorrows. The same may be said of the madness of Lear. Again, the opening of ' Hamlet ' is full of exhausting interest. There is more mind in ' Hamlet ' than in any other play, more knowledge of human nature. The first act is incomparable. There is too much of an every-day sick room in the death-bed scene of Catherine, in ' Henry the Eighth '—too much of leeches and apothecaries' vials.

C. W., Jr. (Grosart, iii, 460). *c.* 1827

50. [*Pericles* should be admitted to the canon on internal evidence alone.] See Criticism 67

51.* . . . the ' Merchant of Venice,' in language . . . almost faultless: with the exception of some little straining in some of the speeches about the caskets, he said, they were perfect, the genuine English expressions of the ideas of their own great minds.

Justice Coleridge (Grosart, iii, 430-1). X. 10, 1836

52. [*Lear*, a masterpiece of genius.] See Copyright Laws 4

53.   See Plato 2

54.*   . . . Shakespeare's fine sonnets.   *I. F.* (*Grosart*, iii, 53).   1843

55.*   . . . Wordsworth found fault with the repetition of the concluding sound of the participles in Shakespeare's lines about bees:

> The *singing* masons *building* roofs of gold.
> [*Henry V*, I, ii, 198.]

This, he said, was a line which Milton would never have written. *Hunt*, ii, 40.   N. D.

56.   These sonnets beginning at CXXVII to his mistress, are worse than a puzzle-peg. They are abominably harsh, obscure, and worthless. The others are for the most part much better, have many fine lines and passages. They are also in many places warm with passion. Their chief faults—and heavy ones they are—are sameness, quaintness, and elaborate obscurity. [W.'s *marginalia* in the Folger Library set of Anderson's *British Poets.*] *C. Miscellaneous Criticism*, p. 454.   N. D.

Shand, [?]

1.   . . . told Mr. Shand how sorry I was that he had been thrown on so unpromising a way of gaining his bread. I was a good deal pleased with the modesty and humility of his manner, when I exhorted him to discard all notion of distinction, for the present at least, to controul his inclinations, and write or labour merely for his bread, till he should put himself at ease; and that *then* it would be time enough for his thinking about indulging his Genius—. . . . It seemed to me possible that something might be procured for his translations from the German, from some Editor of a magazine. There is also merit in his Poems, they are free from false ornaments, but not striking enough to attract attention in their presentation, where poetry finds so little favor with the Publick. . . . *To Moxon*,   VI-VII, 1838

Sharp, Richard.   See W. 172

Sharp, [? Charles Kirkpatrick]

1.   Mr. Sharpe is entitled to the gratitude of the Poets of England for the elegant, and above all for what I am told is the case the very correct Editions published by him—*To A. Cunningham*,   II. 26, 1828

Sheffield, John.   See Johnson 11

Shelley, Percy Bysshe (General Criticism)

1.*   [Said in 1819 that he thought nothing of Shelley as a poet] . . . A poet who has not produced a good poem before he is twenty-five we may conclude cannot, and never will do so. [Asked about *The Cenci*, he replied,] Won't do. . . . [Trelawney adds that W. later read more of S.'s poetry and] admitted that Shelley was the greatest master of harmonious verse in our modern literature. *Trelawney*, pp. 13-14.   summer, 1819

2.*   [W. spoke well of Shelley who] was a greater genius than Byron (*i. e.* a less successful one). *Letters of Scott*, ii, 342.   VIII. 25, 1825

3.* Shelley is one of the best *artists* of us all: I mean in workmanship of style. *C. W., Jr.* (*Grosart*, iii, 463).   *c.* 1827

4.* I recollect Wordsworth places him [Shelley] above Lord Byron. *H. C. R.*, i, 351.   XII. 20, 1827

5. See Byron 9, 15, 23A

6.* [W.] thought Shelley had the greatest native powers in poetry of all the men of this age. . . . Saw in Shelley the lowest form of irreligion, but a later progress towards better things. Named the discrepancy between his creed and his imagination as the marring idea of his works. . . . *Gladstone*, i, 136.   1836

7.* . . . looks on all things with an evil eye. *H. C. R.*, ii, 485.   I. 29, 1936

8.* [Shelley suffered in trying] to out-soar the humanities. . . . *De Vere* (*Grosart*, iii, 489).   1842-46

9. [W. objected to Shelley's opposition and ill-humour toward established opinions and institutions.] See Coleridge, Hartley 6

10.* [One general comment on Keats and Shelley is preserved by Sara Coleridge. They] would ever be favorites with the young, but would not satisfy men of all ages. *Batho*, p. 101.   [*c.* 1845]

Shelley (Works)

11.* Wordsworth spoke of it [Shelley's *Cenci*] as the greatest tragedy of the age. *H. C. R.*, i, 409.   IX. 9, 1832

12.* Wordsworth had said that Shelley's poem on the Lark was full of imagination, but that it did not show the same observation of nature as his [Wordsworth's] own poem on the same bird did. *Maurice*, i, 199.   1836

13.* [*The Skylark*] was greatly admired by the older poet, though for the most part he considered that Shelley's works were too remote from the humanities. *De Vere's Essays*, i, 201.   1842-46

Shelley, Mary

1.* Wordsworth especially admired her *taste* in poetry. He praised her Lives of the Italian poets in the Cabinet Library. *Remains*, p. 69.   *c.* 1840

Shenstone, William

1. . . . I had spoken inaccurately in citing Shenstone's Schoolmistress as the character of an individual. I ought to have said of individuals representing classes. *D. W. and W. to Coleridge*,   II. 27, 1799

2. Shenstone, in his *Schoolmistress*, gives a still more remarkable instance of this timidity [see Percy 1]. Of its first appearance (see D'Israeli's 2nd Series of the *Curiosities of Literature*) the Poem was accompanied with an absurd prose commentary, showing, as indeed some incongruous expressions in the text imply, that the whole was intended for burlesque. In subsequent editions, the commentary was dropped, and the People have since

continued to read in seriousness, doing for the Author what he had not courage openly to venture upon for himself.
E. Supp. Pref., p. 949 n.².   1827

3. [*The Schoolmistress.*] See Langhorne 2

Sheridan, Richard Brinsley. See Scott, W. 21

Shewell, [Mrs. J. T.]. [Her article on Thomas Clarkson.] See *Christian Keepsake* 1

Shirley, James. [*The Gamester.*] See Versification 2

Sidney, Philip

1.   Great men have been among us; hands that penned
          And tongues that uttered wisdom—better none. . . .
          " Great men," 1-2.   1802

2. See Johnson 11

Sigourney, Lydia

1. . . . Mrs. Sigourney's volume—which judging from the ' Mother's Sacrifice,' and ' the American Indians,' especially the former, I cannot but expect much pleasure from. To Mackenzie,   XI. 25, 1837

Simonides

1.   Thus was the tenderest Poet that could be,
              Who sang in ancient Greece his moving lay,
          Saved out of many by his piety.
          " I find it written," 12-14.   1803

2.   O ye, who patiently explore
          The wreck of Herculanean lore,
          What rapture! could ye seize
          Some Theban fragment, or unroll
          One precious, tender-hearted, scroll
          Of pure Simonides. [See *Knight*, vi. 204 n.—5.]
          " Departing summer," 49-54.   1819

Skelton, John

1. See Scotch Writers 2

2.   I am glad you have taken Skelton in hand, and much wish I could be of any use to you. In regard to his life, I am certain of having read somewhere (I thought it was in Burns's *Hist. of Cumberland and West*ⁿᵈ, but I am mistaken), that Skelton was born at Branthwaite Hall, in the County of Cumberland. Certain it is that a family of that name possessed the place for many generations; and I own it would give me some pleasure to make out that Skelton was a Brother Cumbrian. . . . Tickell (of the Spectator, one of the best of our minor Poets, as Johnson has truly said) was born

within two miles of the same Town. These are mere accidents it is true, but I am foolish enough to attach some interest to them.

To Dyce,   VII. 23, 1831

3. . . . a Writer deserving of far greater attention than his works have hitherto received. *To Dyce,*   I. 7, 1833

Smith, Adam

1.   how dire a thing
              Is worshipped in that idol proudly named
              " The Wealth of Nations." . . . .

              Prel., xiii, 76-78.   1804-39

2. See Criticism 49; Burke 3A

Smith, Charlotte

1. If a second edition of your *Specimens* should be called for, you might add . . . a few more from Charlotte Smith, particularly,

              I love thee, mournful, sober-suited Night.

To Dyce,   V. 10, 1830

2. The form of stanza in this [*St. Bees' Head*] Poem, and something in the style of versification, are adopted from the " St. Monica," a poem of much beauty upon a monastic subject, by Charlotte Smith: a lady to whom English verse is under greater obligations than are likely to be either acknowledged or remembered. She wrote little, and that little unambitiously, but with true feeling for rural nature, at a time when nature was not much regarded by English Poets; for in point of time her earlier writings preceded, I believe, those of Cowper and Burns. *Oxf. W.,* p. 924.   1835

3. See Scott, W. 14

Smith, Edmund. See Hervey 2

Smith, John T.

1. I have nothing to say of books (Newspapers having employed all the voices I could command) except that the 1st Vol of Smith's ' Nolleken's and his Times ' [1828] has been read to me—and I am indignant at the treachery that pervades it—Smith was once very civil to me, offering to show me anything in the Museum at any and all times when he was disengaged—I suppose he would have made *a Prey* of me as he has done of all his acquaintance, of which I had at that time no suspicion having thought myself not a little obligated to him for his offer—There are however some good Anecdotes in the book, the one which made most impression on me was that of Reynolds who is reported to have taken from the print of a half-penny ballad in the Street an effect in one of his Pictures which pleased him more than anything he had produced—*To C. R.* (*Corr. C. R.,* i, 207),   IV. 26, 1829

Smith, Thomas Southwood

1.*   Wordsworth was not incapable of appreciating the value of reason in its application to theology. He praised Southwood Smith's book on the Divine Government as the only reasonable view of the subject.

H. C. R., ii, 711.   [*c.* 1838]

2. . . . present my sincere acknowledgements to Dr. Smith for his valuable Work, Divine Government, both for its own sake and the Compliment paid in sending it to me as a Stranger. *To T. Powell*,   VI. 28, 1838

Smollett, Tobias George

1.* Mr. Wordsworth expressed his regret that neither of these great masters [S. and Fielding] of romance appeared to have been surrounded with any due marks of respect in the close of life.

Memoirs of Scott, p. 731.   IX. 17, 1831

2. [Smollett] wrote good pure English. See Style 68

Sophocles

1.* [No] finer dramatic poetry, next to Shakespeare, than that of Æschylus and Sophocles, not to speak of Euripides.

Ellis Yarnall (*Grosart*, iii, 479) .   VIII. 18, 1849

Sotheby, William

1.* [W. approved of *Saul.*] *L. of Coleridge*, i, 373.   IV. 18, 1807

Southey, Cuthbert

1.   In considering the difficulty of the Editorship of the Papers, you ask what opportunities I have had of judging of Cuthbert's competence to undertake it. *Directly* I have had scarcely more than was afforded while he read to me in MSS his own Portion, which is not little, of the life of Dr. Bell [*v. M. Y.*, p. 251]. I have no hesitation in saying that I was satisfied with his work, but this gives but slender ground for concluding that he is equal to the arduous office of determining what part of his Father's papers is fit for publication, and what ought to be held back—or destroyed. . . . But then his education has been altogether irregular, he is unpractised in Literature, and cannot possibly, were it from his youth merely, be competent to decide finally upon the merits of writings so numerous and various in their matter and style, as his Father's must be. He has inherited much of his Father's quickness, and possesses I am told a great deal of information, gathered up, I should think, in a desultory way. But on the whole I cannot entertain the opinion that justice to Southey's memory will be done, if the papers are not for the most part to be looked over by some one of more experience. And to do this, if they be numerous, as there is reason to believe they are, would require more time and labour than any but Cuthbert himself is likely to have to spare. . . .

Mr. Hill has *studied* literature in several of its branches much more carefully I believe than it is possible Cuth[bert] can have done, and could he find time and did opportunity favor, for his uniting his endeavours with Cuthbert's, they might jointly put the papers into such a state that without any unwarrantable demand upon your own time and health you might pass a final judgment upon them with reference to publication.

To H. Taylor,   III. 31, 1843

2. [W. considered Cuthbert Southey " quite equal to " the task of publishing Southey's letters.] *To H. Taylor,*   VIII, 1846

Southey, Robert (General Criticism)

1. See Books 26; Poetry 61; Versification 11; Clarkson 6; Coleridge 22; White, K. 1; W. 117

4.* . . . he is one of the cleverest men that is now living, at the same time he [W.] justly denied him ideality in his works. He never inquires . . . on what idea his poems is to be wrought; what feeling or passion is to be excited; but he determines on a subject, and then reads a great deal and combines and connects industriously, but he does not give anything which impresses the mind strongly and is recollected in solitude.

H. C. R., i, 87.   V. 24, 1812

6. [Southey's prose good.] *To J. Scott.*   III. 11, 1816

7.   Perhaps some of Southey's friends may think that his tranquillity is disturbed by the late and present attacks upon him—not a jot—Bating inward sorrow for the loss of his only son he is cheerful as a Lark, and happy as the day. Prosperous in his literary undertakings, admired by his friends, in good health, and honoured by a large portion of the Public, and as he thinks infinitely the wisest and best part of the Public, busily employed from morning to night, and capable from his talents of punishing those who act unjustly towards him, what cause has he to be disturbed.

To Haydon,   IV. 7, 1817

10.   And this too from the Laureate's Child [Edith May],
              A living lord of melody!
        How will her Sire be reconciled
              To the refined indignity?

        Needlecase, 13-6.   1827

11.* [Landor's *Satire*] will fall ineffectual if it were intended to wound. He [W.] had heard that the pamphlet imputed to him a depreciation of Southey's genius, but as he felt a warm affection for Southey and an admiration for his genius he never could have said that he would not give five shillings for all Southey had ever written. He had in consequence written a few lines to Southey. Notwithstanding his sense of the extreme injustice of Landor towards him, he willingly acknowledged his sense of Landor's genius. As to the image of the sea-shell, he acknowledged no obligation to Landor's *Gebir* for it.   *H. C. R.,* ii, 516.   III. 22, 1837

12.* . . . Wordsworth spoke of him with great feeling and affection. He said: ' It is painful to see how completely dead Southey is become to all but *books*; when he comes here he seems restless, as if from a sense of duty, and out of his element. . . . ' If I must,' said Wordsworth, ' lose my interest in one of them I would rather give up books than men.'

H. C. R., ii, 565.   I. 18, 1839

13.   That the amended [Copyright] Bill would take away from venal Publishers the liberty of re-publishing such things as the Author might have discarded—whereas, as the law now is, when an Author who has begun early and lived to a good age dies—they can reprint those Pieces and pass off *their* injurious editions as the only complete collection of the Writers Works—The fear of this, absolutely prevented Southey from throwing overboard in his last Ed: several minor pieces that were written merely for the newspapers when he wanted money.

To C. R. (Corr. C. R., i, 379),   II. 19, 1839

14.*   [A.] Of the narrative poems of his friend, well executed as he considered them, and of the mainly external action of imagination or fancy in which they deal, I have certainly heard him pronounce a very depreciatory opinion; whether I ever heard him use the hard words attributed to him, ' I would not give five shillings for a ream of them,' I cannot now assert, but if used, they were said in reference to the nobler kind of imaginative power which reveals to man the deep places and sublimer affinities of his own being. But to some others of Southey's verses, as well as to the lines above quoted, and [B] to his prose writings in general, he was wont to give liberal praise; and no one could doubt the sincerity and warmth of his admiration of the intellect and virtues of the man, or the brotherly affection towards him which he not unfrequently expressed. *Graves (Grosart,* iii, 475).   *c.* 1840

16.*   Southey deficient in felicity and comprehension. . . . *Aubrey de Vere,* p. 70.   III. 9, 1841

17.*   Wordsworth lamented the loss of so fine a mind as Southey's " to his numerous friends and to the nation whose literature he has benefited so largely." *A Day with Wordsworth,* p. 734.   VIII or IX, 1841

19.   And ye, lov'd books, no more
                Shall Southey feed upon your precious lore,
                To works that ne'er shall forfeit their renown,
                Adding immortal labours of his own—
                Whether he traced historic truth, with zeal
                For the State's guidance, or the Church's weal,
                Of Fancy, disciplined by studious art,
                Inform'd his pen, or wisdom of the heart,
                Or judgments sanctioned in the Patriot's mind
                By reverence for the rights of all mankind.
                Crosthwaite Church, 3-12.   1843

20.   His Genius and abilities are well known to the world. . . . *To Wm. Gomm,*   III. 24, 1843

21.   For though, as you are aware, the formal task-work of New Year and Birthday Odes was abolished, when the appointment was given to Mr Southey, he still considered himself obliged in conscience to produce, and did produce, verses—some of very great merit—upon important public occasions. He failed to do so upon the Queen's Coronation, and I knew that this omission caused him no little uneasiness. The same might happen to

myself upon some important occasion, and I should be uneasy under the possibility; I hope, therefore, that neither you nor Lord Lonsdale, nor any of my friends, will blame me for what I have done.
To Lady Bentwick, IV. 1, 1843

22. Southey's claim to be so commemorated [burial in Westminster Abbey] for his genius and attainments. . . .
To John T. Coleridge, VI. 27, 1843

22A.* He says it is most gratifying to fill the same station [laureateship] that Dryden and Southey have done. *Old Friends*, p. 200. VII. 21, 1843

23. Southey and I were of one mind on this subject [the importance of agriculture in relation to commerce] and in his writings he has frequently expresst himself with genuine feelings upon it.
To C. R. (Corr. C. R., ii, 624), V. 20, 1846

24.* . . . he had had the misfortune to outlive his faculties.
Ellis Yarnall (Grosart, iii, 482). VIII. 18, 1849

Southey (Works)

25. I met with Southey also, his manners pleased me exceedingly and I have every reason to think very highly of his powers of mind. He is about publishing an epic poem on the subject of the Maid of Orleans. From the specimens I have seen I am inclined to think it will have many beauties.
To Wm. Mathews (L. Y., pp. 1333-4), X. 24, 1795

26. The two best verses of this extract were given me by Southey, a friend of Coleridge: Who sees Majesty, and etc. He supplied me with another line which I think worth adopting; we mention Lord Courtnay. Southey's verse is 'Whence have I fallen alas! what have I done?' A literal translation of the Courtnay motto, *Unde lapsus quid feci?*
To Wm. Wrangham, XI. 20, 1795

27. You were right about Southey; he is certainly a coxcomb, and has proved it completely by the preface to his *Joan of Arc*, an epic poem which he has just published. This preface is indeed a very conceited performance, and the poem, though in some passages of first rate excellence, is on the whole of very inferior execution. *To Wm. Mathews,* III. 26, 1796

28. Southey's review [see *E. L.*, pp. 229-30] I have seen. He knew that I published those poems for money and money alone. He knew that money was of importance to me. If he could not conscientiously have spoken differently of the volume, he ought to have declined the task of reviewing it.
The bulk of the poems he has described as destitute of merit. Am I recompensed for this by vague praises of my talents? I care little for the praise of any other professional critic, but as it may help me to pudding.
To J. Cottle (pp. 229-30), 1799

29. We have read *Madoc,* and been highly pleased with it; it abounds in beautiful pictures and descriptions, happily introduced, and there is an animation diffused through the whole story; though it cannot, perhaps, be

said that any of the characters interest you much, except, perhaps, young Llewellyn, whose situation is highly interesting, and he appears to me the best conceived and sustained character in the piece. His speech to his Uncle at their meeting in the Island is particularly interesting. The Poem fails in the highest gifts of the poet's mind, imagination in the true sense of the word, and knowledge of human nature and the human heart. There is nothing that shows the hand of the great Master; but the beauties in description are innumerable; for instance, that of the figure of the Bard, towards the beginning of the convention of the bards, receiving the poetic inspiration; that of the wife of Talala, the Savage going out to meet her husband; that of Madoc and the Aztecan king with a long name, preparing for battle; everywhere, indeed, you have beautiful descriptions, and it is work which does the Author high credit, I think. *To Beaumont,*   VI. 3, 1805

30.   I am glad you like the passages in *Madoc* about Llewellyn. Southey's mind does not seem strong enough to draw the picture of a Hero. The character of Madoc is often very insipid and contemptible; for instance, when he is told that the Hoamen have surprized Caermadoc, and of course (he has reason to believe) butchered or carried away all the women and children, what does the author make him do? Think of Goervyl and Llayan very tenderly forsooth; but not a word about his people! In short, according to my notion, the character is throughout languidly conceived, and as you observe, the contrast between her and Llewellyn makes him look very mean. I made a mistake when I pointed out a beautiful passage as being in the beginning of the meeting of the bards; it occurs before, and ends thus:

> His eyes were closed;
> His head, as if in reverence to receive
> The inspiration, bent; and as he raised
> His glowing Countenance and brighter eye
> And swept with passionate hands the ringing harp.

To Beaumont.   VII, 29, 1805

31.*   I have not yet read Southey's Curse of Kehama; but I believe, from William's account, that it has great merit.
D. W. to C. Clarkson,   XII. 30, 1810

32.   Southey is a Fellow labourer [on works dealing with liberty]. I have seen but little of his performance, but that little gave me great pleasure.
To J. Scott,   II. 25, 1816

33.   There is a maxim laid down in my Tract on the Convention of Cintra which ought never to be lost sight of. It is expressed, I believe, nearly in the following words. ' There is, in fact, an unconquerable tendency in all power, save that of knowledge, acting by and through knowledge, to *injure the mind* of him by whom that power is exercised.' I pressed this upon Southey's consideration with a wish that his excellent Letter to Mr. W. Smith, in which he proposed to state his opinions and to recommend measures, might contain some wholesome advice to Ministers grounded upon this law of our infirm nature. *To D. Stuart,*   VI. 22, 1817

34. He [Southey] is about to publish a Poem [*Vision of Judgment*], occasioned by the death of his late Majesty, which will bring a nest of hornets about his ears; and will satisfy no party. It is written in English Hexameter verse, and in some passages with great spirit. But what do you think; in enumerating the glorified spirits of the reign of George 3d admitted along with their earthly sovereign into the New Jerusalem, neither Dr. Johnson nor Mr. Pitt are to be found. . . . Woe to the Laureate for this treasonable judgment! will be the cry of the Tories.
To C. R. (Corr. C. R., i, 97), I. 23, 1821

35. He [Southey] is as busy as ever, and about to publish a political Poem [*A Vision of Judgment*] which will satisfy no party. George the Third is represented as entering the true Jerusalem with the deceased worthies of his reign, and neither Charles Fox, Wm. Pitt, nor Dr. Johnson are of the Party! ! ! *To J. Kenyon,* II. 5, 1821

36. If our Productions [*Ecc. Sonn.*, and Southey's *History of Church of England*] thus unintentionally coinciding, shall be found to illustrate each other, it will prove a high gratification to me, which I am sure my friend will participate. *Oxf. W.*, p. 920. 1822

37. Mr. Southey, in the " Poet's Pilgrimage," speaks of it [the city of Bruges] in lines which I cannot deny myself the pleasure of connecting with my own [" Bruges I saw "]. *Oxf. W.*, p. 905. 1822

38.* He [W.] is not satisfied with my account of the Con. of Cintra: the rest of the book [*History of the Peninsular War*, vol. i] he likes well. Our difference here is, that he looks at the principle, abstractedly, and I take into view the circumstances.
Southey to C. R. (Corr. C. R., i, 125), II. 22, 1823

39. I have read the whole with great pleasure; the work will do you everlasting honour. I have said the whole forgetting, in that contemplation, my feelings upon one part, where you have tickled with a feather when you should have branded with a red hot iron. You will guess I mean the Convention of Cintra. *To Southey* (p. 167), 1824

40. . . . the ' Peninsular War.' I have read it with great delight: it is beautifully written, and a most interesting story. I did not notice a single sentiment or opinion that I could have wished away but one—where you support the notion that, if the Duke of Wellington had not lived and commanded, Buonaparte must have continued the master of Europe. I do not object to this from any dislike I have to the Duke, but from a conviction—I trust, a philosophic one—that Providence would not allow the upsetting of so diabolical a system as Buonaparte's to depend upon the existence of any individual. *To Southey,* II-III, 1827

41. Many thanks for the Review; your article is excellent. I only wish that you had said more of the deserts of government in respect to Ireland; since I do sincerely believe that no government in Europe has shown better dispositions to its subjects than the English have done to the Irish, and that no country has improved so much during the same period.
To Southey, XII, 1828

42. [*Sir Thomas More.*] He is about to publish a book, two volumes of Dialogues—between the Ghost of Sir Thomas More—and Montesino—himself—It is an interesting work—and I hope will attract some attention. But periodicals appear to have swallowed up so much money—that there is none left for more respectable Literature.

To C. R. (Corr. C. R., i, 201),   I. 27, 1829

43.   There is, perhaps, not a page of them [*Colloquies on the Progress and Prospects of Society,* 1829] that he did not read to me in MS.; and several of the Dialogues are upon subjects which we have often discussed. I am greatly interested with much of the book, but upon its effect as a whole I can yet form no opinion as it was read to me as it happened to be written. I need scarcely say that Mr. Southey ranks very highly, in my opinion, as a prose writer. His style is eminently clear, lively, and unencumbered, and his information unbounded; and there is a moral ardour about his compositions which nobly distinguishes them from the trading and factious authorship of the present day.   *To Geo. H. Gordon,*   V. 14, 1829

44.   I observed that Mr. Southey in his extracts from Skelton affirms that he was born at Dis in Norfolk, but I have heard, or read, that he was born at Branthwaite Hall near Cockermouth in Cumberland which place was un-doubtedly possessed for many generations by a family of his name—but on the above I lay no stress as I have no means of verifying the report.

To Dyce,   VII. 21, 1832

45.   I like your Book [*The Doctor*] much, and have only one objection to what I have seen: viz. the notice of Mr. Wilberforce by name. My wish is that you should adopt it as a general rule, not to allude (in the mention of public men),—to their *private* habits, otherwise your book will be so far degraded to the level of the magazine-writers—but probably this may be the only instance, and as it is so good natured there is little or no harm in it. A public man's public foibles are fair game! The Popes allusion is also well struck out—it is astonishing how queerly in these fantastic times the sale of a Book may be checked by what might seem the arrantest trifle.

To Southey,   V. 1833

46.   Southey's Sonnet to Winter [' A wrinkled, crabbed man they picture thee, Old Winter,' (*Oxf. Southey,* p. 350), written in 1799] pleases me much. . . . *To Dyce*   spring, 1833

47.   I was glad to see Mr. Southey's Sonnet to Winter. A Lyrical Poem of my own, upon the disasters of the French army in Russia [*The French Army in Russia*], has so striking a resemblance to it, in contemplating winter under two aspects, that, in justice to Mr. S., who preceded me, I ought to have acknowledged it in a note, and I shall do so upon some future occasion.

To Dyce,   XII. 4, 1833

48.   In the class entitled ' Musings,' in Mr. Southey's Minor Poems, is one upon his own miniature picture, taken in childhood, and another upon a landscape painted by Gaspar Poussin. It is possible that every word of the above verses [" Among a Grave "], though similar in subject, might have

been written had the author [W.] been unacquainted with those beautiful effusions of poetic sentiment. But, for his own satisfaction, he must be allowed thus publicly to acknowledge the pleasure those two Poems of his friend have given him, and the grateful influence they have upon the mind as often as he reads them or thinks of them. *Grosart*, iii, 172.   1835

49.* The transition from the grave to comic scenes [*The Doctor*] is in Wordsworth's eyes abrupt and uncomfortable, and he, as well as myself, thinks the comic passages much less pleasing than the serious.
H. C. R., ii, 537.   IX. 10, 1837

50.* Wordsworth not only sympathised with the feelings expressed in Southey's touching lines upon The Dead, but admired very much the easy flow of the verse and the perfect freedom from strain in the expression by which they are marked. Yet in the first two stanzas he noted three flaws, and suggested changes by which they might have been easily avoided. I have underlined the words he took exception to:

> ' My days among the dead are past;
>   Around me I behold,
> Where'er *these casual eyes* are cast,
> . . .
> With whom I *converse* day by day.
>
> With them I take delight in weal,
>   And seek relief in woe;
>   And while I understand and feel
>   How much to them I owe,
> My cheeks have often been bedew'd
>   With tears of thoughtful gratitude.'

In the first stanza, for ' Where'er *these casual eyes* are cast,' which he objected to as not simple and natural, and as scarcely correct, he suggested ' Where ' er *a casual look I* cast; ' and for ' *converse*,' the accent of which he condemned as belonging to the noun and not to the verb, he suggested ' commune.' In the second stanza he pointed out the improper sequence of tenses in the third and fifth lines, which he corrected by reading in the latter ' *My cheeks are oftentimes dedew'd.*'
Graves (*Grosart*, iii, 474-75).   c. 1840

51.* Wordsworth thinks the finest thing Southey has ever written is the graver part of a book, published anonymously, called *The Doctor*, the jocose parts of which he does not altogether admire or approve of, and the whole of which taken together shows, he thinks, a little too much bookmaking; while the sequence of quotations, though done with beautiful taste and a profound knowledge of the literature not only of England, but of the world in general, might have been done nearly as well by other persons than S. if they had chosen to devote their time to it. But of the graver parts he spoke with an admiration. . . . *A Day with Wordsworth*, p. 735.   VIII. 31, 1841

53. Dear Southey one of the most eminent is just added to the list. . . .

13

As to his literary Remains, they must be very considerable, but except his Epistolary correspondence none are left unfinished. His Letters cannot but be very numerous, and if carefully collected and judiciously selected will I doubt not, add greatly to his reputation. He had a fine talent for that species of Composition and took much delight in throwing off his mind in that way. *Reed*, pp. 95-6.   III. 27, 1843

65. . . . his Letters . . . will prove highly interesting to the Public, they are so gracefully and feelingly written. *Reed*, p. 110.   VIII. 2, 1843

55. . . . 'Oliver Newman ' . . . . I have however read the Volume and most of it more than once. The beautiful parts of Oliver are I think fully equal to any preceding work of their Author, and the whole of it with some correction and softening from his pen, which he undoubtedly would have given, would have met the desires of his most judicious Friends. The speech of the Governor is too long and somewhat dry and prosaic, and a few expressions in Randolph's mouth partake in my opinion of vulgarity; with these exceptions, I like the fragment exceedingly and several parts of it cannot be overestimated. *To H. Hill*,   I. 22, 1846

56. [Southey's] letters: and I, who cannot be long in this world, am much grieved that there is no prospect of their being collected and a selection of them published, a duty which would naturally devolve upon his Son [Cuthbert], and which I cannot but think he is quite equal to. How untoward has been our dear Friend's fate in these later years.
To H. Taylor,   VIII, 1846

Spedding, James

1. . . . a man of first rate talents. *To Moxon*,   IV. 28, 1836

Spenser, Edmund (General Criticism)

1.   And that gentle Bard,
     Chosen by the Muses for their Page of State—
     Sweet Spenser, moving through his clouded heaven
     With the moon's beauty and the moon's soft pace,
     I called him Brother, Englishman, and Friend!
     Prel., iii, 278-82.   1804-39

2.* . . . Spenser [finest writer] of stanzas. . . .
Collier's Preface, p. lii.   II. 10, 1814

4. [Spenser, a greater genius than *even* Ariosto, hardly known out of England, where his works are underestimated:]

     The laurel, meed of mighty conquerors
     And poets *sage*—

are his own words; but his wisdom has, in this particular, been his worst enemy: while its opposite, whether in the shape of folly or madness, has been *their* best friend. But he was a great power, and bears a high name: the laurel has been awarded to him. *E. Supp. Pref.*, p. 946.   1815

5. See Drama 15; Imagination 33G; Poetry 78; Versification 13B; Godwin, C. Grace 1; Goethe 7, 8; Johnson 11; Shakespeare 16

10.* [Spenser is always sincere.] *C. W., Jr. (Grosart,* iii, 465). c. 1827

12.* . . . Spenser, whom he loves, as he himself expresses it for his " earnestness and devotedness." *Mrs. Hemans,* ii, 92.   1830

13. The Poetic Genius of England with the exception of Chaucer, Spenser, Milton, Dryden, Pope, and a very few more, is to be sought in her Drama. *To Dyce,*   IV. 30, 1830

14. . . . the divine Spenser. . . . *Lakes (Grosart,* ii, 274).   1835

16.* [As a poet W. feared] competition . . . with . . . Spenser. . . . *H. C. R.,* ii, 776.   [*c.* 1845]

Spenser (Works)

17. Tell John when he buys Spenser, to purchase an edition which has his ' State of Ireland ' in it. This is in prose. This edition may be scarce, but one surely can be found. *To ? ,*   XI. 1802

18. [*F. Q.,* one his favorites.] See Books 12

19. . . . as that sovereignty [the Fairy Queen] was conceived to exist by the moral and imaginative genius of our divine Spenser. *Ans. to Mathetes (Grosart,* i, 322).   I. 4, 1810

20. . . . This Legend of Courtesy [Book vi of the *F. Q.*], taking it all together, is to me exceedingly delightful. [W.'s *marginalia* in the Folger set of Anderson's *British Poets,* p. 352.] *C. Miscellaneous Criticism,* p. 454 n.[3]   [*c.* 1810]

21.* . . . Wordsworth pronounced the Twelfth Canto of the Second Book of the ' Fairy Queen ' unrivalled in our own, or perhaps in any language, in spite of some pieces of description imitated from the great Italian poets. The allegory, he said, was miraculous and miraculously maintained, yet with the preservation of the liveliest interest in the impersonations of Sir Guyon and the Palmer, as the representatives of virtue and prudence. I [Collier] collected, however, that Spenser was not in all respects a great favourite with Wordsworth, dealing, as he does so much, in description and comparatively little in reflection. *Collier's Preface,* p. xxxii.   X. 20, 1811

22. [W. describes the appeal of the fanciful and inspiring story of Una.] *White Doe: Dedication,* 2-64 (see *Prel.,* ix, 440-60).   IV. 20, 1815

23. [*F. Q.*] See Poetry 78

24.* But I instance Spenser's ' Marriage ' [as proof that good poetry can be written on contemporary persons and events]. [See Introduction, note 11.] *C. W., Jr. (Grosart,* iii, 461).   *c.* 1827

Sprat, Thomas. See Johnson 11

Staël, Anne Louise Germaine de. See Macpherson 2

Stapleton, Thomas

1.   [Edited *The Plumpton Correspondence.*] See Camden Society 1

Steevens, George.   See Shakespeare 46

Stepney, George.   See Johnson 11

Sterling, John

1.*   John Sterling! Oh, he has written many very beautiful poems himself; some of them I greatly admire. . . . A man of such learning and piety! *Old Friends*, p. 214.   X. 6, 1844

Stillingfleet, Edward

1.   Stillingfleet adduces many arguments in support of this opinion [" Did Holy Paul a while in Britain dwell "] but they are unconvincing.
Oxf. W., p. 920.   1822

Stolberg, Frederic Leopold.   See Coleridge 46

Stuart, Daniel.   See *Courier* 1

Swift, Jonathan

1.   . . . theories as fanciful as Swift's in his Gullivers travels.
To C. R. (Corr. C. R., ii, 623),   V. 20, 1846

2.   . . . *Gulliver's Travels*, and the *Tale of the Tub*, being both much to my taste. *Grosart*, iii, 221.   XI. 1847

Sympson, Joseph

1.   These two lines [9-10 of *Flowers*] are in a great measure taken from ' The Beauties of Spring, a Juvenile Poem,' by the Rev. Joseph Sympson . . . his poems are little known, but they contain passages of splendid description; and the versification of his ' Vision of Alfred ' is harmonious and animated. In describing the motions of the Sylphs, that constitute the strange machinery of his Poem, he uses the following illustrative simile: [Book VII, lines 15-30, *Science Revised, or the Vision of Alfred*, London, 1802. See *Oxf. W.*, p. 908, for these lines.]
He was a man of ardent feeling, and his faculties of mind, particularly his memory, were extraordinary. Brief notices of his life ought to find a place in the History of Westmoreland. *Grosart*, iii, 101.   1820

Talfourd, Thomas N.

1.   . . . delighted with his Drama—[*Ion*] . . . he has pleased us.
To Moxon,   XI. 20, 1835

2.   You have most ably fulfilled your own purpose [in *Ion*], and your poem is a distinguished contribution to English literature. I reserve the sonnets as a *bonne bouche* for tomorrow. But I must tell you that Mrs. Wordsworth read me the second preface, which is written with much elegance of style and a graceful modesty. I cannot help catching at the hope

that, in the evening of life, you may realize those anticipations which you throw out. Chaucer's and Milton's great works were composed when they were far advanced in life. So, in times nearer our own, were Dryden's and Cowper's; and mankind has ever been fond of cherishing the belief that Homer's thunder and lightning were kept up when he was an old man and blind. Nor it is unworthy of notice that the leading interest attached to the name of Ossian is connected with gray hairs, infirmity, and privation.
To Talfourd,   XI. 28, 1836

3.* [At a performance of *Ion,* W.] thumped with his stick most lustily and if Talfourd saw him, he must have been not a little gratified by *such* approval of his *Tragedy.*
John Dix, Pen and Ink Sketches (ed. 1846), pp. 202-3.   1836

4.   I am not surprised at the effect of Sergeant Talfourd's speech [for the Copyright Bill] which I had read at length in the Times. It is judiciously and eloquently done, and I trust it will produce its effect, and that you all . . . may derive some little benefit from the measure it will lead to, after I am gone. The notice the Sergeant kindly took of me may excite some envy and spite, but upon the whole it will tend to swell the stream of my reputation and so widen the circulation of my works; for the good of readers I hope and also for Mr Moxon's sake, for I shall be delighted when he gets his money back. *To Dora,*   VI. 4, 1837

5.* Wordsworth says it [Talfourd's ed. of Lamb's letters] is the only book of the kind he knows, executed with delicacy and judgment.
H. C. R., iii, 853.   VIII. 7, 1837

6. . . . he is an interesting man—for talents, Genius, and energy of mind. *To Moxon,*   V. 21, 1838

7.* Do you not defend . . . [Sergeant Talfourd's] books more warmly than my slight (not slighting) expression of opinion about some portions of them warrants? *To C. R. (Corr. C. R.,* i, 399),   I. 23, 1840

Taliesin [The Book of Taliesin]

1.   Taliesin's unforgotten lays. . . .
              1 Ecc. Sonn, v, 10.   1821
2.   *The oppression of the tumult—wrath and scorn—*
              The tribulation—and the gleaming blades—
              Such is the impetuous spirit that pervades
              The song of Taliesin. . . .
              1 Ecc. Sonn., xii, 1-4.   1821

Tasso, Torquato

1.* . . . Wordsworth seemed disposed to think low of him.
H. C. R., i, 89.   V. 29, 1812

2. Now Tasso's [*Jerusalem Delivered*] is a religious subject, and in my opinion, a most happy one; but I am confidently of opinion that the movement of Tasso's poem rarely corresponds with the essential character of the subject; nor do I think it possible that, written in stanzas, it should. The celestial

movement cannot, I think, be kept up, if the sense is to be broken in that despotic manner at the close of every eight lines. Spenser's stanza is infinitely finer than the *ottava rima*, but even Spenser's will not allow the epic movement as exhibited by Homer, Virgil, and Milton. How noble is the first paragraph of the *Aeneid* in point of sound, compared with the first stanza of the *Jerusalem Delivered!* The one winds with the majesty of the Conscript Fathers entering the Senate House in solemn procession; and the other has the pace of a set of recruits shuffling on the drill-ground, and receiving from the adjutant or drill-serjeant the command to halt at every ten or twenty steps. *To Southey*,   1815

   3. See Ariosto 3

Taylor, Miss [sister of John Taylor (1757-1832); see *E. L.* p. 268
    n. 1.]

   1. . . . and the Pamphlet which dear Miss Taylor, in her pride, sent me, though cleverly written upon the whole, impressed me unfavorably in spite of the soundness of its opinions. There was in style an air of conceit and a flippancy which I could not but dislike.—*To I. Fenwick*,   X. 19, 1846

Taylor, Sir Henry

   1.* . . . a great admirer of *Philip van Artevelde.*
De Vere (*Grosart*, iii, 492).   1842-46

   2. In all that you condemn [in *Edwin the Fair*] I entirely concur, and approve of the reverence with which your disapprobation is expressed; as I am pretty sure that it arose out of your personal relations to the author, and from an unwillingness to hurt Miss Fenwick's feelings. Of the impression which the whole play has made upon my mind, with much pain, I must tell you, that I regret that it was ever written. It shews great command of language, however, and in the versification there is much skill, though, owing to the want of trochaic endings in the lines, it is very often rather fit for didactic or epic poetry than the dramatic. [In] the play also are some particular passages that are very happy, but they are rather incidental than a part of the action, and throughout the whole there are striking manifestations of talent; but alas it is talent prostrated or thrown away. The subject is most unfortunately chosen, and it is still more unfortunately treated, in fact, it has betrayed the Author. Religion he has truly said in his preface is a source which will naturally be looked to by one who would deal with the profound feelings of the human heart and the worthiest aspirations of the Soul. Something to this effect he has said; but it is not such religion as this play is conversant with. A dispute between Regulars and Seculars if conducted with ten times Mr. Taylor's knowledge of the question would but little affect the Reader or Spectator in these days, and as it is managed by him it is wholly uninteresting. You care for neither side; you have neither wish nor anxiety about them. And as to Dunstan the hero he is a piece of incongruity, nay of impossibility throughout. His mode of proceeding as you mention is taken from reports of dealings ascribed to him by his enemies; and these wretched tricks and devices are wholly incompatible with that compass and even

grandeur of mind with which Mr. Taylor has endeavoured to endow him; I say endeavoured for nothing can be more vague and obscure than the speeches put into Dunstan's mouth where he gives vent to his notions of a spiritual and everlasting Church. On my judgment such meanness as he works by cannot coexist with elevation of mind; or if it be possible, we may confidently affirm that the character is utterly unfit for dramatic exhibition. That scene of the mimic cross is unendurably profane in itself, and still more if possible is the Author to be condemned, for making the Almighty a party to his own dishonour by representing him (Dunstan does it) as sanctioning such mechanical expedients by his own practice. . . . and again I say that I deeply lament that Mr. Taylor should have produced such a work. Of other faults there is abundance; the love-concerns are mere excrescences; and there are far too many of them, though Lyulf's account of his own passion is the gem of the Play. Wolstan and his daughter, a wanton Lyar and Impostor [?] are both excrescences, though Wolstan's speech about the voice of the wind is very pretty, and in fact the most poetical thing in the play; but enough. How Mr. Taylor could think that with a story so uninteresting, people would take the trouble of learning who was who, in such a mob of dramatis Personae, I should be at a loss to conceive were I not aware that Shakespeare has seduced him into the practice. . . . *To E. Q.*, X. 18, 1842

Taylor, Isaac (1787-1865)

1.* Even Wordsworth, so intolerant of novelties, allowed his remark on the *imaginative powers* to be pretty; but would have them, like his *Ode*, in a poem rather than in prose. *H. C. R.*, ii, 563. I. 6, 1839

2.* Wordsworth admires the *Physical Theory* [1836], but he said ' It would read better in verse.'
C. R. to T. R. (Corr. C. R., ii, 651), VI. 25, 1847

Taylor, Jeremy. See Fancy 14; Montagu, B. 5

Taylor, John (1757-1832)

1. . . . thank you for your obliging Letter and the elegant Sonnet with which you have honored me. . . . *To John Taylor*, XI. 21, 1826

Taylor, William (1765-1836)

1. . . . took the trouble of versifying Blue Beard some years ago. . . . He is a Man personally unknown to me, and in his literary character doubtless an egregious coxcomb, but he is ingenious enough to do this if he could be prevailed upon to undertake it [to versify a tale of the Beauty and the Beast type for Godwin]. *To Godwin*, III. 9, 1811

2. [*British Synonyms.*] See Imagination 33A

3. See Letters 10

Tegg, Thomas

1. It is now high time to thank you my dear Friend for the valuable, and what will be to us the most useful present, of Tegg's (you see I can bring

my Pen upon this occasion to write the name) *Tegg's* Cyclopedia [*sic*]. It is a sort of Book which all my life I have wanted, but on account of expense never thought it right to buy.
To C. R. (Corr. C. R., i, 431),   IV. 18, 1841

Tennyson, Alfred

1.*   . . . young a poet as he then was, there was a man of the highest promise. *Hamilton*, iii, 187 n-88.   1830

2.   We have also a respectable show of blossom in poetry. Two brothers of the name of Tennyson, in particular, are not a little promising.
To W. R. Hamilton,   XI. 26, 1830

3.*   The danger for both Keats and Tennyson . . . was over-lusciousness. *Batho*, pp. 101-2.   *c.* 1840

4.*. . . . [W.] spoke slightingly of Tennyson's first performance [*Juvenalia*]. .*Gladstone*, iii, 483.   *c.* 1840

5.*   'You ask me why?' Of which Mr. Wordsworth praised the manly diction. *Aubrey de Vere*, p. 68.   III. 6, 1841

6.   See Literature 17

7.*   Mr. Tennyson, I have been endeavoring all my life to write a pastoral like your 'Dora' and have not succeeded. *Tennyson*, i, 265.   *c.* 1845

8.   He is decidedly the first of our living Poets, and I hope will live to give the world still better things. You will be pleased to hear that he [Tennyson] expressed in the strongest terms his gratitude to my writings. To this I was far from indifferent though persuaded that he is not much in sympathy with what I sh[o]uld myself most value in my attempts, viz the spirituality with which I have endeavored to invest the material Universe, and the moral relation under which I have wished to exhibit its most ordinary appearances.
Reed, p. 144.   VII. 1, 1845

9.*   [Little contemporary poetry can be called high poetry.] Mr. Tennyson affords the richest promise. He will do great things yet; and ought to have done greater things by this time. . . . The perception of harmony lies in the very essence of the poet's nature; and Mr. Tennyson gives magnificent proofs that he is endowed with it. [That Tennyson possessed as fine a sense of music in syllables as Keats, and even Milton, W. agreed.]
Thomas Cooper, p. 292.   1846

10.*   . . . a right poetic genius, though with some affectation. He [W.] had thought an elder brother of Tennyson at first the better poet, but must now reckon Alfred the true one. *English Traits*, p. 295.   III, 1848

Tennyson, Charles.   [See Turner, Charles Tennyson-]

Thelwall, John

1.   Thelwall the Politician many years ago lost a Daughter about the age of Scott's child. I knew her she was a charming creature. Thelwall's were the agonies of an unbeliever, and he expressed them vigorously in several

copies of harmonious blank verse, a metre which he wrote well for he has a good ear. These effusions of anguish were published, but though they have great merit, one cannot read them but with much more pain than pleasure.

To Haydon (*L. Y.*, p. 1368), I. 20, 1817

2. Mr. Coleridge and I were of opinion that the modulations of his blank verse were superior to those of most writers in that metre.

To Mrs. Thelwall, XI. 16, 1938

3. He really was a man of extraordinary talent. . . .

I. F. (*Grosart*, iii, 20). 1843

Theocritus. See Manners 2

Thomson, James (General Criticism)

1.* [W. has] a fondness for Thomson. . . . *Hazlitt*, iv, 277. *c.* 1800

2. See Collins 5, 8; Godwin, C. Grace 1; Macpherson 2; Peace 2

3.   The sweet-souled Poet of the Seasons stood—
       Listening, and listening long, in rapturous mood,
       Ye heavenly Birds! to your Progenitors.
       " Fame tells," 12-14. 1820

5. I had once a hope to have learned some unknown particulars of Thomson, about Jedburgh, but I was disappointed—had I succeeded, I meant to publish a short life of him, prefixed to a Volume containing The Seasons, The Castle of Indolence, his minor pieces in rhyme, and a few Extracts from his plays, and his Liberty; and I feel still inclined to do something of the kind. These three Writers, Thomson, Collins, and Dyer, had more poetic Imagination than any of their Contemporaries, unless we reckon Chatterton as of that age—I do not name Pope, for he stands alone—as a man most highly gifted—but unluckily he took the Plain, when the Heights were within his reach. *To Dyce,* I. 12, 1829

6. I know not what to say about my intended Edition of a portion of Thomson. There appears to be some indelicacy in one poet treating another in that way [see 5 above]. The Example is not good, though I think there are few to whom the Process might be more advantageously applied than to Thomson; but so sensible am I of the objection, that I should not have entertained the thought, but for the Expectation held out to me by an Acquaintance, that valuable materials for a new Life of Thomson might be procured. In this I was disappointed. *To Dyce,* X. 16, 1829

7.* Thomson he spoke of as a real poet, though it appeared less in his ' Seasons ' than in his other poems. He had wanted some judicious adviser to correct his taste; but every person he had to deal with only served to injure it. He had, however, a true love and feeling for Nature, and a greater share of poetical imagination, as distinguished from dramatic, than any man between Milton and him. As he stood looking at Ambleside, seen across the valley, embosomed in wood, and separated from us at sufficient distance, he quoted from Thomson's ' Hymn on Solitude,' and suggested the addition, or rather insertion, of a line at the close, where he speaks of glancing at London from

Norwood. The line, he said, should have given something of a more favourable impression [see Tickell 1A]:

'Ambition—[Coleridge could not fill the blank] and pleasure vain.'
Justice Coleridge (*Grosart*, iii, 431).   X. 10, 1836

9.*   With Thomson's Seasons he is delighted, and even more so, at
least in point of finish of execution and polish of numbers, with his Castle of
Indolence. Of the Seasons he has a copy of the first edition, throughout
which he has interlined the alterations subsequently made; and he looks upon
the author as one whom Nature had admitted to share in many of her highest
enjoyments and most retired pleasures, and who had received the boon with
the keenest feelings and a warm and exquisite sensibility. Then for the
circumstances of the man he has always felt great compassion; almost
unfriended even in his own country, struggling with poverty and adversity in
another one, which was then more foreign than it is now; suffering the dis-
advantages of a style not free from imperfections, and not quite pure as
English, at a time when the classical diction and refinement of Pope were
familiar to the reading public, and looked down upon in consequence, and
treated with undue disregard, if not harshness and contempt, by Pope and all
the band of authors and critics who then associated so much together, and
thought so much alike on matters of taste and learning. The want of perfect
English style has, he [W.] thinks, been a great hindrance to the reputation of
many of Thomson's countrymen—indeed, more than we can now perhaps
form any adequate idea of; and as an instance of this he mentioned the great
sensation excited by the first appearance of Robertson's works—good English,
written by a Scotchman. *A Day with Wordsworth*, p. 737.   VII. 1, 1841

Thomson, James (Works)

10. . . . these beautiful lines [*Hymn to Solitude*, 41-8, Oxford ed.]. . . .
To Lady Beaumont (p. 91),   XII. 23, 1806

11.* [Some] of Thomson's stanzas in 'Castle of Indolence' were quite
equal to Spenser. See also 13, below.
Collier's Preface, p. lii.   II. 10, 1814

13. [*Seasons*.] It is a work of inspiration; much of it is written from
himself, and nobly from himself. [Quoting a biographer of Thomson on the
popularity of *The Seasons*, W. says that here we do not have an exception to
his opinion that great works must undergo long neglect, for] we must distinguish between wonder and legitimate admiration. The subject of the work
is the changes produced in the appearances of nature by the revolution of the
year; and, by undertaking to write in verse, Thomson pledged himself to
treat his subject as became a Poet. Now, it is remarkable that, excepting the
nocturnal *Reverie of Lady Winchelsea*, and a passage or two in the *Windsor
Forest* of Pope, the poetry of the period intervening between the publication
of the *Paradise Lost* and the *Seasons* does not contain a single new image of
external nature; and scarcely presents a familiar one from which it can be
inferred that the eye of the Poet had been steadily fixed upon his object, much
less that his feelings had urged him to work upon it in the spirit of genuine

imagination. To what a low state knowledge of the most obvious and important phenomena had sunk, is evident from the style in which Dryden has executed a description of Night in one of his Tragedies [*The Indian Emperor*, III, ii, 1-6], and Pope his translation of the celebrated moonlight scene in the *Iliad*. A blind man, in the habit of attending accurately to descriptions casually dropped from the lips of those around him, might easily depict these appearances with more truth. Dryden's lines are vague, bombastic, and senseless; those of Pope, though he had Homer to guide him, are throughout false and contradictory. The verses of Dryden, once highly celebrated, are forgotten; those of Pope still retain their hold upon public estimation,—nay, there is not a passage of descriptive poetry, which at this day finds so many and such ardent admirers. Strange to think of an enthusiast, as may have been the case with thousands, reciting those verses under the cope of a moonlight sky, without having his raptures in the least disturbed by a suspicion of their absurdity!—If these two distinguished writers could habitually think that the visible universe was of so little consequence to a poet, that it was scarcely necessary for him to cast his eyes upon it, we may be assured that those passages of the elder poets which faithfully and poetically describe the phenomena of nature, were not at that time holden in much estimation, and that there was little accurate attention paid to those appearances.

Wonder is the natural product of Ignorance; and as the soil was *in such good condition* at the time of the publication of the *Seasons*, the crop was doubtless abundant. Neither individuals nor nations become corrupt all at once, nor are they enlightened in a moment. Thomson was an inspired poet, but he could not work miracles; in cases where the art of seeing had in some degree been learned, the teacher would further the proficiency of his pupils, but he could do little *more*; though so far does vanity assist men in acts of self-deception, that many would often fancy they recognized a likeness when they knew nothing of the original. Having shown that much of what his biographer deemed genuine admiration must in fact have been blind wonderment—how is the rest to be accounted for?—Thomson was fortunate in the very title of his poem, which seemed to bring it home to the prepared sympathies of every one: in the next place, notwithstanding his high powers, he writes a vicious style; and his false ornaments are exactly of that kind which would be most likely to strike the undiscerning. He likewise abounds with sentimental commonplaces, that, from the manner in which they were brought forward, bore an imposing air of novelty. In any well-used copy of the *Seasons* the book generally opens of itself with the rhapsody on love, or with one of the stories (perhaps ' Damon and Musidora ') ; these also are prominent in our collections of Extracts, and are the parts of his Work which, after all, were probably most efficient in first recommending the author to general notice. Pope, repaying praises which he had received, and wishing to extol him to the highest, only styles him ' an elegant and philosophical Poet '; nor are we able to collect any unquestionable proofs that the true characteristics of Thomson's genius as an imaginative poet were perceived, till the elder Warton . . . pointed them [The most striking passages Warton admires were improvements later than the second edition of the *Seasons*.

W. later (1820) added this note.] out by a note in his Essay on the *Life and Writings of Pope*. In the *Castle of Indolence* (of which Gray speaks so coldly) these characteristics were almost as conspicuously displayed, and in verse more harmonious, and diction more pure. Yet that fine poem was neglected on its appearance, and is at this day the delight only of a few! See Fame 12 and 13

E. Supp. Pref., pp. 948-49 and n 1.   1815

14.* . . . Thomson's *Winter* . . . is praised by Wordsworth.

H. C. R., i, 206.   IV. 9, 1817

15.* [A beautiful instance of the modifying and investive power of imagination] in Thomson's description of the streets of Cairo [*Summer*, 980]. . . . *C. W., Jr. (Grosart*, iii, 465).   *c.* 1827

16.   See Scotch Writers 2

Thornton, B.

1.   British Poetesses make but a poor figure in the *Poems by Eminent Ladies* [ed. B. Thornton, 2 vols., 1755]. But observing how injudicious that Selection is in the case of Lady Winchelsea, and of Mrs. Aphra Behn, from whose attempts they are miserably copious, I have thought something better might have been chosen by more competent Persons, who had access to the Volumes of the several writers. *To Dyce*,   IV. 30, 1830

Thucydides

1.   [Hopes Dora will soon read Thucydides.]

W., M. W., and D. W. to C. R. (Corr. C. R., i, 268),   XI. 24, 1834

2.* [W. thought less of Thucydides than of Herodotus.]

Ellis Yarnall (Grosart, iii, 479).   VIII. 18, 1849

Tickell, Thomas

1.   See Scotch Writers 2

1A.   [Brown's verses on a night-scene suggested by the Vale of Keswick, show] a dawn of imaginative feeling. . . . Tickel, a man of no common genius, chose, for the subject of a Poem, Kensington Gardens, in preference to the Banks of the Derwent, within a mile or two of which he was born. [Little progress evident since in nature-description,] except in the works of Thomson and Dyer. . . . *Lakes (Grosart*, ii, 256n.).   1809-35

2.   . . . I think there is a good deal of resemblance in her [Lady Winchilsea's style and versification to that of Tickell, to whom Dr. Johnson justly assigns a high place among minor Poets, and of whom Goldsmith rightly observes, that there is a strain of ballad-thinking through all his Poetry, and it is very attractive. *To Dyce*,   V. 10, 1830

3.   (. . . one of the best of our minor poets, as Johnson has truly said). . . . *To Dyce*,   VII. 23, 1831

Todd, Henry J.

1. Like you, I had been sadly disappointed with Todd's *Spenser*; not with the Life, which I think has a sufficient share of merit; though the matter is badly put together; but three parts of four of the Notes are absolute trash. That style of compiling notes ought to be put an end to.

To W. Scott, XI. 7, 1805

Townsend, Chauncey H.

1. . . . is as pretty a rascal as ever put on a surplice. . . . The thing as an intellectual production is safe in its own vileness. Who that ever felt a line of my poetry would trouble himself to crush a miserable maggot crawled out of the dead carcass of the Edinburgh review. [To *Blackwood's Magazine*, Sept.–Dec. 1829, he contributed four anonymous articles on W. which as Southey pointed out to him were 'obnoxious,' and, as W. said truly, 'contained much scoffing, much literary misrepresentation and personal disparagement.' De Sel.] *To E. Q.,* II. 4, 1830

2. Not long ago I made mention in a Letter to you of a certain Critic, the only one whose strictures on my writings had ever given me concern worth speaking of. I was hurt and even wounded by his unworthy mode of proceeding. He has lately written to me a long Letter of penitential recantation to which I have replied as, I trust, it became me.

To T. Powell, V. 1, 1840

Trench, Richard C.

1. . . . with the utmost sincerity [tell him his poems have pleased us].
To Moxon, XI. 20, 1835

2.* . . . W. was charmed with French's poems. . . .
Gladstone, i, 136. 1836

3. [Take] Trench's Vol. of Poems with you, and read them, as I am sure from . . . his former productions, they must be of no common merit.
To Dora W., early IV, 1838

4. See Kenyon 4, 5, 7

Tupper, Martin F.

1. [Derived great pleasure from Tupper's *Proverbial Philosophy.*]
To Tupper (L. of W. Family, p. 82), XII. 10, 1842

Turner, Charles Tennyson-. See Tennyson 2, 10

Turner, Sharon

1. Turner's valuable history [*History of the Anglo-Saxons*].
Oxf. W., p. 921. 1822

Vanbrugh, Sir John. Manners 2

Vane, Henry (1613-62)

1.   Great men have been among us; hands that penned
        And tongues that uttered wisdom—better none:
        The later Sidney, Marvel, Harrington,
        Young Vane. . . .
        " Great men," 1-4.   1802

Vanhomrigh, Esther

1. . . . that ever-to-be-pitied Victim of Swift, ' Vanessa.' I have somewhere a short piece of hers upon her passion for Swift, which well deserves
to be added [to Dyce's *Specimens*]. *To Dyce,*   V. 10, 1830

Virgil

1. Virgil gives a high place in Elysium to the *improvers* of life, and it is
neither the least philosophical or least poetical passage of the *Æneid* [vi,
663-5]. *To F. Wrangham,*   XII. 3, 1808

2. See Ancient Writers 11; Imagination 33B and D; Poetry 78; Translation 4, 9; Dryden 2, 21-2; Wrangham 10; W. 201, 242, 291, 293-4

5. The Eaglogues of Virgil appear to me, in that in which he was most
excellent, polish of style and harmony of numbers, the most happily finished
of all his performances. *To F. Wrangham* (p. 704),   I. 18, 1816

6. [*Aeneid.*] See Biography 2B; Poetry 78; Tasso 2

10.   I began my translation [of part of the *Aeneid*] by accident. I continued it, with a hope to produce a work which would be to a certain degree
affecting, which Dryden's is not to me in the least. Dr. Johnson has justly
remarked that Dryden had little talent for the pathetic, and the tenderness
of Virgil seems to me to escape him. Virgil's style is an inimitable mixture of
the elaborately ornate and the majestically plain and touching. The former
quality is much more difficult to reach than the latter, in which whosoever
fails must fail through want of ability, and not through the imperfections of
our language.

In my last I troubled you with a quotation from my own translation, in
which I found a failure—' fuimus Troes,' etc., ' we have been Trojans,' etc.
It struck me afterwards that I might have found still stronger instances.
At the close of the first book Dido is described as asking several questions of
Venus,

        Nunc, quales Diomedis equi, nunc quantus Achilles,

which Dryden translates very nearly, I think, thus,

        The steeds of Diomede varied the discourse, etc.

My own translation is probably as faulty upon another principle:

        Of Hector asked, of Priam o'er and o'er,
        What arms the son of bright Aurora wore,
        What horses there of Diomede, had great
        Achilles—but, O Queen, the whole relate.

These two lines will be deemed, I apprehend, hard and bald. So true is Horace's remark, ' in vitium ducet culpae fuga,' etc.

To Lord Lonsdale,   II. 17, 1819

12.*   I admire Virgil's high moral tone: for instance, that sublime Aude, hospes, contemnere opes,' etc. and ' his dantem jura Catonem!' What courage and independence of spirit is there! There is nothing more imaginative and awful than the passage,

> ' ――――――――――――――― Arcades ipsum
>   Credunt se vidisse Jovem,' etc.

In describing the weight of sorrow and fear on Dido's mind, Virgil shows great knowledge of human nature, especially in that exquisite touch of feeling,

> ' Hoc visum nulli, *non ipsi effata sorori.'*

C. W., Jr. (*Grosart,* iii, 459).   *c.* 1827

13.*   Lucretius . . . a far higher poet than Virgil, not in his system, which is nothing, but in his power of illustration.

English Traits, p. 21.   VIII. 28, 1833

14.   Virgilian haunt,
> Illustrated with never-dying verse,
> And, by the Poet's laurel-shaded tomb,
> Age after age to Pilgrims from all lands
> Endeared.

> *Aquapendente,* 265-69.   1837

15.*   He was a very great admirer of *Virgil,* not so much as a creative poet, but as the most consummate master of language, that, perhaps, ever existed. From him, and Horace, who was an especial favourite, and Lucretius, he used to quote much. *Graves* (*Grosart,* iii, 469).   *c.* 1840

16.   [Implied preference for Virgil over Ovid.]

I. F. (*Grosart,* iii, 168).   1843

Voltaire, François Marie Arouet de

1.   See Rousseau 1; Scott, W. 18

2.   . . . this dull product [*Candide*] of a scoffer's pen,
> Impure conceits discharging from a heart
> Hardened by impious pride.
> *Exc.,* ii, 484-6.   1814

3.   Him I mean
> Who penned, to ridicule confiding faith,
> This sorry Legend; which by chance we found
> Piled in a nook, through malice, as might seem
> Among more innocent rubbish.
> *Exc.,* iv, 1005-9.   1814

4.*   [Lamb asked W.] Why do you call Voltaire dull?

Life of B. R. Haydon from his Autobiography and Memoirs, ed. Tom Taylor, 2 vols. (N. Y., 1853), i, 340.   XII. 8, 1817

6.*   His moral and religious feelings added to a spice of John Bullism have utterly blinded him for instance to the marvellous talent of Voltaire. . . . Let me remark too as to censure that I do not believe I ever heard him speak against any one (except Gothe) whom I have not heard you attack in much more vehement language. Indeed I thought I had remarked a general concurrence in your critical opinion.
C. R. to Landor (*Corr. C. R.*, i, 328),   XII. 7, 1836

Voss, Johann Heinrich

1.   See Milton 47
2.*   Wordsworth [liked] . . . his *Luise.*
H. C. R., i, 447.   IX. 16, 1834
3.   [*Louise.*] See Longfellow 2

Waldie, Jane [Mrs. George A. Watts].   See Watts, A. 4

Waller, Edmund.   See Milton 48

Walpole, Horace

1.   See Winchilsea, Lady 3
2.   . . . that cold and false-hearted Frenchified Coxcomb—Horace Walpole. *To Dyce.*   III. 20, 1833

Walsh, William.   See Johnson 11

Walton, Isaac

1.*   He approves of Walton's Angler. . . . *Hazlitt*, iv, 277.   *c.* 1800
2.*   My brother has seized upon the book [Walton's *Compleat Angler*] for his own reading this night, as he fancies that the imagery and sentiments accord with his own train of thought at present, in connection with his poem [*White Doe*]. . . . *D. W. to Lady Beaumont*,   I. 3, 1808
3.   See Currie 2; Plato 2
4.   [*The Compleat Angler.*]

> While flowing rivers yield a blameless sport,
> Shall live the name of Walton: Sage benign!
> Whose pen, the mysteries of the rod and line
> Unfolding, did not fruitlessly exhort
> To reverend watching of each still report
> That Nature utters from her rural shrine.
> "While flowing rivers," 1-6.   1819

5.   [*Lives.*]

> There are no colors in the fairest sky
> So fair as these. The feather, whence the pen
> Was shaped that traced the lives of these good men,
> Dropped from an Angel's wing. With moistened eye
> We read of faith and purest charity
> In Statesman, Priest, and humble Citizen:

—like stars on high,
Satellites burning in a lucid ring
Around meek Walton's heavenly memory.
3 Ecc. Sonn., v, 1-6; 12-14. 1821

Warton, Jane

1. A beautiful Elegy of Miss Warton (sister to the Poets of that name) upon the death of her father. . . . *To Dyce*, IV. 30, 1830

Warton, Joseph. [*Essay on Pope.*] See Thomson 13

Waterson, Robert C.

1. He also sent me a Copy of verses addressed by himself to me, I presume some little time ago, and printed in the " Christian Souvenir["]. You have probably seen the Lines, and if so I doubt not you will agree with me that they indicate a true feeling of the leading characteristics of my Poems. At least I am sure that I wished them such as he represents them to be, *too* partially no doubt. *Reed*, p. 109. VIII. 2, 1843

Waterton, Charles

1.* . . . the Book [*Wanderings in S. America*] . . . has interested us very much. *D. W. to Jane Marshall*, XII. 23, 1825

Watts, Alaric

1. Of the poems . . . notwithstanding the modest manner in which you speak of their merits, I must be allowed to say that I think the volume one of no common promise, and that some of the pieces are valuable, independent of such consideration. My sister tells me she named the *Ten Years Ago*. It is one of this kind; and I agree with her in rating it more highly than any other of the collection. Let me point out the thirteenth stanza of the first poem as—with the exception of the last line but one—exactly to my taste, both in sentiment and language. Should I name other poems that particularly pleased me, I might select the *Sketch from Real Life*, and the lyrical pieces, the *Serenade* and *Dost thou love the Lyre?* The fifth stanza of the latter would be better omitted, slightly altering the commencement of the preceding one. In lyric poetry the subject and simile should be as much as possible lost in each other.

It cannot but be gratifying to me to learn from your letter that my productions have proved so interesting; and, as you are induced to say, beneficial, to a writer whose pieces bear such undeniable marks of sensibility as appear in yours. I hope there may not be so much in my writings to mislead a young poet as is by many roundly asserted.

. . . the respect I entertain for your sensibility and genius.
To A. Watts, XI. 16, 1824

2. . . . his Poems have the stamp of genuine sensibility, and his opinions, as far as I am acquainted with them, are sound.
To Maria Jewsbury, V. 4, 1825

3. . . . should be happy to converse with you upon certain principles of style, taking for my text any one of your own animated poems, say the last in your *Souvenir*, which along with your other pieces in the same work I read with no little admiration. *To Watts,*　　　　　　VIII. 5, 1825

4. . . . *The Souvenir* for 1832, just received. I have been much pleased with Mrs Watt's *Choice*, Mrs Howitt's *Infancy, Youth, and Age*, and your own *Conversazione*—a great deal too clever for the subjects which you have here and there condescended to handle. *To Watts,*　　　　　　1832

5.* . . . Mrs. Coleridge's declaration that she herself heard Wordsworth declare that there is better poetry in Watts than in Keble. I have also heard him speak slightly of the mechanical talents of Keble, but he esteemed the tendency of his poems. *H. C. R.*, ii, 803.　　　　　　*c.* 1835

6.* . . . Watts wrote better poems than those of the Christian Year. *Sara Coleridge and Reed*, p. 122.　　　　　　*c.* 1840

Way, Benjamin

1. . . . the Memoirs of Mr. B. L. Way and his son, the Rev. Lewis Way, I have read with great interest. . . .

The whole of the little volume (with the exception that for ordinary perusal too much space is given to Mr. B. L. Way's literary pursuits) I found so interesting as earnestly to desire to see it printed in some shape that would give it a wide circulation; and this would perhaps be most effectually done, if it could be included in some collection of brief biographies confined exclusively to the lives of men of remarkable virtues and talents, though not universally or generally known. The number of these, if sought for, would be found considerable, and I cannot but think they would tend more to excite imitation than accounts of men so pre-eminent in genius and so favoured by opportunity as rather to discourage than inspire emulation. *To ?*　　　　　　IV. 22, 1845

Way, Lewis.　See Way, B. 1

Webster, Daniel

1.* . . . the ablest man in America. *H. C. R.*, i, 430.　　　VI. 20, 1833

Webster, John.　See Dyce 4

Weever, John

1. The invention of epitaphs, Weever, in his *Discourse of Funeral Monuments*, says rightly, ' proceeded from the presage or fore-feeling of immortality, implanted in all men naturally, and is referred to the scholars of Linus the Theban poet, . . . who first bewailed this Linus their Master, when he was slain, in doleful verses, then called of him Oelina, afterwards Epitaphia, for that they were first sung at burials, after engraved upon the sepulchres.' *Epitaph 1*, p. 928.　　　　　　1810

2. [Gives] an example of the manner in which an epitaph ought to have been composed. . . . *Epitaph 2 (Grosart*, ii, 50).　　　　　　1810

West, Thomas

1. [West's *Guide* is the authoritative work on the lake region.]
Lakes (*Grosart*, ii, 300). 1835

Whewell, William

1. . . . In the *Quarterly Review* lately was an article, a very foolish one I think, upon the decay of science in England, and ascribing it to the want of patronage from the government—a poor compliment this to science! Her hill, it seems, in the opinion of the writer, cannot be ascended unless the pilgrim be ' stuck o'er with titles and hung round with strings,' and have his pockets laden with cash; besides a man of science must be a minister of state or a privy councillor, or at least a public functionary of importance. Mr. Whewell [Wm. Whewell, 1794-1866, mathematician and philosopher] of Trinity College, Cambridge, has corrected the mis-statements of the reviewer in an article printed in the *British Critic* of January last, and vindicated his scientific countrymen. *To W. R. Hamilton,* I. 24, 1831

2.* Wordsworth would not tolerate his English hexameters. . . .
H. C. R., ii, 584. V. 22, 1840

3.* When asked whether he [W.] would like to go hear Lord Monteagle (Mr. Spring Rice), Mr. Whewell, and Mr Carlyle lecture on " Astronomy, Universal Philantropy, etc." " Go! " said he, " I would as soon go to see so many carrion crows." *A Day with Wordsworth,* p. 740. VIII. 31, 1841

Whitaker, Thomas D.

1.* . . . how much pleasure my Brother has already received from Dr. Whitaker's Books [*The History of the Original Parish of Whalley, and Honour of Clitheroe,* 1801, and *The History and Antiquities of the Deanery of Craven,* 1805], though they have been only two days in his possession. Almost the whole time he has been greedily devouring the History of Craven, and (what is of more importance) he has found all the information which he wanted for the prosecution of his plan [of *The White Doe*].
D. W. to Jane Marshall, X. 18, 1807

2. . . . I have lately read Dr. Whitaker's history of Craven and Whalley both with profit and pleasure. *To F. Wrangham,* X. 2, 1808

3. If you have not seen White's and Whitaker's books [*History of Craven, and History of Walley*], do procure a sight of them.
To F. Wrangham, IV. 1809

4. . . . his excellent book, *The History and Antiquities of the Deanery of Craven.* . . . *Grosart,* iii, 121. 1815

5. . . . Dr. Whitaker's *History of Craven,* a topographical writer of first-rate merit in all that concerns the past; but such was his aversion from the modern spirit, as shown in the spread of manufactories in those districts of which he treated, that his readers are left entirely ignorant, both of the progress of these arts, and their real bearing upon the comfort, virtues, and happiness of the inhabitants. *I. F.* (*Grosart,* iii, 166). 1843

White, Gilbert

1. [Read] White's *Natural History and Antiquities of Selborne* with great pleasure when a boy at school. . . . *To F. Wrangham,*   X. 2, 1808

2. See Whitaker 2, 3

White, Henry Kirke

1.* Wordsworth talked at his ease, having confidence in his audience. . . . He spoke of Kirke White. Both he and Rough agreed in considering him as a man of more talents than genius, and that the great correctness of his early writings was a symptom unpromising as to his future works. He would probably have been rather a man of great learning than a great poet. He would not have been more than a Southey, said Rough. " And that would have been nothing after all," said Wordsworth, " —when speaking of the highest excellence," he added. He however spoke afterwards of the " genius " of Southey. *H. C. R.,* i, 82.   V. 13, 1812

2. See Poetry 119

Wieland, Christoph Martin

1. See Gillies 3; Goethe 1

2.* . . . I thought the story [of *Oberon*] began to flag about the seventh or eighth book; . . . that it was unworthy of a man of genius to make the interest of a long poem turn entirely upon animal gratification. . . . I thought the *passion* of love as well suited to the purposes of poetry as any other passion; but that it was a cheap way of pleasing to fix the attention of the reader through a long poem on the mere *appetite.* . . . it was the province of a great poet to raise people up to his own level, not to descend to theirs. [W. thought little of the style, though he had read it only in translation.] *Biog. Lit.* (" Satyrane's Letters "), ii, 177-8.   [*c.* IX, 1798]

Wilberforce, Robert and Samuel

1. . . . Wilberforce' life by his Sons as a specimen [of idolatrous biography]. See Gillman 1

Wilkinson, Thomas

1. . . . a little of a Poet. . . . *To Beaumont* (p. 526),   X. 17, 1805

2. . . . a little poem of yours upon your Birds which gave us all very great pleasure. *To Wilkinson,*   VII. 7, 1809

3. . . . some [of his verses are] worthy of preservation; one little poem in particular, upon disturbing, by prying curiosity, a bird while hatching her young in his garden. *I. F.* (*Grosart,* iii, 163).   1843

Williams, Helen Maria

1. If a 2nd edition of your Specimens should be called for, you might add from H. M. Williams the Sonnet to the Moon, and that to Twilight. . . . *To Dyce,*   V. 10, 1830

2. . . . Sonnet upon Twilight is pleasing; that upon Hope of great merit.
To Dyce,   spring, 1833

Wilson, John

1. I was pleased to find that I had given so much pleasure to an ingenuous and able mind, and I further considered the enjoyment which you had had from my Poems as an earnest that others might be delighted with them in the same, or a like manner. It is plain from your letter that the pleasure which I have given you has not been blind or unthinking; you have studied the poems, and prove that you have entered into the spirit of them. They have not given you a cheap or vulgar pleasure. . . .
To John Wilton (p. 292),   VI, 1802

2. See W. 395

3.* And of Wilson, whom the Edinb. Rev[iewer]s had most disingenuously set above Words. W. did not hesitate to say ' Wilson's poems are an attenuation of mine. He owes everthg. to me and this he acknowledges to me in private, but he ought to have said it to the public also.'
Remains, p. 50.   V. 13, 1812

4.* . . . when Wilson was a candidate for the professorship of Moral Philosophy in the Univ. Edinb., Wil. applied to Wordsw. for a testimonial. Words. repeated to me the one he sent—I quote from memory. It imported that if a delicate perception of the subleties of Ethics as a science and ability in developing what he thought and making it intelligible and impressing it on others constituted the qualification, he knew no one more highly qualified than Wilson. *Remains*, p. 50.   after 1812

5. I am glad to hear so good an account of Mr. Wilson's poem [*The City of the Plague*]. . . . But Mr. W. knows that Ladies for the most part are very sorry Critics, and the person in question is, perhaps, not an exception, though I have no doubt that in this case she is in the right, knowing Mr. Wilson's genius. . . . *To Gillies*,   IV. 9, 1816

6. I have not yet seen his *City of the Plague*; the more the pity for I quarrel with the title, it not being English and being unintelligible. The English phrase, is, the City *in* the Plague; if the subject be a City suffering under the Plague. *To Gillies*,   IV. 15, 1816

7. I have seen the Article in Blackwood alluded to in your last—it is undoubtedly from the pen of Mr. Wilson himself. He is a perverse Mortal,—not to say worse of him. Have you peeped into his Trials of Margaret Lyndsay [1823]—you will there see to what an extent he has played the Plagiarist—with the very tale of Margaret in the Excursion, which he abuses—and you will also, with a glance learn, what passes with him for poetical Christianity—more mawkish stuff I never encountered.—I certainly should think it beneath me to notice that Article in any way—my Friends and admirers I hope will take the same view of it. Mr W's pen must be kept going at any rate—I am at a loss to know why—but so it is—he is well paid twice as much, I am told as any other Contributor.
To C. R. (*Corr. C. R.*, i, 200-1),   I. 27, 1829

8.   If you can lay your hands upon Mr. Coleridge's ' Friend,' you will find some remarks of mine upon a letter signed, if I recollect right, ' Mathetes,' which was written by Professor Wilson, in which, if I am not mistaken, sentiments like yours are expressed; at all events, I am sure that I have long retained those opinions, and have frequently expressed them either by letter or otherwise. *To W. R. Hamilton,*   IX. 26, 1830

9.*   . . . his quality both as a prose and as a verse writer, in both of which he [W.] thinks diffuseness his fault, and cheerful, natural, warm-hearted vigour his excellence. . . .

A Day with Wordsworth, p. 738.   VIII. 31, 1841

Winchilsea, Anne Finch, Countess of

1.   See Montagu, Mary W. 1; Thomson 13; Thornton, B. 1

2.   There is one Poetess to whose writings I am especially partial, the Countess of Winchelsea. I have perused her Poems frequently, and should be happy to name such passages as I think most characteristic of her Genius, and most fit to be selected. *To Dyce,*   X. 16, 1829

3.   [Her poems.] I will transcribe a note from a blank leaf of my own Edition written by me before I saw the scanty notice of her in Walpole. (By the bye, that book has always disappointed me, when I have consulted it upon any particular occasion.)   The note runs thus: ' The Fragment, page 280, seems to prove that she was attached to James 2nd, as does page 42, and that she suffered by the Revolution. The most celebrated of these poems, but far from the best, is the " Spleen." The Petition for an Absolute Retreat and A Nocturnal Reverie are of much superior merit. See also for favorable Specimens, page 156, on the Death of Mr. Thynne, 263; and 280, Fragment. The fable of Love, Death, and Reputation, page 29, is ingeniously told.' Thus far my own note. I will now be more particular. Page 3, ' Our vanity,' etc., and page 163 are noticeable as giving some account from herself of her Authorship. See also 148 where she alludes to the Spleen. She was unlucky in her models—Pindaric odes and French Fables. But see page 70, The Blindness of Elymas, for proof that she could write with powers of a high order when her own individual character and personal feelings were not concerned. For less striking proofs of this power, see page 4, ' All is Vanity,' omitting verses 5 and 6, and reading ' clouds that are lost and gone,' etc. There is merit in the 2 next Stanzas, and the last Stanza towards the close contains a fine reproof for the ostentation of Louis 14, and one magnificent verse, ' Spent the astonished hours, forgetful to adore.' . . . As far as ' For my garments,' page 36, the poem is charming—it then falls off—revives at 39, ' give me there ' page 41, etc., reminds me of Dyer's Gronger Hill; it revives on page 47, towards the bottom, and concludes with sentiments worthy of the writer, though not quite so happily expressed as in other parts of the Poem. See pages 82, 92. ' Whilst in the Muses' paths I stray.' 113. The ' Cautious Lovers,' page 118, has little poetic merit, but is worth reading as characteristic of the author. 143, ' Deep lines of honour,' etc., to ' maturer age.' 151, if shortened, would be striking; 154 characteristic; 159, from ' Meanwhile ye living parents,' to the close, omitting ' Nor could we hope,'

and the five following verses, 217, last paragraph, 259, *that* you have. 262, 263, 280. Was Lady Winchelsea a R Catholic? 290, ' And to the clouds proclaim thy fall '; 291, omit ' When scattered glow-worms,' and the next couplet—*To Dyce,*   IV. 30, 1830

5.   I observed . . . Lady Winchelsea was unfortunate in her models— *Pindarics* and *Fables*; nor does it appear from her Aristomenes that she would have been more successful than her contemporaries, if she had cultivated Tragedy. She had sensibility sufficient for the tender parts of dramatic writing, but in the stormy and tumultuous she would probably have failed altogether. She seems to have made it a moral and religious duty to control her feelings, lest they should mislead her. Of Love as a passion she is afraid, no doubt from a conscious inability to soften it down into friendship. I have often applied two lines of her Drama (p. 318) to her affections:

> Love's soft Bands,
> His gentle cords of Hyacinths and roses,
> Wove in the dewy spring when storms are silent [Act II, Scene i].

. . . in the next page are two impassioned lines spoken to a person fainting—

> Then let me hug and press thee into life,
> And lend thee motion from my beating heart.

From the style and versification of this so much her longest work I conjecture that Lady W. had but a slender acquaintance with the drama of the earlier part of the preceeding Century. Yet her style in rhyme is often admirable, chaste, tender, and vigorous; and entirely free from sparkle, antithesis, and that overculture which reminds one by its broad glare, its stiffness, and heaviness, of the double daisies of the garden, compared with their modest and sensitive kindred of the fields. Perhaps I am mistaken but I think there is a good deal of resemblance in her style and versification to that of Tickell. . . . *To Dyce,*   V. 10, 1830

7.   Without some additional materials, I think I should scarcely feel strong enough to venture upon any species of publication connected with this very interesting woman. . . . *To Dyce,*   VII. 23, 1831

Winckelmann, Johann Joachim

1.   . . . Abbé Winkelman on the study of the Antique, in Painting and sculpture. He enjoys a high reputation among the most judicious of the German Criticks—His Works are unknown to me, except a short treatise entitled Reflections concerning the imitation of the Grecian Artists in Painting and Sculpture, in a series of Letters. A translation of this is all I have read having met with it the other day upon a Stall at Penrith.—It appears to me but a slight thing; at the best superficial, and in some points, particularly what respects allegorical Painters, in the last Letter, very erroneous. . . . Probably the Author has composed other works upon the same subject, better digested; and to these his high reputation may be owing.

To Haydon,   XII. 21, 1815

Wither, George

1. [Great respect for the poetry of the Beaumonts and of Wither.]
Reed, pp. 96, and 85.   III. 27, 1843

Wolcot, John [Peter Pindar]. See Satire 1

Woodford, A. Montagu

1. . . . the Selection [*The Book of Sonnets*, edited by Woodford] seems
such as will do you credit for taste and discrimination.
To Mrs. A. M. Woodford,   IV. 19, 1842

Wordsworth, Charles

1. We have been reading, with very much pleasure, dear Charles's book
[*Catechetical Questions*, 1842]. *To C. W., Jr.*,   III. 22, 1843

Wordsworth, Christopher, Jr.

1. I have read Chris's Work [*Theophilus Anglicanus*] both with profit
and pleasure. I have not thanked him for it yet, except through the medium
of the *Morning Post*, in a Sonnet printed in that journal, Friday or Saturday
last. . . .
    . . . I hope Chris's valuable Book will meet with the reception it so amply
deserves. *To C. W.*,   XII. 20, 1843

Wordsworth, Christopher

1. I cannot speak of your sermons comparatively with other *modern* ones,
for I read none; but in themselves I can say that they are admirable, both for
the matter and the manner. *D. W. to Priscilla Wordsworth (with a PS.
from W. W. to C. W.)*,   II. 27, 1815

2.   We thank you for your Consecration Sermon [see *M. Y.*, p. 715
n 1.], which we received free of expense. We have read it with much pleasure,
and unite in thinking it excellently adapted to the occasion. For my own
part, I liked it still better upon the second than the first reading.—At first I
felt it somewhat disproportioned . . . afterwards I was less sensible of this
defect (if it really exist) and could feel the strength of the thoughts and
dignity of the sentiments, without discomposure. Your style is grave and
authentic; and wants neither grace nor harmony. . . .
To C. W.,   III. 12, 1816

3. [C. W.'s valuable sermons.] *To C. W.*,   III. 12, 1816

5. . . . the Icon [In 1824 C. W. published *Who wrote Eikon Basilike?
a letter to the Archbishop of Canterbury*, supporting the authorship of Charles
I. In 1825 he published *A Documentary Supplement*, and in 1828 a further
book on the subject. De Sel.] . . . I . . . find it improve upon me in effect.
You ask for remarks—I have only one—that when you argue from the
inherent baseness of Gauden's mind that he was incapable of entertaining
the noble sentiments of the Icon, and therefore of personating the King,
sufficient allowance is not made, I think, for his dramatic talent, as I may

call it, as exhibited in the hyprocrisy of his espiscopal Charge, and his other works; yet, I own, it would be little less than marvellous that Gauden had kept the Icon so clear from stains of vicious moral sentiment and bad taste. In that, I think, would lie the wonder, and not in the production of any *strains* of piety and purity that may be found there. *To C. W.*,   I. 4, 1825

5A.   We reckon it [C. W.'s *Eikon Basilike*] convincing.
To Merewether (*L. of W. Family*, p. 63),   I. 10, 1825

6.   I am very glad you thought the answer [*King Charles the First, the author of ' Icon Basilike '* (1828)] appeared to you triumphant, for it had struck me as, in the main points, knowledge of the subject, and spirit in the writing, and accuracy in the logic, one of the best controversial tracts I ever read.   *To Southey*,   XII, 1828

Wordsworth, Dora.   See under Quillinan, Dora

Wordsworth, Dorothy

1.*   Indeed for other reasons William values it [Dorothy's *Journal*] so highly. . . . *D. W. to C. Clarkson*,   Christmas Day, 1805
2.*   [W.] very much pleased [with *Address to a Child* (*Oxf.* p. 80), and *The Cottager to her Infant* (*Oxf. W.*, pp. 117-18)].
D. W. to Lady Beaumont,   IV. 20, 1806
3.*   My brother is interested when I read it [her *Journal*] to him—
D. W. to C. R. (*Corr. C. R.*, i, 116).   III. 3, 1822
4.   See W. 27
5.   [Coleridge] and my beloved sister are the two beings to whom my intellect is most indebted. . . . *To W. R. Hamilton*,   VI. 25, 1832
6.   Details in the spirit of these sonnets [*Oxf. W.*, p. 335] are given both in Mary's Journal and my sister's; and the reperusal of them has strengthened a wish long entertained, that somebody would put together, as in one work, the notes contained in them, omitting particulars that were written down merely to aid our memory, and bringing the whole into as small a compass as is consistent with the general interests belonging to the scenes, circumstances, and objects touched on by each writer.
Grosart, iii, 77.   1843[K.]

Wordsworth, John

1.   [C. W.'s eldest son, John] I have reason to believe was one of the best scholars in Europe. *To Lady Bentinck*,   I. 3, 1840

Wordsworth, Mary.   See Wordsworth, Dorothy 6; W. 80-1

Wordsworth, William, Jr.

1.   One thing is remarkable, that his Letters are written in a most easy fluent, and sometimes elegant Style, though he has scarcely written half a dozen in his whole life. . . . *To C. W.*,   III. 15, 1829

Wrangham, Francis

1.   I suppose you were too busy to go on with *The Destruction of Babylon.* I don't think you have much occasion to regret your having been otherwise employed. The subject is certainly not a bad one, but I cannot help thinking your talents might be more happily employed.
To Wrangham,   XI. 20, 1795

2.   . . . and hope you will not suffer your *promotion* to interfere with the advancement of your Literary reputation, or to rob your friends and the public of the pleasure to be derived from the pieces you are possessed of.
To Wrangham,   III. 7, 1796

3.   Your verses are good, but having lost my Juvenal I cannot compare them with the original. There is one weak line, ' Urged by avarices,' etc. ' murderers shall *die*,' after ' whips racks and torture,' sounds weak.
To Wrangham (p. 161),   1796

4.   I read with great pleasure a very elegant and tender poem of yours in the 2nd vol: of the Anthology. It is a pity but that you could have avoided in the last Stanzas of that poem a vulgar use of the word ' charms ': in other respects the poem is very pleasing and as I recollect altogether unobjectionable. *To Wrangham,*   I or II, 1801

5.   I have hurried through your songs which I think admirably adapted for the intended purpose. ' A song or a story may drive away care,' etc., pleased me best, but I shall be able to judge better upon a more leisurely perusal. *To Wrangham* (p. 355),   early in 1804

6.   Your epigrams were amusing enough; the last, I think, was the best. . . . *To Wrangham,*   VII. 12, 1807

7.   Your . . . prose translations from Milton are excellent [see Milton 40].
To Wrangham,   IV. 17, 1808

8.   Is there any topographical History of your neighbourhood? would it not be worth your while to give some of your leisure hours to a work of this kind? I remember reading White's *Natural History and Antiquities of Selborne* with great pleasure when a Boy at school, and I have lately read Dr. Whitaker's history of Craven and Whalley both with profit and pleasure. Making these partly your models, and adding thereto from the originality of your own mind [   ] with your activity you might [? produce] some thing of this kind and general interest, taking for your limits any division in your neighbourhood, natural, ecclesiastical, or Civil. . . . I am induced to mention it from belief that you are admirably qualified for such a work [topographical history]; that it would pleasantly employ your leisure hours; and from a regret in seeing works of this kind which might be made so very interesting, utterly marred by falling into the hands of wretched Bunglers, e. g. the *History of Cleveland* which I have just read, by a Clergyman of Yarm of the name of Grave, the most heavy performance I ever encountered. . . .
To Wrangham,   X. 2, 1808

9.   Your sermon [*Earnest Contention for True Faith*]. . . . I believe we have all read it, and are much pleased with it. Upon the whole I like it better than the last. . . . *To Wrangham,*   XII. 3, 1808

10.   . . . your versions of Virgil's Eclogues, [fifty copies printed in 1815, published in 1830] which reached me at last. I have lately compared it line for line with the original, and think it very well done. I was particularly pleased with the skill you have shewn in managing the Contest between the Shepherds in the third Pastoral, where you have included in a succession of couplets the sense of Virgil's paired hexameter. I think I mentioned to you that these poems of Virgil have always delighted me much; there is frequently in them an elegance and a happiness which no translation can hope to equal. In point of fidelity your translation is very good indeed.
To Wrangham,   II. 19, 1819

Wycliffe, John

1.   . . . Wicliffe, like the sun, shot orient beams through the night of Romish superstition!
Ans. to Mathetes (*Grosart,* i, 314).   I. 4, 1810

2.   How the bold Teacher's Doctrine, sanctified
         By truth, shall spread, throughout the world dispersed.
         2 Ecc. Sonn., xvii, 13-14.   1821

Young, Edward

1.   Meanwhile the Evangelists, Isaiah, Job,
     Moses, and he who penned, the other day,
     The death of Abel [Gessner's], Shakespeare, and the Bard
     Whose genius spangled o'er a gloomy theme
     With fancies thick as his inspiring stars [Young's *Night Thoughts*],
     And Ossian (doubt not—'tis the naked truth)
     Summoned from a streamy Morven—each and all
     Would, in their turns, lend ornaments and flowers
     To entwine the crook of eloquence that helped
     This pretty Shepherd, pride of all the plains,
     To rule and guide his captivated flock.
     Prel., vii, 562-72.   1804-39

2.   Out of the three last [philosophical satire, didactic, and idyllic poetry] has been constructed a composite order, of which Young's *Night Thoughts*, and Cowper's *Task*, are excellent examples. *Pref., 1815*, p. 954.   1815

3.   'Zanga' [*The Revenge*] is a bad imitation of ' Othello.'
C. W., Jr. (*Grosart,* iii, 460).   *c.* 1827

Zoilus.   See Jeffrey 10

PART THREE

WORDSWORTH ON HIS OWN WORKS

WORDSWORTH ON HIS OWN WORKS

Poems Written in Youth

Extract

1. . . . the first verses which I wrote were a task imposed by my master; the subject, ' The Summer Vacation '; and of my own accord I added others upon ' Return to School.' There was nothing remarkable in either poem. . . . These verses were much admired, far more than they deserved, for they were but a tame imitation of Pope's versification, and a little in his style. This exercise, however, put it into my head to compose verses from the impulse of my own mind, and I wrote, while yet a schoolboy, a long poem running upon my own adventures, and the scenery of the country in which I was brought up. The only part of that which has been preserved is the conclusion of it, which stands at the beginning of my collected Poems [' Dear native regions,' etc.]. *Grosart*, iii, 221. XI, 1847

2. See W. 289

An Evening Walk

3. It was with great reluctance I huddled up those two little works [*An Evening Walk*, and *Descriptive Sketches* (1793)], and sent them into the world in so imperfect a state. But as I had done nothing by which to distinguish myself at the University, I thought these little things might shew that I could do something. They have been treated with unmerited contempt by some of the periodical publications, and others have spoken in higher terms of them than they deserve. I have another poem [*Guilt and Sorrow*] written last summer, ready for the press, though I certainly should not publish it unless I hope to derive from it some pecuniary recompense.
To Wm. Mathews, V. 23, 1794

4. See W. 9

5. There is not an image in it which I have not observed; and, now in my seventy-third year, I recollect the time and place where most of them were noticed. . . . I will mention another image:

> ' And fronting the bright west, yon oak entwines
> Its darkening boughs and leaves in stronger lines.'

This is feebly and imperfectly exprest; but I recollect distinctly the very spot where this first struck me. It was on the way between Hawkshead and Ambleside, and gave me extreme pleasure. The moment was important in my poetical history; for I date from it my consciousness of the infinite variety of natural appearances which had been unnoticed by the poets of any age

389

or country, so far as I was acquainted with them; and I made a resolution to supply in some degree the deficiency. I could not have been at that time above fourteen years of age. . . . I will conclude my notice of this poem by observing that the plan of it has not been confined to a particular walk, or an individual place; a proof (of which I was unconscious at the time) of my unwillingness to submit the poetic spirit to the chains of fact and real circumstance. The country is idealized rather than described in any one of its local aspects. *I. F.* (*Grosart*, iii, 4-5).   1843

Descriptive Sketches

6.   See Picturesque 1; Ramond 1; W. 3

9.   . . . in truth my life has been unusually barren of events, and my opinions have grown slowly, and I may say insensibly.

You ask me if I have always throught so independently. To this question I am able to give a satisfactory answer by referring you to two poems, which I published in the beginning of the year 1793. The one is entitled ' Descriptive Sketches made during a Pedestrian Tour in the Italian, Grison, Swiss and Savoyard Alps,' the other ' an Evening Walk, an Epistle addressed to a Young Lady.' . . . They are juvenile productions, inflated and obscure, but they contain many new images, and vigorous lines; and they would perhaps interest you, by shewing how very widely different my former opinions must have been from those which I hold at present.

To Miss Taylor,   IV. 9, 1801

10.   [" Stanzas upon Einsiedeln " in *Descriptive Sketches*, 545-68.] See W. 172

Guilt and Sorrow

11.   You inquired after the name of one of my poetical bantlings. Children of this species ought to be named after their characters, and here I am at a loss, as my offspring seems to have no character at all. I have however christened it by the appellation of Salisbury Plain [The poem named *The Female Vagrant* in the *Lyrical Ballads* (1798); afterwards, *Guilt and Sorrow; or Incidents upon Salisbury Plain.*]; though, A night on Salisbury plain,—were it not so insufferably awkward—would better suit the thing itself. *To Wm. Mathews*,   XI. 7, 1794

12.   . . . I have made alterations and additions so material as that it may be looked on almost as another work. Its object is partly to expose the vices of the penal law and the calamities of war as they affect individuals.

To F. Wrangham,   XI. 20, 1795

13.   I also took courage to devote two days (O Wonder) to the Salisbury Plain. I am resolved to discard Robert Walford and invent a new story for the woman. The poem is finished all but her tale. Now by way of a pretty moving accident and to bind together in palpable knots the story of the piece I have resolved to make her the widow or sister or daughter of the man whom the poor Tar murdered. So much for the vulgar. Further· the Poet's invention goeth not. This is by way of giving a physical totality to

the piece, which I regard as finished minus 24 stanzas, the utmost tether allowed to the poor Lady. *To Coleridge,* II. 27, 1799

14. See Style 17

15.* . . . it was addressed to coarse sympathies, and had little or no imagination about it, nor invention as to story. . . . it is one of my worst poems, nevertheless—merely descriptive, although the description is accurate enough. *Collier's Preface,* p. li. II. 10, 1814

16. The monuments and traces of antiquity, scattered in abundance over that region, led me unavoidably to compare what we know or guess of those remote times with certain aspects of modern society, and with calamities, principally those consequent upon war, to which, more than other classes of men, the poor are subject. In those reflections, joined with particular facts that had come to my knowledge, the following stanzas originated. *Oxf. W.*, p. 24. I. 24, 1842

17. Mr. Coleridge, when I first became acquainted with him, was so much impressed with this poem, that it would have encouraged me to publish the whole as it then stood; but the Mariner's fate appeared to me so tragical, as to require a treatment more subdued, and yet more strictly applicable in expression, than I had at first given to it. This fault was corrected nearly fifty years afterwards, when I determined to publish the whole. It may be worth while to remark, that though the incidents of this attempt do only in a small degree produce each other, and it deviates accordingly from the general rule by which narrative pieces ought to be governed, it is not therefore wanting in continuous hold upon the mind, or in unity, which is effected by the identity of moral interest that places the two personages upon the same footing in the reader's sympathies. *I. F.* (*Grosart*, iii, 11). 1843

The Borderers

18. See Character Analysis 6

19. Having, however, impressions upon my mind which made me unwilling to destroy the MS., I have determined to undertake the responsibility of publishing it during my own life, rather than impose upon my successors the task of deciding its fate. Accordingly it has been revised with some care; but, as it was at first written, and is now published, without any view to its exhibition upon the stage, not the slightest alteration has been made in the conduct of the story, or the composition of the characters; above all, in respect to the two leading Persons of the Drama, I felt no inducement to make any change. The study of human nature suggests this awful truth, that, as in the trial to which life subjects us, sin and crime are apt to start from their very opposite qualities, so there are no limits to the hardening of the heart, and the perversion of the understanding to which they may carry their slaves. During my long residence in France, while the Revolution was rapidly advancing to its extreme of wickedness, I had frequent opportunities of being an eye-witness of this process, and it was while that knowledge was fresh upon my memory that the Tragedy of the *Borderers* was composed. *Grosart*, iii, 14. 1842

14

20.   I am glad you like the tragedy. I was myself surprised to find the interest so kept up in the fourth and fifth Acts. Of the third I never doubted, and quite agree with you that Herbert's speech is much the finest thing in the drama; I mean the most moving, or rather, the most in that style of the pathetic which one loves to dwell upon, though I acknowledge it is not so intensely dramatic as some parts of the fifth act especially.

As to the first, my only fear was that the *action* was too far advanced in it. I think the scene where the vagrant tells her false story has great merit; it is thoroughly natural and yet not commonplace nature.

Some of the sentiments which the development of Oswald's character required will, I fear, be complained of as too depraved for anything but biographical writing. *To Dora*,   IV. 7, 1842

21.   Had it been the work of a later period of life, it would have been different in some respects from what it is now. The plot would have been something more complex, and a greater variety of characters introduced, to relieve the mind from the pressure of incidents so mournful; the manners also would have been more attended to. My care was almost exclusively given to the passions and the characters, and the position in which the persons in the drama stood relatively to each other, that the reader (for I never thought of the stage at the time it was written) might be moved, and to a degree instructed, by lights penetrating somewhat into the depths of our nature. In this endeavour, I cannot think, upon a very late review, that I have failed. As to the scene and period of action, little more was required for my purpose than the absence of established law and government, so that the agents might be at liberty to act on their own impulses. Nevertheless, I do remember, that having a wish to colour the manners in some degree from local history more than my knowledge enabled me to do, I read Redpath's *History of the Borders*, but found there nothing to my purpose. . . . For myself, I had no hope, nor even a wish (though a successful play would in the then state of my finances have been a most welcome piece of good fortune), that he should accept my performance; so that I incurred no disappointment when the piece was *judiciously* returned as not calculated for the stage. In this judgment I entirely concurred; and had it been otherwise, it was so natural for me to shrink from public notice, that any hope I might have had of success would not have reconciled me altogether to such an exhibition. . . . In conclusion, I may observe, that while I was composing this play, I wrote a short essay, illustrative of that constitution and those tendencies of human nature, which make the apparently *motiveless* actions of bad men intelligible to careful observers. This was partly done with reference to the character of Oswald, and his persevering endeavour to lead the man he disliked into so heinous a crime; but still more to preserve in my distinct remembrance what I had observed of transitions in character, and the reflections I had been led to make, during the time I was a witness of the changes through which the French Revolution passed.

I. F. (Grosart, iii, 12-13).   1843

Poems Referring to the Period of Childhood

21A.   It may be proper in this place to state, that the extracts in the second class, entitled " Juvenile Pieces," are in many places altered from the printed copy, chiefly by omission and compression. The slight alterations of another kind were for the most part made not long after the publications of the Poems from which the extracts were taken. These extracts seem to have a title to be placed here, as they were the productions of youth, and represent implicitly some of the features of a youthful mind, at a time when images of nature supplied to it the place of thought, sentiment, and almost of action; or, as it will be found expressed, of a state of mind when [see *Tintern Abbey*, 76-83]. I will own that I was much at a loss what to select of these descriptions: and perhaps it would have been better either to have reprinted the whole, or suppressed what I have given.

Pref., 1815 (*K. Prose*, ii, 206-7). [Omitted 1845.]   1815

Alice Fell

22.   The humbleness, meanness if you like, of the subject, together with the homely mode of treating it, brought upon me a world of ridicule by the small critics, so that in policy I excluded it from many editions of my Poems, till it was restored at the request of some of my friends, in particular my son-in-law, Edward Quillinan. *I. F.* (*Grosart*, iii, 15).   1843

Lucy Gray

23.   The way in which the incident was treated, and the spiritualising of the character, might furnish hints for contrasting the imaginative influences, which I have endeavoured to throw over common life, with Crabbe's matter-of-fact style of handling subjects of the same kind. This is not spoken to his disparagement, far from it; but to direct the attention of thoughtful readers into whose hands these notes may fall, to a comparison that may enlarge the circle of their sensibilities, and tend to produce in them a catholic judgment. *I. F.* (*Grosart*, iii, 16). [See also W. 345A.]   1843

We are Seven

23A.   See Aim of Writing 7

24.   My friends will not deem it too triffling to relate, that while walking to and fro I composed the last stanza first, having begun with the last line.

I. F. (*Grosart*, iii, 17-18).   1843

25.*   [Coleridge wrote the first verse beginning " A simple child."]

Whately, p. 205.   *c.* 1843

The Idle Shepherd-boys

26.   In describing a tarn under Helvellyn, I say,

> ' There sometimes doth a leaping fish
> Send through the tarn a lonely cheer.'

This was branded by a critic of those days, in a review ascribed to Mrs. Barbauld, as unnatural and absurd, I admire the genius of Mrs. Barbauld, and am certain that, had her education been favourable to imaginative influences, no female of her day would have been more likely to sympathise with that image, and to acknowledge the truth of the sentiment.

I. F. (Grosart, iii, 19).   1843

Rural Architecture

27.   From the meadows of Armath, etc. [line 1, ed. 1827]. My sister objected so strongly to this alteration at the time that—her judgment being confirmed by yours—the old reading may be restored.

To B. Field,   X. 24, 1828

The Norman Boy

28.   . . . not improbably the fact is illustrative of the boy's early piety, and may concur, with my other little pieces on children, to produce profitable reflection among my youthful readers. This is said, however, with an absolute conviction that children will derive most benefit from books which are not unworthy the perusal of persons of any age. I protest with my whole heart against those productions, so abundant in the present day, in which the doings of children are dwelt upon as if they were incapable of being interested in anything else. On this subject I have dwelt at length in the Poem on the growth of my own mind [*Prelude*].

I. F. (Grosart, iii, 21-2).   1843

POEMS FOUNDED ON THE AFFECTIONS

29.   . . . omitting to speak of them [" Poems Founded on the Affections "] individually, do they not, taken collectively, fix the attention upon a subject eminently poetical, viz., the interest which objects in nature derive from the predominance of certain affections more or less permanent, more or less capable of salutary renewal in the mind of the being contemplating these objects? This is poetic, and essentially poetic, and why? because it is creative. *To Lady Beaumont,*   V. 21, 1807

30.   See Poetry 68

The Brothers

31.   . . . I have begun the pastoral of Bowman [Bowman: the name of the youth called James Ewbank in *The Brothers*. On the previous Nov. 12, W. had been with C. at Ennerdale, and there heard of Bowman's tragic fall. De Sel.]: in my next letter I shall probably be able to send it to you. I am afraid it will have one fault, that of being too long.

To Coleridge (p. 237),   1799

32.   See Aim of Writing 7; Gilbert 1; W. 48, 364A

33.   [W. states that in *The Brothers* and in *Ruth* he is exhibiting the influence of nature on the character of man.] But it seems that to produce these effects, in the degree in which we frequently find them to be produced, there must be a peculiar sensibility of original organization combining with moral accidents [as exhibited in these poems]. . . .

To John Wilson (p. 294).   VI, 1802

Artegal and Elidure

34.   What wonder then, if in such ample field
    [Geoffrey of Monmouth's *Chronicle*]
    Of old tradition, one particular flower
    Doth seemingly in vain its fragrance yield,
    And bloom unnoticed even to this late hour?
    Now, gentle Muses, your assistance grant,
     While I this flower transplant
    Into a garden stored with Poesy;
    Where flowers and herbs unite, and haply some weeds be,
    That, wanting not wild grace, are from all mischief free!
    Artegal and Elidure, 57-65.   1815

35. This was written in the year 1815, as a token of affectionate respect for the memory of Milton. *Grosart*, iii, 22.   1843 [K.]

"She dwelt among the untrodden ways"

36. In the last stanza of this little poem [earlier form of "She dwelt among the untrodden ways." See *E. L.*, p. 204-5] you will consider the words 'Long time' as put in merely to fill up the measure but as injurious to the sense. *W. and D. W. to Coleridge*,   XII, 1798 or I, 1799

The Complaint of a Forsaken Indian Woman. See Aim of Writing 7

The Emigrant Mother

37.* 'Once in a lonely hamlet I sojourned' . . . displays, he says, more than other of his poems a profound knowledge of Womans heart—he could feel no respect for the Mother who could read it with-[out] emotion & admiration—Wordsworth quotes his own Verses with pleasure And seems to attach to the approbation of them a greater connection with moral worth which others may deem the effect of vanity. . . .

C. R. to T. R. (Corr. C. R., i, 53),   III, 1808

38. See Poetry 47

Vaudracour and Julia

39. See Subjects 13

40.   . . .
    For Vaudracour and Julia (so were named
    The ill-fated pair) in that plain tale will draw
    Tears from the hearts of others, when their own
    Shall beat no more.
    Prel. ix, 565-68.   1804-39

41. The following tale was written as an Episode, in a work [*Prelude*, ix, 553-85] from which its length may perhaps exclude it. The facts are true; no invention as to these has been exercised, as none was needed.

Oxf. W., p. 121.   1820

The Idiot Boy

42. See Aim of Writing 7; Hine, J. 2; W. 87

43. [In discussing *The Idiot Boy*, and whom poetry should please, W. remarks on the variety of tastes, and of prejudices against expressions in "Her eyes are wild" and *The Thorn*, and adds that a poem should please those] who lead the simplest lives, and those most according to nature; men who have never known false refinements, wayward and artificial desires, false criticisms, effeminate habits of thinking and feeling, or who, having known these things, have outgrown them. This latter class is the most to be depended upon, but it is very small in number. [To understand *The Idiot Boy* one must understand the life of the cottage, of the fields, and of children.] A man must have done this habitually before his judgment upon *The Idiot Boy* would be in any way decisive with me. I *know* I have done this myself habitually; I wrote the poem with exceeding delight and pleasure, and whenever I read it I read it with pleasure.

To John Wilson (p. 295),   VI, 1802

44. . . . You have given me praise for having reflected faithfully in my Poems the feelings of human nature. I would fain hope that I have done so. But a great Poet ought to do more than this; he ought, to a certain degree, to rectify men's feelings, to give them new compositions of feeling, to render their feelings more sane, pure, and permanent, in short, more consonant to nature, that is, to eternal nature, and the great moving spirit of things. He ought to travel before men occasionally as well as at their sides. I may illustrate this by a reference to natural objects. What false notions have prevailed from generation to generation as to the true character of the Nightingale. As far as my Friend's Poem in the *Lyrical Ballads*, is read, it will contribute greatly to rectify these. You will recollect a passage in Cowper, where, speaking of rural sounds, he says,

> And *even* the boding owl
> That hails the rising moon has charms for me.

Cowper was passionately fond of natural objects, yet you see he mentions it as a marvellous thing that he could connect pleasure with the cry of the owl. In the same poem he speaks in the same manner of that beautiful plant, the gorse; making in some degree an amiable boast of his loving it, *unsightly* and unsmooth as it is. There are many aversions of this kind, which, though they have some foundation in nature, have yet so slight a one that, though they may have prevailed hundreds of years, a philosopher will look upon them as accidents. So with respect to many moral feelings, either of love or dislike. . . . So with regard to birth, and innumerable other modes of sentiment, civil and religious. But you will be inclined to ask by this time how all this applies to *The Idiot Boy*. To this I can only say that the loathing and disgust which many people have at the sight of an idiot, is a feeling which, though having some foundation in human nature, is not necessarily attached to it in any virtuous degree, but is owing in a great measure to a false delicacy, and, if I may say it without rudeness, a certain want of comprehensiveness of thinking and feeling. . . . [Now follows a discussion of

the reverence felt for idiots among certain social classes and national groups.]
A friend of mine, knowing that some persons had a dislike to the poem,
such as you have expressed, advised me to add a stanza, describing the person
of the boy so as entirely to separate him in the imaginations of my readers
from that class of idiots who are disgusting in their persons; but the narration
in the poem is so rapid and impassioned, that I could not find a place in
which to insert the stanza without checking the progress of the poem, and
so leaving a deadness upon the feeling. This poem has, I know, frequently
produced the same effect as it did upon you and your friends; but there are
many also to whom it affords exquisite delight, and who, indeed, prefer it to
any other of my poems. This proves that the feelings there delineated are such
as men *may* sympathize with. This is enough for my purpose. It is not enough
for me as a Poet, to delineate merely such feelings as all men *do* sympathize
with; but it is also highly desirable to add to these others, such as all men
may sympathize with, and such as there is reason to believe they would be
better and more moral beings if they did sympathize with.

To John Wilson,   VI, 1802

46. Let me add, that this long poem was composed in the groves of
Alfoxden, almost extempore; not a word, I believe, being corrected, though
one stanza was omitted. I mention this in gratitude to those happy moments,
for, in truth, I never wrote anything with so much glee.

Grosart, iii, 27.   1843 [K.]

47.* [W. demanded its publication in every edition of his poems.]

C. R. to J. Mottram (Corr. C. R., ii, 819),   IX. 12, 1857

Michael

48.   But were I assured that I myself had a just claim to the title of a
Poet, all the dignity being attached to the Word which belongs to it, I do
not think that I should have ventured for that reason to offer these volumes to
you: at present it is solely on account of two poems in the second volume,
the one entitled ' *The Brothers,*' and the other ' *Michael,*' that I have been
emboldened to take this liberty.

. . . In the two poems, ' *The Brothers* ' and ' *Michael* ' I have attempted
to draw a picture of the domestic affections as I know they exist amongst a
class of men who are now almost confined to the North of England. They are
small independent *proprietors* of land here called statesmen, men of respectable education who daily labour on their own little properties. The domestic
affections will always be strong amongst men who live in a country not
crowded with population, if these men are placed above poverty. But if
they are proprietors of small estates, which have descended to them from
their ancestors, the power which these affections will acquire amongst such
men is inconceivable by those who have only had an opportunity of observing
hired labourers, farmers, and the manufacturing Poor. Their little tract of
land serves as a kind of permanent rallying point for their domestic feelings,
as a tablet upon which theu are written which makes them objects of memory
in a thousand instances when they would otherwise be forgotten. It is a
fountain fitted to the nature of social man from which supplies of affection,

as pure as his heart was intended for, are daily drawn. [See all of this letter for additional details.] *To Chas. J. Fox,*   I. 14, 1801

49.   In the last Poem of my 2nd Vol. I have attempted to give a picture of a man, of strong mind and lively sensibility, agitated by two of the most powerful affections of the human heart; the parental affection, and the love of property, *landed* property, including the feelings·of inheritance, home, and personal and family independence. This Poem has, I know, drawn tears from the eyes of more than one—persons well acquainted with the manners of the Statesmen, as they are called, of this country; and, moreover, persons who never wept, in reading verse, before. This is a favourable augury for me. . . . I had a still further wish that this poem should please you, because in writing it I had your character often before my eyes, and sometimes thought I was delineating such a man as you yourself would have been under the same circumstances. *To T. Poole,*   IV. 9, 1801

50.   See W. 364A

The Armenian Lady's Love.   See Digby 2; Percy 4

Her Eyes are Wild [*earlier **The Mad Mother***].   See Aim of Writing
    7; W. 43

POEMS ON THE NAMING OF PLACES

55.   This class of poems I suppose to consist chiefly of objects most interesting to the mind not by its personal feelings or a strong appeal to the instincts or natural affections, but to be interesting to a meditative or imaginative mind either from the moral importance of the pictures or from the to employment they give to the understanding affected through the imagination and to the higher faculties. *To Coleridge,*   early V, 1809

POEMS OF FANCY

A Morning Exercise.   See W. 102

To the Daisy

57.   This Poem, and two others to the same flower, were written in the year 1802; which is mentioned, because in some of the ideas, though not in the manner in which those ideas are connected, and likewise even in some of the expressions, there is a resemblance to passages in a Poem (lately published) of Mr. [James] Montgomery's, entitled a 'Field Flower.' This being said, Mr. Montgomery will not think any apology due to him. . . .
I. F. (Grosart, iii, 32).   1843

To a Skylark.   See Passion 51; Shelley 12

The Seven Sisters

60.   I had almost forgotten to request you would employ somebody to transcribe for me those Verses ' Seven Daughters had Lord Archibald ' etc.,

I mean if you think they would have any effect in my intended Vol: either for their own sakes or for the sake of variety. I stumbled upon the first draught of that Poem some little time since and it seemed to me sad stuff; perhaps the more finished Copy which I think you said you have may turn out better. If it gives you any pleasure your judgment shall decide and I will print it. . . . *To W. Scott,* XI. 10, 1806

" Who fancied what a pretty sight." See W. 79

The Kitten and Falling Leaves

62.* . . . merely fanciful. . . . *H. C. R.,* i, 89. V. 31, 1812

Address to my Infant Daughter, Dora. See Fancy 14A

The Waggoner

63.* *Benjamin the Waggoner* has far less meaning. It is, says Wordsworth, purely fanciful. *H. C. R.,* i, 101. VI. 4, 1812

64. See W. 118

65. The 'Waggoner' was written con amore, as the Epilogue states almost in my own despite; I am not therefore surprised that you read it with pleasure; composing widely as you do from unborrowed feelings.
To Hans Busk, VII. 6, 1819

66. When the Poem was first written the note of the bird was thus described [see Canto i, l. 3]:

> ' The Night-hawk is singing his frog-like tune,
> Twirling his watchman's rattle about '

but from unwillingness to startle the reader at the outset by so bold a mode of expression, the passage was altered as it now stands.
Grosart, iii, 37. 1836

67.* It seems a very favourite poem of his, and he read me splendid descriptions from it. He said his object in it had not been understood. It was a play of the fancy on a domestic incident and lowly character: he wished by the opening descriptive lines to put his reader into the state of mind in which he wished it to be read. If he failed in doing that, he wished him to lay it down. He pointed out, with the same view, the glowing lines on the state of exultation in which Ben and his companions are under the influence of liquor. Then he read the sickening languor of the morning walk, contrasted with the glorious uprising of Nature, and the songs of the birds.
Justice Coleridge (Grosart, iii, 429-30). X. 10, 1836

68. The character and story from fact. *I. F. (Grosart,* iii, 36). 1843

POEMS OF THE IMAGINATION

69. See Imagination 32A

There was a Boy. See Imagination 34

To the Cuckoo

70.   See Poetry 58

71.*   He afterwards spoke of his own poem, ' The Cuckoo,' with such warm praise as to make it evident to me that, if he did not consider it his best of its kind, it was a favorite with him, especially the opening [first stanza] . . . the merit did not so much consist in that thought which must be familiar to all, but in the power of recording what struck all as true, but what had never before been remarked upon; the Cuckoo was always heard, but never seen, and therefore poetically termed ' a wandering voice.' [Collier adds this note: See the Preface to the edition of Wordsworth's Poems, 6 vols. 12mo, 1836, I, p. xvi., where the poet quotes two of the lines (3-4) I have above extracted, and remarks upon them that " this concise interrogation characterises the seeming ubiquity of the voice of the cuckoo, and disposses the creature almost of corporeal existence."] I mentioned that I had several times seen the cuckoo, but Wordsworth observed that that made no difference as to the general accuracy.

Collier's Preface, pp. lii-liii and note.   II. 10, 1814

A Night-piece.   See Versification 30; W. 75

Yew-trees

75.*   Wordsworth particularly recommended to me among his Poems of Imagination *Yew Trees* and a description of Night [*A Night-piece*]. These, he says, are among the best for the imaginative power displayed in them.   *H. C. R.*, i, 166.   V. 9, 1815

76.   See Versification 30

She was a Phantom of Delight

77.*   The Poet expressly told me that the Verses [" She was a phantom of delight "] were on his Wife.

C. R.'s Note on L. from Mrs. Clarkson (*Corr. C. R.*, i, 464).   V, 1842

78.   The germ of this poem was four lines composed as a part of the verses on the Highland Girl. Though beginning in this way, it was written from my heart, as is sufficiently obvious.   *I. F.* (*Grosart*, iii, 39).   1843

"I wandered lonely as a cloud"

79.   [' The Daffodils,' and ' The Rock crowned with Snowdrops.'] I am sure that whoever is much pleased with either of these quiet and tender delineations must be fitted to walk through the recesses of my poetry with delight, and will there recognize, at every turn, something or other in which, and over which, it has that property and right which knowledge and love confer. *To Lady Beaumont*,   V. 21, 1807

80.   . . . two lines in that little Poem which if thoroughly felt, would annihilate nine tenths of the Reviews of the Kingdom, as they would find no Readers; the lines I alluded to, were those

> They flash upon that inward eye,
> Which is the bliss of Solitude.

To F. Wrangham, XI. 4, 1807

81. The two best lines [21-2] in it are by Mary. [See *Grosart*, iii, 39 and 40; also see 80 above.] *I. F. (Grosart*, iii, 39). 1843 [K.]

The Reverie of Poor Susan. See W. 270

Beggars

83. See Poetry 47

84.* . . . It is a poetical exhibition of the power of physical beauty & the charm of health & vigor in childhood even in a state of the greatest moral depravity. *C. R. to T. R. (Corr. C. R.*, i, 53), III, 1808

85. I will state the faults, real or supposed, which put me on the task of altering it [a long list of faults in diction follows].
To B. Field, X. 24, 1828

Ruth. See W. 33

Resolution and Independence

87. [W. writes Sara that he cannot take much satisfaction from pleasing her with the first part if the last part of the poem does not please her. He describes his feeling in writing the poem.] I describe myself as having been exalted to the highest pitch of delight by the joyousness and beauty of Nature and then as depressed, even in the midst of those beautiful objects, to the lowest dejection and despair. A young Poet in the midst of the happiness of Nature is described as overwhelmed by the thought of the miserable reverses which have befallen the happiest of all men, viz, Poets—I think of this till I am so deeply impressed by it, that I consider the manner in which I was rescued from my dejection and despair almost as an interposition of Providence. ' Now whether it was by peculiar grace A leading from above' . . . A person reading this Poem with feelings like mine will have been awed and controuled, expecting almost something spiritual or supernatural—What is brought forward? ' A lonely place, a Pond' ' by which an old man *was* far from all house or home '—Not stood, not sat, but ' *was* '—the figure presented in the most naked simplicity possible. This feeling of spirituality or supernaturalness is again referred to as being strong in my mind in this passage—' *How came he here* thought I or what can he be doing?' I then describe him, whether ill or well is not for me to judge . . . , but this I can *confidently* affirm, that, though I believe God has given me a strong imagination, I cannot conceive a figure more impressive than that of an old Man like this, the survivor of a Wife and ten children, travelling alone among the mountains and all lonely places, carrying with him his own fortitude, and the necessities which an unjust state of society has entailed upon him. [He adds that if the poem is not good until after the introduction of the old man, as Sara said, then it is a bad poem.] . . . there is no intermediate state. You speak of his speech as tedious: everything is tedious when one

does not read with the feelings of the Author—'*The Thorn*' is tedious to hundreds; and so is the *Idiot Boy* to hundreds. It is in the character of the old man to tell his story in a manner which an *impatient* reader must necessarily feel as tedious. But Good God! Such a figure in such a place a pious selfrespecting, miserably infirm, and [?] Old Man telling such a tale! . . . it is of the utmost importance that you should have had pleasure from contemplating the fortitude, independence, preserving spirit, and the general moral dignity of this old man's character. [See also the remarks on this poem in *Grosart*, ii, 206-7.]

D. W. and W. to Mary and Sara H. (pp. 305-6),   VI. 14, 1802

88.   Your objection to the word *view* ['view' only occurs in *Resolution and Independence*, stanza 9, omitted after 1815. It is there used as a noun. M. H. must have criticized its use as a verb in the early (lost) draft of the poem. De Sel.] is ill founded; substitute the word *see*, and it does not express my feeling. I speak as having been much impressed, and for a *length of time*, by the sight of the old man—*view* is used with propriety because there is continuousness in the thing—for example had I seen a man shoot at a bird, with the point of his gun behind his back, the action being instantaneous, I should say, The like I did never *see*—I speak in this place with the feeling upon me of having been, and being absolutely then, *viewing* the old man—'Sickness had by him' [*Res. and Ind.*, l. 69],I know not why you object to—The poem is throughout written in the language of men—'I suffered much by a sickness had by me long ago' is a phrase which anybody might use, as well as 'a sickness which I had long ago.'

In the Poem on leaving Grasmere in a stanza which I am sure none of you have understood. I find neither D. nor C. understand it. But first correct the first stanza thus:

> Farewell, thou little nook of mountain ground,
> Thou rocky corner in the lowest stair
> Of that magnificent temple which doth bound
> One side of our whole Vale with grandeur rare.

After the words 'blessed life which we lead here' insert the following stanza—

> Dear spot! which we have watched [etc. as *Oxf. W.*, p. 106]
> And oh most constant, yet most fickle Place
> That hast a wayward heart, as thou dost shew
> To them who look not daily on thy face,
> Who, being loved, in love no bounds dost know,
> And say'st when we forsake thee, let them go etc.

I have been obliged to alter the last stanza thus for both C. and D. supposed the word 'scorner' not to apply to myself, as I meant it, but any casual visitor, Tourist for example. This idea is as wretchedly mean as the other is beautiful. I have no doubt however that you certainly understood it as C. and D. have done, as my Idea was not developed as it ought to have been, and as I hope it is now. I am for the most part uncertain about my success in *altering* Poems; but in this case by the additional stanza I am sure I have produced a great improvement—Tell me your opinion—' Primrose vest ' cannot stand. I should never have thought of such an expression but in a Spenserian poem, Spenser having many such expressions—But here it cannot stand, if it were only on account of ' saffron coat,' an expression beautiful and appropriate. Let it stand thus:

> Here with its primroses the steep rock's breast
> Glittered at evening like a starry sky—

and thus the beautiful line is preserved.

D. W. and W. to Mary and Sarah Hutchinson (pp. 304-5),   VI. 14, 1802

89.* . . . the Old Man in his Leech Gatherer and the simile of the stone on the eminence [ll. 57-63] as an instance of an imaginative creation.

H. C. R., i, 90.   V. 31, 1812

The Thorn

90. The poem of *The Thorn*, as the reader will soon discover, is not supposed to be spoken in the author's own person: the character of the loquacious narrator will sufficiently show itself in the source of the story.

Adv. L. B. (*K. Prose*, i, 32).   1798

91. It was my wish in this poem to show the manner in which such men cleave to the same ideas; and to follow the turns of passion, always different, yet not palpably different, by which their conversation is swayed. I had two objects to attain; first, to represent a picture which should not be unimpressive, yet consistent with the character that should describe it; secondly, while I adhered to the style in which such persons describe, to take care that words, which in their minds are impregnated with passion, should likewise convey passion to readers who are not accustomed to sympathize with men feeling in that manner or using such language. It seemed to me that this might be done by calling in the assistance of lyrical and rapid metre. It was necessary that the poem, to be natural, should in reality move slowly; yet, I hoped that, by the aid of the metre, to those who should at all enter into the spirit of the poem, it would appear to move quickly. The Reader will have the kindness to excuse this note, as I am sensible that an introductory Poem is necessary to give this Poem its full effect. *Oxf. W.*, p. 899.   1800-5

92. See Wordiness 1; W. 43, 87

95. [*The Thorn*] is a favourite with me. . . . *To Beaumont*,   V. 1, 1805

Brougham Castle

96.* *Passion in Poetry.*—One day, speaking of passion as an element of poetry, he referred to his own poems, and said that he thought there was a stronger fire of passion than was elsewhere to be found among them in the lyrical burst near the conclusion of [*The Song at the Feast of Brougham Castle*]. *Graves* (*Grosart*, iii, 473-74).   *c.* 1840

Lines Composed a Few Miles above Tintern Abbey

97. This line [106-7] has a close resemblance to an admirable line

[*Night-Thoughts* (*Night*, vi, 427). K.] of Young's, the exact expression of which I do not recollect.   *Oxf. W.*, p. 207 note 1.   1798

98.   I have not ventured to call this Poem an Ode; but it was written with a hope that in the transitions and the impassioned music of the versification, would be found the principal requisites, of that species of composition. *Oxf. W.*, p. 901.   1802-5

99.   [Lines on the Wye (49-57).] See   Byron 6A; Gillies 6

100.*   [Emerson said that more contemplative readers preferred the first books of *The Excursion* and the sonnets to *Tintern Abbey*.] Yes, they are the better. *English Traits*, p. 23.   VIII. 28, 1833

French Revolution

101.   It was first published by Coleridge in his *Friend*, which is the reason of its having had a place in every edition of my poems since.
I. F. (*Grosart*, iii, 45).   1843 [K.]

" Yes, it was the mountain Echo "

101A.   The word ' rebounds ' [l. 17] I wish much to introduce here; for the imaginative warning turns upon the echo, which ought to be revived as near the conclusion as possible.   This rule of art holds equally good as to the theme of a piece of music, as in a poem. *To B. Field*,   X. 24, 1828

To a Skylark

102.   After having succeeded in the second *Skylark*, and in the conclusion of the poem entitled *A Morning Exercise* [*Oxf. W.*, p. 153] in my notice of this bird, I became indifferent to this poem. . . . I like, however, the beginning of it so well that, for the sake of that, I tacked to it the respectably-tame conclusion. *To B. Field*,   X. 24, 1828

Laodamia

103.   I have sent to the Printer another Stanza to be inserted in Laodamia after,

> ' While tears were thy best pastime, day and night: '

(not a full Stop as before) [*Laodamia*, ll. 115-126] . . . so I fear it must be altered from The oracle, lest these words should seem to allude to the other answer of the oracle which commanded the sacrifice of Iphigenia.
To De Quincey,   II. 8, 1815

104.   . . . that dialogue of yours, in which he [Southey] is introduced as a speaker with Porson. It had appeared (something I must say to my regret) in a Magazine, and I should have had the pleasure to hear the whole. . . . You have condescended to minute criticism upon the *Laodamia*. I concur with you in the first stanza, and had several times attempted to alter it upon your grounds. I cannot, however, accede to your objection to the ' second birth,' merely because the expression has been degraded by Conventiclers. I certainly meant nothing more by it than the *eadem cura*, and the *largior aether*, etc.,

of Virgil's 6th Æneid. All religions owe their origin or acceptation to the wish of the human heart to supply in another state of existence the deficiencies of this, and to carry still nearer to perfection whatever we admire in our present condition; so that there must be many modes of expression, arising out of this coincidence, or rather identity of feeling, common to all Mythologies; and under this observation I should shelter the phrase from your censure; but I may be wrong in the particular case, though certainly not in the general principle. This leads to a remark in your last, ' that you are disgusted with all books that treat of religion.' I am afraid it is a bad sign in me, that I have little relish for any other—even in poetry it is the imaginative only, viz., that which is conversant with, or turns upon infinity, that powerfully affects me,—perhaps I ought to explain: I mean to say that, unless in those passages where things are lost in each other, and limits vanish, and aspirations are raised, I read with something too much like indifference—but all great poets are in this view powerful Religionists, and therefore among many literary pleasures lost, I have not yet to lament over that of verse as departed.

To Landor,   I. 21, 1824

105.* Of his own poems he expressed himself with a confidence not unlikely to be misunderstood by strangers. . . . He asked me what I thought the finest elegiac composition in the language; and, when I diffidently suggested *Lycidas*, he replied, " You are not far wrong. It may, I think, be affirmed that Milton's *Lycidas* and my *Laodamia* are twin Immortals."

Life of Alaric Watts, i, 240.   *c.* 1840

107. . . . No stanza is omitted. The last but one is, however, substantially altered. . . . As first written the heroine was dismissed to happiness in Elysium. To what purpose then the mission of Protesilaus? He exhorts her to moderate her passion; the exhortation is fruitless, and no punishment follows. So it stood; at present she is placed among unhappy ghosts for disregard of the exhortation. Virgil also places her there; but compare the two passages, and give me *your* opinion. *To John W.,*   Autumn, 1831

108. The incident of the trees growing and withering put the subject into my thoughts, and I wrote with the hope of giving it a loftier tone than, so far as I know, has been given it by any of the ancients who have treated of it. It cost me more trouble than almost anything of equal length I have ever written. *I. F. (Grosart,* iii, 46).   1843

Dion

109. This poem was first introduced by a stanza that I have since transferred to the notes, for reasons there given; and I cannot comply with the request expressed by some of my friends, that the rejected stanza should be restored. I hope they will be content if it be hereafter immediately attached to the poem, instead of its being degraded to a place in the notes.

The ' reasons ' (*supra*) are thus given: This poem began with the following stanza, which has been displaced on account of its detaining the reader too long from the subject, and as rather precluding, than preparing for, the due effect of the allusion [I, 7-17] to the genius of Plato.

I. F. (Grosart, iii, 46).   1843

The Triad

110.   How strange that any one should be puzzled with the name *Triad, after* reading the poem! I have turned to Dr Johnson, and there find '*Triad, three united*,' and not a word more, as nothing more was needed. I should have been rather mortified if *you* had not liked the piece, as I think it contains some of the happiest verses I ever wrote. It had been promised several years to two of the party before a fancy fit for the performance struck me; it was then thrown off rapidly, and afterwards revised with care.
To Geo. H. Gordon,   XII. 15, 1828

111.   . . . the Triad is my *own* favorite. *To C. R.*,   XII. 18, 1828

The Wishing-gate

112.   [Has merit.] *To M. and Dora W.*,   III, 1828

Suggested by a Picture of the Bird of Paradise. See W. 249

On the Power of Sound

114.   I cannot call to mind a reason why you should not think some passages in ' The Power of Sound ' equal to anything I have produced; when first printed in ' Yarrow Revisited,' I placed it at the end of the Volume, and in the last edition of my poems, at the close of the Poems of Imagination, indicating thereby my *own* opinion of it. *To Dyce*,   XII. 23, 1837

Peter Bell

115.   Wishing not to be in debt when I return to England I have been lately employed in hewing down Peter Bell, with another dressing I think he will do, He has risen in my esteem. Heaven knows there was need. The third part I think *interesting*, a praise which I give myself with more pleasure as I know that in general I can lay little claim to it.
To Coleridge,   II. 27, 1799

116.   . . . remember that no Poem of mine will ever be popular. . . . I say not this in modest disparagement of the Poem, but in sorrow for the sickly taste of the Public in verse. The *People* would love the poem of ' Peter Bell,' but the *Public* (a very different Being) will never love it.
To Beaumont,   I or II, 1808

117.   . . . it first saw the light in the summer of 1798. During this long interval, pains have been taken at different times to make the production less unworthy of a favourable reception; or, rather, to fit it for filling *permanently* a station, however humble, in the Literature of our Country. This has, indeed, been the aim of all my endeavours in Poetry, which, you know, have been sufficiently laborious to prove that I deem the Art not lightly to be approached; and that the attainment of excellence in it may laudably be made the principal object of intellectual pursuit by any man who, with reasonable consideration for circumstances, has faith in his own impulses.

The Poem of ' Peter Bell,' as the Prologue will show, was composed under a belief that the Imagination not only does not require for its exercise the intervention of supernatural agency, but that, though such agency be excluded, the faculty may be called forth as imperiously and for kindred results of pleasure, by incidents, within the compass of poetic probability, in the humblest departments of daily life. Since that Prologue was written, *you* [Southey] have exhibited most splendid effects of judicious daring, in the opposite and usual course. Let this acknowledgment make my peace with the lovers of the supernatural; and I am persuaded it will be admitted that to you, as a Master in that province of the art, the following Tale, whether from contrast or congruity, is not an unappropriate offering. Accept it, then, as a public testimony of affectionate admiration from one with whose name yours has been often coupled (to use your own words) for evil and for good; and believe me to be, with earnest wishes that life and health may be granted you to complete the many important works in which you are engaged, and with high respect. . . . *To Southey (Oxf. W.,* p. 236),   IV. 7, 1819

118.   When I sent you, a few weeks ago, ' The tale of Peter Bell,' you asked ' why " The Waggoner " was not added? '—To say the truth,—from the higher tone of imagination, and the deeper touches of passion aimed at in the former, I apprehended, this little Piece could not accompany it without disadvantage. . . . Being therefore in some measure the cause of its present appearance, you must allow me the gratification of inscribing it to you; in acknowledgment of the pleasure I have derived from your writings. . . .
Oxf. W., p. 173.   V. 20, 1819

119.   A Book came forth of late, called PETER BELL:
    Not negligent the style;—the matter?—good
    As aught that song records of Robin Hood;
    Or Roy, renowned through many a Scottish dell;
    But some (who brook those hackneyed themes full well,
    Nor heat, at Tam o' Shanter's name, their blood)
    Waxed wroth, and with foul claws, a harpy brood,
    On Bard and Hero clamorously fell.
    Heed not, wild Rover once through heath and glen,
    Who mad'st at length the better life thy choice,
    Heed not such onset! nay, if praise of men
    To thee appear not an unmeaning voice,
    Lift up that grey-haired forehead, and rejoice
    In the just tribute of thy Poet's pen!
    " A Book came forth," 1-14.   1820

MISCELLANEOUS SONNETS, PART I

Upon the Sight of a Beautiful Picture

120.   The images of the smoke and the Travellers are taken from your Picture; the rest were added, in order to place the thought in a clear point of view, and for the sake of variety. *To Beaumont* (p. 468),   VIII. 28, 1811

121.   It is a favorite of mine, and I think not unworthy of the subject, which was a picture painted by our Friend Sir George Beaumont. . . . My

poems are not so extensively known but that a Reprint of this piece would be new to a great majority of the Readers of the Champion.
To Haydon,   I. 13, 1816

To Sleep. A flock of sheep

122. The line,

Come, blessed barrier, &c.,

in the 'Sonnet upon Sleep,' . . . had before been mentioned to me by Coleridge, and indeed by almost everybody who had heard it, as eminently beautiful. *To Lady Beaumont,*   V. 21, 1807

"Where lies the land." See Poetry 61

"With ships the sea"

124. [W. denies that he has fallen below himself in the sonnet, "With ships the sea."] . . . and will attempt now to illustrate it by a comment, which, I feel, will be inadequate to convey my meaning. There is scarcely one of my Poems which does not aim to direct the attention to some moral sentiment, or to some general principle, or law of thought, or of our intellectual constitution. For instance, in the present case, who is there that has not felt that the mind can have no rest among a multitude of objects, of which it either cannot make one whole, or from which it cannot single out one individual, whereupon may be concentrated the attention, divided among or distracted by a multitude? After a certain time we must either select one image or object, which must put out of view the rest wholly, or must subordinate them to itself while it stands forth as a Head:

> Now glowed the firmament
> With living sapphires; Hesperus, that *led*
> The starry host, rode brightest; till the Moon,
> Rising in clouded majesty, at length,
> Apparent *Queen,* unveiled *her peerless* light,
> And o'er the dark her silver mantle threw.

Having laid this down as a general principle, take the case before us. I am represented in the Sonnet as casting my eyes over the sea, sprinkled with a multitude of Ships, like the heavens with stars, my mind may be supposed to float up and down among them, in a kind of dreamy indifference with respect either to this or that one, only in a pleasurable state of feeling with respect to the whole prospect. 'Joyously it showed,' this continued till that feeling may be supposed to have passed away, and a kind of comparative listlessness or apathy to have succeeded, as at this line, 'Some veering up and down, one knew not why.' All at once, while I am in this state, comes forth an object, an individual, and my mind, sleepy and unfixed, is awakened and fastened in a moment. 'Hesperus, that *led* The starry host' is a poetical object, because the glory of his own Nature gives him the pre-eminence the moment he appears; he calls forth the poetic faculty, receiving its exertions as a tribute but this Ship in the Sonnet may, in a manner still more appropriate, be said to come upon a mission of the poetic Spirit, because in its own appearance and attributes it is barely sufficiently distinguished to rouse the creative faculty of the human mind to exertions at all times welcome, but doubly so when they come upon us when in a state of remissness. The mind being once fixed and roused, all the rest comes from itself; it is merely a lordly Ship, nothing more:

> This ship was naught to me, nor I to her,
> Yet I pursued her with a lover's look.

My mind wantons with grateful joy in the exercise of its own powers, and, loving its own creation,

> This ship to all the rest I did prefer,

making her a sovereign or a regent, and thus giving body and life to all the rest; mingling up this idea with fondness and praise—

> where she comes the winds must stir;

and concluding the whole with,

> On went She, and due north her journey took.

Thus taking up again the Reader with whom I began, letting him know how long I must have watched this favourite Vessel, and inviting him to rest his mind as mine is resting.

To Lady Beaumont, V. 21, 1807

Miscellaneous Sonnets, Part II

"How sweet it is, when." See Poetry 61

To B. R. Haydon

126. In regard to that addressed to yourself, you deserve a much higher Compliment; but from the nature of the subject it may be found pretty generally interesting. The two others ["While not a leaf" and "How clear, how keen"], particularly the Snow-crested Mountain, full surely are morsels only for the few. *To B. R. Haydon,* I. 13, 1816

Composed after a Journey across the Hambleton Hills

127. The subject was our own confinement contrasted with hers; but it was not thought worthy of being preserved.

I. F. (Grosart, iii, 58). 1843

"While not a leaf." See W. 126

129. In the Champion, another weekly journal, have appeared not long since five sonnets of mine, all of them much superior to the one ["While not a leaf"] you have sent me. *To Gillies,* IV. 9, 1816

130. This conclusion [ll. 9-14] has more than once, to my great regret, excited painfully sad feelings in the hearts of young persons fond of poetry and poetic composition by contrast of their feeble and declining health with

that state of robust constitution which prompted me to rejoice in a season of frost and snow as more favourable to the Muses than summer itself.
I. F. (*Grosart*, iii, 58).   1843

"How clear, how keen."   See W. 126

Composed upon Westminster Bridge.   See W. 217

MISCELLANEOUS SONNETS, PART III

To the Author's Portrait

133.   The six last lines of this sonnet are not written for poetical effect, but as a matter of fact, which in more than one instance could not escape my notice in the servants of the house.
I. F. (*Grosart*, iii, 64).   1843

"Why art thou silent!"

133A.*   [Merely] an act of the intellect.
Corr. Taylor, p. 73.   VI. 11, 1836

134.   . . . a bird's-nest half filled with snow. Out of this comfortless appearance arose this Sonnet, which was, in fact, written without the least reference to any individual object, but merely to prove to myself that I could, if I thought fit, write in a strain that poets have been fond of.
I. F. (*Grosart*, iii, 64).   1843

"A Poet! He hath put"

135.   I was impelled to write this Sonnet by the disgusting frequency with which the word *artistical*, imported with other impertinencies from the Germans, is employed by writers of the present day. For ' artistical ' let them substitute ' artificial,' and the poetry written on this system, both at home and abroad, will be, for the most part, much better characterised.
I. F. (*Grosart*, iii, 64).   1843

On a Portrait of the Duke of Wellington

136.   As the Sonnet first stood, there was a pleonasm. . . .
To Haydon (p. 1038),   IX. 11, 1840

Composed on a May Morning.   See W. 217
"Hark! 'tis the thrush."   See W. 217

"Oh what a Wreck!"

139.   The thought in the sonnet as it now stands has ever been a consolation to me, almost as far back as I can remember, and hope that, thus expressed, it may prove so to others makes one wish to print it; but your mother seems to think it would be applied at once to your dear aunt. I own I do not

see the force of this objection; but if you and Miss Fenwick and others should be of the same mind, it shall be suppressed. *To Dora,*   II-III, 1838

"Wansfell: this Household"

140.*   . . . he declares to be one of his most perfect as a work of art.
H. C. R., ii, 628.   I. 1, 1843

"While beams of orient light." See W. 217

MEMORIALS OF A TOUR IN SCOTLAND, 1803

141.   See Imagination 32A

Ellen Irwin

142.   It may be worth while to observe, that as there are Scotch poems on this subject, in the simple ballad strain, I thought it would be both presumptuous and superfluous to attempt treating it in the same way; and accordingly, I chose a construction of stanza quite new in our language; in fact, the same as that of Bürgher's 'Leonora,' except that the first and third lines do not in my stanzas rhyme. At the outset, I threw out a classical image, to prepare the reader for the style in which I meant to treat the story, and so to preclude all comparison. *I. F.* (*Grosart,* iii, 66).   1843

142A.   See W. 242

To a Highland Girl

143.*   . . . of the highest kind being imaginative. . . .
H. C. R., i, 89.   V. 31, 1812

144.   See Rogers 2

Yarrow Unvisited

145.   See W. 151

146.*   . . . Scott misquoted in one of his novels my lines [43-4] on *Yarrow.* He makes me write,

> " The swans on sweet St. Mary's lake
> Float double, swans and shadow; "

but I wrote

> " The *swan* on *still* St. Mary's lake."

Never could I have written " swans " in the plural. The scene when I saw it, with its still and dim lake, under the dusky hills, was one of utter loneliness: there was *one* swan, and one only, stemming the water, and the pathetic loneliness of the region gave importance to the one companion of that swan, its own white image in the water. It was for that reason that I recorded the Swan and the Shadow. Had there been many swans and many shadows, they would have implied nothing as regards the character of the scene; and I should have said nothing about them.

De Vere (*Grosart,* iii, 487-8).   1842-4

Sonnet. In the Pass of Killicranky. See W. 156

The Blind Highland Boy

148. [For Coleridge's criticism, *v. Animae Poetae*, pp. 207-8; for Lamb's, *v.* his letter to W. W. of April 7, 1815. De Sel.]

The 'shell' was substituted for the 'washing-tub,' on the suggestion of Coleridge; and, greatly as I respect your opinion and Lamb's, I cannot now bring myself to undo my work; though if I had been aware before hand that such judges would have objected, I should not have troubled myself with making the alteration. *To B. Field,*   X. 24, 1828

MEMORIALS OF A TOUR IN SCOTLAND, 1814

148A.   See Imagination 32A

The Brownie's Cell

149.* [*The Brownie's Cell*] his favorite [in new volume of poems of 1820.] *H. C. R.,* i, 240.   VI. 2, 1820

Yarrow Visited

150.   You are a most indulgent and good-natured critic, or I think you would hardly have been so much pleased with *Yarrow Visited*; we think it heavier than my things generally are, and nothing but a wish to show to Mr. Hogg that my inclination towards him, and his proposed work were favourable, could have induced me to part with it in that state. I have composed three new stanzas in place of the three first, and another to be inserted before the two last, and have made some alterations in other parts; therefore, when you see Mr. Hogg, beg from me that he will not print the poem till he has read the copy which I have added to Miss E. Wilson's MSS, as I scarcely doubt, notwithstanding the bias of first impressions, that he will prefer it. *To Gillies,*   XI. 12, 1814

151.   I sent the alterations of *Yarrow Visited* to Miss Hutchinson and my sister, in Wales, who think them great improvements, and are delighted with the poem as it now stands. Second parts, if much inferior to the first, are always disgusting, and as I had succeeded in *Yarrow Unvisited*, I was anxious that here should be no falling off; but that was anavoidable . . . from the subject, as imagination almost always transcends reality.
To Gillies,   XI. 23, 1814

151A.   . . . we declined going in search of this celebrated stream, not altogether, I will frankly confess, for the reasons assigned in the poem on the occasion. *I. F.* (*Grosart,* iii, 70).   1843

Poems Dedicated to National Independence and Liberty

"I grieved for Buonaparté"

152.   . . . one afternoon in 1801, my sister read to me the sonnets of Milton. I had long been well acquainted with them, but I was particularly struck on that occasion with the dignified simplicity and majestic harmony that runs through most of them—in character so totally different from the Italian, and still more so from Shakespeare's fine sonnets. I took fire, if I may be allowed to say so, and produced three sonnets the same afternoon—the first I ever wrote, except an irregular one at school. Of these three, the only one I distinctly remember is ' I grieved for Buonaparte,' &c. One was never written down; the third, which was I believe preserved, I cannot particularise.
I. F. (*Grosart*, iii, 52-3).   1843

Thought of a Briton on the Subjugation of Switzerland

153.   See Passion 51; Poetry 47

154.*   The Sonnet which he is most anxious to have popular because he says, were it generally admired it would evince an elevation of mind and strength & purity which [*sic*] fancy which we had not yet witnessed.
C. R. to T. R. (*Corr. C. R.*, i, 53),   III, 1808

155.   The Sonnet beginning ' Two voices are there,' you will remember is the one which I mentioned to you as being the best I had written.
To R. Sharp,   IX. 27, 1808

To the Men of Kent

156.   They are however heavy-armed Troops [*To the Men of Kent*, and *Anticipation* and " Six thousand Veterans "], and might perhaps stand in the way of the movements of your flying artillery.
To F. Wrangham,   early in 1804

Anticipation. See W. 156

"Hail, Zaragoza!"

158.   In this sonnet I am under some obligations to one of an Italian author, to which I cannot refer. *Oxf. W.*, p. 903.   1815

Indignation of a High-minded Spaniard

159.*   [Preferred the sonnet, " Indignation of a Highminded Spaniard."]
English Traits, p. 23.   VIII. 28, 1833

"Here pause"

160.   Here pause: the poet claims at least this praise,
                That virtuous Liberty hath been the scope

> Of his pure song, which did not shrink from hope
> In the worst moment of these evil days. . . .
> "Here pause," 1-4.

1811

The French Army in Russia. See Southey 47

Occasioned by the Battle of Waterloo. See W. 164

Siege of Vienna. See W. 164

Occasioned by the Battle of Waterloo

164.   I know not that the three following Sonnets ['Intrepid Sons of Albion' (*Oxf. W.*, p. 325), 'The Bard—whose soul is meek' (*Oxf. W.*, p. 326), and 'Oh, for a kindling touch' (*Oxf. W.*, p. 326)], occasioned by the Battle of Waterloo will do any credit to your journal; but perhaps the subject may make up with your Readers (if it does not tell the contrary way) for the deficiencies of the execution. *To J. Scott,*   I. 29, 1816

"Imagination—ne'er before content." See W. 168

Ode, Thanksgiving

166.   . . . I threw off a sort of irregular Ode upon this subject, which spread to nearly 350 lines; the longest thing of the Lyrical Kind, I believe, except Spenser's *Epithalamion*, in our language. Out of this have sprung several smaller pieces, effusions rather than Compositions, though in justice to myself I must say that upon the correction of the Style I have bestowed, as I always do, great Labour. I hope that my pains in this particular have not been thrown away, and that in their several degrees the things will not be found deficient in spirit. But I do not like to appear as giving encouragement to a lax species of writing, except where the occasion is so great as to justify an aspiration after a state of freedom beyond what a succession of regular Stanzas will allow. But, as I before hinted, these smaller pieces are but offsets of the larger; and their defects in this point may be charged upon their parent; though I shall not call upon the public to be so indulgent.— From my Country I solicit no mercy; I have laboured intensely to merit its approbation, and in some smaller degree to secure, in the future times at least, its gratitude; and for the present I am well contented with my portion of distinction. If I wish for more, I can honestly affirm it is mainly from a belief that it would be an indication that a better taste was spreading, and high and pure feelings becoming more general.

To J. Scott,   III. 11, 1816

167.   The principal poem is 300 Lines long, a Thanksgiving Ode, and the others refer almost exclusively to recent public events. The whole may be regarded as a *Sequel* to the Sonnets dedicated to Liberty, and accordingly I have given directions for its being printed uniform with my Poems, to admit of being bound up along with them. . . . I ought to tell you that the Sonnet ["While not a leaf," *Oxf. W.*, p. 263] you have sent me is thus corrected.

For me *who under kindlier laws belong*
To Nature's tuneful quire, this rustling etc
Mid frost and snow *the instinctive* joys of song
And nobler cares etc.

When these little things will be permitted to see the light, I know not; as
my Publisher has not even condescended to acknowledge the Receipt of the
MSS, which were sent three weeks ago; from this you may judge of the
Value which the Goods of the author of the Excursion at present bear in the
estimation of the Trader. N'importe, if we have done well we shall not miss
our reward. . . . *To Gillies,* IV. 9, 1816

168.   I am glad that you were pleased with my Odes [*Thanksgiving
Ode*] &c [?] They were poured out with much feeling, but from mismanagement of myself the labour of making some verbal corrections cost me more
health and strength than anything of that sort ever did before. I have written
nothing since—and as to Publishing I shall give it up, as nobody will buy
what I send forth: nor can I expect it seeing what stuff the public appetite is
set upon. *To C. R. (Corr. C. R.,* i, 87),   VIII. 2, 1816

169.   Wholly unworthy of touching upon the momentous subject here
treated would that Poet be, before whose eyes the present distress under which
this kingdom labours could interpose a veil sufficiently thick to hide, or even
to obscure, the splendour of this great moral triumph. . . . [p. 73] . . .
I should feel little satisfaction in giving to the world these limited attempts
to celebrate the virtues of my country, if I did not encourage a hope that a
subject, which it has fallen within my province to treat only in the mass, will
by other poets be illustrated in that detail which its importance calls for, and
which will allow opportunities to give the merited applause to PERSONS as
well as to THINGS [p. 75]. *Grosart,* iii, 73 and 75.   1816

170.   Had it been a hymn, uttering the sentiments of a *multitude,* a *stanza*
would have been indispensable. But though I have called it a *Thanksgiving
Ode,* strictly speaking it is not so, but a poem composed, or supposed to be
composed, on the morning of the thanksgiving, uttering the sentiments of
an individual upon that occasion. It is a dramatized ejaculation; and this, if
any thing can, must excuse the irregular frame of the metre. . . . [See
Versification 13B.]

If Gray's plan be adopted, there is not time to become acquainted with
the arrangement, and to recognize with pleasure the recurrence of the
movement.

Be so good as to let me know where you found most difficulty in following
me. The passage which I most suspect of being misunderstood is,

And thus is missed the sole true glory;

and the passage, where I doubt most about the reasonableness of expecting
that the reader should follow me, in the luxuriance of the imagery and the
language, is the one that describes—under so many metaphors—the spreading
of the news of the Waterloo victory over the globe. Tell me if this displeased
you. *To Southey,* 1816

171.   The view taken of Napoleon's character and proceedings is little in accordance with that taken by some Historians and critical philosophers. I am glad and proud of the difference, and trust that this series of Poems, infinitely below the subject as they are, will survive to counteract in unsophisticated minds the pernicious and degrading tendency of those views and doctrines that lead to the idolatry of power as power, and in that false splendour to lose sight of its real nature and constitution, as it often acts for the gratification of its possessor without reference to a beneficial end. . . .
I. F. (Grosart, iii, 75).   1843

MEMORIALS OF A TOUR ON THE CONTINENT, 1820

172.*   In the 'Memorials' he himself likes best the Stanzas upon Einsiedeln, the three Cottage Girls, and, above all, the Eclipse upon the Lake of Lugano; and, in the 'Sketches' the succession of those on the Reformation, and those towards the conclusion of the third part. Mr. Sharpe liked best the poem on Enterprise, which surprized my Brother a good deal.
D. W. to S. Rogers,   I. 3, 1823

Dedication

173.   Dear Fellow-travellers! think not that the Muse,
               To You presenting these memorial Lays,
               Can hope the general eye thereon would gaze,
               As on a mirror that gives back the hues
               Of living Nature; no—though free to choose
               The greenest bowers, the most inviting ways,
               The fairest landscapes and the brightest days—
               Her skill she tried with less ambitious views.
               For You she wrought: Ye only can supply
               The life, the truth, the beauty; she confides
               In that enjoyment which with You abides
               Trusts to your love and vivid memory;
               Thus far contented, that for You her verse
               Shall lack not power the " meeting soul to pierce! "
               " Dear Fellow-travellers," 1-14.   XI, 1821

The Eclipse of the Sun. See Gray 6; W. 172

The Three Cottage Girls. See W. 172

MEMORIALS OF A TOUR IN ITALY, 1837

At Albano

176.   This sonnet is founded on simple fact, and was written to enlarge, if possible, the views of those who can see nothing but evil in the intercessions countenanced by the Church of Rome.
I. F. (Grosart, iii, 90).   1843

At Florence—From Michael Angelo

177. . . . one of the party who had lived much in Italy pointed out & transcribed for me a sonnet of Michael Angelo; & seemed to regret that I had not translated it. This I have done today, and send it with my compts for his gratification; or to show at least my good will. It is as literal as two languages so different will allow, without more pains than I felt inclined to bestow; and probably had I endeavoured to give it word for word I should have succeeded no better with the spirit.

To C. R. (Corr. C. R., i, 385),   VI. 22, 1839

178.   I forget how the first line of the translated sonnet stood; I know however it is much improved in the correction so is the third; & upon the whole I think the translation is not now inferior to the original. The eighth line I cannot but thing [*sic*] greatly superior—

To C. R. (Corr. C. R., i, 390-1),   VII. 7, 1839

179. See Michelangelo 6

The Egyptian Maid

180. . . . is a sort of Romance with no more solid foundation than the word—Water lily but don't mention it—it rose out of my mind like an exhalation—no better, probably, you will say for that.

To E. Q.,   XI. 28, 1828

180A.   My little Romance is an odd thing and I can scarcely guess how anyone could relish it—I do not consider *that* my own nor any detached Poem which I am now writing.

To Gordon (L. of W. Family, p. 11),   XII. 15, 1828

181. The form of the stanza is new, and is nothing but a repetition of the first five lines as they were thrown off, and is, perhaps, not well suited to narrative, and certainly would not have been trusted to had I thought at the beginning that the poem would have gone to such a length.

I. F. (Grosart, iii, 96).   1843

THE RIVER DUDDON. A SERIES OF SONNETS

182. . . . the above series of Sonnets was the growth of many years; the one which stands the 14th was the first produced; and others were added upon occasional visits to the Stream, or as recollections of the scenes upon its banks awakened a wish to describe them. In this manner I had proceeded insensibly, without perceiving that I was trespassing upon ground pre-occupied, as least as far as intention went, by Mr. Coleridge; who, more than twenty years ago, used to speak of writing a rural Poem, to be entitled ' The Brook,' of which he has given a sketch in a recent publication. But a particular subject cannot, I think, much interfere with a general one; and I have been further kept from encroaching upon any right Mr. C. may still wish to exercise, by the restriction which the frame of the Sonnet imposed upon me,

narrowing unavoidably the range of thought, and precluding, though not without its advantages, many graces to which a freer movement of verse would naturally have led. *Grosart*, iii, 97-98.   1820

Flowers. See Sympson, J. 1

Return

185.   The reader who may have been interested in the foregoing Sonnets [*Return* and *Seathwaite Chapel*], (which together may be considered as a Poem), will not be displeased to find in this place a prose account of the Duddon, extracted from Green's comprehensive *Guide to the Lakes*. . . . *Grosart*, iii, 102.   1820

Seathwaite Chapel. See W. 185

YARROW REVISITED AND OTHER POEMS

186.   See W. 194

Yarrow Revisited

187.   [W. Scott] was our guide to Yarrow. The pleasure of that day induced me to add a third to the two poems upon Yarrow, *Yarrow Revisited*. It is in the same measure, and as much in the same spirit as matter of fact would allow. You are artist enough to know that it is next to impossible entirely to harmonize things that rest upon their poetic credibility, and are idealised by distance of time and space, with those that rest upon the evidence of the hour, and have above them the thorny points of actual life.
To W. R. Hamilton,   X. 27, 1831

188.   The circumstances under which Yarrow was *re*visited by me, viz in company with Sir W. Scott not more than two or three days before his departure from Abbotsford, forced my thoughts into a more Personal channel than would otherwise have happened, and this perhaps notwithstanding the illustrious character of the Individual and his poetical connection with the scene, may have interfered with the romantic idealization which would naturally have pervaded a Poem on such a subject.
To T. Kelsall,   X. 31, 1833

189.   . . . a friendly notice of my late Vol.—Is it discreditable to say that these things interest me little, but as they may tend to promote the sale; which with the prospects of unavoidable expense before me, is a greater object to me [three words deleted here] much greater than it would otherwise have been.—The private testimonies which I receive very frequently of the effect of my writings upon the hearts & minds of men, are indeed very gratifying— because I am sure *they* must be written under *pure* influences—but it is not necessarily or even probably so with strictures intended for the public. The one are *effusions*, the other *compositions*, and liable in various degrees to intermixtures that take from their value—It is amusing to me to have proofs how Critics & Authors differ in judgment, both as to fundamentals and

Incidentals.—As an instance of the latter—see the passage where I speak of Horace [*Liberty*, 100-7 (*Oxf. W.*, p. 528)],—quoted in the Examiner. The Critic marks in Italics for approbation, certain passages—but he takes no notice of three words, in delicacy of feeling worth in my estimation, all the rest—'he only listening'! Again what he observes in praise of my mode of dealing with Nature, as opposed to my treatment of human life, which as he says is not to be trusted, would be reversed as it has been by many who maintain that I run into excess in my pictures of the influence of natural objects, and assign to them an importance which they are not entitled to; while in my treatment of the intellectual instincts affections & passions of mankind, I am nobly distinguished by having drawn out into notice the points in which they resemble each other, in preference to dwelling, as dramatic Authors must do, upon those in which they differ. If my writings are to last, it will I myself believe, be mainly owing to this characteristic. They will please for the single cause, 'That we have all of us one human heart!'

To C. R. (*Corr. C. R.*, i, 272-3), spring, 1835

190. You will find in it some political verses, which highflying critics will not allow to be poetry—enough for me, if they be admitted to be good rhetoric and enlightened patriotism. . . . *To Liddell*, III, 30, 1835

191. . . . the verses, 'Yarrow Revisited' are a memorial. Notwithstanding the romance that pervades Sir Walter's works, and attaches to many of his habits, there is too much pressure of fact for these verses to harmonise, as much as I could wish, with the two preceding poems.

I. F. (*Grosart*, iii, 140). 1843

Composed in Roslin Chapel during a Storm

192. Here this sonnet was composed, and [I shall be fully satisfied] if it has at all done justice to the feeling which the place and the storm raging without inspired. I was as a prisoner. A Painter delineating the interior of the chapel and its minute features, under such circumstances, would have no doubt found his time agreeably shortened. But the movements of the mind must be more free while dealing with words than with lines and colours. Such, at least, was then, and has been on many other occasions, my belief; and as it is allotted to few to follow both arts with success, I am grateful to my own calling for this and a thousand other recommendations which are denied to that of the Painter. *I. F.* (*Grosart*, iii, 142). 1843

The Trosachs

193. The sentiment that runs through this sonnet was natural to the season in which I again saw this beautiful spot; but this, and some other sonnets that follow, were coloured by the remembrance of my recent visit to Sir Walter Scott, and the melancholy errand on which he was going.

I. F. (*Grosart*, iii, 142). 1843

Apology

194. No more: the end is sudden and abrupt,
Abrupt—as without preconceived design

Was the beginning; yet the several Lays
Have moved in order, to each other bound
By a continuous and acknowledged tie
Though unapparent. . . .
" No more," 1-6.   1831

THE WHITE DOE OF RYLSTONE

195.   As to the reception which the Doe has met with in Mitre Court I
am much more sorry on Lamb's account than on my own. I had no wish that
they should see the Poem by an act of private courtesy on my part, because
as I knew it could not please them, I did not think that I had the right to
subject them to the disagreeable feeling of owing to my kindness this sight of
a Work which they could not approve of. I also told Lamb that I did not
think the Poem could ever be popular first because there was nothing in it
to excite curiosity, and next, because the main catastrophe was not a material
but an intellectual one; I said to him further that it could not be popular
because some of the principal objects and agents, such as the Banner and the
Doe, produced their influences and effects not by powers naturally inherent
in them, but such as they were endued with by the Imagination of the human
minds on whom they operated: further, that the principle of action in all the
characters, as in the Old Man, and his Sons, and Francis, when he has the
prophetic vision of the overthrow of his family, and the fate of his sister, and
takes leave of her as he does, was throughout imaginative; and that all
action (save the main traditionary tragedy), i. e. all the action proceeding
from the will of the chief agents, was fine-spun and inobstrusive, consonant
in this to the principle from which it flowed, and in harmony with the
shadowy influence of the Doe, by whom the poem is introduced, and in whom
it ends. It suffices that everything tends to account for the weekly pilgrimage
of the Doe, which is made interesting by its connection with a human being,
a Woman, who is intended to be honoured and loved for what she *endures*,
and the manner in which she endures it; accomplishing a conquest over
her own sorrows (which is the true subject of the Poem) by means, partly, of
the native strength of her character, and partly by the persons and things with
whom and which she is connected; and finally, after having exhibited the
' fortitude of patience and heroic martyrdom,' ascending to pure etherial
spirituality, and forwarded in that ascent of love by communion with a
creature not of her own species, but spotless, beautiful, innocent and loving,
in that temper of earthly love to which alone she can conform, without violation to the majesty of her losses, or degradation from those heights of heavenly
serenity to which she had been raised.
    Let Lamb learn to be ashamed of himself in not taking some pleasure in
the contemplation of this picture, which supposing it to be even but a sketch,
is yet sufficiently made out for any man of true power to finish it for himself—
As to the principal characters doing it is false and too ridiculous to be dwelt
on for a moment. When it is considered what has already been executed in
Poetry, strange that a man cannot perceive, particularly when the present

tendencies of society, good and bad, are observed, that this is the time when
a man of genius may honourably take a station upon different ground. If
he is to be a Dramatist, let him crowd his scene with gross and visible action;
but if a narrative Poet, if the Poet is to be predominant over the Dramatist,—
then let him see if there are no victories in the world of spirit, no changes, no
commotions, no revolutions there, no fluxes and refluxes of the thoughts
which may be made interesting by modest combination with the stiller actions
of the bodily frame, or with the gentler movements and milder appearances
of society and social intercourse, or the still more mild and gentle solicitations
of irrational and inanimate nature. But too much of this—of one thing be
assured, that Lamb has not a reasoning mind, therefore cannot have a comprehensive mind, and, least of all, has he an imaginative one.

To Coleridge,   IV. 19, 1808

196.* . . . he is sure it will not sell, nor be admired more than the
[?] he has already published. *D. W. to C. Clarkson,*   V. 10, 1808

197.* He wishes to know, what your feelings were—whether the *tale*
itself did not interest you—or whether you could not enter into the conception of Emily's Character, or take delight in that visionary communion which
is supposed to have existed between her and the Doe. . . . Now as his sole
object for publishing this poem at present would be for the sake of the money,
he would not publish it if he did not think from the several judgments of his
Friends that it would be likely to have a Sale. He has no pleasure in publishing—he even detests it—and if it were not that he is *not* over wealthy
he would leave all his works to be published after his Death. William himself is sure that the *White Doe* will not sell or be admired except by a very
few at first. . . . *D. W. to Jane Marshall,*   V. 11, 1808

198.   Thank you for the interesting particulars about the Nortons; I
shall like much to see them for their own sakes; but so far from being
serviceable to my Poem [i. e. *The White Doe of Rylstone*] they would stand
in the way of it; as I have followed (as I was in duty bound to do) the
traditionary and common historic records. Therefore I shall say in this case,
a plague upon your industrious Antiquarianism that has put my fine story to
confusion. *To W. Scott* (p. 458e),   V. 14, 1808

198A.* I have not learnt with what motive Wordsworth omitted the
original advertisement prefixed to his White Doe, that the peculiar metre and
mode of narrative he had imitated from the Christabel.

L. of Coleridge, ii, 148.   X, 1815

199. . . . hope it will be acceptable to the intelligent, for whom alone
it is written. It starts from a high point of imagination, and comes round
through various wanderings of that faculty to a still higher; nothing less
than the Apotheosis of the Animal, who gives the first of the two titles to the
Poem. And as the Poem thus begins and ends with pure and lofty Imagination, every motive and impulse that actuates the persons introduced is from
the same source, a kindred spirit pervades, and is intended to harmonize,
the whole. Throughout, objects (the Banner, for instance) derive their
influence not from properties inherent in them, not from what they are

actually in themselves, but from such as are bestowed upon them by the minds of those who are conversant with or affected by those objects. Thus the Poetry, if there be any in the work, proceeds whence it ought to do, from the soul of Man, communicating its creative energies to the images of the external world. *To F. Wrangham,*   I. 18, 1816

200.   Do you know who reviewed *The White Doe* in the *Quarterly?* After having asserted that Mr. W. uses his words without any regard to their sense, the writer says, that on no other principle can he explain that Emily is *always* called ' the consecrated Emily.' Now, the name Emily occurs just fifteen times in the poem; and out of these fifteen, the epithet is attached to it *once*, and that for the express purpose of recalling the scene in which she had been consecrated by her brother's solemn adjuration, that she would fulfil her destiny, and become

> A soul, by force of sorrow high,
> Uplifted to the purest sky
> Of undisturbed humanity.

The point upon which the whole moral interest of the piece hinges, when that speech is closed, occurs in this line,

> He kissed the consecrated maid;

and to bring this back to the reader I repeated the epithet.
To Southey (p. 718),   1816

201.   As to the Nortons [i. e. *The White Doe, or the Fate of the Nortons*] the Ballad is my authority, and I require no more. It is much better than Virgil had for his Æneid.
To F. Wrangham,   II. 19, 1819

201A.*   [W. published *The White Doe* in quarto] To show the World my own opinion of it. *Moore's Diary*, p. 31.   X. 27, 1820

202.*   He said he considered ' The White Doe ' as, in conception, the highest work he ever produced. The mere physical action was all unsuccessful; but the true action of the poem was spiritual—the subduing of the will, and all inferior passions to the perfect purifying and spiritualising of the intellectual nature; while the Doe, by connection with Emily, is raised as it were from its mere animal nature into something mysterious and saint-like. He said he should devote much labour to perfecting the execution of it in the mere business parts, in which, from anxiety ' to get on ' with the more important parts, he was sensible that imperfections had crept in, which gave the style a feebleness of character.
Justice Coleridge (*Grosart*, iii, 430).   X. 10, 1836

203.   See Character Analysis 7

204.   Poetic excitement, when accompanied by protracted labour in composition has throughout my life brought on more or less bodily derangement. . . .

Let me here say a few words of this Poem, by way of criticism. The subject being taken from feudal times has led to its being compared to some of Walter Scott's poems that belong to the same age and state of society. The comparison is inconsiderate. Sir Walter pursued the customary and very natural course of conducting an action, presenting various turns of fortune, to some outstanding point on which the mind might rest as a termination or catastrophe. The course I attempted to pursue is entirely different. Everything that is attempted by the principal personages in the ' White Doe' fails, so far as its object is external and substantial: so far as it is moral and spiritual, it succeeds. The heroine of the poem knows that her duty is not to interfere with the current of events, either to forward or delay them; but—

' To abide
The shock, and finally secure
O'er pain and grief a triumph pure.'

This she does in obedience to her brother's injunction, as most suitable to a mind and character that, under previous trials, had been proved to accord with his. She achieves this, not without aid from the communication with the inferior creature, which often leads her thoughts to revolve upon the past with a tender and humanising influence that exalts rather than depresses her. The anticipated beatification, if I may so say, of her mind, and the apotheosis of the companion of her solitude, are the points at which the poem aims, and constitute its legitimate catastrophe; far too spiritual a one for instant or widely-spread sympathy, but not therefore the less fitted to make a deep and permanent impression upon that class of minds who think and feel more independently than the many do of the surfaces of things, and interests transitory because belonging more to the outward and social forms of life than to its internal spirit.

I. F. (Grosart, iii, 123-24).   1843

Ecclesiastical Sonnets

205. . . . it struck me that certain points in the Ecclesiastical History of our Country might advantageously be presented to view in verse.
For the convenience of passing from one point of the subject to another without shocks of abruptness, this work has taken the shape of a series of Sonnets: but the Reader, it is to be hoped, will find that the pictures are often so closely connected as to have jointly the effect of passages of a poem in a form of stanza to which there is no objection but one that bears upon the Poet only—its difficulty. *Grosart, iii, 126-27.*   I. 24, 1822

206. See Southey 36

207.   The *Ecc. Sketches* labour under one obvious disadvantage, that they can only present themselves as a whole to the reader, who is pretty well acquainted with the history of this country; and, as separate pieces, several of them suffer as poetry from the matter of fact, there being unavoidably in all history, except as it is a mere suggestion, something that enslaves the Fancy. But there are in those Poems several continuous strains, not in the least degree liable to this objection. I will only mention two: the sonnets on the Dissolution of the Monasteries, and almost the whole of the last part,

15

from the picture of England after the Revolution, scattered over with Protestant churches, till the conclusion. *T. R. Sharp,*   IV. 16, 1822

209.   [I have written] a couple of sonnets upon subjects recommended by you to take place in the Ec[c]lesiastical Series. They are upon the marriage ceremony, and the funeral sermon. I have also . . . added two others, one upon visiting the sick, and the other upon the than[k]sgiving of women after childbirth, both subjects taken from the services of our Liturgy. To the second part of the same series I have also added two, in order to do more justice to the Papal Church for the services which she did actually render to Christianity and humanity in the middle ages. By the bye, the Sonnet beginning Men of the western world &c was slightly altered after I sent it to you, not in the hope of substituting a better verse, but merely to avoid the repetition of the word, " brook " which occurs as a Rhyme in the ["] I Pilgrim Fathers." *Reed,* p. 81.   IX. 4, 1842

210.   My purpose in writing this Series [*Ecc. Son.*] was, as much as possible, to confine my view to the introduction, progress, and operation of the CHURCH in ENGLAND, both previous and subsequent to the Reformation. *I. F. (Grosart,* iii, 127).   1843

Saxon Conquest

212.   The last six lines of this Sonnet [*Ecc. Son.* XI, " Nor wants the cause "] are chiefly from the prose of Daniel. . . . *Grosart,* iii, 131.   1822

"I saw the figure of a lovely maid "

213.   [W. says he never revised this rapidly written sonnet.] I wish I could say the same of the five or six hundred I have written: most of them were frequently retouched in the course of composition, and not a few laboriously. *I. F. (Grosart,* iii, 128).   1843

Acquittal of the Bishops

214.   And upon the acquittal of the Seven Bishops [*Oxf. W.,* p. 442] I have done little more than versify a lively description of that event in the MS. Memoirs of the first Lord Lonsdale. *Grosart,* iii, 131.   1822

EVENING VOLUNTARIES

By the Sea-Side.   See Landor 7

Composed upon an Evening of Extraordinary Splendor and Beauty

216.   Allusions to the Ode, entitled ' Intimations of Immortality,' pervade the last stanza of the foregoing Poem. *Grosart,* iii, 147.   1820

217.   . . . among the Miscellaneous Sonnets are a few alluding to morning impressions, which might be read with mutual benefit in connection with these Evening Voluntaries. See for example that one on Westminster Bridge, that on May 2d, on the song of the Thrush, and the one beginning ' While beams of orient light.' *I. F. (Grosart,* iii, 147).   1843

POEMS COMPOSED OR SUGGESTED DURING A TOUR, IN THE SUMMER OF 1833

218. . . . produced between 30 and 40 sonnets, some of which, I think, would please you. *To Dyce,*   XII. 4, 1833

To a Friend

219. . . . which you may perhaps read with some interest at the present crisis. *To Lady Beaumont* (p. 691),   1834

Stanzas Suggested in a Steamboat off Saint Bees' Heads

220. See Smith, Charlotte 2

222. . . . two of the stanzas exceeded the others in length—a fault which was afterwards corrected in the edition of 1837 as the lines have stood since.—The last stanza I wish you would print thus, that being the only alteration I purpose to make in future [see this letter]. . . .
To F. W. Faber,   VIII. 6, 1844

By a Retired Mariner

223.   This unpretending sonnet is by a gentleman [Hutchinson] nearly connected with me, and I hope, as it falls so easily into its place, that both the writer and the reader will excuse its appearance here.
Oxf. W., p. 924.   *c.* 1833

Cave of Staffa [XXVIII, XXIX, and XXX]

224.   The reader may be tempted to exclaim, 'How came this and the two following Sonnets [XXIX and XXX, *Oxf. W.,* pp. 473-74] to be written after the dissatisfaction expressed in the preceding one?' In fact, at the risk of incurring the reasonable displeasure of the master of the steamboat, I returned to the cave, and explored it under circumstances more favourable to those imaginative impressions which it is so wonderfully fitted to make upon the mind. *Grosart,* iii, 155.   1835

Iona. Upon Landing

225.   The four last lines of this Sonnet are adapted from a well-known Sonnet of Russel [Sonnet no. X of *Sonnets and Miscellaneous Poems*], as conveying my feeling better than any words of my own could do.
Grosart, iii, 155.   1835

The River Eden

226.   It is to be feared that there is more of the poet than the sound etymologist in this derivation of the name Eden.
Grosart, iii, 156.   1835

Lowther

227.   It may be questioned whether this union was in the contemplation

of the Artist when he planned the edifice. However this might be, a Poet may be excused for taking the view of the subject presented in this Sonnet.
I. F. (*Grosart*, iii, 157).   1843

Poems of Sentiment and Reflection

Expostulation and Reply

229.   The lines entitled *Expostulation and Reply*, and those which follow, arose out of conversation with a friend who was somewhat unreasonably attached to modern books of moral philosophy.
Adv. L. B. (*K. Prose*, i, 32).   1798

230.   This poem is a favourite among the Quakers, as I have learnt on many occasions. *Grosart*, iii, 158.   1843 [K.]

Simon Lee. See Aim of Writing 7

To the Daisy

231.   Thou wander'st the wide world about. Etc. etc.
I was loath to part with this stanza. *To B. Field*.   X. 24, 1828

232.   I have been censured for the last line but one, ' thy function apostolical,' as being little less than profane. How could it be thought so? The work is adopted with reference to its derivation, implying something sent on a mission; and assuredly, this little flower, especially when the subject of verse, may be regarded, in its humble degree, as administering both to moral and to spiritual purposes.
I. F. (*Grosart*, iii, 161).   1843

Matthew

233.   This and other poems connected with Matthew would not gain by a literal detail of facts. Like the wanderer in the ' Excursion,' this school-master was made up of several, both of his class and men of other occupations. I do not ask pardon for what there is of untruth in such verses, considered strictly as matters of fact. It is enough if, being true and consistent in spirit, they move and teach in a manner not unworthy of a Poet's calling.
I. F. (*Grosart*, iii, 161).   1843

Two April Mornings. See Aim of Writing 7

The Fountain. See Aim of writing 7

Personal Talk

234.   The last line but two stood at first, better and more characteristically, thus:

            ' By my half-kitchen and half-parlour fire.'

I. F. (*Grosart*, iii, 162).   1843

Tribute to the Memory of the same Dog

235. Walter Scott heard of the accident, and both he and I, without either of us knowing that the other had taken up the subject, each wrote a poem in admiration of the dog's fidelity. His contains a most beautiful stanza:

' How long didst thou think that his silence was slumber!
When the wind waved his garment how oft didst thou start!

I will add that the sentiment in the last four lines of the last stanza of my verses was uttered by a shepherd with such exactness, that a traveller, who afterwards reported his account in print, was induced to question the man whether he had read them, which he had not. *Grosart*, iii, 164. 1843 [K.]

Ode to Duty

236. [Speaking in his (W.'s)] character of philosophical poet, having thought of morality as implying in its essence voluntary obedience, and producing the effect of order, he transfers in the transport of imagination, the law of moral to physical natures, and having contemplated, through the medium of that order, all modes of existence as subservient to one spirit, concludes his address to the power of Duty in the following words:—
[ll. 49-56, *Oxf. W.*, pp. 492-3].
Ans. to Mathetes (*Grosart*, i, 326). I. 4, 1810

237. This Ode, written in 1805, is on the model of Gray's ' Ode to Adversity.' which is copied from Horace's ' Ode to Fortune.' [In pencil on the MS—But is not the first stanza of Gray's from a chorus of Aeschylus? And is not Horace's Ode also modelled on the Greek?]
I. F. (*Grosart*, iii, 164-65). 1843

Character of the Happy Warrior

238. . . . I kept them by me from week to week with a hope (which has proved vain) that in some happy moment a new fit of inspiration would help me to mend them. . . .

You will find that the Verses are allusive to Lord Nelson, and they will shew that I must have sympathized with you in admiration of the Man, and sorrow for our loss. . . . The Old Ballad [from ' The more modern Ballad of Chevy Chase ' in Percy's *Reliques*. De Sel.] has taught us how to feel on these occasions:

> I trust I have within my realm
> Five hundred good as he.

To Beaumont, II. 11, 1806

239.* . . . *The Happy Warrior* as appertaining to reflection.
H. C. R., i, 89. V. 31, 1812

240.* . . . does not best fulfil the conditions of poetry, but it is a chain of extremely *valooable* thoughts.
Martineau Autobiography, i, 507. 1845

A Fact, and an Imagination

241.   The first and last four lines of this poem each make a sonnet, and were composed as such. But I thought that by intermediate lines they might be connected so as to make a whole. One or two expressions are taken from Milton's *History of England. I. F. (Grosart,* iii, 166).   1843

Ode to Lycoris

242.   The discerning reader who is aware that in the poem of ' Ellen Irwin ' I was desirous of throwing the reader at once out of the old ballad, so as if possible to preclude a comparison between that mode of dealing with the subject and the mode I mean to adopt, may here, perhaps, perceive that this poem originated in the four last lines of the first stanza. These specks of snow reflected in the lake, and so transferred, as it were, to the subaqueous sky, reminded me of the swans which the fancy of the ancient classic poets yoked to the car of Venus. Hence the tenor of the whole first stanza and the name of Lycoris, which with some readers, who think mythology and classical allusion too far-fetched, and therefore more or less unnatural or affected, will tend to un-realize the sentiment that pervades these verses.   But surely one who has written so much in verse as I have done may be allowed to retrace his steps into the regions of fancy which delighted him in his boyhood, when he first became acquainted with the Greek and Roman Poets. Before I read Virgil I was so strongly attached to Ovid, whose *Metamorphoses* I read at school, that I was quite in a passion whenever I found him, in books of criticism, placed below Virgil. As to Homer, I was never weary of travelling over the scenes through which he led me. Classical literature affected me by its own beauty. But the truths of Scripture having been entrusted to the dead languages, and these fountains having been recently laid open at the Reformation, an importance and a sanctity were at that period attached to classical literature that extended, as is obvious in Milton's *Lycidas,* for example, both to its spirit and form in a degree that can never be revived. No doubt the hackneyed and lifeless use into which mythology fell towards the close of the 17th century, and which continued through the 18th, disgusted the general reader with all allusion to it in modern verse. And though, in deference to this disgust, and also in a measure participating in it, I abstained in my earlier writings from all introduction of pagan fable,—surely, even in its humble form, it may ally itself with real sentiment—as I can truly affirm it did in the present case. *I. F. (Grosart,* iii, 167-68).   1843

Humanity.   See Digby 3

The Warning

244.   . . . a sober and sorrowful sequel [*The Warning. A Sequel to the Foregoing, Oxf. W.,* p. 503] to it which I fear none of you will like. . . . Bear in mind with respect to 2nd especially that this will be its first appearance on paper and no doubt it will require altering.

W. to his Family (pp. 645 and 646),   III, 1833

245.   These lines were composed during the fever spread through the

nation by the Reform Bill. As the motives which led to this measure, and the good or evil which has attended or has risen from it, will be duly appreciated by future historians, there is no call for dwelling on the subject in this place. I will content myself with saying that the then condition of the people's mind is not, in these verses, exaggerated.

I. F. (*Grosart*, iii, 170).   1843

Ode, composed on May Morning

246. . . . my first intention was to write only one Poem; but subsequently I broke it into two [see *To May*], making additions to each part, so as to produce a consistent and appropriate whole.

I. F. (*Grosart*, iii, 171).   1843

To May.   See W. 246

The foregoing Subject resumed.   See Southey 48

Upon seeing a coloured Drawing of the Bird of Paradise

249. [There are] two Poems on pictures of this bird among my Poems. I will here observe, that in a far greater number of instances than have been mentioned in these Notes one Poem has, as in this case, grown out of another, either because I felt the subject had been inadequately treated or that the thoughts and images suggested in course of composition have been such as I found interfered with the unity indispensable to every work of art, however humble in character.

I. F. (*Grosart*, iii, 172).   1843

SONNETS DEDICATED TO LIBERTY AND ORDER

250. . . . those to Liberty, at least, have a connexion with, or a bearing upon, each other; and, therefore, if individually they want weight, perhaps, as a Body, they may not be so deficient, at least, this ought to induce you to suspend your judgment, and qualify it so far as to allow that the writer aims at least at comprehensiveness. . . . these Sonnets, while they each fix the attention upon some important sentiment, separately considered, do at the same time collectively make a Poem on the subject of civil Liberty and national independence, which, either for simplicity of style or grandeur of moral sentiment, is, alas! likely to have few parallels in the Poetry of the present day. *To Lady Beaumont*,   V. 21, 1807

251. See W. 167

SONNETS UPON THE PUNISHMENT OF DEATH

"Not to the object specially designed."   See Repetition 2

Miscellaneous Poems

Upon Perusing the Foregoing Epistle

255.   The ' Epistle,' to which these notes refer, though written so far back as 1811, was carefully revised so late as 1842, previous to its publication. I am loath to add, that it was never seen by the person to whom it is addressed. So sensible am I of the deficiencies in all that I write, and so far does everything that I attempt fall short of what I wish it to be, that even private publication, if such a term may be allowed, requires more resolution than I can command. I have written to give vent to my own mind, and not without hope that, some time or other, kindred minds might benefit by my labours; but I am inclined to believe I should never have ventured to send forth any verses of mine to the world, if it had not been done on the pressure of personal occasions. Had I been a rich man, my productions, like this ' Epistle,' the ' Tragedy of the Borderers,' &c., would most likely have been confined to MS. *I. F. (Grosart*, iii, 178).   1843

Liberty.   See W. 189

The Gleaner

257.   [Has merit.]   *To M. and Dora W.,*   III, 1828

Goody Blake and Harry Gill

258.   The tale of *Goody Blake and Harry Gill* is founded on a well-authenticated fact which happened in Warwickshire.

Adv. L. B. (K. Prose, i, 32).   1798

258A.   See Pope 1A

" In desultory walk "

259.   The best news I have of myself is my having done I trust with that . . . troublesome prefatory Poem [" In desultory walk," *Oxf. W.*, pp. 537-8]; never was I so hampered with anything, the chief difficulty rising out of the simultaneous actions of both the Bird and the Poet being engaged in singing and the word ' while' not being manageable for both—that having done this to my own mind and Mary's and having improved, I cannot but think, the little I now send. . . . *To I. Fenwick,*   XII. 2, 1841

260.   [This poem is] too restricted in its bearing to serve as a Preface for the whole [of his poetry]. The lines towards the conclusion allude to the discontents then fomented thro' the country by the Agitators of the Anti-Corn-Law League: the particular causes of such troubles are transitory, but disposition to excite and liability to be excited, are nevertheless permanent and therefore proper objects of the Poet's regard.

I. F. (Grosart, iii, 3).   1843

The Russian Fugitive

261.   See Bruce, Peter Henry 1

261A.   I lately wrote a Tale (350) verses the Scene of which is laid in Russia, though it is not even tinged with Russian imagery—It will give me great pleasure to shew it you—I think your Russian Friends would be pleased with it. *To Gordon* (*L. of W. Family*, p. 14),   I. 29, 1829

262.   Early in life this story had interested me; and I often thought it would make a pleasing subject for an Opera or musical drama.
I. F. (*Grosart*, iii, 182).   1843

INSCRIPTIONS

"In these fair vales hath many a tree"

263.   . . . following serious Inscription, you will forgive its Egotism.
To J. Kenyon,   IX. 9, 1831

"If thou in the dear love of some one Friend"

264.   . . . the subject is elevated and serious.
To Beaumont (p. 475),   XI. 16, 1811

SELECTIONS FROM CHAUCER MODERNIZED

265.   See Chaucer 11-20

The Prioress's Tale

266.   In the following Poem no further deviation from the original has been made than was necessary for the fluent reading and instant under-standing of the Author: so much, however, is the language altered since Chaucer's time, especially in pronunciation, that much was to be removed, and its place supplied with as little incongruity as possible. The ancient accent has been retained in a few conjunctions, as *alsò* and *alwày*, from a conviction that such sprinklings of antiquity would be admitted, by persons of taste, to have a graceful accordance with the subject [1820]. The fierce bigotry of the Prioress forms a fine back-ground for her tender-hearted sympathies with the Mother and Child; and the mode in which the story is told amply atones for the extravagance of the miracle [1827].
Grosart, iii, 185.   1820 and 1827

267.   [*Prioress's Tale*, ix, 61.] See Chaucer 19

The Cuckoo and the Nightingale

268.   . . . I felt as if they wanted something of solidity, and am now tempted, my beloved Friend, to send you, in Joanna's writing, a copy slightly revised, with an additional stanza toiled at unsuccessfully yesterday evening, but thrown off in a few minutes this morning. We all like it and hope you and Dora will do the same. But it is too lately born for sound judgment, and I never sent to any one verses immediately after they were composed without some cause for regret I had been so hasty.
To I. Fenwick,   III. 26, 1840

Poems Referring to the Period of Old Age

The Old Cumberland Beggar

269.   I am loath to object to any mode of circulating the Cumberland Beggar, as I believe that Poem has done much good. But your general object being what it is, it does not seem sufficiently appropriate—there is little I hope in my poetry that does not breathe more or less in a religious atmosphere; as these verses certainly do, but if you were to take as wide a range as this Ex: leads to, one scarcely sees why it should be selected in preference to many others. Would you object to substitute for it the beginning of the 6th Book of the Excursion—or an Ex: from the close of the preceding one, as having a more strict connection with your title.

To S. Wilkinson,   IX. 21, 1842

269A.   See Aim of Writing 7

The Farmer of Tilsbury Vale

270.   With this picture, which was taken from real life, compare the imaginative one of " The Reverie of Poor Susan,' and see (to make up the deficiencies of the class) ' The Excursion' *passim.*

Grosart, iii, 186.   1837

271.   The latter part of the poem, perhaps, requires some apology, as being too much of an echo to the ' Reverie of Poor Susan.'

Grosart, iii, 186.   1843 [K.]

The Two Thieves

272.   This is described from the life, as I was in the habit of observing when a boy at Hawkshead School.

I. F. (*Grosart*, iii, 186).   1843

272A.   See Aim of Writing 7

Animal Tranquillity and Decay

273.   If I recollect right, these verses were an overflow from the ' Old Cumberland Beggar.' *I. F.* (*Grosart*, iii, 187).   1843

Epitaphs and Elegiac Pieces

Epitaphs Translated from Chiabrera

274.   Chiabrera has been here my model—though I am aware that Italian Churches, both on account of their size and the climate of Italy, are more favourable to long inscriptions than ours—His Epitaphs are characteristic and circumstantial—so I have endeavoured to make this of mine—but I have not ventured to touch upon the most striking feature of our departed friend's character and the most affecting circumstance of his life, viz. his faithful and intense love of his Sister. Had I been pouring out an Elegy or Monody, this would and must have been done; but for seeing and feeling the sanctity of

that relation as it ought to be seen and felt, lights are required which could scarcely be furnished by an Epitaph, unless it were to touch on little or nothing else.—The omission, therefore, in my view of the case was unavoidable: and I regret it the less, you yourself having already treated in verse the subject with genuine tenderness and beauty.

To Moxon, XI. 20, 1835

"Six months to six years"

275.   These verses I have transcribed because they are imbued with that sort of consolation which you say Scott is deprived of.

To Haydon (*L. Y.*, p. 1368), I. 20, 1817

"By playful smiles"

276.   I find no fault with it myself, the circumstances considered, except that it is too long for an Epitaph, but this was inevitable if the memorial was to be as conspicuous as the subject required, at least according to the light in which it offered itself to my mind.

To C. W., VIII. 11, 1841

Peele Castle

277.   . . . I could not but write them with feeling with such a subject, and one that touched me so nearly. . . . *To Beaumont,* VIII. 1, 1806

Elegiac Musings

278.   As it often recurs to my memory, in the trials to which grief has subjected me, it will be taken by you, (by which I mean understood and felt,) in its true degree and meaning. *To Lord Monteagle,* XII. 30, 1839

Written after the Death of Charles Lamb

279.   It was composed yesterday—and, by sending it immediately, I have prepared the way, I believe, for a speedy repentance—as I do not know that I ever wrote so many lines without some retouching being afterwards necessary. If these verses should be wholly unsuitable to the end Miss Lamb had in view, I shall find no difficulty in reconciling myself to the thought of their not being made use of, though it would have given me great, *very* great pleasure to fulfill, in all points, her wishes.

The first objection that will strike you, and every one, is its extreme length, especially compared with epitaphs as they are now written—but this objection might in part be obviated by engraving the lines in double column, and not in capitals. *To Moxon,* XI. 20, 1835

280.   [Revisions of W.'s *Lamb* in the letter to Moxon, XI. 23, 1835.]

281.   I have sent you the Epitaph again revised. Yesterday I went through it to make a few alterations, those which the present sheet contains being added, I send the whole [?] I hope the changes will be approved of. At all events, they better answer my purpose. The lines, as they now stand, preserve better the balance of delicate delineation, the weaknesses are not so

prominent, and the virtues placed in a stronger light; and I hope nothing is said that is not characteristic. . . . If the length makes the above utterly unsuitable, it may be printed with his Works as an effusion by the side of his grave. . . . *To Moxon,*   XI. 24, 1835

282.   As to the lines [*Written after the Death of Charles Lamb*] sent— the more I think of them, the more do I feel that their number renders it little less than impossible that they should be used as an Epitaph—so convinced am I of this, that I feel strongly impelled, as I hinted to Moxon in my yesterday's letter, containing a revised copy of the lines, to convert them into a Meditation supposed to be uttered by his Graveside; which would give me an opportunity of endeavoring to do some little justice to a part of the subject, which no one can treat *adequately*—viz—the sacred friendship which bound the Brother and sister together, under circumstances so affecting. Entertaining this view, I have *hoped* rather than expected that I might be able to put into ten or twelve couplets, a thought or feeling which might not be wholly unworthy of being inscribed upon a stone—consecrated to his memory & placed near his remains. Having however thrown off my first feeling already, in a shape so different—I wish that some one else, Mr Talfourd, Mr Moxon, Mr Southey, or any other of his friends accustomed to write verse would write the Epitaph.—Miss L. herself, if the state of her mind did not disqualify her for the undertaking.—*She* might probably do it better than any of us. *To C. R. (Corr. C. R., i, 284),*   XI. 25, 1835

283.   I wrote them [verses on Lamb] (how could it be otherwise?) with feeling for the subject. *To Moxon,*   I. 30, 1836

284.   This way of indicating the *name* [" From the most gentle creature nursed in fields "] of my lamented friend has been found fault with; perhaps rightly so; but I may say in justification of the double sense of the word, that similar allusions are not uncommon in epitaphs. One of the best in our language in verse, I ever read, was upon a person who bore the name of Palmer [see *Epitaph* 2 (*Grosart*, ii, 46)]; and the course of the thought, throughout, turned upon the Life of the Departed, considered as a pilgrimage. Nor can I think that the objection in the present case will have much force with any one who remembers Charles Lamb's beautiful sonnet addressed to his own name, and ending,

"No deed of mine shall shame thee, gentle name!"
Oxf. W., p. 926.   1837

Ode, Intimations of Immortality from Recollections of Early Childhood

285.   [Two kinds of impediments to the sympathy of the reader.] See W. 329

286.*   In my Ode on the 'Intimations of Immortality in Childhood,' I do not profess to give a literal representation of the state of the affections and of the moral being in childhood. I record my own feelings at that time— my absolute spirituality, my 'all-soulness,' if I may so speak. At that time I

could not believe that I should lie down quietly in the grave, and that my body would moulder into dust.
C. W., Jr. (Grosart, iii, 464).   *c.* 1827

287. Two years at least passed between the writing of the four first stanzas and the remaining part. To the attentive and the competent reader the whole sufficiently explains itself, but there may be no harm in adverting here to particular feelings or *experiences* of my own mind on which the structure of the poem partly rests. Nothing was more difficult for me in childhood than to admit the notion of death as a state applicable to my own being. I have said elsewhere

> 'A simple child
> That lightly draws its breath,
> And feels its life in every limb,
> What should it know of death?'

But it was not so much from the source of animal vivacity that *my* difficulty came as from a sense of the indomitableness of the spirit within me. I used to brood over the stories of Enoch and Elijah, and almost to persuade myself that, whatever might become of others, I should be translated in something of the same way to heaven. With a feeling congenial to this, I was often unable to think of external things as having external existence, and I communed with all that I saw as something not apart from, but inherent in, my own immaterial nature. Many times while going to school have I grasped at a wall or tree to recall myself from this abyss of idealism to the reality. At that time I was afraid of such processes. In later periods of life I have deplored, as we have all reason to do, a subjugation of an opposite character, and have rejoiced over the remembrances, as is expressed in the lines, ' Obstinate questionings,' &c. To that dreamlike vividness and splendor which invests objects of sight in childhood, every one, I believe, if he would look back, could bear testimony, and I need not dwell upon it here; but having in the Poem regarded it as presumptive evidence of a prior state of existence, I think it right to protest against a conclusion which has given pain to some good and pious persons, that I meant to inculcate such a belief. It is far too shadowy a notion to be recommended to faith as more than an element in our instincts of immortality. But let us bear in mind that, though the idea is not advanced in Revelation, there is nothing there to contradict it, and the fall of man presents an analogy in its favour. Accordingly, a pre-existent state has entered into the popular creeds of many nations, and among all persons acquainted with classic literature is known as an ingredient in Platonic philosophy. Archimedes said that he could move the world if he had a point whereon to rest his machine. Who has not felt the same aspirations as regards the world of his own mind? Having to wield some of its elements when I was impelled to write this poem on the 'Immortality of the Soul,' I took hold of the notion of pre-existence as having sufficient foundation in humanity for authorising me to make for my purpose the best use of it I could as a Poet. *I. F. (Grosart, iii, 194-95).*   1843

288.* . . . proposed another alteration of his Ode, with a view to rescue himself from a charge—possible or impossible—of paganism.
Aubrey de Vere, p. 69.   III. 9, 1845

Supplement of Pieces not Appearing in Edition
of 1849-50

Lines Written as a School Exercise at Hawkshead

289. The verses were much admired, far more than they deserved, for they were but a tame imitation of Pope's versification, and a little in his style. This exercise, however, put it into my head to compose verses from the impulse of my own mind, and I wrote, while yet a schoolboy, a long poem running upon my own adventures, and the scenery of the country in which I was brought up. The only part of that poem which has been preserved is the conclusion of it, which stands at the beginning of my collected Poems.
Oxf. W., p. 618.   1847

George and Sarah Green

290. . . . I stopped at the grave of the poor Sufferers and immediately afterwards composed the following stanzas; *composed* I have said, I ought rather to have said effused, for it is the mere pouring out of my own feeling. . . . *To Coleridge*,   IV. 19, 1808

Translation of Part of the First Book of the Æneid

291. I shall be much gratified if you happen to like my translation, and thankful for any remarks with which you may honour me. I have made so much progress with the second book, that I defer sending the former till that is finished. It takes in many places a high tone of passion, which I would gladly succeed in rendering. When I read Virgil in the original I am moved; but not so much by the translation; and I cannot but think this owing to a defect in the diction, which I have endeavoured to supply, with what success you will easily be enabled to judge. *To Lord Lonsdale*,   I, 1819

292. See Virgil 10

293.   My own translation runs thus . . .

> 'Tis come, the final hour,
> Th' inevitable close of Dardan power
> Hath come! we *have* been Trojans, Ilium *was*,
> And the great name of Troy; now all things pass
> To Argos. So wills angry Jupiter,
> Amid a burning town the Grecians domineer.

I cannot say that 'we *have* been,' and 'Ilium *was*,' are as sonorous sounds as 'fuimus' and 'fuit'; but these latter must have been as familiar to the Romans as the former to ourselves. . . . I have one word to say upon ornament. It was my wish and labour that my translation should have far more of the *genuine* ornaments of Virgil than my predecessors. Dryden has been very careful of these, and profuse of his own, which seem to me very rarely to harmonize with those of Virgil; as, for example, describing Hector's appearance in the passage above alluded to,

> *A bloody shroud,* he seemed, and *bath'd* in tears.
> I wept to see the *visionary* man.

Again,

> And all the wounds he for his country bore
> Now streamed afresh, and with *new purple ran.*

I feel it, however, to be too probable that my translation is deficient in ornament, because I must unavoidably have lost many of Virgil's and have never without reluctance attempted a compensation of my own. Had I taken the liberties of my predecessors, Dryden especially, I could have translated nine books with the labour that three have cost me. The third book, being of humbler character than either of the former, I have treated with rather less scrupulous apprehension, and have interwoven a little of my own. . . . See Translation 4; Dryden 22. *To Lord Lonsdale,* II. 5, 1819

294.   At last, however, I have sent off the two first books of my translation [i. e. of the *Æneid. v. M. Y.,* pp. 836-40. De Sel.] to be forwarded by Mr Beckett. I hope they will be read with some pleasure, as they have cost me a good deal of pains. Translation is just as to labour what the person who makes the attempt is inclined to. If he wishes to preserve as much of the original as possible, and that with as little addition of his own as may be, there is no species of composition which costs more pains. A literal translation of an ancient poet in verse, and particularly in rhyme, is *impossible.* Something must be left out, and something added. I have done my best to avoid the one and the other fault. I ought to say a prefatory word about the versification, which will not be found much to the taste of those whose ear is exclusively accommodated to the regularity of Pope's Homer. I have run the couplets freely into each other, much more even than Dryden has done. This variety seems, to me, to be called for, if anything of the movement of the Virgilian versification be transferable to our poetry; and, independent of this consideration, long narratives in couplets with the sense closed at the end of each are to me very wearisome. *To Lord Lonsdale,* XI. 23, 1824

295.   See Translation 4, 9; Virgil 10

296.   . . . I had abandoned the thought of ever sending into the world any part of that experiment—it was nothing more—an experiment begun for amusement, and, I now think, a less fortunate one than when I first named it to you. Having been displeased, in modern translations, with the additions of incongruous matter, I began to translate with a resolve to keep clear of that fault, by adding nothing; but I became convinced that a spirited translation can scarcely be accomplished in the English language without admitting a principle of compensation.

To Ed. of Philological Museum (p. 611), 1832

A Cento made by Wordsworth

297.   For printing (the following piece) some reason should be given, as not a word of it is original: it is simply a fine stanza of Akenside, connected with a still finer from Beattie, by a couplet from Thomson [*Hymn on Solitude* (" Hail, everpleasing Solitude ")]. This practice, in which the

author sometimes indulges, of linking together in his own mind, favourite passages from different authors, seems in itself unobjectionable: but, as the *publishing* such compilations might lead to confusion in literature, he should deem himself inexcusable in giving this specimen, were it not from a hope that it might open to others a harmless source of *private* gratification.

Oxf. W., p. 626.   1835

A Poet to his Grandchild

298.   It was thought by some of my Friends that the other conclusion took the mind too much away from the subject.

Reed, p. 147,   VII. 31, 1845

Lines inscribed in a Copy of his Poems sent to the Queen

299.   Deign, Sovereign Mistress! to accept a lay,
            No Laureate offering of elaborate art. . . .
        "Deign, Sovereign," 1-2.   I. 9, 1846

Ode on the Installaton of His Royal Highness

300.*   Wordsworth said that the Installation Ode contained only superficial thought, and that it is not worth much.

L. Sara Coleridge, ii, 54.   IV. 26, 1847

THE PRELUDE

300A.*   Then the plan [of *The Prelude*] laid out, and I believe, partly suggested by me, was, that Wordsworth should assume the station of a man in mental repose, one whose principles were made up, and so prepared to deliver upon authority a system of philosophy. He was to treat man as man,—a subject of eye, ear, touch, and taste, in contact with external nature, and informing the senses from the mind, and not compounding a mind out of the senses; then he was to describe the pastoral and other states of society, assuming something of the Juvenalian spirit as he approached the high civilization of cities and towns, and opening a melancholy picture of the present state of degeneracy and vice; thence he was to infer and reveal the proof of, and necessity for, the whole state of man and society being subject to, and illustrative of, a redemptive process in operation, showing how this idea reconciled all the anomalies, and promised future glory and restoration. Something of this sort was, I think, agreed on.

Table Talk (*C. Miscellaneous Criticism*, pp. 411-12).   [1798]

301.   I have written 1300 lines of a poem in which I contrive to convey most of the knowledge of which I am possessed [the projected *Recluse*]. My object is to give pictures of Nature, Man, and Society. Indeed I know not any thing which will not come within the scope of my plan. If ever I attempt another drama, it shall be written either purposely for the closet, or purposely for the stage. There is no middle way. But the work of composition is carved out for me, for at least a year and half to come. The essays of which I have spoken to you must be written with eloquence, or not all.

My eloquence, speaking with modesty, will all be carried off, at least for some time, into my poem. If you could collect for me any books of travels you would render me an essential service, as without much of such reading my present labours cannot be brought to a conclusion. I have not yet seen the life of Mrs. Godwyn [*Memoirs of the Author of a Vindication of the Rights of Woman*, by William Godwin, 1798]. I wish to see it, though with no tormenting curiosity. *To J. Tobin,* III. 6, 1798

302. . . . a poem which I hope to make of considerable utility. Its title will be *The Recluse; or, views of Nature, Man, and Society.* *To J. Losh,* III. 11, 1798

303. . . . I have great things in meditation, but as yet I have only been doing little ones. At present I am engaged in a Poem on my own earlier life, which will take five parts or books to complete, three of which are nearly finished. My other meditated works are a Philosophical Poem, and a narrative one. These two will employ me some, I ought to say several, years, and I do not mean to appear before the world again as an Author, till one of them at least be finished. *To F. Wrangham,* early in 1804

304. . . . love Nature and Books; seek these, and you will be happy; for virtuous friendship, and love, and knowledge of mankind must inevitably accompany these, all things thus ripening in their due season.—I am now writing a poem on my own earlier life; and have just finished that part in which I speak of my residence at the University; it would give me great pleasure to read this work to you at this time, as I am sure, from the interest you have taken in the L. B., that it would please you, and might also be of service to you. This Poem will not be published these many years, and never during my lifetime, till I have finished a larger and more important work to which it is tributary. Of this larger work I have written one Book and several scattered fragments; it is a moral and philosophical Poem; the subject whatever I find most interesting in Nature, Man, and Society, and most adapted to poetic illustration. To this work I mean to devote the prime of my life, and the chief force of my mind. I have also arranged the plan of a narrative Poem; and if I live to finish these three principal works I shall be content. That on my own life, the least important of the three, is better than half complete, viz., 4 books, amounting to about 2500 lines. They are all to be in blank verse. *To De Quincey,* III. 6, 1804

305. . . . am advancing rapidly in a Poetical Work [*Prelude*], which though only introductory to another of greater importance [*The Recluse*], will I hope be found not destitute of Interest. *To W. Sotheby,* III. 12, 1804

306. I am at present in the 7th book of this work, which will turn out far longer than I ever dreamt of; it seems a frightful deal to say about one's self; and, of course, will never be published (during my lifetime, I mean) till another work has been written and published, of sufficient importance to justify me in giving my own history to the world. I pray God to give me life to finish these works, which I trust, will live, and do good; especially the

one to which that, which I have been speaking of as far advanced, is only supplementary. *To R. Sharp,*   IV. 29, 1804

307.   You will be pleased to hear that I have been advancing with my work; I have written upwards of 2,000 verses during the last ten weeks. I do not know if you are exactly acquainted with the plan of my poetical labour: it is twofold; first, a Poem, to be called *The Recluse*; in which it will be my object to express in verse my most interesting feelings concerning Man, Nature, and society; and next, a Poem (in which I am at present chiefly engaged) on my earlier life or the growth of my own mind taken up upon a large scale. This latter work I expect to have finished before the month of May; and then I purpose to fall with all my might on the former, which is the chief object upon which my thoughts have been fixed these many years. Of this poem, that of 'The Pedlar,' which Coleridge read you, is part, and I may have written of it altogether about 2,000 lines. It will consist, I hope, of about 10 or 12 thousand. *To Beaumont,*   XII. 25, 1804

308.   Six changeful years have vanished since I first
                Poured out (saluted by that quickening breeze
                Which met me issuing from the City's walls)
                A glad preamble to this Verse: I sang
                Aloud, with fervour irresistible
                Of short-lived transport, like a torrent bursting,
                From a black thunder-cloud, down Scafell's side
                To rush and disappear. But soon broke forth
                (So willed the Muse) a less impetuous stream,
                That flowed awhile with unabating strength,
                Then stopped for years; not audible again
                Before last primrose-time.
                Prel., vii, 1-12.   1804-39

309.   . . . this history is brought
                To its appointed close: the discipline
                And consummation of a Poet's mind,
                In everything that stood most prominent,
                Have faithfully been pictured; we had reached
                The time (our guiding object from the first)
                When we may, not presumptuously, I hope,
                Suppose my powers so far confirmed, and such
                My knowledge, as to make me capable
                Of building up a Work that shall endure.
                Yet much hath been omitted, as need was;
                Of books how much! and even of the other wealth
                That is collected among woods and fields,
                Far more: for Nature's secondary grace
                Hath hitherto been barely touched upon,
                The charm more superficial that attends
                Her works, as they present to Fancy's choice
                Apt illustrations of the moral world,
                Caught at a glance, or traced with curious pains.
                Prel., xiv, 302-20.
                                                                                1804-39

310.   Anon I rose
        As if one wings, and saw beneath me stretched
        Vast prospect of the world which I had been
        And was; and hence this Song, which like a lark
        I have protracted, in the unwearied heavens
        Singing, and often with more plaintive voice
        To earth attempered and her deep-drawn sighs,
        Yet centring all in love, and in the end
        All gratulant, if rightly understood.
        Prel., xiv, 379-87.   1804-39

311. It will be not much less than 9000 lines,—not hundred but thousand
lines long,—an alarming length! and a thing unprecedented in literary history
that a man should talk so much about himself. It is not self-conceit, as you
will know well, that has induced me to do this, but real humility; I began
the work because I was unprepared to treat any more arduous subject, and
diffident of my own powers. Here, at least, I hoped that to a certain degree
I should be sure of succeeding, as I had nothing to do but describe what I
had felt and thought; therefore could not easily be bewildered. This might
certainly have been done in narrower compass by a man of more address, but
I have done my best. If, when the work shall be finished, it appears to the
judicious to have redundancies, they shall be lopped off, if possible; but this
is very difficult to do, when a man has written with thought; and this defect,
whenever I have suspected it or found it to exist in any writings of mine, I
have always found incurable. The fault lies too deep, and is in the first conception. If you see Coleridge before I do, do not speak of this to him, as I
should like to have his judgment unpreoccupied by such an apprehension.
To Beaumont,   V. 1, 1805

312. . . . when I looked back upon the performance it seemed to have a
dead weight about it, the reality so far short of the expectation; it was the
first long labour that I had finished, and the doubt whether I should ever
live to write *The Recluse*, and the sense which I had of this poem being so
far below what I seemed capable of executing, depressed me much. . . .
This work may be considered as a sort of *portico* to *The Recluse*, part of the
same building, which I hope to be able, ere long, to begin with in earnest; and
if I am permitted to bring it to a conclusion, and to write, further, a narrative
Poem of the Epic kind, I shall consider the *task* of my life as over. I ought
to add that I have the satisfaction of finding the present Poem not quite of so
alarming a length as I apprehended. *To Beaumont,*   VI. 3, 1805

313. The above [*Prelude*, viii, 1-61 (1805 text)] is from one of the
books upon my own earlier life. It has been extracted not so much from any
notion of its merit, as from its standing more independent of the rest of the
poem than any other part of it. *To Beaumont,*   VI-VII, 1805

314. [Relationship between *The Prelude* and *The Excursion*.] See
W. 340

315. See Passion 47; Power 4; Revisions 3, 9; Coleridge 12; W. 368A,

317. . . . in the year 1805, I concluded a long poem upon the formation

of my own mind. . . . That book still exists in manuscript. Its publication has been prevented merely by the personal character of the subject. Had it been published as soon as it was finished, the copyright would long ago have expired in the case of my decease. Now I do honestly believe that that poem, if given to the world before twenty-eight years had elapsed after the composition, would scarcely have paid its own expenses. If published now, with the aid of such reputation as I have acquired, I have reason to believe that the profit from it would be respectable. *To T. Talfourd,* IV. 11, 1839

THE EXCURSION

319.   A Portion of a long Poem from me will see the light ere long. I hope it will give you pleasure. It is serious, and has been written with great labour. *To F. Wrangham*   IV. 26, 1814

321.   I am glad that it has interested you; I expected no less, and I wish from my Soul that it had been a thousand times more deserving of your regard. In respect to its final destiny I have neither care nor anxiety being assured that if it be of God it must stand; and that if the spirit of truth, 'The Vision and the Faculty divine,' be not in it, and so do not pervade it, it must perish. So let the wisest and best of the present generation and of Posterity decide the question. Thoroughly indifferent as I am on this point, I will acknowledge that I have a wish for the *sale* of the present Edition, partly to repay the Expense of our Scotch Tour, and still more to place the book within the reach of those who can neither purchase nor procure it in its present expensive shape.   . . . I mentioned the Philanthropist because it circulates a good deal among Quakers, who are wealthy and fond of *instructive* Books. Besides, though I am a professed admirer of the Church of England, I hope that my religious sentiments will not be offensive to *them*. *To C. Clarkson,*   XII. 31, 1814

322.   . . . I it belongs to the second part of a long and laborious Work, which is to consist of three parts.   . . . . [Had the first part been completed, W. would have preferred the natural order of publication], but, as the second division of the Work was designed to refer more to passing events, and to an existing state of things, than the others were meant to do, more continuous exertion was naturally bestowed upon it, and greater progress made here than in the rest of the poem; and as this part does not depend upon the preceding, to a degree which will materially injure its own peculiar interest, the Author, complying with the earnest entreaties of some valued Friends, presents the following pages to the Public. *Pref. Exc.,* 754.   1814

325.   See Aim of Writing 28; Character Analysis 8; Passion 40; Versification 35-6; Gifford 1; Jeffrey 4-6, 8-10; W. 100, 340.

328.   IV. V. *Prospectus* of the design and scope.   . . . See *Oxf. W.,* p. 755.

329.   . . . . the Excursion has one merit if it has no other, a versification to which for variety of musical effect no poem in the language furnishes a parallel.

Miss — s notion of poetical imagery is probably taken from the Pleasures of Hope or Gertrude of Wyoming—See for instance Stanza the first of said poems—There is very little imagery of that kind, But I am far from subscribing to your conception that there is little imagery in the Poem Either collateral in the way of metaphor colouring the style, illustrative in the way of Simile, or directly under the shape of description or incident [p. 78]. . . . The construction of the language is perspicuous, at least I have taken every possible pains to make it so. Therefore you will have no difficulty here—The impediments you may meet with will be of two kinds; such as exist in the Ode which concludes my second Volume of Poems—This poem rests entirely upon two recollections of Childhood One that of a Splendour in the objects of Sense which is passed away, and the other an indisposition to bend to the law of death as applying to our own particular case—A Reader who has not a vivid recollection of these feelings having existed in his mind in Childhood cannot understand that poem. So also with regard to some of those elements of the human soul whose importance is insisted upon in the Excursion, and some of those images of Sense which are dwelt upon as holding that relation to immortality & infinity which I have before alluded to—If a person has not been in the way of receiving these images, it is not likely that he can form such an adequate conception of them as will bring him into vivid sympathy with the Poet—For instance one who has never heard the Echoes of the flying Ravens voice in a mountainous country as described at the close of the fourth Book will not perhaps be able to relish that illustration; Yet every one must have been in the way of perceiving similar effects from different causes [p. 80]. . . . The reason of the thing being so bad [a criticism of the *Excursion*] is that your friends remarks were so monstrous To talk of the Offence of writing the Excⁿ & the difficulty of forgiving the author is carrying audacity & presumption to a height of which I did not think any *Woman* [a Unitarian] was capable. Had my poem been much coloured by books as many parts of what I have to write must be I should have been accused as Milton has been of Pedantry and of having a mind which could not support itself but by other mens labours——

Do you not perceive that my conversations [in *The Excursion*] almost all take place out of Doors. And all with grand objects of nature surrounding the speakers, for the express purpose of their being alluded to in illustration of the subjects treated of —— *Much* imagery from books would have been an incumbrance. Where it was wanted, it is found. [See all this letter.]

To Mrs. Clarkson (*Corr. C. R.*, i, 78, 80, 82),   1814

330. And, as it is in some places a little abstruse, and in all, serious, without any of the modern attractions of glittering style, or incident to provoke curiosity, it cannot be expected to make its way without difficulty, and it is therefore especially incumbent on those who value it to exert themselves in its behalf. My opinion as to the execution of the minor parts of my works is not in the *least altered. To Poole,*   III. 13, 1815

331. Let me beg out of kindness to me that you would relinquish the intention of publishing the Poem addressed to me after hearing *mine* to you. The commendation would be injurious to us both, and my work when it appears, would labour under a great disadvantage in consequence of such a precursorship of Praise.

I shall be thankful for your remarks on the Poems, and also upon the Excursion, only begging that whenever it is possible references may be made to some passages which have given rise to the opinion whether favourable or otherwise; in consequence of this not having been done (when indeed it would have been out of Place) in your Letter to Lady B— [For Coleridge's Letter to Lady B., here referred to, and his answer to W. W.'s letter, *v. Letters of S. T. Coleridge*, ed. E. H. Coleridge, 1895, pp. 641-50. Coleridge assures W. that 'I had never determined to print the lines addressed to you. . . . Most assuredly, I never once thought of printing them without having consulted you.' But two years later he included them in *Sybilline Leaves*. De Sel.] I have rather been perplexed than enlightened by your *comparative* censure. One of my principal aims in the Exn: has been to put the commonplace truths, of the human affections especially, in an interesting point of view; and rather to remind men of their knowledge, as it lurks inoperative and unvalued in their own minds, than to attempt to convey recondite or refined truths. Pray point out to me the most striking instances where I have failed, in producing poetic effect by an overfondness for this practice, or through inability to realize my wishes.
To Coleridge,   V. 22, 1815

332.   In the edition of [18]27 it was diligently revised; and the sense in several instances got into less room, yet still it is a long Poem for these feeble and fastidious times. *To Dyce,*   IV. 30, 1830

334.   When you read the Excursion do not read the Quarto,—it is improved in the octavo edition,—but the quarto may have its value with you as a collector. *To Dyce,*   IV. 7, 1841

335.   . . . I am here called upon freely to acknowledge that the character I have represented in his person ['Pedlar'] is chiefly an idea of what I fancied my own character might have become in his circumstances.

Nevertheless much of what he says and does had an external existence, that fell under my own youthful and subsequent observation. . . .
I. F. (Grosart, iii, 196).   1841

THE RECLUSE

337.   See W. 301-7, 312, 372

338.   . . . I wrote one book of the Recluse nearly 1000 lines, then had a rest, last week began again, and have written 300 more; I hope all tolerably well, and certainly with good views. *To Beaumont,*   IX. 8, 1806

339.   . . . I have at last resolved to send to the Press a portion of a Poem which, if I live to finish it, I hope future times will 'not willingly let die.' These you know are the words of my great Predecessor, and the depth of my feelings upon some subjects seems to justify me in the act of applying them to myself, while speaking to a Friend, who I know has always been partial to me. *To T. Poole,*   IV. 28, 1814

340.   It may be proper to state whence the poem, of which *The Excursion*

is a part, derives its Title of THE RECLUSE.—Several years ago, when the Author retired to his native mountains, with the hope of being enabled to construct a literary Work that might live, it was a reasonable thing that he should take a review of his own mind, and examine how far Nature and Education had qualified him for such employment. As subsidiary to this preparation, he undertook to record, in verse, the origin and progress of his own powers, as far as he was acquainted with them. That Work, addressed to a dear Friend, most distinguished for his knowledge and genius, and to whom the Author's Intellect is deeply indebted, has been long finished; and the result of the investigation which gave rise to it was a determination to compose a philosophical poem, containing views of Man, Nature, and Society; and to be entitled, *The Recluse*; as having for its principal subject the sensations and opinions of a poet living in retirement.—The preparatory poem is biographical, and conducts the history of the Author's mind to the point when he was emboldened to hope that his faculties were sufficiently matured for entering upon the arduous labour which he had proposed to himself: and the two Works have the same kind of relation to each other, if he may so express himself, as the ante-chapel has to the body of a gothic church. Continuing this allusion, he may be permitted to add, that his minor Pieces, which have been long before the Public, when they shall be properly arranged, will be found by the attentive Reader to have such a connexion with the main Work as may give them claim to be likened to the little cells, oratories, and sepulchral recesses, ordinarily included in those edifices.

The Author would not have deemed himself justified in saying, upon this occasion, so much of performances either unfinished, or unpublished, if he had not thought that the labour bestowed by him upon what he has heretofore and now laid before the Public entitled him to candid attention for such a statement as he thinks necessary to throw light upon his endeavours to please and, he would hope, to benefit his countrymen.—Nothing further need be added, than that the first and third parts of *The Recluse* will consist chiefly of meditations in the Author's own person; and that in the intermediate part (*The Excursion*) the intervention of characters speaking is employed, and something of a dramatic form adopted.

It is not the Author's intention formally to announce a system: it was animating to him to proceed in a different course; and if he shall succeed in conveying to the mind clear thoughts, lively images, and strong feelings, the Reader will have no difficulty in extracting the system for himself.

Pref. Exc., pp. 754-55.   1814

342. [*The Recluse* and its relation to *Poems, 1815.*] See Poetry 68

POEMS NOT IN THE "OXFORD WORDSWORTH"

343.   I shall not consume much paper in defending myself against your criticisms; in general I think them just, others might be added to them with equal propriety. For the 2 poems [see *E. L.*, p. 222 and note 1] 'How sweet where crimson colours etc. and ' One day the darling of my heart' I do not care a farthing. Of the rest we will talk when we meet.

D. W., and W. to Coleridge (p. 222),   II. 27, 1799

446   *The Critical Opinions of William Wordsworth*

LYRICAL BALLADS (GENERAL)

343A.   See Coleridge 61A; W. 364A, 368A

344.   [Reputation increases] though slowly, as might be expected from
a work so original. *W., and D. W. to R. W.*,   VI. 26, 1803

345.*   . . . most of his Lyrical Ballads were founded [on fact].
H. C. R., i, 190.   IX. 11, 1816

LYRICAL BALLADS, 1798

345A.*   During the first year [1797] that Mr. Wordsworth and I were
neighbours, our conversations turned frequently on the two cardinal points of
poetry, the power of exciting the sympathy of the reader by a faithful adherence to the truth of nature, and the power of giving the interest of novelty
by the modifying colors of imagination. The sudden charm, which accidents
of light and shade, which moon-light or sun-set diffused over a known and
familiar landscape, appeared to represent the practicability of combining both.
These are the poetry of nature. The thought suggested itself (to which of us
I do not recollect) that a series of poems be composed of two sorts. In the
one, the incidents and agents were to be, in part at least, supernatural; and the
excellence aimed at was to consist in the interesting of the affections by the
dramatic truth of such emotions, as would naturally accompany such situations,
supposing them real. And real in *this* sense they have been to every human
being who, from whatever source of delusion, has at any time believed himself under supernatural agency. For the second class, subjects were to be
chosen from ordinary life; the characters and incidents were to be such, as
will be found in every village and its vicinity, where there is a meditative
and feeling mind to seek after them, or to notice them, when they present
themselves.

In this idea originated the plan of the "Lyrical Ballads"; in which it
was agreed, that my endeavours should be directed to persons and characters
supernatural, or at least romantic; yet so as to transfer from our inward nature
a human interest and a semblance of truth sufficient to procure for these
shadows of imagination that willing suspension of disbelief for the moment,
which constitutes poetic faith. Mr. Wordsworth, on the other hand, was to
propose to himself as his object, to give the charm of novelty to things of
every day, and to excite a feeling analogous to the supernatural, by awakening
the mind's attention from the lethargy of custom, and directing it to the
loveliness and the wonders of the world before us; an inexhaustible treasure,
but for which, in consequence of the film of familiarity and selfish solicitude
we have eyes, yet see not, ears that hear not, and hearts that neither feel nor
understand. *Biog. Lit.*, ii, 5-6.   [1797]

346.   The majority of the following poems are to be considered as
experiments. They were written chiefly with a view to ascertain how far the
language of conversation in the middle and lower classes of society is adapted
to the purposes of poetic pleasure. Readers accustomed to the gaudiness and

inane phraseology of many modern writers, if they persist in reading this book to its conclusion, will perhaps frequently have to struggle with feelings of strangeness and awkwardness: they will look round for poetry, and will be induced to inquire by what species of courtesy these attempts can be permitted to assume that title. It is desirable that such readers, for their own sakes, should not suffer the solitary word Poetry, a word of very disputed meaning, to stand in the way of their gratification; but that, while they are perusing this book, they should ask themselves if it contains a natural delineation of human passions, human characters, and human incidents; and if the answer be favourable to the author's wishes, that they should consent to be pleased in spite of that most dreadful enemy to our pleasures, our own pre-established codes of decision. *Adv. L. B. (K. Prose*, i, 31). 1798

347. Of the other poems in the collection [*L. B.* (1798)] it may be proper to say that they are either absolute inventions of the author, or facts which took place within his personal observation or that of his friends. *Adv. L. B. (K. Prose*, i, 32). 1798

349. See Aim of Writing 10, 11; Style 3; Coleridge 61A; W. 368A

349A.* [W.] would not object to the publishing of " Peter Bell," or the " Salisbury Plain " singly; but to the publishing of his poems in two volumes, he is decisively repugnant and oppugnant.

He deems that they want variety, etc, etc. . . . We deem that the volumes offered to you, are, to a certain degree, one work in kind, though not in degree, as an ode is one work; and that our different poems are, as stanzas, good, relatively rather that absolutely . . . in kind, though not in degree. *Coleridge to Cottle (Reminiscences of S. T. Coleridge and R. Southey,* Joseph Cottle, New York, 1847, p. 135), V, 1798

350. The first volume of these Poems [*L. B.* 1798] has already been submitted to general perusal. It was published, as an experiment, which, I hoped, might be of some use to ascertain, how far, by fitting to metrical arrangement a selection of the real language of men in a state of vivid sensation, that sort of pleasure and that quantity of pleasure may be imparted, which a Poet may rationally endeavour to impart.

I had formed no very inaccurate estimate of the probable effect of those Poems: I flattered myself that they who should be pleased with them would read them with more than common pleasure: and, on the other hand, I was well aware, that by those who should dislike them, they would be read with more than common dislike. The result has differed from my expectation in this only, that a greater number have been pleased than I ventured to hope I should please. *Pref. L. B.*, p. 934. 1800

351.* The first volume [of *L. B.*] sold much better than we expected, and was liked by a much greater number of people, not that we had ever much doubt of its finally making its way, but we knew that poems so different from what have in general become popular immediately after their publication were not likely to be admired all at once.

D. W. to Jane Marshall (p. 250). IX. 10, 1800

352. . . . we began to talk of a volume which was to consist, as Mr.

Coleridge has told the world, of Poems chiefly on natural subjects, taken from common life, but looked at, as much as might be, through an imaginative medium. Accordingly I wrote ' The Idiot Boy,' ' Her Eyes are wild,' &c., and ' We are Seven,' ' The Thorn,' and some others.

I. F. (Grosart, iii, 17).   1843

LYRICAL BALLADS, 1800

353.   Several of my Friends are anxious for the success of these Poems, from a belief, that, if the views with which they were composed were indeed realized, a class of Poetry would be produced, well adapted to interest mankind permanently, and not unimportant in the quality, and in the multiplicity of its moral relations: and on this account they have advised me to prefix a systematic defence of the theory upon which to undertake the task [W. feared: (1) some one might think he was reasoning the reader into approval of the poems; (2) he would require more space than the proper length of a preface] . . . it would be necessary to give a full account of the present state of the public taste in this country, and to determine how far this taste is healthy or depraved; which, again, could not be determined, without pointing out in what manner language and the human mind act and re-act on each other, and without retracing the revolutions, not of literature alone, but likewise of society itself. I have therefore altogether declined to enter regularly upon this defence; yet I am sensible, that there would be something like impropriety in abruptly obtruding upon the Public, without a few words of introduction, Poems so materially different from those upon which general approbation is at present bestowed. *Pref. L. B.*, p. 934.   1800

354.   The principal object, then, proposed in these Poems [*L. B.*, 1800] was to chose incidents and situations from common life, and to relate or describe them, throughout, as far as was possible in a selection of language really used by men, and, at the same time, to throw over them a certain colouring of imagination, whereby ordinary things should be presented to the mind in an unusual aspect; and, further, and above all, to make these incidents and situations interesting by tracing in them, truly though not ostentatiously, the primary laws of our nature: chiefly, as far as regards the manner in which we associate ideas in a state of excitement. Humble and rustic life was generally chosen, because, in that condition, the essential passions of the heart find a better soil in which they can attain their maturity, are less under restraint, and speak a plainer and more emphatic language; because in that condition of life our elementary feelings coexist in a state of greater simplicity, and, consequently, may be more accurately contemplated, and more forcibly communicated; because the manners of rural life germinate from those elementary feelings, and, from the necessary character of rural occupations, are more easily comprehended, and are more durable; and, lastly, because in that condition the passions of men are incorporated with the beautiful and permanent forms of nature. The language, too, of these men has been adopted (purified indeed from what appear to be its real defects, from all lasting and rational causes of dislike or disgust) because

such men hourly communicate with the best objects from which the best part of language is originally derived; and because, from their rank in society and the sameness and narrow circle of their intercourse, being less under the influence of social vanity, they convey their feelings and notions in simple and unelaborated expressions. Accordingly, such a language, arising out of repeated experience and regular feelings, is a more permanent, and a far more philosophical language, than that which is frequently substituted for it by Poets, who think that they are conferring honour upon themselves and their art, in proportion as they separate themselves from the sympathies of men, and indulge in arbitrary and capricious habits of expression, in order to furnish food for fickle tastes, and fickle appetites, of their own creation. (It is worth while here to observe, that the affecting parts of Chaucer are almost always expressed in language pure and universally intelligible even to this day.)
Pref. L. B., p. 935 and n¹.   1800

355. . . . with reference solely to these particular poems, and to some defects which will probably be found in them. I am sensible that my associations must have sometimes been particular instead of general, and that, consequently, giving to things a false importance, I may have sometimes written upon unworthy subjects; but I am less apprehensive on this account, than that my language may frequently have suffered from those arbitrary connexions of feelings and ideas with particular words and phrases, from which no man can altogether protect himself. Hence I have no doubt, that, in some instances, feelings, even of the ludicrous, may be given to my Readers by expressions which appeared to me tender and pathetic. Such faulty expressions, were I convinced they were faulty at present, and that they must necessarily continue to be so, I would willingly take all reasonable pains to correct. But it is dangerous to make these alterations on the simple authority of a few individuals, or even of certain classes of men; for where the understanding of an Author is not convinced, or his feelings altered, this cannot be done without great injury to himself: for his own feelings are his stay and support; and, if he set them aside in one instance, he may be induced to repeat this act till his mind shall lose all confidence in itself, and become utterly debilitated. To this it may be added, that the critic ought never to forget that he is himself exposed to the same errors as he Poet, and, perhaps, in a much greater degree: for there can be no presumption in saying of most readers, that it is not probable they will be so well acquainted with the various stages of meaning through which words have passed, or with the fickleness or stability of the relations of particular ideas to each other; and, above all, since they are so much less interested in the subject, they may decide lightly and carelessly. *Pref. L. B.*, p. 941.   1800

356. [The reader of the *L. B.*, and of the *Pref. L. B.* will perceive the object and] will determine how far it has been attained; and, what is a much more important question, whether it be worth attaining: and upon the decision of these two questions will rest my claim to the approbation of the Public.
Pref. L. B., p. 942.   1800

357. See Imagery 5; Pleasure 2, 3; Style 6-17; Versification 2

359. . . . the feeling therein developed gives importance to the action and situation. . . . See Passion 7

361. [Each poem has a worthy purpose.] See Aim of Writing 10, 11

362. [Wordsworth writes that he will probably accept eighty pounds for the second edition of the *Lyrical Ballads* with the hope that they will sell rapidly and bring a better price at their next market] when their merit will be known. *To Richard W.,*   V. 8, 1800

364.   Several of the poems contained in these Volumes are written upon subjects, which are the common property of all Poets, and which, at some period of your life, must have been interesting to a man of your sensibility, and perhaps may still continue to be so. It would be highly gratifying to me to suppose that even in a single instance the manner in which I have treated these general topics should afford you any pleasure; but such a hope does not influence me upon the present occasion; in truth I do not feel it. Besides, I am convinced that here must be many things in this collection, which may impress you with an unfavorable idea of my intellectual powers. I do not say this with a wish to degrade myself; but I am sensible that this must be the case, from the different circles in which we have moved, and the different objects with which we have been conversant.
To Chas. J. Fox,   I. 14, 1801

364A.* [W. regretted that Lamb had not enjoyed the second volume of *L. B.*] "was compelled to wish that my range of sensibility was more extended, being obliged to believe that I should receive large influxes of happiness and happy Thoughts . . ." — [There was] a deal of stuff about a certain Union of Tenderness and Imagination, which in the sense he used Imagination was not the characteristic of Shakespeare, but which Milton possessed in a degree far exceeding other Poets: which Union, as the highest species of Poetry, and chiefly deserving that name, "He was most proud to aspire to"; then [W. had illustrated that union by two quotations from his poems: the first was from "Michael," 340-43; W. had indicated lines 342-3 as] "combining in an extraordinary degree that Union of Imagination and Tenderness" which I am speaking of, I consider as one of the Best I ever wrote!" [The second quotation was from "The Brothers," 98-9.]
L. of Lamb, i, 246.   II. 15, 1801

365. [Relationship between the minor poems and *The Recluse*.] See W. 340

366.* Wordsworth was of opinion that posterity will value most those lyrical ballads which were most laughed at. . . . This he said to me when I remarked that no metrical form of his various poems afforded me so great pleasure as the Sonnets. 'You are quite wrong,' he replied.
C. R. to J. Mottram (*Corr. C. R.,* ii, 818-9),   *c.* 1840

367.*   His first publication worth notice was *The lyrical ballads* that which in his own opinion posterity will value the most. . . .
C. R.'s notes (*Corr. C. R.,* ii, 836),   *c.* 1840

POEMS IN TWO VOLUMES, 1807

368. It would look like affectation if I were to say how indifferent I am to its [*Poems in Two Volumes, 1807*] present reception; but I have a true pleasure in saying to you that I put some value upon it; and hope that it will one day or other be thought well of by the Public.

To W. Scott,   XI. 10, 1806

368A.   The short Poems, of which these volumes consist, were chiefly composed to refresh my mind during the progress of a work of length and labour, in which I have for some time been engaged; and to furnish me with employment when I had not resolution to apply myself to that work, or hope that I should proceed with it successfully. Having already, in the Volumes entitled Lyrical Ballads, offered to the World a considerable collection of short poems, I did not wish to add these to the number, till after the completion and publication of my larger work; but, as I cannot even guess when this will be, and as several of these Poems have been circulated in manuscript, I thought it better to send them forth at once. They were composed with much pleasure to my own mind, and I build upon that remembrance a hope that they may afford profitable pleasure to many readers.

" Advertisement " to 1807 edition, *Longman MSS*, pp. 71-2.   1807

368B.   This Book, which strives to express in tuneful sound
          The joys and sorrows which through life abound,
          (Some great, some small, some frequent, and some rare,
          Yet all observ'd or felt and truly there)
          May in the following pages, which are penn'd
          From general motives, gain a private end:
          This little wandering Book (for who can say
          Into what coverts it shall find its way)
          May reach, perchance, the very Man, whose ear
          Knows nothing of what many Strangers hear,
          Whether through his mishap or his neglect:
          A doleful plaint it is, to this effect.
          [Prefatory lines written for *The Lyrical Ballads,* 1807.]
Longman MSS, p. 63.   1807

369. . . . I have expressed my calm confidence that these Poems will live, I have said nothing which has a particular application to the object of it, which was to remove all disquiet from your mind on account of the condemnation they may at present incur from that portion of my contemporaries who are called the Public. . . . [Have no] fear that this present blame is ominous of their future or final destiny . . . be assured that the decision of these persons has nothing to do with the Question; they are altogether incompetent judges. These people in the senseless hurry of their idle lives do not *read* books, they merely snatch a glance at them that they may talk about them. And even if this were not so, never forget what I believe was observed to you by Coleridge, that every great and original writer, in propor-

tion as he is great or original, must himself create the taste by which he is to be relished; he must teach the art by which he is to be seen; this, in a certain degree, even to all persons, however wise and pure may be their lives, and however unvitiated their taste; but for those who dip into books in order to give an opinion of them, or talk about them to take up an opinion—for this multitude of unhappy, and misguided, and misguiding beings, an entire regeneration must be produced; and if this be possible, it must be a work *of time*. To conclude, my ears are stone-dead to this idle buzz, and my flesh as insensible as iron to these petty stings. . . . I doubt not that you will share with me an invincible confidence that my writings (and among them these little Poems) will co-operate with the benign tendencies in human nature and society, wherever found; and that they will, in their degree, be efficacious in making men wiser, better, and happier.

To Lady Beaumont,   V. 21, 1807

370. . . . these breathings of simple Nature, the more so, because I conclude, from the character of the Poems which you have particularized, that the Volumes cannot but improve upon you. I see that you have entered into the spirit of them. *To F. Wrangham,*   XI. 4, 1807

POEMS, 1815

371. [The reader who can remember the prevailing taste in 1798, the effect these poems have had, and the unremitting hostility toward them, will understand the relation between these poems and the *E. Supp. Pref.*]
E. Supp. Pref., p. 951.   1815

372. [W.] . . . by assuring them—that, if he were not persuaded that the contents of these Volumes, and the Work to which they are subsidiary, evince something of the ' Vision and the Faculty divine '; and that, both in words and things, they will operate in their degree, to extend the domain of sensibility for the delight, the honour, and the benefit of human nature, notwithstanding the many happy hours which he has employed in their composition, and the manifold comforts and enjoyments they have procured to him, he would not, if a wish could do it, save them from immediate destruction;—from becoming at this moment, to the world, as a thing that had never been. *E. Supp. Pref.*, p. 953.   1815

373. I cannot but flatter myself that this publication will interest you. The pains which I have bestowed on the composition can never be known but to myself, and I am very sorry to find, on reviewing the work, that the labour has been able to do so little for it. *To Gillies,*   IV. 25, 1815

374. See Fame 13; Poetry 68

THE SONNETS OF W. W. COLLECTED IN ONE VOLUME, 1838

376. See Aim of Writing 37

POEMS, 1845

377. . . . there will be no small demand for it [*Poems, 1845*]; partly for its own sake, & partly to class with Byron & Southey &c who are already in the same forms. The alterations of which you heard, are almost exclusively confined to a few of the Juvenile Poems—

To C. R. (Corr., C. R., ii, 606),   VIII. 7, 1845

   378. [Classification of poems.] See Imagination 48

PREFACE TO " LYRICAL BALLADS," 1800

378A.* But I will apprise you of one thing, that although Wordsworth's Preface is half a child of my own brain, and arose out of conversations so frequent that, with few exceptions, we could scarcely either of us, perhaps, positively say which first started any particular thought (I am speaking of the Preface as it stood in the second volume), yet I am far from going all lengths with Wordsworth. . . . On the contrary, I rather suspect that somewhere or other there is a radical difference in our theoretical opinions respecting poetry. . . . *Letters (Coleridge),* i, 386-7.   VII. 29, 1802

   379. [As a guide to *L. B.*] See W. 353-56

   379A. [As a guide to object of *L. B.*] See Pleasure 3

   380. [Purpose in writing.] See Poetry 16; W. 354

   380. See Criticism 57, 59, 77; W. 381A, 388-90A

   381. [Revolutionary criticism therein.] See Aim of Writing 11

   381A. The observations prefixed to that portion of these Volumes, which was published many years ago, under the title of " Lyrical Ballads," have so little of a special application to the greater part, perhaps, of this collection, as subsequently enlarged and diversified, that they could not with any propriety stand as an Introduction to it. Not deeming it, however, expedient to suppress that exposition, slight and imperfect as it is, of the feelings which had determined the choice of the subjects, and the principles which had regulated the composition of those Pieces, I have transferred it to the end of the second Volume, to be attended to, or not, at the pleasure of the Reader. *Pref., 1815* [*W.'s Works,* ii, 431n.²].   1815-36

   382. . . . I never cared a straw about the ' theory ' and the ' preface ' was written at the request of Mr. Coleridge, out of sheer good nature.

Letters K., iii, 121.   1836 or after

APPENDIX TO " LYRICAL BALLADS "

   382A. [For two passages cancelled in MS from the *Appendix,* see Style 22, and Criticism 39A.]

   382B. See Pope 14; W. 388

PREFACE TO THE EDITION OF 1814 (" THE EXCURSION ")

383.   In the Preface to that part of " The Recluse," lately published under the title of " The Excursion," I have alluded to a meditated arrangement of my minor Poems, which should assist the attentive Reader to perceiving their connection with each other, and also their subordination to that Work. I shall here say a few words explanatory of this arrangement, as carried into effect in the present Volumes.

Pref., 1815 [*W.'s Works*, ii, 431n.²].   1815-36

PREFACE, 1815

383A.   See W. 381A, 388

ESSAY, SUPPLEMENTARY TO THE PREFACE

383B.   See W. 371, 388

POSTSCRIPT, 1835

384.   See also W. 388

385.   [His remarks on subjects of national interest were uttered] in the spirit of reflective patriotism. . . .   [There are many objects of general concern, and changes going forward that affect the lower social classes] . . . in reference to these, I wish here to add a few words in plain prose. [Publication in the present edition of poems will have the advantages of permanence and of the weight of his name.] *Postscript, 1835*, p. 959.   1835

386.   [The thoughts and feelings in the *Postscript* have been expressed in his verse, and W. concludes with an illustrative quotation from *The Prelude*, xiii, 224-78. Willing to sacrifice his credit as a poet with the critics] if the sober-minded admit that, in general views, my affections have been moved, and my imagination exercised, under and *for* the guidance of reason. *Postscript, 1835*, p. 966.   1835

PREFACE TO " THE BORDERERS "

387.   See W. 21, 388

PREFACES (GENERAL)

388.   Much the greatest part of the foregoing Poems has been so long before the Public that no prefatory matter, explanatory of any portion of them, or of the arrangement which has been adopted, appears to be required; and had it not been for the observations contained in those Prefaces upon the

principles of Poetry in general they would not have been reprinted even in an Appendix in this Edition.

Oxf. W., p. 934. [Prefatory note to ed. 1849-50.] 1849

389. Having long wished that an Edition of my Poems should be published without the Prefaces and supplement, I submit to your consideration whether that would not be well, (printing, however, the prose now attached to the Volumes as a portion of the Prose Volume which you meditate). The Prefaces, etc contain many important observations upon Poetry—but they were written solely to gratify Coleridge; and, for my own part, being quite against anything of the kind, and having always been of opinion that Poetry should stand upon its own merits, I would not even attach to the Poems any explanation of the grounds of their arrangement. I should however by all means wish that the Vol. of prose should be printed uniform with the Poems. . . . *To Moxon,* IV. 10, 1845

390. In respect to the prefaces my own wish w[o]uld be that now the Poems sh[o]uld be left to speak for themselves without them, but I know that this w[o]uld not answer for the purposes of sale. They will therefore be printed at the end of the Volume, and to this I am in some degree reconciled by the matter they contain relating to Poetry in general, and the principles they inculcate. *Reed,* p. 152. IX. 27, 1845

390A. [Will hereafter print the prefaces at the end of the volume] the poems should be left to speak for themselves. . . .
To Moxon, XI. 5, 1845

LITERATURE OF KNOWLEDGE AND LITERATURE OF POWER

391.* [De Quincey stated in *Letters to a Young Man*, (Boston, 1853), p. 93 n.[7]]: For which distinction, as for most of the sound criticism on poetry, or any subject connected with it that I have ever met with, I must acknowledge my obligations to many years' conversation with Mr. Wordsworth. Upon this occasion it may be useful to notice that there is a rhetorical use of the word "power" very different from the analytic one here introduced, which, also, is due originally to Mr. Wordsworth, and will be found in no place before 1798. . . . [De Quincey explains the distinction]: The function of the first is—to teach; the function of the second is—to *move*: the first is a rudder, the second an oar or a sail. The first speaks to the mere discursive understanding; the second speaks ultimately, it may happen, to the higher understanding or reason, but always through affections of pleasure and sympathy. . . . [De Quincey speaks of] *power*, or deep sympathy with truth [p. 150, and of] *power*, that is exercise and expansion to your own latent capacity of sympathy with the infinite, where every pulse and each separate influx is a step upwards . . . from earth to mysterious altitudes above the earth [p. 151]. De Quincey's *Essays on the Poets*, pp. 149-51 (see also pp. 149-56; and *Letters to a Young Man*, pp. 47-51).

[1807-17]

THE CONVENTION OF CINTRA

392. What I have written has been done according to the best light of my Conscience. It is indeed very imperfect, and will, I fear, be little read; but, if it is read, it cannot I hope fail of doing some good, though I am aware it will create me a world of enemies, and call forth the old yell of Jacobinism.

To F. Wrangham (p. 290),   IV, 1809

394.   You said that Mr. Canning could not deny that I had spoken with the bone of truth [i. e. in the *Convention of Cintra*]. The misfortune is, with persons in Mr. Canning's situation, it is impossible to know when *they* speak with *sincerity*. But this I am assured of, that the events which have since taken place prove that I had at least some portion of the gift of prescience. In fact, everything that has been done in Spain, right or wrong, is a comment upon the principles I have laid down.

To Lady Beaumont,   V. 10, 1810

394A. . . . I think myself with some interest upon its being reprinted hereafter, along with my other writings. But the respect, which in common with all the rest of the rational parts of the world, I bear for the Duke of Wellington, will prevent my reprinting the Pamphlet during his life-time.

Reed, p. 36.   IX. 14, 1840

ANSWER TO THE LETTER OF MATHETES

395. The Friend might rest satisfied that his exertions thus far have not been wholly unprofitable, if no other proof had been given of their influence, than that of having called forth the foregoing letter, with which he has been so much interested, that he could not deny himself the pleasure of communicating it to his readers. . . . one of the main purposes of his work is to weigh, honestly and thoughtfully, the moral worth and intellectual power of the age in which we live; to ascertain our gain and our loss; to determine what we are in ourselves positively, and what we are compared with our ancestors; and thus, and by every other means within his power, to discover what may be hoped for future times, what and how lamentable are the evils to be feared, and how far there is cause for fear. If this attempt should not be made wholly in vain, my ingenuous correspondent, and all who are in a state of mind resembling that of which he gives so lively a picture, will be enabled more readily and sorely to distinguish false from legitimate objects of admiration: and thus may the personal errors which he would guard against be more effectually prevented or removed by the developement of general truth for a general purpose, than by instructions specifically adapted to himself or to the class of which he is the able representative. There is a life and spirit in knowledge which we extract from truths scattered for the benefit of all, and which the mind, by its own activity, has appropriated to itself,—a life and a spirit, which is seldom found in knowledge communicated by formal and direct precepts, even when they are exalted and endeared by reverence and love for the teacher.

Ans. to Mathetes (*Grosart*, i, 309).   XII. 14, 1809

GUIDE TO THE LAKES

396.   I am very happy that you have read the Introduction [to Wilkinson's *Select Views*] with so much pleasure, and must thank you for your kindness in telling me of it. I thought the part about the cottages well done; and also liked a sentence where I transport the reader to the top of one of the mountains or, rather, to the cloud chosen for his station, and give a sketch of the impressions which the country might be supposed to make on a feeling mind contemplating its appearance before it was inhabited. But what I wished to accomplish was to give a model of the manner in which topographical descriptions ought to be executed, in order to their being either useful or intelligible, by evolving truly and distinctly one appearance from another. In this I think I have not wholly failed.

To Lady Beaumont,   V. 10, 1810

397.   I have in the press a little book on the Lakes, containing some illustrative remarks on Swiss scenery. If I have fallen into any errors, I know no one better able to correct them than yourself, and should the book (which I must mention is chiefly a *re*publication) meet your eye, pray point out to me the mistakes. The part relating to Switzerland is new.

To R. Sharp,   IV. 16, 1822

398.   In the book on the Lakes, which I have not at hand, is a passage rather too vaguely expressed, where I content myself with saying, that after a certain point of elevation the effect of mountains depends much more upon their form than upon their absolute height. This point, which ought to have been defined, is the one to which fleecy clouds (not thin watery vapours) are accustomed to descend. I am glad you are so much interested with this little tract; it could not have been written without long experience.

To Geo. H. Gordon,   XII. 15, 1828

ON EPITAPHS

400.   [See the essays *On Epitaphs* for W.'s purpose in writing these essays; Criticism 59 and Johnson 14.]

LETTER TO A FRIEND OF BURNS

401.   The subject is delicate, and some of the opinions are of a kind, which, if torn away from the trunk that supports them, will be apt to wither, and, in that state, to contrast poisonous qualities. . . . [W. suggests no publicity be given to his opinions, unless they are considered useful.]

L. to Friend of Burns (Grosart, ii, 19).   1816

402.   . . . not that I mean you to present the prose [*Letter to a Friend of Burns*] to the Archbishop; it is a little too profane for his Grace's acceptance.

To C. W.,   III. 25, 1816

Two Addresses to the Freeholders of Westmoreland

403.   My object in writing this work was to give the *rationale* of the question, for the consideration of the upper ranks of society, in language of appropriate dignity. It shall be followed up with brief essays, in plain and popular language, illustrating the principles in detail, for the understanding of the lower orders.   *To Lord Lonsdale,*   IV. 6, 1818

Isabella Fenwick Notes

1.   Once more, in excuse for so much egotism, let me say, these notes are written for my familiar friends, and at their earnest request.
I. F. (W.'s Works, iii, 423).   1843

INDEX

PART ONE

(The last numeral after each heading is always a page-reference; all other numerals refer to sections. For example, *Abuse* appears on page 3, but 9 indicates a section under *Criticism*.)

SUBJECTS

PART TWO

PART THREE

WORDSWORTH ON HIS OWN WORKS

For Reference

Not to be taken from this room